Victor Houliston, D. Phil. (1986) in English
Literature, Oxford University, teaches
English at the University of Witwatersrand,
Johannesburg. His publications include a
critical edition of Thomas Moffet's *The
Silkewormes and their Flies* (Renaissance
English Text Society, 1989).

ROBERT PERSONS, S.J.
THE CHRISTIAN DIRECTORY
(1582)

STUDIES IN THE HISTORY
OF
CHRISTIAN THOUGHT

EDITED BY

HEIKO A. OBERMAN, Tucson, Arizona

IN COOPERATION WITH

HENRY CHADWICK, Cambridge

JAROSLAV PELIKAN, New Haven, Connecticut

BRIAN TIERNEY, Ithaca, New York

ARJO VANDERJAGT, Groningen

VOLUME LXXXIV

VICTOR HOULISTON (ED.)

ROBERT PERSONS S.J.
THE CHRISTIAN DIRECTORY
(1582)

ROBERT PERSONS S.J.
THE CHRISTIAN DIRECTORY
(1582)

THE FIRST BOOKE OF
THE CHRISTIAN EXERCISE, APPERTAYNING
TO RESOLUTION

EDITED BY

VICTOR HOULISTON

BRILL
LEIDEN · BOSTON · KÖLN
1998

This book is printed on acid-free paper.

Library of Congress Cataloging-in-Publication Data

Parsons, Robert, 1546–1610.
  [Christian directory]
  Robert Persons S.J. : the Christian directory (1582)
; the first booke of the Christian exercise,
appertayning to resolution / edited by Victor
Houliston.
    p.   cm. — (Studies in the history of Christian
thought, ISSN 0081–8607 ; v. 84)
  Includes bibliographical references and index.
  ISBN 9004110097 (hardcover : alk. paper)
  1. Christian life—Catholic authors—Early works to
1800.   I. Houliston, Victor, 1954–   .   II. Title.
III. Series.
BX1750.P33   1998
248.4'82—dc21

98–25291
CIP

Die Deutsche Bibliothek - CIP-Einheitsaufnahme

Robert Persons S.J.: The Christian Directory (1582) : the first
booke of the Christian exercise, appartayning to resolution / ed. by
Victor Houliston. – Leiden ; Boston ; Köln : Brill, 1998
  (Studies in the history of Christian thought ; Vol. 84)
  ISBN 90–04–11009–7

ISSN   0081-8607
ISBN   90 04 11009 7

PRINTED IN THE NETHERLANDS

CONTENTS

THE SECOND PART OF THIS FIRST BOOKE

ACKNOWLEDGEMENTS

In preparing this edition I have been greatly indebted to the friendly interest, support and advice of Fr John W. Padberg, S.J., and his colleagues at the Institute of Jesuit Sources in St Louis. Others whose assistance I should like to acknowledge include the staff of Duke Humfrey's Library (Oxford), the British Library and St Louis University Library; Mr Anthony Allison, now sadly deceased, Professor Brian Cheadle, Miss Katherine Duncan-Jones, Professor John Gouws, Professor Geoffrey Hughes, Fr Geoffrey Holt, S.J. (formerly Archivist of the British Province of the Society of Jesus), Fr Thomas McCoog, S.J. (Archivist of the British Province of the Society of Jesus), Fr Joseph Munitiz (Master of Campion Hall), Professor Martin Orkin, Professor Nancy Pollard Brown, Dr Michael Questier, Dr Nigel Smith, Fr Norman Tanner, S.J. (Archivist of Campion Hall), and Mr Michael Walsh (Archivist, Heythrop College). None of these, of course, can be held responsible for any of the errors or shortcomings in this addition.

I should like to thank Dr Heiko A. Oberman for accepting this edition for the series Studies in the History of Christian Thought, and Mr Theo Joppe of Brill whose friendly advice has been much appreciated.

The research involved in preparing this edition was made possible by a grant from the Centre for Scientific Development and by sabbatical leave granted by the University of the Witwatersrand.

V.H.
Johannesburg, South Africa
April, 1997

SHORT REFERENCES

ARCR I and II — *The Contemporary Printed Literature of the English Counter Reformation between 1558 and 1640*, ed. A.F. Allison and D.M. Rogers, 2 vols. (Aldershot: Scholar Press, 1989–94), Vol. 1: Works in Languages other than English (1989), Vol. 2: Works in English (1994).

Bunny — *A Book of Christian exercise, appertaining to Resolution . . . Perused, and accompanied now with a Treatise tending to pacification*, by Edmund Bunny (London, 1584; STC 19355) = B.

Bunny, *Briefe answer* — Edmund Bunny, *A briefe answer, vnto those idle and friuolous quarrels of R.P. against the late edition of the Resolution* (London, 1589; STC 4088).

Christian directorie, A — Robert Persons, *A Christian directorie guiding men to their saluation* (Rouen, 1585; STC 19354.1) = R2.

Christian directory, The — Robert Persons, *The Christian directory, guiding men to eternall saluation* (St Omer, 1607; STC 19354.5) = R4.

CRS — Publications of the Catholic Record Society (London, 1905, *etc.*).

Gregory — Brad S. Gregory, 'The "True and Zealouse Seruice of God": Robert Parsons, Edmund Bunny, and *The First Book of the Christian Exercise*', *Journal of Ecclesiastical History*, 45 (1994): 238–68.

McNulty — Robert McNulty, 'The Protestant Version of Robert Parsons' *The First Booke of the Christian Exercise*', *Huntington Library Quarterly*, 22 (1959): 271–300.

Persons Letters	*Letters and Memorials of Father Robert Persons, S.J.: Vol. I (to 1588)*, ed. L. Hicks, S.J., CRS 39 (1942).
Persons Memoirs	'The Memoirs of Father Robert Persons', ed. J.H. Pollen, S.J., in *Miscellanea II*, CRS 2 (1906): 12–218.
Persons Notes	'Father Persons' Memoirs (Concluded) . . . Punti per la Missione d'Inghilterra', ed. and trans. J.H. Pollen, S.J., as 'Notes Concerning the English Mission', in *Miscellanea IV*, CRS 4 (1907): 1–161.
Resolution	Robert Persons, *The first booke of the Christian exercise, appertayning to resolution* (Rouen, 1582; STC 19353) = R.
STC	*A Short-title Catalogue of Books Printed in England, Scotland, & Ireland and of English Books Printed Abroad, 1475–1640*, ed. A.W. Pollard and G.R. Redgrave (1926), rev. ed. by W.A. Jackson, F.S. Ferguson and Katharine F. Pantzer, 3 vols. (London: The Bibliographical Society, 1976–91).
Wing	*A Short-title Catalogue of Books Printed in England, Ireland, Scotland, Wales, and North America and of English Books Printed in Other Countries, 1641–1700*, ed. Donald Wing, 3 vols. (New York: Columbia University Press for the Index Society, 1945).

INTRODUCTION

Historical Significance

If we include all versions, authorised and unauthorised, *Parsons'
Resolution* (as the various versions of *The Christian Directory* were usually called) was probably the most popular devotional work to appear
in English before 1650. The *Short-title Catalogue, 1485–1640* lists some
forty editions of the book in whole or part (1582–1640), a record that
was matched not even by *The foundation of Christian religion* by William
Perkins (nineteen editions, 1590–1638) or *The plaine man's path-way to
heaven* by Arthur Dent (twenty-five editions, 1601–1640).[1] In 1584,
two years after the first, anonymous but identifiably Roman Catholic,
publication of the *Resolution*, a Protestant adaptation by Edmund
Bunny caused a sensation: by the end of the following year it had
been reprinted no fewer than sixteen times, provoking a squabble
between rival printers and giving momentum to the newly-founded
Oxford university press.

As a phenomenal best-seller the *Resolution* bears witness to an
important aspect of contemporary taste. Thomas Middleton could
expect his playhouse audience to recognize the title *Resolution* instantly
in 1608: the book was the obvious choice for a jealous husband
wanting to reform his coquettish wife:

> *Harebrain.* Do, labour her, prithee; I have convey'd away all her wan-
> ton pamphlets, as *Hero and Leander, Venus and Adonis*; oh, two luscious
> mary-bone pies for a young married wife. Here, here, prithee take the
> *Resolution*, and read to her a little.
>
> *Courtesan.* Sh'as set up her resolution already, sir.
>
> *Harebrain.* True, true, and this will confirm it the more. There's a chap-
> ter of Hell, 'tis good to read this cold weather. Terrify her, terrify her;
> go, read to her the horrible punishments for itching wantonness, the
> pains allotted for adultery; tell her her thoughts, her very dreams are

---

[1] See Gregory, pp. 239–40. The name is variously spelt 'Persons' and 'Parsons';
I normally use 'Persons' in accordance with the weight of the evidence of his correspondence, except when citing authors who prefer 'Parsons'.

answerable, say so; rip up the life of a courtesan, and show how loath-
some 'tis.[2]

In due course it was superseded in the Protestant tradition by Jeremy
Taylor's *Holy Living* (1650), John Bunyan's *Pilgrim's Progress* (1678) and
William Law's *Serious Call to a Devout and Godly Life* (1728),[3] but the
Catholic version remained in print until 1861. This 'text book of
sturdy piety', as Evelyn Waugh put it, has been described as 'one
of the simplest, sweetest, soundest books of devotion in the English
tongue'.[4]

Of the book's persuasiveness we have several testimonies. The
adventurous Jesuit missionary John Gerard claimed that it had 'converted more souls to God than it contains pages'.[5] Several famous
readers found it hard to resist, such as Robert Greene in his final
illness:

> sodainly taking the booke of Resolution in my hand, I light vpon a
> chapter therein, which discouered vnto mee the miserable state of the
> reprobate, what Hell was. . . . After that I had with deepe considera-
> tion pondered vpon these points, such a terrour stroke into my con-
> science, that for very anguish of minde my teeth did beate in my head,
> my lookes waxed pale and wan, and fetching a great sigh, I cried vnto
> God, and said: If all this be true, oh what shall become of me?[6]

Thomas Nashe believed it had no rival as an antidote to atheism.[7]
Sir John Harington was anxious to distinguish his translation of
Orlando Furioso from the kinds of works that Persons warned would
continue, after the author's death, to accumulate demerit for the

---

[2] *A Mad World, My Masters*, I.ii.47–59, in *The Selected Plays of Thomas Middleton*,
ed. D.L. Frost (Cambridge: Cambridge University Press, 1978), pp. 14–15.
[3] William T. Costello, introduction to *The Judgement of a Catholic Englishman*, by
Robert Persons, S.J. (Gainesville, Flo.: Scholars' Facsimiles and Reprints, 1957), p. vii.
[4] Evelyn Waugh, *Edmund Campion: Jesuit and Martyr* (1946; reprint, New York:
Image Books, 1956), p. 82; Garrett Mattingly, *The Defeat of the Spanish Armada* (London:
Jonathan Cape, 1959), p. 72.
[5] John Gerard, *The Autobiography of an Elizabethan*, trans. Philip Caraman (London:
Longmans, Green & Co., 1951), p. 2.
[6] Robert Greene, *The Repentance of Robert Greene* (1592), in *The Life and Complete
Works of Robert Greene*, ed. A.B. Grosart, 15 vols. (London, 1881–86), 12: 164–70. I
am indebted for several of the following references to Robert McNulty, 'Robert
Parsons's *The First Booke of the Christian Exercise* (1582): An Edition and a Study' (Unpublished Ph.D. thesis, Columbia University, 1955).
[7] Thomas Nashe, *Christ's Tears over Jerusalem* (1593), in *The Works of Thomas Nashe*,
ed. R.B. McKerrow (1908), rev. F.P. Wilson, 2d ed., 5 vols. (Oxford: Blackwell,
196), 2: 121.

Day of Judgement.[8] Richard Baxter eloquently testified to the peculiar power of the book:

> I had before heard some Sermons, and read a good Book or two, which made me more love and honour Godliness in the General; but I had never felt any other change by them on my heart. Whether it were that till now I came not to that maturity of Nature, which made me capable of discerning; or whether it were that this was God's appointed time, or both together, I had no lively sight and sense of what I read until now. And in the reading of this Book (when I was about Fifteen years of Age) . . . it pleased God to awaken my Soul, and shew me the folly of Sinning, and the misery of the Wicked, and the unexpressible weight of things Eternal, and the necessity of resolving on a Holy Life, more than I was ever acquainted with before. The same things which I knew before came now in another manner, with Light, and Sense, and Seriousness to my Heart.[9]

These responses, subject though they are to their authors' own falsifying rhetoric, nevertheless suggest that Persons had an extraordinary gift, for his time, of giving familiar doctrines a new and personal application.

The appeal of the *Resolution* to readers who were themselves major authors suggests that it had stylistic distinction as well as rhetorical power. Gabriel Harvey, indeed, noted that it was 'elegantly and pathetically penned', while Jonathan Swift—perhaps contrasting Persons with the 'enthusiastic jargon' of the revolutionary period—expressed the opinion that the passing of time had rendered all Elizabethan prose writers unreadable except Richard Hooker and the Jesuit Parsons.[10] The readers just cited were Protestant, and probably most of them were reading Bunny's version,[11] but it was surely the force of Persons's underlying prose style that engaged them.

The *Resolution* is a key document in the understanding of the impact of the Catholic reformation on England. Many Jesuits were subsequently to claim that they owed their vocation to a reading of the

---

[8] Sir John Harington, preface to *Orlando Furioso* (1591), ed. R. McNulty (Oxford: Clarendon Press, 1972), p. 558; see commentary to p. 43 below.

[9] Richard Baxter, *Reliquiae Baxterianae* (London, 1696), p. 3.

[10] Gabriel Harvey, *Pierces Supererogation* (1593), extracted in *Elizabethan Critical Essays*, ed. G. Gregory Smith, 2 vols. (London: Oxford University Press, 1904), 2: 280; Jonathan Swift, in *The Tatler*, no. 230; cf. his 'Proposal for Correcting, Improving, and Ascertaining the English Tongue' (1712) for comments on the language of religious controversy.

[11] Harington, however, quotes from Persons's revised version, *A Christian directorie*, p. 354.

Resolution.[12] With its secure foundation in Scripture, St Augustine and St Bernard, the work implicitly promoted the Roman church's post-Tridentine claims of continuity and authority and challenged the Anglicans to produce their credentials. That challenge was in turn made explicit and reinforced by Persons's directly polemical works. The influence of all this on the Anglo-Catholic movement of the early seventeenth century can only be guessed at. Certainly John Donne was painfully aware of Persons's presence, and his sermons used similar authorities to present an image of a deeply-rooted, reformed church that was recognizably one with the catholic tradition of Christendom.[13]

The propaganda value of the *Resolution* touches on the question of Persons's own spirituality. Many observers have been tempted to dismiss his most famous work as a piece of Jesuitical cunning. Persons's contemporary opponents, if they were Protestant, tended to treat it as a Trojan horse, deliberately smuggling in a corrupt doctrine of works under the guise of uncontroversial devotion.[14] The anti-Jesuit party amongst the Catholics, loth to give credit to the author, relegated it to the status of a compilation.[15] The originality and sincerity of the book thus have a bearing on our interpretation of Persons's career and personality. Many historians—including John Bossy and A.L. Rowse—have struggled to find 'the heart of Robert Persons' and confess to puzzlement.[16] Francis Edwards, author of the long-

---

[12] See Thomas H. Clancy, 'Spiritual Publications of English Jesuits, 1615–40', *Recusant History*, 19 (1988): 426–46.

[13] Janel M. Mueller, introduction to *Donne's Prebend Sermons* (Cambridge, Mass.: Harvard University Press, 1971), pp. 8–9. References to Persons are to be found in Donne's *Pseudo-Martyr* (1610), ed. Anthony Raspa (Montreal: McGill-Queen's University Press, 1993), pp. 9, 11, 160–62, 217–18.

[14] E.g. Matthew Sutcliffe, *A brief reply to a certain odious and slanderous libel . . . entitled A temperate wardword* (London, 1600, STC 23453), sig. A3v.

[15] E.g. Anthony Copley, *An answere to a letter of a Iesuited gentleman* (London, 1601; STC 5735), p. 98; William Watson, *A decacordon of ten quodlibeticall questions concerning religion and state* (London, 1602), pp. 71–73. See also J.C.H. Aveling, *The Handle and the Axe: The Catholic Recusants in England from Reformation to Emancipation* (London: Blond & Briggs, 1976), p. 73.

[16] John Bossy, 'The Heart of Robert Persons', in *The Reckoned Expense: Edmund Campion and the Early English Jesuits*, ed. Thomas McCoog, (Woodbridge, Sussex: Boydell and Brewer, 1996), pp. 141–58; A.L. Rowse, 'Father Parsons the Jesuit', in *Eminent Elizabethans* (London: Macmillan, 1983), pp. 41–74. See also Ethelred L. Taunton, *The History of the Jesuits in England, 1580–1773* (London: Methuen, 1901), pp. 96–97; Peter Guilday, *The English Catholic Refugees on the Continent, 1558–1795* (London: Longmans, Green & Co., 1914), 1: 127–34; Bernard Basset, *The English*

awaited first biography of Persons, claims that 'his primary vocation was that of priest; his avocation, politics', but pays scant attention to the evidence that this book might give to support his case.[17] One of the purposes of this edition, therefore, is to contribute to the understanding of Persons as a controversial and enigmatic major figure in the history of early modern England.

The Authorship of the Resolution

Although the only clue to the author's identity in the first edition of the *Resolution* is the initials R.P. at the end of the preface 'to the Christian reader', the hand of Robert Persons was quickly recognized. He referred to it frequently in his correspondence, and his authorship was acknowledged publicly by both his supporters and his opponents. His name finally appeared on the title page in 1620, some ten years after his death.[18]

Robert Persons was one of the ablest of the 'second wave' of Catholic exiles from Elizabethan England.[19] Born of Somerset yeomanry stock in 1546, he was the product of Taunton Free School and Balliol College, Oxford.[20] Evidently he was an outstanding scholar and became a popular tutor: Henry More, Jesuit Provincial in the mid-seventeenth century, claimed that pupils flocked to him from all over the country.[21] In 1573 he was expelled from the college after a clash with the Master, Adam Squire, in circumstances that are still unclear. Ostensibly he was charged, as bursar, with financial irregularity;

Jesuits: From Campion to Martindale (New York: Herder & Herder, 1968), pp. 55–96; E.E. Reynolds, *Campion and Parsons: The Jesuit Mission of 1580–1* (London: Sheed & Ward, 1980).

[17] Francis Edwards, *Robert Persons, S.J.* (St Louis: Institute of Jesuit Sources, 1995), p. 62.

[18] ARCR II 621 ff. For Persons's own references to his authorship, see notes 29, 34, 37, 42. Contemporary printed references to the *Resolution* are too numerous to list here; a good example is John Mush, *A dialogue betwixt a secular priest, and a lay gentleman* (1601; STC 25124), pp. 85–86.

[19] The 'first wave' included those who, like William Allen, left soon after the religious settlement of 1558/9; the 'second wave' followed in the 1570s, many attracted to the seminary at Douay. See Eamon Duffy, 'William, Cardinal Allen, 1532–1594', *Recusant History* 22 (1995): 265–90.

[20] For early biographical details, see L. Hicks, introduction to *Persons Letters*, and *Persons Memoirs*, pp. 12–47.

[21] Henry More, *The Elizabethan Jesuits: Historia Missionis Anglicanae Societatis Jesu* (1660), ed. and trans. Francis Edwards (London: Phillimore & Co., 1981), pp. 47–49.

More believed that he was proceeded against as a known or sus-
pected papist. There is also some evidence that he was disposed
towards Puritanism during some of his time at Balliol.[22] What is certain is that he had incurred the antagonism of Christopher Bagshaw,
one of the fellows, who later converted to Catholicism himself and
pursued Persons with his malice, justified or not, for the rest of his
life. He gloated: '[T]here was such lamentation at his departure from
the Colledge, as for joye he was rung thence with Bels'.[23] After this
reversal, Persons decided to go to Padua, like many Elizabethans,
to study medicine. The critical moment in his religious development
occurred en route in 1575, when he made the spiritual exercises with
the Jesuit William Good in Louvain. That experience, as described by
Henry More, would later inform his book of *Resolution*:

> As [Fr Good] worked through them, he roused in Persons a distaste
> for the mundane which eventually overcame every other feeling. . . .
> Good hoped that he would send down deep roots into goodness, and
> offered him sound advice to that end. . . . [He should] put every other
> thought aside save that of getting nearer to God. He should think over
> what he ought to do now, and come to his decision in calm and tran-
> quillity. . . . He had now set his mind on a more spiritual life, and
> in his fresh awareness of the transitoriness of things took a new and
> strange delight. [In Rome, after an interview with the General, Mer-
> curian, he] fell on his knees and made the total offering to God. He
> so overflowed with inner joy that then and there he made away all
> he possessed. With no hesitant afterthought, he adopted the Society's
> way of life. In it he lived henceforth in complete peace of mind.[24]

Soon afterwards he joined the Society of Jesus in Rome, and in due
course became involved in preparations for a mission to England.

The *Resolution* emerged from the experiences and constraints of
the Mission itself. Persons and Edmund Campion left Rome for
England in April 1580.[25] After the initial flurry of activity in London

---

[22] This was William Camden's view, in his *Annales* (Frankfurt, 1616), p. 319,
reported by Edward Gee, introduction to *The Jesuit's memorial for the intended reformation of England* (London, 1690; Wing P569), pp. xii–xiii. Cf. J.H. Pollen, ed., *Persons
Memoirs*, p. 22n.

[23] Christopher Bagshaw, *A sparing discouerie of our English Iesuits, and of Fa. Parsons
proceedings vnder pretence of promoting the Catholike faith in England* (London, 1601; STC
25126), p. 41. All quotations from contemporary sources, unless cited from modern editions, have been regularized according to the editorial policy for this edition. Titles are given as in the appropriate catalogue.

[24] Henry More, *The Elizabethan Jesuits*, pp. 15, 49–53.

[25] For details of the mission, see Richard Simpson, *Edmund Campion: A Biography*,

in June and July, leading up to the Southwark synod (when the Jesuit missionaries met the existing Catholic leaders), Persons left for a tour of the west midlands, returning to London for the beginning of the law term at Michaelmas. From then until April 1581 he was urgently engaged in writing three books—*Reasons of refusal, A brief censure* and *A discouerie of I. Nichols*—on the two main controversial issues of the day: whether Catholics should be permitted to attend Anglican services, as they were by law required to do, and whether the mission could be judged a purely spiritual venture. He had to deal with Protestant attacks on 'Campion's Brag', a prematurely publicised declaration of intent, and with a government propaganda ploy involving an apostate scholar from the English College in Rome, John Nichols, who had made a public recantation in the Tower of London.[26]

It was during this winter of 1580/1 that Persons also began writing the *Resolution*, apparently as the guest of a gentlewoman named Bellamy, at Uxenden Manor near Harrow, which at that time was a thickly-wooded retreat, ideal for the purpose.[27] Meanwhile, the three completed books were printed in secret by Persons and his printer, Stephen Brinkley, at various venues in London and Stonor Park, near Henley-on-Thames. From about March 1581 they were preparing also for the publication of Campion's *Decem rationes*, the primary academic thrust of the mission. This formal defence of Catholic doctrine was daringly distributed in Oxford in late June.[28] Within weeks, Campion was arrested at Lyford Grange and Persons fled to France via Michelgrove, Sussex.

Once he got to Rouen and was settled in the house of the Archdeacon, Monsignor de Monsi, Persons was able to continue with the *Resolution*, one of three further books that (he later recalled) he had

---

2d ed. (London: John Hodges, 1896), chapters 5–11; E.E. Reynolds, *Campion and Parsons: The Jesuit Mission of 1580–1* (London: Sheed & Ward, 1980); and *Persons Notes*.

[26] *A brief discours contayning certayne reasons why Catholiques refuse to goe to church* (London, 1580; STC 19394), *A brief censure vppon two bookes written in answere to M. Edmonde Campions offer of disputation* (London, 1581; STC 19393), *A discouerie of I. Nichols minister, misreported a Iesuite, lately recanted in the Tower of London* (Stonor Park, 1581; STC 19402). See *Persons Letters*, p. 75, n. 9; p. 76, n. 14; p. 77, n. 18; and ARCR II, p. 225. On the question of church attendance, see Alexandra Walsham, *Church Papists: Catholicism, Conformity and Confessional Polemic in Early Modern England* (Woodbridge, Sussex: Boydell and Brewer, 1993).

[27] William Weston, *The Autobiography of an Elizabethan*, trans. Philip Caraman (London, 1955), p. 3 and n. 10.

[28] E.E. Reynolds, *Campion and Parsons*, pp. 102–03.

already 'either begun to write, or at least projected'.[29] Even then, leisure was at a premium. He was concerned, first, to stabilise the English mission and make plans for Scotland. Already his mind may have been turning to an alliance with the Duke of Guise through de Monsi's relative, the Bourbon Archbishop Charles of Rouen.[30] His most pressing literary task was the Latin tract *De persecutione anglicana* which was used primarily to raise funds for the seminary at Rheims;[31] indeed, he was establishing at Rouen a vital link between the exiles at Rheims and the recusants in England. Throughout the winter of 1581/2 he was uncertain whether he should return immediately to England, make a venture to Scotland, or remain where he was. The Spanish Ambassador in London, Mendoza, applied pressure to him to hasten to Scotland, arguing (as Persons recalled) that 'it was no time to be occupied in writing books when it was a question of the salvation of kingdoms'.[32] Fortunately for Persons, the Jesuit General Claudio Aquaviva intervened to keep him in Rouen by recommending the senior Scottish priest, William Crichton (Creighton), to go in his stead.[33] By 11 April 1582 he was able to report the completion of the work to Aquaviva with some satisfaction: 'A book has been published in English on resolution suited to our [present] needs'.[34]

We may take the immediate needs to have been primarily pastoral, the 'helping of souls' to which the Jesuits were devoted. To write a spiritual handbook, 'some one sufficient direction for matters of life and spirit' (as he put it in his preface), rather than become embroiled in controversy, was in line with Jesuit practice throughout Europe, relying on moral regeneration for the establishment of Catholic orthodoxy.[35] As Persons himself wrote of those who differed

---

[29] *Persons Notes*, pp. 26–27, and *Persons Memoirs*, p. 30. The other two books were *De persecutione Anglicana, epistola* (Rouen, 1581) and *A defence of the Censure, gyven upon two bookes of William Charke and Meredith Hanmer* (Rouen, 1582; STC 19401).

[30] A. Lynn Martin, *Henry III and the Jesuit Politicians* (Geneva: Librairie Droz, 1973), pp. 63–74; John Bossy, 'The Heart of Robert Persons', in *The Reckoned Expense*, ed. Thomas McCoog.

[31] *Persons Letters*, p. xliii.

[32] *Persons Notes*, pp. 56–57. Mendoza was prompted by Mary Queen of Scots.

[33] L. Hicks (introd.), *Persons Letters*, p. xlix.

[34] '*Liber quidam editus de resolutione anglice accomodatus temporibus nostris*', R. Persons to C. Aquaviva, 11 April 1582. In an earlier letter, 21 October 1581, he describes the book as 'most pertinent to our purpose' ('*unum, qui ad propositum nostrum maxime pertinet*').

[35] John W. O'Malley, *The First Jesuits* (Cambridge, Mass.: Harvard University Press, 1993), pp. 70–71.

from him doctrinally: '[if we] joyne together in amendment of our lyves ... God (no doubt) will not suffer us to perishe finallye for want of right faithe' (p. 4). Yet he also intended the book to reinforce the missionary campaign against compromise. In his correspondence he was consistently to link resolution with recusancy and consequent persecution,[36] and he later explained that the *Resolution* as published in 1582 contained motives 'to encourage Catholics to virtue and specially to patience and firm resolve to bear the present persecution'.[37]

From April 1582 until the summer of 1584 Persons was almost continuously engaged in diplomatic missions to promote the plans orchestrated by the Duke of Guise for the invasion of England. He was initially dispatched to Portugal to approach Philip II about taking advantage of the ascendancy of the pro-Catholic Duke of Lennox in Scotland; the raid of Ruthven on 23 August 1582 dashed hopes of an early Franco-Spanish invasion, but a valuable and long-lasting rapport between Persons and the King of Spain was established. When he arrived back in Paris in July 1583, delayed for several months by a serious illness en route, a new military plan had already been devised. He had time to draw encouragement from reports from England of the 'increase of Catholics in the last year, after they had read certain spiritual books', no doubt including the *Resolution*,[38] before leaving for Rome to seek support from Pope Gregory XIII. This time it was the arrest of Throckmorton in November that undid the plan, and Persons's attention was next directed to the Prince of Parma in Tournai, where he spent the first few months of 1584.

In the hope that the Duke of Guise could engineer an early Catholic restoration in England Persons had virtually functioned as his agent, but as invasion prospects receded the connection became more compromising. The Duke of Anjou (formerly Alençon) died and the Prince of Orange was assassinated within weeks of each other in June–July 1584, with the result that Guise was preoccupied with French internal politics: the contest of the 'three Henries' (Henry III Valois, Henry of Guise and Henry of Navarre). Persons contributed to this through his involvement in the notorious publication

---

[36] E.g. letter to Alfonso Agazzari (Rector of the English College, Rome), 24 August 1583, in *Persons Letters*, pp. 172–82.
[37] *Persons Notes*, pp. 26–27.
[38] '*Vix est credibile quod narrant nostri de augmento catholicorum hoc ultimo anno posteaquam libros quosdam legerint de rebus spiritualibus scriptos*': Persons to Alfonso Agazzari (Rector of the English College Rome), Paris, 24 August 1583 (*Persons Letters*, pp. 173, 179).

known as *Leicester's Commonwealth*, an immensely effective and popular Catholic attack on the person and politics of the Queen's favourite. The book was of dubious benefit to the English mission, but it was translated into French as propaganda against the pro-English tendencies of Henry III. It seems unlikely that Persons wrote it himself, but he had a hand in its printing and distribution at least, and was forced into hiding at Rouen in November 1584 in consequence.[39] It was about this time that he indicated to Mary Queen of Scots that he and Allen had decided to abandon the military option: 'uppon consyderation of . . . the small successe owr former labors had browght forth wee had resolved I say to leave cogitation of soch matters and to follow only owr spiritual cowrse wheruppon all dependeth thowgh in longer time'.[40]

Even after this, Persons was seldom unwilling to support the use of force or diplomacy to transform the conditions of English Catholics. But for the time being he concentrated on the spiritual work of the mission and particularly on the revision of the *Resolution*. In mid-1584 he spent time preparing William Weston to take over as superior in England. They were probably together in the professed house in Paris during June and July, and Weston, who had been lecturer in Greek at the English College in Seville, gave Persons some assistance with his books, very likely the new material for the *Resolution*.[41] But he began in earnest with the revision in February 1585, as is evident from a recently-uncovered letter he wrote to Aquaviva. He appealed to the General, who wanted him in Rome, for two or three months in which to complete the work. For one thing, all the original copies had been read to pieces, and although the book had been reprinted at Rouen, this had been done without his permission; he would like to review and correct it before reprinting. Second, he had heard of a government-sponsored adaptation containing heretical passages, which needed to be refuted. Finally, he wanted to write the second and third books as originally projected.[42] The

---

[39] Persons to Agazzari, Rouen, 12 November 1584 (*Persons Letters*, pp. 259–60).

[40] *Persons Letters*, p. 246.

[41] For Weston's arrival in Paris, see *Persons Letters*, pp. 203, 205; for consultation on works being prepared for the press, see *Persons Notes*, pp. 156–57.

[42] '*Illius tamen primi libri impressa fuerunt 2500 exemplaria, et statim distracta* [read to pieces] . . . *quidam Barbitonsor Rothomagi, eundem librum, me inscio, lucri solius causa, denuo imprimendum curavit . . . Quibus rationibus impulsus fui, ut librum illum primum, revisum, correctum et nonnihil amplificatum cum haereticae nequitiae reprehensione his diebus denuo praelo per-*

letter also expresses a longing to leave off diplomacy and other business, and complete his Jesuit training. He begged to be 'allowed to make the third year of probation in order to recollect myself. . . . I feel myself very weakened as a result of these dealings with the world; and although I have had keener desires [i.e. for personal consolation in retreat], nevertheless, the importunity of affairs in no way allows me to satisfy myself'.[43]

As it happened, Persons was soon interrupted again by urgent business: it was likely that France would go to war with Spain, so new arrangements would have to be made about the Belgian routes to England; this kept him busy intermittently until July, and explains why he made no progress on Books Two and Three. In late August the revised work, now entitled A Christian directorie, went to press and the author was free at last to proceed to Rome, in company with William Allen. There he completed his tertianship by going into retreat at the novitiate of San Andrea.[44] It was another twenty years before he turned his hand once again to the Resolution. From 1588 he was based in Spain, establishing English seminaries at Seville and Valladolid, but was recalled to Rome in 1597 to help resolve the difficulties at the Venerable English College. He remained there as rector of the college, enjoying international prestige as the confidant of Pope Paul V, until his death in 1610. Pressure of business still kept him from completing the Resolution, but in 1607 he had a newly-revised version of Book One printed in St Omer. It was singularly appropriate that this should be the final edition in his lifetime, for he had been responsible for the founding, in 1593, of an English College at St Omer. This college (the original of Stonyhurst) took over the printing of his works in 1608, and soon became an internationally famous centre of Jesuit schoolboy theatre.[45] Persons could not have been better pleased.

---

mitterem': Persons to Aquaviva, 12 February 1585, Archivum Romanum Societatis Iesu, MS. Fondo Gesuitico 651/640.

[43] '[L]iceat mihi ad me recolligendum, tertium novitatus annum, secundum Societatis constitutiones, facere. . . . Sentio enim me diuturnis his cum saeculo commerciis debilitatum valde, et licet nunquam acriora habuerim desideria; tamen negotiorum importunitas nullo modo mihi ipsi satisfacere me permittit.'

[44] Persons Letters, p. lxxii.

[45] See William H. McCabe, An Introduction to the Jesuit Theater (St Louis: Institute of Jesuit Sources, 1983).

Stages of Composition, Adaptation and Revision

1 The first booke of the Christian exercise (1582)

The *Resolution* began in 1580 as a modest project of adaptation. In the preface 'to the Christian reader' Persons explained his original intention:

> But the principall cause and reason was, to the ende our countrye men might have some one sufficient direction for matters of life and spirit, among so manye bookes of controversies as have ben writen, and are in writinge dailye. (p. 5)

His own printer, Stephen Brinkley, had recently produced a translation of a work, Gaspar de Loarte's *Esercitio della vita christiana* (Genoa, 1557), that went some way towards meeting this need, and at first Persons simply planned an expansion of it.[46] Gaspar de Loarte was a Spanish Jesuit writing in Italian, whose *Esercitio* was the first serious Jesuit attempt to provide practical guidance for lay people on prayer and religious discipline.[47] It did not, however, challenge the reader to that initial change of heart which is the *sine qua non* of Ignatian spirituality. Persons therefore decided to amplify the book by writing two introductory parts, on the motives for resolution and the way of entering into resolution, with Loarte's work forming the basis of the third part, on persevering in resolution. He soon found that he would effectively need to write a new book altogether:

> *But yet notwithstanding, when I had sett downe an other order and method to my selfe, than that booke foloweth: and had begunne this first booke of resolution: wherof no parte is handled in that treatise: I found by experience, that I could not well joyne that with this: to satisfie, ether the order or argument by me conceyved: and therfore was I inforced, to resolve upon a further labour, than at the first I intended: whiche was, to drawe out the whole three bookes myself.*[48]

Looking back on this process in 1585, he noted that his first few chapters were written 'upon a purpose of greate brevitie which in the beginning was conceaved, (but afterwardes could not be held)'.[49] This suggests that he began work on expanding Loarte in haste on

---

[46] Stephen Brinkley, trans. *The exercise of a Christian life. Written in Italian by . . . Gaspar Loarte* (London, 1579: STC 16642). See *Persons Memoirs*, p. 35.

[47] John W. O'Malley, *The First Jesuits*, pp. 115, 139 and *passim*.

[48] 'An advertisement to the reader', p. 4. This preliminary section of the book (sig. A) was printed last.

[49] Preface to *A Christian directorie*, fol. 20r.

the Mission in 1580/1, and perhaps wrote the first three chapters
(which are very short), but postponed the project once he realized
what it would entail. The bulk of the first edition, in the two parts
devoted to motives and hindrances, was therefore probably written
in Rouen in the winter of 1581/2.

2 *A booke of Christian exercise (1584)*: Edmund Bunny's Perusal

In the 'Advertisement to the Reader' in 1582 Persons promised to
write the second and third books 'as time, healthe and libertie shall
permit me' (sig. A2r). But the projected completion of the *Resolution*
was much affected by the editorial intervention of Edmund Bunny,
who produced his own Protestant version of the first book in 1584.
Bunny had a creditable history of godly Protestantism: a graduate
of Magdalen College, Oxford (where the radical Puritan Laurence
Humphrey was soon to be welcomed as president), he had won a
fellowship at Merton College on the strength of his reputation as
a preacher. He published works of Calvinist theology and sought
the patronage of Archbishop Grindal.[50] Now, as chaplain to Edwin
Sandys, Archbishop of York, he responded to the *Resolution* with
mixed feelings:

> . . . first by a frind of mine, and after by mine own experience, I per-
> ceived, that the booke insuing was willingly read by divers, for the
> persuasion that it hath to godlines of life, which notwithstanding in
> manie points was corruptly set down. . . .[51]

The book had evidently won a considerable Protestant readership.
While Bunny conceded that those who read the book even in its
original form might eventually become Puritans,[52] he was alarmed
by its many unobtrusive but inescapable indications that the godly
life so powerfully urged on the reader was not a natural outcome
of salvation but its unremitted condition. This would undermine the
very basis of Protestant faith.

Other Protestant critics accused Persons of sugaring over an implied
gospel of good works with the attractions of a holy life, claiming

---

[50] Edmund Bunny (1540–1618), author of *The summe of the Christian religion* (London,
1576), *Of divorce for adulterie, and marrying again* (Oxford, 1610), etc. See his entry in
DNB.
[51] Bunny, sig. *2.
[52] Dedicatory Epistle (1584), sig. *2v–3.

that 'he laboureth altogether to draw men from faith to works making them the cause of justification, breathing out his poyson with a
sweet breath, and with sweete words covering his deadly venome'.[53]
Bunny seems to have accepted Persons's good faith, but did not
underestimate the potential damage. As Robert McNulty points out,
it would not be sufficient to attack the book directly and expose its
theological flaws, for the *Resolution* was attracting an unprecedented
number of readers. The answer was to reproduce it in a harm-
less form.

McNulty has provided a full and reliable analysis of Bunny's alterations, which need only be briefly summarised here.[54] All references
to merit attaching to good works are omitted or altered: 'the good
man ... by resisting [sin] encreaseth in the favor of God'; he does
not increase in merit, as Persons fondly supposed (p. 35). The sphere
of independent human action is further restricted by close censorship
of words suggesting that things may happen by chance or fortune:
'better were it a great deal to say, that such things are of the hand
of God' (p. 251). Bunny intervenes to steer his reader away from
acts of penance and satisfaction towards repentance, from quantifiable
devotions to sincere spirituality, from bodily self-chastisement to 'painful labour in his vocation' (p. 31). Out go a few rare glances at
auricular confession and the intercession of saints, a longish description of purgatorial fire, the colloquial expletive 'marry', and papist
idiom such as 'Our Lord' or 'Palm Sunday'. He prefers 'worldly' to
'secular', lest religious experience be restricted to a 'sacred' category
dominated by priestcraft. The Epistle to the Hebrews becomes apos-
tolic rather than Pauline, and Biblical quotations are purged of the
Latinate terms used by the Rheims New Testament.[55] Other Roman
practices and doctrines glanced at are monasticism, priestly celibacy,
and categories such as mortal sin and the six sins against the Holy
Spirit.[56]

In addition to these omissions and alterations, Bunny frequently

---

[53] *An answeare for the time, vnto that foule, and wicked defence of the censure* (London,
1583; STC 5008), sig. B2v-3.
[54] Most of the examples given below are cited by McNulty, with a few added
by Gregory, pp. 246–52. For a more extensive discussion of the Bunny-Persons controversy, see my essay, 'Why Robert Persons would not be pacified', in *The Reckoned
Expense*, ed. Thomas McCoog, pp. 159–78. See also Ceri Sullivan, 'Cannibalizing
Persons's *Christian Directorie*, 1582', *Notes and Queries*, 239 (1994): 445–46.
[55] *The New Testament of Iesus Christ* (Rheims, 1582: STC 2884).
[56] *Resolution*, pp. 55, 174, 177, 275.

guarded against impure doctrine by adding a qualification in paren-
thesis or a warning in the margin. Jesus gave the rich young ruler
no other hope of salvation but keeping God's commandments, wrote
Persons, Bunny adding '(so long as he sought salvation by his works)'
(p. 40). He queried interpretations of scripture and the Fathers, commented on Persons's dubious scientific knowledge, and in one place
dared to find fault with the Blessed Virgin herself (p. 290).

While some of the annotations stamped Bunny's version as aggres-
sively Protestant, for the most part he could claim with some justification that he had merely reduced the original to a scrupulous
neutrality. He assumed that Persons had intended to separate 'amendment of life' from distinctively Roman (or, for that matter, Protestant)
formulations, and he, Bunny, would perfect this ecumenical work.
When, for example, he changed 'those which attend in the Catholique
Churche, to deale with soules in the holie sacrament of confession' to
'those which are known to be skilful, and to deal so sincerely withal,
that others disburden their consciences unto them for their comfort
or counsel', his professed intention was to leave the description
'as indifferent to you (if so you could imploy your selves) as I did
unto us'.[57]

As a fairly characteristic Elizabethan Protestant editor of a Catholic
work of devotion, then, Bunny was more concerned with his readers'
spiritual health than the integrity of his author's text. Nor was he
reluctant to display the superiority of his own erudition. The Vulgate
comes in for much criticism, as the inadequacy of traditional readings both literal and allegorical are exposed by reference to scriptural context. Bunny's trump card is to endorse Persons's point while
denying its basis in the text cited. 'The slouthefull man, is stoned to
death with a stone of durt,' writes Persons, quoting from Ecclesiasticus
22. Comments Bunny, 'The vulgar translation so readeth: but now
it is found, that therin it misseth the sense of the text in both these
places heer alledged. And yet the matter it selfe is tru, though it
have no warrant hence' (p. 307). Again, he goes out of his way to
identify relatively innocuous statements that might conceivably lead
Protestant readers into error: for example, he queries an observa-
tion that choler may be usefully transmuted into zeal, in case this
might imply that 'the soul doth follow the temperature of the bodie'.

---

[57] *Resolution*, p. 170; Bunny, *Briefe answer*, sig. D4. See McNulty, pp. 290–91.

While Persons is merely concerned to show that rebellious passions may be turned to virtuous uses, Bunny is anxious lest such recognition of the body's influence on the state of the soul might make plausible the doctrine of the immaculate conception (p. 147). A pious assertion that there was no earthly reason for Jesus to lower himself to become man elicits the patronising remark: 'although God hath given to this our Author a very good gift in persuading to godlines of life (for which we have to æsteem of him accordingly:) yet hath he not given him therwithal so ful a knowlege of the mysterie of our redemption in Christ' (p. 189).

Some of Bunny's verbal substitutions, less obviously related to theological differences, call out for explanation. He consistently finds fault with the word 'motyves', as in 'important reasons and motyues, to prouoke a man to this resolution', preferring 'persuasions' or 'reasons' (pp. 11, 112). This may reflect an uneasiness with a rhetoric that seeks to move the emotions and will rather than persuade the reason. He regularly replaces 'majesticall' with 'of great majestie' or 'ful of majestie' when the reference is to God or His handiwork. According to the *OED*, 'majestical' was a fairly recent coinage (1579), to be replaced in 1601 by 'majestic', so one may place it in the category of unusual words associated with the Rheims New Testament, such as 'pressure' meaning 'distress', that Bunny eschewed.[58]

Bunny's 'perusal' provides intriguing evidence of an embattled and ambiguous meeting place between Rome and the English Reformation. His intention was not only to give Protestants safe access to the *Resolution*, but also to invite moderate Roman Catholics to join him on this putative middle ground. To the adapted *Resolution* he added a 126-page 'Treatise tending to pacification' addressed to the papists, attempting to explain why they need have no scruples about conforming to the Church of England. Generously, he conceded that they were already members of the true church of Christ, something which had been denied by earlier Anglican apologists.[59] If they would only grant the same to Anglicans and come to church, they could enjoy the benefits of the English Protestant settlement and live at peace with their consciences.

---

[58] *Resolution*, pp. 113 (majesticall), 43 (pressure).

[59] See Richard Hopkins, 'Translatours dedicatorie epistle' to *A memoriall of a Christian life*, by Luis de Granada (Rouen, 1586; STC 16903), referring to Bunny

3   *A Christian directorie (1585)*

Bunny's 'neutralising' of the *Resolution* was not the only, nor indeed
the main, stimulus to Persons to revise the book. He was influenced
by the need for reprinting, a certain dissatisfaction with what he felt
to be a hasty, unpolished first edition, the comments and criticisms
of his colleagues, and a desire for a more reflective kind of devotion. By the summer of 1584, when he resumed work on the *Resolution*,
he was patently tired of ceaseless political manoeuvrings and resigned
himself to a long patient struggle.

The preface to the re-titled *Christian directorie guiding men to their saluation* gives an efficient synopsis of the revision. Persons had reviewed
and amplified some chapters, wholly altered some others, and added
four new ones. Two of these, 'of the certaintie of one God', and 'of
our Christian faith and religion', were added because the heat of
religious controversy was inducing an atmosphere of indifference and
atheism: 'a certaine contempt and carles insensibilitie in thes affaires,
esteeming al things to stand upon probabilitie only of dispute to and
fro'. Another chapter was added, 'against dispaire of Godes mercie',
to correct an alleged over-emphasis on God's judgement. He also
'inserted divers chapters and discourses of matters more plausible,
and of them selves more indifferent' for the benefit of readers who
might be discouraged by the unmitigated vehemence of the *Resolution*.
This would presumably apply to the new chapter of 'examples of
true resolution', which was entertaining (in the precise sense) rather
than intimidating.[60]

These additions reflected a change in the overarching design. Persons still thought of the projected work as containing three books,
but in two volumes. Book One, now complete, would form fully half
of the entire treatise, a 'speculative' volume containing 'matter of
discourse, knowledge, speculation, and consideration, to move us to
resolve', while the projected second volume, 'practive' by nature,
would comprise Books Two and Three and handle the rule of life
by which resolution could be put in execution.[61]

A table comparing the contents of the 1582 and 1585 editions
will clarify the expansions:

---

and John Jewel, *An apologie or aunswer in defence of the Church of England* (London, 1562;
STC 14590).

  [60] Preface to *A Christian directorie*, fols. 20–21.
  [61] Preface to *A Christian directorie*, fol. 4v–5.

RESOLUTION	A CHRISTIAN DIRECTORIE
Part 1	Part 1
1 Of the end and parts of this book	1 Perils that ensue by inconsideration
2 How necessary it is to enter into earnest consideration and meditation of our estate	
	2 That there is a God
3 Of the end for which man was created	3 Why man was created
	4 Confirmations of Christian religion
	5 How a man may judge whether he be a true Christian
4 Two special things required at [man's] hands in this life	6 Two principal points of a Christian life
5 The severe account that we must yield to God	7 The account which Christians must yield to God
6 The nature of sin	8 The nature of sin
7 The majesty of God and his benefits towards us	9 The majesty of him whom we offend
8 The time of our death	10 The time of our death
9 Pains after this life	11 Punishments after this life
10 Rewards proposed to all them that truly fear God	12 Rewards ordained for such as truly serve God
Part 2	Part 2
	1 Mistrust and diffidence in God's mercies
1 Difficulty or hardness, which seemeth to be in virtuous life	2 Supposed hardness and asperity of virtuous life
2 Persecution, affliction, and tribulation	3 Fear of persecution
3 The love of the world	4 Love of the pleasures of this world

4 Too much presuming of the mercy of God

5 Delay of resolution, upon hope to doe it better afterwards

6 Three other impediments

5 Examples of true resolution

6 Over much presumption in the mercy of our Saviour

7 Deceitful hope to do it better afterward

8 Slothfulnes, negligence and hardness of heart

It will be noticed that the most extensive revision applies to the first half of the first Part. Not only does the addition of the two long chapters contribute largely to the doubling of the length of the work as a whole, it also blunts the edge of the governing argument, replacing urgency with solidity. Instead of challenging the reader on the account to be rendered to God, and passing swiftly to the actual reckoning, *A Christian directorie* systematically sets out the philosophical and theological basis for Christian belief and practice. One further significant 'improvement' was the addition, at the end, of a scheme which the reader could follow in order to use *A Christian directorie* for regular meditation over ten days or two weeks, dividing the material into readings for morning and evening.

While this expansive, more cumbersome but stately work was going to press in August 1585, Persons received the actual text of Bunny's perusal. With forme Dd imposed, he squeezed an annotation into a space at the end of chapter five: 'THE PRINT BEING come to this place, M. Bunneys edition of this booke was delivered to me, out of whose infinite corruptions, maymes, and manglings, divers things shalbe noted hereafter in the margents.'[62] Some aspects of his revision had already been designed as a response to the rumour of a Protestant adaptation: indeed, in the very chapter standing in print before him, he had added some careful explanation of the Catholic doctrine of faith and works so as to make such adaptation more difficult in future.[63] He had also included much stronger suggestions of a whole panoply of ecclesiastical and sacramental 'helps' to the keeping of one's resolution, anticipating the projected second and third books. But now, seeing his words altered and his meaning

---

[62] *A Christian directorie*, p. 322.
[63] See esp. Part One, chapter 5, 'How a man may judge or discerne of him self, whether he be a true Christian or not'.

redirected, he adopted a different mode of responding to the threat of misunderstanding. Using not only the marginal notes from forme Ee onwards but also the Preface, which as usual was printed after the main body of the text, he adopted the acerbic style of his most aggressive controversy: full of satirical mockery, personal insult and unfair argumentative manoeuvres.

These last-minute additions were written in haste, without careful consideration of the points at issue. As McNulty has commented, '[A] much better answer could have been made'.[64] Yet this is to discount the contrast in style between the text of *A Christian directorie* and its marginal and prefatory overlay. Under pressure of time, Persons simply mounted a virtuoso display of debating finesse for the benefit of his Catholic readers, participating in an *agon* rather than engaging in serious, measured dialogue. He rejected the claim of Anglican neutrality, saying caustically that Bunny made him 'speake like a good minister of England'.[65] Had Bunny merely toned down the Roman idiom and left the substance intact and scrupulously in-different? No, for although Bunny conceded that 'the Protestantes faith . . . and ours is al one in substance, and we al are members of one true Catholique and Apostolique Churche', the purified terms reflected his assurance that 'some of us be somewhat better members in that Church then others'.[66]

It may be inferred from Persons's explosive reaction that in the 1580s there was little scope for a neutral idiom; the language could not disguise its allegiance to Rome or Geneva. If centrist Anglican apologists from Hooker onwards struggled to create just such an idiom, we should not be surprised if a Calvinist, trying his best to be indifferent and inoffensive, should have failed to find it in 1584. Bunny replied to Persons in his *Briefe answer* of 1589, and again in 1610, in an appendix to his *Of divorce for adulterie, and marrying again . . . With a note at the end, that R.P. many yeares since was answered*. But Persons paid him no further attention except to retain, in later editions, those parts of his Preface which addressed the Protestant version and the Treatise of Pacification.

---

[64] McNulty, p. 299.
[65] Preface to *A Christian directorie*, fol. 12r.
[66] Preface, fol. 19r.

4   *The Christian directory (1607)*

The 1585 revision was reprinted faithfully in Louvain in 1598, but thereafter was subjected to critical reconsideration. Persons decided to drop the chapters proving the existence of God and the truth of the Christian religion. As apologetics, these chapters evidently met a contemporary need and put the case as well as the average educated person of the day could expect.[67] Of arguments 'to confirme the Deity', Thomas Nashe judged that 'In the *Resolution* most notably is thys tractate enlarged. He which peruseth that, & yet is *Diagoriz'd*, will never be Christianiz'd.'[68] Yet they formed a dubious part of the 'one sufficient direction for matters of life and spirit' as originally designed. If the 1582 *Resolution* was too 'vehement', a rhetorical exhortation rather than the first part of a comprehensive handbook of Catholic spirituality, *A Christian directorie* lacked the focus of 'principall reasons that ought to move a man to this resolution'.[69] By 1607 Persons was persuaded that he had allowed his conception of Book One's 'matter of discourse, knowledge, speculation, and consideration' to become too accommodating. 'To the studious reader' he wrote:

> I thought good to passe over this first Booke againe, and by *displacing certaine Chapters* which seemed to some not to be so necessary to the end heere proposed (but fitter to goe in some other worke of that argument a part) and by adding and altering divers other thinges, to reduce the bulk of this Booke to a very moderate bignesse, fit to joyne with the other two promised, when leasure and health shall yeeld commodity to finish them. . . . (my italics)[70]

The meditational 'method' was also cut, the entire text reviewed for minor verbal alterations and re-arrangement of material, and the Preface revised accordingly.

Allison and Rogers conclude that *The Christian directory* of 1607 represents the final authorial revision of the *Resolution*, and it is so reproduced in the facsimile series of English Recusant Literature.[71] Yet Persons would not give up his intention to complete the work. In

---

[67] See J.M. Stone, 'Atheism under Elizabeth and James I', *The Month*, 81 (May/August 1894): 174–87.

[68] See note 7 above; Nashe glosses, '*Diagoras primus Deos negans*'.

[69] *Resolution*, 'The Summarie of the Christian exercise, as it is intended'.

[70] *The Christian directory*, sig. §5v.

[71] ARCR II 620; *The Christian directory*, English Recusant Literature series 41 (Menston: Scholar Press, 1971).

1609, according to his secretary Edward Coffin, he decided to ignore an attack on his *Iudgment of a Catholicke English-man* (1608) 'and in lieu of refuting this answere to set forth the other two parts of Resolution, so long before promised by him'. In the event he was obliged to write his *Discussion of the answere of M. William Barlow*, and died in April 1610 before he could give undivided attention to the *Resolution*.[72] Nevertheless, significant changes appeared in the edition of 1622. The text generally follows that of 1607, but the meditational method is restored, as well as the two apologetic chapters, shortened to about one third of their previous length. This revision may be substantially the work of Thomas Fitzherbert, who saw *A discussion of the answere of M. William Barlow* through the press in 1612. Yet we cannot discount the possibility that Persons, realizing that he had no other obvious home for those admired chapters, decided to try to reintroduce them without disturbing the balance of the book. The abbreviation is certainly skilful. The explanation 'to the studious reader' was changed to:

> I thought good to passe over this first Booke agayne, and by *adding some necessary examples*, fitly applyed for the purpose, in divers places; and by altering some other things, to make the same fit to joyne with the other two promised, when leasure and health shall yield commodity to finish them. (my italics)

This accurately reflects the changes of 1622 but yields no clue to the authorship. The next edition, of 1633, reverts to what is effectively the 1607 text, and is similarly accompanied by minor alterations to the preliminary material: for example, the 'studious reader' now learns that the two apologetic chapters have been 'omitted' (1633) rather than 'displaced' (1607). The question whether the 1622 edition represents Persons's final intention thus remains open.

Sources and Influences

There has been much confusion about the nature of the *Resolution* and its indebtedness to previous authors. Helen C. White believed it was no more than a free translation of Loarte, although there are only localised traces of the *Esercitio della vita christiana* to be found in

---

[72] Edward Coffin, Preface to *A discussion of the answere of M. William Barlow* (1612; STC 19409); see ARCR II 626.

the *Resolution* of 1582.[73] Maria Hagedorn, followed by A.C. Southern, identified the Dominican Luis de Granada as the main source, but J.P. Driscoll dismissed the cases of apparent borrowing as mere coincidence.[74] John R. Roberts endorsed Driscoll's conclusion without pursuing the matter.[75] William T. Costello categorised the book as 'ascetical', grouping it with Richard Baxter's *Saints' Everlasting Rest* and Jeremy Taylor's *Holy Dying*, despite the fact that Persons offers little counsel on making a good end and mentions ascetic practices only in passing.[76]

The Book of Resolution is not a work of spirituality or devotion in the normally accepted sense, offering practical steps to holiness, directed prayer or mystical insights. Robert McNulty has claimed that it was 'something almost completely new in godly literature . . . a work aimed deliberately and with all Parsons' considerable powers of forceful eloquence at the crucial point in the process of salvation where the individual must resolve to serve God, to turn to Him and live in His ways rather than in the ways of the world'.[77] As McNulty's circumlocution itself suggests, the term 'resolution' as Persons uses it has no traditional gloss. It gives a specific application to the meaning defined by *OED* as 'the solving of a doubt or difficulty', viz. removing all uncertainty or reserve from one's commitment to God's service, and is closely associated with the idea of reducing a complex entity to a simpler state: what J.B. Leishman irreverently described (in relation to John Donne) as exchanging 'the complexity of a personality for the singleness and simplicity of a soul'.[78]

In Jesuit practice, this settled determination or 'new and happier orientation at the very core of [one's] being' was the fundamental aim of the first week of the *Christian Exercises*.[79] In a letter to Isabel

---

[73] *English Devotional Literature [Prose] 1600–1640* (Madison: University of Wisconsin Press, 1931), p. 144.

[74] Maria Hagedorn, *Reformation und Spanische Andachtsliteratur: Luis de Granada in England* (Leipzig: Bernhard Tauchnitz, 1934); A.C. Southern, *Elizabethan Recusant Prose 1559–1582* (London: Sands & Co., 1950), p. 186; J.P. Driscoll, 'The Supposed Source of Persons's "Christian Directory"', *Recusant History*, 5 (1959–60): 236–45.

[75] John R. Roberts, ed., *A Critical Anthology of English Recusant Devotional Prose* (Pittsburgh: Duquesne University Press, 1966), p. 71, n. 4.

[76] William T. Costello, introduction to *The Judgement of a Catholic Englishman* (1608), by Robert Persons (Gainesville, Flo.: Scholars Facsimiles & Reprints, 1957), p. vii.

[77] McNulty, pp. 272–73.

[78] J.B. Leishman, *The Monarch of Wit*, 5th ed. (London: Hutchinson University Library, 1962), p. 261.

[79] John W. O'Malley, *The First Jesuits*, p. 40.

Roser in 1532, Ignatius described it thus: 'deliberately chosen and ...
utterly resolved to engage themselves on behalf of God our Lord's
glory, honour and service.'[80] This was the effect Persons's book was
designed to duplicate, using continuous prose rather than directed
meditation. The *Resolution*, therefore, can best be described as a full
prose realization, the first in Europe, of the first week of *The Spiritual
Exercises*, incorporating and adapting to this purpose a wide range
of scriptural, patristic and modern materials, most notably from the
Guía de Pecadores (1556–67) by Luis de Granada. Of Ignatius' original
it has been said:

> [The book fails to entice because] it consists of interspersed pieces
> from different literary genres—directives, meditations, prayers, decla-
> rations, procedures, sage observations, and rules.... [T]he very diver-
> sity of genres at first glance suggests a scissors-and-paste composition.
> The book is not laid out in continuous discourse and lacks literary
> grace.[81]

Herein lies the value of Persons's fluent, coherent argument—no
doubt enhanced, as A.L. Rowse (ignoring Ignatius) suggests, by his
Oxford training[82]—elaborating the Ignatian themes of the purpose
of life, the nature of virtue and vice, judgement, death and hell, all
directed towards a radical and permanent inner change.[83] The process
of 'consideration' which Persons demands of his reader at the very
beginning is a readerly equivalent to the examination of conscience
required in the *Exercises*. In this way Persons is able to transmit the
mentality and approach of *The Spiritual Exercises* to readers who for
the most part did not have access to a Jesuit priest. The *Resolution*
is not, however, a handbook or guide to *The Spiritual Exercises*, and
the fact that its title was later changed to *A Christian directorie* should
not lead one to confuse it with other Jesuit directories which were
intended to assist priests in conducting the exercises.[84]

Once one has recognized that the *Resolution* approximates to the

---

[80] St Ignatius of Loyola, *Personal Writings*, ed. and tr. Joseph A. Munitiz and Philip
Endean (Harmondsworth: Penguin, 1996), p. 126.

[81] O'Malley, p. 37.

[82] A.L. Rowse, 'Father Parsons the Jesuit', in *Eminent Elizabethans* (London: Macmillan, 1983), pp. 41–74, esp. pp. 59–61.

[83] *The Spiritual Exercises of St Ignatius*, trans. Louis J. Puhl (Chicago: Loyola University
Press, 1951), paragraphs 23, 65, 71. See also Pierre Janelle, 'English Devotional
Literature in the Sixteenth and Seventeenth Centuries', in *English Studies Today*, 2d
series, ed. G.A. Bonnard (Bern: Francke Verlag, 1961), pp. 159–71.

[84] E.g. The *Directory of the Spiritual Exercises*, published in definitive form under the
auspices of Aquaviva in 1599. See Joseph de Guibert, *The Jesuits: Their Spiritual*

first week of the *Exercises*, its relationship to Gaspar de Loarte's *Esercitio* becomes clear. At the end of the first week the exercitant is expected to confirm the inner change by a formal general confession of the whole previous life of sin. This is the point at which Loarte begins, continuing with practical instructions for prayer and religious discipline. We have seen how Persons, originally planning a modest preface to Loarte, found himself writing extensively on the motives for resolution, quite independently of him. Instead, he turned for much of his detail to Luis de Granada, whose writings he would have encountered during his training in Rome before embarking on the English mission.[85] The first book of *The Sinner's Guide* consists of 'A full and ample exhortation to the pursuit of virtue', including reasons why man is bound to seek after virtue (part one), temporal and spiritual blessings in this life (part two) and answers to excuses (part three).[86] Similarly, the *Resolution*'s Part One deals with 'causes and reasons that should move a man to resolve hym selfe to the service of God', while Part Two covers Luis' second and third parts by showing in its first chapter that the virtuous life is blessed even if full of hardship, and then removing the 'impediments' to virtue.

Persons borrowed not only his general scheme, many of his chapter headings and sub-headings from Luis, but also dozens of illustrations and arguments, for the Dominican author had been highly successful in addressing the needs of a new audience of lay people.[87] John Mush, a contemporary anti-Jesuit catholic author, alleged that the *Resolution* 'woon him all the credit which was due to *Granada*, that laid the platforme to Father *Parsons* hand, and gaue him the principall grounds and matter thereof'.[88] It is impossible to maintain, with Driscoll, that these were only 'minor' borrowings. That

---

Doctrine and Practice, trans. W.J. Young (1964; rpt. St Louis: Institute of Jesuit Sources, 1986), pp. 243–47.

[85] De Guibert, p. 218.

[86] Luis de Granada, *Guía de Pecadores* (Salamanca, 1556/7, rev. edn 1567), trans. Francis Meres as *The sinners guide: a worke contayning the whole regiment of a Christian life* (London, 1598; STC 16918); modern translation (anon.), *The Sinner's Guide* (Philadelphia: Eugene Cummiskey, 1833; rpt. Dublin: James Duffy, 1856). His *Memorial de lo que debe hacer el cristiano* (Lisbon, 1561), trans. Richard Hopkins as *A memoriall of a Christian life* (Rouen, 1586), begins with a much shorter 'Exhortation to Good Life' from which Persons also borrowed some details.

[87] Alvaro Huerga, introduction to *Summa of the Christian Life: Selected Texts from the Writings of Venerable Louis of Granada, O.P.*, trans. Jordan Aumann, 3 vols. (St Louis/London: B. Herder Book Co., 1954).

[88] John Mush, *A dialogue betwixt a secular priest, and a lay gentleman* (Rheims, 1601; STC 25124), p. 107.

Persons was conscious of the suitability of Luis for English readers is clear from his association with translations of two other works of his, published in Rouen in 1584 and 1586.[89] Yet the *Resolution* is not a translation or close adaptation of *The Sinner's Guide*, for the argument is entirely recast to correspond with the first week of *The Spiritual Exercises*. Instead of beginning with the inherent goodness of God and his benefits, as Luis does, progressing methodically to the consideration of the 'four last things'—death, judgement, heaven and hell—, Persons develops his argument from the purpose of human life and man's accountability to God as his servant (chapters 3–4). This foregrounds final judgement as evidence of God's severity in calling us to account (chapter 5); his goodness and benefits are invoked afterwards (chapter 7) to justify that severity. Only then does Persons move on to death, hell and heaven (chapters 8–10). He further simplifies and unifies the structure of the book by subsuming the blessings of virtuous life under his removal of impediments: such blessings repudiate the excuse that virtue is too difficult (Part Two, chapter 1).

In order to impress on his readers the urgency of resolving to serve God truly, Persons adapts the method of applying the three powers of the soul (memory, understanding and will), ultimately derived from Augustine. Unlike Luis, he is not content to prove that man is 'bound' to follow virtue; he must move the affections. In his presentation of judgement, death, heaven and hell, for example, he proceeds from theological exposition (understanding) to vivid imaginative projection (memory) and concludes with powerful exhortation (will). This alters the familiar Ignatian sequence, which begins with memory,[90] but since the book is cast in the form of a continuous argument from chapter one to the end, consideration of the 'last things' has to be introduced logically rather than broken up into a series of detached meditations.

The influence of early Jesuit tradition is readily detectable. In accordance with the catechisms of Peter Canisius, just service is formally divided between shunning evil and doing good (Part One, chapter 4).

---

[89] *Of prayer, and meditation*, trans. Richard Hopkins (Rouen, 1584; STC 16908), and *A memoriall of a Christian life*, trans. Hopkins (Rouen, 1586; STC 16903). On Persons and the press of George L'Oyselet, who printed these two translations, see below, 'Printing History'.

[90] *The Spiritual Exercises of St Ignatius*, trans. Louis J. Puhl (Chicago: Loyola University Press, 1951), paragraphs 45–53 (The First Exercise of the First Week).

Persons strongly emphasises the consolations of the Christian life (Part Two, chapter 1), a recurring theme in early Jesuit ministry.[91] It would be a mistake, however, to regard the *Resolution* as narrowly Ignatian, for it draws heavily on the Augustinian and Bernardine traditions of spirituality whose influence was so widely dispersed during the Reformation. Lengthy translations from both authors are a feature of the second part, most notably the account of St Augustine's conversion, which is strategically placed as the climax of Part Two, chapter 1, 'Of the difficultie or hardnesse, whiche seemeth to many to be in vertuouse lyfe'. Since that narrative is the prototype for the act of resolution, its appearance exactly half way through the whole book is designed not only to illustrate the theme of the chapter, that passion can be overcome with less pain than one might imagine, but also to provide a model of diligence in examining one's vocation and using violence to execute the conversion. Appropriately, it is followed by St Bernard's discourse on the 'feigned labour' of virtue.

Thus Persons associates his plea for resolution with the acknowledged central core of Christian experience. Though clearly Ignatian in origin, 'resolution' as a subjective experience was open to appropriation by Protestants, and especially a Puritan like Edmund Bunny. Persons's earnestness, his unsparing subordination of all worldly things to the saving of souls, and his emphasis on the value of deep 'consideration' of man's estate as created for God's service have led critics to comment on the similarities between the Puritan and Jesuit programmes.[92] Moreover, his book is saturated with scriptural quotations and references. If it is true that the sixteenth century in England was 'not, by and large, an age of sermons or of interpretations of Scripture for any but controversial and polemical purposes',[93] Persons's skilful deployment of Biblical material to add force to his non-controversial but challenging prose is striking. Biblical language, in Latin, English translation or paraphrase is assimilated into the sentence structure, not to be dissected and expounded after the manner of Andrewes or Donne but to arouse wonder and awe or to

---

[91] See John W. O'Malley, *The First Jesuits*, pp. 123–25, on Canisius, and 82–84 on consolation.

[92] E.g. Elizabeth K. Hudson, 'The Catholic Challenge to Puritan Piety, 1580–1620', *Catholic Historical Review*, 77 (1991): 1–20, and Brad S. Gregory.

[93] Janel M. Mueller, introduction to *Donne's Prebend Sermons* (Cambridge, Mass.: Harvard University Press, 1971), p. 21; see also pp. 30–35.

command assent. The reader is in a sense intimidated by Scripture into accepting the inescapable and dreadful fact of accountability. It is no wonder that the book made such an impact.

The distinguishing characteristic of the *Resolution*, finally, is its rhetorical disposition. In concentrating the reader's mind on a single, crucial choice, Persons adopted the form of a deliberative oration—a speech designed to persuade the audience to a certain course of action—and extended it over sixteen chapters. The necessity of 'consideration' (chapters 1–2) acts as the exordium; the purpose of human life—to serve God (chapters 3–4)—is the proposition; the motives for serving God (chapters 5–10) provide the confirmation; and the removing of impediments (part two) serves as the refutation. These are approximations rather than formal divisions, and the correspondence is obscured somewhat by the internal structure of the chapters, each of which has a well-defined introduction and concluding appeal, but the basic rhetorical configuration survives. There is no superfluous material, nothing that does not contribute to the advance of the argument. Persons's lucid, vigorous prose style, which has attracted its admirers, was well suited to the purpose. He eschewed the conspicuous ornamentation and schematic parallelism of literary fashion, relying on clearly explained 'similitudes' drawn from war, commerce, travel and domestic life, many of them strikingly effective. There is little specialized vocabulary—a feature which made Bunny's task easier—except for some Latinisms derived from the Rheims New Testament project completed in the same year. In adopting this immediately accessible idiom Persons was following the example (and sometimes borrowing the instances) of Luis de Granada, but the emotional temperature is much higher, with repetitive devices and lengthy amplifications. Set pieces of highly-charged exhortations or imaginary scenes are frequent. Yet the argument carries weight, and Persons commands a wide range of tones: calmly reasonable, combative, imperious, satirical (when exposing the folly of those who make excuses) and compassionate.[94]

---

[94] See my article, 'The Polemical *Gravitas* of Robert Persons', *Recusant History*, 22 (1995): 291–305.

Printing History

The apparently tireless Robert Persons—called *polypragman*, or 'busy-body', 'Jack-of-all-trades' by his many enemies—supervised the publication and distribution of Roman Catholic propaganda both while he was on the mission in England and when he retired to Rouen. His first book, *A brief discours contayning certayne reasons why Catholiques refuse to goe to church* was secretly printed in December 1580 by his close associate Stephen Brinkley at the so-called 'Greenstreet House' press in East Ham, London. This had to be dismantled and hastily re-assembled in January at the house of Francis Browne in Southwark for the printing of *A brief censure vppon two bookes written in answere to M. Edmonde Campions offer of disputation* (STC 19393).[95] They next moved from London to Stonor Park near Henley-on-Thames in March 1581 to await the arrival of Edmund Campion from Lancashire with his *Rationes decem*. In the mean time they printed *A discouerie of I. Nichols minister* (STC 19402).[96] Campion duly arrived at Stonor in Whit-week; on 27 June the freshly-printed copies of his book were distributed on the benches of St Mary's, the university church of Oxford. When the dons arrived for the annual academic disputations, the *Rationes decem* caused a sensation.[97] Soon afterwards the press and the printer Brinkley were seized.

Deprived of his press and on the run himself, Persons quickly took steps to remedy the situation. Writing to the Rector of the English College in Rome soon after fleeing to Rouen, he gave as one of his reasons: 'to set up some sort of printing press in some place nearby where the books could be printed which are brought out by our fathers in English as circumstances call for them'.[98] He was able to replace Brinkley, now in the Tower of London, with 'a very pious and zealous merchant, named George Flinton',[99] for the printing of *De persecutione anglicana* (1581), *A defence of the Censure* (1582) and the *Resolution*.[100] His assistant, the lay brother Ralph Emerson, smuggled large numbers of these books into England.

---

[95] *Persons Letters*, p. 75, n. 9, and p. 76, n. 14. For details of 'Presses operating secretly in England', see ARCR II, p. 225.

[96] *Persons Letters*, p. 77, n. 18.

[97] E.E. Reynolds, *Campion and Parsons*, pp. 102–03.

[98] Persons to Agazzari, 21 Oct. 1581, *Persons Letters*, p. 107.

[99] *Persons Notes*, pp. 30–31.

[100] *De persecutione Anglicana, epistola* (Boulogne, *scil.* Rouen, 1581: ARCR I 874); *A*

A.C. Southern has argued, on the basis of the use of ornaments, that these books were actually printed for Persons by George L'Oyselet, who produced several English Catholic books during the 1580s, including a reprint of the *Resolution* in 1584.[101] Allison and Rogers suggest, instead, that the ornaments in question could have been borrowed, especially while Flinton was establishing his press.[102] Comparison of several books printed by L'Oyselet with those normally attributed to 'Father Persons' Press' shows that the decorative initials in common are chiefly those of a fairly common metal-cast intaglio set.[103] The only identical woodcut initial is an M (distinguished by a break in the right descender), appearing on sig. Ll2r of the 1582 *Resolution*, A7v of the *Defence of the Censure*, and O4v of L'Oyselet's 1584 *Resolution*. There are a very few woodcut initials of different letters but similar decoration, for instance the N (*Resolution*, sig. I9r) and the B (L'Oyselet's *Memoriall of a Christian life*, sig. T4v), both with a stippled background. There is also is a horizontal rectangular woodblock which appears twice in L'Oyselet's *Of prayer, and meditation* (sig. A2r, 3C2r) and corresponds to the lower panel of the title-page compartment of the *Resolution*. This shows a seated winged figure surrounded by cornucopiae and rabbits in a garden, possibly representing the presence of God in the garden of Eden and thus more suitable to a book of meditation than the *Resolution*. Differences in detail, however, indicate that they are impressions of different woodcuts from the same design, likely enough in the case of two printers in the same town. Nor is there any paper in common. The compilers of the *Short-title Catalogue, 1475–1640* conclude: 'Although at least some of the printing material belonged to George Loyselet, the items below were apparently produced at a separate press by George Flinton, later joined by Stephen Brinkley, both of whom were aides to Robert Parsons'.[104]

defence of the Censure, gyuen vpon two bookes of William Charke and Meredith Hanmer mynysters (Rouen, 1582; STC 19401).

[101] A.C. Southern, *English Recusant Prose 1559–82*, pp. 359–63.

[102] A.F. Allison and D.M. Rogers, review of *Elizabethan Recusant Prose 1559–1582*, *The Library*, 5th series, 5 (1951): 48–57.

[103] Titles examined: *Of prayer, and meditation*, by Luis de Granada, trans. Richard Hopkins (1584; STC 16908); *The firste booke of the Christian exercise*, by Robert Persons (1584; STC 19354); *A memoriall of a Christian life*, by Luis de Granada, trans. Richard Hopkins (1586: STC 16903); *Du droict et tiltre de la Serenissime Princesse Marie Royne d'Escosse . . . à la succession du Royaume d'Angleterre*, by John Leslie (1587; ARCR I 724).

[104] STC, 3: 132 *sub* 'Fr. Parsons' Press'.

The evidence of L'Oyselet's 1584 reprint of the *Resolution* supports this conclusion. Persons described it in his Preface to *A Christian directorie*:

> I was enformed of two other editions come forth . . . without my knowledge, the one by a Catholique (as it seemeth) who perceiving al copies of the former print to be spent; for satisfying of them that desired the booke, procured the same to be set forth againe, albeit somewhat incorrected, and very disorderly, not having the consent or advise of such, as therin should have geven him best direction. (fol. 5r)

It was, in fact, a fairly accurate reprint, but in black letter, which for the most part Persons avoided. The term 'procured' suggests that L'Oyselet had no copy for the work. More forthrightly, Persons complained to Aquaviva that 'a certain barber in Rouen has seen to a reprinting of the same book without my knowledge and solely for profit. In many ways he has falsified the book.'[105] One must ask why, if L'Oyselet had printed the first edition of the *Resolution*, his reprint should have drawn such criticism. No previous collaboration over the *Resolution* is hinted at in these references, although they do not preclude the possibility that Flinton borrowed or bought materials from L'Oyselet. Another of L'Oyselet's productions in 1584 was also a reprint of a work in which Persons had an interest: Hopkins's translation, first printed in Paris, of Luis de Granada's *Of prayer, and meditation*. Persons claimed to have seen to the translations of Luis de Granada,[106] so he may subsequently have decided to entrust the next one to L'Oyselet directly. At all events, L'Oyselet was the first to print *A memoriall of a Christian life* (1586).

There seems little reason, then, to question Persons's later report (referring to himself in the third person) that 'the heretics saw . . . an abundance of good books, both devotional as well as controversial, from the printing press that Persons had established in France for that purpose'.[107] He seems always to have taken a personal interest in printing matters. At Stonor Park in March 1581, for example, when *The discouerie of I. Nichols* was in press, he hastily added some new material '[t]hat the pages folowinge shoulde not be emptie' (sig.

---

[105] See note 42 above.
[106] '*Traduci curavi multa ex Granatensi Loarte et aliis.*' Persons to Aquaviva, 21 Oct. 1581, ARSI FG 651, *ad finem*; this passage is not in the version of the letter in *Persons Letters*, pp. 91–115.
[107] *Persons Notes*, p. 129.

M7v). Presumably he was the one to ensure, now, that the appearance of the *Resolution* effectively disguised its origins. Unlike many other Catholic English books of the time, including those printed by L'Oyselet, it lacks any characteristically Catholic or Jesuit devices and ornaments. The title-page compartment is striking but neutral, and the words 'with privylege' are presumably meant to allay suspicion. It was, therefore, eminently suitable to be smuggled by daring Catholic youths into the stalls of unsuspecting booksellers in London, and so find its way into the hands of browsers. In this way, according to Persons himself, the entire first edition of 2500 copies was dispersed.[108]

The *Resolution* as printed in 1582 was not, however, altogether satisfactory: reviewing it, Persons decided that *A Christian directorie* 'should passe forth in better print, paper, and character, then the former did, (wherin by some errour, as also by difficultie of the time, greate defect was found;)'.[109] This probably refers to the difficulty he had had with the letter *w*: for most of the book the compositor(s) opted for *vv* or made do with an outsize *w*. Only on sig. Q2r was a suitably sized *w* introduced.[110] From the pattern of *w* and *vv* it appears that the book was composed *seriatim*, for the predominance of one or the other continues over several consecutive pages rather than being confined to an inner or outer forme. The ten signatures E to O alternate regularly between signatures where *w* is used almost exclusively (signatures E, G, I, L, N) and those where a few pages of predominantly *vv* intrude (F, H, K, M, O). The transitions from *w* to *vv* or vice versa are gradual and usually begin mid-page. This suggests that the type was normally distributed after both formes of a signature were worked off. The compositor would begin the next signature, composing *seriatim*, while the previous signature was being printed, using *w* until the stock ran low, when he would switch to *vv* for a while until more type was made available by distribution.

These are signs of a makeshift operation. When Persons returned to Rouen in the autumn of 1584 to revise the book, conditions were more favourable. He now enjoyed once more the services of Stephen Brinkley, released from the Tower the previous year.[111] Together

---

[108] See note 42 above.
[109] Preface to *A Christian directorie*, fol. 4v.
[110] A.C. Southern, *English Recusant Prose*, p. 362.
[111] *Persons Notes*, pp. 120–21.

with Flinton they retreated to 'a voyde house given to the Society in a garden' and presumably there set up their press.[112] Despite the interruption of the printing of *A Christian directorie* and the appropriation of margins and preface to lambast Bunny, the result was a more handsome volume than the *Resolution*: the type face is larger (71 mm per 20 lines instead of 67/8), there is a plethora of rules and type ornaments separating chapters and sub-divisions, and although the initial ornaments are once again a miscellany of woodcut and metalcast, the woodcuts are large and eye-catching. The format is again duodecimo, but gathered, unusually, in 8s and 4s. The title-page is more informative and pugnacious, obviously entering into the battle for men's souls: it advertises the intended three books, the improvements made, the 'reprofe of the corrupt and falsified edition' of Edmund Bunny, the addition of two tables and a preface 'necessarie to be reade'. Where the title-page epigraph of the *Resolution* invited its readers to share in a single-minded desire to dwell forever in the house of the Lord and do his will, *A Christian directorie* asks pointedly, 'You children of men why love you vanitie' and declares 'But one thing is necessarie'.

After Persons left Rouen a few months later in 1585, Antwerp became the centre for the printing and distribution of his works. His printer there was Arnout Conincx, who produced seven English books for him between 1592 and 1602. He then turned to St Omer as an even better base of cross-channel operations, using as printer François Bellet for several books, including the revised *Christian directory* of 1607. Copies of this edition were seized at the house of the Venetian ambassador in London in July 1609.[113] Evidently Persons was still taking a deep interest in the printing itself, for he sent his secretary, the secular priest John Wilson, from Rome to St Omer to establish the English College Press. This became the most productive of the recusant presses from 1608 to 1640, printing several of Persons's own works.[114]

---

[112] *Letters and Memorials of Cardinal Allen*, ed. T.F. Knox (London: David Nutt, 1882), p. 222n, cited by Southern, p. 362 and Allison and Rogers, art. cit. (note 102 above).

[113] ARCR II 620.

[114] See the list in ARCR II, p. 221. For the foundation of the college and the printing press, see A.C.F. Beales, *Education under Penalty: English Catholic Education from the Reformation to the Fall of James II, 1547–1689* (London: University of London Athlone Press, 1963), and Hubert Chadwick, *St Omers to Stonyhurst* (London: Burns & Oates, 1962).

The competitive language of the book trade on the title-page of *A Christian directorie* of 1585 probably reflects the scramble for Bunny's version that was then exciting the printers and publishers in London. Bunny entrusted his book to the bookseller John Wight, in whose name it was entered in the Stationers' Register on 28th August, 1584. The printers were a newly-formed syndicate often referred to as the Eliot's Court Press: Nynian Newton and Arnold Hatfield (identified on the title-page), John Jackson and Edmund Bollifant. This was their first combined production, and they chose an octavo format. There appeared in the same year a duodecimo edition at Middelburg in the Netherlands, presumably intended to compete with the original *Resolution* among English exiles in the Low Countries. The Eliot's Court Press reprinted their octavo three times in 1585, but their good fortune was soon under threat. As Edmund Bollifant put it in a memorial to the Privy Council, dated 'winter of 1585–6':

> where a booke called *the Resolution* . . . was entred in our hall boke [i.e. the Stationers' Register] to be the Copye of JOHN WIGHTE Bookseller, vppon condicion that we your poore Orators . . . shoulde be the onelye woorkemen thereof; which beinge the moste vendible Copye that happened in our Companie theis manie yeeres, woulde haue kepte vs in worke for a longe tyme: But to our greate preiudice and hindraunce . . . JOSEPH BARNES Prynter at Oxford ymmediatelye printed one ympression of the saide booke; Notwithstandinge ye said JOHN WIGHTE for reverence and good will to the vniuersitye then sente his sonne to Oxford, to buye the saide ympression of the said BARNES, and paide him readye monney for yt to his contentement: Wherevppon the saide BARNES made faithfull promise yat he would henceforthe never reprinte the same booke: And yett notwithstandinge the said WIGHTES curteous dealinge the saide BARNES beinge furnished with monney by him, forthwith ymprinted twoe ympressions more, contrarye to all honestye and reason, and contrarye to his faithe and promise: which others perceyuinge to passe without Controlment, printed alsoe ye said booke to our great hindrance, and thereby disfurnished vs of woorke for the moste parte euer since.[115]

The appeal failed, possibly because of Barnes's privileged position as the University printer. The very fact that Wight tried to buy him off rather than resort immediately to law suggests that he put little confidence in the protection of the Company. Yet the circumstances

---

[115] E. Arber, *Transcript of the Registers of the Company of Stationers of London, 1554–1640*, 5 vols. (London, 1875–91), 2: 793–94.

are mysterious. The compilers of the *Short-title Catalogue* claim, without providing any evidence, that the Oxford editions were probably forgeries. The standard histories of the Oxford University Press shed no light on the matter except to note vaguely that there was some conflict between Barnes and the London book trade.[116] The question of forgery is confused by the fact that Barnes's two octavo editions bear a close resemblance to those of the Eliot's Court Press, using similar factotum initials. This may give the impression that Bollifant and his partners forged the 'Oxford' editions in order to stimulate sales. But H.R. Plomer, illustrating these factotums, comments that they 'were very probably stock patterns, as they are found in numerous printing offices'. In any case, the printing materials of the Eliot's Court Press, including these factotums, were taken over from Henry Bynneman after his death in December 1583, not long before Joseph Barnes set up his press in Oxford, so it would not be surprising if he obtained similar materials.[117] Several other books unquestionably printed by Barnes exhibit the same factotums.[118]

Whether or not Barnes was as much the villain of the piece as Bollifant's memorial suggests, he quickly recognized, after printing two octavo editions, that the duodecimo was the ideal format for the book, and flooded the market with no fewer than seven editions, each completely reset. Presumably he did not have enough type to keep the book standing in print. John Windet followed suit, printing one duodecimo edition in 1585 and another in 1586. Meanwhile, two more octavo editions appeared in 1585 under the imprint of Thomas Dawson.

Even given that the London print runs were considerably smaller than Persons's on the continent (750/1000 against 2500 or more), 1585 was the *annus mirabilis* of the *Resolution*. After that the Bunny version remained more or less within the Wight family, passing to Thomas Wight from 1594 until 1602, and then to Edmund and

---

[116] F. Madan, *Oxford Books: A Bibliography of Printed Works Relating to the University and City of Oxford or Printed or Published There*, 3 vols. (Oxford: Clarendon Press, 1895–1931), 1: 16–17; H. Carter, *A History of the Oxford University Press: Vol. 1: To the year 1780* (Oxford: Clarendon Press, 1975).

[117] H.R. Plomer, 'Eliot's Court Press: Decorative Blocks and Initials', *The Library*, 4th series, 3 (1922/3): 194–209, esp. p. 208, and figures 30 and 32. See also his 'The Eliot's Court Printing House, 1584–1674', *The Library*, 4th series, 2 (1921/2): 175–84.

[118] E.g. John Case, *Speculum moralium quaestionum in uniuersam ethicen Aristotelis* (1585: STC 4759).

Thomas Weaver. The printers were generally Bollifant and his partners, but a new name enters the story in 1589, when John Charlewood
printed an octavo edition. He had been branded a 'popish printer'
in one of the Marprelate tracts for allegedly printing Robert Southwell's
Epistle of comfort in 1587, but this was probably a wild charge based
on the fact that he had once used the title 'printer to the right honourable Earl of Arundel'.[119] Whatever the case, this was the second
time he was involved with a book that offended Persons, for in 1581
he had printed *The oration and sermon made at Rome . . . the xxviij day of
Maie 1578*, by the John Nichols whom Persons immediately proceeded to 'discover' (see 'Authorship of the *Resolution*', above).

Again, it was Charlewood who printed the first edition of a second Protestant adaptation of Persons. The latter's ruthless attack on
Bunny did not deter others from pirating the fresh material added
in 1585, which offered an outstanding publishing opportunity, for
the readers of the *Resolution* were expecting a continuation.[120] An
anonymous imitator of Bunny gathered three of the entirely new
chapters and three expanded chapters, adapted them and brought
them out in 1590 as *The seconde parte of the booke of Christian exercise,
appertayning to Resolution. Or a Christian directorie, guiding all men to their
saluation*, printed by Charlewood for Simon Waterson.[121] From then
until 1640 Waterson's various printers (including Jaggard) kept pace
with new editions of Bunny's *Resolution*, so that the two parts could
be bound together. There were five duodecimo editions of Bunny
and six of the 'Second Part' from 1591–1602;[122] six duodecimo editions of each between 1607 and 1633. Finally, in 1640 appeared the
first edition of Bunny to be published by Waterson, who advertised
on the title-page that '[b]oth parts [were] joyned together'.

Caveat emptor. The 'Second Part' bound with the 1640 Bunny turned
out in practice to be an unsold copy of the edition of 1631 or 1633.

---

[119] See James H. McDonald and Nancy Pollard Brown, introduction to *The Poems
of Robert Southwell, S.J.* (Oxford: Clarendon Press, 1967), pp. xxvi–xxvii.

[120] See *Resolution*, 'An Aduertisement to the Reader'.

[121] *The seconde parte of the Booke of Christian exercise, appertayning to Resolution* (London,
1590; STC 19380; several times reprinted). See J.P. Driscoll, S.J., '*The Seconde Parte*:
Another Protestant Version of Robert Persons' *Christian Directorie*', *Huntington Library
Quarterly*, 25 (1962): 139–46. The contents are: 1. Of inconsideration; 2. That there
is a God; 3. Why man was created; 4. Proofs of Christianity; 5. Who is a true
Christian; 6. Of despair of God's mercy.

[122] An octavo was printed for Wight in 1599, but in the previous year P. Short
had printed a duodecimo for F. Kyngston, who himself took over the printing of
the *Resolution* for Weaver in 1607.

Many different books in late Elizabethan England might be called the Resolution: there was little to distinguish the enlarged *Christian directorie* from the combined protestant version; both were thick duodecimo volumes and contained a similar bulk of writing. But whereas one consisted of two parts as planned by Persons with the new chapters inserted, the other had the two parts corresponding to the 1582 *Resolution*, followed by another second part containing most of the additional chapters. The modern reader who finds a reference to the *Resolution* will also need to be alert.

Bibliographical Description

Extended bibliographical description is given for all editions of the *Resolution* until 1622 (the final revision); this is followed by a list of all editions until 1700. The first edition of Bunny's adaptation is fully described, followed by a list of reprints up to 1640, including the adaptation of the so-called 'second part'.

THE CATHOLIC TRADITION

1582 *The first booke of the Christian exercise, appertayning to resolution*

[within a compartment: 105 × 65 enclosing 77 × 45: head enclosed in flowing headdress above, seated winged figure, also with headdress, below, in a garden flanked on each side by an outward-facing rabbit and a cornucopia; a scroll supporting an urn in left and right corners above, a lobster outside a scroll in left and right corners below; an inward-facing mage with book just above centre left and right.] **THE FIRST BOOKE OF** ¦ THE CHRISTIAN EXER- ¦ ci∫e, appertayning to re- ¦ ∫olution. ¦ [blank] ¦ VVherein are layed downe the ¦ cau∫es & rea∫ons that ∫hould moue ¦ a man to re∫olue hym selfe to the ¦ ∫eruice of God: And all the impe- ¦ dimentes remoued, which may lett ¦ the ∫ame. ¦ P∫al. 62. ver∫. 4. ¦ *Vnam petii a domino, hanc requiram:* ¦ *vt inhahitem in domo domini omni-* ¦ *bus diebus vitæ meæ: vt videam vo-* ¦ *luntatem domini.* ¦ [blank] ¦ One thing haue I reque∫ted at¦gods hãndes, & that will I demaunde ¦ ∫tille: which is, to dwell in his hou∫e ¦ all the daies of my life: to the ende, ¦ I maye knowe and doe his vvill. ¦ [outside the compartment] *Anno.* 1582. ¦ VVITH PRIVYLEGE. ¦ [signed] A

[Rouen: Father Persons' Press]

Coll.: 12° (435 × 360, crown): A⁶ B–T¹² [$5 (–C4, F2, G3; +B6, B7) signed]; 222 leaves, pp. [*12*] 1–431 *432*.

RT] THE CHRISTIAN EXERCISE [EXERSISE L1, NPR2, D5, F6, H8, BS9, I10, G12; AXERCISE B11; CHRITIAN L2, C3, R5, E6, IMT7, P9; CRISTIAN F2, H6, DN7, K11, IM12; THEH CRISTIAN H11; EXRECISE M3; CRITIAN O4]

Type: 34 ll. with marginal nn. (D12), 114 (122) × 57 (69); text, ordinary Garamond-derived roman (and some italic) 67/8 mm for 20 ll.; advertisement italic 81 mm (A2); headline as text with small caps. Outsize *w* used almost exclusively in signatures E, G, I, L, N; *vv* used for passages of two to four pages in signatures B, C, D, F, H, K, M, O, P with outsize *w* elsewhere in these signatures; introduction of right size *w* and disuse of outsize *w* occurs gradually from 2r to 4r in signature Q; right size *w* and *vv* used in signatures R, S, T and A.

Contents: A1r title; A1v Summarie; A2 Aduertisement to the reader; A3–6 Contentes; B1r–3r (pp. 1–5) [Preface] to the Cristian reader towchinge two editions of this booke; B3v–5r (pp. 6–9) Induction to the three bookes followinge; B5v blank; B6r–I8v (pp. 15–184) Part 1 chapters 1–10; I9r–T12r (pp. 185–431) Part 2 chapters 1–6; T12v blank.

Copies: Bodleian Library (Mar. 392); British Library (C.111 f.11); Huntington Library (microfilm: Films STC 347).

Notes: STC 19353; ARCR II 616. The preface 'to the Cristian reader towchinge two editions of this booke' (sig. B) reflects an earlier intention (of reprinting *The exercise of a Christian life* by Gaspar Loarte in expanded form) than the 'aduertisement to the reader' (sig. A).

1584   *The first booke of the Christian exercise, appertayning to resolution*

[within a frame of printer's flowers: 112 × 64 enclosing 100 × 52] **THE FIRST BOOKE** ǀ OF THE CHRISTIANǀ exerciſe, appertayning to ǀ reſolution. ǀ [blank] ǀ Corrected and newlye Imprinted. ǀ Anno 1584. ǀ [blank] ǀ [Gothic] Wherein are layed down the ǀ cauſes and reaſons that ſhould ǀ moue a man to reſolue him ſelfe ǀ to the ſeruice of God: And all ǀ the impedimentes remoued, ǀ which may let the ſame. [Gothic ends] ǀ [blank] ǀ *Psal.* 62. *verſ.* 4. ǀ Vnam petij a domino, hanc requi- ǀ ram: vt inhabitem in domo domini om- ǀ nibus diebus vitæ meæ: vt videam vo- ǀ luntatem domini. ǀ [blank] ǀ [Gothic] One thinge haue I requeſted at gods handes, and that will I ǀ demaunde ſtill: which is, to ǀ dwell in his houſe all the dayes ǀ of my lyfe: to the ende, I maye ǀ knowe and doe his will. [Gothic ends] ǀ WIHT PRIVYLEGE. ǀ

[Rouen: George L'Oyselet.]

Coll.: 12° (450 × 320): A–2A¹² [$5 (–A1, B4, F3, G2, L4, N5, O4, P2, P3) signed; H4 as I4, K3 as K2, M5 as M3]; 288 leaves, pp. [*24*] 1–547 *548–52*.

Type: 32 ll. with marginal nn. (L6v), 114 (121) × 55 (68); text, black letter 71 mm for 20 ll.; some roman in text 65 mm for 20 ll.; roman for chapter headings 80 mm for 20 ll.; headline as text, chiefly roman.

Copy: British Library (C.111 f.8).

Notes: STC 19354, ARCR II 617. The text is an unauthorized, uncorrected black-letter reprint. Contents as in 1582, except that the 'Summarie' is displaced to the end (see note on sig. A7r).

1585   *A Christian directorie guiding men to their saluation*

A CHRISTIAN ǀ **DIRECTORIE** ǀ **GVIDING MEN TO** ǀ THEIR SALVATION. ǀ [blank] ǀ DEVIDED INTO THREE BOOKES ǁ *THE* firſt *wherof apperteining to* Reſolu- ǀ tion, *is only conteined in this volume, deui-* ǀ *ded into tvvo partes, and* ſet *forth novv* ǀ *againe vvith many corrections, and ad-* ǀ *ditions by th'Authour him* *ſelf, vvith re-* | *profe of the corrupt and falſified edition* | *of the ſame booke lately publiſhed by M.* | *Edm. Buny.* | THER is added alſo a methode for the vſe | of al; with two tables, and a prefa- | ce to the Reader, which is ne- | ceſſarie to be reade. | [blank] | Pſal. 4. v. 3 ‖ [blank] | *Filij hominum vt quid diligitis vanitatem.* | You children of men why loue you vanitie. | [blank] | Luc. I. v. 22 ‖ [blank] *Porró vnum est neceſſarium.* | But one thing is neceſſarie ‖ ANNO. 1585. AVUGVSTI. 30.

[Rouen: Father Persons' Press]

Coll.: 12° (8s and 4s: 495 × 372): a⁸b⁴ c⁸d⁴ A⁸B⁴–Yy⁸Zz⁴ AA⁸BB⁴–ZZ⁸AAA⁴ BBB⁸CCC⁴ DDD–EEE⁸ FFF⁴ [$3 (–Xx3, EEE2, FFF3 + $4 in all 8s) signed; a3–a5 as a2–a4, OO1 as Oo, ZZ1 as Zz]; 476 leaves, ff. 1–24, pp. 1–883 *884–904*.

RT] THE PREFACE TOGETHER WITH | CERTAINE INSTRVCTIONS a4v–d4r [THE PRE. TOGE. WITH CER. INST. d4v] CHRIST. DIRECT. LIB. I. A2v–EEE1v [CHRIST-IAN DIRECTORIE. LIB. I. A1v] A BREEF METHODE | FOR THE VSE OF THINGS EEE3v–FFF1v [A BREEF MET. FOR THE VSE OF THINGS EEE2v] THE TABLE FFF2r–FFF4v.

Type: 35 ll. with marginal nn. (Ee1), 124 (131) × 59 (73); text, ordinary Garamond-derived roman (and some italic) 71 mm for 20 ll.; headline as text with small caps and italics; preface roman 67 mm (b3); table of contents italic 84 mm (a2v); index roman 49 mm (FFF2v).

Contents: a1r title; a1v blank; a2r–3v (ff. 2–3) Table of contents; a4r–d4v (ff. 4–23) Preface containing the causes and reasons of this new edition; A1r–Vv8v (pp. 1–520) Part 1 chapters 1–12; Xx1 Preface to Part 2; Xx2r–EEE2r (pp. 523–883) Part 2 chapters 1–8; EEE2v–FFF2r A breefe methode how to use the former treatises; on FFF2r–FFF4v A table of the principal matters handled in this booke.

Copies: Bodleian Library (Th. 8° P 145), British Library (C.111 f.5), Yale University Library (microfilm: Films STC 1149).

Notes: STC 19354.1, ARCR II 618. The second edition, a major revision and expansion, adding four completely new

chapters (Part 1 chapters 2 and 4, Part 2 chapters 1 and 5).
A note is inserted on sig. Dd5v, at the end of part 1, chapter 5, signalling Persons's intention of noting some of Bunny's
'infinite corruptions, maymes, and manglings' in the margins
thereafter. These marginal notes begin in the next signature (Ee) and are supplemented by an extended attack on
Bunny's procedure in the Preface.

1598 *A Christian directorie guiding men to their saluation*

A CHRISTIAN ¦ **DIRECTORIE** ¦ GVIDING MEN TO ¦
THEIR SALVATION ¦ [blank] ¦ DEVIDED INTO THREE
BOORES. ¦ *THE firſt whereof apperteining to Reſolution, is* ¦ *only
conteyned in this volume, deuided into tvvo* ¦ *partes, and ſet forth novv
again vvith many cor-* ¦ *rections, and additions by th'Athour him ſelf,
vvith* ¦ *reprofe of the corrupt and falſified edition of the* ¦ *ſame booke lately
publiſhed by M. Edmu. Buny.* ¦ [blank] ¦ [double rule enclosing
horizontal ladder design] ¦ [blank] ¦ THER is added alſo a
methòde for the vſe of al; ¦ vvith tvvo tables, and a preface
to the Reader, ¦ vvhich is neceſſarie to be reade. ¦ [blank] ¦ pſal.
4. v. 3. ¦ *Filij hominum vt quid diligitis vanitatem.* ¦ You children
of men why loue you vanitie. ¦ [blank] ¦ Luc. I. v. 22. ¦ *Porro
vnum eſt neceſſarium.* ¦ But one thing is neceſſarie. ¦ [blank] ¦ AT
LOVAN, ¦ Imprinted by Laurence Kellam, ¦ cum priuilegio.
1598. ¦

Coll.: 8° (380 × 310): *⁴ a–b⁸ A–2Z⁸ [$4 (–*1, *2, F4,
+A–F5, I5, K5, M5) signed; B5 as A5, G5 as E5, K3 as
I3, R3 as R5, 2E3 as 2E2, 2Q3 as 2Q4; *3, *4 as *]; 388
leaves, ff. *1*–20, pp. *1*–719, *720–46* (pp. 718 and 719 cross-
paginated).

Copies: Bodleian Library (Antiq. f. N.1598.1: made up from two
imperfect copies), British Library (C.111 f.1), Huntington
Library (microfilm: Films STC 347).

Notes: STC 19354.3 (formerly 19368), ARCR II 619. The
third edition, an exact reprint of the 1585 text, including
references in the Preface to better paper, etc., and the last-
minute marginal references to Bunny. Contents as in 1585.
British Library copy has extensive MS. annotations to Part
One chapters 2 and 4 (added in 1585).

1607 *The Christian directory guiding men to eternall saluation*

THE | **CHRISTIAN** | DIRECTORY | Guiding men to eter-
nall ſaluation, | [blank] | *Deuided into three Bookes.* | [blank] | The
FIRST vvherof teacheth hovv to makeſa good Reſolution.
The SECOND, hovv | to begin vvell. The THIRD, hovv to
per- | ſeuere and end happily. | [blank] | *In this volume is onely
contayned the first Booke,* | *conſiſting of tvvo Partes, vvherof the former
lay-* | *eth dovvne the motiues to Reſolution; and the other* | *remoueth
the impedimentes: both of them hauing* | *byn lately reuievved, corrected,
and not a little al-* | *tered by the Author himſelfe, for the greater com-* |
modity and vtility of the Reader. | [blank] | *Matth.* 16. *verſ.* 26 |
What auaileth it a man if he could gaine the | whole world
by looſing his ſoule? Or what ex- | change will a man giue
for his owne ſoule? | [blank] | One thing is neceſſary. *Luc.* 10.
v. 42 | [blank] | [horizontal fleuron] | [vertical leaf] | [blank]
| *Superiorum permissu.* 1607. |

[St Omer: François Bellet]

Coll.: 12° (450 × 370): §¹² *⁸ **⁸ ***⁶ A–2C¹² 2D–2G⁸ 2H⁶
[$5 (–§1, ***5) signed; §3–6 as §2–5]; 384 leaves, pp. [*68*]
1–684 *685–700*.

Contents: §1 blank; §2r title; §2v The particular contents [i.e.
summary] of the three designed bookes; §3r (signed §2r)
–7v [Epistle] to the studious reader; §8r–12r Table of chapters; §12v IHS ornament; *1r–***6r Preface [of 1585 somewhat altered]; *6v blank; A1–N6v (pp. 1–299) Part 1 chapters
1–10; N7r title of Second part; N7v blank; N8 Argument;
N9r–2G6v (pp. 305–684) Part 2 chapters 1–8; 2G7r–2H6v
Table of particular matters.

Copies: British Library (C.111 f.6), Heythrop College (BQ
7095.C4 PER 1607); personal copy of D.M. Rogers (facsimile reprint in English Recusant Literature series, ed.
D.M. Rogers, no. 41, Menston, Yorkshire: Scholar Press, 1970).

Notes: STC 19354.5, ARCR II 620. The fourth edition, abbreviating the 1585/1598 text by the omission of two chapters in Part 1 and the meditative 'method', and incorporating
numerous verbal revisions. Possibly the final authorial revision, but see 1622 text below.

1620 *A Christian directory guiding men to eternall saluation, commonly called the Resolution*

[St Omer: English College Press + François Bellet]

Copy: The Heythrop College copy (BQ 7095.C4 PER 1620), the only one listed in ARCR II and STC, has gone missing, but the catalogue card confirms the change of title page from 1607, including the identification of Persons as author.

Notes: STC 19354.6, ARCR II 621. The fifth edition, a re-issue of the 1607 text printed by Bellet, with a new title page printed by the English College Press.

1622 *A Christian directory guiding men to eternall saluation: commonly called the Resolution*

A⎪**CHRISTIAN** ⎪ **DIRECTORY,** ⎪ Guiding men to Eternall Saluation: com- ⎪ monly called the RESOLVTION. ⎪ [blank] ⎪ *Deuided into three Bookes.* ⎪ [blank] ⎪ The firſt wherof, teach-eth how to make ⎪ a good Reſolution. The ſecond, how ⎪ to begin well. The third, how to per- ⎪ ſeuere, and end hap-pily. ⎪ [blank] ⎪ WRITTEN ⎪ [blank] ⎪ *By the R. Father* ROBERT PERSONS, ⎪ *Priest of the Society of IESVS.* ⎪ [blank] ⎪ The Sixt, and laſt Edition. ⎪ [IHS ornament] ⎪ One thing is neceſſary. *Luc.* 10. verſ. 41. ⎪ Permiſſu Superiorum, M.DC. XXII. ⎪

[St Omer: English College Press]

Coll.: 12° in 6s (448 × 320): §⁶ §§⁶ A–3Y⁶ [$4 (–§1, S4, 2E3, 2H3, 3Y3, 3Y4, + 2L5 as 2L4) signed, 2E4 as 2E3, 3V2 as 2V2]; 420 leaves, pp. [24] 1–517 528–826.

Contents: §1r title; §1v blank; §2r Aduertisement [material from 1607 title page]; §2v Particuler contents; §3r–§§2r [Epistle] to the studious reader; §§2v–§§6v Table of chapters; A1–2N6v (pp. 1–432) Part 1 chapters 1–12; 2O1 Argument of Part 2; 2O2r–3Y3r (pp. 435–819) Part 2 chapters 1–8; 3Y3v–3Y6v (pp. 820–826) A briefe methode.

Copies: Bodleian Library (Antiq. f. F.1622.1), British Library (C.111 f.10), Cambridge University Library (microfilm: Films STC 1492), Heythrop College (BQ 7095.C4 PER 1622).

Notes: STC 19354.7, ARCR II 622. The sixth edition, revised either by the author (who died in 1610) or a close associate, e.g Thomas Fitzherbert. The two chapters omitted in 1607 are restored but abbreviated, and there are some verbal revisions. The preface is omitted entirely, but the 'method' restored. The Heythrop College copy also contains a MS. abbreviation of the 'method'.

1633   *The Christian directory, guiding men to eternall saluation. . . . The seauenth, and last Edition*

[St Omer: English College Press]

Copies: British Library (C.111 f.9): copy owned by Henry Francis Lyte; Cambridge University Library (microfilm: Films STC 1458).

Notes: STC 19354.9, ARCR II 623. Follows 1607 text, omitting the two chapters restored in 1622, and abbreviating the 1607 preface.

1650   *A Christian directory, guiding men to eternall salvation, commonly called the Resolution*

[Antwerp]

Copies: Bodleian Library (Vet. B3 f. 294), British Library (852.F.3).

Notes: Wing P563. The text and preface follow 1607 but the two chapters then omitted are re-inserted, using full 1585 text for these chapters, not the 1622 abbreviation. Later reprints, up to 1861, substantially follow this, the eighth edition.

1660   *A Christian directory, guiding men to eternal salvation; commonly called the Resolution*

[Antwerp]

Copy: Bodleian Library (Linc. 8° G.8)

Notes: Wing P564. Wing inaccurately gives this as a re-issue of the 1650 edition, but it omits all the Bunny references, in the preface and margins.

1673 *A Christian directory guiding men to their eternal saluation*

[no place]

Copy: Bodleian Library (k.7.23).

The Protestant Tradition

1584 *A booke of Christian exercise, appertaining to resolution*

[within a frame of printer's flowers: 137 × 84 enclosing 100 × 46] A ¦ **Booke of Chriſtian ex-** ¦ erciſe, appertaining to RE- ¦ SOLVTION, *that is, ſhew-* ¦ ing how that we ſhould re- ¦ ſolve our ſelves to become ¦ Chriſtians in deed: ¦ *by R.P.* ¦ *Peruſed, and accompanied now* ¦ with a Treatiſe tending ¦ *to Pacification:* ¦ by Edm. BVNNY. ¦ [two blank lines] ¦ *Heb.* 13,8. ¦ Ieſus Chriſt yesterday, and to ¦ day, and the ſame ¦ for ever ¦ [blank] ¦ *Imprinted at London by N. New-* ¦ ton, and A. Hatfield, for ¦ *Iohn Wight.* ¦ [blank] ¦ 1584.

Coll: 8° (420 × 310): *⁸ A⁴ B–2M⁸ [$4 (–A4) signed; A3 signed 3, C2 as G2, P4 as B4; E2 and several others signed in italics]; 284 leaves, pp. [24] *1–412 413–18* 1–126.

Contents: *1r title; *1v arms of the archbishop of York; *2r–4v epistle dedicatory to Edwin Sandys, archbishop of York; *5r–8r Preface to the reader, dated Bolton-Percy, 9 July 1584; *8v–A4v contents; B1r–2D6v (pp. 1–412) A booke of Christian exercise; 2D7 blank; 2D8r title of Treatise tending to pacification; 2D8v–2E1r table declaring the method of the treatise; 2E1v blank; 2E2r–2M8v (pp. 1–126) The treatise tending to pacification.

Copies: Bodleian Library (141 m. 149), lacking *1–3, replaced by A1–3 of STC 19357 and, in addition, *1–3 in facsimile from British Library copy; British Library (C.111 f.3).

Notes: STC 19355. Entered 28 August 1584 (Arber 2: 435); for Bollifant's memorial, see Arber 2: 793–94 and Calendar of State Papers (Domestic) Elizabeth 1581–1590, p. 296 (185 art. 73).

1584	12°: Middelburg, Netherlands: R.P. [Painter = Schilders] (STC 19356)
1585a	8°: London: N. Newton and A. Hatfield for John Wight (STC 19356.5)
1585b	8°: London: N. Newton for John Wight (STC 19357)
1585c	8°: London: [N. Newton] for John Wight (STC 19357.5)
1585d	8°: London: Thomas Dawson (STC 19358)
1585e	8°: London: Thomas Dawson (STC 19358.5)
1585f	8°: Oxford: Joseph Barnes (STC 19359.1)
1585g	8°: Oxford: Joseph Barnes (STC 19359.3)
1585h	12°: Oxford: Joseph Barnes (STC 19359.5)
1585k	12°: Oxford: Joseph Barnes (STC 19359.7)
1585m	12°: Oxford: Joseph Barnes (STC 19359.9)
1585n	12°: Oxford: Joseph Barnes (STC 19360)
1585p	12°: Oxford: Joseph Barnes (STC 19360.3)
1585q	12°: Oxford: Joseph Barnes (STC 19360.5)
1585r	12°: Oxford: Joseph Barnes (STC 19360.7)
1585s	12°: London: John Windet (STC 19359)
1586	12°: London: John Windet (STC 19363)
	For later 12° editions, see table below
1589	8°: London: J. Charlewood for John Wight (STC 19364)
1599	8°: London: Thomas Wight (STC 19368.5)

The Second Part

1590   8°: *The seconde parte of the booke of Christian exercise, appertayning to Resolution. Or a Christian directorie, guiding all men to their saluation*

London: J. Charlewood for Simon Waterson
STC 19380: Bodleian Library (Antiq. f. E.1590/3)

1591–1640 : 12° editions

A booke of Christian exercise	*The seconde parte*
	1591 J. Charlewood for S. Waterson (STC 19381)
	1592 J. Charlewood for S. Waterson (STC 19382)
1594 Edmund Bollifant for Thomas Wight (STC 19365)	1594 J. Roberts for S. Waterson (STC 19383)

1596   J. Jackson for T. Wight
       (STC 19365.5)
1597   A. Hatfield for T. Wight
       (STC 19366)
1598   ?P.Short for F. Kingston   1598   J. Roberts for S. Waterson
       (STC 19367)   (STC 19384)
                                         1599   J. Roberts for S. Waterson
                                                (STC 19384.5)
                                         1601   J. Roberts for S. Waterson
                                                (STC 19385)

1602   Thomas Wight
       (STC 19369)
1607   Felix Kingston for
       Edmund Weaver
       (STC 19370)
                                         1608   W. Jaggard for S. Waterson
                                                (STC 19385.5)

1609   F. Kingston for
       E. Weaver (STC 19372)
                                         1610   W. Jaggard for S. Waterson
                                                (STC 19386)

1612   F. Kingston for
       E. Weaver (STC 19373)
1615   F. Kingston for   1615   W. Jaggard for S. Waterson
       E. Weaver (STC 19374)   (STC 19387)
                                         1619   W. Jaggard for S. Waterson
                                                (STC 19388)

1621   John Dawson for
       E. Weaver (STC 19375)
1630   G. Purslowe for Thomas
       Weaver (STC 19376.5)
1631   A. Matthews for   1631   A. Matthews for
       S. Waterson   S. Waterson (STC 19388a)
       (STC 19377)
                                         1633   T. Cotes for S. Waterson
                                                (STC 19389)

1640   Thomas Harper for
       J. Waterson (STC 19379):
       Films STC 1690

Note: Tp claims 'both
parts joyned together . . .
1640' but this copy
(Illinois) is bound with
the 1631 Second Part

Editorial Policy

This is an old-spelling edition of *The first booke of the Christian exercise,
appertayning to Resolution* of 1582. Since there is no certainty about
Persons's final intentions, and the 1607 edition is in any case available in facsimile, it seems wise to make available a reliable edition
of the first version, which initiated both the Catholic and Protestant
traditions. Historical value apart, it is arguable that the brevity and
coherence of the 1582 version make it a more satisfactory literary
achievement, or at least better adapted to modern tastes. In so doing,
I have followed the example of Robert McNulty, whose unpublished
edition (1955) has proved extremely useful. McNulty's highly con-
servative edition is very sound and informative, but I believe I have
been able to improve on it by examining the later editions more
thoroughly and by checking and tracing the sidenote references to
the Bible and the Church Fathers. Often these have disclosed errors
in the 1582 text of which McNulty was not aware.

My intention has been to interfere as little as possible with the
original conventions of the printed work, especially since Persons was
so closely involved in its production. Standard editorial practice has
been followed in silently modernising *u/v*, *i/j*, long *s* and *vv*. I have
also expanded contractions, including *&*, and given an initial capital to the name *God* throughout. Latin quotations have not been
modernised except in the use of initial *v* (as in *ubi*).

Although the 1582 punctuation is in all likelihood not authorial,
I have retained it for the sake of rhetorical consistency, occasionally
lightening it in the direction of the 1607 practice.[123] The use of punctuation and capital letters surrounding quotations is irregular in the

---

[123] An example of *R*'s heavy pointing is: 'so muche, as he knoweth well, how to
discharge, the next morning, at his departure' (p. 256). Each of these commas
(except the first) is omitted by *R2* and *R4*. In this case, however, I have retained
R's punctuation.

1582 text, and some emendations have been necessary for the sake of clarity. I have not interfered with the positioning of major punctuation marks inside brackets (thus;) nor have I regularized the use of capital letters after colons. In the case of question marks, I have substituted a subsequent capital letter only when it is clear that a rhetorical run of questions is complete. The critical apparatus records all these departures from the copy-text (including punctuation) except in the case of turned letters.

I have taken far greater liberty with the sidenotes than with the body of the text. Where scripture references are wrong, I have emended them even though it may have been Persons rather than the compositor who made the mistake. These corrections are recorded in the critical apparatus. Where necessary I have silently interfered with the hyphenation and position of sidenotes, and added full stops.

The text is based on a collation of the 1582, 1585 and 1607 editions of the *Book of Resolution*. Although this includes three copies of the 1582 edition (Bodleian Library, British Library, Huntington Library), only one press variant has been identified (p. 53.4). In some instances Persons's later editions are used as authority for an emendation when it seems clear that they correct rather than revise the 1582 text. The revisions of 1585 and 1607 are too extensive to be incorporated into the apparatus but some interesting cases are discussed in the commentary.

It is assumed that many who use this edition will be interested in the alterations, omissions and additions made by Edmund Bunny. Fortunately these have proved to be quite easily accommodated in a separate apparatus, following Bunny's spelling. In this apparatus, omissions are indicated as such, and substitutions are recorded by quoting the word immediately preceding and following the substitution (which itself is given in full). Where identical substitutions are made frequently throughout the text, only the first is recorded, followed by *and passim*. Bunny's marginal notes are included in this apparatus, preceded (where appropriate) by square brackets indicating the positioning of the asterisk in his text. I have for the most part refrained from offering commentary on these alterations unless they attracted remarks from Persons himself or shed light on his original intentions. For ease of comparison, the Bunny apparatus appears at the foot of the page of the main text, while the critical apparatus is to be found at the end. The commentary is chiefly intended to provide objective glosses on the historical, biblical, patristic and theological/scholastic allusions and references. In the interests of efficiency I have appended indices to Biblical, classical and patristic references in the sidenotes, and a guide to the parallel passages in Luis de Granada.

Sigla

R   *The first booke of the Christian exercise, appertayning to resolution* (Rouen, 1582)

R2   *A Christian directorie guiding men to their saluation* (Rouen, 1585)

R4   *The Christian directory guiding men to eternall saluation* (St Omer, 1607)

B   *A booke of Christian exercise, appertaining to resolution*, 'perused' by Edmund Bunny (London, 1584)

M   'Robert Parsons's *The First Booke of the Christian Exercise* (1582): An Edition and a Study', by Robert McNulty (Unpublished Ph.D. thesis, Columbia University, 1955)

THE FIRST BOOKE OF THE
CHRISTIAN EXERCISE,
APPERTAYNING TO RESOLUTION
(1582)

THE SUMMARIE OF THE CHRISTIAN EXERCISE, AS IT IS INTENDED.

FOR THAT three thyngs are necessarie to a man in this lyfe, for the attayning of salvation: that is, to resolve
5 hym selfe to serve God in deed: to begynne a right: and to persevere unto the ende: therfore this whole treatise shalbe devided into three bookes.

THE FIRST booke shalbe of resolution, devided into two partes. And in the first parte shalbe layed downe
10 all the principall reasons that ought to move a man to this resolution. In the second shalbe removed all the impedimentes that commonlie doe hynder men from the same.

THE SECONDE booke shall treate of the waye how
15 to begynne well, and shall lykewyse be devided into two partes: wherof the fyrst shall shew the waye how to delyver ourselves from sinne, and from the custome, bondage or delectation therof. The second shall open the meanes, how to joyne our selves perfectlie to God,
20 and to make a right entrance into his service.

THE THIRDE booke shall handle the meanes of per-severance, so farre forthe as it concerneth our habilitie, for thogh this gyft be onelie of God: yet are there two thinges left by his grace to be performed of us: the one,
25 to aske his ayde: the other, to joyne our endevour with the same. According to which two pointes, this booke shalbe devided also into two partes: The first wherof shall intreate of all kynde of prayer, bothe mentall and vocall. The second shall declare the wayes and meanes,
30 how (by help of Gods grace) we may resist and over-come all sortes of sinne, and the temptations therof.

AN ADVERTISEMENT TO THE READER.

I hadde purposed (gentle reader) at the beginning, to have printed againe, the Exercise of a Christian lyfe, composed by D. Loartes,
35 *and translated (not long since) into our tongue: as may appeare by the preface foloweing. And albeit I minded to adde certaine*

matters and treatises unto the same: yet ment I not, but to retayne
so much as therin was done before, esteeming it so well done (as
in deed it is) as no alteration needed therein. But yet notwithstanding,
when I had sett downe an other order and method to my selfe,
than that booke foloweth: and had begunne this first booke of resolution: wherof no parte is handled in that treatise: I found by
experience, that I could not well joyne that with this: to satisfie,
ether the order or argument by me conceyved: and therfore was I
inforced, to resolve vpon a further labour, than at the first I
intended: whiche was, to drawe out the whole three bookes myself:
not omitting any thing, that is in the sayd Exercise, or other like
bookes, to this effect. Which thing by Gods holy assistance, I
meane to doe, as time, healthe and libertie shall permit me.

    Now I am constrayned to breake of, for the present, and to
send thee onelie this first booke of resolution: which I beseeche our
Lord may so worke in thy hart by his heavenlie grace, as I maye
be incouraged therby the sooner to dispache the other two. God
for our better triall permitteth many difficulties, disturbances, lettes,
and hynderances, in everie thing that is taken in hand for his
service: but yet, alwayes after, he helpeth us out agayne: as I
know he will doe from tyme to tyme: the cause being his: and
much more importing hym than us. The onelie thing that he desireth
at our handes is, that we should once resolve our selves throughelie to serve hym in deede: and consequentlie cast our selves wholie
into his holy armes: without reservation of any one jote that we
have, unto our selves: and then should we see, how good and
mercifull a lord he is: as now also we prove dailie, beyond all
desertes, or expectation. Our lord blesse and preserve thee (gentle
reader) and enriche thee with the guyftes of his holie grace: and
when thou art amiddest thy deepest devotions, I beseeche thee to
have some memorie of me also, poore sinner: as I shall not be
forgetfull of thee. But above all others, lett us bothe be myndfull
to praye for our persecutors: who finallie will prove to be our best
freendes: being in deed the hammers which beate and polish us,
for makyng us fytt stones, for the buylding of Gods new Jerusalem
in heaven.

TO THE CHRISTIAN READER TOWCHINGE
TWO EDITIONS OF THIS BOOKE

Abowt three yeres past (good reader) a certaine learned
and devout gentilman, consideringe the greate want of
5 spirituall bookes in Englande, for the direction of men
to pietie and devotion (whiche ought to be the cheefest
point of our exercise in this lyfe) tooke the paines to
translate a godlye treatise to that effect, named, *the Exercise of a Christian life*, writen in the Italian toung, by a
10 reverende man of the societie of Jesus, named Gasper
Loartes, Doctor in divinitie, and of greate experience in
the handlinge and managinge of sowles to that purpose.
Whiche booke because I understande of certaintie, to
have done greate good, and to have wrought forcebly
15 in the hartes of manye persons, towards the foresayed
effect of pietie and devotion: I was moved to cause the
same to be printed againe, and that in muche more
ample manner than before, havinge added unto it, two
partes of three, which were not in the former booke.
20   The reason of this so large an addition shall appeare
in the Induction followinge, where shalbe shewed the
partes of this booke, with the causes and contentes therof.
But the principall cause and reason was, to the ende
our countrye men might have some one sufficient direc-
25 tion for matters of life and spirit, among so manye bookes
of controversies as have ben writen, and are in writinge
dailye. The whiche bookes, albeit in thes our troublesome and quarrelous times be necessarie for defence of
our faithe, againste so manye seditious innovations, as
30 now are attempted: yet helpe they litle oftentymes to
good lyfe, but rather do fill the heades of men with a
spirite of contradiction and contention, that for the most
parte hindereth devotion, which devotion is nothinge els,   A descrip-
but a quiet and peaceble state of the sowle, endewed   tion of
35 with a joyful promptnes to the diligent execution of all   devotion.
thinges that appartayne to the honour of God. In respect
wherof, S. Paule geeveth this counsayle to his scholer
Timothie: *contende not in wordes, for it is profitable to nothinge,*   2.Ti.2.
but to subvert the hearers. The lyke counsayle he gevethe

in divers other places, in respect of this quiet devotion, whiche is trowbled by contention.

But yet (as I have saide) these bookes of controversies are necessarie for other considerations, especialie in thes our tymes, when everye man almost is made of a fancie, and apte to esteeme the same great wisdome, except it be refuted. Suche are our dayes, most unhappie truelye in respect of our forefathers, whoe receavinge the grownde of faithe peaceably, and without quarelinge from their mother the Churche, did attend onlye to builde uppon the same, good woorkes and Christian life, as their vocation required. But we spendinge all the tyme in janglinge abowte the foundation, have no leysure to think upon the building, and so we wearye out our spirites without commoditie, we dye with muche doe and litle profit, greate disquiet and small rewarde. For whoe knoweth not, that what faithe so ever a man hathe, yet without good lyfe it helpeth hym litle?

I am therfore of opinion (gentle reader) that albeit trew faithe be the grownde of Christianitie, without which nothinge of it selfe can be meritorious before God: yet that one principall meane to come to this trew faithe, and right knowledge, and to ende all thes our infinite contentions in religion, were for eche man to betake him selfe to a good and vertuous life, for that God could not of his unspeakeable mercie suffer suche a man to erre longe in religion. We have a cleare example of Cornelius a Gentile to whome God in respect of his religious lyfe, prayer and almes deedes, (as the scripture affirmeth) sent his Apostle S. Peter to instruct him in the right faithe. So mercifull is God to those whiche applye them selves to vertue and pietie, albeit they erre as yet in pointes of faithe.

And on the contrarie side, as loose lyfe and worldlye ambition, was the first cause of all heresye in Christian religion from the beginninge: so is it the continuance of the same, and it is verie harde for him that is so affected to be recalled from his error. For that (as the scripture saithe) *the wisdome of God will not entre into a malitious minde, nor dwell in a bodye subject to sinne.* And our Saveoure in

Marginal notes:

Bookes of controversie, necessarie though not profitable to devotion.

1.Cor.3.

Jaco.2.
1.Co.1.
Heb.11.
Good life a meane to right faithe.

Act.10.

Sap.1.

the gospell askethe a question of certaine ambitious world-
lynges, whiche geevethe greate light to the thinge we
talke of: *how* (sayeth he) *can you beleeve, which seeke glorye* John.5.
one of an other? as whoe woulde saie, that this worldly
5 ambition and evill life of theirs, did make it impossible
for them to come to the trewe faithe.

   Wherfore (gentle reader) if thow be of an other religion than I am, I beseche the most hartelye, that layenge
a side all hatred, malice and wrathfull contention, let
10 us joyne together in amendment of our lyves, and pray-
eng one for an other: and God (no doubt) will not suffer
us to perishe finallye for want of right faithe. And to
Catholiques I must saye further withe S. Paule and 1.Co.13.
S. James, that all their faith will profitt them nothinge, Jaco.2.
15 except they have charitie allso, bothe towardes God and
man, and therby doe directe their lyves accordinglye.
Whiche God of his holye mercye geeve them grace to
doe, to his honour and their eternall saluation. And I
most humblye request the (good Christian reader) to
20 praie for me allso, (if thow take any commoditie by this
booke) that I be not like the Conduit pipe whiche bringeth
water to the citie, without drinkinge anye it selfe, or as
S. Paule withe muche lesse cause than I have, feared of 1.Cor.9.
hym selfe, to witt, leste that after preachinge to other,
25 I become perchaunce a reprobate my selfe. Remembre
allso I beseeche the, that most vertuous good gentilman,
whoe by his first translation, was the cause of this labour
now taken againe. He hathe suffered much sence for
the cause of his conscience, and is at this present under
30 indurance for the same, and by that meanes, so muche
the more in disposition to receave fruite by thy prayer,
by howe muche the more he hathe suffered for righteousnes sake, and is nearer joined to God by his sepa-
ration from the world. Our lorde blesse him and the
35 allso (good reader) and sende us all his holy grace, to
doe his will in this woorld, that we maye raigne with
him in the world to come. Amen.

Thy hartie welwiller and servant in Christ.
R.P.

AN INDUCTION TO THE THREE BOOKES FOLLOWINGE

Al Christian divinitie (good reader,) that is, all the busines that man hath withe God in this lyfe standethe in two poyntes. The one to knowe: the other to doe. This first parte containeth principally our beleefe, set forth to us in our Creede, and other declarations abowt our faith, delivered us by the Catholique churche to know and beleeve onlie. The other parte containethe the ten commaundementes, the uses of holye Sacramentes, and the like, prescribed unto Christians not onlye to knowe or beleeve, but allso to exercise and execute in this lyfe. The first of thes two partes is called theorike or speculatyve, because it consisteth in speculation, that is, in understandinge and discourse of the minde, wherby a man comprehendeth the thinges he hath to knowe and beleeve. The second parte is called practique or active, because it standeth not onlye in knowledge, but also in action and execution of those thinges whiche by the first parte he hath conceaved and understoode.

    In the first parte there is lesse labour and difficultie a greate deale than in the seconde. Because it is easier to know, then to doe: to beleeve aright, then to lyve accordinglie: and the thinges that a man hathe to beleeve are muche fewer, than the thinges he hathe to doe, and therfore Christ in the Ghospels, and the Apostles in their writinges, spake muche more of thinges to be donne, than of thinges to be knowen: of good lyvinge, than of right understandinge: And amongest Christians few are damned for lacke of knowledge, which commonlye all men baptised have sufficient: (except in tymes of heresies,) but many thowsandes for evill life dailye. Wherfore Christ in the Ghospell tellinge the reason of suche as shoulde be damned, putteth lacke of good lyfe, as the reason of their damnation. *Departe from me* (saieth he) *into everlastinge fire: I was hungrie and you gave me not to eate, et ce.*

    And the reason of this is, for that the thinges which a man is bounde to beleeve (as I saide before) are fewe, in respect of the thinges whiche a man hathe to doe,

5
10
15
20
25
30
35

Two partes of Christian divinitie.

Theorike.

Practike.

Active divinitie harder then speculative.

Mat.25.

or the vices that he hath to avoyed. Againe, the partes
in man whiche appertaine to understandinge and knowledge, were not so hurte by the fall of Adam, as the
partes appertayninge to action, whereby it commeth,
5   that a man hath lesse difficultie, payne, and resistance
in hym selfe to knowledge, than to good lyfe, where
our owne corrupt affections make warre against us, and
so doe make the matter unpleasant for a tyme, untill
they be conquered. For whiche cause we see manie
10 greate lerned men not to be the best lyvers, for that to
know muche is a pleasure to them, but to doe muche
is a payne.

The partes of action more hurte than the partes of understadinge by the fall of Adam.

For thes causes, not onlye the scriptures (as I noted
before) but allso the auncient holye fathers, have made
15 greate and longe discourses, ample volumes, and manye
bookes, about this second parte of Christian divinitie,
whiche consisteth in action, owt of whose worckes, thes
three bookes followinge for the most parte are gathered,
containinge a perfect and exact instruction or direction,
20 for all them that meane to leade a trew Christian life,
as also divers helpes for them which have not yet fullye
that determination. For what so ever is necessarie to
a Christian after he hathe once receaved the faithe, is
contained in this worcke. And to speake in particuler,
25 three thinges are necessarie. The first is a firme resolution to serve God for the time to come, and to leave
vice. The second is how to begynne to doe this. The
third is how to persever and continew unto the ende.

Three thinges necessarie to a Christian in this lyfe.

These three thinges whoe so ever hath, no doubt but
30 he shall bothe lyve and dye a good Christian, and enjoye
everlastinge life in the world to come. And for lacke of
all or some one of thes thinges, manie thowsandes (the
more is the pittie) doe perishe daylie. For some men are
ether so carelesse, or so carnallie geeven, as they never
35 resolve them selves to lyve in deed well, and to forsake
wickednes: and thes are farof from the state of salvation. Other resolve them selves often, but they never
beginne, or at least way they beginne not as they shoulde
doe, wherby they never come to any perfection. Other
40 doe both resolve and begyn well, but they persever not

unto the ende, ether for lacke of instruction, or helpes
necessarie to the same: and thes also can not attayne to
lyfe everlastinge, but rather doe leese their labour, for
that Christ hath not promised salvation, but onlie to
5 such as persever to the ende.

 For helpinge therfore Christians in thes three poyntes,
this worcke is devided into three bookes. In the first
booke there are shewed manye meanes and helpes,
wherby to bringe a man to this necessarie resolution, of
10 leavinge vanities to serve God, with a Christian lyfe,
accordinge to his profession. In the second booke is
declared in particuler, how a man shall begin to putt
this resolution in practise, and without errour to begyn a new trade of lyfe. In the third booke are layed
15 downe, the meanes and helpes to perseverance unto the
ende. The which beinge done, there remaineth nothinge,
but the reapinge of glorie in the lyfe to come, which we
shalbe able to doe without instructions, yf it be our good
happe to come to it, which God graunte, and send us
20 his grace, that we maye be as well content to labour
for it in this lyfe, as we will be joyfull to possesse it in
the next, and to avoyde the dreadfull tormentes, which
those must needes fall into, who for slowth, pleasure, or
negligence, omitt in this worlde, to procure the kyng-
25 dome prepared for Godes servantes, in the next.

Mat.10.
& 24.

The divi-
sion of this
worcke.

The first
booke.

The
second
booke.

The third
booke.

THE FIRST BOOKE AND FIRST PARTE.

*Of the end and partes of this booke, withe a necessarie adver-
tissement to the reader.*

CHAP. I

5   The first booke (as I have shewed before) hathe for
his proper end, to perswade a Christian by name, to
become a trewe Christian in deed, at the leaste, in resolution of mynde. And for that there be two principall
thinges necessarie to this effect: therfore this first booke
10   shalbe devided into two partes. And in the first shalbe
declared important reasons and strong motyves, to provoke a man to this resolution. In the second shalbe
refuted all the impedimentes, whiche our spirituall enymies (the fleshe the world and the devyll) are wont to
15   laye for the stoppinge of the same, knowinge very well,
that of this resolution dependethe all our good in the
life to come. For he that never resolveth hym selfe to
doe well and to leave the dangerous state of synne wherin
he lyvethe, is farof from ever doynge the same. But he
20   that sometymes resolveth to doe it, althoughe by frayltie
he performethe it not at that tyme, yet is that resolution much acceptable before God, and his mynd the
rediar to returne after to the like resolution againe, and
by the grace of God, to putt it manfully in execution.
25   But he that willfully resistethe the good motions of the
holly ghost, and uncurteouslie contemnethe his Lorde,
knockinge at the doore of his conscience, greatly pro-
vokethe the indignation of God agaynst hym, and commonlye growethe harder and harder daylye, untill he be
30   given over into a reprobate sense, which is the next
doore to damnation it selfe.

One thinge therfore I must advertyse the reader before

The ende
of this
booke.

Two
partes of
this
booke.

The
necessitie
of resolu-
tion.

Act.7.

Apoc.3.

Rom.1.

An

Bunny's Adaptations
5 This first booke hath   8 *omits* And   11 strong persuasions, to   16
dependeth all our whole service of GOD. For

I goe any further, that he take greate heede of a certayne principall deceyt of our ghostlye adversarie, whereby he drawethe many millions of soules into hell daylye.
Whiche is, to feare and terrifie them from hearinge or
5   readinge any thinge contrarye to theyre present humor
or resolution. As for example, a usurer, from readinge
bookes of restitution: a lecherer, from readinge discourses
against that synne: a worldlinge, from readinge spirituall bookes or treatyses of devotion. And he usethe com-
10 monlye this argument to them for his purpose: Thow
seest how thow art not yet resolved to leave this trade of
lyfe, wherin thow art: and therfore the readinge of these
bookes will but trouble and afflict thy conscience, and
caste the into sorrowe and melancholye, and therfore
15 reade them not at all. This (I saye) is a cunninge sleyght
of Satan, wherby he leadethe manye blyndfolded to
perdition, even as a faulkener carriethe many hawkes
quyetly beinge hooded, whiche other wyse he could not
doe, yf they hadd the use of their sight.

20   If all ignorance dyd excuse synne, than this might be
some refuge for them that would lyve wickedlye: But
this kinde of ignorance, (beinge voluntarie and willfull)
increasethe greatlye bothe the sinne and the synners evell
state. For of this man the holye ghost speakethe in great
25 dysdayne. *Noluit intelligere vt bene ageret.* He would not understande to doe well. And agayne: *quia tu scientiam repulisti,*
repellam te. For that thou hast rejected knoledge, I will reject the.
And of the same men in an other place the same holye
ghost sayethe: *they doe leade their lyves in pleasure, and in a*
30 *moment goe downe unto hell, whiche saye to God, goe from us,*
we will not have the knowledge of thy wayes. Let every man
therfore be ware of this deceyt, and be contente at the
least, to reade goode bookes, to frequent devoute com-
panye and other lyke goode meanes, of his amendment,
35 albeit he were not yet resolved to follow the same: yea
althoughe he should fynde some greeff and repugnaunce
in hym selfe to doe it. For these things can never doe

Marginal notes:

advertise-
ment.

The
devyles
argument.

Wilfull
ignorance
increas-
ethe
sinne.

Psal.36.
Ose.4.

Job.21.
See S. Au-
sten of
this sinn:
de gra. &
lib.arbi.
cap.3.
& S. Chri-
sostome.
homi.26.
in epist.
ad Rom.

---

6 an usurer *and passim* (an *before* u/h)   20 If ignorance

hym hurte, but maye chaunce to doe hym very muche goode: and perhappes the very contrarietie and repugnance which he bearethe in frequentinge these thinges against his inclination, may move our mercifull lorde, whiche seethe his harde case, to gyve hym the victorye over hym selfe in the ende, and to send hym much more comforte in the same, than before he hadd dislyke. For he can easelie doe it onelie by alteringe our taste withe a litle droppe of his holye grace, and so make those thinges seeme most sweet and pleasant, whiche before tasted bothe bitter and unsaverye.

Wherfore as I would hartelye wyshe every Christian soule, that comethe to reade these considerations folowinge, should come with an indefferent mynde, layed downe wholly into Godes handes, to resolve and doe as it should please his holy spirite to move hym unto, althoughe it were to the losse of all worldlye pleasures what so ever: (whiche resignation is absolutlie necessarye to every one that desirethe to be saved:) so yf some can not presentlye wynne that indifferencie of them selves: yet would I counsayle them in any case to conquer theyr myndes to so much patience, as to goe throughe to the ende of this booke, and to see what maye be sayde at leaste to the matter, althoughe it be withoute resolution to followe the same. For I doubt not, but God maye so pearse these mennes hartes before they come to the ende, as their myndes maye be altered and they yealde them selves unto the humble and sweete service of theyr lorde and saviour, and that the Angells in heaven (whiche will not ceasse to praye for theym whyle they are readinge) maye rejoyce and triumphe of theyr regayninge, as of sheepe most dangerouslye loste before.

What mynde a man should bringe to the readinge of this booke.

Luc.15.

---

1 *omits* chaunce to   2 and it may be, that the   4 move the merciful Lord *and passim* (the Lord *for* our Lord)   29 *omits* (whiche will not ceasse to praye for theym whyle they are readinge)

Howe necessarie it is to enter into earnest consideration and meditation of our estate.

CHAP. II

The prophet Jeremie after a long complaynte of the miseries of his tyme, fallen upon the Jewes by reason of their sinnes, utterethe the cause therof in these wordes: *All the earthe is fallen into utter desolation for that there is no man which considereth deepely in his harte.* Signifieng hereby, that yf the Jewes would have entered into deepe and earnest consideration of their lyves and estate, before that greate desolation fell uppon them: they might have escaped the same, as the Ninivites dyd by the forewarninge of Jonas: albeit the sworde was nowe drawen, and the hande of God stretched out, within fourtye dayes to distroye them. So important a thing is this consideration. In figure wherof all beasts in old tyme, whiche dyd not ruminate or chewe theyre cudde, were accounted uncleane by the lawe of Moyses, as no dowt but that soule in the sight of God muste nedes bee, whiche revolvethe not in harte, nor chewethe in often meditation of mynde the thinges required at her handes in this lyfe.

For of want of this consideration, and due meditation, all the foule errors of the woorlde are committed, and many thowsand Christians doo fynde them selves within the very gates of hell, before they mystrust anye suche matter towardes them, beinge carryed thorowghe the vale of this lyfe blyndfolded, withe the veyle of negligence and inconsideration, as beastes to the slawghter howse, and never suffred to see theyr owne daunger, untill it be to late to remedie the same.

For this cause the holly scripture dothe recommende unto us most carefully, this exercyse of meditation, and diligent consideration of our deutyes, to delyver us therby from the perill which inconsideration leadethe us unto.

Moyses havinge delyvered to the people his embassage from God, towchinge all particulars of the lawe, addethe this clause also from God, as most necessarye:

5   10   15   20   25   30   35

Jere.12.

Jon.3.

Lev.11.
Deu.14.

Thes wordes must remaine in thy harte, thou shalt meditate uppon   Deut.6.
them bothe at home and abroade, when thou goest to bedde, and
when thou rysest agayne in the morninge. And agayne in an
other place: *teache your childeren thes thinges, that they maye*   Deu.11.
5   *meditate in their hartes uppon them.* The lyke commande-
ment was geeven by God hym selfe, to Josue at his first
election, to governe the people: to witt, *that he should*   Josu.1.
meditate upon the lawe of Moyses bothe daye and night, to the
ende, he might keepe and performe the thinges writen therein. And
10   God addethe presentlie the commoditie he should reape
therof. *For then* (saythe he) *shalt thou direct thy waye aryght,*
and shalt understand the same. Signifyinge that without this
meditation, a man goethe bothe amysse, and also blynd-
lye, not knowinge hym selfe whether.
15   Saint Paule havinge discribed unto his scholler Tym-
othye, the perfect dewtye of a prelate, addethe this advertisement in the ende: *hæc meditare. Meditate, ponder and*   1.Tim.4.
consider uppon this. And finallie whensoever the holye scripture describethe a wyse, happy, or juste man (for all
20   these are one in scripture, for that justice is onlye trewe   Psal.1.
wisdome and felicitie:) one cheefe pointe is this. *He will*   Pro.15.
meditate upon the lawe of God, bothe daye and night. And for   Eccl.14.
examples in the scripture howe good men dyd use to
meditate in tymes past, I might here rekon upp great
25   store, as that of Isaac, whoe was wonte to goe forth into   Gen.24.
the feeldes towardes night to meditate: also that of
Ezechias the kynge, whoe (as the scripture sayeth) dyd   Esa.38.
meditate lyke a dove, that is, in silence, withe his harte
onely, without noyse of wordes. But above all other, the
30   example of holye David is singuler herein, who every
where almoste, makethe mention of his continuall exer-
cise in meditation, sayeng to God. *I dyd meditate uppon*   Psal.119.
thy commandementes whiche I loved. And agayne: *I will med-*   Psal.63.
itate uppon the in the morninges. And agayne, *O lorde howe*   Psal.119.
35   *have I loved thy lawe? it is my meditation all the daye long.*
And with what fervoure and vehemencie he used to
make these his meditations, he sheweth when he saythe

---

25 who went foorth   26 [* meditate] *mn*: B. Or moorn: for it was
in the way of sorrowing or lamentation

of hym selfe: *my harte dyd waxe hoote within me, and fire dyd*   Psal.39.
kyndle in my meditations.

    This is recorded by the holy ghost of these auncient
good men, to confounde us which are Christians, whoe
5   beynge farr more bounde to fervour than they, by reason of the greater benefytes we have receyved: yet doe
we lyve so lazelye, (for the most parte of us) as we never
almoste enter into the meditation and earneste consideration of Godes lawes and commaundementes, of the
10   mysteries of our faithe, of the lyfe and deathe of our
Savyour, or of our dewtye towardes hym, and muche
lesse do we make it our dayly studdye and cogitation, as
those holy kinges dyd, notwithstandinge all their great
busines in the commen wealthe.

15   Whoe is there of us now a dayes, which makethe the   Psa.119.
lawes and commandementes or justifications of God (as
the scriptures learnethe hym) his dayly meditations, as
kinge Davide dyd? neyther onely in the daye tyme dyd
he this, but also *by night in his harte*, as in an other place   Psal.77.
20   he testyfiethe of hym selfe. Howe many of us doe passe
over whole dayes, and monethes, without ever entringe
into theise meditations? nay God graunte there be not
manye Christians in the worlde, which knowe not what
these meditations doe meane. We beleeve in grosse the   Beleef in
25   mysteryes of our Christiane faythe, as that there is a   grosse.
hell, a heaven, a rewarde for vertue, a punyshement for
vice, a judgement to come, an accompt to be made,
and the lyke: but for that we chue them not well by
depe consideration, nor doe not digest them well in our
30   hartes, by the heate of meditation: they helpe us litle to
good lyfe, no more than a preservative putt in a mans
pockett can helpe his healthe.

    What man in the world would adventure so easelye   Marvelous
upon mortall synne (as commonlye men doe which drynk   effectes of
35   them upp as easely as beastes drynk water) yf he dyd   inconsid-
consider in particuler the greate daunger and losse that   eration.

---

16 (as the scripture termeth them)   29 consideration, and do   34
omits mortall   34 drink it up   36 *omits* losse that commethe by the
same, as the

commethe by the same, as the losse of grace, the losse
of Gods favour, and purchassinge his eternall wrathe,
also the deathe of Gods owne sonne sustayned for sinne,
the inestymable tormentes of hell for the everlastinge
5   punishement of the same? which albeit everye Christian
in summe doethe beleyve: yet because the moste parte
doe never consider them withe due circunstances in their
hartes: therefore they are not moved withe the same,
but doe beare the knoweledge thereof locked uppe in
10 their breastes, without any sense or feelinge, even as a
man carryethe fyre aboute hym in a flynte stone withoute heate, or perfumes in a pommander withoute smell,
except the one be beaten and the other be chafed.

And (now to come neare our matter whiche we meane
15 to handle in this boke:) what man lyvinge would not
resolve hym selfe thorowlye to serve God in deede, and
to leave all vanities of the world, yf he dyd consider
as he should doe, the wayghtie reasons he hathe to
move hym therunto, the rewarde he shall receyve for
20 it, and his infinite daunger yf he doe it not? but because
(as I have saide) scarce one among a thousande doethe
enter into these considerations, or yf he doe, it is with
lesse attention or contynuance than so greate a matter
requirethe: hereof it commethe, that so many men peryshe
25 dayly, and so fewe are saved: for that, by lack of consideration, they never resolve them selves to lyve as they
should doe, and as the vocation of a Christian man
requirethe. So that we maye also complayne withe holy   Jere.12.
Jeremie, alleaged in the begyninge, that our earthe also
30 of Christianitie, is brought to desolation, for that men
doe not deepely consider in their hartes.

Consideration is the keye whiche openethe the doore   The
to the closet of our harte, where all our bookes of ac-   nature of
compte doe lye. It is the lookinge glasse, or rather the   consideration.
35 very eye of our soule, wherby shee seethe her selfe, and
lookethe into all her whole estate, her riches, her debtes,
her duetyes, her negligences, her good gyftes, her defectes,
her safftie, her daunger, her waye she walkethe in, her

---

36 *omits* her debtes, her duetyes, her negligences

pase shee holdeth, and finallye, the place and ende which
shee drawethe unto. And without this consideration, shee
runnethe on blindlye into a thousande brakes and bryers,
stumblinge at every steppe into some one inconvenience
5   or other, and continualie in perill of some great and
deadlie mischiefe. And it is a wounderfull matter to
thincke, that in other busines of this lyfe, men bothe see
and confesse, that nothinge can be eyther begonne, pros-
ecuted, or well ended, without consideration, and yet in
10   this greate busines of the kyngedome of heaven, no man
almoste usethe or thinkethe the same necessarie.

  If a man had to make a journeye but from Englande   A fitt
to Constantinople, albe it he had made the same once   similitude.
or twyse before, yet would he not passe it over withe
15   oute greate and often consideration, especially whether
he were right, and in the waye or no, what pase he
helde, howe neere he was to his wayes ende, and the
lyke. And thinkest thou (my deare brother) to passe from
earthe to heaven, and that by so many hills and dales,
20   and daungerouse places, never passed by the before, and
this without any consideration at all? thou arte deceived
if thou thinckeste so, for this journey hath farr more
neede of consideration than that, beinge much more
subjecte to bypathes and daungers, everie pleasure of
25   this world, every lust, everye dissolute thought, every
alluringe sight and temptynge sownde, every devill uppon
the earthe, or instrument of his (which are infinite,)
beynge a theefe, and lyenge in wayte to spoyle the, and
to distroie the uppon this waye towardes heaven.
30   Wherefore I would gyve counsayle to every wyse pas-
senger, to looke well aboute hym, and at leaste wyse
once a daye, to enter into consideration of his estate, and
of the estate of his treasure, whiche he carryethe with
hym, in a brickle vessell, as Sainct Paule affirmethe, I   2.Cor.4.
35   meane his soule, whiche maye as soone be lost by inconsideration, as the smalleste and nysest Jewell in this
world, as partlye shall appeare by that which heerafter
I have writen for the helpe of this consideration, whereof
bothe I my selff and all other Christians doe stande in

so great neede in respect of our salvation. For suerly if
my soule or anye other dyd consider attentyvelye but a
fewe thinges of many which shee knowethe to be trewe:
shee could not but speedilie reforme hir selfe, with in-
5   finite myslyke and detestation of hir former course. As
for example, if she considered thorowghly that her onely   Deut.6.
commynge into this lyfe was to attende to the serv-   Luc.1.
ice of God, and that shee notwithstandinge attendethe
onely or the moste parte, to the vanyties of this world:
10   that shee must geeve accompt at the last daye of every   Mat.12.
ydle worde, and yet that shee makethe none accompt
not onely of wordes, but also, nor of evyll deedes: That   1.Cor.5.
no fornicator, no adulterer, no usurer, no covetouse or   Eph.5.
uncleane persone shall ever enjoye the kingdome of
15   heaven, as the scripture saiethe, and yet she thincketh
to goe thither, lyvinge in the same vices: That one onely   Gen.6.
sinne hathe bene sufficient to damne many thousandes   Gen.19.
togither, and yet shee beinge looden withe manye, thinckethe to escape: that the waye to heaven is harde, strayte,   Mat.7.
20   and paynefull, by the affirmation of God hym selfe, and
yet shee thinckethe to goe in, lyvinge in pleasures and
delytes of the worlde: that all hollye saintes that ever
were (as the Apostles, and mother of Christ her selff,   Act.1.
withe all good men since) chose to them selves to lyve   1.Cor.4.
25   an austere lyfe, in fastinge, prayenge, punishinge there   2.Cor.4.6.
bodyes, and the lyke, and for all this, lyved in feare and   11.12.
tremblinge of the judgmentes of God: and shee attendinge   1.Cor.9.
to none of thes thinges, but folowinge her pastimes,   Phili.2.
makethe no doubt of her owne estate. If (I saye) my   1.Cor.2.
30   soule or any other, dyd in deede, and in earneste consider these thinges, or the leaste parte of a thousand
more that might be considered, and which our Christian
faithe doethe teache us to be true: she wold not wan-
der (as the moste parte of Christian soules doe) in suche
35   desperat perill thorowe want of consideration.

---

1 respect of our acceptable service to God. For   12 not of evil deeds
25 life (in painful labour, profitable to others, fasting

What makethe theives to seeme madde unto wyse
men, that seinge so manye hanged dayly for theefte
before their eyes, will yet notwithstandinge steale agayne,
but onlye lacke of consideration? and the verie same
5   cause makethe the wisest men of the world to seeme
very fooles, and worse than frantickes unto God and
good men, that knowinge the vanities of the world and
daunger of sinnfull lyfe, doe folowe soe muche the one,
and feare so litle the other. If a lawe were made by the
10 authoritie of man, that whoe soever should adventure
to drincke wyne, should without delaye holde his hand
but halfe an houre in the fyre, or in boylinge leade for
a punyshement: I thincke many would forbeare wyne,
albeit naturallie they loved the same: and yet a lawe
15 beynge made by the eternall majestie of God, that whoe
so ever commitethe sinne, shall boyle everlastinglye in
the fire of hell, withoute ease or end: Many men for
lacke of consideration doe committ sinne, withe as litle
feare, as they do eate or drincke.

20   To conclude therfore, consideration is a moste necessarie thinge to be taken in hande, especially in these
our dayes, wherein vanitie hathe so muche prevayled
withe the moste, as it semethe to be true wisdome, and
the contrarie thereof to be mere follye, and contemptible
25 simplicitie. But I doubt not by the assistance of God,
and helpe of consideration, to discover in that whiche
followethe, the erroure of this matter unto the discrete
reader, whiche is not willfully blynded, or obstinatlye
geven over unto the captivitie of his ghostly ennemye
30 (for some suche men therebe,) of whome God sayethe
as it were pytyeng and lamentinge their case: *they have
made a league withe deathe, and a covenant withe hell it selfe*:
that is, they will not come oute of the daunger wherin
they be, but will headelonglye caste them selves into
35 everlastinge perdition, rather than by consideration of
their estate, to recover to them selves eternall lyfe and
glorie, from which deadly obstinacie our Lorde of his
mercye deliver us all.

A com-
parison.

Mat.7.
Luc.12.
Rom.1.
1.Cor.1.
2.3.

Gal.3.

The con-
clusion of
this
chapter.

Esa.28.

---

4 *omits* onlye   34 headlong   38 all, that belong unto him.

Of the ende for which man was created and placed in
this world.

CHAP. III

Nowe then, in the name of almightie God, and with
5   the assistance of his most holy spirite, let the Christian
man or woman desirous of salvation, first of all consider
attentyvely, as a good marchand factour is wonte to doe,
when he is arrived in a strange countrye: or as a captaine sent by his prince to some great exployte is accus-
10   tomed, when he comethe to the place appointed: that
is, to thinke for what cause he came thither? why he
was sent? to what ende? what to attempt? what to prosecute? what to performe? what shalbe expected and
required at his handes upon his returne by hym that
15   sent hym thither? for these cogitations (no doubt) shall
styrre hym upp to attende to that which he came for,
and not to employe hym selff in impertinent affayres.
The lyke (I saye) would I have a Christian to consider,
and to aske of hym selfe, whye, and to what ende was
20   he created of God, and sent hither into this worlde?
what to doe? wherin to bestowe his dayes? he shall finde
for no other cause or ende, but onely to serve God in   Deu.6.
this life, and by that service to gayne everlastinge glorye   Josu.22.
in the life to come. This was the condition of our cre-   Deu.14.
25   ation, and this was the onelie consideration of our redemption, prophesied by Zacharie before we were yet
redeemed, *that we beinge delivered from the handes of our*   Luc.1.
enymyes, might serve hym in holynes and justice all the dayes
of our lyfe.
30   Of this it foloweth first, that seinge the ende and finall   The first
cause of our beynge in this worlde, is to serve God in   conse-
this lyfe and therby to gayne heaven in the next: that   quence.
what so ever we doe, or endevour, or bestowe our tyme
in, eyther contrarie or impertinent to this ende, whyche
35   is only to the service of God, thoughe it were to gayne

---

5 *omits* most   23 *omits* and by that service to gayne everlastinge glorye in the life to come   26 *omits* we were yet redeemed   28 *holynes*
and righteousnes al   32 *omits* and therby to gayne heaven in the next

all the kyngdomes of the earthe: yet is it meere vanitie, follie, and lost labour: and will turne us one daye to grefe, repentance, and confusion: for that it is not the matter for whiche we came into this lyfe, or of whiche
5   we shalbe asked accompt at the last daye, except it be to receave Judgement for the same.

Secondlie it folowethe of the premisses, that seinge our onely ende and busines in this worlde, is to serve God, and that all other earthelye creatures are putt here
10   to serve us to that ende: we should for our partes be indifferent to all these creatures, as to riches or povertie, to healthe or sicknes, to honour or contempt: and we should desire onely so muche or litle of the same, as were best for us to our sayd ende that we entende:
15   that is, to the service of God: for whoe soever desirethe or seekethe thes creatures more than this, runnethe from his ende for the which he came hither.

By this nowe maye a carefull Christian take some scantelinge of his owne estate withe God, and make a
20   conjecture whether he be in the right waye or no. For yff he attende onely or principallye to this ende, for whiche he was sent hither, that is, to serve God, and gayne heaven, yf his cares, cogitations, studies, endevours, labours, talke, and other his actions, runne upon
25   this matter, and that he careth no more for other creatures, as honour, riches, learninge, and the lyke, then they are necessarie unto hym for this ende, whiche he pretendethe. If his dayes and lyfe (I saye) be spent in this studie of the service of God, and procuringe his sal-
30   vation in feare and tremblinge as the Appostle willethe us: then is he doubtles a most happye and blessede man, and shall at lengthe attayne to the kyngedome whiche he lookethe for.

But yf he finde hym selff in a contrarie case, that is,
35   not to attende to this matter for which onelye he was sent hither, nor to have in his harte and studie this service of God, and gayninge of heaven, but rather some

The second consequence.

Phili.2.

---

16 the creatures   22 *omits* and gayne heaven   29 *omits* and procuringe his salvation in feare and tremblinge as the Appostle willethe us 32 kingdom of God   37 *omits* and gayninge of heaven

other vanitie of the world, as promotion, wealthe, pleasure, sumptuous apparell, gorgious buyldinges, bewtie, or any other thinge els that partaynethe not to this ende: yf he spende his tyme (I saye) abowt these tryfles, havinge his
5 cares and cogitations, his talke and delight, more in thes, then about the other great busines of gayninge heaven for which he was sent: Then is he in a perilouse course, leadinge directlie to perdition, except he alter and change the same. For most certaine it is, that who soever shall
10 not attende unto the service he came for, shall never attayne to the rewarde promised to that service.

And because the most parte of the world not only of infidels, but also of Christians, doe amisse in this pointe, and doe not attende to this thinge for which they were
15 onely created and sent hyther: Hence it is that Christ   Luc.13.23.
and his holye saintes have alwayes spoken so hardly of the small number that shalbe saved even amonge Christians, and have uttered some speeches which seeme very rigorous to fleshe and bloode, and scarce trewe,
20 albeit they must be fulfilled: as, *that it is easier for a camell*   Mat.19.
to goe thorowghe a needles eye then for a riche man to enter into   Mar.10.
heaven. The reason of which sayenge and many more stand-ethe in this, that a riche man or worldlinge attendinge to heape riches, can not attende to doe that whiche he
25 came for into this worlde, and consequently never attayne heaven, except God worke a miracle, and so cause hym to contemne his riches, and to use them onely to the service of God as some tymes he dothe: and we have a rare example in the gospell of Zacheus, whoe beinge
30 a very riche man, presently upon the enteringe of Christ into his house, and muche more into his harte, gave   Luc.19.
half his goodes unto the poore, and whome so ever he hadd injuried, to hym he made fower tymes so muche restitution. And so entered into heaven whiche other-
35 wyse he hadd not done.

But hereby now maye be seene the lamentable state   The

---

5 in them   6 *omits* of gayninge heaven   15 thence   17 that are in state of salvation even   31 hart by faith, gave   32 and offered withal, that whomsoever he had injuried, to him he would make four-times so much restitution   34 *omits* And so entered into heaven whiche otherwyse he hadd not done

of manye a thowsande Christians in the world, which
are so farr of from bestowinge there hole tyme and
travell in the service of God and the gayninge of heaven,
as they never almost thincke of the same, or yf they
5　doe, it is with very litle care or attention. Good Lorde,
howe manye men and women be there in the world
which bearinge the name of Christians, scarse spende
one houre of fower and twentie in the service of God?
howe manye doe beate their braynes about worldly
10　matters, and how fewe are troubled withe this care?
howe manye finde tyme to eate, drinke, sleepe, disporte,
deck and painte them selves out to the worlde, and
yet have no tyme to bestowe in this greatest busines of
all other? howe manye spend over whole dayes, weekes,
15　monethes, and yeares, in hauking, hunting, and other
pastymes, without any care or earnest cogitation of these
thinges? Other in ambition and promotion without makinge accounte or regarde of the matter? what shalbe
come of these people? what will they saye at the daye
20　of judgment? what excuse will they have?

If the marchand factour (which I spake of before) after
manye yeares spent beyond the seas, returninge home
to geeve accountes to his maister, should yeald a recon-
ninge of so muche tyme spent in singinge, so much in
25　daunsinge, so muche in courtinge, and the lyke: who
would not laughe at his accountes? but beinge further
asked by his maister, what tyme he bestowed on his mar-
chandise which he sent hym for: yf he should answere,
none at all, nor that he ever thought or studyed uppon
30　that matter: whoe wold not thynke hym worthie of all
shame and punishement? and surelye withe muche more
shame and confusion shall they stande at the daye of
judgement, whoe beinge placed here to so great a busines,
as is the service of almightie God and the gayninge of
35　his eternall kyngdome of heaven, have not withstandinge
neglected the same, bestowinge their studies, labours and

lament-
able state
of men of
the world.

A com-
parison.

---

1 manie thousand　3 *omits* and the gayninge of heaven　16 *omits*
without any care or earnest cogitation of these thinges? Other in
ambition and promotion　34 *omits* and the gayninge of his eternall
kyngdome of heaven

cogitations in the vaine trifles of this world: which is as
muche from the purpose, as yf men beinge placed in a
course to runne at a golden game of infinite price, (as
we are all placed to runne at heaven, as S. Paule sayeth)   1.Cor.9.
5   they should leave their marke and some steppe a side
after flyes or fethers in the ayre, and some other stande
styll gatheringe upp the dunge of the grounde: and how
were these men worthie (trowe you) to receave so greate
a rewarde as was proposed to them?

10   Wherfore (deare Christian) yf thow be wyse, consider
thy case whyle thou haste tyme. Followe the Apostles
counsaile: examine thy owne worke and wayes, and   Gal.6.
deceyve not thy selfe. Yet thowe maiste reforme thy
selfe, because the daye tyme of lyfe yet remayneth. The
15   dreadfull night of deathe will overtake thee shortly, when   Joh.9.
there wilbe no more tyme of reformation. What will all
thy labour and toyle in procurynge of worldlie wealthe,
profitt or comfort thee, at that hower, when it shalbe
sayed to thee, as Christ sayed to thy lyke in the ghos-
20   pell, when hee was nowe come to the topp of his worldly
felicitie: *thow foole, this nyght shall they take awaye thy soule,*   Luc.12.
and then whoe shall have the thinges which thou haste gotten
together? Beleve me (deare brother) for I tell the no un-
trewth, one howre bestowed in the service of God, will
25   more comforte the at that tyme, than a hundrede yeares
bestowed in advauncinge thy selfe and thy familie in
the world. And yf thou mightest feele nowe the case,
wherein thy poore harte shalbe then, for omittinge of
this thinge, whiche it should most have thought uppon:
30   thow wouldest take from thy sleepe, and from thy meate,
also, to recompence thy negligence for the tyme past.
The difference betwyxt a wyse man and a foole is this,
that the one prouidethe for a mischeef whyle tyme
serveth: but the other when it is to late.

35   Resolve thy self therfore good Christian whyle thow
hast tyme. Resolve thy selfe without delay, to take in
hande presentlye and to applye for the tyme to come,

---

3 *omits* (as we are all placed to runne at heaven as, S. Paule sayeth)
12 works   13 Yet maist thou have grace to reform   26 thy house in

the great and weyghtie busines for which thow wast sent
hither, which onely in deede is wayghtie and of importance, and all other are meere tryfles and vanities, but
onely so far furthe as they concerne this. Beleeve not
5   the world, whiche for runninge a wrie in this pointe,
is detested by thy Saviour, and every frend therof, pronounced an enemye to hym by his Appostle. Saye at
lenght unto thy Savyour, I doe confesse unto the o Lorde,
I doe confesse and can not denye, that I have not hith-
10   erto attended to the thinge for which I was created,
redeemed, and placed here by thee: I doe see my error,
I can not dissemble my greevous faulte, and I doe
thancke the ten thowsande tymes, that thou hast geeven
me the grace to see it whyles I maye yet amend it:
15   which by thy holye grace I meane to doe and without
delaye to alter my course, beseechinge thy divine majestie
that as thou hast geeven me this light of understandinge
to see my daunger, and this good motion to reforme
the same: So thow wilt continew towardes me thy blessed
20   assistance, for performance of the same, to thy honour
and my soules healthe. Amen.

Joh.7.8.12.
1.Joh.2.

*Of the ende of man more in particuler, and of two speciall
thinges required at his handes in this lyfe.*

CHAP. IV

25   Havinge spoken of the ende of man in generall, in the
former chapter, and shewed that it is to serve God in
this lyfe, and therby to gayne heaven in the next: it
semethe convenient (for that the matter is of greate and
singuler importance) to treate some what more in par-
30   ticuler, wherin this service of God dothe consist, that
therby a Christian may judge of him selfe, whether he
performe the same or no, and consequentlye whether

---

3 al others *and passim* (others *for* other)   14 while I may yet by thy
grace amend   22 *omits more*   26 *omits* in this lyfe, & therby to gayne
heaven in the next

he doe the thinge for whiche he was sent into this worlde.

First therfore it is to be understood, that the whole service whiche God requireth at a Christian mans handes in this lyfe, consisteth in two thinges. The one to flye evill, and thother to doe good. And albeit thes two thinges were required of us also before our redemption by Christ, as appeareth by David whose commaundement is generall: *declyne from evill and doe good*: and by Esay the prophet whose wordes are: *leave to doe perverslie, and learne to do well*: yet muche more particulerlye and with farr greater reason are they demaunded at the handes of Christian people, whoe by the death and passion of their redemer, doe receave grace and force to be able to performe thes two thinges, which the old lawe did not gyve, albeit it commaunded the same.

But nowe we beinge redeemed by Christ, and receavinge from him not onlye the renewinge of the same commaundement, for the performance of thes two thinges, but also force and habilitie by his grace, wherby we are made able to doe the same: we remayne more bounde therto in reason and dewtie than before, for that this was the fruite and effect of Christ his holye passion, as S. Peter sayeth, *that we beinge dead to sinne, shoulde live to justice*. Or as S. Paule more plainelye declareth the same when he sayeth, *the grace of God our Saveour hath appeared to all men, instructinge us to this end, that we renouncinge all wickednes and seculer desires, should live soberlye, justlye, and godlye, in this worlde.*

Thes two thinges then are the service of God, for whiche we were sent into this world: the one, to resist sinne, the other to follow good woorkes. In respect of the first we are called souldiers, and our lyfe a warfare uppon the earthe. For that as souldiers doe alwaies lye in waite to resist theire enimies: so ought we to resist sinne, and the temptations therof. And in respect of the seconde, we are called labourers, sowers, workemen,

Two partes of our ende in this lyfe.

Psal.37.
Esa.1.

Rom.6.

1.Pet.2.
Tit.2.

Two partes of the service of God.
Job.7.
2.Cor.10.
1.Tim.1.
2.Tim.2.
Phil.1.
Heb.10.

---

6 before the coming of Christ   13 able in some measure to perform   20 made somwhat able   23 *live unto righteousnes.* Or   27 *and worldly desires*   36 *omits* sowers, workemen, marchantes, bankers,

marchantes, bankers, stewardes, farmers, and the like, for
that as thes men attende diligentlye to their gayne and
increace of substance in this lyfe, so should we to good
workes, for the encrease of our treasure in the world
5 to come.

Thes two thinges are the pointes which a Christian
man should meditate uppon: the exercises wherin he
should be occupied: the two legges wheruppon he muste
walke towardes his countrie: the two armes wherwith he
10 must apprehende and lay holde on Gods eternall kingdome: and fynally the two wynges wherby he must flie
and mounte to heaven. And whosoever wanteth any one
of thes, though he had the other: yet can he not ascend
to heaven, no more than a byrde can flye lackinge one
15 of her wynges. I say, that nether innocencie is sufficient
with out good woorkes: nor good workes anye thing
availeable, where innocencie from sinne is not: the latter is evident by the people of Israell, whose sacrifices,
oblations, prayers and other good workes commended
20 and commaunded by God hym selfe, were often tymes
abhominable to God: for that the doers thereof lyved
in sinne and wickednes, as at large the prophet Esaye
declareth: the former also is made apparent by the parable of the foolishe virgines, whoe albeit they were inno-
25 cent from sinne, yet because they lacked the oyle of
good workes, they were shutt owt of doores. And at the
last daye of judgement Christ shall saye to the damned,
because you clothed me not, fed me not, and did not
other deedes of charitie appointed to your vocation: ther-
30 fore goe you to everlastinge fire, et ce. Bothe thes poyntes
then are necessarie to a Christian for his salvation: and

& 12.
Math.9.10.
20.

Luc.10.
1.Tim.5.

Psal.126.
Mat.13.

Esa.1.
Mat.25.

Luc.13.
Mat.25.

---

4 *omits* for the encrease of our treasure in the world to come; *substitutes* to the glorie of God, and benefit of others here in this life
6 These therfore are two special points which a Christian man should
meditate upon; two special exercises wherin he shuld be occupied:
two special legs wherupon he must walk in the service of God: and
finally two wings wherby he must flie and mount up unto a Christian
life. And 12 wanteth either of 13 ascend to any tru godlines, no
more 25 bicause they gave not attendance, they were shut out of
the doores. Christian to the service of God: and

so necessarie, as one without the other avayleth not, as
I have sayed.

And towchinge the first, whiche is resistinge of sinne:
we are willed to doe it (by S. Paule) even unto deathe
5   and with the last of our blood (yf it were neede:) and in
divers other places of scripture, the holie ghost willeth
us most diligentlye to prepare our selves, to resist the
devill manfullye, whiche tempteth us to sinne: and this
resistance ought to be made in suche perfect maner, as
10   we yealde not wittinglye and willinglie to any syn what
soever, ether in worke, worde, or consent of harte: in
so muche, that whoe so ever should geeve secret consent of minde to the performance of a sinne yf he had
time, place, and abilytie therunto: is condemned by the
15   holye scripture in that sinne, even as yf he had committed the same now in acte. And touchinge the second, which is good woorkes, we are willed to doe them
abundantlie, diligentlie, joyfullye, and incessantlie, for so
saieth the scripture. *What soever thy hand can doe, doe it*
20   *instantlie.* And againe: *walke worthie of God, fructyfiynge in*
everie good woorke. And againe S. Paule sayeth: *Let us doe*
good workes unto all men. And agayne in the verie same
place, *let us never leave of to doe good, for the tyme will come*
when we shall reape without end. And in an other place he
25   willeth us to *be stable, immoveable, and abundant in good*
woorckes, knowinge that our laboure shall not be unprofitable.

By this it may be seene (deare brother) what a perfect
creature, is a good Christian, that is, as S. Paule describeth hym, *the handworke of God and creature of Christ to*
30   *good workes, wherin he hathe prepared that he should walcke.* It
appeareth (I saye) what an exacte lyfe the trew lyfe of
a Christian is: which is a continuall resistance of all
sinne, bothe in thought, word and deede, and a performance or exercise of all good woorkes, that possiblie
35   he can devise to doe. What an Angelicall lyfe is this?
nay more than Angelicall, for that Angels beinge now
placed in their glorie, have neither temptation of sinne

How we
ought to
resist
sinne.
Heb.12.
Eph.5.
Jaco.4.
1.Pet.5.

Math.5.

Exod.20.
Deut.5.
How we
must doe
good
woorkes.
Eccle.9.
Col.1.
Gal.6.

1.Cor.15.

A descrip-
tion of a
Christian.
Ephe.2.

---

4 *omits* (by S. Paule)   6 divers places

to resist, nor can doe any meritorious worke as we maye.

If Christians did live accordinge to this their dewtie, that is, in doinge all good that they might, and never consentinge to evill: what needed there almost any tem- porall lawes? what a goodlye common wealth were Chris- tianitie? Whoe will not marvaile of the happy dayes of our forefathers, wherin such simplicitie, such trueth, such conscience, suche almes deedes, such sinceritie, such vertue, such religion and devotion, is reported to have ben? the cause was, for that they studied uppon thes two pointes of a Christian mans dewtie, and laboured for the performance therof, everye man as God gave hym grace. And we, because we looke not into thes matters, are become as loose and wicked in lyfe, as ever the gentiles or infidels were. And yet is God the same God still, and will accept at our handes, no other accounte, than he did of our forefathers, for the per- fourmance of thes two partes of our dewtie towardes hym. What than shall become of us, which doe not lyve in anye parte as they did? And to enter yet some what more into the particuler consideration of thes thinges, whoe is there now a dayes amongest common Christians, (for no dout there be in secrette, manye servauntes of God which doe it) but of those which beare the name of Christians and most sturr abrode in the world, whoe is there (I saye) that taketh any payne aboute the first pointe, that is, towchinge the resistinge of the concu- piscence of sinne? which concupiscence or naturall motion to sinne, remayninge in us, as a remnant of our natu- rall maladie in punishment of the sinne of our first father Adam, is left in us now after baptisme, *ad agonem*, that is, to stryve withall, and to resist, and by resistinge, to merit increase of glorie in heaven. But alas how manie be there which doe resist (as they should) thes evill motions of concupiscence? whoe dothe ever examine

The per- fection of a Christian life.

Aug.lib.2. cont. Julian & li.I.de peccat. mer. ca.vl. Jo. Cassian.l. 5.c.12. & deinceps.

---

1 do any work (as we may) for to encrease their further glorie   6 wil not marvel at the rare examples of many good forefathers of ours 17 those forefathers of ours   28 natural motion of sin   32 *omits* and by resistinge, to merit increase of glorie in heaven

his conscience of the same? whoe doth not yelde commonlye consent of harte, to everye motion that commeth with pleasure, of covetousnes, of anger, of revenge,
of pryde, of ambition, and above all, of lecherie, and
5   other filthye synnes of the fleshe: knowinge notwithstandinge (by the protestation of our Saveour Christ him   Mat.5.
selfe) that everye such consent of harte, is as much in substance of synne, as the act, and maketh the soule guiltie
of eternall damnation?

10   It is a wounderfull matter to consider, and able to
make a man astonnyed to thincke, what greate care,
feare, diligence and laboure, good men in old tymes did
take about this matter of resistinge synne, and how lytle
we take now. Job the just, havinge lesse cause to feare   Job.9.
15   than we, saieth of hym selfe: *I did feare all my doinges (o
lord) consideringe that thow doest not pardon such as offende the.*
But the good kynge David whiche had now tasted Gods
heavie hande for consentinge to sinne before, shewethe
him selfe yet more carefull and fearefull in the matter,
20   when he saieth: *I did meditate in the night tyme together with*   Psal.77.
*my harte, and it was my whole exercise, and I did brushe or
sweepe myne owne spirite withe in me*: what a diligent examination of his conscience, thoughtes and cogitations was
this in a kynge? and all this was for the avoidinge and
25   resistinge of synne: as allso it was in S. Paule, whoe
examined his conscience so narrowly, and resisted all
temptations with suche diligence and attention, as he
could pronounce of hym selfe, that to his knoledge he   1.Cor.4.
was guyltie of nothinge, albeit he doth confesse in an
30   other place, that he had most vile and strong temptations of the fleshe layed uppon him of the devill, by
Gods permission: marye yet by the grace of Christ he   2.Cor.12.
resisted and overcame all. For the better performance
wherof it is liklye that he used also these externall helpes
35   and remedies of much fastinge, longe prayinge, painefull   2.Cor.6.

---

29 was in his ministerie guiltie   31 by Gods appointment. Yet by
35 remedies of tru fasting, earnest praieng, diligent watching, and
severe chastising of his body, by continual and most painful labour
in his vocation, wherof

watchinge, and severe chastisinge of his bodie, wherof   & 11.
he maketh mention in his writinges. As also all godlye   2.Tim.1.
men by his example, have used the lyke helpes sence,   1.Cor.9.
for the better resistinge of synfull temptations when neede
5 requyred, I meane the helpes of abstinence, fastinge,   Remedies
watchinge, prayer, chastisinge of the bodie by heare-   used by
clothe, lyinge on the grownde, beatinge, and the like.   the aun-
Wherof I coulde here recite greate store of examples   cient
out of the holye fathers.   fathers for
  resistynge
10 But he which would reade many heaped togyther in   of synne.
everye one of thes particuler pointes, let him reade the
worckes of John Cassian the Eremite, which wrote almost   Jo.Cassian.
twelve hundred yeres past, of the doinges of mounkes   de instit.
and other the best Christians in his dayes: or let him   renun-
  ciant. &
15 reade Marcus Marulus examples of the lyves of the aun-   collat.
cient fathers gathered owt of this Cassian, S. Jherome   patrum.
and others: where he shall reade manye thinges that will   M. Maru-
make hym wounder, and afeard also (if he be not past   lus de
feare) to see what extreame payne and diligence these   factis
  dictisque
20 first Christians tooke, in watchinge everye litle sleight of   memora-
the devill, and in resistinge everie litle temptation or   bilibus.
cogitation of synne, wheras we never thincke of the matter, nor make accounte ether of cogitation, consent of
harte, worde or worke, but doe yelde to all what soever
25 our concupiscence moveth us unto, doe swallow downe
everie hooke layed us by the devill, and most greedelye
doe devoure everie poysened pleasant bayte, which is
offered by the enimye for the destruction of our sowles:
and thus muche aboute resistinge of synne.

30 But now touchinge the second poynte, whiche is con-   How
tinuall exercisinge our selves in good workes, it is evi-   much we
dent in it selfe, that we utterlie fayle (for the most parte   fayle in
of us) in the same. I have shewed before how we are   doinge
in scripture commaunded, to doe them, without ceassinge,   good
35 and most diligentlye whiles we have tyme of daye to   workes.

---

5 *omits* I meane the helpes of abstinence, fastinge, watchinge, prayer,
chastisinge of the bodie by heareclothe, lyinge on the grownde,
beatinge 10 *omits* But he which would reade . . . where he shall
reade manye thinges; *continues* fathers: which would make a man to
woonder 18 if he were not

doe them in, for as Christ sayth, *the night will come when*   Jo.9.
no man can worke anye more. I might also shew how our
forefathers the sainctes of God, were most diligent and
carefull in doinge good workes in their daies, even as
5   the husbandman is carefull to caste seede into the grownde
whyles fayre weather lasteth, and the marchante to laye
out his monye whiles the good markytt endureth: they
knew the tyme woulde not last longe, which they had to   Gal.6.
worke their owne salvation in: and therfore they bestirred   Phili.2.
10   them selves whiles opportunitie served: they never ceased
but came from one good worke to an other, well knowinge
what they did, and what gayne they hoped for.

If there were nothinge els to prove their wounderfull care and diligence herein: yet the infinite monu-
15   mentes of their almes deedes, yet extant to the worlde,
are sufficient testimonies of the same: to wit, the infinite churches builded and indowed with greate and
abundant maintenance, for the ministers of the same:
so manye bishopprickes, deaneryes, archdeaconryes, Can-
20   onryes, prebendes, chauntryes, and the like: So manye
hospitalles and houses of orphanes and poore people: so
many scholes, Colledges, universities: so manye bridges,
high wayes, and publique commodities, so manye Abbayes, Nunries, Priaries, hermitages, and the like, for
25   the service of God, and repose of holye people, whiche
would leave the world and betake them selves onlye to
the contemplation of heavenlye thinges. Which charita-
ble deedes all (and a thowsand more bothe private and
publique, secrete and open, which I can not reporte)
30   came owt of the purses of our good auncesters: whoe

---

2 how certein of our forefathers   9 *omits* their owne salvation   12
did, and how good and acceptable service it was unto God.   14
[* monuments] *mn:* B. Although many such things wer doon to super-
stitious and very il uses: yet even then also were they somtimes
sufficient testimonies of a great care to do wel (so far as their knowledge served them) in so manie as did not wilfully er; but were
desirous to know the truth, and to do accordingly. And so may those
also be (in such a sense) examples to us.   19 *omits* so manye bishopprickes . . . houses of orphanes and poore people   23 *omits* so
manye Abbayes . . . contemplation of heavenlye thinges   28 deeds
(and

oftentimes not onlye gave of their abundance, but also
saved from their owne mouthes and plucked from their
owne children and posteritie, and bestowed it uppon
deedes of charitie for behoofe of their sowels. Wheras
5   we are so farof from geevinge awaye our necessaries, as
we will not bestow our verie superfluities, but will im-
ploye them rather, upon haukes and dogges, and other
brute beastes, and some times also upon much viler uses,
then to the reliefe of our poore brethren, and to the
10   ease of our sowles in the lyfe to come.

Alas (deare brother) to what a carelesse and senseles
estate are we come towchinge our owne salvation and
damnation? S. Paule cryeth owt unto us, *worke your owne*   Phili.2.
salvation with feare and tremblinge: And yet no man for that
15   maketh accounte therof. S. Peter warneth us gravelye
and ernestlye: *brethren take you great care to make your voca-*   2.Pet.1.
tion and election suer by good workes, and yet whoe almost
will thinke upon them? Christ him selfe thundereth in
thes wordes: *And I tell you make your selves frindes, (in this*   Luc.16.
20   *woorld) of unjust mammon, that when you fainte they maye receave*
you into eternall tabernacles. That is, by your riches of this
worlde, purchase unto you the prayers of good people,
that by their intercession, you may enjoye lyfe everlastinge. And yet for all that, we are not moved here-
25   withall: so deade we are and lumpyshe to all goodnes.

If God did exhorte us to good deedes for his owne
commoditie, or for any gayne that he is to take therby:
yet in reason we ought to pleasure him therin, seinge
we have receaved all from his onlye liberalitie before.
30   But seinge he asketh it at our handes for no neede of
his owne, but onlye for our gayne, and to paye us home
agayne with usury: it is more reason we should harken
unto him. If a common honest man upon earthe shoulde
invite us to do a thinge, promisinge us of his honestie
35   a sufficient rewarde, we woulde beleeve him: but God

---

2 *omits* plucked from their owne children & posteritie   4 charitie, to
the glorie of God; and benefit of others. Wheras   9 *omits* and to the
ease of our sowles in the lyfe to come   21 *omits* That is, by your
riches . . . enjoye lyfe everlastinge.   32 with advantage: it   35 reward
to our wel doing

makinge infinite promises unto us in scripture of eternall rewarde for our well doinge, as that we shall eate
with him, drincke with him, raigne with him, possesse
heaven with hym, and the like, can not move us notwith-
5   standinge to workes of charitie. Marie because our forefathers were moved here withall, as havinge hartes of
softer metall than ours are of: therfor they brought
forth such abundant fruite as I have shewed.

Of all this then that I have sayde, the godlie Christian
10   maie gather, first, the lamentable estate of the world at
this daye, when amongest the small number of those
whiche beare the name of Christians, so manye are like
to perishe, for not perfourminge of thes two principall
pointes of theire vocation. Secondly he maye gather the
15   cause of the infinite difference of rewarde for good and
evill in the lyfe to come, whiche some men will seeme
to mervaille at: but in deede is most just and reasonable, consideringe the greate diversitie of lyfe in good
and evill men whiles they are in this worlde. For the
20   good man dothe not onlye lyve voide of mortall syn:
but also by resistinge the same, daylie and howerlye encreaseth his merit. The loose man, by yeldinge consent
to his concupiscence, dothe not onlye lose all merit, but
also doubleth synne upon synne without number. The
25   good man, besides avoydinge syn, dothe infinite good
worckes, at the least wise in desyre and harte, where
greater abilitie serveth not. But the wicked man, neyther
in hart or deede dothe anye good at all, but rather seeketh in place therof to doe hurte. The good man im-
30   ployeth all his mynde, harte, wordes, and handes, to
the service of God and of his servauntes for his sake.
But the wicked man bendeth all his force and powers
bothe of bodye and mynde, to the service of vanities,
the world, and his fleshe: in so muche, that as the
35   good man encreaseth howerlye in merit, to whiche is
due encrease of grace and glorye in heaven: so the evyl

Luc.22.
Mat.13.
Rom.8.
Apo.22.

The
different
state of a
good &
evel man
at the
daye of
deathe.

---

5 charitie. But bicause those forefathers of ours were   20 only endevor to avoid sin   21 encreaseth in the favor of God. The   23
lose the favor of God, but   35 hourly in the favor of God

from tyme to tyme, in thought, worde or deede, or in all at once, heapeth up sinne and damnation uppon him selfe, to whiche is due vengeance, and encrease of tormentes in hell: and in this contrarie course they passe over their lyves for twentie, thirtie, or fortie yeres, and so come to dye. And is it not reason now, that seinge there is so great diversitie in their estates: there shoulde be as greate or more diversitie also in their rewarde? especiallye seinge God is a great God, and rewardeth small thinges with greate wages, ether of everlastinge glorye, or everlastinge payne.

Thirdlye and lastlye the diligent and carefull Christian may gather of this, what greate cause he hath to put in practyse the godlie counsaile of S. Paule which is, *that everie man shoulde prove and examine his owne worke* and so be able to judge of hym selfe, in what case he standeth. And yf uppon this examination, he finde him selfe a wrye: to thanke God of so greate a benifite, as is the reveilinge of his daunger, whyles yet there is tyme and place to make amendes for all. No doubt manye perishe dailie by Gods justice in theire owne grosse ignorance, whoe if they had receaved this speciall favoure, as to see the pitt before they fell in: happylye they woulde have escaped the same. Use Goddes mercie to thy gayne then (gentle brother) and not to thy further damnation. If thow see by this examination that hitherto thow hast not led a trew Christian lyfe: resolve thy selfe to begynne now, and cast not awaye wilfullye that precious sowle of thyne, whiche Christ hath bought so dearlye, and which he is most readie to save and endew with grace and eternall glorye, if thow wouldest yelde the same into his handes, and be content to direct thy lyfe accordinge to his most holye, easie, and sweete commaundementes.

Gal.6.

---

15 *his own works* 20 place to amend. No 23 in, it may be they
30 and to indu

Of the severe accounpte that we must yelde to God of the
matters aforesayed.

CHAP. V

Amongest other pointes of a prudent servant, this is to be

5   esteemed one principall, to consider in everye thinge committed to his charge, what accounpte shalbe demaunded
towchinge the same: also what maner of man his maister is: whether facile, or rigorous: mylde, or sterne: careles or exquisite in his accountes. Also whether he be

10   of abilitie to punishe hym at his pleasure, findinge him
faultie: and finallye, how he hathe dealt with other before in like matters. For accordinge to thes circumstances (if he be wise) he will governe hym selfe and
use more or lesse diligence in the charge committed.

15   The like wisdome woulde I counsaile a Christian to
use, in the matters before recited: to witt, towchinge our
ende for which God sent us hither, and the two principall pointes therof, enjoyned for our exercise in this life:
to consider (I saye) what accounte we shalbe demaunded

20   for the same: in what maner: by whome: with what severitie: with what daunger of punishment, if we be founde
negligent and recheles therin.

For better understandinge wherof, it is to be noted,
first, with what order and with what ceremonies and

25   circumstances God gave us this charge, or rather made
and proclaimed this lawe of our behaveoure and service
towardes him. For albeit he gave the same commaundement to Adam in his first creation, and imprinted it
afterwardes by nature into the hartes of eche man before

30   it was writen (as S. Paule testifyeth:) yet for more plaine
declarations sake, and to convince us the more of our
wickednes, (as the same Apostle noteth,) he published
the same lawe in writen tables, uppon the mounte Synay:
Marie withe suche terrour, and other circumstances of

Marginal notes:

A princi-
pall point
of wyse-
dome in
a servant.

A neces-
sarie con-
sideration.

Rom.2.
Rom.7.
Gal.3.

---

8 whether gentle, or rigorous   33 in writing tables   33 Synay: but
with *and passim* (but *for* Mary)

Majestie, (as also S. Paule noteth to the Hebrews) as may   Heb.12.
greatly astonishe the breakers therof. Let anye man reade
the nynetenthe chapter of Exodus, and there he shall   Exo.19.
see, what a preparation there was for the publishinge of
5   this lawe. First, God calleth Moyses up to the hill, and   The
there reckoneth upp all the benefites which he ever had   dreadfull
bestowed upon the people of Israell: and promiseth them   publica-
manye more, yf they would keepe the lawe which he   tion of
was then to geve them. Moyses went to the people, and   the lawe.
10   returned aunswere againe, that they would keepe it.
Then caused God the people to be sanctified against
the thirde daye, to washe all their garmentes, and that
no man shoulde companie with his wife: also to be
charged that none upon payne of death should presume
15   to mounte up to the hyll but Moyses alone, and that
whoe soever should dare but to touche the hill, should
presentlie be stoned to death. When the third daye was
come, the Angels (as S. Steven interpreteth it) were readie   Act.7.
there to promulgate the lawe. The trompettes sounded
20   mightilye in the ayre: greate thunder brake owt from
the skye, with fearse lightninges, horrible clowdes, thicke
mystes, and terrible smoke rysinge from the mountaine.
And in the middest of all this Majestie, and dreadfull
terror, God spake in the hearinge of all: *I am thy Lorde*   Exo.20.
25   *God which have brought the out of the lande of Egypt, me onlie*   Deut.5.
shalt thow serve: and the rest which foloweth, containinge
a perfect description of our dewtie in this lyfe, commonlye called the ten commaundementes of God.
    All which terror and majestie, S. Paule hym selfe as
30   I have sayde, applyeth to this meaninge, that we should   Heb.12.
greatlye tremble to breake this lawe, delyvered us with
such circumstances of dread and feare: signifiyinge also
hereby, that the exaction of this lawe, must needes be
with greater terrour at the daye of judgement, seinge
35   that the publication therof, was with such astonishment
and dreade. For so we see alwaies great princes lawes

---

1 also the Apostle noteth *and passim* (the Apostle *for* S. Paule *as author
of Heb*)   6 up many of benefits which he had bestowed   18 were
readie to

to be executed upon the offenders with much more terror than they were proclaimed. And this maye be a forcible reason to move a Christian to looke unto his dewtie.

5   Secondlye if we consider the sharpe execution used by God upon offenders of this lawe, bothe before it was writen and synce: we shall fynde greate cause of feare also, as the wounderfull punishement upon Adam and so manye millions of people besydes, for his one fault: the drowninge of all the worlde together: the burninge

10   of Sodome and Gomorra with brimstone: the reprobation of Saul: the extreme chastisement of David: and the like. Which all beinge done by God with suche rigour for lesse and fewer synnes than ours are, and allso uppon them whome he had more cause to spare

15   than he hath to tollerate with us: may be admonishmentes what we must looke for at Gods handes, for breache of this law of servinge him in this lyfe.

     Thirdlye if we consider the speeches and behavyour of our lord and maister Christ in this matter: we shall

20   have yet more occasion to doubte our owne case: whoe albeyt he came now to redeeme us and to pardone all, in all mildenes, humilitie, clemencie and mercye: yet in this point of our accounte he never shewed but austeritie and greate rigour, not onlie in wordes and familiar

25   speeche with his Apostles, but also in examples and parables to this purpose. For so in one parable he damneth that poore servaunte to hell, (where should be weepinge and gnashinge of teeth) onlye for that he had not augmented his talent delivered hym. And Christ confesseth

30   there of him selfe, that he is a hard man, reapinge where he sowed not, and gathering where he cast not abrode: expectinge also usurye at our handes, for the talentes lent us, and not accepting onlye his owne againe. And consequentlie threatning much more rigour to them

35   which shall mispende his talentes, as the most of us doe. Agayne he damneth the servant whome he founde asleepe: he damned the poore man which was compelled to come

Marginal notes:

Gods punishments.

Gen.3.

Gen.7.
Gen.19.
1.Re.28.
2.Re.12.

Christes speches.

Mat.25.

Mat.24.
Mat.22.

---

15 tollerate us   23 point of taking accounts, he is not woont to shew but   24 familiar speeches   32 also advantage at our hands

into the weddinge, onlye for that he came without a
wedding garment: he damned the fyve foolishe virgynes,   Mat.25.
for that they had not theire oyle with them, and were
not readie jumpe at the verie hower to goe in with hym,
5   and would not know them when they came after: and
finallie he promiseth to damne all those (without exception) which shall worke iniquitie, as S. Mathew testifieth.   Matt.13.

   Moreover beinge asked by a certaine prince on a tyme
how he might be saved: he woold geeve hym no other
10   hope, though he were a prince, but onlye this, *yf thow*
wilt enter into lyfe, keepe the commaundements of God. And   Luc.18.
talkinge with his Disciples at an other tyme of the same   Mat.19.
matter, he geeveth them no other comfort but this: *yf*
ye love me keepe my commaundements. As whoe should saye, if   Joh.14.
15   you were never so much my Disciples, and yf ye breake
my commaundements: there is no more love nor frend-
shippe betwixt us. And S. John (which best of all other
knew his meaninge herein) expoundeth it in this sense,
when he saythe: *if a man* (sayeth he) *knoweth God, and yet*   1.Joh.2.
20   *keepeth not his commaundementes, he is a lyar, and the trueth is*
not in him. And more yet (to take awaye all hope or
expectation from his disciples of any other waye of
salvation, than by keepinge his commaundementes) he
saieth in an other place, that *he came not to take awaye the*   Math.5.
25   *law but to fulfill it,* and streight waie he inferreth upon
the same, *whoe soever therfore shall breake one of the least of*
thes commaundementes, shalbe called the least in the kingdome of
heaven. For whiche cause, at his departure out of the
worlde, the verie last wordes that he spake to his Apostles
30   were these: that they should teach men *to observe all his*   Mat.28.
commaundementes what soever.

   By which appeareth the severe meaninge that Christ
had towchinge our accounte for the keepinge of his commaundementes in this lyfe. The whiche also may be
35   gathered by that beinge asked whether the number were   Luc.13.
small of them that should be saved: he aunswereth yea,

---

10 hope (so long as he sought salvation by his works) though   13
other rule of their life, but   15 disciples, if   17 of al others knew
22 way pleasing him than   36 *omits* aunswereth yea, and

and counsaileth men to stryve to goe into the straite
gate: for that manie should be shut out, yea even of
them, which had eaten and dronken with him, and had
enjoyed the corporall presence of his blessed bodye, but
5   had not lyved as he commaunded them. In whiche case
he signifieth that no respect or frindshippe must take
place with hym at the last day. For whiche cause he
saide to the man whome he had healed at the fishepools
side in Jerusalem, *beholde now thow art hole, see thow synne*   Joh.5.
10 *no more, least worse happen to the than before.* And general-
lye he warneth us in S. Mathews ghospell, that we agree   Matt.5.
with our adversaries, and make our accountes streight
in this lyfe, otherwise we shall paye the uttermost fardinge
in the life to come. And yet more severelye he sayth in
15 an other place: *that we shall render account at the daye of*   Mat.12.
judgement for everie ydle worde whiche we have spoken.

Whiche daie of judgement he warneth us of before,
and foretelleth the rigour and daunger in sundrie places
of holye scripture to the end we should prevent the
20 same, and so direct our lyves while we have time in this
world: as we may present our selves at that daye without feare and daunger, or rather with greate joye and
confort when so manie thowsands of whicked people
shall appeare there, to their eternall confusion.

25 And because there is nothinge which so fitlye sheweth   Of the
the severitie of Christ in taking our accounte at the last   daye of
daye, as the order and maner of this judgement described   judge-
most diligentlie by the holye scripture it selfe: it shall   ment.
make muche for our purpose, to consider the same. And
30 first of all, it is to be noted, that there be two judge-   Two
mentes appointed after death: the one called particuler,   judge-
wherby eche man presentlie upon his departure from   ments after
this worlde, receaveth particuler sentence, ether of pun-   death.
ishement or of glorie, accordinge to his deedes in this   Joh.5.
35 life (as Christes owne words are:) wherof we have ex-   Mat.25.
amples in Lazarus and the riche gloutton, whoe were   & 16.
presentlie caried, the one to payne, thother to rest, as
S. Luke testifieth. And to doubt of this, were obstinacie,   Luc.16.

---

5 had not regarded to live as   31 death; wherof the one is called

as S. Austen affirmeth. The other judgement is called generall, for that it shalbe of all men together in the end of the world, where shall a finall sentence be pronounced, (eyther of reward, or punishment) upon all men that ever lived, accordinge to the workes which they have done, good or bad, in this life: and afterward never more question be made of alteringe their estate: that is, of easinge the paine of the one or endinge the glorie of the other.

Now as towchinge the first of these two judgements, albeit the holye auncient fathers, especiallie S. Austen, doe gather and consider divers particulers of greate severitie and feare (as the passage of our soule from the bodye to the tribunall seate of God, under the custodie both of good and evill Angels: the feare she hath of them: the sodeine straungenes of the place where she is: the terror of Gods presence, the strayte examination she must abyde, and the lyke) yet for that the moste of thes thinges are to be considered also in the seconde judgement which is generall: I will passe over to the same: notinge onlye certaine reasons yealded by the holye fathers, why God after the first judgement, (wherin he had assigned to eche man accordinge to his desertes in particuler) would appoint moreover this second generall judgement. Wherof the first is, for that the bodie of man rysinge from his sepulcher, might be partaker of the eternall punishement or glorie of the sowle, even as it hath bene partaker with the same, eyther in vertue or vice in this lyfe. The seconde is, that as Christ was dishonored and put to confusion heere in the world publikelye: so muche more he might shew his majestie and power, at that daye in the sight of all creatures, and especiallie of his enimyes.

The third is, that both the wicked and good might receave theire rewarde openlye, to more confusion and harte greefe of the one, and triumphe of the other, whoe commonlie in this world have ben overborne by the wicked. The fourth is, for that evill men when they dye,

Lib.2.de anima. chap.4.

2.Cor.5.

The particuler judgement.
Aug.tra. 49. In Jo.

Why there be two judgements appointed.
1.

2.

3.

4.

---

36 and to the greater joy and triumph

do not commonlie carie with them all theire demerite
and evill: for that they leave behynde them ether theire
evill example, or theire children and familiars corrupted
by them, or els bookes and meanes which maie in time
5 corrupt other. All which beinge not yet done, but comminge to passe after theire death, they can not so con-
venientlie receave their judgement for the same presentlie:
but as the evill falleth out: so their paines are to be
encreased. The like may be saied of the good. So that
10 (for examples sake) S. Paules glorie is increased dailie,
and shalbe unto the worldes ende, by reason of them
that daylye profit by his writinges and example: and the
paines of the wicked are for the lyke reason dailye augmented. But at the last daye of judgement, shalbe an
15 end of all meryt and demerit, and then it shalbe seene
evidentlye what eche man hathe deserved.

To speake then of this second judgement, generall
and common for all the worlde, wherin as the scripture
saith, *God shall bringe into judgement everie errour which hath*
20 *bene committed*: there are divers circunstances to be considered, and divers men doe set downe the same diver-
slye, but in myne opinion, no better, playner, or more
effectuall declaration can be made therof, than the verye
scripture maketh it selfe, settinge furthe unto us in most
25 significant wordes, all the maner, order, and circunstances, with the preparation therunto as followeth.

At that daye, there shalbe signes in the Sunne and in
the moone, and in the starres: the Sunne shalbe darckened: the moone shall geeve no light: the starres shall
30 fall from the skyes: and all the powers of heaven shalbe
moved: the firmament shall leave his situation with a
greate violence: the elementes shalbe dissolved with heate:
and the earth with all that is in it shalbe consumed with
fire: the earthe also shall move of her place, and shall
35 flye like a litle deare or sheepe. The pressures of nations upon the earthe shalbe greate, by reason of the

Consider
well this
reason
good
reader.

Of the
generall
day of
judge-
ment.
Eccl.12.

Luc.21.
Mat.24.
Marc.13.

Esa.13.

---

14 shal be an end of al our dooings, and then   16 evidently, what
ech man is to have in the justice, and mercie of God.   35 The distresse of nations

confusion of the noyse of the sea and fluddes, and men
shall wither a waye for feare and expectation of thes
thinges, that then shall come upon the whole world. Then
shall the signe of the Sonne of man appeare in the skye,
and then shall all the tribes of the earthe mourne and
wayle: and they shall see the sonne of man comminge
in the clowdes of heaven, with muche power and glorie,
great authoritie and majestie. And then in a moment, in   1.Cor.15.
the twynklynge of an eye, he shall send his Angels with
a trumpet and with a greate crie at midnight, and they   Mat.25.
shall gather together his elect, from the fower partes of
the world, from heaven to earth. All must be presented   2.Cor.5.
before the tribunall of Christ: whoe will bringe to light   1.Cor.4.
those thinges which were hidden in darcknes, and will
make manifest the thoughtes of mens hartes: and what
soever hath bene spoken in chambers in the eare, shalbe
preached upon the house toppe: Accounte shalbe asked   Lu.12.
of everye ydle worde, and he shall judge our verie right-   Psal.75.
eousnes it selfe. Then shall the just stande in greate constancie, against those which have afflicted them in this
lyfe. And the wicked seeinge that, shalbe trowbled with   Sap.5.
a horrible feare, and shall saye to the hilles, fall uppon   Luc.23.
us, and hyde us from the face of hym that sitteth uppon   Apoc.6.
the throne, and from the angre of the lambe, for that
the greate daye of wrath is come. Then shall Christ sep-   Mat.25.
arate the sheepe from the goates, and shall put the
sheepe on his right hande, and the goates on the left,
and shall saye to those on the right hand, come ye
blessed of my father, possesse the kingdome prepared
for you, from the beginninge of the worlde: I was hungry, and you gave me to eate: I was a straunger, and
you gave me harboure: I was naked, and you clothed
me. I was sycke, and you visited me: I was in prison,
and you came to me. Then shall the just saye, o lorde
when have we donne thes thinges for the? and the kinge
shall aunswere: trewlye when you dyd them to the least
of my brothers, you did it to me. Then shall he saye
to them on his left hand: departe from me (you accursed)

---

13 the judgement seat of   33 *omits* I was sycke, and you visited me

into everlastinge fyre, prepared for the devill and his angels: for I was hungrie, and you fed me not: I was a straunger, and you harboured me not: I was naked, and you clothed me not: I was sicke and in prison, and you
5   visited me not. Then shall they saye, o lorde, when have we seene thee hungrie, or thirstie, or a straunger, or naked or sicke, or in pryson, and did not minister unto the? and he shall aunswere, verylye I tell you: seeinge you have not donne it to one of thes lesser, you have
10   not done it to me. And then thes men shall goe into eternall punishment, and the just into lyfe everlastinge.

Tell me what a dreadfull preparation is heere layed doune? how manye circumstances of feare and horrour? it shalbe (saythe the scripture) at midnight when com-
15   monlie men are a sleepe: it shalbe with hydeous noyse of trumpetts, sounde of waters, motion of all the ele-mentes. What a night will that bee trowest thow, to see the earthe shake, the hilles and dales moved from their places, the moone darckened, the starrs fall downe from
20   heaven, the whole element shivered in peeces, and all the world in a flaminge fire?

Sainct John sawe it in vision, and was marvailous a   Apoc.6.
feard. I saw (saithe he) when the lambe had opened one of the seven seales: and I harde one of the fower beastes
25   saye (lyke the voyce of a thunder) come and see, and I sawe: and beholde a white horse, and one that satte upon him had a bowe, and he went out to conquere. Then went there furthe a blacke horse, and he that sate upon him had a payre of balances in his hand: then
30   went there forthe a pale horse, and he that satte upon hym was named *death*: and *hell* folowed behynde hym: and he had authoritie geeven hym to kyll by sworde, by death, and by beastes of the earth. The earth did shake, the sunne grew blacke lyke a sacke: the moone
35   like bloode: the starres fell from heaven: the skye dou-bled it selfe like a folded booke: everie hyll and Ilande was moved from his place: the kynges of the earth and

_____

22 *omits* Sainct John sawe it in vision ... sence men dwelt uppon the grounde. [47.19]

princes and tribunes, and the riche and stoute hid them
selves in dennes, and in the rockes of hylles. Then appeared there seven Angels with seven trumpettes, and
eche one prepared hym selfe to blow his blast. At the
5   first blast came there hayle and fyre mixt with bloode.
At the second blast came there a whole mountaine of
burnynge fyre into the sea, and the thyrd part of the
sea was made bloode. At the thyrd blast fell there a
greate starre from heaven named Absinthium, burninge
10   like a torche, and infected the ryvers and fountaines. At
the fourth blast was striken doune the third parte of
the sunne, moone, and starres: and an egle flewe in the
element cryeinge with a hydeous voice: woe, woe, woe
to all them that dwell uppon the earth. At the fyfthe   Apoc.9.
15   blast fell a starre from heaven which had the keye of
the pytt of hell, and he opened the pitt, and there arose
a smoke as from a greate furnace, and there came forth
(besydes) certaine Locustes lyke scorpions, to torment
them that had not the marcke of God in their fore-
20   heades. And at thes dayes men shall seeke deathe and
shall not fynde it. And these Locustes were like barbed
horses, with crownes on their heades. Their faces like
men, theire heare lyke wemen, their teeth lyke lyons:
and the noyse of their wynges lyke the noyse of manye
25   chariottes running together: their tayles like scorpions,
and theyre stinges were in their tayles: their kynge was
an Angel of hell, named Abbadon, whiche signifieth an
utter destroyer. At the sixth blast of the triumpet, were
loosed fower angels tyed before, and then rushed forth
30   an armye of horsemen in number twentie hundred times
ten thowsand, and I sawe the horses, and they which
satte upon them had breastplates of fyre and brymstone.
The heades of these horses were as lyons, and out of
their mouthes came fyre and smoke and brymstone,
35   wherby they slewe the third parte of men which had
not repented, and their strength was in their tailes, whiche
were like serpentes. Then was there an angel whiche
puttinge one foote uppon the sea, and an other uppon
the land, did sweare by hym that lyvethe for ever and
40   ever, that after the blast of the seventh trumpett there

should be no more tyme. And so when the seventh   Apo.11.
angell had sounded, their came greate voyces from heaven
sayinge, the kyngdome of this world is made to our
lorde and his Christ, and he shall raigne for ever. And   Apo.16.
5   I hearde a great voice sayinge to the seven angels: goe
and powre out seven cuppes of Godes wrath upon the
earth: and so they did. And the first brought foorth
cruell wounds uppon men: the second turned the sea
into reade bloode: the thirde turned the rivers and foun-
10   taines into bloode: the fowrth afflicted men with fyre
and made them blaspheme God: the fifthe made them
eate their owne tongues for sorowe: the sixth dried up
the water. And I sawe three foule spirites lyke frogges
issew out of the mouth of a dragon. And finallie the
15   seventh cuppe beinge powred out there came a mightie
voyce from the throne of God, sayinge, it is dispatched.
And there followed lyghtninges, and thunders, and voices,
and earthquakes, such as never were, sence men dwelt
uppon the grounde.
20   Can any tongue in the world expresse a thinge more
forcybly than this matter is expressed by the holie Apostle
him selfe? What mortall harte can but tremble in the
middest of this unspeakeable terrour? is it mervaile yf
the verie just men and the Angels them selves are sayde
25   to feare it? and then (as S. Peter reasoneth) *yf the just*   1.Pet.4.
shall scarse be saved: where shall the wicked man and sinner
appeare? what a dreadfull daye wil it be for the careles
and loose Christian, (which hath passed his tyme pleasantlye in this worlde) when he shall see so infinite a sea
30   of feares and miseries to rushe upon hym?
        But besides all thes most terrible and fearce prepara-
tions, there wilbe many other matters, of no lesse dreadfull consideration: as to see all sepulchres open at the
sounde of the trumpett, and to yelde forth all their dead   The
35   bodies which they have receaved from the beginninge of   demandes
the world: to see all men, wemen, and children, kynges   at the last
and Queenes, princes and potentates, to stand there   day.
naked in the face of all creatures: their sinnes reveiled,

---

21 expressed by Christ, the Apostles, and Prophets themselves? What

their secrete offences laide open, done and committed
in the closettes of their palacies, and they constrayned
and compelled to geeve a counpte of a thowsande matters, wherof they would disdaine to have ben tolde in
5   this lyfe: as how they have spent the tyme: how they
have imployed their wealth: what behavyour they have
used towardes their brethren: how they have mortifyed
their senses: how they have ruled their appetites: how
they have obeied the inspirations of the holie ghost: and
10   finallye how they used all Godes gyftes in this life?

    Oh (deare brother) it is unpossible to expresse, what
a great treasure a good conscience wilbe at this daye:
it wilbe more worth then tenne thowsande worldes. For
wealth will not helpe: the judge will not be corrupted
15   with monye: no intercession of worldly frindes shall prevaile for us at that daye, no not of the Angels them
selves: whose glorie shalbe then as the prophet saieth,   Psa.149.
to binde kynges in fetters, and noble men in yron manacles, to
execute upon them the judgment prescribed, and this shalbe glorie
20   *to all his sainctes.* Alas what will all those wyse people do
then, that now lyve in delites, and can take no paine
for their salvation? what shyft will they make in those
extremities? whether will they turne them? whose helpe
will they crave? they shall see all thinges crye vengeance
25   about them, all thinges yelde cause of feare and terror:
but nothinge to yelde them anye hope or comforte.   A pitifull
Above them shalbe their judge offended with them for   case.
their wickednes: beneath them hell open, and the cruell fornace readie boilynge to receave them: on their
30   right handes shalbe their sinnes accusinge them: on their
left handes the devilles redye to execute Gods eternall
sentence upon them: within them their conscience gnaw-
inge: without them, their frendes bewaylinge: on everie
side the world burninge. Good Lorde what will the sin-
35   ner doe, environed with all thes miseries? how will his

---

3 to geeve accounts of   10 al good gifts   21 pain in the service of
God? What   24 al things yeeld them cause   28 *mn: Anselm.*   29 on
the right hand   30 on the left hand   33 them, al damned soules
bewailing

harte sustaine thes anguishes? what waie will he take? to goe backe is impossible: to goe forwarde is intollerable: what then shall he doe, but (as Christ foretelleth) he shall drie up for verie feare: seeke death, and death

5　shall flye from him: crye to the hilles to fall upon him, and they refusinge to doe hym so much pleasure, he shall stande there as a most desperate forlorne, and miserable caytife wretch, untill he receave that dreadfull and irrevocable sentence: *Goe you accursed into ever-*

10　*lastinge fyre.*

Which sentence once pronunced, consider what a dolefull crye and shout will streight follow. The good rejoysinge and singinge prayses in the glorie of their Savyour: the wicked bewailinge, blaspheminge, and cursinge the daye

15　of their nativitie. Consider the intollerable upbraydinge of the wicked infernall spirites, against these miserable condemned soules, now delyvered to them in pray for ever. With how bitter scoffes and tauntes will they hale them on, to tormentes. Consider the eternall seperation

20　that then must be made of fathers and children, mothers and daughters, frindes and companions: the one to glorie, the other to confusion, without ever seinge one the other agayne, and (that whiche shalbe as great a greefe as anye other) the sonne goinge to heaven shall

25　not pitie his owne father or mother goinge to hell, but shall rejoyse at the same, for that it turneth to Godes glorie, for the execution of his justice. What a seperation (I say) shall this be? what a farewell? whose harte woulde not breake at that daye, to make this separa-

30　tion, yf a harte could breake at that tyme, and so end his paines? but that will not be lawfull. Where are all our delites now? all our pleasant pastimes become? our braverie in apparell, our glisteringe in golde, our honour done to us with cappe and knee? all our delicat

35　fare, all our musicke, all our wanton daliances and recreations we were wount to have? all our good frindes and

Mat.24.
Apoc.6.
Apo.9.

Mat.25.

The last
sentence
pro-
nunced.

---

15 upbraieng   24 other: if it be tru that some conceave, that our
knowledge one of another here on earth shal so far remain) the son
32 now! Where are al our pleasant

merie companions, accustomed to laugh and disporte
the tyme with us? where are they become? Oh (deare
brother) how sower will all the pleasures past of this
worlde seeme at that howre? how dolefull will their mem-
5   orie be unto us? how vaine a thinge will all our dignities, our riches, our possessions appeare? and on the
contrarie side, how joyfull will that man be, that hath
attended in this lyfe to lyve vertuouslie, albeit with paine
and contempt of the world? happie creature shall he be,
10   that ever he was borne, and no tongue, but Godes, can
expresse his happenesse.

And now to make no other conclusion of all this, but   The con-
even that which Christ him selfe maketh: let us consider   clusion.
how easie a matter it is now for us (with a litle paine) to
15   avoide the daunger of this daye, and for that cause it
is foretolde us, by our most mercifull judge and Savyour,
to the ende we should by our diligence avoyde it. For
thus he concludeth after all his former threatenings: *Videte*   Mar.13.
vigilate etc. Looke about you, watch and praye, for you know not
20   *when the tyme shalbe. But as I say to you, so I saie to all, be*
watchfull. And in an other place, havinge reckonede upp
all the particulers before recited, least anye man should
doubt that all should not be fulfilled: he sayeth, *heaven*   Mat.24.
and earth shall passe, but my wordes shall not passe. And then
25   he addeth this exhortation. *Attend therfore unto your selves,*   A goodlie
that your hartes be not overcome with banquettinge and dronkennes,   exhorta-
and with the cares of this lyfe, and so that daye come uppon you   tion of
sodenlye. For he shall come as a snare uppon them which inhab-   Christ.
ite the earth: be you therfore watchfull, and alwayes praye, that
30   *you may be worthie to escape all thes thinges which are to come,*
and to stande confidentlie before the sonne of man at this daye.
What a frindlye and fatherlie exortation is this of Christ?
whoe could desire a more kinde, gentle or effectuall forewarninge? is there anie man that can pleade ignorance
35   hereafter? The verie lyke conclusion gathereth S. Peter
out of the premisses: when he saith: *The daye of our*   2.Pet.3.
lorde shall come as a theefe, in which the elements shalbe dis-
solved: &c. Seinge then all these thinges, must be dissolved: what

---

19 *and praie ye, for*

maner of men ought we to be in holye conversation and pietie,
expectinge and goinge on to meete the comminge of that daye of
our lorde? &c. This meetinge of the daye of judgement
(which S. Peter speaketh of) is dewe examination of our
5 estate, and speedye amendment of our lyfe past. For
so saithe most notablie the wise man, *provide thee of a*   Eccl.18.
medicine before the sore come, and examyne thy selfe before judge-
ment, and so shalt thow finde propitiation in the sight of God.
To which S. Paule agreeth when he saieth, *if we woold*   1.Co.11.
10 *judge our selves, we should not be judged.* But because no man
entreth into dew judgement of him selfe, and of his
owne lyfe: therof it commeth, that so fewe doe prevent
this latter judgement: so fewe are watchfull, and so manie
fall a sleepe in ignorance of their owne daunger. Our
15 lord geeve us grace to looke better about us.

A consideration of the nature of sinne, and of a sinner:
for the justifyng of Godes rigour shewed in the
chapiter before.

CHAP. VI

20 To the ende that no man may justly complayne of the
severe accounpte which God is to take of us at the last
daye, or of the rigour of his judgment set doune in the
chapiter before: it shall not be amisse to consider in this
chapter, the cause whye God doth shew such severitie
25 against sinne and sinners: as bothe by that which hath   Godes
bene sayde doth appeare, and also by the whole course   hatred to
of holye scripture: where he in everie place almost   synners.
denounceth his extreme hatred, wrath and indignation
against the same: as where it is sayed of hym, *that he*   Psal.5.
30 *hateth all those that worke iniquitie. And that both the wicked*   Sap.14.
man and his wickednes, are in hatred with hym. And finallie,   Pro.15.
that the whole lyfe of sinners, their thoughts, wordes,   Job.11.

---

4 is an earnest longing after it, which never is had until first there
go before a du examination   5 past. Therfore saith   17 *Gods severitie*
shewed   20 the severitie of   32 words and works, yea

yea and their good actions also, are abhomination in
his sight whyles they lyve in sinne. And that (which yet
is more) he can not abide nor permit the sinner to prayse
him, or to name his testament with his mouthe, as the
5 holye ghost testifieth: and therfore no mervaile yf he
shew suche rigour to hym at the last daye whome he
so greatlye hateth and abhorreth in this lyfe.

Esa.1.
Psal.14.
Psal.49.
Eccl.15.

There might be manye reasons alleaged of this: as
the breach of Godes commaundementes: the ingratitude
10 of a sinner in respecte of his benifites, and the lyke:
which might justifie sufficientlie his indignation towards
hym. But there is one reason above the rest, which
openeth the whole fountaine of the matter: and that is,
the intollerable injurie donne unto God, in everie mortall
15 sinne committed: whiche in deede is suche an oppro-
brious injurie and so dishonorable, as no meane poten-
tate could beare the same at his subjectes handes: and
much lesse God hym selfe (whoe is the God of majestie)
may abide to have the same so often iterated against
20 hym, as commonly it is by a wicked man.

The rea-
son why
God so
hateth a
synner.

And for the understandinge of this injurie, we must
note that everie tyme we committ a mortall sinne, there
dothe passe thorowgh our hart (though we marcke it
not) a certaine practick discourse of our understandinge,
25 (as there doth also in everie other election) whereby we
lay before us, on the one side, the profit of that sinne
which we are to committ, that is, the pleasure that
draweth us to it: and on thother parte, the offence of
God, that is, the leesinge of his frindshippe by that sinne
30 yf we doe it: and so havinge as it were the balances
there before us, and puttinge God in one end, and in
the other the aforesayde pleasure: we stande in the middest deliberatinge and examininge the wayght of both
partes, and finallie we doe make choise of the pleasure
35 and doe reject God: that is, we doe chuse rather to leese
the frindshipp of God, with his grace, and whatsoever
he is worth besides, than to lose that pleasure and delec-

The
injurie
done to
God by
synne.

---

1 abhominations   14 everie sin that wittingly we do commit; which
22 commit such a sin, there   23 mark it not

tation of sinne. Now what thinge can be more horrible
than this? what can be more spitefull to God, than to
prefer a most vile pleasure before his majestie? is not
this worse than that intollerable injurie of the Jewes, Mat.17.
5 whoe chose Barrabas the murderer, and rejected Christ Mar.15.
their Savyour? surelye, how haynous soever that sinne
of the Jewes were, yet in two pointes this doth seeme
to exceede it: the one, in that the Jewes knew not whome
they refused in their choise, as we doe. The other, in
10 that they refused Christ but once, and we doe it often,
yea dailye and howerlye, when we geve consent in our
hartes to mortall sinne.

And is it mervaile then that God dealeth so severely
and sharplye in the worlde to come with wicked men,
15 whoe doe use hym so opprobriouslye and contemptu-
ouslye in this lyfe? surelye the malice of a sinner is greate
towardes God, and he dothe not onlye dishonour hym The
by contempt of his commaundementes, and by prefer- malice of
ringe most vyle creatures before hym: but also beareth a sinner
                    towardes
20 a secrete hatred and grudge against his majestie, and God.
woulde (yf it lay in his power) pull hym out of his seate,
or (at the least wise) wishe there were no God at all to
punish sinne after this lyfe. Let everie sinner examine
the botome of his conscience in this point, whether he
25 could not be content, there were no immortalitie of the
sowle, no reckoninge after this lyfe, no judge, no punishment, no hell, and consequentlye no God, to the ende
he might the more securelie enjoye his pleasures?

And because God (which searcheth the harte and Sap.1.
30 reynes) seethe well this trayterous affection of sinners Rom.8.
towardes hym, lurkinge within their bowels, how smothe Psal.7.
so ever their wordes are: therfore he denounceth them
for his enemies in the scripture, and professeth open Rom.5.
warre and hostilitie against them. And then suppose you, Jac.4.
35 what a case thes unfortunate men are in, (beinge but 1.Joh.3.
seely wormes of the earth) when they have suche an
enemye to fight against them, as doth make the verie

---

4 worse than intollerable 11 when with advisement we give consent in our harts unto sin 35 thes miserable men

heavens to tremble at his looke. And yet that it is so: heare what he sayeth, what he threatneth, what he thundreth against them. After he had by the mouth of Esaye the prophet repeated many synnes abhominable in his 5 sight, as the takinge of bribes, oppressinge of poore people, and the lyke: He defieth the doers therof, as his open enymies, saying: *This saieth the lorde of hoostes, the stronge lord of hoostes of Israell: Beholde I wilbe revenged uppon my enimies, and will comfort my selfe in their destruction.* 10 And the prophet David, as he was a man in most high favour with God, and made preevie to his secretes above all other: so he (more than any other) doth utter this severe meaning and infinite displeasure in God against synners, calling them his enemies, vessels of his wrath, 15 and ordayned to eternall ruyne and destruction: and complaineth that the world will not beleeve this point. *An unwise man* (saieth he) *will not learne this, nether will the foole understand it.* What is this? *how synners (after they are spronge up) and workers of iniquitie (after they have appeared to 20 the worlde) doe perishe everlastingly.* And what is the reason of this? he aunswereth immediatly: *because thy enimies (o lorde), behold o Lorde thy enimies shall perishe, and all those that worcke iniquitie shalbe consumed.* By this we see, that all synners be enemyes to God, and God to them, and we see 25 also upon what grounde and reason. But yet (for the further justifyinge of Godes severitie) let us consider in what measure his hatred is towardes synne: how greate: how far it proceedeth: within what boundes it is comprehended: or yf it hath any lymites or bondes at all, 30 as in deede it hath not, but is infinit, that is, without measure or limitation. And (to utter the matter as in trueth it standeth) if all the tongues in the worlde were made one tongue and all the understandinges of all creatures (I meane of angels and men) were made one under- 35 standinge: yet, could nether this tongue expresse nor this understandinge conceive, the great hatred of Gods harte

Synners enemyes to God & God to them. Esa.1.

Psal.92.

Godes hatred infinite against sinners.

---

7 *Thus saith* 8 mn: *Such like also.* Isa.26.11 11 made very privy to his secrets: so he very much doth utter 18 after they be sprong 22 *Lord, thine enimies*

towards every mortall synne which we committ. And
the reason hereof standeth in two poyntes. First for that
God by how much more he is better than we are: by
so muche more he loveth goodnes and hateth synne,
than we doe. And because he is infinitelie good: therfore his love to goodnes is infinite, as also his hatred to
evill, and consequentlye his rewardes to them bothe are
infinite, the one in hell, the other in heaven.

Secondlie we see by experience, that how much more
greate and worthie the person is, against whome an
offence is committed, so much greater the offence is: as
the selfe same blow geven to a servant and to a prince
differeth greatlye in offence, and deservethe different
hatred and punishment. And for that everie mortall sinne
which we committ, is donne directlye against the person of God hym selfe, as hath bene declared before, whose
dignitie is infinite: therfore the offence or guylt of every
such sinne is infinite, and consequently deserveth infinite
hatred and infinite punishment at Gods handes. Hereof
foloweth the reason of divers thinges both sayed and
donne by God in the scriptures, and taught by divines
towchinge matter of mortall sinne, whiche seeme straunge
unto the wisedome of the worlde, and in deede scarce
credible: as first of all, that dreadfull punishment of
eternall and irrevocable damnation of so manie thowsandes, yea millions of Angels created to glorie, with
almost infinite perfection, and that for one onlye sinne,
once committed, and that onlye in thought, as divines
doe holde.

Secondlye, the rigourous punishment of our first parents Adam and Eve and all their posteritie, for eatinge
of one seely aple: for whiche fault besides the chastysinge
of the offenders them selves, and all the creatures of the
earth for the same, and all their children and ofspring
after them, bothe before our redemption and sence (for

Why every synne deserveth infinite punishe-ment.

Rom.1. 1.Cor.1.

The pun-ishment of angels.

Of Adam and Eve.

---

1 every sin, which we do wittingly commit   14 every sin which we
advisedly commit   21 Divines touching the punishment of sin, which
31 for eating of the tree forbidden: for   35 before the incarnation
of Christ, and since

albeit we are delivered from the guilte of that sinne, yet
temporall punishmentes remaine upon us for the same,
as hunger, thirst, cold, sicknes, death, and a thowsand
miseries more,) besides also the infinite men damned for
5   the same before the comming of Christ, by the space
of fower thowsand yeres, and also synce, as infidels which
are not baptized, and others: besides this, I say, (which
in mans reason maye seeme severe enough) Godes wrath
and justice could not be satisfied, except his owne soone
10   had come downe into the worlde, and taken our flesh
upon hym, and by his paines satisfied for the same. And
when he was come downe and had in our fleshe subjected hym selfe unto his fathers justice, albeit the love
his father bare hym were infinite, and every litle paine
15   that he tooke for us, or at leastwise every litle dropp of
bloode which he shed, had ben sufficient for the satisfiynge
of the whole offence, for that his fleshe being united to
his godhead made everie such satisfactorie action of his,
of infinite value and merite, and consequently of infinite
20   satisfaction, for the infinitnes of Adams sinne: yet that
God might shew the greatnes of his hatred and justice   Esa.53.
against sinne, he never left to laye on, upon his owne
blessed deare sonne, untill he had left no one whole
peece of skynne on his fleshe, nor droppe of bloode
25   within his bodie: no not then, when he saw hym sorowfull unto death, and bathed in a sweate of bloode and   Mat.26.
water, and cryinge, *o father myne, if it be possible, let this*   Mar.14.
cupp passe from me. And yet more pitifully after upon the   Luc.22.
crosse. *O my God, why hast thow forsaken me?* Notwithstanding   Mat.27.
30   all this (I say,) his father delivered hym not, but layed   Psal.22.
on strype upon stripe, paine upon paine, torment after   Esa.53.
torment, untill he had rendred up his lyfe and soule into
his sayed fathers handes: which is a wounderfull and
dreadfull document of Godes hatred against sinne.

---

2 temporal chastisements remain   5 *omits* before the comming of
Christ, by the space of fower thowsand yeres, and also synce, as
infidels which are not baptized, and others   14 *omits* and every litle
paine ... for the infinitnes of Adams sinne   23 *omits* untill he had
left no one whole peece of skynne on his fleshe, nor droppe of bloode
within his bodie

I might heere mention the sinne of Esau in selling
his inheritance for a litle meate: of whiche S. Paule
sayeth, *he founde no place of repentance after, though he sought
the same with teares.* Also the sinne of Saule whoe (his
5   sinne beinge but one synne, and that onlye of omission,
in not killinge Agag the kynge of Amalech and his catell,
as he was willed) was utterlie cast of by God for the
same, (though he were his annointed and chosen servant before): and could not get remission of the same,
10   though both he and Samuell the prophet did greatly
lament and bewaille the same synne.

Also I might alleage the example of kinge David,
whose two synnes (albeit uppon his hartie repentance)
God forgave: yet, besides all the weepinge, fastinge,
15   watchinge, lyeinge on grownde, wearinge of sackcloth,
and other punishement of bodye that David did use,
God punished the same with marvaylous severitie, as
with the death of Davides sonne, and other continuall
afliction unto him as longe as he lived. And all this to
20   shew his hatred against synne, and thereby to terrifie us
from committinge the same.

Of this also doe proceede all those harde and bitter
speeches in scripture towching sinners, which comming
from the mouthe of the holye ghost, (and therfore beinge
25   most trewe and certaine) may justlye geeve all them
greate cause of feare which lyve in synne, as where it
is saied: *death, bloode, contention, edge of sworde, oppression,
hunger, contrition, and whyppes: all thes thinges are created for
wicked sinners.* And againe: *God shall rayne snares of fyre
30   uppon sinners: brimstone with tempestuous wyndes shalbe the portion
of their cupp.* Agayne, God wilbe known at the day of
judgement uppon the synner, whoe shalbe taken in the
worckes of his owne handes: manye whippes belonge
unto a synner: let synners be turned into hell: God shall
35   scatter all sinners: God shall dashe the teeth of synners
in their mouthes: God shall scoffe at a sinner when he

The sinne
of Esau.
Gen.25.
& 27.
Heb.12.
Of Saul.

1.Re.15.
& 16.

1.Re.10. &
15. & 16.

2.Re.12.
Psal.6.35.
69.109.
102.30.

2.Re.12.

Eccl.40.

Psa.11.

Psa.9.

Psal.3.
Psal.37.

---

11 same sin, or at least, that he was rejected.   14 forgave: yet
notwithstanding al the sorrow that David conceaved for the same,
God chastised him with marvelous severitie: as with the death of his
son   19 affliction on himselfe

seethe his daye of destruction cometh on: the sworde of   Psa.145.
sinners shall turne into their owne hartes: thow shalt see   Psal.58.
when sinners shall perishe. The armes of sinners shalbe   Psal.37.
crushed and broken: sinners shall wither from the earth: Psa.104.
5   desire not the glorye and riches of a synner, for thow   Psa.141.
doest not know the subversion which shall come upon
hym: God hath geeven him riches to deceave him ther-   Eccle.2.
with: beholde the daye of our lorde shall come, (a cruell   Psal.73.
daye and full of indignation, wrath and furye) to make   Esa.13.
10   desolate the earth and to crushe in peeces her synners   Psal.58.
within her. The just man shall rejoyse seinge this revenge,
and then shall he washe his handes in the blood of sinners. These and a thowsande suche sentences more of
scripture, which I omitt, uttered by the holye ghost
15   against synners, maye instruct us of their pitifull estate,
and of the unspeakable hatred of God against them, as
long as they persist in synne.

Of all these considerations the holy scriptures doe
gather one conclusion greatlye to be noted and consid-
20   ered by us: which is, *miseros facit populos peccatum. Synne*   Prov.14.
bringeth men to miserie. And againe: *Qui diligit iniquitatem*   Psal.11.
odit animam suam: he which loveth iniquitie hateth his owne
soule: Or (as the Angel Raphaell uttereth it in other   Tob.12.
wordes) *they which committ sinne, are open enemyes to their*
25   *owne sowles.* Wherfore they laye downe to all men, this
generall, severe, and most necessarie commaundement,
upon all the paines before recited. *Quasi a facie colubri*   Eccl.21.
fuge peccata. Flee from sinne as from the face of a snake. And
againe: *cave ne aliquando peccato consentias. Beware thow never*   Tob.4.
30   *consent to sinne.* For how soever the worlde doeth make
litle accounte of this matter, of whome (as a scripture
noteth) *the sinner is praysed in his lustes, and the wicked man*   Psal.10.
is blessed, yet most certaine it is (for that the spirite of   1.Joh.3.
God avoucheth it) *qui facit peccatum ex diabolo est. He which*
35   *committeth sinne is of the devill*, and therfore is to receave
his portion amonge devills at the latter daye.

And is not all this sufficient (deare brother) to make   The
us detest sinne, and to conceave some feare in com-   obstinacie
of sinners.

---

28 *omits Flee from sinne as from the face of a snake.*   31 as the scripture
noteth

mittinge therof? nay is not all this strong enough to
batter their hartes which live in state of sinne, and doe
committ the same daylie without consideration or scruple? what obstinacie and hardnes of harte is this? sure-
5 lye we see the holye ghost prophesied trewlye of them
when he sayede, *sinners alienated from God are possessed with*
a furye like a serpent and like a deafe cocatrise which stoppeth
her eares to the enchaunter: this furie (I saie) is the furye or
madnesse of willfull synners, which stoppe their eares
10 lyke serpentes, to all the holy enchauntmentes that God
can use unto them for their conversion, that is, to all
his internall motions and good inspirations, to all remorse
of their owne consciences, to all threatninges of holye
scriptures, to all admonishmentes of Gods servauntes,
15 and to all the other meanes which God can use for their
salvation.

Good Lorde, whoe would committ a mortall sinne for
the gayninge of ten thowsande worldes, yf he considered
the infinite dommages, hurtes, inconveniences and mis-
20 eries which doe come by the committinge of one sinne?
for first, he that sinneth mortallie, leeseth the grace of
God inherent in his sowle: (which is the greatest gift
that God can geeve to a creature in this lyfe) and consequentlye he leeseth all those thinges which dyd accom-
25 panye that grace: as the vertues infused, and the seven
giftes of the holy ghost, wherby the sowle was bewtyfied
in the sight of her spouse, and armed against the assaultes
of her enemies. Secondlie, he leesethe the favour of God,
and consequentlye his fatherlye protection, care and
30 providence over hym, and gayneth hym to be his professed enemie. Which, how great a losse it is we may
esteeme by the state of a worldley courtier, which should
leese the favour of an earthlie prince, and incurre mortall hatred by the same.
35 Thirdly he leeseth all inheritance, clayme, and title to
the kyngdome of heaven, whiche is dew onlye by grace,

Psal.58.

1.
The losses
that come
by everye
mortall
sinne.
Esa.11. &
Jero.ibid.
2.

3.

---

10 God doth use   17 would wittingly commit any sin,   21 that in
such sort sinneth, leeseth the grace of God, which was given him:
which   22 *mn: came by sin.*   25 as the vertues and gifts of the holy
Ghost

as S. Paule noteth: and consequentlye deprivethe hym   Rom.6.
selfe, of all dignities and commodities folowinge the same
in this lyfe: as the condition and high priveledge of a
sonne of God, the communion of sainctes, the protection of Angels, and the lyke. Fowerthlye, he leeseth the   4.
quiet, joye, and tranquilitie of a good conscience, and
all the favours, cherishmentes, consolations, and other
cumfortes, wherwithe the holie ghost is wont to visite
the mindes of the Just. Fyvethlye, he leeseth the merit   5.
and reward of all his good woorkes done sence he was
borne, and whatsoever he doth or shall doe while he
standeth in that state. Sixthlye he maketh hym selfe   6.
guyltie of eternall punishment, and engrosseth his name
in the booke of perdition, and consequentlie byndeth
hym selfe to all these inconveniences wherto the reprobate are subject, that is, to be inheritour of hell fyre,
to be in the power of the devill and his Angels, to be
subject to all synne and temptation of sinne, and his
sowle (which was before the temple of the holy ghost,
the habitation of the blessed trinitie, and place of repose
for the Angels to visit) now to be the nest of scorpions,
and dongeon of devilles, and hym selfe a companion of
the miserable damned.

Lastlye he abandoneth Christ, and renounceth the   7.
portion he had with hym, makinge hym selfe a perse-
cuter of the same by treadinge him under his feete. And   Heb.10.
crucifyinge hym againe, and defylinge his bloode (as   Heb.6.
S. Paule sayeth) in synninge against hym whiche dyed   Rom.6.
for synne, and therfor the same Apostle pronounceth a
marvailous hevie sentence against suche in these wordes:
If we synne willfullye now after we have receaved knowledge of   Heb.10.
the trewth: there remaineth no more sacryfice for synnes, but rather   Rom.6.
a certaine terrible expectation of judgement, and emulation of fyre
whiche shall consume the adversaries. To which S. Peter
agreeth, when he saieth: *It had ben better not to have knowen*   2.Pet.2.
the way of justice, than after such knowledge to slyde backe agayne
from the holye commaundement which was geeven.

---

9 *omits* the merit and

Now then let our worldlinges goe and solace them   Excuse of
selves with sinne as muche as they will: let them excuse   sinne.
and pleasantlye defend the same, sayinge, pryde is but
a pointe of gentrye: glouttonie good fellowship, lecherye
5   and wantonnes a trycke of yowth: and the lyke: they
shall finde one daye that these excuses will not be receaved: but rather that these pleasant devises, wilbe
turned into teares. They shall prove that God will not
be jested with, but that he is the same God still, and   Gal.6.
10 will aske as severe accounte of them as he hathe done
of other before, although it please not them now to
keepe any accounte of their lyfe at all: but rather to
turne all to disporte and pleasure, persuadinge them
selves, that how soever God hath delt with other before,
15 yet he will forgeeve all to them: but the holye scripture
reasoneth after an other manner, which I would have
everie wise Christian to consider.

S. Paule comparinge the Jewes sinnes with ours, maketh
this collection. *If God spared not the naturall boughes, take*   Rom.11.
20 *heede least he spare not the.* And ther upon he inferreth this
admonition, *noli altum sapere sed time. Be not to high minded,*
but feare. Againe, he reasoneth thus upon the olde and
the new lawe: he that broke the lawe of Moyses, beinge   Heb.10.
convicted by two or three witnesses, died for the same
25 without commiseration or mercye: and how much more
greevous punishment doth he deserve which breaking
the law of Christ by wilfull sinne, treadeth the sonne of
God under his feete, polluteth the bloode of the new
testament, and reprocheth the holye ghost? In lyke maner
30 reasoneth S. Peter and S. Jude towchinge the sinne of   2.Pet.2.
Angels and ours: yf God spared not the Angels, when   Ep.Jud.
they sinned, but did thrust them downe to hell there
to be tormented, and to be kept unto judgement with
eternall chaines under darckenes: how much lesse will
35 he spare us? And agayne: yf the Angels which passe us   2.Pet.2.
in power and strength, are not able to beare Gods
execrable judgement against them, what shall we doe?
Agayne in an other place, he reasoneth thus: yf the just   1.Pet.4.

24 dieth   36 to bear Gods

man shall hardlye be saved, where shall the wicked man A good maner of rea- soninge.
and sinner appeare? By which examples we are instructed
to reason in lyke sorte: yf God have punished so severelie one sinne in the Angels, in Adam, and in other before
5   recited: what shall I looke for which have committed so
manie sinnes agaynst hym? yf God have damned so
manye for lesser sinnes then myne be: what will he do
to me for greater? yf God hath borne longer with me,
then he hath done with many other whome he hath cut
10   of without geving them time of repentance: what reason is there, that he should beare longer with me? yf
David and other after their synnes forgeeven them, tooke
suche paynes in afflictinge them selves for satisfaction of
the temporall punishement in this lyfe, what punishe-
15   ment remaineth for me either heere or in the world to
come, for satisfaction of so manie synnes committed? If
it be trew that our savyour saithe, that the waie is harde,   Math.7.
and the gate narrow wherby men goe into heaven, and   Luc.13.
that they shall aunswere for everye ydle worde before   Mat.12.
20   they enter there: what shalbe come of me which doe
lyve so easie a lyfe, and doe keepe no accounte of my
deedes, and muche lesse of my wordes? yf good men in
olde time did take suche paynes for theyr salvation, and
yet (as S. Peter saieth) the verye just were scarce saved:
25   what a state am I in which take no payne at all, but
doe lyve in all kynde of pleasure and worldly delytes?

These kyndes of consequentes were more trew and
profitable for us, wherby we might enter into some consideration of our owne daunger, and into some feare of
30   the judgementes of God, for want wherof the moste
parte of synnes amongest Christians are committed. For
so the holye scripture describinge dyvers causes of
wickednes among men, putteth thes two for principall.
Fyrst, the flatterye of the world: *Quoniam laudatur pecca-*
35   *tor in desideriis animæ suæ. For that the sinner is praysed in his*   Psal.10.
lustes: And secondly, *quia auferuntur iudicia tua a facie eius.*

---

12 them, were nevertheles so sharply chasticed, what punishment
16 come; for so many, and so greevous sins committed?   23 pains
in the way of their

For that thy judgementes (o lorde) are not before his face. And
in the contrarye side speaking of him selfe he saieth: *I
have kept the waies of our lorde and have not behaved my selfe
impiouslie towardes God.* And he geeveth the reason therof

5   immediatlie. *For that all his judgementes are in my sight.* And
againe, *I have feared thy judgementes o lorde.* And againe, *I
have ben mindfull of thy judgementes.* And how profitable this
feare is, he sheweth in the same place, demaundinge
this feare most instantlye at Godes handes: for so he

10 prayeth, *stryke my fleshe thorough, with thy feare o lorde.* And
S. Paule (after he had shewed to the Corinthians, that
we must all be presented before the tribunall of Christ),
maketh this conclusion. *We knoweinge therfore thes thinges
doe perswade the feare of our lorde unto men.* And S. Peter

15 after a longe declaration of the majestie of God and Christ
now rayning in heaven, concludeth thus, *yf then you call
him father which doth judge everye man accordinge to his workes
without exception of persons: doe you lyve in feare duringe the
tyme of this your habitation uppon earth.* A necessarie lesson

20 (no doubt) for all men, but speciallie for those which by
reason of their synnes and wicked lyfe, doe remaine in
displeasure and hatred of God, and howerlye subject (as
I have shewed) to the furye of his judgementes, whiche
if they once fall into, they are both irrevocable and

25 intollerable, and they may be fallen into as easelye, and
by as manie wayes, as a man may come to death, which
are infinite, especiallie to them whoe by their wickednes
have lost the peculier protection of God and good Angels
(as I have shewed) and have subjected them selves to

30 the feendes of darckenes, whoe do nothinge els but seeke
their destruction both of bodye and sowle, with as greate
diligence as they can. What wise man then would but
feare in such a case? whoe coulde eate or drincke, or
sleepe quietlye in his bedd untill by the holye sacrament

35 of penance, he had discharged his conscience of mortall

Psal.18.
How nec-
essarie it is
to feare.

Psa.119.

2.Cor.5.

1.Pet.1.

The
daunger

---

1 And on the contrarie side speaking of himselfe   12 *before the judge-*
ment seat of Christ   28 of God, and so consequently of his angels too
(as   34 until by tru and hartie repentance, he had discharged his
conscience of sin?

synne? a litle stone fallinge from the howse upon his head, or his horse stumblinge under him as he rydeth, or his enymie meetinge hym on the highe waye, or an agew comminge with eatinge or drinckinge a litle to

5   muche, or ten thowsande chaunces besydes (wherof he standeth dailie and howerlye in daunger) may ridd him of this lyfe and put hym in that case, as no creature of this world, nor anye continuance of time shalbe able to delyver hym thence againe. And whoe then wolde not

10   feare? whoe wolde not tremble? Our lorde of his mer-cye geeve us his holye grace, to feare hym as we should doe, and to make suche accounte of his justice, as he by threatninge the same wolde have us to doe. And then shall not we delay the tyme, but resolve our selves to

15   serve hym whiles he is content to accept of our service, and to pardon us all our offences, if we woulde once make this resolution from our harte.

An other consideration for the further justifyinge of Godes judge-
mentes and declaration of our demerit, taken from the majestie
20   *of God and his benefites towardes us.*

CHAP. VII

Albeit the most parte of Christians through their wicked lyfe arrive not to that state wherin holy David was, when he sayed to God, *thy judgementes o Lord are pleasant unto*   Psal.119.
25   *me,* as in deed they are to all those that lyve vertuouselye and have the testimonie of a good conscience: yet at least wise, that we maye saye withe the same prophet, *the judgementes of our Lorde are trew and justified in them selves:*   Psal.19.
And againe, *thow art just o Lorde and thy judgement is right:*
30   I have thought good to add a reason or two more in this chapter, wherby it maye appeare how greate our offence is towardes God by sinninge as we doe, and how righteous his judgementes and justice are against us for the same.

of them whiche lyve in synne.

---

5 thousand means besides   23 estate

And first of all is to be considered the majestie of
hym agaynst whome we sinne: for most certaine it is,
(as I have noted before) that everie offence is so muche
the greater, and more greevous, by how muche greater
5   and more noble the person is against whome it is done,
and the partie offendinge more base and vile. And in
this respect God (to terrifie us from offendinge hym)
nameth hym selfe often with certayne titles of majestie,
as to Abraham, *I am an omnipotent Lorde*: And agayne,
10   *heaven is my seate, and the earth is my footestoole.* And againe,
he commaunded Moyses to say to the people in his
name, this ambassage, *harden not your neckes any longer, for*
that your Lord and God, is a God of godes and a Lorde of lordes,
a greate God both potent and terrible, which accepteth nether per-
15   *son nor brybes.*

    First then I saye, consider (gentle Christian) of what
an infinite majestie he is, whome thow a poore woorme
of the earth, hast so often and so contemptuousely
offended in this lyfe. We see in this worlde, that no man
20   dareth to offende openly, or say a worde against the
majestie of a prince within his owne dominions: and
what is the majestie of all the princes upon earthe, compared to the thowsandth parte of the majestie of God,
whoe with a worde made both heaven and earthe and
25   all the creatures therin, and with halfe a worde can
destroie the same againe: whome all the creatures which
he made, as the Angels, the heavens, and all the ele-
mentes besides, doe serve at a becke and dare not offend?
onlye a sinner is he which emboldeneth hym selfe against
30   this majestie, and feareth not to offend the same, whome
(as the holye Catholique Churche dothe professe daylie,
in her preface to the blessed sacrifice) the Angels do
praise, the dominations doe adore, the powers do tremble, and the highest heavens, together with Cherubins
35   and Seraphins, doe daylie honour and celebrate.

    Remember then (deare brother) that everie tyme thow

The
majestie
of God.

Gen.17.
Esa.66.

Deu.10.

Psa.148.

Job.9.

---

9 *I am the almightie Lord:*   14 *both mightie and*   31 *omits* (as the holye
Catholique Churche dothe professe daylie, in her preface to the
blessed sacrifice)

doest committ a sinne thow geevest a blow in the face
to this greate majesticall God, whoe (as S. Paule sayeth)
dwelleth in an unaccessible light, which no man in this world,   1.Tim.6.
can abyde to looke upon: As also it appeareth by the exam-
5   ple of S. John evangelist, whoe fell downe dead for
very feare at the appearance of Christ unto hym, as him   Apoc.1.
selfe testifieth: and when Moyses desired to see God
once in his lyfe, and made humble petition for the same:
God aunswered, that no man could see hym and lyve:
10   but yet (to satisfie his request, and to shew hym in parte
what a terrible and majesticall God he was,) he tolde   Exo.33.
Moyses, that he should see some peece of his glorie:
mary he added, that it was needfull he shoulde hyde
hym selfe in the hole of a rocke, and be covered with
15   Godes owne handes for his defence, while God, (or rather
an Angell sent from God as all devines doe interprete)
dyd passe by in glorie. And when he was past: God
tooke awaye his hande and suffered Moyses to see the
hynder partes onlye of the Angell, which was notwith-
20   standinge, most terrible to beholde.

    The prophet Daniell also describeth the majestie of
this God, shewed unto hym in vision, in these wordes.   Dani.7.
I did see (saieth he) when the thrones were set, and the olde of
man manye dayes sat downe: his apparell was as white as snow:
25   *his heare lyke unto pure woolle, his throne was of a flame of fyre,*
and his chariottes were burninge fyre, a swifte fludd of fyre came
from his face: a thowsand thowsandes did serve hym, and ten
thowsand hundred thowsands did assist him, he sat in judgement,
and the bookes were opened before hym. All this and much
30   more is recorded in scripture, to admonishe us therby
what a prince of majestie he is whome a synner offendeth.

    Imagine now (brother myne) that thow seest this greate   A con-
kynge sittinge in his chaire of majestie, with chariottes   templation
of fire, unspeakable light, and infinite millions of Angels   of the
35   aboute hym, as the scripture reporteth. Imagine further,   majestie
of God.

---

1 givest as it were a blow in the face, to this God of great majestie
11 and glorious God   12 glorie: but he   15 God (in some measure
of his majestie) did   18 see his hinder parts only, which   23 *old of*
many dais

(which is most trew) that thow seest all the creatures in
the world stand in his presence, and tremblinge at his
majestie, and most carefullie attendinge to doe that for
which he created them: as the heavens to move aboute:
5   the Sonne, moone, and starres to geeve light: the earth
to bringe foorth sustenance: and the lyke. Imagine further that thow seest all these creatures (how bigge or
litle soever they be) to hange and depende onlye of the
power and vertue of God: wherby they stande, move,
10   and consist: and that there passeth from God, to eche
creature in the world, yea to everie parte that hath motion or beinge in the same, some beame of his vertue:
as from the sunne, we see infinite beames to passe into
the ayer. Consider (I say) that no one parte of anye
15   creature in the world, (as the fishe in the sea, the grasse
on the grounde, the leaves of the trees, or the partes of
man upon the face of the earth) can grow, move, or
consist, without some litle streame of vertue and power
come to it continuallie from God. So that thow must
20   imagine God to stand as a most majesticall sunne in the
middest: and from hym to passe foorth infinite beames
or streames of vertue to all the creatures that are eyther
in heaven, earthe, the ayer, or the water, and to everie
parte thereof: and upon thes beames of his vertue, all
25   creatures to hange: and yf he should stopp but any one
of them, it would destroye and annihilate presentlie some
creature or other. This (I saye) yf thow shalt consider
towchinge the majestie of God, and the infinite dread
that all creatures have of hym, except onlye a sinner:
30   (for the devills also doe feare hym as S. James saieth:)   Jac.2.
thow wilt not mervaile of the severe judgement of God,
appointed for his offence. For sure I am, that very shame
of the world maketh us to have more regarde in offendinge the poorest frinde we have in this lyfe, then a
35   wicked man hath in offendinge God: which is an intollerable contempt of so greate a majestie.

    But now if we adjoine to this contemplation of majestie,   A consid-

---

5 *omits* the Sonne, moone, and starres to geeve light   20 most glorious sun   22 al creatures

an other consideration of his benefites bestowed uppon us: our defaut will grow to be far greater, for that to in-jurey hym whoe hathe done us good, is a thinge moste detestable even in nature it selfe. And there was never

5   yet so fearce a harte, no not amongest brute beastes, but that it might be wonne with curtesie and benefites: but muche more amongest reasonable creatures dothe beneficence prevaile, especiallie if it come from greate personages, whose love and frindshippe (declared unto

10   us but in small gyftes) doth greatlye bynde the hartes of the receavers to love them agayne.

Consider then (deare Christian) the infinite good turnes and benefites which thow hast receaved at the handes of this great God, therby to winne the to his love, and

15   that thow shouldest leave of to offende and injurie him. And albeit no tongue created ether of man or Angel, can expresse the one halfe of thes gyftes which thow hast receaved from hym, or the valew of them, or the greate love and hartie goodwill wherewith he bestowed

20   them uppon the: yet for some memorie sake, I will repeate certaine generall and principall pointes therof, wherunto the rest may be referred.

First then he hathe bestowed uppon the, the benifite of thy creation, wherby he made the of nothinge to the

25   likenes of hym selfe, and appointed the to so noble an ende as is to serve hym in this lyfe, and to raigne with hym in the lyfe to come, furnishinge the for the pre-sent with the service and subjection of all creatures. The greatnes of this benefite may partlye be conceaved, yf

30   thow doe imagine thy selfe to lacke but any one parte of thy bodie, as a legge, an arme, an eye, or the lyke: and that one should freelie geeve the same unto the: or yf thow wantest but any one sense, as that thow were deafe or blynde, and one should restore sight or hearinge

35   unto the: howe wooldest thow esteeme of this benefite? how muche wouldest thow professe thy selfe beholdinge unto him for the same? and yf the gyft of one of these partes onlye would seeme such a benefite unto thee:

eration of the benefites of God.

The benefite of creation.

---

8 if he come

how greate oughtest thow to esteeme the free gyfte of
so manye partes together?

Add to this now, (as I have sayde) that he hath created the to the lykenes of no other thinge, but of hym
5   selfe, to no other ende, but to be his honorable servante
in this world, and his compartener in kynglie glorie for
all eternitie to come: and this he hath done to the, beinge only a peece of durte or claye before. Now ymagine thow of what maner of love proceeded this. But yet
10   add further, how he hathe created all this magnificent
world for the, and all the creatures therof to serve thee
in this busines: the heaven to gouverne the, and geeve
the light: the earthe and ayer and water to minister most
infinite varietie of creatures for thy use and sustenance:
15   and hath made thee Lord of all, to use them for thy
comforte and his service: and what magnificent gyftes
are these: and what shamefull ingratitude is it, to turne
the same to the dishonour and injurie of so lovinge a
geever as thow doest, by usinge them to serve the in sinne.
20   But yet consider a litle furder, the benefite of thy
redemption, much greater then all the former: which is,
that thow havinge lost all those former benefites agayne,
and made thy selfe guyltie by synne of eternall punishement wherto the Angels were now delivered for their
25   synne committed before: God chose to redeeme the, and
not the Angels, and for satisfyinge of thy fault, to delyver
his owne onlie sonne to deathe for the. O lorde, what
harte can conceave the greatnes of this benefite? Imagine thy selfe, (beinge a poore man,) haddest committed
30   a greevous cryme against a kynges majestie together with
some great man of his cheefest nobilitie, and that the
kynge beinge offended highlye with you bothe, shoulde
notwithstandinge pardon the, and put the noble man to
death: and furder also, (beinge no other waye to save
35   thy lyfe) should laye the paynes of deathe dew to the,
uppon his onlye sonne and heyre, for thy sake: how
muche wouldest thow thincke, that this kinge loved the?
how greatlye wooldest thow esteeme thy selfe beholdinge

The bene-
fite of
redemp-
tion.
2.Pet.2.

---

12 heaven to distinguish times and seasons, and to geeve thee

and bounden to that yonge prince, which should offer
hym selfe to his fathers justice to dye for the a poore
worme, (and not for the noble man as he would not
dye for the Angels:) and to put his head in the haulter
5 for thyne onlye offences? couldest thow ever have the
harte to become enimie to this man after, or willinglye
and wittingly to offend hym: and yet such is our case,
and much more bounden towardes Christ and his father,
whome the moste of us notwithstandinge doe dailie offend,
10 dishonour, and injurey by synne.

But yet there follow on more benefites of God unto
us, as our vocation and justification: vocation, wherby he
hath called us from infidelitie, to the state of Christians:
and therby made us partakers of this our redemption,
15 which infidels are not: for albeit he payed the ransome
for all in generall: yet he hath not imparted the benefite
therof to all, but to such onlie as best it pleased his
devine goodnes to bestow it upon. After which followed
our justification wherby we were not onlye set free from
20 all our synnes committed before, and from all payne
and punishement dew to the same: but also our sowles
beutified and enriched with the infusion of his holie
grace, accompanied with the vertues theologicall, as faith,
hope and charitie, and with the gyftes of the holye ghost:
25 and by this grace we are made just and righteous in
the sight of God, and entitled to the most blessed enher-
itance of the kyngdome of heaven.

After these doe ensew a greate number of benefites
together, (as to us beinge now made the children and
30 deare frindes of God) and everie one of them, of infinite
price and valew. As the gyft of the holy sacramentes, left
for our comforte and preservation, beinge nothinge els
but conduits to convey Godes grace unto us, especialie
these two which appertaine to all, to witt, the sacrament
35 of penance, and of his blessed bodye and bloode, wherof
the first, is to purge our sowles from sin, the seconde
to feede and comforte the same after she is purged. The
first is as a bathe made of Christ his owne bloode, to

Marginal notes:

The benefites of voca- tion & justifi- cation.

Rom.8.
1.Co.1.

Rom.5.
1.Co.13.
Esa.11.

The benefite of the sacra- mentes.

The use of sacra- mentes.

---

22 *omits* the infusion of 34 sacrament of Baptism, and 38 is a bath

washe and bath our woundes therein: the seconde as a
most comfortable and riche garment, to cover our sowle
withall after she is washed. In the first, Christ hath left
all his authoritie withe his spouse the church, which he
5   hath in heaven to remit sinnes: in the seconde he hath
left him selfe and his owne fleshe and bloode to be a
pretious foode, to cherishe her withall.

Besides all these, there is yet an other gift named our
preservation, wherby God hath preserved us from so
10   manie daungers into whiche other have fallen, and wherin
we had fallen also, yf Gods holye hande had not stayed
us: as from heresie and infidelitie, and manie other greevous sinnes: and especiallie from death and damnation,
which longe agoe by our wickednes, we deserved to have
15   bene executed upon us. Also there are the benefites of
godlie inspirations and admonitions, whereby God hath
often both knocked inwardlye at the dore of our conscience, and .warned us outwardley by so many wayes
and meanes: as are good bookes, good sermons, good
20   exhortations, good compagnie, good example of others,
and a hunderd meanes els, which he at divers tymes
hath and doth use, thereby to gaine us and our sowles
unto his eternall kingdome, by stirringe us to abandon
vitious lyfe, and to betake our selves to his holy and
25   sweete service.

All whiche rare and singuler benefites beinge measured, ether accordinge to the valew of them selves, or
accordinge to the love of that harte from which they
do proceede, ought to move us most vehementlie, to gra-
30   titude towardes the geever. Which gratitude shoulde be,
to resolve our selves at length to serve hym unfayned-
lie, and to prefer his favoure before all worldlye or mortall respectes what soever. Or yf we can not obtaine so
muche of our selves, yet at leastwise not to offende hym
35   anye more by our sinnes and wickednes.

The benefite of preservation and inspiration.

Apoc.3.

---

3 Christ hath substituted in his place his spouse the church, to pronounce in his name remission of sins: in the second he hath left
himselfe, and his own flesh and blood Sacramentally to be a precious food, to cherish hir withal.   12 as from superstition, heresie,

There is not so feerse or cruell a nature in the worlde, (as I noted before) but is mollified, allured, and wonne by benefites: And stories do make reporte of straunge examples in this kynde, even among brute beastes, as of the gratitude of lyons, dogges, and the lyke, towardes their maisters and benefactours. Onlie an obstinate sinner is he, among all the savage creatures that are, whome nether benefites can move, nor curtisies can mollifie, nor promises can allure, nor gyftes can gayne to the faithfull service of God his Lorde and maister.

Aelian. in hist. animal.

The greatest synner that is in the worlde, if he geeve his servaunte but twentie nobles a yere, or his tennant some litle farme to lyve uppon, and yf for this they serve hym not at a becke: he cryeth out of their ingratitude: and yf thei shoulde further malitiouslie seeke to offende hym, and to joyne with his professed enimye against him: how intollerable a matter woolde it seeme in his sight? and yet he hym selfe, dealinge muche more ingratfullie and injuriouslie with God thinketh it a matter of no consideration, but easely pardonable. I saie, he dealeth more ingratfullie with God, for that he hath receaved a thowsand for one, in respect of all the benefites that a mortall man can geeve to an other. For he hathe receaved all in all from God: the bread which he eateth, the grounde which he treadeth, the light which he beholdeth, together with his eyes to see the sunne, and fynallye what so ever is within or without his bodie: as also the mynde with the spirituall gyftes therof, wherof eche one is more worth then a thowsand bodies: I say also that he dealeth more injuriouslie with God, for that notwithstandinge all thes benefites he serveth Godes open enemie the devill, and committeth dailie synne and wickednes, which God hateth more then anye harte created can hate a mortal enemye, beinge that in verye deede whiche persecuted his Sonne our Saveoure, with such hostilitie, as it tooke his most precious lyfe from hym, and nayled hym fast to the woode of the crosse.

The intollerable ingratitude of a synner.

Sinne persecuted Christ unto death.

Of this extreme ingratitude and injurie, God hym selfe is enforsed to complaine in divers places of the scripture, as where he saithe. *Retribuebant mihi mala pro bonis.*

Godes complaint against synners.

They returned me home evill for good. And yet much more   Psa.35.
vehementlie in an other place, he calleth the heavens
to witnes of this iniquitie, sayinge: *Obstupescite coeli super*   Jere.2.
hæc. O you heavens be you astonished at this. As yf he should
5   saye by a figurative kynde of speeche, goe out of your
wittes you heavens with mervaile, at this incredible iniquitie of man towardes me. For so he expoundeth the   Esa.1.
whole matter more at large in an other place: *Audite cæli*
and auribus percipe terra: harken ye heavens, and thow earth bende
10   *hither thine eares: filios enutriui & exaltaui, ipsi autem spreuerunt*
me. I have norished up children and have exalted them, and now
they contemne me. What a pitefull complainte is this of God
against most vile and base wormes of the earth? But yet
God amplyfieth this iniquitie more by certaine examples
15   and comparisons. *The oxe (sayeth he) knoweth his owner, and*
the asse knoweth the maunger of his Lord and maister: but yet
my people knoweth not me. Wo be to the synfull nation, to
the people loden with iniquitie, to this naughtie seede, to wicked
children. What complaint can be more vehement then
20   this? what threatninge can be more dreadfull then this
woe, commynge from the mouth of hym which may
punishe us at his pleasure?

Wherefore (deare brother) if thow have grace, cease to
be ungratefull to God any longer: cease to offend hym
25   whiche hath by so many waies prevented the withe benefites: cease to render evill for good, hatred for love,
contempt for his fatherlie affection towardes the. He
hath done for the all that he can: he hath geeven the   Isa.4.
all that thow art: yea and (in a certayne maner) all that
30   he is worthe hym selfe: and meaneth besydes to make
the partaker of all his glorie in the world to come, and
requireth no more for all this at thy handes, but love
and gratitude. O (deare brother) why wilt thow not yelde
hym this? why wilt thow not doe as muche to him, as
35   thow wooldst have an other man to doe to the, for lesse
then the ten thowsanthe parte of thes benefites which
thow hast receaved? for I dare well saye, that if thow

---

17 *my people know not me*   36 thousand

haddest geeven a man but an almes at thy dore, thow
wooldest thinke hym bounde to love the for it, albeit
thow haddest nothinge in thee worthe love besydes. But
now thy lorde (besydes thes his gyftes,) hath infinite
5   causes to make the love hym, that is, all the causes
which any thinge in the worlde hath to purchase love,
and infinite more besydes. For, yf all the perfections of
all thinges created in heaven and in earth, (which doe
procure love) were put together in one: as all their bewtie,
10 all their vertue, all their wisedome, all their sweetnes,
all their nobilitie, all their goodnes, and the lyke: yet
thy lorde and Savyour whome thow contemnest, doth
passe all this, and that by infinite, and infinite degrees:
for that he is not onlie all thes thinges together: but also
15 he is verie bewtie it selfe, vertue it selfe, wisedome it
selfe, sweetenes it selfe, nobilitie it selff, goodnes it selff,
and the verie fountaine and welspringe, where hence,
all thes thinges are derived by litel peeces and parcels
unto his creatures.
20   Be a shamed then (good Christian) of this thy ingratitude, to so greate, so good, and bountifull a Lord: and
resolve thy selfe for the tyme to come, to amende thy
course of lyfe and behavyour towardes hym. Say with
the prophet, which had lesse cause to saye so then thow.
25 *Domine propitiare peccato meo multum est enim. O lord pardon me*
myne offence for it is greate in thy sight. I know there is nothinge (o lorde) which dothe so muche displease the, or
drye upp the fountaine of thy mercye, and so byndeth
thy handes from doinge good, as ingratitude in the re-
30 ceyvers of thy benefites: wherin hetherto I have exceeded
all others: but I have done it (o lord) in myne ignorance, not consideringe thy gyftes unto me, nor what
accounte thow wouldest demaunde againe of the same.
But now seinge thow hast vouchsafed to make me woor-
35 thie of this grace also, wherby to see and knowe myne
owne state and defaut: I hope hereafter by direction of
the same grace of thyne, to shew my selfe a better childe

Causes of
love in
God
besides
his
benefites.

Psal.25.

---

10 *omits* all their wisedome, all their sweetnes   13 by many and
infinite degrees   23 *mn: A praier.*   31 other

towardes the. O lord I am overcome at the lengthe with consideration of thy love: and how can I have the harte to offend thee hereafter, seinge thow hast prevented me so manye wayes with benefites, even when I demaunded
5 not the same? can I have handes evermore to sinne against thee, whiche hast geeven upp thyne owne most tender handes, to be nayled on the crosse for my synnes heretofore? no, no, it is to greate an injurie against thee (o lord) and woe worth me that have donne it so often
10 heretofore. But by thy holye assistance, I trust not to returne to suche iniquitie for the tyme to come: to which (o lord) I beseeche the for thy mercie sake, from thy holie throne of heaven, to saie amen.

Of what opinion and feelinge we shalbe, towchinge these
15 *matters, at the tyme of our deathe.*

CHAP. VIII

The holy scriptures doe teach us, and experience maketh it plaine, that duringe the tyme of this lyfe, the commodities, preferments, and pleasures of the worlde, doe
20 possesse so stronglye the hartes of manye men, and doe holde them chayned with so forcible enchauntmentes, beinge forsaken also upon their just desertes of the grace of God: saye and threaten what a man can, and bringe against them all the whole scripture even from the be-
25 gynninge of Genesis to the end of the Apocalips, (as in deede it is all against synne and synners): yet will it prevaile nothinge with them, beinge in that lamentable case, as ether they beleeve not, or esteeme not, what so ever is saide to that purpose, against their setled lyfe and res-
30 olution to the contrarye. Of this we have infinite examples in scripture: as of Sodome and Gomorra, with the cities aboute, which could not heare the warninges that good Lot gave unto them. Also of Pharao, whome all that ever Moyses could doe, ether by signes or sayinges,
35 moved nothinge. Also of Judas, whoe by no faire meanes or threatninges, used to him by his maister, would change

The indura-cion of some hartes.

Gen.19.

Exo.6.7.8. 9.

Mat.26.

his wicked resolution. But especialye the prophets sent
from God, from tyme to tyme, to disswade the people
from their naughtie lyfe, and consequentlye from the
plagues hanginge over them, doe geeve abundant testi-
5   monie of this, complaininge everie where, of the hardnes
of synners hartes, that wold not be moved with all the
exhortations, preachings, promisses, allurementes, exclamations, threatnings, thunderinges that they could use.
The prophet Zacharie shall testifie for all in this matter,
10   whoe saieth of the people of Israell a litle before theire
destruction. *Hoc ait dominus exercituum et ce. This sayeth the*   Zach.7.
Lorde of hostes: judge justlie: and so forthe. And presentlie
he added: *And they would not attende, but turninge their backes
went awaye, and stopped their eares, to the ende they might not*
15   *heare, and they did put their hartes as an adamant stone, to the
end they might not heare the lawe and the wordes which God did
send in his spirite, by the handes of the former prophetes, wherby
Godes greate indignation was sturred upp.*

This then is and always hath ben the fashion of
20   worldinges, and reprobate persons, to harden their hartes
as an adamant stone, against anye thinge that shalbe
tolde them for the amendement of their lives, and for
the savinge of their soules. Whyles they are in healthe
and prosperitie, they will not know God, as in an other
25   place he complaineth. Marye yet as the prophet saieth: Esa.1.
God will have his daye withe thes men also, when he   Psal.9.
wilbe knowen. And that is, *cognoscetur dominus iudicia faciens.
God wilbe knowen when he begynneth to doe judgment*, and this
is at the daye of deathe, which is the next dore to judge-
30   ment, as S. Paule testifieth, sayinge, *it is appointed for all*   Heb.9.
men once to dye, and after that enseweth judgement.

This I saye is the day of God, most terrible, sorowfull,   Isa.2.3.34.
and full of tribulation, to the wicked, wherin God wilbe   37.61.
knowen, to be a righteous God, *and to restore to everye man*   2.Cor.5.
35   *accordinge as he hath donne while he lived*, as S. Paule sayeth:
or as the prophet describeth it, *he wilbe knowen then to be*   Psal.76.
a terrible God, and such a one, as taketh awaye the spirite of

---

7 *omits* allurements, exclamations, threatnings; *continues* and thunderings
25 *omits* Marye   30 *for al men*

princes, a terrible God to the kynges of the earthe. At this daye, as there wilbe a greate change in all other thinges, as mirth wilbe turned into sorow, laughinges into weepinges, pleasures into paynes, stoutnes into feare, pryde into dis-

5 paire, and the like: so especiallie will there be a straunge alteration in judgement and opinion: for that the wise-dome of God, wherof I have spoken in the former chap-ters, and which (as the scripture saieth) *is accounted folye of the wise of the world,* will then appeare in her likenes,

10 and, as it is in verie deede, wilbe confessed by her great-est enimyes, to be onlie trew wisedome: and all carnall wisdome of worldlinges, to be meere folye, as God call-ethe it.

    This the holye scripture setteth downe clerelye when

15 it describeth the verie speeches and lamentations of the wise men of this worlde at the last daye, sayinge towchinge the vertuous whome they despised in this life. *Nos insen-sati etc. we senseles men* did esteeme their lyfe to be madnes, and their end to be dishonorable: but looke howe they

20 are now accounted amonge the children of God, and their portion is with the sainctes. We have erred from the waye of trewth, and the light of righteousnes, hath not shyned before us, nether hath the sunne of under-standinge appeared unto us. We have weried out our

25 selves in the waye of iniquitie and perdition, and we have walked craggye pathes: but the waye of our lord we have not knowen. Hytherto are the wordes of scrip-ture: wherby we may perceyve, what great chaunge of judgement there wilbe, at the last daye, from that which

30 men have now, of matters: what confessinge of folye, what acknowledginge of errour, what hartie sorow for laboure lost, what fruiteles repentance for havinge runne a-wrie. Oh that men would consider these thinges now. *We have weried out our selves* (saye thes miserable men) *in*

35 *the waye of iniquitie and perdition, and we have walked craggie pathes.* What a description is this of lamentable worldlinges, whoe beate their braynes dailie, and wearie out them selves in pursuyte of vanitie and chaffe of this worlde, for which they suffer notwithstandinge more paine often

The greate change of thinges at the daye of deathe.

1.Cor.2.

Rom.8.
1.Cor.1.

Sap.5.

---

30 al such matters

times, than the just doe in purchasinge of heaven? and
when they arrive at the last daie, to the gate of death,
weryed and worne owt with trouble and toyle, they finde
that all their laboure is lost, all their vexation taken in
5   vaine. For that the litle pelfe which they have gotten in
the worlde, and for which they have strugled so sore,
will helpe them nothinge, but rather greatly afflicte and
torment them. For better understandinge wherof, it is to
be considered, that three thinges will principallie molest
10   these men at the daye of their death, and unto these
maye all the rest be referred.

The first is the excessyve paynes whiche commonlye
men suffer in the seperation of the sowle and bodie,
which have lyved so longe together as two deare frendes,
15   united in love and pleasure, and therfore most lothe to
parte now, but onlye that they are enforced therunto.
This payne may partlye be conceaved by that, yf we
would dryve out lyfe, but from the least parte of our
bodye, (as for example owt of our litle finger, as surgeans
20   are wont to doe when they will mortifye any place, to
make it breacke): what a payne doth a man suffer before
he be dead? what raginge greefe dothe he abyde? and
yf the mortyfyinge of one litle parte onlye, dothe so
much afflicte us: Imagine, what the violent mortyfiinge
25   of all the partes together will doe. For we see that first
the sowle is driven by death to leave the extreamest
partes, as the toes, feete and fyngers: then the legges
and armes, and so consequentlye one parte dyeth after
an other, untill lyfe be restrained onlye to the harte, which
30   holdeth out longest as the principall parte, but yet must
finallye be constrained to render it selfe, though with
never so much payne and resistance. Which paine how
greate and stronge it is, may appeare by the breakinge
in peeces of the verye stringes and holdes wherwith it
35   was envyroned, thorough the excessyve vehemencie of
this deadlye torment.

The first
matter of
miserie in
deathe.

---

12 *mn: Of the souls parting frow the bodie the first matter of miserie in death.*
[* pains] *mn:* B. *Those paines in death are especially to be restreined
to the death of the worldlie: for the godlie have for the most part
a singular comfort therin.   21 before it be dead   36 torment. But yet

Marye yet before it come to this pointe to yelde, no man can expresse the cruell conflict that is betwixt death and her, and what distresses she abydeth in tyme of her agonie. Imagyne that a prince possessed a goodlye citie in all peace, wealth and pleasure, and greatlie frinded of all his neighbours aboute hym, whoe promise to assiste hym in all his needes and affayrs, and that upon the sudden, his mortall enymie should come and besyege this citie, and takinge one holde after an other, one wall after another, one castell after an other, should dryve this prince onlye to a litle tower and besiege him therin, all his other holdes beinge beaten downe, and his men slaine in his sight: what feare, anguishe, and miserie woold this prince be in? how often would he looke owt at the windowes and loope holes of his tower, to see whether his friendes and neighboures would come to help hym or no? and yf he saw them all to abandone hym, and his cruell enemye even readie to breake in upon hym: would he not be in a pityfull plight trow you? And even so fareth it with a poore soule, at the hower of death. The bodye wherin she raigned lyke a jolye princesse in all pleasure, whiles it florished, is now battered and overthrowen by her enemye, which is death: the armes, legges, and other partes where with she was fortified, as with walles and wardes duringe tyme of health, are now surprised and beaten to the grounde, and she is driven onlye to the harte, as to the last and extremest refuge, where she is also most fearcelye assayled in suche sorte as she can not hold owt longe. Her deare frendes which soothed her in tyme of prosperitie, and promised assistance, as yowth, phisicke, and other humane helpes, doe now utterlye abandone her: the enemye will not be pacified or make any league, but night and daye assaulteth this turret where in she is, and whiche now begynneth to shake and shiver in peeces, and she looketh howerlye when her enemye in most raginge and dreadfull maner, will enter upon her.

What thinke you is now the state of this afflicted

A similitude expressinge the paynes of death.

---

21 raigneth

sowle? It is no marvaile yf a wise man become a foole,
or a stowte worldlinge most abject, in this instant of
extremitie, as we often see they doe in such sorte, as
they can dispose of nothinge well ether towardes God
5   or the world at this hower: the cause is the extremitie
of paines, oppressinge their myndes, as S. Austen also
proveth, and geeveth us therwithall a most excellent forewarninge, yf men were so happie as to follow it. When
you shalbe in your last sicknes deare bretheren (sayeth
10   he) o how harde and painfull a thinge will it be for you
to repent of your faultes committed, and of good deedes
omitted, and whye is this? but onlye for that, all the
intention of your mynde wil runne thither, where all the
force of your paine is. Manie impedimentes shall let men
15   at that day. As the payne of the bodye, the feare of
deathe, the sight of children, for the which their fathers
shall often tymes thinke them selves damned, the weepinge of the wife, the flattrie of the world, the temptation
of the devill, the dissimulation of phisitions for lucre
20   sake, and the lyke. And beleeve thow (o man) which
readest this, that thow shalt quickelye prove all this trew
uppon thy selfe, and therfore I beseeche the that thow
wilt doe penance before thow come unto this last daye:
dispose of thy house and make thy testament whyle thow
25   arte whole, while thow art wise, while thow art thyne
owne man: for if thow tarye untill the last daie, thow
shalt be ledd whether thow wouldest not. Hitherto are
S. Austens woords.

The seconde thinge whiche shall make death terrible
30   and greevous to a worldlye man is the sudden partinge,
(and that for ever and ever) from all the thinges which
he loved most dearely in this lyfe, as from his ryches,
possessions, honours, offices, fayre buildinges, with their
commodities, goodlye apparell with rych jewels: from
35   wyfe, and children, kyndred and frindes, and the lyke:
wherewith he thought hym selfe a blessed man in this

Ser.48.ad
Frat.in
eremo.

The
second
matter of
miserie in
deathe.

---

7 proveth (or some other under his name) and   8 so gracious as
9 deer brother   11 *omits* and of good deedes omitted   23 wilt repent
before   24 *omits* whyle thow arte whole, while thow art wise   27 are
the Authors words.

lyfe, and now to be plucked from them uppon the sudden, without ever hope to see or use them agayne, oh what a greefe, what a torment will this be? for which cause the holye scripture saieth: *O mors quam amara est memoria* Eccl.41. *tua, homini pacem habenti in substantiis suis?* O deathe how bytter is thy memorie unto a man, that hath peace and rest in his substaunce and riches? as whoe would saye, there is no more bytternes or greefe in the world to such a man, than to remember or thinke on death onlye, but muche more to goe to it hym selfe, and that owt of hande, when it shalbe saied unto hym, as Christ re-porteth it was to the greate wealthie man in the ghos-pell, whiche had his barnes full and was come now to the hyghest topp of felicitie. *Stulte hac nocte animam tuam* Luc.12. *repetunt a te, quæ autem parasti, cuius erunt?* thow foole, even this night they will take thy sowle from the, and then whoe shall have all that thow hast scraped together?

It is unpossible I saye for anye tongue to expresse the dolefull state of a worldlye man in this instant of death, when nothinge that ever he hath gathered together with so muche labour and toyle, and wherin he was wont to have so much confidence, will now doe hym good any longer, but rather afflict hym with the memorie therof, consideringe that he must leave all to other and goe hym selfe to geeve accounte for the gettynge and usinge of the same, (perhaps to his eternall damnation) whiles in the meane tyme other men in the world do lyve merylye and plesantlie uppon that he hath gotten, litle remembringe and lesse caringe for hym, which lyeth perhapps burninge in unquencheable fyre for the ryches left unto them. This is a wofull and lamentable point, which is to bringe manie a man, to greate sorow and anguyshe of harte at the last daye, when all earthlie joyes must be left, all pleasures and commodities for ever abandoned. Oh what a dolefull daye of partinge will this be? what wilt thow saie, (my frende) at this daye? when all thy glorye, all thy welth, all thy pompe, is come to an ende. What art thow the better now to

The sorow of leavinge all.

---

24 al to others

have lived in credit with the world? in favour of princes?
exalted of men? feared, reverenced, and advaunced,
seinge now all is ended, and that thow canst use these
thinges no more?

5   But yet there is a third thinge whiche more then all
the rest will make this daie of deathe to be trowblesome
and miserable unto a worldlye man, and that is, the
consideration what shall become of him, both in bodye,
and sowle. And for his bodie it wilbe no small horrour

10   to think that *it must inherite serpentes, beastes and wormes,*
as the scripture saieth: that is, it must be cast out to
serve for the foode of vermen. That bodie, I meane,
which was so delicatelie handled before, with varietie of
meates, pillowes, and beddes of downe, so trymlye set

15   foorthe in apparell, and other ornamentes, where uppon
the wynde might not blow, nor the sunne shyne: that
bodye (I saye) of whose beawtie there was so muche
pride taken, and wherby so greate vanitie and sinne was
committed: that bodie, which in this world was accus-

20   tomed to all pamperinge, and could abide no austeritie
or discipline, must now come to be abandoned of all
men, and left onlye to be devoured of wormes. Whiche
thing albeit it can not but breede much horrour in the
hart of hym that lyeth a dyinge: yet is it nothinge in

25   respect of the dreadfull cogitations, which he shall have
towchinge his sowle: as what shal become of it? whether
it shall goe after her departure out of the bodie? and
then consideringe that it must goe to the judgement
seate of God, and there to receyve sentence, ether of

30   unspeakeable glorye, or insupportable paynes: he falleth
to consider more in particuler, the daunger therof, by
comparinge Godes justice and threates (set downe in
scripture against sinners) with his owne lyfe: he begynneth to examine the witnes which is his conscience, and

35   he findeth it readie to laye infinite accusations against
hym, when he commeth to the place of justice.

And now (deare brother) begynneth the miserie of this
man. For there is not a severe saynge of God in all the

The third
matter of
miserie in
death.

Eccl.10.

The cogi-
tation of
the bodie.

---

38 For scantly there

scripture, whiche commeth not now to his mynde to
terrify hym withall at this instant: as, if thow wilt enter   Mat.19.
into lyfe, keepe the commaundementes. He that sayeth   1.Joh.2.
he knoweth God and keepeth not his commaundementes,
5   is a liar. Manie shall saie unto me at that daye, Lord   Matt.7.
Lord, &c. Not the hearers of the law, but the doers of   Rom.2.
the lawe shalbe justifyed. Goe from me all workers of   Luc.13.
iniquitie into everlastinge fyar. Doe not you know that   1.Cor.6.
wicked men shall not possesse the kyngdome of God?
10 be not deceyved, for nether fornicatours, nor Idola-
tours, nor adulterers, nor uncleane handlers of theire
owne bodies, nor Sodomites, nor theeves, nor covetous
men, nor dronkardes, nor backbyters, nor extorsioners,
shal ever possesse the kingdome of God. Yf you lyve   Rom.8.
15 accordinge to the fleshe you shall dye: and the workes   Gal.5.
of the fleshe are manifest, as fornication, uncleannes,
wantonnes, luxurie, poyseninges, enimities, contentions,
emulations, hatred, stryfe, dissentions, sectes, envie, murder, dronkenes, glouttonie, and the lyke. Wherof I fore-
20 tell you as I have tolde you before, that they whiche
doe thes thinges shall never attaine to the kyngdome of
God. We must all be presented before the tribunall of   2.Cor.5.
Christ, and everie man receyve particularlie, accordinge   Jere.2.
as he hathe donne in this lyfe good or evill: everye man   Apo.20.
25 shall receyve accordinge to his woorkes: God spared not   2.Pet.2.
the Angels when they sinned. You shall geeve accounte
of everye idle worde at the daye of judgement. If the   1.Pet.4.
juste shall scarce be saved, where shall the wicked man
and synner appeare? Few are saved, and a riche man   Mat.19.
30 shall hardlie enter into the kyndome of heaven.
   All these thinges (I saye) and a thowsand more towchinge the severitie of Godes justice, and the accounte
which shalbe demaunded at that daye, will come into
his minde that lieth a dyinge, and our ghostlye enimie
35 (which in this lyfe laboured to keepe these thinges from
our eyes, therby the easier to draw us to sinne) will now
laye all and more too, before our face, amplyfiynge and
urginge everie pointe to the uttermost, alleaginge alwayes

---

23 *the judgment seat of Christ*

our conscience for his witnes. Which when the poore sowle in dieinge can not deny, it must needes terrifie her greatlie: for so we see that it dothe daylie, even manie good and vertuous men. S. Jereme reported of holie

5 S. Hillarion, whose sowle beinge greatlie afeard, upon these considerations, to goe out of the bodie, after longe conflict, he tooke courage in the end and sayde to his soule: *Goe out my sowle, goe out: why art thow afeard: thow hast served Christ almost threescore and ten yeres, and art thow*

10 *now a fearde of deathe?* And to lyke effect the holye martyr, Saint Cyprian telleth of a vertuous and godlie bishoppe, which dyinge in his tyme, was greatlye a feard notwith-standinge his good lyfe, untill Christ appeared unto hym in the forme of a goodlye yonge man, and did chyde

15 hym for it, sayinge: *You are a feard to suffer, and you will not goe out of this lyfe: what shall I doe to you?* which example saint Austen did often use to recounte talkinge of this matter, as his scholar Possidonius dothe write in his lyfe.

Now then, if good men, and saintes are so a fearde

20 at this passage, yea such as had served God with all puritie of lyfe, and perfect zeale for three score and ten yeres together: what shall they be, which scarce have served God trewlie one daye in all their lyves, but rather have spent all theire yeres in sinne and vanitie of the

25 world? must not these men be needes in great extrem-itie at this passage? surely S. Augusten dothe describe the same marvailouslie in a certaine sermon of his. And (accordinge to his manner) dothe geeve a notable exhor-tation upon the same. Yf you wil know dearlie beloved

30 (saithe he) with what greate feare and paine the sowle passeth from the bodie: marke diligently what I will saie. The Angels at that hower, doe come to take the sowle and to bringe her before the judgement seate of a most dreadfull judge: and then she callinge to mynde

35 her wicked deedes beginneth greatlye to tremble, and

Jerom.in vita Hilarionis abba. Cyp. lib. de mortal.

Possidon. in vita August.

Ser.50.ad fratres in Eremo & cap.1.de vanitate seculi.

---

10 *omits* And to lyke effect the holye martyr ... as his scholar Possidonius dothe write in his lyfe; *continues [no paragraph break]* But if so good a man was so afeard   20 such an one as   26 *omits* surely S. Augusten dothe describe the same marvailouslie ... not for theirs which dyed, whome they profited nothinge. [86.27]

would gladlie seeke to flye and to leave her deedes behynde her, seekinge to entreate the Angels and to request but one hower space of delaye. But that will not
be graunted: and her evill woorkes cryeinge out all
5 together shall speake against her, and saye, we will not
staye behynde or parte from the, thow hast donne us,
and we are thy workes, and therfore we wil follow the
whether soever thow goest, even unto the seate of judgment. And this is the state of a sinners soule which
10 partinge from his bodye, with most horrible feare, goeth
onwardes to judgement loaden with sinnes, and with
infinite confusion. Contrariwise the just mans sowle goeth
out of his bodie with greate joye and comforte, the good
Angels accompaininge her, with exultation. Wherfore
15 brethren seinge these thinges are so, doe you feare this
terrible hower of death now, that you maye not feare
it when you come to it. Foresee it now, that you maye
be secure then. Thus farre S. Augusten.

And because S. Austen maketh mention of good and
20 evill Angels heere, whiche are readie to receyve the
sowles of the just and wicked men, at the hower of
their death: it is to be noted, that often tymes God
doth permit the visions of Angels both good and evill,
as also of other sayntes, to men lyinge on their death
25 beddes, before they departe this lyfe, for a tast ether
of comforte or sorow towchinge that which shall ensewe
after, in the world to come: and this is one singuler
priveledge, belonginge to this passadge also. And so
concerninge the just I have shewed before an exam-
30 ple out of S. Cyprian and S. Austen towchinge one to
whome Christ appeared at the hower of his death. And
S. Gregorie the greate, hath divers other lyke examples
in the fourthe booke of his dialogues for divers chapters
together, as of one Ursinus to whome the blessed Apostles
35 S. Peter and S. Paule appeared, and the lyke: but of
dreadfull apparitions of divers and wicked Angels, which
shewed themselves unto divers synners at the houer of
their deathe, and denounced to them, their eternall
damnation, and their horrible tormentes appointed in
40 hell, we have manie also and most terrible examples,

Appari-
tions to
them that
lye a
dyinge.

Lib.4. ca.
11.12.13.
14. &c.

recorded in the auncient writers. As that in S. Gregorie
of one Chrisorius a greate and riche man, but as full
of sinne as of wealth, as S. Gregorie saieth, to whome
lyinge on his deathbed, the infernall fiendes in most
5   uglye manner appeared, shewinge how now he was delivered into their power, and so never left hym untill he
died, and left his sowle unto them to be caried awaye
to eternall tormentes. The like doth S. Beede write of
divers in Englande at his tyme, as of a courtyer of kyng
10   Coenride, a most wicked man, though in greate favour
of the prince, to whome lyinge in his panges of deathe,
and beinge now a litle recovered, bothe the good and
evill Angels appeared visibly, the one layinge before hym
a litle small booke of his good deedes, the other a greate
15   huge volume of his mischievous factes. The which after
they had caused hym to reade, by the permission of the
good Angels from God, they seazed upon him, appoint-
inge him also what hower he should dye, as hym selfe
confessed openlie to all that came to visit hym, and as
20   by this horrible and desperate deathe ensueinge at the
hower by them appointed, manifestlie was confirmed.
The like storie he sheweth in the chapter folowinge, of
one whome he knew him selfe, and as both he and
S. Gregorie, and S. Cyprian also doe note, all these and
25   the lyke visions, were permitted for our sakes which doe
lyve, and maye take commoditie by the same, and not
for theirs which dyed, whome they profited nothinge.

    Now then (deare Christian) these thinges beinge soe,
that is, this passage of death beinge so terrible, so daun-
30   gerous, and yet so unavoydable as it is: seinge so manye
men perish and are overwhelmed dailye in the same, as
it can not be denied but there doe: and both holie scriptures and auncient fathers do testifie it by examples and
recordes unto us: what man of discretion would not
35   learne to be wise by other mens daungers? or what reasonable creature would not take heede and looke aboute
him, beinge warned so manifestlie, and apparantlie, of
his owne perill? Yf thow be a Christian, and doest beleeve
in deede the thinges which Christian faith doth teache
40   the: then doest thow know and most certainlie beleeve

Lib.4.
dial.c.38.

Lib.5.hist.
Ang.cap.
14.

Beda lib.
5.cap.15.

also, that of what state, age, strength, dignitie, or condition, so ever thow be now, yet that thow thy selfe (I
saye) which now in health and mirth readest this, and
thinkest that it litle pertaineth to thee, must one of these
5   daies (and that perhaps shortlie after the readinge hereof,)
come to prove all these thinges uppon thy selfe, which
I have here writen: that is, thow must with sorow and
greefe be enforced to thy bed, and there after all thy
strugglings with the dartes of deathe, thow must yelde
10   thy bodie which thow lovest so muche, to the baite of
wormes, and thy sowle to the tryall of justice, for her
doinges in this lyfe.

    Imagine then (my freende) thow I saye which art so
freshe and froelicke at this daie, that the ten, twentie, or
15   two yeres, or perhaps two monethes, which thow hast
yet to lyve, were now ended, and that thow were even
at this present, stretched out uppon a bed, wearied and
worne with dolour and paine, thy carnall frindes about
the weepinge and howlinge, the phisitions departed with
20   theire fees, as havinge geeven the over, and thow lyinge
there alone mute and dumme in most pitifull agonie,
expectinge from moment to moment, the last stroake of
death to be geeven the. Tell me in this instant, what
would all the pleasures and commodities of this world
25   doe the good? what comforte would it be to the, to
have bene of honour in this world, to have bene ryche
and purchassed muche, to have borne office, and bene
in the princes favoure? to have left thy children or kynred
wealthye, to have trodden downe thyne enimies, to
30   have sturred much, and borne greate swaye in this lyfe?
what ease (I saye) or comfort would it be to the, to have
ben fayre, to have ben gallant in apparell, goodlie
in personage, glytteringe in golde? would not all thes
thinges rather afflict than profit the at this instant? for
35   now shouldest thow see the vanitie of thes trifles: now
would thy hart begyn to saye within the: o follye and
unfortunate blindenes of myne: Loe, heere is an end

A veri
profitable
considera-
tion.

The cogi-
tation &
speeche of
the sowle
at the last
daye.

5 and it may be shortlie 14 or (it may be) two 36 and miserable
blindnes 37 *mn: at the day of death.*

now of all my delytes and prosperities: all my joyes, all
my pleasures, all my myrth, all my pastymes are now
finished: where are my frindes whiche were wont to
laugh with me? my servantes wont to attende me, my
5   children wont to disporte me? where are all my coches
and horses, wherwith I was wont to make so goodlie a
shew, the cappes and knees of people wont to honour
me, the troupes of suters followinge me? where are all
my daliances and trickes of love? all my pleasant musicke,
10   all my gorgeous buyldinges, all my costlie feastes and
banquettinges? and above all other, where are my deare
and sweete frindes, whoe seemed they would never have
forsaken me? but all are now gone, and have left me
heere alone to aunswere the reckoninge for all, and none
15   of them will doe so muche as to goe with me to judgement, or to speake one worde in my behalfe. Woe worthe
to me, that I had not foreseene this daye rather, and
so have made better provision for the same: it is now
to late, and I feare me I have purchased eternall damna-
20   tion, for a litle pleasure, and lost unspeakable glorie, for
a flootinge vanitie. Oh how happie and twise fortunate
are they whiche so lyve as they maye not be a fearde
of this daye? I now see the difference betwixt the endes
of good and evill, and marvaile not though the scrip-
25   tures saye of the one, *the deathe of sainctes is precious*: And   Psa.116.
of the other, *the death of sinners is miserable*: Oh that I had   Psal.34.
lyved so vertuouslye as some other have donne, or as I
had often inspirations from God to doe: or that I had
done the good deedes I might have donne: how sweete
30   and confortable woold they be to me now in this my
last, and extremest distresse?

     To these cogitations and speeches (deare brother) shall
thy harte be enforced, of what estate soever thow be,
at the hower of death, yf thow doe not prevent it nowe
35   by good lyfe and vertuous actions, whiche onlye can
yeeld the comfort in that sorowfull daye. For of good
men the judge hym selfe sayeth. *His autem fieri incipien-*   Luc.21.

---

17 day sooner, and   21 happie and twise happie are   35 by amendment of life, which only

*tibus, respicite & leuate capita vestra, quoniam appropinquat
redemptio vestra.* When these terrible thinges begyn to come
upon other men doe you looke aboute you, and lyft up
your heades, for that your redemption commeth on,

5 from the laboures and toyles of this worlde. And the
holye prophet sayeth of the vertuous man which hath
done good woorkes in this lyfe, that he shalbe at this
tyme *beatus vir*, a happye man, and he geeveth the cause,   Psal.41.
quia in die mala liberabit eum dominus, & opem feret illi super

10 *lectum doloris eius.* For that God will deliver hym in this
evill daye, and will assist hym uppon the bed of his
sorow. Whiche is ment (no doubt) of the bed of his last
departure, especialye for that of all other beddes this is
the most sorowfull, as I have shewed, beinge nothinge

15 els but a heape of all sorowes together, especiallie to
them whiche are drawen unto it before they are readie
for the same, as commonly all they are, which deferre
their amendement from daye to daie, and doe not attend
to lyve in such sorte now, as they shall wishe they had

20 done when they come to that last passage.

*Of the paines appointed for sinne after this lyfe and of two
sortes of the same.*

CHAP. IX

Amongest all the meanes whiche God useth towardes
25 the children of men, to move them to this resolution,
wherof I entreate, the strongest and most forcible is, the
consideration of punishmentes prepared by hym for rebellious sinners, and transgressours of his commaundements.
Wherfore he useth this motyve often, as maye appeare
30 by all the prophetes, whoe doe almost nothinge els but
threaten plagues and destruction to offenders. And this
meane hath often tyme prevailed more than anye other

---

2 *these things*   3 *omits* looke aboute you, and   21 *omits and of two sortes
of the same*   26 forcible (to the common sort of men) is   29 consideration often   32 oft times

that could be used, by reason of the naturall love which
we beare towardes our selves: and consequentlie the
naturall feare whiche we have of our owne daunger.
So we reade that nothinge could move the Ninivites
5   so much as the foretellinge them of theire imminent
destruction. And S. John Baptist, although he came in
a simple and contemptible maner: yet preachinge unto
the people the *terrour of vengeance to come, and that the axe*
was now put to the tree to cut downe for the fyre all those
10   *which repented not*: he moved the verie publicanes and
souldiers to feare, (which otherwise are people of verie
harde metall) whoe came unto hym uppon this terrible
embassage, and asked what they should doe to avoyde
these punishmentes?

15   After then that we have considered of death and of
Godes severe judgmente, which ensueth after death, and
wherin everie man hath to receyve accordinge to his
woorkes in this lyfe, as the scripture sayeth: it followeth
that we consider also of the punishmentes which are
20   appointed for them that shalbe founde faultie, in that
accounte, hereby at leastwise (yf no other consideration
will serve) to induce Christians to this resolution of
servinge God. For as I have noted before, if everie man
have naturallie a love of him selfe and desire to con-
25   serve his owne ease: then should he also have feare of
perill, wherby he is to fall into the extreame calamitie.
This expresseth S. Bernard excellently according to his
wounte. O man (saiethe he) if thow have left all shame,
(which appertaineth to so noble a creature as thow art:)
30   if thow feele no sorow (as carnall men doe not:) yet leese
not feare also which is founde in very beastes. We use
to loade an asse and to werie him out with laboure and
he careth not, because he is an asse: but yf thow woldest thrust him into fyre, or flynge hym into a ditche, he
35   woold avoide it as muche as he coulde, for that he loveth
lyfe and feareth death. Feare thow then, and be not
more insensible than a beast. Feare death, feare judgement, feare hell. This feare is called the begynninge of
wisdome, and not shame or sorow, for that the spirite

The force
of feare.

Jon.3.

Math.3.

Marc.1.

Luc.3.

2.Cor.5.

In
serm.de
primordiis.

Pro.9.

of feare is more potent to resist sinne, than the spirite
of shame or sorow. Wherfore it is saide, *remember the ende*
and thow shalt never sinne, that is, remember the finall pun-   Eccle.7.
ishmentes appointed for sinne, after this lyfe. Thus far
5   S. Bernarde.

First therfore to speake in generall of the punishmentes
reserved for the lyfe to come, yf the scriptures did not
declare in perticular theire greatnes unto us: yet are
there manie reasons to persuade us that they are most
10 severe, dolorous and intollerable. For first, as God is a   Gods
God in all his woorkes, that is to saye, greate, wounder-   majestie.
full, and terrible: so especialie he sheweth the same in   Psal.76.
his punishmentes, beinge called for that cause in scrip-   Deu.10.
ture, *deus iustitiæ*, God of justice: as also, *deus vltionum*,   Psal.4.
15 God of revenge. Wherfore seinge all his other woorkes,   Psal.94.
are majestical and exceedinge our capacities: we maye
lykewise gather that his hande in punishment, must be
wounderfull also. God hym selfe teacheth us to reason
in this maner, when he sayethe: *And will ye not then feare*   Jere.5.
20 *me? and will ye not tremble before my face, whiche have putt the*
sande as a stopp unto the sea, and have geeven the water a com-
mandement never to passe it, no not when it is most trowbled and
the flooddes most outragious? as who would saye: yf I am
wounderfull and doe passe your imagination, in these
25 woorkes of the sea and other which you see daylie: you
have cause to feare me, consideringe that my punishmentes are lyke to be correspondent to the same.

An other conjecture of the great and severe justice of   Gods
God, maye be the consideration of his infinite and un-   mercye.
30 spekeable mercie: the whiche as it is the verie nature of
God, and without ende or measure, as his godhead is:
so is also his justice. And these two are the two armes
(as it were) of God, embracinge and kyssinge one the   Psal.85.
other, as the scripture saieth. Therfore as in a man of
35 this world, yf we had the measure of one arme, we might
easely conjecture of the other: so seinge the wounderfull examples dailie of Godes infinite mercie towardes

---

1 more mightie to   16 are ful of majestie and exceeding

them, that doe repent: we maye imagyne by the same,
his severe justice towardes them, whome he reserveth to
punishment in the next lyfe, and whome for that cause,   Rom.9.
he calleth in the scriptures *Vasa furoris*: Vessels of his   Esa.13.
5   furye, or vessels to shew his furye uppon.   Psal.7.

A third reason to perswade us of the greatnes of these   Gods
punishmentes, maye be the marvailous patience, and   patience.
longe sufferinge of God in this lyfe, as for example, in
that he sufferethe divers men from one sinne to an other,
10 from one daye to an other, from one yere to an other,
from one age to an other, to spend all (I saye) in dishonoure and dispite of his majestie, addinge offence to
offence, and refusinge all perswasions, allurementes, good
inspirations, or other meanes of frindshipp, that his mer-
15 cie can devise to offer for theire amendment. And what
man in the world could suffer this? or what mortall hart
can shew suche patience? but now yf all this should not
be requited with severitie of punishment, in the worlde
to come, uppon the obstinate: it might seeme against
20 the lawe of justice and equitie, and one arme in God
might seeme longer than the other. S. Paule toucheth
this reason in his epistle to the Romans, where he saithe:
Doest thow not know that the benignitie of God is used to bringe   Rom.2.
thee to repentance? and thow by thy harde and impenitent hart
25 *doest hoord upp vengeance unto thy selfe, in the daye of wrath,*
and appearance of Gods just judgementes, which shall restore to
everie man accordinge to his workes? He useth heere the wordes
of *hoordinge upp of vengeance*, to signifie that even as the
covetous man doth hoorde up monie to monie dailie,
30 to make his heape greate: so the unrepentant synner
dothe hoorde up sinne to sinne: and God on the contrary
side hoordeth upp vengeance to vengeance, untill his
measure be full, to restore in the end, *measure against meas-*   Esa.27.
ure, as the prophet saith, and to paye us home *accordinge*
35 *to the multitude of our owne abhominations.* This God meant   Jere.16.
when he sayde to Abraham *that the iniquities of the Amorrheans*   Gen.15.
were not yet full upp. Also in the revelations unto S. John

---

1 that repent

Evangelist, when he used this conclusion of that booke: *He that doth evill, let hym doe yet more evill: and he that lyeth in filth, let hym yet become more filthie: for beholde I come quick-lye, and my rewarde is with me, to render to everye man accordinge* **Apo.22.**

5 *to his deedes.* By which wordes God signifieth that his bearinge and tolleratinge with sinners in this lyfe, is an argument of his greater severitie in the lyfe to come, which the prophet David also declareth when talkinge of a careles sinner he saieth: *Dominus irridebit eum quoniam* **Psal.37.**

10 *prospicit quod veniet dies eius.* Our God shall scoff at hym foreseinge that his daye shall come. This daye (no dout) is to be understoode the daye of accounte and punishe-ment, after this lyfe, for soo dothe God more at large declare hym selfe in an other place, in these wordes.

15 And thow sonne of man, this saieth thy lord God: the end **Ezec.7.** is come, now (I saye) the end is come uppon the. And I will shew in the my furye, and will judge the accord-inge to thy waies. I will laye against the all thy abom-inations, and my eye shall not spare the, nor will I

20 take anye mercie uppon the, but I will put thyne owne wayes uppon the, and thow shalt know that I am the lord. Behold affliction commeth on, the end is come, the end (I saye) is come: it hath watched against the, and beholde it is come: crusshinge is now come uppon

25 the: the tyme is come: the daye of slaughter is at hand. Shortlie will I poure owt my wrathe uppon the, and I will fill my furye in the, and I will judge the accordinge to thy waies, and I will laye all thy wickednes uppon the: my eye shall not pitie the: nor wil I take any com-

30 passion uppon the, but I will laye thy waies uppon the, and thy abhominations in the middest of the, and thow shalt know that I am the lorde that striketh. Hytherto is the speeche of God hym selfe.

Seinge then now we understande in generall, that the **Of**

35 punishmentes of God in the lyfe to come are moste cer- **paynes in** taine to be greate and severe, to all suche as fall into **particular.** them: for whiche cause S. Paule saithe: *Horrendum est* **Heb.10.** *incidere in manus dei viuentis*: it is a horrible thinge to fall

---

10 *eius. The Lord shal*   19 neither wil I   29 neither wil I

into the handes of our lyvinge God: Let us consider some
what in particular what manner of paines and punishmentes they shalbe. For better conceavinge wherof, it
is to be noted, that as there are two sortes of sinners,
5   the one whiche dye in the guylt of mortall sinne, and
in the disfavoure and displeasure of God, of whome it
is saide, *conuertantur peccatores in infernum*: Let sinners be
turned into hell. And againe: there is a sinne unto deathe,
and I doe not saye that anye man should praye for that.
10   And againe: the portion of wicked men, shalbe in the
lake burninge with fire and brymstone: which is called
the second deathe. An other sorte of sinners there are,
whiche have the guylt of theire sinnes pardoned by their
repentance in this lyfe, but yet have not made that tem-
15   porall satisfaction to Gods justice, nor are so thorough-
lie purged in this lyfe, as they maye passe to heaven
without punishment: and of these it is writen: *Detrimentum
patientur, ipsi autem salui erunt, sic tamen quasi per ignem*. They
shall suffer hurt and dammage but yet they shalbe saved
20   as by fire. Upon which wordes of S. Paul, the holye
father S. Austen writeth thus: Because S. Paul sayeth
that these men shalbe saved by fire, therfore this fire is
contemned. But surely though they shalbe saved by it:
yet is this fire more greevous than what soever a man
25   can suffer in this life: and yet you know how greate and
intollerable thinges men have or maie suffer. The same
S. Austen in an other place sayeth thus: They which
have donne thinges worthie of temporall punishment (of
whome the Apostle sayeth: *They shalbe saved by fire*) must
30   passe thorough a firie river, and most horrible shallowes
of burninge flames, signified by the prophet, when he
saithe, *and a fludd of fyre went before hym*: and looke how
much matter there is in theire synnes, so longe must
they sticke in passinge thorough: how much the fault
35   requireth, so much shall the punishement of this fyre
revenge. And because the word of God dothe compare
the sowle of a synner, to a pott of brasse, sayinge: *put*

Two sort
of synners
that dye.

Psal.9.
1.Joh.5.
Apoc.21.

1.Co.3.

Psal.38.

The
severitie
of pun-
ishement
in purga-
torie.
Hom.16.
ex
50.homi.
1.Co.3.

Dan.7.

---

1 *of the living*   3 *omits* For better conceavinge wherof ... revealed
unto us, concerning this punishement. [97.23]

the pott emptie uppon the coles, untill all the rust be melted of:
therfore in this fyre all ydle speeches, all filthie cogitations, all light synnes, shall boyle out, which by a shorte
waie might have ben seperated from the sowle in this
5   lyfe, by almes and teares. Hitherto S. Austen.

    And the same holie father in an other place hath
these wordes. If a sinner by his conversion escape death,
and obtaine lyfe, yet for all that I can not promise hym,
that he shall escape all payne or punishment. For he
10   that differred the fruites of repentance till the next lyfe,
must be perfited in purgatorie fire: and this fyre (I tell
you) though it be not everlastinge, yet is it passinge
greevous, for it doth far exceede all paines that man
can suffer in this lyfe. Never was there founde out yet
15   so greate a paine in fleshe, as that is, though martyrs
have abydden straunge tormentes, and many wicked
men have suffered exceedinge greate punishmentes. To
lyke effecte dothe S. Gregorie write of the severitie of
this punishment, expoundinge those wordes of David. *O*
20   *Lorde rebuke me not in thy furye nor correct me in thy wrathe.*
This is as yf he sayde (saythe S. Gregorie) I know that
after this lyfe, some must be clensed by purginge fire.
And other must receave sentence of eternall damnation.
But because I esteeme that purginge fyre (though it be
25   transitorie) to be more intolerable, than all the tribulation which in this lyfe maye be suffered: therfore I doe
not onlye desire not to be rebuked in the furie of eternall damnation, but also I greatlie feare to be purged in
the wrathe of transitorie correction: thus far S. Gregorie.
30   And I might add a hundred like sayinges more out of
the holye fathers towchinge the extreame severitie of this
purginge fyre after death, and of the greate feare which
they had of it, but this shalbe sufficient to warne Catholiques which beleeve it, to looke better aboute them than
35   they doe, for the avoydinge of the rigoure of this fyre
by theire good lyfe in this world, especiallie by these
two meanes of almes and teares, whiche S. Austen in
the place before recited, dothe mention: which holye
father also in the same place, maketh this collection:
40   we see what men doe or maye suffer in this life: what

De vera
& falsa
poeniten-
tia.c.18.

In Psal.
tertium
pænitent.

Psa.6.38.

August.in
Psa.37.

rackinge, what tearinge, what burninge and the like: and
yet they are nothinge in respect of that fire: whereof he
inferreth this conclusion, *ista ergo etc.* Thes thinges therfore which we suffer heere, are much easiar than that
5   fire: and yet yow see that men will doe any thinge rather
than suffer them: how much more then ought wee to
doe that litle whiche God commaundeth us, to avoyde
that fyre, farre and muche more greevouse?

It is a straunge matter to consider, what great feare
10 holye men had of this fire, and how litle we have now
a dayes, having much more cause than they. S. Barnarde
hathe these woordes of hym selfe: Oh wold to God some
man wold now before hand provide for my head abundance of water and to my eyes a fountaine of teares,
15 for so perhaps the burninge fire should take no holde,
where running teares had clensed before. And agayne, I
tremble and shake for feare, of falling into Gods hands.
I wolde gladlie present my selfe before his face, alredie
judged of my selfe, and not to be judged then of hym.
20 Therfore I will make a reckonyng whiles I am heere of
my good dedes and of my badde. My evell shalbe corrected with better woorkes: they shalbe watered with
teares: they shalbe punished by fasting: they shalbe
amended by sharp discipline: I will ripp up the verie
25 bottom of my wayes and all my devises, that he may
fynde nothing untryed at that day, or not fullye discussed to his handes. And then I hope in his mercie,
that he will not judge the same faults again, and the
second time, as he hathe promised. The lyke feare uttereth
30 S. Ambrose in thes woordes: O Lorde yf thou reserve
any whit in me to be revenged in the next lyfe: yet I
humblie aske of the, that thow geve me not upp to the
power of wycked spirits, whiles thou wypest awaye my
synnes, by the paynes of purgatorie. And agayn, in an
35 other place: I shalbe searched and examined as leade
(in this fire) and I must burne untill all the lead be
melted away. And yf then there be found no silver matter in me: woe be to me. For I must be thrust doune
to the nethermost partes of hell, or elles whollie waste
40 away as straw in the fyre. But if anie gold or silver be

The feare
that old
saintes
had of
the fyre
of purga-
torie.

Serm.16.
& 55.in
cant.

Naum.1.
Præcat.
præparat.
2.Ad
missam.

Serm.20.
in
Psalm.118.

1.Cor.3.

fownd in me, not throughe my woorkes, but by grace
and Christes mercie, and through the ministerie of my
prestehoode: I shall also once say: *surelie they that trust in*   Psal.31.
the, shall never be confounded. And thus muche of this tem-
5   porall punishement reserved even for the purging of
Gods servants in the lyfe to come.

    But now touching the reprobate and such as for their   Of hell &
wickednesse have to die everlastinglie: we must imagine   the pun-
that the case standeth much more hardlye: for to that   ishment
10   purpose soundeth Christs sayeing to the good wemen of   damned.
Jerusalem, when he was goeing to his passion: *Yf they*
doe these things to grene wood: what shal become of that which   Luc.23.
is drye? which woordes S. Peter seemeth in some parte
to expounde, when he sayeth: *Yf the Judgement of God*   1.Pet.4.
15   *begyn with us which are his servants: what shall the end of wicked*
men be? As who wold say, that in all reason, their ende
must be intollerable. For more particular conceaving
whereof, because the matter is of great importance for
all Christians to know: it shall not be perhaps amisse,
20   to consider breeflie, what the holie scriptures and auncient fathers of the Catholique churche, (directed no
doubt by the holie Ghost) have revealed unto us, concerning this punishement. And first of all, towchinge the   Of the
place of punishement appointed for the damned, com-   name of
25   monlie called hell, the scripture in diverse languages,   hell in
useth diverse names, but all tending to expresse the   tongues.
greevousnesse of punishement there suffered: As in latyn
it is called, *Infernus,* a place beneathe or under ground   Esa.5.
(as most of the old fathers doe interprete). But whether   & 38.
30   it be under ground or no, most certaine it is, that it is
a place most opposit to heaven, which is sayd to be
above, and from which Lucifer was throwne downe. And   Job.11.
this name is used to signifie the miserable suppressing   Esa.14.
and hurling downe of the damned, to be troden under
35   the feet, not onlie of God, but also of good men for
ever. For so sayeth the scripture. *Beholde the daye of the*   Mala.4.
lorde cometh burning like a fornace, and all proud and wicked

---

32 *omits* and from which Lucifer was throwne downe. 36 [* so]
mn: B. *The matter in hand is not by this place substantially prooved.

men shall be straw to that fornace, and you that feare my name shall tread them dowen, and they shalbe as burnt ashes under the soles of your feet in that daye. And this shalbe one of the greatest miseries that can happen to the prowde and
5   stowte potentates of the worlde, to be thrown doune with suche contempt, and to be troden under feet of them, whome they so muche despised in this worlde.

    The Hebrew woord whiche the scripture useth for hell, is *Seol*, whiche signifieth a great ditche or dungeon.
10 In whiche sense it is also called in the Apocalips *lacus iræ Dei*, the lake of the wrathe of God. And again, *Stagnum ardens igne & sulphure*: a poole burning with fyre and brimstone. In greek the scripture useth three woordes for the same place. The fyrst is, *Hades*, used in the
15 gospell, whiche (as Plutarche noteth) signifieth a place where no light is: The second is *zophos*, in S. Peter, which signifieth darknes it selfe. In whiche sense it is called also of Job, *terra tenebrosa & operta mortis caligine.* A darke land and overwhelmed with deadlie obscuritie.
20 Also in the gospell *tenebræ exteriores*, utter darknesse. The thirde greek woorde is *tartaros*, used also by S. Peter: whiche woorde being derived of the verbe *tarasso*, (which signifieth to terrifye, trouble, and vexe) importeth an horrible confusion of tormentors in that place: even as
25 Job sayeth of it, *ibi nullus ordo, sed sempiternus horror inhabitat*, there dwelleth no order, but everlastinge horrour.

    The chaldie woorde (which is also used in hebrew, and translated to the greke) is *gehenna*. First of all used by Christ, for the place of them whiche are damned, as
30 S. Jerom noteth upon the tenth chapiter of S. Mathewes gospell. And this woord being compounded of *gee and hinnom* signifieth a valley nighe to Jerusalem, called the valley of hinnom, in whiche the olde idolatrous Jewes were wont to burne alyve their owne children in the
35 honour of the devill, and to sownd with trumpets, tymprills, and other lowd instruments, whiles they were doeinge therof, that the childerens voyces and cryes might not be heard: whiche place was afterward used also for the receipt of all filthines, as of doung, dead
40 carions, and the like: And it is moste probable, that our

Esa.14.

Apo.14.
Apo.21.
Matt.11.
In com.
supra
verba
uiue
latenter.
2.Pet.2.
Job.10.
Mat.22.
& 25.
2.Pe.2.

Job.10.

Mat.5.10.
18.23.
Mar.9.
Luc.12.
The
valley
hinnom.

Saviour used this woorde above all other for hell, thereby
to signifie the miserable burninge of soules in that place,
the pitifull clamours and cries of the tormented, the confuse and barbarous noyse of the tormentors, together
5   with the moste lothesom fillthynesse of the place, which
is otherwise described in the scriptures, by the names
of adders, snakes, cocatrices, scorpions, and other venemouse creatures, as shalbe afterwards declared.

    Having declared the names of this place and thereby
10 also in some part, the nature: yt remaineth now, that
we consider, what maner of paines men suffer there.
For declaration whereof, we must note, that as heaven
and hell are contrary, assigned to contrary persones, for
contrary causes: so have they in all respectes contrarye
15 properties, conditions, and effects, in suche sorte, as what
soever is spoken of the felicitye of the one, may serve
to inferre the contrary of the other. As when S. Paule
sayeth *that no eye hath seene, nor eare heard, nor hart conceaved*
the joyes that God hathe prepared for them that shalbe saved: We
20 may inferre that the payns of the damned must be as
great. Again, when the scripture saithe that the felicitie
of them in heaven is a perfect felicitie, containing *omne*
bonum, all goodnesse: So that no one kinde of pleasure
can be imagined whiche they have not: we must thinke
25 on the contrary part, that the miserie of the damned,
must be also a perfect miserie, contayning all afflictions
that may be, without wanting any. So that, as the happines of the good is infinite, and universall: so also is
the calamitie of the wicked infinite and universall. Now
30 in this lyfe all the miseries and pains which fall upon
man, are but particular and not universall. As for example: we see one man pained in his eyes, an other in his
teeth, an other in his stomak, an other in his back:
whiche particular pains notwithstandinge some times are
35 so extreame, as lyfe is not able to resist them, and a
man wolde not suffer them long for the gayning of many
worldes to gether. But suppose now, a man were tormented in all the parts of his bodye at once, as in his

The
paynes of
hell uni-
versall.

1.Co.2.

Exo.33.

---

32 *omits* an other in his teeth, an other in his stomak

head, his eyes, his tongue, his teeth, his throote, his stomak, his bellie, his back, his hart, his sides, his thighes, and in all the joynts of his bodye besides: suppose (I say) he were moste cruellie tormented with extreme
5   paines in all these parts together, without ease or intermission. What thing could be more miserable than this? what sight more lamentable? Yf thou shouldest see a dogge lye in the strete so afflicted: I know thou couldest not but take compassion upon him. Well then, consider
10   what difference there is betwene abydinge these pains for a week, or for all eternitie: in suffering them upon a soft bedde, or upon a burning grydyron and boyling fornace: among a mans freendes comforting hym, or among the furies of hell whipping and tormentinge hym.
15   Consider this (I say gentle reader,) and yf thou woldest take a greate deale of labour, rather than abyde the one, in this lyfe: be content to sustain a litle pain rather than to incurre the other in the lyfe to come.

But to consider these things yet further, not onelie all   **Peculiar**
20   these partes of the body which have bene instruments   **torments**
to sinne, shalbe tormented together, but also everie sense   **to every**
bothe externall and internall for the same cause shalbe   **parte.**
afflicted with his particular torment, contrarie to the object wherein it delited moste, and tooke pleasure in
25   this worlde. As for example, the lasciviouse eyes shalbe afflicted with the uglie and fearefull sight of devills: the delicate eares with the horrible noyse of damned spirits: the nyse smell, with poysoned stenche of brimstone and other unsupportable filthe: the dainty taste with most
30   ravynouse hungar and thirst: and all the sensible partes of the body with burning fire. Again, the Imagination shalbe tormented, with the apprehension of paines present, and to come: the memorie, withe the remembrance of pleasures past, the understanding, with consideration
35   of the felicitie lost, and the miserie now come on. O poore Christian, what wilt thou doe amiddest the multitude of so grevouse calamities?

It is a wounderfull matter, and able (as one father   **The pains**

---

11 eternities   25 As if for example, the lascivious eies were afflicted

sayeth) to make a reasonable man goe out of his wittes, to consider what God hathe reveyled unto us in the scriptures, of the dreadfull circumstances of this punishment, and yet to see, how litle the rechelesse men of the worlde doe feare it. For first, touching the universalitie, varietie, and greatnesse of the payne, not onely the reasons before alleaged, but also diverse other considerations in the scriptures do declare. As where it is sayed of the damned, *cruciabuntur die & nocte*, they shalbe tormented day and night. And again, *Date illi tormentum*, *geve her torment*, speaking of Babilon in hell, by whiche is signified that the paines in hell are exercised, not for punishement, but for torment of the parties. And torments commonlie we see in this worlde to be as great and as extreame, as the witt of man can reache to devise. Imagin then, when God shall lay his head to devise torments (as he hathe done in hell) what maner of torments will they be.

Yf creating an element heere for our comfort (I mean the fire) he could create the same so terrible as it is, in such sorte as a man wolde not holde his onelie hand in it one daye, for to gayne a kingdome: what a fire think you hathe he provided for hell, which is not created for comfort, but onelie for torment, of the parties? Our fire hathe a thousand differences from that, and therfore is truelie sayd of the holy fathers, to be but a painted and fained fire in respect of that. For our fire was made to comfort (as I have sayd) and that, to torment. Our fire hathe neede to be fedde continuallie with wood or els it goeth oute: that burneth continuallie, without feeding. Our geveth light: that geveth none: Our is out of his naturall place, and therfore shifteth to ascend, and to get from us, as wee see: but that is in the naturall place, where it was created, and therfore it abydeth there perpetuallie. Our consumeth the matter layed in it, and so quickelie dispatcheth the payne: that tormenteth but consumeth not, to the ende the paine may

Marginal notes:

of hell exercised for torment, not for punishement.

Apo.20. & 14.

Apo.18.

Luc.16.

The fearse nature of the fire of hell.

---

4 *mn: for chastisement.*   12 not for chastisement, but   15 wit of a man
25 many differences   31 Ours *and passim*

be everlasting. Our fire is extinguished with water, and
greatlie abated by the coldenesse of the ayer about it:
that hathe no such abatement, or qualification. Finallie
what a straunge and incredible kynde of fire that is,
5   appeareth by these woordes of our Saviour so often re-   Matt.8.13.
peated: *There shalbe weeping and gnashing of teeth.* Weeping   22.24.
is to be referred to the effect of extreme burning in that   Luc.13.
fire, for that the torment of scalding and burning enforc-
eth tears sooner than any other torment, as appeareth
10   in them, which upon the sodain doe put a hote thing
in to their mouthe, or skalde any other parte of their
body. And gnashing of teeth (as every man knoweth)
proceedeth onelie of great and extreme colde. Imagin
then what a fire this is which hathe suche extreme
15   effects bothe of heate and colde. O mightie Lorde what
a straunge God art thow? how wounderfull and terrible
in all thy woorkes and inventions? how bountifull art
thow to those that love and serve the? and how severe
to them whiche contemne thy commaundements? Hast
20   thow devised a way how they whiche lie burning in a   Apo.21.
lake of fire and brimstone shall also be tormented with
extreame colde? what understandinge of man can conceave how this may be? but thy Judgements (o lorde)   Psal.36.
are a depthe without bottom, and therefore I leave
25   this to thy onelie providence, praysing the eternallye for
the same.

Besides these generall paynes common to all that be   Particular
in that place, the scripture signifieth also that there   pains for
shalbe particular torments, peculiar bothe in qualitie and   particular
offenders.
30   quantitie to the sinnes and offences of eche offender.
For to that ende sayeth the prophet Esay to God, *thou*   Esa.27.
wilt judge in measure against measure. And God saieth of
hym selfe: *I will exercise Judgement in weight, and Justice in*   Esa.28.
measure. And that is the meaning of all those threates of   Jere.2.
35   God to sinners, where he sayeth that he will paie them   Apo.20.
home accordinge to their particular woorkes, and accord-   Psa.28.99.

---

12 [* gnashing] *mn*: B. *Gnashing and chattering of the teeth are
not al one; and proceed of divers causes.   12 teeth or chattering at
least (as everie man knoweth) proceedeth

ing to the inventions of their owne harts. In this sense
it is saied in the Apocalipse, of Babylon, now throwen
downe in to the lake: *Looke how muche she hathe glorified
her selfe, and hathe lived in delites: so muche torment and affliction*
5   *geve her.* Whereof the holy fathers have gathered the
varietie of torments that shalbe in that place. As there
be differences of sinnes: so shall there be varietie of
torments, (sayeth olde Ephraem) for the adulterer shall
have one kynde of torment, the murderer an other,
10   the theefe an other, the drunkarde an other: the lyar
an other: And so he foloweth on, shewinge how the
prowde man shall be trodden under feet to recompence
his pryde: the gloutton suffer inestimable hungar: the
drunkarde extreme thirst: the delitiouse mouthe filled
15   up with gaule: and the delicate bodie seared with hote
burning yrons.

The holie Ghoste signifieth such a thing when he
sayeth in the scriptures, of the wicked worldling: *His*
breade in his belly shalbe turned in to the gaul of serpents: he
20   *shall be constrayned to spue out again the riches which he hathe*
devoured: Nay, God shall pull them out of his belly again: he
shallbe constrayned to sucke the gaules of cocatrices, and tongue
of an adder shall kill hym: he shall pay swetelie for all that ever
he hathe done: and yet shall he not be consumed, but shall suffer
25   *according to the multitude of all his devises: utter darkenesse lyeth*
in wayt for hym: and fire which needeth no kindling shall eate
hym up: this is the wicked mans portion from God. By whiche
woordes is plainlie shewed, that woorldlings shall receyve
particular torments for their gluttonie, for their delicate
30   fare, for extorsion, and the like. Which torments shall
be greater than any mortall tongue can expresse: As
may appeare by the vehement and horrible woordes
whiche the holie ghoste here useth to insinuate the same.

There is reported (by men of good credit) a vision of
35   a servant of God, that he had in his prayers of the

Marginal notes:

Eze.24.
Osee.12.
Zach.1.
Apo.18.

Li.de
veri.
poen.c.2.

Job.20.
A mar-
vailous
descrip-
tion used
by the
scripture.

A vision
of the

---

8 as if the adulterer should have   11 another. As if the proud man
should be   22 *and the tong*   28 words and such like, it is plainlie
shewed, that worldlings shall receive as it were particular and proper
30 for their extortion   34 *omits* There is reported ... though in dede
he be invisible. [104.37]

handling of a certain wicked man in hell. Yt is not unlike to some whiche the holie prophets recount of other matters. And therfore I will rehearse it, for that it maketh to our purpose. This servant then of God sawe, that as

5   sone as this riche worldling was dead, he was brought by the damned spirits to the place of torment, and there a captain devell sitting in a chaire of burning hote yron, rose up for reverence, and tolde hym, for that he had bene a man of honour and state in the worlde, he wolde

10   geve hym that place, and so perforce made hym syt downe. Whereat he cryeing out horriblie, there came two other devells with two huge trompetts full of wylde fyre and brimstone, and sayd they wolde make hym some musicke to his song, for that he had loved musick

15   well in the worlde, and so blew the fire and brimstone in to his eares. Then for that he cried he was drie: there came a devill and put in to his mouthe a pot of venemouse liquore made of the gauls of toads and serpents, sayeing, this must be your drink in steade of your del-

20   icate wines whiche you were accustomed to tast in the world. And eftsons folowed two other uglie feendes with a greate companie of foule and fearse snakes, whiche clasped hym about the mydle, and fastned their teeth in his bodye, the devills sayeing, that for so muche as

25   he liked so well to embrace dames in the worlde, he should not want embrasements now also: And after that folowed a greate route of furiouse spirits, with whippes and hookes in their hands, which all assaulted hym, renting and tearing his fleshe, and sayeing, that

30   these recreations were reserved for hym in that place for ever and ever.

These things God suffred this holy man to see, not for that perhaps these materiall thinges are there, in dede, but that by these we might conceave the insup-

35   portable torments prepared for the wicked in that place: even as he shewed hym selfe and his glorie, by visible things to Daniel: though in dede he be invisible.

Beside this, the scripture sheweth unto us not onelie the universalitie, particularitie and severitie of these paines,

40   but also the straitnesse thereof, without ayde, help, ease,

handling of a wicked man in hell.

Dan.7.

The straitnes of paines

or comfort, when it sayeth, *we shall be cast in bownde bothe*   in hell.
hand and feete: for it is some kynde of comfort in this   Mat.22.
worlde, to be able to resist or strive against our afflictions,
but heere we must lye still and suffer all. Again, when
5   it sayeth: *clausa est ianua*, the gate is shutt: that is, the   Mat.25.
gate of mercie, of all pardon, of all ease, of all intermission, of all comfort, is shutt upp from heaven, from
earthe, from the creator, and from creatures: in so muche
as no consolation is ever to be hoped for more: as in
10   all the miseries of this lyfe there is alwaies some. This
straytnesse is likewise most lyvelie expressed in that dreadfull parable of the riche gloutton in hell: who was driven   Luc.16.
to that necessitie, as he desired that Lazarus might
dypp the topp of his fingar in water to coole his tongue,
15   in the myddes of that fire wherein he sayeth he was:
and yet could not he obtain yt. A small refreshing it
semeth it wold have bene unto hym, yf he had obtained
the same. But yet to shew the straitnesse of the place,   The won-
it was denied hym. Oh you that live in sinfull welthe   derfull
20   of the worlde, consider but this one example of Gods   example
severitie, and be afearde. This man was in that Royaltie   of the
a litle before as he wolde not geve the crommes of his   ryche
table to Lazarus, to buy heaven withall: and now wolde   gloutton.
he geve a thowsand worldes (yf he had them) for one
25   dropp of water to coole his tongue. What demaund
could be lesse than this? he durst not aske to be delivered thense, or to have his torments diminished, or to
aske a great vessel of water to refreshe his whole bodie
therein: but onely so muche as woold sticke on the topp
30   of a mans fingar, to coole his tongue. To what neede was
this poore man now driven? what a great imagination
had he of the force of one dropp of water? to what pitifull chaunge, was his tongue now come unto, that was
wount to be so diligentlie applied with all kyndes of
35   pleasant liquours? Oh that one man can not take example by an other: ether this is true or els the sonne

---

13 desireth   19 in the sinful wealth   21 This man was in great
roialtie a litle before, and nothing regarded the extreme miserie that
Lazarus was in: but now   31 this rich man

of God is a lyar. And then what men are we, that seing
our selves in daunger of this miserie, doe not seeke with
more diligence to avoyde the same?

In respect of these extremities and strait dealings of
5   God in denyeing all comfort and consolation at this day:
The scripture sayeth, that men shall fall into rage, furie,   Apo.16.
and utter impatience, blaspheming God, and cursing the   Eccl.23.
day of their nativitie, with eating their own tongues for   Luc.23.
greefe, and desiring the rockes and mountaines to come
10   and fall on them, to ende their paynes.

Now yf we add to this the eternitie and everlasting   The
continuance of these torments: we shall see that it en-   eternitie
creaseth the matter greatlie. For in this worlde there is   of the
no torment so great, but that tyme ether taketh away or   paynes.
15   diminisheth the same. For ether the tormentor, or the
tormented dyeth, or some occasion or other happeneth
to alter or mitigate the matter. But heere is no suche
hope or comfort: but *cruciabuntur* (saythe the scripture)   Apo.20.
in secula seculorum, in stagno ardente igne & sulphure: They   & 21.
20   shalbe tormented for ever and ever, in a poole burning with fire and brimstone. As long as God is God, so
long shall they burne there: Nether shal the tormen-
tour nor the tormented dye, but bothe live eternallie,
for the eternall miserie of the parties to be punished.

25   Oh (sayeth one father in a godlie meditation) yf a   A won-
sinner damned in hell dyd know that he had to suffer   derfull
those torments there no more thousand yeres, than there   sayeing.
be sandes in the sea, and grasse in the ground: or no
mo thousand millions of ages than there be creatures in
30   heaven, and in earthe: he wold greatlie rejoyce thereof,
for he wolde comfort hym selfe at the least with this
cogitation, that once yet the matter wold have an ende.
But now (saieth this good man) this woord *Never*, breaketh his hart, when he thinketh on yt, and that after a
35   hundred thousand millions of worldes there suffered, he
hath as farre to his end as he had at the first day of
his entrance to these torments. Consider (good Christian)
what a lengthe one houre wolde seme unto the, yf thou

---

27 no mo thousands of yeres   28 gras piles in the ground

haddest but to holde thy hand in fire and brimstone onelie during the space thereof. We see yf a man be grevouslie sick, though he be layd upon a verie soft bedd, yet one night seemeth a long time unto hym. He

5 turneth and tosseth hym selfe from syde to syde, telling the clock, and counting everie houre, as it passeth, which semeth to hym a whole day. And yf a man should saye unto hym, that he were to abyde that pain but seven yeres to gether: he wolde goe nighe to dispare for greefe.

10 Now yf one night seeme so long and tediouse to hym that lyeth on a good soft bedd, afflicted onelie with a litle ague: what will the lyeing in fire and brimstone doe, when he shall know evidentlie, that he shall never have ende thereof? Oh (deare brother) the satietie of contin-

15 uance is lothesome, even in things that are not evell of them selves. Yf thow shouldest be bound allways to eat one onelie meate: yt wold be displeasant to the in the ende. Yf thow shouldest be bound to sitt still all thy lyfe in one place, without moving: yt wold be grevouse unto

20 the, albeit no man dyd torment the in that place. What then will it be to lye eternally, that is worlde without ende, in moste exquisite torments? ys it any way toler- able? What judgement then, what witt, what discretion is there left in men, which make no more account of

25 this matter than they doe?

I might heere add an other circumstance, which the scripture addeth, to witt, that all these torments shalbe in darkenesse: A thinge dreadfull of it selfe, unto mans nature, for there is not the stowtest man in the

30 worlde, yf he found hym selfe alone, and naked in extreme darkenesse, and should heare a noyse of spir- its commyng towards hym, but he wold feare, albeit he felt never a lashe from them, on his bodye. I might also add an other circumstance, that the prophet addeth,

35 which is, that God and good men shall laugh at them that daye, which will be no small affliction. For as to be moned by a mans freende in time of adversitie, is some comfort: so to be laughed at, speciallie by them,

(marginal notes) Darckenes in hell. Matt.8.22.

Psal.37.

---

38 by him who

who onelie may help hym, is a great and intolerable
encrease of his miserie.

And now all this that I have spoken of hitherto, is
but one part of a damned mans punishement onelie,
5   called by divines *pæna sensus*, the paine of sense or feeling, that is, the paine or punishment sensiblie inflicted
upon the sowle and bodye. But yet beside this, ther is
an other part of his punishement called *pæna damni*, the
payne of losse or dammage: which (by all learned mens
10   opinion) is either greater, or no lesse than the former.
And this is, the infinite losse which a damned man hathe   Paynes of
in being excluded for ever and ever, from the sight of   damage
his creator, and his glorie. Which sight onelie, being   which the
sufficient to make happie and blessed all them that are   damned
    suffer.
15   admitted unto it, must nedes be an infinite miserie to
the damned man to lack yt eternallye. And therfore this
is put as one of the first and chiefest plagues to be layed
upon hym: *Tollatur impius ne videat gloriam dei*: Lett the   Esa.26.
wicked man be taken away to hell, to the ende he may
20   not see the glorie of God. And this losse contayneth all
other losses and dammages in yt: as the losse of eternall blysse and Joye (as I have sayd,) of eternall glorie,
of eternall societie with the Angels, and the like: whiche
losses when a damned man considereth (as he can not
25   but consider them still,) he taketh more greef thereof (as
divines doe prove) than by all the other sensible torments that he abydeth besides.

And therefore here foloweth now the last and one of   The
the greatest torments of all, and for that cause so often   worme
30   repeated in scripture. Which is, *the worme of our conscience*,   of con-
    science.
so called, for that, as a worme lyeth eating and gnaw-
ing the wood where in she abydeth: so shall the remorse   Mar.9.
    Esa.66.
of our owne conscience, lye within us griping and tor-   Eccle.7.
menting us for ever. And this worme or remorse shall   Judit.16.
35   principallie consiste in bringing to oure myndes, all the

---

16 lak that   25 (as Divines do hold) than   28 *omits* And therefore
here foloweth ... so often repeated in scripture. *Paragraph begins*
Wherunto apperteineth the worm of conscience: in scripture so called,
for that

meanes and causes of our present extreame calamities: **The cogi-**
as our negligences, whereby we lost the felicitie whiche **tations**
other men have gotten. And at every one of these con- **of the**
siderations, this worme shall geve us a deadlie bite, even **damned.**
5   unto the hart. As when it shall lay before us all the
occasions that we had offered to avoyde this miserie,
wherin now we are fallen, and to gayne the glorie which
we have lost: how easye yt had bene to have done yt:
how nighe we were oftentimes to resolve our selves to
10   doe yt: and yet how unfortunatlie we left of that cogitation again: how many times we were foretolde of this
daunger, and yet how litle care and feare we tooke of
the same. How vaine the worldlie trifles were, wherein
we spent our time, and for which we lost heaven, and
15   fell in to this intolerable miserie: howe they are exalted,
whome we thought fooles in the worlde: And how we
are now proved fooles and laughed at, whiche thought
our selves wyse. These things (I saye) and a thowsand
more beinge layed before us by our own conscience,
20   shall yelde us infinite greefe. For that it is now to late
to amend them. And this greefe is called the worme
or remorse of our own conscience: whiche worme shall
more enforce men to weepe and houle, than any torment else, consideringe how negligentlie, foolishlie, and
25   vainlie they are come in to those so insupportable torments, and that now there is no more time to redresse
their errors.

Now onelie is the time of weeping and lamenting for
these men: but all in vaine. Now shall they begynne to
30   freat and fume, and marvaile at them selves, sayeing:
where was our witt? where was our understanding? where
was our Judgement, when we folowed vanities, and contemned these matters? This is the talke of sinners in hell
(sayeth the scripture) *What hathe our pride, or what hathe*   Sap.5.
35   *the glorie of our riches profited us? they are all now vanished like*
a shadow: we have wearied out our selves in the way of inqui-
tie and perdition, but the way of our Lorde we have not knowne.
This (I saye) must be the everlasting song of the damned

---

7 to have gotten the   10 how ungratiously we

wormeaten conscience in hell: Eternall repentance without profitt. Whereby he shalbe brought to such desperation (as the scripture noteth) as he shall turne into furie
against hym selfe, teare his own flesh, rent his own soule

5   (yf it were possible) and invite the feendes to torment
hym, seyng he hathe so beastlie behaved hym selfe, in
this worlde, as not to provide in time for this principall
matter, onlie in deede to have bene thought upon. Oh
yf he could have but an other lyfe to lyve in the worlde

10   again, how wold he passe it over? with what diligence?
with what severitie? but it is not lawfull: we onelie which
are yet alive have that singular benefit, yf we knew, or
wolde resolve our selves to make the moste of yt. One
of these dayes, we shalbe past it also, and shall not re-

15   cover it agayn, no not one houre, yf we wolde geve a
thowsand worldes, for the same, as in deede the damned
wolde doe, yf they might. Lett us now therfore so use the
benefite of our present time, as when we are past hense,
we have not neede to wishe our selves heere againe.

20   Now is the time we may avoyde all: now is the time
we may put our selves out of daunger of these matters:
now (I say) yf we resolve our selves out of hand. For
we know not what shall become of us to morrow. Yt
may be to morrow our harts will be as hard and care-

25   lesse of these things as they have bene heretofore, and
as Pharao his hart was, after Moyses departure from
hym. Oh that he had resolved hym selfe throwghlie
while Moyses was with hym, how happie had he bene?
Yf the riche glutton had taken the time while Lazarus

30   lay at his dore, how blyssed a man had he bene? he
was foretolde of his miserie (as we are now) by Moyses
and the prophets, as Christ signifieth: but he wolde not   Luc.16.
heare. Afterward he was in suche admiration of his own
foly, that he wolde have had Lazarus sent from Abrahams

35   bosome unto his bretheren to warne them of his successe. But Abraham tolde hym, it was bootelesse, for
they wolde not have beleeved Lazarus, but rather have
persecuted hym as a lyar and defamer of their honor-

---

12 if we know it   28 while he was in prosperitie, how

able brother deade, yf he should have come and tolde
them of his torments. In dede so wolde the wicked of
the world doe now yf one should come and tell them
that their parents or freends are damned in hell, for
5   such and such things: and doe beseech them to looke
better to their lives, to the end by their comming thither
they doe not encrease the others paynes, for being some
cause of their damnation (for this is onelie the cause of
care whiche the damned have towardes the living, and
10   not for anie love they now beare them:) yf (I say) suche
a message should come from hell, to the florishing synners of this world, wolde they not laugh at yt? wolde
they not persecute eagarlie the parties that should bring
such newes? What then can God devise to doe for the
15   saving of these men? what way, what means may he
take, when nether warning, nor example of others, nor
threats, nor exhortations will doe any good? We know,
or may know, that leading the lyfe whiche we doe, we
can not be saved. We know or ought to know, that
20   many before us have bene damned for lesse matters.
We knowe and can not chuse but know, that we must
shortlie dye, and receave our selves, as they have received:
living as they dyd, or worse. We see, by this layd down
before, that the paynes are untolerable, and yet eternall,
25   whiche doe expect us, for the same. We confesse them
most unfortunate that for anie pleasure or commoditie
of this worlde, are now fallen in to those paynes. What
then should let us to resolve, to dispache our selves
quicklie of all impediments? to breacke violentlie from
30   all bonds and chaynes of this wicked worlde, that doe
lett us from this true and zealouse service of God? why
showld we sleepe one night in sinne, seing that night
may chaunce to be our last, and so the everlastinge cut-
ting of, of all hope for the time to come?
35   Resolve thy selfe therefore (my deare brother) yf thou
be wise, and cleare thy selfe from this daunger, while
God is willing to receave the, and moveth the therunto
by these meanes, as he dyd the riche man by Moyses

---

26 most miserable, that

and the prophets while he was yet in his prosperitie.
Let his example be often before thine eyes, and consider it throughlie, and it shall doe the good. God is a
wounderful God, and to shew his patience and infinit
5   goodnesse, he woweth us in this lyfe, seeketh unto us,
and layeth hym selfe (as it were) at our feet, to move
us to our owne good, to wynne us, to drawe us, and to
save us from perdition. But after this lyfe he altereth his
course of dealing: he turneth over the leafe, and chaungeth
10   his style. Of a lambe he becometh a lyon to the wicked:
and of a Saviour, a just and severe punisher. What can
be sayd or done more to move us? he that is forewarned
and seeth his own daunger before his face, and yet is
not stirred nor made the more wary or fearefull there by,
15   but notwithstanding will come or slyde in to the same:
may well be pityed, but surelie by no meanes can he
be helped, making hym selfe incapable of all remedies,
that may be used.

Of the moste honorable and munificent rewardes proposed to all
20   *them that truelie serve God.*

CHAP. X

The motives and considerations layed downe before, in
the former chapiters might well suffice, to sturre up the
hart of anye reasonable Christian to take in hand this
25   resolution, whereof we talke, and whereunto I so much
covet to persuade the (for thy onelie good, and gayne)
gentle reader. But for that all hartes are not of one con-
stitution in this respect, nor all drawen and stirred with
the same means: I purpose to adjoyne heere a consid-
30   eration of commoditie, whereunto commonlie, eche man
is prone by nature. And therfor I am in hope it shall
be more forcible to that we go about than anye thinge
else that hitherto hath bene spoken. I meane then to
treate of the benefits whiche are reaped by service of

_____

22 The reasons and

God, of the gayne drawn thence, and of the good pay
and most liberall rewarde which God performeth to his
servants, above all the maisters created, that may be
served. And though the just feare of punishment, (yf we
5   serve hym not) might be sufficient to drive us to this
resolution: and the infinite benefites allredie receaved,
might induce us to the same, in respect of gratitude, (of
bothe which somewhat hath bene sayed before:) yet am
I content so farre to enlarge this libertie to thee, (good
10   reader,) that except I shew this resolution, whiche I
crave, to be more gainfull and profitable than any thinge
els in the worlde that can be thought of: thow shalt not
be bound unto yt for anye thing that hitherto hath bene
sayde in that behalfe. For as God in all things is a ma-
15   jesticall God, full of bountie, liberalitie and princelie
magnificence: so in this point above all other: in suche
sort, as albeit what so ever we doe or can doe, is but
due dett unto him: and of it selfe deserveth nothing:
yet of his munificent Majestie, he letteth passe no one
20   jote of our service, unrewarded, no not so muche as *a*
cuppe of colde water.

    God commaunded Abraham to sacrifice unto hym
his onelie sonne Isaac, whiche he loved so muche. But
when he was redie to doe the same: God sayed, doe it
25   not: it is enoughe for me that I see thy obedience. And
because thow hast not refused to doe it I sweare to thee
(sayeth he) by my selfe, that I will multiplie thy seed
as the starres of heaven, and the sands of the sea: and
among them also one shalbe Christ the Saviour of the
30   worlde. Was not this a good paye for so litle paynes?
King David one night, beganne to thinke with hym selfe,
that he had now a howse of Cedar, and the arcke of
God lay but under a tent, and therfore resolved to build
a house for the sayd Arcke. Whiche onelie cogitation
35   God tooke in so good parte, as he sent Nathan the
prophet unto hym presentlie, to refuse the thing, but
yet to tell hym, that for so muche as he had determined
such a matter: God wolde build a house, or rather a

Marginal notes:
God the
best pay-
maister.

Mat.10.
Marc.9.
Gen.22.

2.Re.7.

---

6 received, induce us   14 is a God of great majestie, ful

kingdome, to hym, and his posteritie, whiche should last
for ever, and from whiche he wold never take away his   Psal.89.
mercie, what sinnes or offences so ever they committed.
Whiche promisse we see now fullfilled, in Christ his
5   Churche, raysed out of that familie. What shoulde I recite many like examples? Christ geveth a generall note
hereof, when he calleth the workemen and payeth to
eche man his wages so duelie: as also when he sayeth   Matt.20.
of him selfe, *beholde I come quicklie, and my rewarde is with*   Apo.22.
10   *me.* By which places is evident, that God suffereth no
labour in his service to be lost or unpayed. And albeit
(as after in place convenient shalbe shewed) he payeth
also, (and that abundantlie) in this lyfe: yet (as by these
two texts appeareth) he deferreth his cheefe paye, unto
15   his comming in the end of the day, that is, after this
lyfe, *in the resurrection of the just,* as hym selfe sayeth in an   Luc.14.
other place.

Of this payment then reserved for Gods servants in
the lyfe to come, we are now to consider, what, and
20   what maner a thing it is, and whether it be woorthe so
muche labour and travail, as the service of God requireth
or no. And first of all, yf we will beleeve the holie scripture, calling it a kingdome, a heavenlie kingdome, an   Mat.25.
eternall kingdome, a most blessed kingdome: we must   2.Tim.4.
25   nedes confesse it to be a marvailous great rewarde: for   2.Pet.1.
that worldlie princes doe not use to geve kingdomes to   Luc.14.
their servants for recompence of their labours. And yf
they did, or were able to doe it: yet could it be nether
heavenlie nor eternall, nor blessed kingdome. Secondlie,
30   yf we credit that which S. Paul saieth of it, *that nether*   1.Cor.2.
eye hath seene, nor eare heard, nor hart of man conceaved, how   Esa.64.
great a matter it is: then must we yet admitt a greater
opinion thereof. For that we have seen many wounderfull things, in our dayes: we have heard more wounder-
35   full: we may conceave moste wounderfull, and almost
infinite. How then shall we come to understand the
greatnesse and value of this rewarde? surelie no tongue
created ether of man or Angell can expresse the same,

---

13 by those two examples   23 an heavenly   24 a blessed kingdome

no imagination conceave, no understanding comprehend
it. Christ hym selfe hathe sayd, *nemo scit nisi qui accipit*:   Apoc.2.
No man knoweth it but he that enjoyeth yt. And there-
fore he calleth it *hidden manna*, in the same place. Notwith-
5   standing, as it is reported of a learned Geometrician
that fynding the lengthe of Hercules foote, upon the
hill Olimpus, drewe out his whole bodie, by the proportion of that one parte: so wee by some things sett
downe in scripture, and by some other circumstances
10   agreing thereunto, may frame a conjecture of the matter, though it come farre behinde the thing it selfe.

I have shewed before how the scripture calleth it
heavenlie, everlasting and most blessed kingdome. Whereby is signified, that all must be kinges that are admit-
15   ted thither. To like effect it is called in other places, *a*   Apoc.2.
crown of glorie, a throne of majestie, a paradise, or place of   & 3.
pleasure, *a lyfe everlasting.* S. John the Evangelist beinge   Mat.16.
in his banishement, by speciall privilege, made pryvie   Luc.10.
to some knowlege and feeling thereof, aswell for his
20   own comfort, as for oures, taketh in hand to describe it,
by comparison of a citie: Affirming, that the whole citie   Apo.21.
was of pure golde, with a great and high wall of the   & 22.
pretiouse stone, called Jaspis. This wall had also twelve   The
foundations, made of twelve distinct pretiouse stones   discrip-
25   which he there nameth: also twelve gates made of twelve   tion of
riche stones called margarits, and everie gate was an   paradise.
entire margarit. The streetes of the citie were paved with
golde, interlayed also with pearls and pretiouse stones.
The light of the citie was the clearenesse and shinyng
30   of Christ hym selfe, sitting in the middest thereof: from
whose seat proceded a river of water, as cleare as cristall,
to refresh the citie: and on bothe sides of the bankes,
there grew the tree of lyfe, geving out continuall and
perpetuall fruit: there was no night in that citie, nor any
35   defiled thing entered there: but they which are within
shall raigne (sayeth he) for ever and ever.

---

8 some thing set   13 an heavenly, an everlasting, and a most

By this description of the moste riche and pretiouse things that this worlde hathe, S. John wolde geve us to understand the infinite value, glorie and Majestie of this felicitie, prepared for us in heaven: though (as I have noted before) it being the princelie inheritance of our Saviour Christ, the kingdome of his father, the eternall habitation of the holie Trinitie, prepared before all worldes to sett out the glorie, and expresse the power of hym that hath no end or measure, ether in power or glorie: we may verie well thinke with S. Paul, that nether tongue can declare it, nor hart imagin it.

When God shall take upon hym to doe a thing for the uttermoste declaration (in a certain sorte) of his power, wisdome, and Majestie: imagine you what a thing it wilbe. It pleased hym at a certain time, to make certain creatures to serve hym in his presence, and to be witnesses of his glorie: and thereupon with a woorde, created the Angels, bothe for number and perfection so straunge and wounderfull, as maketh mans understanding astonished to think of it. For as for their number they were almost infinite, passing the number of all the creatures of this inferiour woorlde, as divers learned men and some auncient fathers doe think: though Daniel (according to the fashion of the scripture) doe putt a certain number for an uncertain, when he sayeth of Angels, *a thousand thowsands dyd minister unto hym* (that is unto God) *and tenn thowsand tymes a hundred thowsand dyd stand abowt hym to assist.* And for their perfection of nature, it is suche, (being, as the scripture sayeth, spirits and like burning fire) as they farre surpasse all inferiour creatures, in naturall knowledge, power, and the like, wherein one Angel doeth exceede all men in the worlde put together. What an infinit Majestie doeth this argue in the creator?

After this, when many of these Angels were fallen: it pleased God to creat an other creature, farre inferiour to this, for to fill up the places of such as had fallen:

Marginal notes:
Heb.1.
Mat.13.

The creation of Angels.

Dan.7.

Psa.104.

The creation of the

---

18 [* perfection] *mn:* B. *Great excellency of gifts may be ascribed unto them: but not perfection   31 *omits* wherein one Angel doeth exceede all men in the worlde put together   37 [* fill] *mn:* B. *We

and there upon created man of a peece of claye as you know, appointing hym to lyve a certain time in a place distant from heaven, created for this purpose, which is this worlde: a place of entertainment and triall for a
5   tyme, which afterwarde is to be destroyed againe. But yet in creating of this transitorie worlde, (whiche is but a cotage to his own eternall habitation) what power, what magnificence, what Majestie hath he shewed? what heavens and how wounderfull hath he created? what
10   infinit starres and other lights hath he devised? what elements hath he framed? and how marvailouslie hathe he compacte them together? The seas tossing and tumbling without rest, and replenished with infinite sortes of fishe: the ryvers running incessantlie through the earth like
15   veins in the bodie, and yet never to be emptie nor overflow the same: the earthe it selfe so furnished with all varietie of creatures, as the hundredth part thereof, is not employed by man, but onelie remaineth to shew the full hand, and strong arme of the creator. And all
20   this (as I saied) was done in an instant, with one woord onelie: and that for the use of a small time, in respect of the eternitie to come. What then shall we imagin that the habitation prepared for that eternitie shall be? Yf the cotage of his meanest servant (and that made onelie
25   for a time to bear of as it were a shower of rayne), be so princelie, so gorgeouse, so magnificent, so Majesticall, as we see this worlde is: what must we think that the kings palace it selfe is, appointed for all eternitie, for hym and his freends to raigne together? We must needs
30   think it to be as great, as the power and wisdome of the maker could reache unto, to perfourme: and that is, incomparablie, and above all measure infinite.

The greate king Assuerus, which raigned in Asia over a hundred twentie and seven provinces, to discover his
35   power and riches to his subjects, made a feast (as the scripture sayeth) in his citie of Susa, to all princes, states

Side notes: worlde, to expresse the power of God.

Side note: Ester.1.

---

may not wel restrein the purpose of God only to this: besides that, it may be dowted likewise, by what warrant that opinion doth stand.
17 hundred   26 magnificent, so ful of majestie, as

and potentates, of his dominions, for a hundred and
fowerscore dayes together. Esay the prophet sayeth, that   Esa.25.
our God and lorde of hoosts, will make a solemne banquet to all his people upon the hill and mount of heaven,
5   and that a harvest banquet, of fatt meates and pure
wines. And this banquet shalbe so solemne, as the very
sonne of God hym selfe, cheefe Lorde of the feast, shal-   Lu.12.
be content to gyrd hym selfe, and to serve in the same,
as by his own woordes he promiseth. What maner of
10   banquet then shall this be? how magnificent? how majesticall? especiallie seing it hath not onely to endure a
hundred and fower score dayes, (as that of Assuerus
dyd,) but more than a hundred and fourscore millions
of ages: not served by men (as Assuerus feaste was) but
15   by angels, and the verie sonne of God hym selfe: not
to open the power and riches of a hundred twentie and
seven provinces, but of God hym selfe, king of kings,
and lorde of lordes, whose power and riches are without end, and greater than all his creatures together can
20   conceave? How gloriouse a banquet shall this be then?
how triumphant the joy of this festivall day? O miserable and foolish childeren of men, that are borne to so
rare and singular a dignitie, and yet can not be brought
to consider, love, or esteeme of the same.
25   Other such considerations there be to shew the great-   The
nesse of this felicitie: as that, yf God hathe geven so   pleas-
many pleasures and comfortable gyfts in this lyfe, (as   ures and
we see are in the worlde) being a place notwithstanding   commodi-
of banishment, a place of sinners, a vale of miserie, and   ties of
30   the time of repenting, weeping, and wayling: what will   this lyfe.
he doe in the lyfe to come, to the just, to his freends,
in the time of joye, and mariage of his sonne? This was   Apo.19.
a moste forcible consideration with good S. Augustin,   In solilo-
whoe in the secret speeche of his soule with God, said   quiis
35   thus: O Lord, yf thou for this vile bodie of oures, geve   animæ ad
us so great and innumerable benefites, from the fir-   Deum.
mament, from the ayer, from the earth, from the sea:
by light, by darkenesse, by heate, by shadow: by dewes,

---

10 ful of majestie

by showers, by windes, by raines: by byrds, by fishes,
by beasts, by trees: by multitude of hearbes, and varietie of plants, and by the ministerie of all thy creatures:
O sweet lorde what maner of things, how great, how
5   good, and how innumerable, are those which thou haste
prepared in our heavenlie countrie, where we shall see
thee face to face? yf thou doe so greate things for us in
our prison: what wilt thou geve us in our palace? yf
thou gevest so many things in this world, to good and
10   evill men together: what hast thou layd up for onelie
good men in the world to come? yf thine enemies and
freends together are so well provided for in this lyfe:
what shall thy onelie freends receave in the lyfe to come?
yf there be so great solaces in these dayes of teares:
15   what joye shall there be in that day of Mariage? yf our   Apo.19.
jayle contain so great matters: what shall our countrie
and kingdome doe? O my lord and God, thou art a
great God, *and great is the multitude of thy magnificence and*   Psal.31.
sweetnesse. And as there is no end of thy greatnes, nor
20   number of thy wisdom, nor measure of thy benignitie:
so is there nether end, number, nor measure of thy
rewardes, towards them that love and fight for thee.
Hither to S. Augustin.

An other way to conjecture of this felicitie is, to con-   Howe
25   sider the great promises whiche God maketh in the scrip-   muche
tures, to honour and glorifie man in the lyfe to come.   God
Who so ever shall honor me (sayeth God) *I will glorifie hym.*   honoreth
And the prophet David, as it were complaineth joyful-   man.
lie, that Gods freends were to much honoured by hym.   1.Re.2.
    Psa.139.
30   Whiche he might with muche more cause have sayd, yf
he had lived in the new testament, and had heard that
promisse of Christ whereof I spake before, that his ser-   Luc.12.
vants should sitt down and banquet, and that him selfe
wolde serve and minister unto them in the kingdome of
35   his father. What understanding can conceave, how great
this honour shall be? But yet in some part it may be
gessed, by that he sayeth, that they shall sitt in judge-   Ma.19.
ment with hym: and (as S. Paul addeth,) shall be Judges   Luc.22.

---

29 so much honored

not onelie of men, but also of Angels. It may also be   1.Co.6.
conjectured by the exceedinge greate honour whiche
God at certain times hathe done to his servants, even   Mat.10.
in this lyfe. Wherin notwithstanding they are placed to
5 be despised and not to be honoured. What great hon-   Gen.12.
our was that he dyd to Abraham in the sight of so many   14.20.
kings of the earth, as of Pharao, Abimalech, Melchisee-   Exo.5.6.7.
dech, and the like? What honour was that he dyd to   8.
Moyses and Aaron in the face of Pharao and all his
10 court, by the wonderfull signes that they wrought? What
excessive honour was that he dyd to holie Josue, when
in the sight of all his armie he stayed the sunne and
Moone in the middest of the firmament, at Josue his   Josu.10.
appointement, obeyng therein (as the scripture sayeth)
15 to the voice of a man? what honour was that he dyd
to Esay in the sight of kinge Ezechias, when he made   Esa.38.
the sunne to goe backe tenne degrees in the heavens?
what honour was that he did to Helias in the sight of   3.Re.17.
wicked Achab, when he yelded the heavens in to his
20 hands, and permitted hym to say, that nether raine nor
dewe should fall uppon the ground (for certain yeres)
but by the woordes of his mouthe onely? what honour
was that he dyd to Elizeus in the sight of Naaman the   4.Re.5.
noble Syrian, whome he cured onelie by his woorde
25 from the Liprosie? and his bones after his death raysed   4.Re.13.
(by onelie touching) the dead to lyfe? finallie (not to
alleage more examples heerin,) what singular honour
was that, he gave to all the Apostles of his sonne, that
as many as ever they layd hands on, were healed from   Act.5.
30 all infirmities, as S. Luke sayeth? Nay (whiche is yet
more) the verie girdles and napkins of S. Paul did the   Act.19.
same effect: and yet more than that also, as many as
came within the onelie shadow of S. Peter, were healed   Act.5.
from their diseases. Is not this marvailous honour even
35 in this lyfe? was there ever Monarche, prince, or poten-
tate of the worlde, whiche coulde vaunt of suche points
of honor? And yf Christ dyd this, even in this worlde
to his servants, whereof notwithstanding he saith his

---

6 was it that

kingdome was not: what honour shall we think he hath
reserved for the worlde to come, where his kingdome
shall be, and where all his servants shall be crowned as
kings with hym?

5 An other declaration yet of this matter is layd down
by divines for opening of the greatnesse of this beatitude in heaven: and that is, the consideration of three
places, whereto man by his creation is appointed. The
first is his mothers wombe, the second this present world,
10 the third is *coelum Empireum,* whiche is the place of blysse
in the lyfe to come. Now in these three places, we must
holde the proportion (by all reason) whiche we see sensiblie to be observed betwene the first two. So that,
Looke in what proportion the second doeth differ from
15 the first: in like measure must the third differ from the
second, or rather muche more: seing that the whole
earth put together, is by all Philosophie, but as a pricke
or small point in respect of the marvailouse greatnesse
of the heavens. By this proportion then we must say,
20 that as farre as the whole worlde dothe passe the womb
of one private woman: so muche in all beautie, delites,
and majestie dothe the place of blisse passe all this whole
worlde. And as muche as a man living in the worlde
dothe passe a child in his mothers bellie, in strength of
25 bodie, beautie, witt, understanding, learning and knowlege: so muche and farre more, doeth a Saint in heaven
passe men of this worlde, in all these things, and many
more besides. And as muche horrour as a man wolde
have, to turne into his mothers wombe againe: so muche
30 wolde a glorified soule have, to returne into this worlde
againe. The nyene moneths also of lyfe in the mothers
wombe, are not so litle in respect of mans lyfe in the
world, as is the longest lyfe upon earth, in respect of
the eternall lyfe in heaven. Nor the blyndenesse, igno-
35 rance, and other miseries of the childe in his mothers
wombe, are any way comparable to the blyndenesse,
ignorance, and other miseries of this lyfe, in respect of

Joh.18.
2.Ti.4.
Apo.4.

The three
places
wherto
a man is
appointed.

---

11 [* must] *mn*: B. *It is rather a conjecture, than grounded upon
any sufficient warrant, to set down so just a proportion herin.

the light, cleare knowlege, and other felicities of the lyfe to come. So that by this also, some conjecture may be made of the matter whiche we have in hand.

But yet to consider the thing more in particular, it is to be noted, that this glorie of heaven shall have two partes, the one called essentiall, belonging to the soule: the other called accidentall, belonging to the bodie. The essentiall consisteth in the vision of God, as shalbe shewed after. The accidentall consisteth in the chaunge and glorification of our flesh, after the generall resurrection, that is, wherby this corruptible bodie of ours, shall put on incorruption (as S. Paul sayeth) and of mortall become immortall. All this flesh (I saye) of oures, that now is so combersome and aggreeveth the mynde: that now is so infested with so many inconveniences: subject to so many mutations: vexed with so many diseases: defilede with so many corruptions: replenished with so infinite miseries and calamities: shall then be made gloriouse, and most perfect to endure for ever, without mutation, and to raigne with the soule worlde without end. And for this purpose (as divines doe prove) it shalbe endewed with certayne qualities and gyftes from God, which holy S. Anselm (whome in this matter I will folow) doeth reckon to be seven, to wit, beawtie, agilitie, fortitude, penetrabilitie, health, pleasure, and perpetuitie, all whiche, ether want in the damned bodies, or else the contraries thereof are fownd in the same.

And first touching the beautie of glorified bodies, how great it shal bee, our Saviour hym selfe declareth, when he sayeth. *At that daie shall the Just shine as the sunne in the kingdome of their father.* A marvailouse sayeing of Christ,

Marginal notes:
Two partes of felicitie in heaven.

The accedentall parte.

1.Co.15.

Sap.9.
Eph.4.

In lib. de similitudinibus c.48. 49. & sequentibus.

1. Beautie.

Mat.13.

5

10

15

20

25

30

6 *omits* called essential   7 *omits* called accidentall   7 bodie. That which belongeth to the soul, consisteth   7 *mn: That which concerneth the bodie.*   9 after: that which belongeth to the bodie, consisteth   20 *omits* And for this purpose ... our Saviour hym selfe declareth, when he sayeth; *substitutes* For it shal be delivered from this lumpish hevines, wherewith it is pestered in this life: from al diseases likewise and pains of this life, and from al trobles and incombrances belonging to the same, as sin, eating, drinking, sleeping, and such like. And it shal be set in a most florishing estate of health, never deceaveable again. So florishing, that our Savior Christ saith; that *At that daie*

and in humane sense almost incredible, that our putrified
bodies should shine and become as cleare as the sunne.
Whereas in the contrarie parte, the bodies of the damned
shall be as black and uglie, as filthe it selfe. The second qualitie is agilitie or velocitie, whereby the glorified
bodie is delyvered from this lumpishe hevinesse, wherewith it was pestered in this lyfe, and made as light as
the Angels them selves, whiche are spirits, and doe passe
frome place to place with infinite swiftnesse, as also doe
ascend and descend of them selves, against the nature
of corruptible bodies: whereas in the mean space, the
damned bodies shall be bound both hand and foote, not
able to move, as the scripture signifieth.

The third qualitie is strengthe, where withe the glorified
bodie shall so abunde (as Anselmus sayeth) as he shall
be able to move the whole earth yf he wolde: and con-
trarywise, the damned body shall be so weake and impo-
tent, as he shal not be able to remove the verie wormes
frome his own face and eyes. The fowerth qualitie shall
be penetrabilitie, or libertie of passage, whereby the
glorified bodie shalbe able to pearse and penetrate any
other bodie: as to goe thorough walles, doores, the earth
or firmament without resistance, contrarie to the nature
of a corruptible bodie. So we see that Christ his bodie
glorified, after his resurrection, passed in to his disciples,
the dores being shut, and pearsed also the heavens at his
ascension, as the scripture sayeth. The fyfthe qualitie is
healthe, whereby the glorified body shall be delyvered
from all diseases and paines of this lyfe, and from all
troubles and encombrances belonging to the same: as
sinne, eating, drinking, sleeping, and the like: and shalbe
sett in a moste perfect and florishing state of healthe,
never decayable again: whereas the damned bodie in
contrarye maner, shall be filled and stuffed with as many
diseases paines and torments bothe inwardlie and owtwardlie as by the wisdome of God maye be devised.

5
10
15
20
25
30
35

2. Agilitie.

Mat.22.

3.
Strengthe.
Cap.52.

4. Pene-
trabilitie.

Joh.20.
Heb.4.
5. Health.

---

4 *omits* The second qualitie is agilitie . . . the glorified bodie above
all measure shalbe replenished; *continues* So likewise al the senses togither, finding then

The sixthe qualitie is pleasure, wherewith the glorified bodie above all measure shalbe replenished, all his senses together finding now their proper objects, in muche more excellencie than ever they could in this worlde (as shalbe 5 shewed after). Now (I say) everie parte, sense, member, and joint shall be filled with exceeding pleasure: even as the same shall be tormented in the damned. I will heere alleage Anselmus his woordes for that they expresse livelie this matter. All the glorifyed body (sayeth he) 10 shall be filled with abundance of all kynde of pleasure: the eyes, the eares, the nose, the mouth, the hands, the throote, the lungs, the hart, the stomacke, the back, the boones, the marowe, the entrales them selves, and every parte thereof, shalbe replenished with suche unspeakable 15 swetenesse and pleasure, that truelie it may be sayed, that the whole man *is made to drinke of the river of Gods divine pleasures, and made dronken with the abundance of Gods house.* In contrarie wyse the damned bodie shalbe tormented in all his partes and members: even as yf you 20 sawe a man that had a burning yron thrust in to his eyes, an other into his mouth, an other into his breest, an other into his ribbes, and so through all the joints, partes, and members of his bodie. Wolde you not thinke hym miserable, and the other man happie?

25 The last qualitie is perpetuitie of lyfe, whereby the bodie is made sure now never to die, or alter from his felicitie, according to the sayeing of scripture, that *the just shall live for ever.* This is one of the cheefest prerogatives of a glorified bodye. For by this, all care and feare 30 is taken away, all daunger of hurt and noyance, for if all the worlde should fall uppon a glorified bodie, it could not hurt or harme it any thing at all: where as the damned bodie lyeth alway in dyeing, and is subject to the greefe of every blow and torment layed upon it, 35 and so must remayn world without end. These seven

6. Pleasure.

Cap.57.

Psal.36.

7. Perpetuitie.

Sap.5.

---

5 even everie part 6 joint, shal be replenished with singular comfort, as the same 18 *omits* In contrarie wyse the damned bodie . . . and the other man happie? *continues* Besides al which, it hath perpetuitie, wherby it is made 28 *ever.* Which is 29 for that by 30 and noiance remooved from us; *omits* for if all the worlde . . . none allmoste will take any paynes

qualities then doe make a glorified bodie happie. And
albeit this happynesse be but accidentall (as I have sayed)
and nothing in deede to the essentiall felicitie of the
soule: yet is it no small matter as you see, but suche as
5   yf any bodie in this lyfe had but one of these seaven
qualities, we should thinke him moste happie, and rather
a God than a man. And to obtayne one of them in this
worlde, many men wolde spend muche and adventure
farre: whereas to gett them all in the lyfe to come, none
10 allmoste will take any paynes.

But now to come to the essentiall poynt of this felic-   The
itie which pertayneth to the soule, as the principall parte: essentiall
it is to be understoode, that albeit there be many things   felicitie of
that doe concurre in this felicitie, for the accomplish-   the soule.
15 ment and perfection of happinesse: Yet the fontaine of
all is but one onelie thing, called by divines *Visio dei*
beatifica: the syght of God that maketh us happie. *Hæc*
sola est summum bonum nostrum, sayeth S. Augusten: this   Aug.l.de
onelie syght of God, is our happynesse. Which Christ   trin.c.13.
20 also affirmeth, when he sayeth to his father, *this is lyfe*   Joh.17.
everlasting, that men know the true God, and Jesus Christ whome
thou hast sent. S. Paul also putteth our felicitie, *in seing*   1.Co.13.
God, face to face. And S. John, *in seing God, as he is.* And
the reason of this is, for that all the pleasures and con-
25 tentations in the world being onlie litle sparkles and par-
cells sent out from God: they are all contayned muche
more perfectlie and excellentlie in God hym selfe, than
they are in their owne natures created: as also all the
perfections of his creatures are more fullie in hym, than
30 in them selves. Whereof it foloweth, that whoe soever
is admitted to the vision and presence of God, he hathe
all the goodnesse and perfections of creatures in the
worlde united together, and presented unto hym at once.
So that what soever deliteth ether bodie or soule, there
35 he enjoyeth it wholye knit up together as it were in one
bundle, and with the presence thereof is ravished in all
partes bothe of mynde and bodie: as he can not imagine,

---

11 to that point   11 *mn: That which concerneth the soul.*   25 only sparkles
32 perfection

thinke, or wishe for anie joye what soever, but there he
findeth it in his perfection: there he findeth all knowlege, all wisedome, all beautie, all riches, all nobilitie, all
goodnesse, all delite, and what so ever beside deserveth
5   ether love and admiration, or woorketh ether pleasure
or contentation. All the powers of the mynde shalbe
filled with this sight, presence, and fruition of God: all
the senses of our bodie shalbe satisfied. God shalbe the
universall felicitie of all his saints, contaning in hym selfe
10   all particular felicities, without end, number, or measure. He shalbe a glasse to our eyes, musike to our eares,
honie to our mowthes, moste sweete and pleasaunt balme
to our smell: he shalbe light to our understanding, contentation to our will, continuation of eternitie to our
15   memorie. In hym shall we enjoye all the varietie of
thinges that delite us heer: all the beautie of creatures
that allure us heer: all the pleasures and Joyes that content us heer. In this vision of God (sayeth one doctor)
wee shall know, we shall love, we shall rejoyse, we shall   Hug.lib.4.
20   prayse. We shall know the verie secrets and judgements   de anima.
of God, which are *a depthe without bottome*: Also, the causes,   ca.15.
natures, beginnings, ofsprings, and ends of all creatures.   Know-
We shall love incomparablie, bothe God, (for the infinite   leige.
causes of love that we see in hym:) and oure compan-   Psa.36.
25   ions as much as our selves, for that we shall see them   Love.
as muche loved of God as our selves, and that also for
the same for which we are loved: whereof enseweth,
that our joye shalbe without measure: bothe for that we
shall have a particular joye for every thing we love in
30   God (which are infinite:) and also for that, we shall   The
rejoyse at the felicitie of everie one of our companions,   greatenes
as much as at our owne: and by that meanes we shall   of joye in
have so many distinct felicities, as we shall have distinct   heaven.
companions in our felicitie: which being without num-
35   ber: it is no marvaile thoughe Christ sayed, *goe in to the*   Mat.25.
joye of thy Lord, and not, let the lordes joye enter in to
thee: for that no one hart created can receyve the fullnesse and greatnesse of this joye. Hereof it foloweth

---

4 either deserveth love   5 worketh pleasure

lastlie, that we shall prayse God without end or weari-
nesse, with all our harte, with all our strengthe, with all
our powers, with all our partes: according as the scrip-
ture sayeth: *Happie are they that live in thy house (o lord) for* Psal.84.
5 *they shall prayse the eternallye without end.*

Of this moste blessed vision of God, the holie father Tra.4.in
S. Austen writeth thus: *Happie are the cleene of harte, for* ep.Joh.
they shall see God (sayeth our saviour:) then is there a
vision of God (deare bretheren) which maketh us hap- Matt.5.
10 pie: A vision (I say) whiche nether eye hath seene in
this world, nor eare hath heard, nor hart conceaved. A 1.Co.2.
vision, that passeth all the beautie of earthlie things, of
golde, of silver, of woodes, of feeldes, of sea, of ayer, of Aug.c.36.
sunne, of moone, of starres, of Angels: for that all theese soliloq.
15 things have their beautie from thence. *We shall see hym* 1.Co.13.
face to face (sayeth the Apostle,) *and we shall knowe hym, as*
we are knowen. We shall know the power of the father:
we shall know the wisdome of the sonne: we shall know
the goodnes of the holie ghoste: we shall know the indi-
20 visible nature of the moste blessed trinitie. And this *seing*
of the face of God, is the joye of Angels, and all saints in
heaven. This is the rewarde of life everlasting: this is
the glorie of blessed spirites, their everlasting pleasure,
their croune of honour, their game of felicitie, their riche
25 rest, their beautifull peace, their inward and outward
joye, their divine paradise, their heavenlie Jerusalem,
their felicitie of lyfe, their fullnesse of blysse, their eter- Phil.4.
nall joye, their peace of God, that passeth all understanding. This sight of God, is the full beatitude, the
30 totall glorification of man, to see hym (I saye) that made
bothe heavene and earth, to see him that made the,
that redemed the, that glorified the. For in seeyng hym,
thow shalt know him, in knoweing him, thow shalt possesse hym, in possessing hym, thow shalt love hym, in
35 loving hym thow shalt prayse hym. For he is the inheritance of his people, he is the possession of their felicitie, he is the rewarde of their expectation. *I wilbe thy* Gen.15.

---

33 *omits* thow shalt know him, in knoweing him; *continues* thou shal
possesse

great reward (sayeth he to Abraham). O lord thou art great, and therfore no marvaile yf thow be a great reward. The sight of thee therfore is all our hyare, all our reward, all our joye and felicitie, that we expect:

5   seing thou hast sayed, that this is lyfe everlasting, to see and know thee our true God, and Jesus Christ whome   Jo.17. thou hast sent.

Having now declared the two generall partes of heav- enlie felicitie, the one appertayning to our soule, the

10   other to our bodie: it is not hard to esteeme, what excesse of joye, bothe of them joined together shall woorke, at that happie daye of our glorification. O joye above all   Ca.35. joyes passing all Joye, and without whiche there is no   solilo- joye, when shall I enter in to thee (sayeth S. Austen?)   quiorum.

15   when shall I enjoye thee to see my God that dwelleth in thee? O everlasting kingdome, o kingdome of all eter-   Phil.4. nities, o light without end, o peace of God that passeth all understandinge, in whiche the soules of Saintes doe rest with thee, *and everlasting joye is upon their heades, they*   Esa.51.

20   *possesse joye and exultation, and all payne and sorow is fledde*   Esa.35. *from them.* O how gloriouse a kingdome is thyne (o lord) wherein all Saintes doe raigne with thee, *adorned with*   Ps.104. *light as with apparell, and having crownes of pretiouse stones on*   Ps.21. *their heades?* O kingdome of everlasting blesse, where thow

25   o lord the hope of all saintes art, and the diademe of their perpetuall glorie, rejoysing them on everie syde, with thy blessed sight. In this kingdome of thine, there is infinite joye, and myrthe without sadnesse: healthe without sorow: lyfe without labour: light without dark-

30   nesse: felicitie withoute abatement: all goodnesse with- out any evill. Where youthe florisheth that never waxeth olde: lyfe that knoweth no end: beautie that never fadeth: love that never cooleth: healthe that never diminisheth: joye that never ceaseth. Where sorow is never fealt, com-

35   plaint is never heard, matter of sadnesse is never seene, nor evill successe is ever feared. For that they possesse thee (o Lorde) whiche art the perfection of their felicitie.

---

3 sight and fruition of thee therfore

If we wolde enter into these considerations, as this
holie man, and other his like dyd: no doubt but we
should more be inflamed with the love of this felicitie,
prepared for us, than we are: and consequentlie should
5   strive more to gayne it than we doe. And to the ende
thow mayest conceave some more feeling in the matter
(gentle reader:) consider a litle with me, what a joyfull
day shall that be at thy howse, when having lived in
the feare of God, and atchived in his service the end
10   of thy peregrination, thow shalt come (by the meanes
of deathe) to passe from miserie and labour to immortalitie: and in that passage (when other men beginne to
feare) thou shalt lyft up thy head in hope, accordinge
as Christ promiseth, for that the time of thy salvation
15   commeth on: tell me, what a day shall that be when
thy soule stepping furth of prison, and conducted by the
Angeles to the tabernacle of heaven, shall be receyved
there with the honorable companies and troupes of that
place? with all those hierarchies of blessed spirites men-
20   tioned in scripture, as Principalities, Powers, Vertues,
Dominations, Thrones, Angels, Archeangels, Cherubines,
and Seraphines? also with the holie Apostles and Disciples
of Christ, Patriarches, Prophets, Martyrs, Virgines, Inno-
centes, Confessors, Bishopes, Preestes, and Saints of God?
25   All which, as they dyd rejoyse at thy conversion from
sinne: so shall they triumphe now at thy coronation and
glorification. What joye will thy soule receyve in that
day, when she shalbe presented by her good Angell, in
the presence of all these states, before the seat and
30   Majestie of the blessed Trinitie, with recitall and declaration of all thy good woorkes, and travailes suffered for
the love and service of God? when (I saye) those blessed
spirites shall laye doune in that honorable consistorie,

Marginal notes:
A com-
fortable
considera-
tion.

Luc.21.

Ephe.1.
Colos.1.
2.The.1.
Esa.6.

Luc.15.

---

16 *omits* by the Angeles   19 *omits* hierarchies of   23 *omits* Virgines;
omits Bishopes, Preestes   25 *omits* as they dyd rejoyse at thy conversion from sinne: so *and continues* shal triumph now   28 *omits* by
her good Angell   30 [* recital] *mn*: B. *This must needs be warily
taken: otherwise, with the comfort that is sought therby, there may
be danger of error also.   32 *omits* when (I saye) those blessed spirites
shall laye doune; *continues* when there shal be laid down in

all thy vertuouse deedes in particular, all thy almes, all
thy prayers, all thy fastinges, all thy innocencie of lyfe,
all thy patience in injuries, all thy constancie in adversities, all thy temperance in meates, all the vertues of
5   thy whole lyfe? when all (I saye) shall be recounted there,
all commended, all rewarded: shalt thou not see now
the value and profite of vertuouse lyfe? shalt thou not
confesse that gaynefull and honorable is the service of
God? shalt thou not now be glad and blesse the hower,
10   wherein first thou resolvedst thy selfe to leave the service of the woorlde, to serve God? shalt thou not think
thy selfe beholden to hym or her that persuaded thee
unto yt? yes verilie.

But yet more than this, when thou shalt consider in   The joye
15   to what a porte and haven of securitie thou art come,   of securi-
and shalt looke backe upon the daungers whiche thou   tie.
hast passed, and wherein other men are yet in hazarde:
thy cause of joye shall greatlie be encreased. For thou
shalt see evidentlie how infinite times thow were to per-
20   ishe in that journey, yf God had not held his speciall
hand over thee. Thow shalt see the Daungers wherein
other men are, the death and damnation whereinto many
of thy freends and acquayntance have fallen: the eternall paynes of hell incurred by many that used to laughe
25   and be merye with thee in the worlde. All whiche shall
augment the felicitie of this thy so fortunate a lott. And
now for thy selfe, thow mayst be secure, thow art out
of all daunger for ever and ever. There is no more neede
now of feare, of wache, of labour, or of care. Thou
30   maiest lay downe all armoure now, as the children of   Josu.21.22.
Israel dyd when they came into the land of promisse: Gene.3.
for there is no more enemie to assaile thee: there is no   Sap.17.
more wyelie serpent to beguile thee: all is peace, all is
rest, all is joye, all is securitie. Good S. Paul hathe no
35   more neede now to fast, to wache, to punishe his bodie: 1.Co.9.

---

1 deeds, all the labors that thou hast taken in thy calling; al thy
almes   14 when as being so neèr thy passage heer, thou shalt   26
this thy blessed estate. And now   30 now, better than the children
of Israel might have done, when they had gotten the land   35 now

Good olde Jerome, may now cease to afflict hym selfe
bothe night and daye for the conquering of his spirituall enemie. Thy onelie exercise must be now to rejoyse, to triumphe, to sing *alleluya* to the Lambe, whiche
5 hathe brought the to this felicitie, and will keepe thee
in the same, worlde without end. What a comfort will it
be to see that Lambe sittinge on his seat of state? Yf the
three wise men of the East, came so farre of, and so rejoysed to see hym lyeing in a Manger: what will it be
10 to see hym sitting in his glorie? If S. John Baptist dyd
leape at his presence in his mothers belly: what shall
his presence doe in this his royall and eternall kingdome?
It passeth all other glorie that saintes have in heaven
(sayeth S. Austen) to be admitted to the inestimable sight
15 of Christ his face, and to receave the beames of glorie
from the splendoure of his majestie. And yf we were to
suffer tormentes everie day, yea to tolerate the verie
paines of hell for a time, therbye to gayne the sight of
Christ, and to be joyned in glorie to the number of his
20 saintes: it were nothing in respect of the rewarde. O
that we made suche accompt of this matter as this holie
and learned man dyd: we wolde not lyve as we doe,
nor leese the same for suche tryfles as moste men doe.

But to goe forwarde yet further in this consideration:
25 Imagine besides all this, what a joye it shall be unto thy
soule at that daye, to meet with all her godlie freendes
in heaven, with father, with mother, with brothers, with
sisters: with wyfe, with husband, with maister, with scholares: with neyghboures, with familiares, with kynred,
30 with acquayntance: the welcomes, the myrthe, the sweete
embracementes that shall be there, the joye whereof (as
noteth well S. Cyprian) shalbe unspeakable. Add to this,

Marginal notes:
Jero.ep.
22. ad
Eusto.

Apo.19.

Mat.2.

Luc.1.

Serm.37.
de sanc-
tis.

Meetinge
with our
fryndes in
heaven.

Cyp. lib.
de mor-
talitate.

---

to labor in the ministerie of the word, neither yet to fast, to watch,
or to punish his bodie   4 *Halleluias*   7 the wise men   9 him in the
manger   16 the brightnes of   27 [* father] *mn*: B. *There be divers
of this mind: but seeing that the knowledge of father, and mother,
and such like is earthlie knowledge; and al earthly knowledge shal
then be abolished: I see not how it may be warranted that we shal
then have remembrance or knowledge of any such; saving only as
they are members of one bodie, and not as our father, kinsman, or
frind.

the daylye feasting and inestimable triumphe, whiche
shalbe there, at the arivall of new bretheren and sisters
coming thither from time to time with the spoyles of
their enemies, conquered and vanquyshed in this world.

5 O what a comfortable sight will it be to see those seates
of Angells fallen, filled upp agayne with men and wemen
from day to day? to see the crownes of glorie sett upon
their heades, and that in varietie, according to the vari- 2.Ti.4.
etie of their conquestes. One for martyrdome, or con- Apoc.2.3.

10 fession against the persecutor: an other for virginitie or 4.
chastitie against the flesh: an other for povertie or humilitie against the world: an other for many conquestes
together against the devill? There the gloriouse quyar Lib. de
of Apostles, (sayeth holie Cyprian) there the number of mortali-

15 rejoysing prophets, there the innumerable multitude of tate.
Martyrs shall receyve the crounes of their deathes and
sufferinges. There, triumphing virgines which have overcome concupiscence with the strengthe of continencie:
there, the good aulmners whiche have liberallie fedd the

20 poore, and (keping Goddes commaundements) have trans-
ferred their earthly riches to the storehowse of heaven,
shall receave their due and peculiar rewarde. O how
shall vertue shew her selfe at this daye? how shall good
deedes content their doers? And among all other joyes

25 and contentations, this shall not be the least, to see the
poore soules that come thither at a jumpe, ether from
the miserie of this lyfe, or from the torments of the purging fyre, how they (I saie) shall remayne astonished, and
as it were, beside them selves, at the suddain mutation,

30 and excessive honour donne unto them. If a poore man, A com-
that were out of his waye, wanderinge alone in a durtie parison.
lane, in the myddest of a darke and tempestuous night,
farre from companie, destitute of money, beaten with
rayne, terrified with thunder, styffe with colde, wearied

35 out with labour, almost famished with hungre and thurst,

---

10 *omits* virginitie or 13 glorious companie of 26 thither on the
sudden from the miseries of this life, how they 31 alone upon the
mountains in the midst

and neare brought to despare with multitude of miseries, should upon the suddain, in the twinkling of an
eye, be placed in a goodlie large and riche palace, furnished with all kynde of cleare lightes, warme fyre, sweete
5   smelles, dayntie meates, soft beddes, pleasant musike,
fine apparell, and honorable companie: all prepared for
hym, and attending his commyng, to serve hym, to honour hym, and to annoynt and crowne hym a king for
ever: what wold this poore man doe? how wolde he
10   looke? what could he saye? surelie I think he could saye
nothing, but rather wolde weepe in silence for joye, his
hart being not able to contayne the suddain and exceeding greatnesse thereof.

Well then, so shall it be and much more with these
15   twyse happie sowles, that come to heaven. For never
was there colde shadow so pleasant in a hoate burning
sunnye daye: nor the welspring to the poore travailer in
his greatest thirst of the sommer: nor the repose of an
easy bedde to the wearied servant after his labour at
20   night: as shalbe this rest of heaven to an afflicted sowle
whiche cometh thither. O that we could conceave this,
that we could imprint this in our hartes (deare brother).
Wold we folow vanities as we doe? wold we neglect this
matter as we doe? Surelye our coldenes in purchasing
25   these joyes doeth procede of the finale opinion we doe
conceave of them. For yf we made suche account and
estimate of this Jewell, as other marchants before us
(more skilfull and wyser than our selves) have done: we
wolde bydde for it as they dyd, or at leastwyse wolde

The great
account
that saints
made of
heaven.

30   not lett it passe so negligentlie, whiche they sought after
so carefullye. S. Paul sayeth of Christ hym selfe, *pro-
posito sibi gaudio sustinuit crucem*: He layinge before hys
eyes, the joyes of heaven, susteined the crosse. A great
estimation of the matter, whiche he wolde buye at so

Heb.12.

35   deare a rate. But what counsayle geveth he to other
men about the same? surelie none other, but to *goe and
sell all that ever they have to purchase this treasure*. S. Paul of

Mat.13.

---

24 coldnes in seeking after these

him selfe, what sayeth he? verilie, that *he esteemed all the world as Doung*, in respect of the purchasing of this Jewell. S. Pauls scholar Ignatius, what byddeth he? heare his own woordes. Fire, galowes, beasts, breaking of my bones,
5 quartering of my members, crushing of my bodye, all the tormentes of the devill together, lett them come upon me, so I may enjoye this treasure of heaven. S. Austen that learned byshop, what offereth he? you have now heard before, that he wolde be content to suffer tor-
10 mentes every day, yea the very torments of hel it selfe to gaine this joye. Good Lord, how farre dyd these holy Saints differ from us? how contrarye were their judge-mentes to oures in these matters? whoe will now mar-vayle of the wisdome of the world, judged folie by God,
15 and of the wysdome of God judged foly by the worlde? *Oh children of men* (sayeth the prophet) *why doe ye love van-itie and seeke after a lye?* why doe you embrace strawe and contemne golde? strawe (I say) and most vile chaffe, and such as finally will set your own howse on fyre, and be
20 your ruyne and eternall perdition?

But now to drawe towards an end in this matter (though there be no end in the thing it selfe:) lett the Christian consider wherto he is borne, and whereof he is in possibilitie, yf he will. He is borne heyre appar-
25 ent to the kyngdome of heaven: a kyngdome without end, a kyngdome without measure, a kingdome of blysse, the kyngdome of God him selfe: he is borne to be joynt heyre with Jesus Christ the sonne of God: to raigne with hym: to triumph with hym: to sitt in Judgement of
30 Majestie with hym: to judge the very Angeles of heaven with hym. What more glorie can be thought upon, except it were to become God hym selfe? All the joyes, all the riches, all the glorie that heaven contayneth, shall be poured out uppon hym. And to make this honour
35 yet more: the gloriouse Lambe that sitteth on the throne of Majestie, with his eyes lyke fyre, his feet lyke burning copper, and all his face more shynyng than preciouse stone: from whose seat there procedeth thunder and lightening without end: and at whose feet the fower and
40 twentie elders lay downe their crownes: this Lambe (I

Phil.3.
Jerom.in catalogo.

Ser.37.de sanctis.

1.Cor.1.2. & 3.

Psal.4.

Wherto a Christian is borne by baptisme.

Gal.3. & 4.

Ephe.1. & 5.
Colos.3.
Tit.3.
Rom.8.
Jac.2.
Heb.1.9.
1.Pet.1.3.
2.Pet.3.
Apoc.1.
Mat.19.
Luc.22.
1.Co.6.
Apo.1. & 4.

say) shall ryse and honour him with his own service.   Luc.12.
Whoe will not esteeme of this royall inheritance? especiallie seing the gayning therof by the benefit of our redemption, and grace purchased to us therin, is brought

5   now to be in our own handes? *The kyngdome of heaven*   Mat.11.
suffereth violence (sayeth Christ) *and men lay handes now on*
it by force: That is, by force of Gods covenant made with   Matt.5.
Christians, that lyving vertuouslie, they shall have the   & 19.
same. What soever Christian then, doeth good woorkes   Joh.14.

10   and lyveth vertuouslie, taketh heaven by force (as it were)   2.Co.7.
and by violence. *The matter is put in the power of the doer*   1.Joh.2.
(sayeth S. Austen,) *for that the kyngdome of heaven suffereth*   Serm.37.
violence. This thing (o man) that is, the kingdome of heaven,   de sanctis.
requireth no other price but thy selfe: yt is so muche woorthe

15   *as thou art woorthe: geve thy selfe and thou shalt have it.* By
whiche he signifieth, that every man, how poore or
needye soever he be in this world, may gayne this inheritance to him selfe: may make hym selfe a prince, a
king, a Monarche yf he will: even the meanest and mis-

20   erablest man in the worlde. O wunderfull bountie and
liberalitie of our Saviour: o princelie hart and unspeakable mercie: o incredible prodigalitie (as I may saye) of
God in treasures so inestimable, as are his infinite and
endlesse riches.

25   Tell me now (gentle reader) why wilt thou not accept
of this his offer? why wilt thou not account of this his
kyngdome? why wilt thou not buye this glorie of hym
for so litle a labour as he requireth? *Suadeo tibi emere a*
me aurum ignitum, probatum, vt locuples fias (sayeth Christ:)   Apoc.3.

30   I counsaile the to buye pure and tried golde of me, to
the end thou mayest be riche. Why wilt thou not folow
this counsaile (deare brother?) especialie of a marchant
that meaneth not to deceave thee? Nothing greeveth this
our Saviour more, than that men will seek with such   Exod.5.

35   paynes to buy straw in Egypt, whereas he wolde sell

---

2 Especially seeing that now we have so good opportunity to
the obteining therof, by the benefite of our redemption, and grace
purchased to us therin; *omits* is brought now to be in our own
handes . . . his infinite and endlesse riches.

them fyne gold at a lower price: and that they will
purchase pudle water, with more labour, than he wolde
require for ten tymes as muche pure liquor out of the
verie fontaine it selfe. There is not the wickedst man in
5 the world, but taketh more travaile in gayning of hell,
(as after shallbe shewed) than the moste paynfull servant
of God in purchasing of heaven.

Folow thow not their folie then (deare brother,) for
thow shalt see them doe heavy penance for it one day,
10 when thy harte shal be full glad, thow hast no parte
among them. Let them goe now and bestow their time
in vanitie, in pleasures, in delites of the world. Lett them
buyld palaces, purchase dignities, add peeces and paches
of ground together: let them hunt after honours and
15 buyld castells in the ayer: the daye will come (yf thow
beleeve Christ hym selfe) wherin thow shalt have small
cause to envye their felicitie. Yf they talke baselie of the
glorie and riches of Saintes in heaven: not esteeming
them in deede in respect of their owne, or contemnyng
20 them, for that carnall pleasures are not reckonned therein:
make litle account of theyr woordes. For that *the sensu-
all man understandeth not the things whiche are of God.* Yf
horses were promised by their maisters, a good banquet,
they could imagin nothing els but provander and water,
25 to be their best cheere, for that they have no knowlege
of dayntier dishes: so these men accustomed to the pudle
of their fleshlie pleasures, can mount with their mynde
no higher than the same. But I have shewed thee before
(gentle reader) some wayes and considerations, to con-
30 ceave greater matters, albeit as I have advertised the
often, we must confesse still, with S. Paul, that no humaine
hart can conceave the least parte therof, for whiche
cause also it is not unlike that S. Paul him selfe was
forbidden to utter the thinges whiche he had seene and
35 heard, in his miraculouse assumption unto the third
heaven.

Jere.2.
Apo.21.

The
vanitie of
worldlie
men.

Luc.6.
Luc.12.
Mat.26.

1.Co.2.
Ep.Jud.
A simili-
tude.

1.Cor.2.

2.Co.12.

---

3 price liquor   7 in obteining of heaven.   9 them suffer greevously
for

To conclude then, this game and gole is sett upp for
them that will runne, as S. Paul noteth: and no man is
crowned in this glorie but suche onelie as will fight, as
the same Apostle teacheth. It is not everie one that
5   sayeth to Christ, lord lord, shall enter into the kingdome
of heaven: but they onelie which shall doe the will of
Christ his father in heaven. Thoughe this kingdome of
Christ be sett out to all: yet everye man shall not come
to raigne with Christ, but such onelie as shal be con-
10   tent to suffer with Christ. Thoughe the kingdome of
heaven be subject to violence: yet no man can enter
there by force, but he onelie whose good deedes goe
with hym, to helpe open the gates: that is, except *he*
enter without spott, and hathe wroght justice, as the prophet
15   testifyeth. My meaning is, that as I have shewed the
greatnesse and woorthynesse of this treasure (gentle
reader:) so thow shouldest also conceave the right way
of gayning the same: whiche is no other, but onelie by
holie and vertuouse lyfe, as God hym selfe hathe assured
20   the. Thow art therfore to sitt downe and consider according to thy Saviours counsaile, what thou wilt doe, whether thow have so muche spirituall money as is sufficient
to buyld this tower, and make this warre, or no: that is,
whether thou have so muche good will and holie man-
25   hode in thee, as to bestowe the paynes of a vertuouse
lyfe, (yf it be rather to be called paynes than pleasure)
required for the gayning of this kingdome. This is the
question, this is the verie whole issue of the matter, and
hitherto hath appertayned what soever hath bene spo-
30   ken in this booke before, ether of thy particular end, or
of the Majestie, bowntie and justice of God: and of the
account he will demaund of thee: also of the punishement or rewarde layd up for thee: All this (I saye) was
meant by me to this onelie end, that thou (measuring
35   the one parte and the other,) shouldest finallie resolve

1.Cor.9.
Phil.3.
2.Tim.2.
1.Ti.6.
Heb.12.
Matt.7.19.
25.

Rom.8.
Mat.11.

Apo.14.
& 20.

Psal.15.

Matt.7.
& 19.

Joh.14.
Luc.14.

---

5 *that shal enter*   6 *which do*   10 *omits* Thoughe the kingdome of
heaven . . . as God hym selfe hathe assured the.   25 the pains of
suffering with Christ (if it be rather to be called pains than pleasure) that so thou maist raign with him in his kingdome.

what thou woldest doe, and not to passe over thy time
in careles negligence as manye doe, never spyeing their
own errour untill it be too late to amend yt.

For the love of God then (deare brother) and for the
5   love thou bearest to thy owne soule, shake of this daungerouse securitie, whiche fleshe and bloode is wonte to lulle
men in: and make some earnest resolution, for looking
to thy soule for the lyfe to come. Remember often that
woorthie sentence: *Hoc momentum, unde pendet æternitas*: This
10   lyfe is a moment of time, whereof all eternitie of lyfe
or deathe to come, dependeth. Yf it be a moment, and
a moment of so great importance: how is it passed over
by worldly men with so litle care, as it is? I might have
alleaged here infinite other reasons and considerations
15   to move men unto this resolution, whereof I have talked:
and surelie no measure of volume were sufficient to contayne so much as might be sayd in this matter. For that
all the creatures under heaven, yea and in heaven it
selfe, as also, in hell: all (I saye) from the first to the
20   last, are argumentes and motives unto this poynt: all are
bookes and sermons, all doe preache and crye, (some
by their punishement, some by their glorie, some by
their beautie, and all by their creation,) that we ought
without delay, to make this resolution, and that all is
25   vanitie, all is folye, all is iniquitie, all is miserie, beside
the onelie service of our maker and redymer. But yet
notwithstanding (as I have sayed) I thought good onelie
to chuse out these few considerations before layed downe,
as cheefe and principall among the rest, to worke in any
30   true Christian hart. And yf these can not enter with
thee (good reader) litle hope is there that any other
wolde doe thee good. Wherefore heere I end this first
parte, reserving a fewe things to be sayd in the second,
for removing of some impediments, which our spiritu-
35   all adversarie is wont to cast against this good woorke,
as against the first stepp to our salvation. Our Lord God
and saviour Jesus Christ, which was content to paye his

A saying
to be
remem-
bred.

---

20 and persuasions unto

own bloode for the purchasing of this noble inheritance
unto us, geve us his holy grace, to esteeme of it as the
great waight of the matter requireth, and not by negligence to leese our portions therin

5   The end of the first parte.

---

1 notable inheritance

THE SECOND PART OF THIS FIRST BOOKE

*Of impedimentes that lett men from this resolution: and first,
of the difficultie or hardnesse, whiche seemeth to many to be in
vertuouse lyfe.*

5   CHAP. I

Notwithstanding all the motives and considerations before
sett downe, for inducing men to this necessarie resolution of serving God, for their salvation: there want not
many Christians abrode in the world, whose hartes, ether
10 intangled with the pleasures of this lyfe, or geven over   Ep.Jud.
by God to a reprobate sense, doe yeeld no whit at all   Rom.1.
to this batterie, that hath bene made, but sheweing them
selves more hard than adamant, doe not onelie resist
and contemne, but also doe seek excuses for their slothe   Pro.18.
15 and wickednesse, and do alleage reasons of their own   & 20.
perdition. Reasons I call them, according to the com-   Psa.141.
mon phrase, though in deede, there be no one thing
more against reason, than that a man shoulde become
enemye to his own soule, as the scripture affirmeth obsti-   Tob.12.
20 nate sinners to bee. But yet (as I say) they have their   Pro.29.
excuses: And the first and principall of all ys, that vertuouse lyfe is painfull and harde, and therfore they can
not endure to folow the same: especiallie such as have
bene brought up delicatlye, and never were acquainted
25 with such asperitie, as (they saye) we require at their
hands. And this is a great, large, and universall impediment, which stayeth infinite men from embracinge the
meanes of their salvation. For which cause yt is fullie
to be answered in this place.
30   First then supposing that the way of vertue were so   Lib.de
hard in deede, as the enemie maketh it seeme: yet might   compunct.
I well saye with S. John Chrisostom, that seeyng the   cordis.

---

1 THE SECOND PART OF THIS BOOKE.   6 al the reasons
and   8 *omits* for their salvation   15 to their own perdition   28 their
conversion, for

rewarde is so great and infinite as now we have declared:
no labour should seeme great for gayning of the same.
Agayne, I might say with holy S. Austen, that seeing   Hom.16.
we take dayly so great payne in this worlde, for avoyd-   ex 50.
5   ing of small inconveniences, as of sicknes, imprysonementes, losse of goodes and the lyke: what paynes should
we refuse for avoyding the eternitie of hell fyre sett
downe before? The first of these considerations S. Paul   Rom.8.
used when he sayd, *the sufferinges of this lyfe are not worthie*
10   *of the glorie which shall be revealed in the next.* The second,   2.Pet.3.
S. Peter used, when he sayed, seeing the heavenes must
be dissolved, and Christ come in Judgement to restore
to every man according to his woorkes: what maner of
men ought we to be in holy conversation? As whoe wold
15   say: No labour, no paynes, no travayle ought to seeme
hard or greate unto us, to the ende we myght avoyde
the terrour of that daye. S. Austen asketh this question:
what we thinke the riche gloutton in hell wolde doe, yf   Luc.16.
he were now in this lyfe again? wolde he take paynes
20   or no? wolde he bestyrre hym selfe, rather than turne
into that place of torment againe? I might adde to this,
the infinite paynes that Christ tooke for us: the infinite
benefites he hathe bestowed upon us: the infinite sinnes
we have committed against hym: the infinite examples
25   of Sainctes, that have trooden this pathe before us: in
respect of all whiche, we ought to make no boones at
litle paynes and labour, yf it were true that Gods service were so travailsome as many doe esteeme yt.

   But now in verie deede the matter is nothing so, and   The waye
30   this is but a subtile deceate of the enemie for our dis-   of vertue is
couragement. The testimonie of Christ hym selfe is cleare   not hard.
in this poynte: *Iugum meum suaue est, & onus meum leue:* My   Mat.11.
yooke is sweete, and my burden light. And the dearlie
beloved disciple S. John, who had best cause to know
35   his maisters secret herein, sayeth playnlie. *Mandata eius*   1.Joh.5.
grauia non sunt, hys commaundements are not greevouse.
What is the cause then why so many men doe conceave
suche a difficultie in this matter? surelie, one cause is,

---

2 for obteining of   12 *to judgement*   20 not bestir   27 so little pains

(besyde the subtiltie of the devill which is the cheefest) for that men feele the disease of concupiscence in their bodies, but doe not consider the strengthe of the medicine geven us against the same: they crye with S. Paul,

5 *that they fynde a law in their members repugning to the law of their mynde,* (whiche is the rebellion of concupiscence left in our flesh by originall synne:) but they confesse not, or consider not with the same S. Paul, *that the grace of God, by Jesus Christ, shall delyver them from the same.*

10 They remember not the comfortable sayeing of Christ to S. Paul, in his greatest temptations: *Sufficit tibi gratia mea:* My grace is sufficient to strengthen thee against them all. These men doe as Helizeus his disciple dyd, whoe casting his eyes onelye upon his enemies, that is

15 upon the huge armie of Syrians redie to assault hym, thought hym selfe lost and unpossible to stand in their sight, untill by the prayers of the holye prophet he was permitted from God, to see the Angels that stoode there present to fyght on his syde, and then he well perceaved

20 that his parte was the stronger.

So these men, beholding onelye our miseries and infirmities of nature, wherby daylie, tentations do ryse against us: doe account the battaill paynfull, and the victorie unpossible, having not tasted in deed, nor ever

25 proved (through their own negligence) the manifold helpes of grace and spirituall succours, which God all wayes sendeth to them, who are content (for his sake) to take this conflict in hand. S. Paul had well tasted that ayde, whiche having reckned up all the hardest matters that

30 coulde be, addeth: *Sed in his omnibus superamus propter eum qui dilexit nos:* But we overcome in all these combates, by his assistance, that loveth us. And then falleth he to that wounderful protestation: that nether death, nor lyfe, nor Angels, nor the lyke, should separate him: and all

35 this upon the confidence of spirituall ayd from Christ, wherby he sticketh not to avouch *that he could doe all things.* David also had proved the force of this assistance, whoe sayde, *I dyd runne the way of thy commaundementes,*

Side notes:
The cause of pretended difficulties. Rom.7.

Ibidem.

2.Co.12.

4.Re.6.

1. The force of grace for the easing of vertuous lyfe.

Rom.8.

Phil.4.

Psa.119.

---

15 of the Sirians

when thou dyddest enlarge my hart. This enlargement of hart, was by spirituall consolation of internall unction, wherby the hart drawen together by anguishe is opened and enlarged: when grace is powered in, even as a drye purse
5   ys softened and enlarged by annoynting it with oyle. Which grace being present, David sayed, he dyd not onelye walke the way of Gods commaundements easilie, but that he *ranne them*: Even as a carte wheele whiche crieth and compleyneth under a small burden being
10 drye, runneth merilye and without noyse, when a litle oyle is put unto it. Which thinge aptlye expresseth our state and condition, whoe without Gods help, are able to doe nothing, but with the ayde thereof, are able to conquere and overcome any thing.
15   And surelie I wolde aske these men that imagine the waye of Gods law to be so hard and full of difficultie, how the prophet could saye, *I have taken pleasure (o lord)*   Psa.119. *in the waye of thy commaundementes as in all the riches of the worlde?* And in an other place: *That they were more pleas-*   Psa.19.
20 *ant and to be desyred, than golde or pretious stone, and more sweter than hony or the hony combe?* by which woordes he yeeldeth to vertuouse lyfe, not onely due estimation above all treasures in the world: but also pleasure, delyte, and sweetnesse: therby to confound all those that abandone
25 and forsake the same, upon ydle pretensed and feyned difficulties. And yf David could say this muche in the olde law: how muche more justlie may we say so now in the new, when grace is geven more abundantlie, as the scripture sayeth? And thow poore Christian whiche   Joh.10.
30 deceavest thy selfe with this imagination: tell me, whye   Rom.5. came Christ into this worlde? whye laboured hee and   Heb.6. tooke he so much paines heere? whie shed he his bloode? whie praied he to his father so often for thee? whie appointed he the sacramentes as conduites of grace?
35 whie sent he the holye ghoste into the worlde? what signifieth gospell or good tydings? what meaneth the woords grace and mercie broght with him? what importeth

---

13 able to do whatsoever he now requireth of us. [*New paragraph*]
And surely   31 and why took he   36 this word Gospel

the comfortable name of Jesus? is not all this to dely- | Matt.1.
ver us from sinne? from sinne past, (I say) by his onlye
deathe: from sinne to come, by the same deathe and
by the assistance of his holy grace bestowed on us more

5   abundantlie than before by all these meanes? was not
this one of the principall effectes of Christ his coming
as the prophet noted: that *craggie wayes should be made* | Esa.40.
streight, and hard wayes playne? was not this the cause whie | Esa.11.
he indewed his churche with the seven blessed gyftes of | Et vide

10   the holie ghoste, and with the vertues infused: to make | Jer.ibi.
the yooke of his service sweete, the exercise of good lyfe | Amb.lib.1.
easye, the walking in his commaundementes pleasant, | de sp.S.
in such sort, as men might now sing in tribulations, | c.20. Au.
have confidence in periles, securitie in afflictions, and | ser.209.de

15   asseurance of victorie in all temptations? is not this the | temp.
begynnyng, mydle, and ende, of the gospell? were not | Matt.5.
these the promises of the prophetes, the tydinges of the | Luc.6.
evangelistes, the preachinges of the Apostles, the doc- | Act.4.
trine, beleefe, and practise of all saincts? and finallie is | 2.Co.4.

20   not this *verbum abbreuiatum*: The woord of God abbrevi- | Esa.10.
ated, wherein doe consist all the riches and treasures of
Christianitie?

    If any man will be contentiouse and aske me how | Of the
God doeth this marvailous woorke: I answere hym (as | force of

25   I have done before) that he doeth it by the assistance | grace.
of his holie grace, poured into the soule of man, wherby
it is beautified and strengthened against all temptations
as S. Paul was in particular against temptations of the | 2.Co.12.
fleshe. And this grace is of suche efficacie and force in

30   the soule where it entereth, that it altereth the whole
state thereof, making those thinges cleare which were
obscure before: those thinges pleasant, which were bytter before: those thinges easie, which were hard and
difficult before. And for this cause also it is sayed in

35   scripture, to make a new spirit and a new hart. As where

---

9 with so many blessed gifts of the holie Ghost, and with divers special graces, to make   23 *omits* If any man will be contentiouse . . .
temptations of the fleshe.   32 *omits* those thinges pleasant, which
were bytter before:

Ezechiel talking of this matter sayeth in the persone of
God: *I will geve unto them a new hart, and will put a new*   Eze.ca.11.
spirit in their bowelles, that they may walke in my preceptes and   & 36.
keepe my commaundementes. Can any thing in the worlde
5   be spoken more playnlie?

Now for mortifyeing and conquering of our passions,
whiche by rebellion doe make the way of Gods commaundementes unpleasant: S. Paul testifieth clearlie, that
abundant grace is geeven to us also by the deathe of
10   Christ, to doe the same: for so he sayeth: *This we know,*   Rom.6.
that our olde man is crucified also, to the ende that the bodie of
sinne may be destroyed, and we serve no more unto sinne. By
the olde man and the bodie of Sinne S. Paul understandeth our rebellious appetite and concupiscence, which
15   is so crucified and destroyed by the most noble sacrifice
of Christ, as we may by the grace purchased us in that   So
sacrifice, resist and conquer this appetite, and so keepe   proveth
our selves from servitude of sinne: that is from any con-   S.Au.li.2.
sent or taste of sinne, yf we will our selves. And this is   de pecca.
merit.
20   that noble and intire victorie, whiche God promised so   cap.6.
long agoe to everie Christian soule by the meanes of
Christ, when he sayd: Be not a feard, for I am with   Esa.41.
thee: stepp not aside, for I thy God have strengthened
thee, and have assisted thee: and the right hand of my
25   just man hathe taken thy defence. Beholde all that fight
against thee shalbe confounded and put to shame: thow
shalt seeke thy rebelles, and shalt not find them: they
shalbe as thoughe they were not, for that I am thy Lord
and God.
30   Loe heere a full victorie promised upon our rebelles,
by the helpe of the right hand of Gods just man, that
is upon our disordinate passions by the ayde of grace
from Jesus Christ. And albeit these rebelles are not heere
promised to be taken cleane awaye, but onelye to be
35   conquered and confounded: yet is it sayed *that they shalbe*

---

10 for he saith   17 sacrifice, in some good measure resist and conquer this appetite, being freed so much as we are, from the servitude of sin. And this is that noble and entire victorie (in this world
begun, & to be finished in the world to come) which

as thoghe they were not. Wherby is signified, that they shall
not hynder us in the way of our salvation, but rather
further the same, yf we will. For as wilde beastes which
of nature are fearse, and wold rather hurt than profitt
5 mankinde, being maistred and tamed, become verie com-
modiouse and necessarie for our uses: so these rebel-
liouse passions of ours, whiche of them selves wold utterlie
overthrowe us, being once subdued and mortified by
Gods graces and our owne diligence, doe stand us in
10 singular steade to the practise and exercise of all kynde
of vertues: as choler or angre to the inkyndeling of zeale:
hatred to the pursewinge of sinne: a hautie mynde, to
the rejecting of the world: love, to the embracing of all
great and heroicall attemptes in consideration of the

A simili-
tude.

The use
of pas-
sions
moder-
ated.

---

2 us of our salvation, but rather advance and further the same.
For 8 by the grace of God, do [*omits* and our owne diligence]
11 [* choler] *mn*: B. *A special point to be considered, for the
rectifieng of one point of philosophie: which is; that the soul doth
follow the temperature of the bodie. And this do they hold, for that
by experience it is commonly seen, that the disposition of men is
such, as the nature of their complexion doth seem to import. For
commonly those that are sanguine, are pleasant; those that are
flegmatik, slow; those that are cholerik, earnest; and those that are
melancholie, solitarie: and such like. And yet the truth is, that the
soul doth not follow, but rather doth use such temperature as the
bodie hath: and that very wel, and to good use, if the soul be good;
but otherwise abuseth it il. For the complexions are indifferent: neither good, nor il of themselves; but as they are used. But bicause
that most mens souls are il (as we are al by original corruption) therfore do most men abuse their complexions to il: as bloud, to wantonnes; fleam, to slought; choler, to anger; and melancholie, to secret
practices of deceit, or naughtines. Wheras notwithstanding, those
souls that are good, do use them wel: as blood, to be valiant, and
cheerful in goodnes; fleam, to moderate their affections with sobrietie; choler, to be earnest in the glorie of God; and melancholie, to
studie and contemplation. Which point notwithstanding might easily be pardoned to philosophers (that hold many things els as wrong
as it) but that this one point of error with them, is the cause of
some others besides in weightie matter. For out of this have som of
our Divines taken their opinion, that the fountain of sin is originally
in the bodie, and from it derived to the soul: and were the rather
induced to think that the blessed Virgin was hir self also conceived
without sin, for that otherwise they did not so plainly see, how Christ
taking flesh of hir, should have the same in himselfe without stein
of sin. And of themselves there be that have dowted of the immortalitie of the soul, for that supposing the soul to hang upon the temperature of the bodie, they did not see how it could be immortal,
when as the temperature and bodie it selfe are known to be mortal.

benefites receaved from God. Beside this the verie conflict
and combate it selfe, in subdewing these passions is
left unto us for our greate good: that is, for our patience,
humilitie, and victorie in this lyfe: and for our merit,
5 glorie, and croune in the lyfe to come: as S. Paul affirmed
of hym selfe, and confirmed to all others, by his example.   2.Tim.4.

Now then lett the slothefull Christian *goe putt his handes*
under his gyrdle, as the scripture sayeth, and saye: *There is*   Pro.26.
a lyon in the waye, and a lyonesse in the pathe, redie to devoure
10 *hym,* that he dare not goe furthe of doors. Let hym saye:
It is colde, and therefore he dareth not go to plowe. Let hym   Pro.20.
saye, it is uneasie to labour: and *therfore he can not purge*   Pro.24.
his vyneyarde of nettles and thystles, nor buyld any wall about
the same. That is, let hym saye his passions are strong,
15 and therfore he can not conquere them: his body is delicate, and therfore he dare not put it to travayle: the
way of vertuouse lyfe is hard and uneasie, and therfore
he can not applye hym selfe therunto. Let hym saye all
this, and muche more, which ydle and slothefull Christians
20 doe use to bryng for their excuse: let hym alleage it (I
say) as muche and as often as he will: it is but an excuse,
and a false excuse, and an excuse moste dishonorable
and detractorie to the force of Christ his grace, purchased us by his bytter passion: that now his yoke should
25 be unpleasant, seing he hathe made it sweete: that now   Mat.11.
his burden shoulde be heavie, seing he hathe made it
light: that now his commaundementes should be greev-   1.Joh.5.
ous, seinge the holie ghoste affirmeth the contrarie: that   Joh.8.
now we should be in servitude of our passions, seinge   Rom.7.
30 he hathe by his grace delyvered us, and made us truelie
free. *If God be with us, who will be against us?* sayeth the   Rom.8.
Apostle. *God is my helper and defender* (sayeth holie David,)   Psal.27.28.
whome shall I feare, or tremble? If whole armies should rise
against me: yet will I allway hope to have the victorie.
35 And what is the reason? *for that thow art with me* (o lord:)   Psal.23.
thow fyghtest on my syde: thou assistest me with thy
grace: by helpe whereof I shall have the victorie, thoghe
all the squadrones of my enemies, that is, of the fleshe,

---

4 our glory, and crown   10 of the doores   33 *or at whom shal I tremble?*

the world, and the devill, should ryse against me at once:
and I shall not onelie have the victorie, but also shall
have it easilie, and with pleasure and delite. For, so muche
signifieth S. John, in that (having saied that the com-   1.Joh.5.
5   maundementes of Christ are not greevous:) he inferreth
presentlie, as the cause thereof: *Quoniam omne quod natum
est ex deo vincit mundum.* For that all whiche is borne of
God, conquerith the worlde: that is, his grace and heavenlie assistance sent us from God doeth bothe conquer
10   the world, with all difficulties and temptations therof:
and also maketh the commaundements of God easie,
and vertuous lyfe most pleasant and sweete.

But perhappes you will saye: Christ him selfe confess-   An objec-
eth it to be a yoke, and a burden: how then can it be   tion,
15   so pleasant and easie as you make yt? I answer, that   answered.
Christ addeth that it is a sweete yoke and a light bur-
den. Wherby your objection is taken away: and also is
signified further, that there is a burden whiche greeveth
not the bearer, but rather helpeth and refresheth the
20   same: as the burden of fethers uppon a byrdes backe
beareth upp the byrd, and is nothinge at all greevous
unto her: So also thoghe it be a yoke, yet is it a sweete
yoke, a comfortable yoke, a yoke more pleasant than
hony or hony combe, as sayeth the prophet. And whie   Psa.119.
25   so? because we drawe therin, with a sweete companion,
we drawe with Christ: that is, his grace at one end, and
our endevour at the other. And because when a great
oxe and a litle doe drawe together, the weight lyeth all
uppon the greater oxe his necke, for that he beareth up
30   quite the yoke from the other: therof it cometh, that we
draweing in this yoke together with Christ, whiche is
greater than we are: he lighteneth us of the whole burden, and onelie requireth that we should goe on with
hym comfortablie, and not refuse to enter under the
35   yoke with hym, for that the payne shalbe his, and the

---

13 But it may be you   27 [* endevor] *mn*: B. *The regenerate have
an indevor framed in them by grace: but otherwise the natural children of Adam have none such of themselves but only to evil.   31
yoke with

pleasure oures. This he signifieth expresselie when he
sayeth: *come you to me all that labour and are heavie loden and*   Mat.11.
I will refreshe you. Heere you see that he moveth us to
this yoke, onelie therby to refreshe and disburden us:
5   to disburden us (I saye) and to refreshe us, and not
any waye to loade or agreeve us: to disburden us of
the heavye loadinges and yokes of this world: as from the
burden of a guiltie conscience, the burden of care, the
burden of melancholie, the burden of envye, hatred, and
10   malice, the burden of pryde, the burden of ambition,
the burden of covetousnes, the burden of wrathe, the
burden of feare, the burden of wickednesse, and hell fire
it selfe. From all these burdens and miserable yokes,
Christ wold delyver us, by coveringe our neckes onelie
15   with his yoke and burden, so lightned and sweetned
by his holy grace, as the bearinge therof is not travailsome, but most easie, pleasant, and confortable, as hathe
bene shewed.

An other cause why this yoke is so sweete, this bur-   2. Love
20   den so light, and this waie of Gods commaundementes   maketh
so pleasant to good men, is love: love (I meane) towards   the waye
pleasant.
God, whose commaundementes they are: for every man
can tell, and hathe experienced in hym selfe, what a
strong passion, the passion of love is, and how it maketh   The force
25   easie the verie greatest paynes that are in this world.   of love.
What maketh the mother to take suche paynes in the
bringing upp of her child, but onelie love? what causeth
the wyfe to sytt so attentyve at the bedde syde of her
sycke husbande, but onelie love? what moveth the beastes
30   and byrdes of the ayer, to spare from their owne foode,
and to endaunger their own lyves, for the feedinge and
defendinge of their litle ones, but onelie the force of   Ser.9.de
love? S. Austen doeth prosecute this pointe at large by   verbis
domini.
many other examples, as of Marchantes that refuse no
35   adventure of sea, for love of gayne: of huntars, that
refuse no season of evill weather, for love of game: of
soldiers that refuse no daunger of deathe, for love of

---

7 *omits* the burden of a guiltie conscience   11 *omits* the burden of
wrathe, the burden of feare   37 love of the spoil

spoyle. And he addeth in the end: that yf the love of man can be so greate towardes creatures heere, as to make labour easie, and in deede to seeme no labour, but rather pleasure: how muche more shall the love of
5   good men towardes God make all their labour comfortable, whiche they take in his service.

This extreme love was the cause whie all the paynes and afflictions which Christ suffered for us, seemed nothing unto hym. And this love also was the cause why all
10   the travailes and tormentes whiche many Christianes have suffered for Christ, seemed nothing unto them. Imprisonmentes, tormentes, losse of honour, goodes, and lyfe, seemed tryfles to divers servantes of God, in respect of this burning love. This love drove infinite virgines,
15   and tender children to offer them selves, in tyme of persecution, for the love of him which in the cause was persecuted. This love caused holye Apollonia of Alexandria, beinge broght to the fyre to be burned for Christ, to slypp out of the handes of suche as ledde her, and
20   joyfullie to runne into the fire, of her selfe. This love moved Ignatius, the auncient Martyre to saye (being condemned to beastes, and fearing leste they wolde refuse his bodie, as they had done of divers Martyres before) that he wolde not permitt them so to doe, but wolde
25   provoke and styrre them to come upon hym, and to take his lyfe from hym, by tearing his body in peeces.

These are the effectes then of fervent love, which maketh even the thinges that are most difficult and dreadfull of them selves, to appeare sweete and pleas-
30   ant: and much more the lawes and commaundementes of God, whiche in them selves are moste just, reasonable, holye and easie. *Da amantem* (sayeth S. Austen speaking of this matter,) *& sentit quod dico: Si autem frigido loquor, nescit quid loquar*: Geve me a man that is in love with
35   God: and he feeleth this to be true, whiche I saye: but yf I talke to a colde Christian: he understandeth not what I saye. And this is the cause whie Christ talking of the keeping of his commaundementes, repeateth so

The love of Christ to his saintes, & of his saintes to hym.

Euseb.li.6. c.34.

Jerom.in catalogo.

Psa.1. & 19. Mat.11. 1.Jo.5. Tra.26.in Johan.

---

14 drove many virgins

often this woorde *love*, as the onelye sure cause of keeping the same: for want whereof in the world, the world
keepeth them not, as there he sheweth. *If you love me,*   Joh.14.
keepe my commaundementes: sayeth he: and againe: *He that*
5   *hathe my commaundementes, and keepeth them, he is he, that*
loveth me. Agayne: *He which loveth me, will keepe my com-*
maundement: and he that loveth me not: keepeth not my com-
maundementes. In which last woordes, is to be noted, that
to the lover, he sayeth *his commaundement* in the singular   Marke
10 number: for that to suche a one all his commaunde-   this ob-
mentes are but one commaundement, according to the   servation.
sayeing of S. Paul: *That love is the fullnesse of the lawe*: For   Rom.13.
that it comprehendeth all. But to hym that loveth not,
Christ sayeth *his commaundementes* in the plurall number:
15 signifyeing thereby, that they are bothe many and heavie
to hym: for that he wanteth love, whiche should make
them easie. Whiche S. John also expresseth, when he   1.Jo.5.
sayeth: *this is the love of God, when we keepe his commaunde-*
mentes, and his commaundementes are not heavie. That is, they
20 are not heavye to hym, whiche hathe the love of God:
otherwyse no marvaile thoughe they be moste heavie.
For that everie thing seemeth heavie whiche we doe
against our lyking. And so by this also (gentle reader)
thow mayest gesse, whether the love of God be in thee,
25 or no.

And these are two meanes now, wherby the lyfe of   3.
good men is made easie in this worlde. There folow   Peculiar
divers other to the end that these negligent excusers may   light of
under-
see, how unjust and untrue this excuse of theyrs is con-   standing.
30 cerninge the pretended hardnes of vertuous lyving: whiche
in verie deede is indewed with infinite privileges of comfort, above the lyfe of wicked men, even in this world.
And the next that I will name for example sake after
the former, is a certaine speciall and peculiar light of
35 understanding, pertayning to the just, and called in scrip-

---

1 the surest cause   6 *omits commaundement: and he that loveth me not:*
keepeth not my   9 [* singular] *mn*: B. *But a little before he useth the
plural number in that case also. viz. Joh.14.15.   30 the vertuous life
33 *omits that I will name for example sake*

ture *prudentia sanctorum*. The wisdome of Saintes: which   Prov.9.
is nothing eles but a certayne sparkle of heavenlie wisdome, bestowed by singular privilege upon the vertuouse in this lyfe: wherby they receyve moste comfortable
5   light, and understanding in spirituall matters, especiallie
towching their owne salvation, and thinges necessarie
therunto. Of whiche the prophet David meant, when he
sayed, *notas mihi fecisti vias vitæ*. Thow hast made the   Psal.16.
wayes of lyfe knowen to me. Also when he sayde of
10   hym selfe. *Super senes intellexi*. I have understoode more   Psal.119.
than olde men. And agayne in an other place: *Incerta*
& occulta sapientiæ tuæ manifestasti mihi: Thow hast opened   Psal.51.
to me the unknowen and hydden secretes of thy wise-
dome. This is that light wherwith S. John sayeth that
15   Christ lighteneth his servantes: as also that unction of   Joh.1.
the holye ghoste, whiche the same Apostle teacheth to   1.Jo.2.
be geven to the godlie, to instructe them in all thinges
behoofefull for their salvation. In lyke wyse this is that
writing of Gods lawe in mennes hartes, whiche he prom-
20   iseth by the prophet Jeremie: as also the instruction of   Jero.31.
men immediatlye from God him selfe, promised by the   Esa.54.
prophet Esaye. And finallie this is that soveraigne understanding in the lawe, commaundementes, and justifica-
tiones of God, whiche holy David so muche desired, and
25   so often demaunded in that most divine psalme, whiche
begynneth: *Blessed are the unspotted in the waye*: That is, in   Ps.119.
this lyfe.

By this light of understandinge, and supernaturall
knowlege and feeling from the holie ghost, in spirituall
30   thinges, the vertuouse are greatlie holpen in the waye of
righteousnes, for that they are made able to discerne for
their owne direction in matters that occurre, accordinge
to the sayeing of S. Paul: *Spiritualis omnia iudicat*: A spir-   1.Co.2.
ituall man judgeth of all thinges: *Animalis autem homo non*
35   *percipit quæ sunt spiritus dei*: But the carnall man conceaveth not the thinges whiche appertayne to the spirit of
God. Doeth not this greatlie discover the priviledge of
a vertuous lyfe? the joye, comfort and consolation of the
same? with the exceeding great miserie of the contrarie
40   parte? For yf two should walke together, the one blynde,

and the other of perfect sight, which of them were lyke
to be wearie first? whose journey were like to be more
paynfull? Doeth not a litle grownde wearie out a blynde
man? consider then in howe wearysome darkenesse the
5 wicked doe walke: consider whether they be blynde or
no. S. Paul sayeth in the place before alleaged, that they   1.Cor.2.
can not conceave any spirituall knowlege: is not this a
great darkenesse? Agayne, the prophet Esay describeth
their state further, when he sayeth in the persone of the   Esa.59.
10 wicked, *we have groped lyke blynde men after the walles, and
have stumbled at middaye, even as yf it had beene in darkenesse.*
And in an other place, the scripture describeth the same,
yet more effectuouslie, with the paynfullnesse therof, even
from the mouthes of the wicked them selves, in these
15 woordes: *The light of Justice hathe not shyned unto us, and the*   Sap.5.
sunne of understanding hathe not appeared unto our eyes: we are
wearyed out in the waye of iniquitie and perdition etc. This is
the talke of sinners in hell. By which woordes appeareth,
not onelye that wicked men doe lyve in great darke-
20 nesse: but also that this darkenesse is most paynefull
unto them: and consequently that the contrarie light, is
a great easement to the waye of the vertuous.

An other principall matter which maketh the waye of   4. Inter-
vertue easye and pleasant to them that walke therein,   nall con-
25 is a certaine hidden and secret consolation, which God   solation.
poureth in to the hartes of them that serve hym. I call
yt secret: for that it is knowen but of such onelye as
have felt it: for which cause, Christ hym selfe calleth yt,
hydden manna, knowen onelye to them that receave it. And the   Apo.2.
30 prophet sayeth of yt, *greate is the multitude of thy sweetnes*   Psa.31.
(o Lord,) which thou haste hydden for them that feare thee. And
againe, in an other place, *thou shalt laye asyde (o Lord) a*   Psal.68.
speciall chosen rayne or dewe for thyne inheritance. And an other
prophet sayeth in the persone of God, talking of the
35 devoute soule that serveth hym: *I will leede her a side into*   Ose.2.
a wildernesse, and there I will talk unto her harte. By all which
woordes, of *wildernesse, separating, choyse,* and *hydden* is
signified, that this is a secret privilege bestowed onelie
uppon the vertuouse, and that the carnall hartes of
40 wicked men, have no parte or portion therein. But now,

how great and inestimable the sweetenesse of this heavenlie consolation is, no tongue of man can expresse: but
we may conjecture by these woordes of David, whoe,   Psal.36.
talking of this celestiall wyne, attributeth to yt suche   & 65.
5   force, as to make all those drounken that taste of the
same: that is, to take from them, all sense and feeling
of terrestriall matters, even as S. Peter having drounke
a litle of yt uppon the mounte Thabor, forgate hym   Mat.17.
selfe presentlie, and talked as a man distracted, of build-   Marc.9.
10 ing tabernacles there, and resting in that place for ever.   Luc.9.
This is that *torrens voluptatis*, that sweete streame of pleas-   Psal.36.
ure, as the prophet calleth yt, which comming from the   Esa.29.
mountaynes of heaven, watereth (by secret wayes and
passages) the hartes and spirites of the godly, and maketh
15 them drounken with the unspeakable joye which it
bringeth with yt. This is a litle taste in this life of the
verie Joyes of heaven, bestowed upon good men, to comfort them withall, and to encourage them to goe forwarde. For as Marchantes desirous to sell their wares,   A simili-
20 are content to let you see and handle, and some times   tude.
also to taste the same, therby to induce you to buy: so
God almightie willing to sell us the joyes of heaven, is
content to imparte a certaine taste before hand to such   Apoc.3.
as he seeth are willing to buye: thereby to make them
25 come of roundlye with the price, and not to stycke in
payeinge so muche, and more, as he requireth. This is
that exceding joye and jubilie in the hartes of just men,
which the prophet meaneth, when he saieth: *The voyce*   Psa.118.
of exultation and salvation is in the tabernacles of the just. And
30 agayne, *Blessed is that people that knoweth jubilation*: That is,   Psa.89.
that hath experienced this extreeme joye and pleasure
of internall consolation. S. Paul had tasted it when he
wrote these woordes, amiddest all his laboures for Christ.   2.Cor.7.
I am filled with consolation, I overflowe or superabounde in all
35 *joye, amyddest our tribulations.* What can be more effectually
sayd or alleaged, to prove the service of God pleasant,
than this? Surelye (good reader) yf thow haddest tasted
once, but one droppe of this heavenlie joye: thou woldest

---

22 willing (as it were)   34 *overflow or exceedingly abound in*

geve the whole worlde to have an other of the same, or at the leastwise, not to leese that one agayne.

But thou wilt aske me perhappes, whye thow being a Christian as well as other, hast yet never tasted of this consolation? to which I answere, that (as it hath bene shewed before) this is not meate for everye mouthe: but *a chosen moysture layed asyde for Gods inheritance onelye.* This *is wyne of Gods owne seller, layed up for his spouse,* as the Canticles declare: That is, for the devoute sowle dedicated unto Gods service. This is a teate of comfort, onelye for the chylde to sucke, and fill hym selfe withall, as the prophet Esaye testifieth. The soule that is drouned in synne and pleasures of the world can not be partaker of this benefite: nether the harte replenished with carnall cares and cogitations. For as Gods Arcke and the Idole Dagon could not stand together uppon one Aultar: so can not Christ and the world stand together in one harte. God sent not the pleasant Manna unto the people of Israell as long as their flower and chyboles of Egipt lasted: soe nether will he send this heavenlie consolation unto thee, untill thou have rydde thy selfe of the cogitations of vanitie. He is a wyse marchant, thoughe a liberall. He wil not geve a taste of his treasure, where he knoweth there is no will to buye. Resolve thy selfe once in deede to serve God, and thow shalt then feele this joye, that I talke of, as many thousandes before thee have done, and never yet any man was herein deceaved. Moyses first ranne out of Egypt, to the hilles of Madian, before God appeared unto hym: and so must thy soule doe owt of worldlye vanitie, before she can looke for these consolations. But thou shalt no sooner offer thy selfe thorowghly to Gods service, than thou shalt fynde entertaynement above thy expectation. For that, his love is more tender in deede upon them that come newlye to his service, than upon those whiche have served hym of olde: as he sheweth playnelye by the parable of the prodigall sonne: whome he cheryshed with much more

The waye to come to spirituall consolation.
Psa.68.
Can.1.

Esa.66.

1.Re.5.
Jo.8.14.
15.16.
1.Jo.2.
Exo.16.

Exod.2.

Luc.15.
Begynners

---

3 *omits* perhappes   8 As the Canticle declareth. That is   29 thy soul go out

dalyance and good cheere, than he dyd the elder brother,   cheefelie
which had served hym of long tyme. And the causes   cherished
hereof are two: the one, for the joye of the new gotten   with spir-
servant, as is expressed by S. Luc in the text: the other,   solation.
5   lest he fynding no consolation at the begynnyng, should
turne back to Egypt agayne: as God by a figure in the
children of Israell declareth manyfestlie in these woordes: Exo.13.
*When Pharao had lett goe the people of Israell out of Egypt: God
brought them not by the countrie of Philistines, whiche was the*
10   *nearest waye, thinking with hym selfe, lest perhappes it might
repent them, yf they should see warres streight waye ryse agaynst
them, and so should returne into Egypt agayne.* Upon which
two causes thow mayest assure thy selfe, of singular consolations and comfortes in the service of God (yf thou
15   wooldest resolve thy selfe therunto) as all other men have
founde before thee, and by reason therof have proved
the waye not harde, as worldlye men imagine yt, but   Matt.11.
most easie, pleasant, and comfortable, as Christ hathe
promised.
20   After this privilege of internall consolation enseueth   5. The
an other, making the service of God pleasant, which is   quiet of
the testimonie of a good conscience, wherof S. Paul   conscience.
made so great accounte, as he called it *his glorie.* And   2.Cor.1.
the holie ghoste sayeth of it further, by the mouthe of
25   the wyse man: *Secura mens quasi iuge conuiuium:* a secure   Pro.15.
mynde, or good conscience is as a perpetuall feaste. Of
which we may inferre, that the vertuous man having
allwayes this secure mynde and peace of conscience,
lyveth allwayes in festivall glorie, and gloriouse feasting.
30   And how then is this lyfe harde, or unpleasant, as you
imagine? In the contrary syde, the wicked man, having
his conscience vexed with the privitie of synne, is always
tormented with in it selfe: as we reade that Cayn was,
having killed his brother Abel: and Antiochus for his   Gen.4.
35   wickednesse done to Jerusalem: and Judas for his trea-   1.Ma.6.
son against his maister: and Christ signifieth it general-   Mat.27.
lie of all naughtie men, when he saieth that they have   Act.1.
a worme whiche gnaweth their conscience within. The   Marc.9.

---

9 *of the Philistines*   10 *himselfe that it might*   26 *is a perpetual*

reason wherof, the scripture openeth in an other place, when it sayeth: *All wickednesse is full of feare, geving testimonie of damnation against it selfe: and therfore a troubled conscience alwaies presumeth cruell matters.* That is, it presumeth

5   cruell thinges to be imminent over it selfe, as it maketh account to have deserved. But yet further, above all other, holie Jobe moste livelie setteth furth this miserable state of wicked men, in these woordes: *A wicked man is proved all the dayes of his lyfe, though the tyme be uncertaine*

10   *howe long he shall playe the tyrant: the sounde of terroure is allwayes in his eares: and althoughe yt be in time of peace, yet he alway suspecteth some treason against hym: he beleeveth not that he can ryse againe from darknesse to light: expecting on every syde the swoorde to come uppon hym: when he sitteth downe to eate,*

15   *he remembreth that the day of darkenesse is redy at hand for him: tribulation terrifieth hym, and anguishe of mynde environeth hym, even as a king is environed with soldiers, when he goeth to warre.*

Is not this a marvailous description of a wicked conscience, uttered by the holy ghoste hym selfe? what can

20   be imagined more miserable than this man, which hathe suche a boucherie, and slaughterhouse with in his owne harte? what feares, what anguishes, what desperations are heere touched? S. Chrisostome discourseth notablie upon this point: Suche is the custome of sinners, (sayeth

25   he) that they suspect all thinges, they dowte their owne shadowes, they are afeard at every litle noyse, and they think every man that cometh towardes them, to come against them. If men talke together, they think they speak of their sinnes: suche a thyng sinne is, as it be-

30   wrayeth it selfe, though no man accuse yt: It condemneth it selfe, though no man beare witnesse against it: It maketh always the sinner fearfull, as Justice doeth the contrarie. Heare howe the scripture doeth describe the sinners feare, and the just mans libertie. *The wicked man*

35   *flyeth though no man pursue hym* (sayeth the scripture.) Whie doeth he flye yf no man doe pursue him? Mary, for that he hathe within his conscience an accuser pursue-

Marginal notes:
Sap.17.

Job.15.
The trouble of an evill conscience.

Hom.8.ad pop. Antiochenum.

Pro.28.

---

3 *conscience alway suspecteth cruel maters.* That is, suspecteth   16 *anguish environeth*   22 *omits* what desperations   36 *omits* Mary

ing hym, whome alwayes he carieth aboute with hym.
And as he can not flye from hym selfe: so can he not
flye from this accuser within his conscience, but where
soever he goeth, he is purseued and whipped by the
5   same, and his wounde is incurable. But the just man is
nothing so: *The just man* (sayeth Salamon) *is as confident*   Pro.28.
as a lyon. Hitherto are the woordes of S. Chrisostome.
        Wherby, as also by the scriptures alleaged, we take   6. The
notice yet of an other prerogative of vertuouse lyfe, which   hope of
10   is hope or confidence, the greatest treasure, the rich-   vertuouse
est Jewell, that Christian men have left them in this   men.
lyfe. For by this we passe throughe all afflictions, all
tribulations and adversities, most joyfullye, as S. James   Jacob.1.
signifieth. By this we say with S. Paul: *We doe glorie in*   Rom.5.
15   *our tribulations, knoweing that tribulation worketh patience, and*
patience proofe, and proofe hope, which confoundeth us not. This
is our most strong and mightie comfort: this is our sure
Anckre in all tempestuous times, as S. Paul sayeth. *We*   Heb.6.
have a most strong solace (sayeth he) *which doe flye unto the*
20   *hope proposed, to laye handes on the same, which hope we holde*
as a sure and firme Anckre of our soule. This is that noble   Eph.6.
galea salutis: heade peece of salvation, as the same Apostle   1.The.5.
calleth yt, which beareth of all the blowes that this
worlde can laye upon us. And finallie, this is the onelie
25   rest set upp in the harte of a vertuous man, that come
lyfe, come deathe: come healthe, come sickenesse: come
wealthe, come povertie: come prosperitie, come adversitie: come never so tempestuous stormes of persecution,
he sitteth downe quietlye, and sayeth calmelie with the
30   prophet, *my trust is in God, and therfore I feare not what flesh*   Psal.56.
can doe unto me. Nay further with holy Job, amiddest all   Job.13.
his miseries, he sayeth, *si occiderit me, in ipso sperabo*: yf
God should kill me, yet wolde I trust in hym. And this
is (as the scripture sayed before) to be as confident as
35   a Lyon, whose propertye is, to shew most courage, when
he is in greatest perill, and nearest his deathe.
        But now, as the holy ghoste sayethe, *non sic impii, non*   Psa.1.

---

1 about him   3 his accuser   5 wound incurable   21 *firm armor*   22
the head-peece

sic. The wicked can not saie this, they have no parte in
this confidence, no interest in this consolation: *Quia spes*   Pro.10.
impiorum peribit, sayeth the scripture: The hope of wicked
men is vayne, and shall perish. And againe, *præstolatio*   Pro.11.
5   *impiorum furor*, the expectation of wicked men is furie:
And yet further, *spes impiorum abhominatio animæ*: the hope   Job.11.
of wicked men is abhomination, and not a comfort unto
their soule. And the reason herof is double. First, for
that in verie deede (thoughe they saye the contrarie in
10   woordes) wicked men doe not put their hope and
confidence in God, but in the world, in their riches, in
their strengthe, freendes, and authoritie, and finallie in
the *deceaving arme of man*: even as the prophet expresseth   Jere.17.
in their persone, when he sayeth: *We have put a lye for*   Esa.28.
15   *our hope*: That is, we have put our hope in thinges transitorie, which have deceaved us. And this is yet more
expressed by the scripture, sayeing, *the hope of wicked men*   Sap.5.
is as chaffe, whiche the wynde bloweth awaye: and as a buble
of water whiche a storme disperseth: and as the smoke which the
20   *wynde bloweth abrode: and as the remembrance of a gest that*
stayeth but one daye in his Inne. By all which metaphores,
the holie ghoste expresseth unto us, bothe the vanitie of
the thinges wherein in deede the wicked doe put their
trust, and howe the same fayleth them, after a litle time,
25   uppon every small occasion of adversitie that falleth owte.

This is that also whiche God meaneth when he so
stormeth and thundreth against those which goe into
Egypt for helpe, and doe put their confidence in the   Esa.30. &
strengthe of Pharao: accursing them for the same, and   36.
30   promising, that it shall turne to their owne confusion:
which is properlie to be understoode of all those, which
put their cheefe confidence in worldlie helpes: as all   Jere.17.
wicked men doe, what soever they dissemble in woordes   48.
to the contrarie. For which cause also of dissimulation,
35   they are called hypocrites by Job: for where as the wyse-   Pro.10.
man sayeth, *the hope of wicked men shall perishe*: Job sayeth,   Job.8.
the hope of hypocrites shall perishe, calling wicked men hypocrites: for that, they say, they put their hope in God,

---

11 and in their riches   19 *as a smoke*

where as in deede they doe put it in the world. Which thing, beside scripture, is evident also by experience. For with whome doeth the wicked man consult in his affayres and doubtes? with God principallie, or with the worlde?

5 whome doeth he seeke to in his afflictions? whome doeth he call upon in his syckenes? from whome hopeth he comfort in his adversities? to whome yeeldeth he thankes in his prosperities? When a worldlye man taketh in hande any worke of importance, doeth he first consult with

10 God, about the event thereof? doeth he fall downe on his knees, and aske his ayde? doeth he referre it wholie or principallie unto his honour? Yf he doe not: howe can he hope for ayde therein at his handes? how can he repayre to hym for assistance in the daungers and

15 lettes that fall out about the same? how can he have any confidence in hym, whiche hathe no parte at all in that woorke? It is hypocrisie then (as Job truelye sayeth) for this man to affirme that his confidence is in God: whereas in deede it is in the worlde, it is in Pharao, yt

20 is in Egypt, yt is in the arme of man, it is in a lye. He buyldeth not his house with the wyse man, upon a rocke: but with the foole, upon the sandes: and therfore (as Christ well assureth him) *when the rayne shall come and*   Matt.7. *fluddes descend, and wyndes blowe, and al together shall rushe*

25 *upon that house* (which shalbe at the hower of his deathe:) *then shall this house fall, and the fall of yt shalbe great.* Great, for the great chaunge which he shall see: great, for the great horroure which he shall conceave: great, for the great miserie which he shall suffer: greate, for the unspekable

30 joyes of heaven lost: great, for the eternall paynes of hell fallen into: great every waye, assure thy selfe (deare brother) or els the mouthe of God wolde never have used this woorde great. And this is sufficient for the first reason, whye the hope of wicked men is vayne: for that

35 in deede they putt it not in God, but in the worlde.

The second reason is for that, albeit they should put   Wicked their hope in God, yet (lyving wickedlie) it is vayne and   men can

---

1 they put it   11 wholy and principally to   25 *the house* (which shal be at the hour of death)   27 the change

rather to be called presumption, than hope. For understanding wherof, it is to be noted that, as there are two
kynde of fayethes recounted in scripture, the one a deade
fayeth without good woorkes: that is, whiche beleeveth

5   all you saye of Christ, but yet observeth not his commaundementes: the other a lyvelie, a justifieing fayeth,
which beleeveth not onelie, but also woorketh by charitie, as S. Paules woordes are: So are there two hopes
foloweing these two fayethes: the one of the good, pro-

10   ceding of a good conscience, whereof I have spoken
before: the other of the wicked, resting in a guyltie conscience, which is in deede no true hope, but rather presumption. This S. John proveth playnlie, when he sayeth.
Brethren yf our harte reprehende us not, then have we confidence

15   *with God*: That is, yf our harte be not guyltie of wicked
lyfe. And the woordes immediatlie foloweing doe more
expresse the same, which are these: *What so ever we aske,*
we shall receyve of hym, for that we keepe his commaundementes,
and doe those thinges whiche are pleasing in his sight. The same

20   confirmeth S. Paule, when he sayeth, that *the end of Gods*
commaundementes is charitie, from a pure harte and a good con-
science: Which woordes S. Austen expoundinge in divers
places of his woorkes, proveth at large, that without a
good conscience, there is no true hope can be conceaved.

25   *S. Paul* (sayeth he) *addeth (from a good conscience) because of*
hope: for he which hathe the scruple of an evill conscience dis-
pareth to attaine that which he beleeveth. And agayne, *Every*
mans hope is in his owne conscience according as he feeleth hym
selfe to love God. And agayne in an other booke, *the Apostle*

30   *putteth a good conscience for hope: for he onelie hopeth which*
hathe a good conscience: and he whome the guylt of an evill con-
science doeth prycke, retyreth backe from hope, and hopeth noth-
ing but his owne damnation.

       I might heere repeate a greate many more privileges,
35   and prerogatives of a vertuouse lyfe, which make the
same easie, pleasant, and comfortable, but that this
chapiter groweth to be long: and therfore I will onelie

Marginal notes:

not hope
in God.
Jacob.2.
Mat.7.
1.Co.13.
& 15.
Rom.1.
Gal.3.
Eph.2.

1.Jo.3.

1.Ti.1.

S. Austen.
lib.1.de
doc.chri.
cap.37.

S. Austen
in prefat.
Psal.31.

---

2 two kinds of faith   17 *Whensoever*   22 divers words, and in divers

touche (as it were in passing bye) two or three other pointes of the moste principall: which notwithstanding wold requyre large discourses to declare the same, according to their dignities. And the first is the inestimable privilege of libertie and freedome, which the vertuouse doe enjoye above the wicked, according as Christ promiseth in these woordes: *If you abyde in my commaundementes, you shalbe my scholares in deede, and you shall knowe the trueth, and the trueth shall set you free*: Which woordes S. Paul as it were expounding, sayeth, *where the spirit of our lord is, there is freedome.* And this freedome is meant, from the tyrannye and thraldome of our corrupt sensualitie and concupiscence, called by divines the inferior parte of our minde: whereunto the wicked are so in thraldome, as there was never bondeman so in thraldome to a moste cruell, and mercilesse tyrant. This in parte may be conceaved by this one example.

If a man had marryed a riche, beautifull, and noble gentlewoman, adorned with all gyftes and graces, which maye be devised to be in a woman: and yet notwithstanding should be so sotted and entangled with the love of some fowle and dishonest begger, or servyle mayde of his house, as for her sake to abandone the companie and freendship of his sayed wyfe: to spende his tyme in daliance and service of this base woman: to runne, to goe, to stand at her appoyntment: to putt all his lyving and reveneues into her handes, for her to consume and spoyle at her pleasure: to deny her nothing, but to wayte and serve her at a becke: yea and to compell his sayde wyfe to doe the same: wolde you not think this mans lyfe miserable and most servile? And yet surely the servitude whereof we talke, is farre greater and more intolerable than this. For no woman or other creature in this world, is or can be of that beautie or nobilitie as ladie reason is, to whome man by his creation was espowsed: which notwithstanding wee see abandoned,

marginal notes:

7. Libertie of soule.

Joh.8.

2.Co.3.

An example to expresse the bondage of wicked men to their sensualitie.

---

1 of the other   13 *omits* called by divines the inferior parte of our minde   24 the said wife   25 his base   29 at hir bek   34 the world   34 nobilitie, as the grace of Gods spirit is, to whom

contemned and rejected by hym, for the love of sensualitie, her hand mayde, and a most deformed creature
in respect of reason: in whose love notwithstanding or
rather servitude, we see wicked men so drowned, as they
5   serve her daye and night with all paynes, perills, and
expenses, and doe constrayne also reason her selfe, to
be subject to all the beckes and commaundementes of
this new mistresse. For, wherfore doe they laboure? wherfore doe they wache? wherfore doe they heape riches
10   together, but onelie to serve their sensualitie, and her
desyers? wherfore do they beate their braynes, but onelie
to satisfie this cruell tyrant and her passions?

And yf you will see in deede how cruell and pytifull
this servitude is: consider but some particular examples
15   therof. Take a man whome she over ruleth in anye passion: as for example, in the lust of the fleshe: what
paynes taketh he for her? how doeth he labour, how
doeth he sweate in this servitude? how potent and strong
doeth he feele her tyrannie? Remember the strengthe
20   of Samson, the wisdome of Salomon, the sanctitie of
David overthrowen by this tyrannie: Jupiter, Mars, and
Hercules, whoe for their valiant actes other wyse, were
accounted godes of the panymes: were they not overcome, and made slaves by the enchauntement of this
25   tyrant? And yf you will yet further see of what strengthe
she is, and how cruellie she executeth the same upon
those, that Christ hathe not delyvered from her bondage:
consider (for examples sake in this kynde) the pytyfull
case of some disloyall wyfe, whoe thoughe she know that
30   by comitting adulterie, she runneth into a thowsand
daungers and inconveniences, as the losse of Gods favoure,
the hatred of her husband, the daunger of punishment,
the offence of her freendes, the utter dishonour of her
persone, (if it be knowen) and finallie the ruyne or per-
35   ill of bodie and soule: yet to satisfie this tyrant, she will
venture to committ the sinne, notwithstanding any daungers or perilles what soever.

*The mis-
erie of
a man
ruled by
sensu-
alitie.*

*2.Re.11.
Jud.16.
3.Re.11.*

---

2 hir enemie, and   6 constrain also the good motions of Gods spirit to
give place at every bek and commandement of   16 and what pains
18 How mightie and strong

Nether is it onelie in this one point of carnall lust, but in all other, wherein a man is in servitude to this tirant, and her passions. Looke upon an ambitious or vaynglorious man: see how he serveth this mistresse: with what care and diligence he attendeth her commaunde-mentes: that is, to folowe after a litle wynde of mens mouthes: to pursue a litle fether flyeing before hym in the ayer. You shall see that he omitteth no one thing, no one tyme, no one circumstance for gayning therof. He ryseth betime: goeth late to bedd: trotteth by daye: studieth by night: heere he flattereth, there he dissem-bleth: heere he stoupeth, there he looketh bygge: heere he maketh freends, there he preventeth enemies: and to this onelye end he referreth all his actions, and appli-eth all his other matters: as his order of lyfe, his com-panie keeping, his sutes of apparell, his house, his table, his horses, his servauntes, his talke, his behavyour, his jestes, his lookes, and his verye goeyng in the streete.

An ambitious man.

In likewyse he that serveth this ladie in the passion of covetousnesse: what a miserable slaverie doeth he abyde? his harte beynge so walled into pryson with money, as he must onelye thinke thereof, talke therof, dreame therof, and imagin onelie new waies to gette the same, and nothing else. If you should see a Christian man in slaverie under the great Turke, tyed in a galley by the legge with chaynes, there to serve by rowe-ing for ever: you could not but take compassion of his case. And what then shall we doe of the miserie of this man, whoe standeth in captivitie to a more base crea-ture, than a Turke, or anie other reasonable creature: that is, to a peece of mettall, in whose prison he lyeth bownde, not onelie by the feete, in suche sort, as he may not goe anye where, against the commoditie and com-maundement of the same: but also by the handes, by the mouthe, by the eyes, by the eares, and by the harte: so as he may nether doe, speake, see, heare, or thinke any thing, but in service of the same? Was there ever servitude so greate as this? doeth not Christ saye truely

A covet-ous man.

Joh.8.

21 in prison   37 but the service

now, *qui facit peccatum seruus est peccati*: He that doeth   Rom.6.
synne is a slave unto synne? doeth not S. Peter saye well,   2.Pet.2.
a quo quis superatus est, huius & seruus est: A man is a slave
to that, wherof he is conquered?

5   From this slaverie then are the vertuous delivered, by
the power of Christ, and his assistance: in so muche,
as they rule over their passions and sensualitie, and are
not ruled thereby. This God promised by the prophet
Ezechiel, sayeing. *And they shall know, that I am theyr lorde,*   Eze.34.
10   *when I shall breake the chaynes of their yoke, and shall delyver*
them from the power of those, that over ruled them before. And
this benefit holye David acknowleged in hym selfe, when
he used these most affectuouse woordes to God: *O lorde*   Psal.116.
I am thy servant, I am thy servant, and the childe of thy hand
15   *mayde: thow hast broken my bandes, and I will sacrifice to the,*
a sacrifice of prayse. This benefit also acknowleged S. Paul,
when he sayed, that our olde man was crucified, to the   Rom.6.
end the bodie of synne might be destroyed, and we be
no more in servitude to sinne: understanding by the olde
20   man, and the bodie of synne, our concupiscence, mortified
by the grace of Christ in the vertuouse.

After this privilege of freedome, foloweth an other, of   8. Peace
no lesse importance than this, and that is a certayne   of mynde.
heavenlie peace, and tranquilitie of mynde, according to
25   the sayeing of the prophet: *Factus est in pace locus eius*, his   Psal.76.
place is made in peace. And in an other place: *Pax multa*   Psa.119.
diligentibus legem tuam, there is greate peace to them that
love thy lawe. And on the contrarye syde, the prophet
Esay repeateth this sentence often from God, *non est pax*   Esa.48.57.
30   *impiis dicit dominus*: Our lorde saieth, there is no peace
unto the wicked. And an other prophet saieth of the
same men. *Contrition and infelicitie is in their waies, and they*   Rom.3.
have not knowen the waye of peace. The reason of this difference
hathe bene declared before in that which I have noted
35   of the diversitie of good and evill men touchinge their
passions. For the vertuous having now (by the ayde of

---

7 in sensualitie   15 *bonds*   16 acknowledgeth Saint Paul, when he
saith   21 Christ in the children of God. [*New paragraph begins*] After
27 *them which*   30 *Dominus: The Lord*

Christ his grace) subdewed their sayd passions, doe passe
on their lyfe moste sweetly and calmely under the guyde
of reason, without any perturbations that trouble them
in the greatest occurrents of this lyfe. But the wicked
5   men not having mortified the sayd passions, are tossed   Rom.11.
and tombled with the same as with vehement and contrarye wyndes. And therfore their state is compared by
Esaye to a tempestuouse sea, that never is quiet, and   Esa.57.
by S. James, to a citie, or countrie, where the inhabit-   Jac.4.
10   antes are at warre and sedition among them selves. And
the causes hereof are two: first, for that the passions of   Two
concupiscence beinge many and almoste infinite in num-   causes of
ber, doe lust after infinite thinges, and are never satisfied,   disquietnes
but are lyke those bloodsuckers whiche the wise man   in wicked
men.
15   speaketh of, that crye allwaies *geeve geeve*, and never say   Pro.30.
hoe. As for example: when is the ambitious man satisfied
with honour? or the incontinent man with carnalitie? or
the covetous man with money? never truelie: and therfore as that mother can not but be greatlie afflicted
20   whiche should have many children cryeing at once for
meate, she havynge no bread at all to breake unto them:
so the wicked man being greedilie called uppon without ceasing by almoste infinite passions to yelde them
their desires: must needes be vexed and pitifullie tor-
25   mented, especiallie being not able to satisfie anye one
of their smallest demaundes.

An other cause of vexation is, for that these passions
of disordinate concupiscence, be often times contrarie
one to the other, and doe demaunde contrarie thinges,
30   representing moste lyvelie the confusion of Babel: where
one tongue spoke against an other, and that in diverse   Gen.11.
and contrarie languages. So we see oftentimes that the
desire of honour sayeth, *spend heere*: But the passion of
avarice sayeth, *holde thy handes*. Lecherie sayeth, *venture*
35   *heere*: But pryde sayeth *No, it may turne thee to dishonoure*.

---

1 subdued the greatest force of their   2 guide of his spirit, without
any perturbations that much troble   5 tossed and troubled   7 state
and condition   22 *omits* without ceasing   29 on contrary to   35 to
thy dishonor

Anger sayeth, *revenge thy selfe heere*: But ambition sayeth, *it is better to dissemble*. And finallie, heere is fullfilled that which the prophet sayeth, *vidi iniquitatem & contradictionem in ciuitate*: I have seene iniquitie and contradiction in the selfe same citie: Iniquitie, for that all the demaundes of these passions are most unjust, in that they are against reason her selfe: Contradiction, for that one contradicteth the other in their demaundes. From all which miseries God hathe delyvered the juste by geving them his peace, *which passeth all understanding*, as the Apostle sayeth, and which the worlde can nether geve nor taste of, as Christ hym selfe affirmeth.

Psal.55.

Phil.4.
Joh.14.17.
Matt.10.

And these many causes may be alleaged now (beside many other which I passe over) to justifie Christs woordes, that his yoke is sweete and easie: to witt, the assistance of grace, the love of God, the light of understanding from the holye ghoste, the internall consolation of the mynde, the quiet of conscience, the confidence thereof proceeding, the libertie of soule and bodie, with the sweete rest and peace of our spirites, bothe towardes God, towardes our neighboures, and towardes our selves. By all whiche meanes, helpes, privileges and singular benefites, the vertuous are assisted above the wicked, as hathe bene shewed, and their waye made easie, light and pleasant. To which also we may adde as the last but not the least comfort, the expectation of rewarde: that is, of eternall glorie and felicitie to the vertuous: and everlasting damnation unto the wicked. O how great a matter is this, to comfort the one, yf their lyfe were paynefull, and to afflict the other, amyddest all their greate pleasures? The labourer when he thynketh of his good paye at night, is encouraged to goe thorough, thogh it be paynfull to hym. Two that shoulde passe together towardes their countrie, the one to receave honour for good service done abrode, the other as prisoner to be

9. Expectation of rewarde.

An example.

---

6 against the word of God. Contradiction, for that one crieth against the other in their demands   13 besides many others   20 *omits* and peace   21 neighbour   30 painful in godlines: and to afflict the other, amidst al their great pleasure of sin! The   31 thinketh on   35 the good

arraygned of treasons, committed in forraine dominions
against his Soveraigne, could not be lyke merie in their
Inne upon the waye, as it seemeth to me: and thoughe
he that stoode in daunger should syng, or make shew
5   of courage and innocencie, and sett a good face upon
the matter: yet the other might well thinke that his hart
had manye a colde pull within hym: as no doubt but
all wicked men have, when they thinke with them selves,
of the lyfe to come. If Joseph and Pharaos baker had
10   knowen bothe their distinct lottes in prison: to witt, that
on suche a daye, one shoulde be called furth to be made   Gen.40.
lorde of Egypt, and the other to be hanged on a payre   41.43.
of newe gallowes: they coulde hardlie have bene equal-
lie merye, whiles they lyved together in tyme of their
15   imprisonment. The lyke may be sayed, and muche more
truelie, of vertuous and wicked men in this worlde. For
when the one doe but thinke upon the daye of deathe,
(which is to be the daye of their deliverance from this
prison:) their hartes can not but leape for verye joye,
20   considering what is to ensewe unto them after. But the
other are afflicted, and doe fall into Melancholie, as
often as mention or remembrance of deathe is offered:
for that they are sure, that it bringeth with yt theyr
bane, according as the scripture sayeth: *The wicked man*   Pro.11.
25   *being deade, there remayneth no more hope unto hym.*

     Well then (deare brother) yf all these thinges be so:
what should staye thee nowe at lengthe to make this
resolution, whiche I exhort thee unto? wilt thou yet saye
(notwithstanding all this) that the matter is hard, and
30   the waye unpleasant? or wilt thow beleeve other that
tell thee so, thoughe they know lesse of the matter than
thy selfe? beleeve rather the woorde and promisse of
Christ, whiche assureth thee the contrarie: Beleeve the   Mat.11.
reasons before alleaged, whiche doe prove it evydentlie:
35   Beleeve the testimonies of them whiche have experienced it in them selves: as of king David, S. Paul, S. John
Evangelist: whose testimonies I have alleaged before, of

---

12 paire of gallows   17 the one doth   21 and fal   26 brethren   35
testimony   36 and Saint John the Evangelist

their owne proofe: Beleeve manye hundredes, whiche by
the grace of God, are converted daylie in Christendome
from vicious lyfe, to perfect service of God: all whiche
doe protest, them selves to have fownde more, than I
5   have sayed, or can saye in this matter.

And for that thou mayest perhappes replye heere, and
saye, that suche men are not where thou art to geve
this testimonie of their experience: I can and doe assure
thee upon my conscience before God, that I have talked
10   with no small number of suche my selfe, to my singular comfort in beholding the strong hand and exceeding bountifullnesse of Gods sweetnes towardes them in
this case. Oh deare brother, no tongue can expresse
what I have seene herein: and yet sawe I not the least
15   parte of that whiche they felte. But yet this maye I saye,
that those which attend in the Catholique Churche, to
deale with soules in the holie sacrament of confession,
are in deede those, wherof the prophet sayeth, *that they*   Psa.107.
woorke in multitudes of waters, and doe see the marvailes of God
20   *in the depthe*: In the depthe (I saye) of mens consciences
uttered with infinite multitudes of teares, when God
toucheth the same with his holy grace. Beleeve me (good
reader,) for I speake in trueth before our Lord Jesus, I
have seene so great and exceeding consolations in divers
25   great synners after their conversion, as no harte can
almoste conceave: and the hartes which receaved them,
were hardlie able to contayne the same: so abundantlie
stylled downe that heavenlie dewe from the moste liberall and bowntefull hand of God. And that this may
30   not seme straunge unto thee: thou must knowe, that it   Vide
is recorded of one holy man called Effrem, that he had   pratum

---

3 life, to the tru service of God: 6 *omits* perhappes   7 [* where]
mn: B. *The soundlier that the Gospel is anywhere received, the mo
examples of sound conversion are there to be found: and yet on the
other side, it is not to be denied, but that a kind of remorse and
sorrowing (especially for the external, or grosser offences) is oft to
be found, not only among counterfet Christians but among the hea-
then also.   16 that those which are known to be skilful, and to deal
so sincerely withal, that others disburden their consciences unto them
for their comfort or counsel, are some part of those, wherof the
prophet   28 the heavenly dew

so marvailous great consolations after his conversion, as
he was often constrayned to crye owt to God: *O Lord retyre
thy hand from me a litle, for that my hart is not able to receave
so extreeme joye.* And the lyke is wrytten of S. Barnard:
5　whoe for a certayne tyme after his conversion from the
world, remayned as it were deprived of his senses, by
the excessive consolations he had from God.

　But yet, yf all this can not move thee, but that thou
wilt still remayne in thy distrust: heare the testimonie of
10　one, whome I am sure thou wilt not discredit, especiallie
speaking of his owne experience in him selfe: And this
is the holye martyr and doctor S. Cyprian, who writing of the verie same matter to a secret freend of hys
called Donatus, confesseth that he was before his con-
15　version, of the same opinion that thou art of: to witt,
that it was impossible for hym, to chaunge his maners,
and to fynde such comfort in a vertuous lyfe, as after
he dyd: being accustomed before to all kynde of loose
behaviour. Therfore he begynneth his narration to his
20　freend in this sort: *Accipe quod sentitur antequam discitur, &c.*
Take that, which is first felte before yt be learned: and
so foloweth on with a large discourse, sheweing that he
proved now by experience, which he coulde never beleeve
before his conversion, thoghe God had promised the
25　same. The lyke writeth S. Austen of him selfe in his
bookes of confession: shewing that his passions wold
needes persuade hym, before his conversion, that he
should never be able to abyde the austeritie of a vertuous lyfe, especiallie touching the sinnes of the flesh
30　(wherin he had lyved wantonlie, until that tyme:) it
seemed unpossible that he coulde ever abandon the same,
and lyve chaste: which notwithstanding he fownd bothe
easie, pleasant, and without all difficultye afterward. For
whiche he breaketh into these woordes, to God: my God
35　lett me remember and confesse thy mercyes towardes
me: lett my verie bones rejoyse and saye unto thee: *O
lord who is lyke unto thee?* thow hast broken my chaynes,

Marginal notes:
spirituale
S.patrum.

Gofr.in
vita Barn.

Li.ep.1.

Li.6.con-
fess.c.12.

Li.8.con-
fess.ca.1.

Psal.35.

---

8 but thou　20 *omits* &c.　21 is felt　32 chastly　32 he felt easie
33 without difficultie　34 *omits* to God

and I will sacrifice to thee a sacrifice of thankesgeving.   Psal.116.
These chaines were the chaines of concupiscence, wherby
he stoode bounden in captivitie before his conversion,
as he there confesseth: but presentlie thereupon he was
5   delyvered of the same, by the blessed helpe of Gods most
holye grace.

My counsaile should be therfore (gentle reader) that
seyng thou hast so manye testimonies, examples, reasons,
and promises of this matter: thow shouldest at least prove
10   once, by thyne owne experience, whether this thing
be true or no: especiallie seying it is a matter of so
great importance, and so worthie thy triall: that is, concerning so neare thy eternall salvation as it dothe. If a
meane felowe should come unto thee, and offer for haz-
15   arding of one crowne of golde to make thee a thowsand by Alchymie: thogh thou shouldest suspect hym
for a cousiner: yet the hope of gayne being so great:
and the adventure, of so small losse: thou woldest goe
nighe for once, to prove the matter. And how muche
20   more shouldest thow doe it in this case, where by proofe
thow canste leese nothinge: and if thow speede well,
thow mayest gayne as muche as the everlastinge joye of
heaven is woorthe?

But yet heere by the way I may not lett passe to   Resistance
25   admonishe thee of one thing, which the auncient fathers   at the
and saintes of God that have passed over this ryver   begyn-
before thee (I meane the ryver deviding betwene Gods   ning.
service and the world) doe affirme of their owne experience: and that is, that as soone as thow takest this
30   worke or resolution in hand, thow must expect great
encounters, strong impedimentes, sharpe contradictions,
and fearce temptations: thow must expect assaultes, combates, and open warre within thy selfe. This S. Cyprian,   Cyp.li.1.
S. Austen, S. Gregorie, and S. Barnard doe affirme uppon   ep.1.
35   their owne proofe. This doe Cyrill and Origen shew in   Aug.li.1.
divers places at large. This dothe S. Hillarie proove   doct.c.23.
bothe by reasons and examples. This dothe the scrip-   Greg. li.

---

5 from the same, by the help   32 expect assaults, combats, and
open war within thy selfe, as Saint Cyprian   36 proove by   37 the
wise man forewarn thee of, willing thee; *When thou art come to the service of God, to prepare thy mind unto temptation.*

ture it selfe forewarne thee of: sayeinge, *My sonne when thow art to come to the service of God, stand fast in justice and in feare, and prepare thy mynde unto temptation.* And the reason of this is, for that the devill possessing quietlie thy
5 soule before, laye still, and sought onelie meanes to content the same, by putting in new and new delites and pleasures of the fleshe. But when he seeth thow offerest to goe from hym: he begynneth streight to rage, and to move sedition within thee, and to tosse up and downe
10 bothe heaven and earthe, before he will leese his kyngdome in thy soule. This is evident by the example of hym whome Christ, coming downe from the hyll, after his transfiguration, delyvered from a deafe and dumme spirite. For albeyt this devill wolde seeme nether to heare
15 nor speake, while he possessed that bodye quietlie: yet when Christ commaunded hym to goe out: he bothe hearde and cryed out, and dyd so teare and rent that poore bodie, before he departed, as all the standers by thought it in deede to be deade. This also in figure was
20 shewed, by the storie of Laban, who never persecuted his sonne in law Jacob, untill he wolde depart from hym. And yet more was this expressed in the doeinges of Pharao, whoe after once he perceaved that the people of Israel meant to departe his kyngdome, never ceassed
25 greevouslie to afflict them (as Moyses testifieth) untill God had utterlie delyvered them out of his handes, with the ruyne and destruction of all their enemies. Whiche event all the holie doctors and saintes in Gods churche, have expounded to be a playn figure of the deliverie of
30 soules from the tyrannie of the devill.

And now yf thow woldest have a lyvelie example of all this that I have sayed before, I could alleage thee many: but for brevities sake, one onelie of S. Austens

Mor.4.c. 24. li.32.cap. 18.
Barn.in psa.90.
Cyr.li.de adorat.
Orig.ho.3. in Exo. & 9. in Levit. &11. in Josue.
Hill.in Psa.118.

Eccle.2.
Marc.9.

Gen.31.

Exod.5.

---

14 the devil   19 thought him   20 [* never] *mn*: B. *He was very greevous unto him before: but he did not follow after him in hostile maner til he departed from him.   24 depart from   26 God utterly   27 al Egypt their enemies. Which event the holie doctors and saints of the church   33 brevitie

conversion shall suffice, testified by hym selfe in his
bookes of confession. It is a marvailouse example, and
contayneth many most notable and comfortable poyntes.
And surelie whosoever shall but reade the whole at large,
5   especialie in his sixthe, seventh and eigth bookes of his
confessions, shall greatlie be moved and instructed therby.
And I beseeche the reader that understandeth the latine
tongue, to vewe over at leaste but certaine chapiters of
the eigthe booke, where this Saints finall conversion (after
10 infinit combates) is recounted. It were too longe to repeate
all heere, thoughe in deede it be suche matter, as no
man could ever be wearie to heare yt. There he sheweth,
how he was tossed and tombled in this conflict betweene
the fleshe and the spirite: betwene God draweing on
15 one side, and the worlde, the flesh, and the devill holding backe on the other parte. He went to Simplicianus
a learned olde man and devoute Christian: he went to
S. Ambrose byshope of Millane. And after his conference with them, he was more troubled than before. He
20 consulted with his companions Nebridius and Alipius:
but all wolde not ease hym. One daye after dynner there
came into his house, a Christian courtier and captaine
named Potinian: and finding by chaunce S. Paules epistles upon the boorde, where Austen and his felowes were
25 at playe: by occasion thereof fell into talke of spirituall

The con-
version of
S. Austen.

Li.8.con-
fess. c.1. &
2.

Cap.6.

---

3 [* notable] *mn*: B. *Yet some points of the storie at large are such,
as that a man may aswel dowt the readines of satan to illude and
deceive: as behold to our comfort the goodnes of God in his conversion.   12 man need to be wearie   13 troubled   14 on the one
side   21 *omits* One daye after dynner . . . and after Potinian was
departed, had a moste terrible combate with hym selfe; *substitutes* Til
at the length a Christian courtier and captain, named Pontition, had
by occasion told him and Alipius of the vertuous life that Saint
Anthonie led, who a little before had professed * a private and a
solitarie life in Egypt: as also others (he then heard) did even in
Millan it selfe, where then he was. Which when he had heard, then
with-drawing himselfe aside, he had a most terrible combat with
himselfe; *mn*: B. *This kind of monastical or private life was very
ancient, and such as the time and estate of the church required then:
but that which after in place therof sprang up among us, was of
later time, and being at the first far unlike to the other, the longer
it stood did notwithstanding stil degenerate more and more til at
the length it grew intollerable.

matters: and among other thinges, to recite unto them
the lyfe of S. Anthonie, the monke of Egypt, and the
infinite vertues and miracles of the same, whiche he had
founde in a booke among Christianes, a litle before, and
5   therby was hym selfe converted to Christianitie. Whiche
storie after Austen had heard: as also, that there was a
monasterie of those monkes, without the walles of Millan,
(in which Citie this happened) nourished by S. Ambrose,
the byshope, (wherof Austen before this, knew nothing:)
10   he was muche more afflicted than before: and after
Potinian was departed, withdraweing him selfe a side,
had a moste terrible combate with hym selfe: wherof he
writeth thus. What dyd I not say against my selfe in
this conflict? how dyd I beate and whyppe my owne
15   soule, to make her folow thee (o lord?) But she helde
backe: she refused, and excused her selfe: and when all
her argumentes were convicted, she remained trembling
and fearing as deathe to be restrayned from her loose
custome of sinne: wherby she consumed her selfe even
20   unto death. After this he went into a garden with Alipius,
his companion: and there cryed out unto hym. *Quid hoc
est? quid patimur? surgunt indocti & cælum rapiunt, & nos cum
doctrinis nostris, sine corde, ecce vbi volutamur in carne & sanguine.* What is this? (Alipius) what suffer we under the
25   tyrannie of synne? unlearned men (suche as Anthonie
and other) doe take heaven by violence: and we with
all our learninge, without hartes, beholde, how we lye
groveling in fleshe and bloode? And he goeth forwarde
in that place, sheweing the wounderfull and almoste
30   incredible tribulations that he had in this fight, that daie.
After this, he went further into an orcharde: and there
he had yet a greater conflict. For there, all his pleasures
past represented them selves before his eyes, saieng:
*Demittes ne nos, & a memento isto non erimus tecum vltra in
35   æternum? &c.* What, wilt thou departe from us? and shall
not we be with thee, no more for ever, after this moment?
shall it not be lawfull for the to doe *this* and *that,* no

A monas-
terie of
monkes
at Millan
before
S. Austens
time.

Cap.7.

Cap.8.

Marke
this gentle
reader.

---

26 and others; for he was altogither unlearned) do take   31 forth
35 shal we be   37 this or that

more hereafter? And then (sayeth S. Austen,) O Lorde, turne from the mynde of thy servant, to think of that, whiche they objected to my soule. What filthe, what shamefull pleasures dyd they lay before myne eyes? At

5 lengthe he sayethe that after long and tedyous combates   Cap.12. a marvailous tempest of weeping came upon him: and being not able to resist, he ranne awaye from Alipius, and cast hym selfe on the grounde under a figg tree, and gave full scope unto his eyes, whiche broght forthe

10 presentlye whole fluddes of teares. Whiche after they were a litle past over: he began to speake to God in   Li.8.c.12. this sort: *Et tu domine, vsquequo? quam diu? quam diu, cras, & cras? quare non modo? quare non hac hora finis est turpitudinis meæ?* O Lorde, how long wilt thou suffer me thus?

15 how long, how long, shall I saye to morow, to morow? why shoulde I not doe it now? whie should there not be an end of my filthie lyfe, even at this hower? And after this foloweth his finall and miraculous conversion, together with the conversion of Alipius, his companion:

20 which because it is sett downe breeflie by hym selfe: I will recite his owne woordes, which are, as foloweth immediatlie upon those that went before.

I dyd talke thus to God, and dyd weepe moste bitterlie, with a deepe contrition of my harte: and beholde,   S. Au-

25 I heard a voyce, as yf it had bene of a boye or mayde   stens singing from some house by, and often repeating, *take*   final con- *upp, and reade: take up and reade*: And streight wayes, I   version chaunging my countenance, beganne to think moste   by a earnestlye withe my selfe, whether children were wont   voyce

30 to sing any such thing, in any kinde of game that they   from used: but I could never remember, that I had heard any   heaven. such thing before. Wherfore repressing the force of my teares: I rose up, interpreting no other thing, but that this voyce came from heaven, to bydde me open the

35 booke that I had with me, (which was S. Paules epistles) and to reade the first chapiter that I should finde. For I had heard before of S. Anthonye, how he was

---

27 straightway I changed my countenance, and began   31 I never remember   33 rose, interpreting   37 afore

admonished to his conversion, by hearing a sentence of
the gospell, whiche was redde, when he by chaunce
came into the churche, and the sentence was: *Goe and*
sell all thou hast, and geve to the poore, and thou shalt have a
5   *treasure in heaven, and come and folowe me.* Which sayeing
S. Anthonie taking as spoken to hym in particular: was
presentlie converted to thee (o Lord.) Wherfore I went
in haste to the place where Alipius satt, for that I had
left my booke there when I departed. I snatched it up,
10   and opened it, and redde in silence the first chapiter
that offered it selfe unto my eyes: and therein were these
woordes: *Not in banquettinges, or in dronkennes: not in wan-*
tonnes, and chamber workes: not in contention and emulation: but
doe you put on our Lorde Jesus Christ: and doe you not performe
15   *the providence of fleshe, in concupiscences.*
Further than this sentence I wolde not reade: nether
was it needfull. For presentlie with the end of this sentence, as yf the light of securitie had bene poured into
my hart: all the darkenes of my doutfullness fledd away.
20   Where upon, putting in my finger, or some other signe,
(which now I remember not,) upon the place: I closed
the booke, and with a quiet countenance opened the
whole matter to Alipius. And he by this meanes, uttered
also that whiche now wroght in hym, (which I before
25   knew not:) he desired that he might see what I had
redde: and I shewed hym. He marked it all, and went
further also than I had redde. For it folowed in S. Paul,
(which I knew not) *take unto you hym, that is yet weake in*
faith. Whiche sayeing, Alipius applied unto hym selfe,
30   and opened his whole state of doutefulnes unto me. But
by this admonition of S. Paul, he was established, and
was joyned to me in my good purpose, but yet calmelie,

S. Antho-
nies con-
version.
Athanasius
in vita
Antonii.
Mat.19.

Rom.13.

Rom.14.

---

2 by occasion came   7 [* thee] *mn:* B. *In such things as are peculiar or proper to som (as this was) there can be no general rule drawn
unto others, that can stand by undowted warrant, without some special calling besides: and so may it wel be dowted, whether S. Anthonie
had on that place sufficient ground-work of those his doings, unlesse
he had som special motion besides. It was otherwise with Saint
Augustine, whose conversion was not, but to such things as we are
al bounden unto, and upon such a place as speaketh to al.   29 *omits*
sayeing

and without any troublesome cunctation, according to his nature and maners, wherby he differed alwayes greatlie from me, in the better parte.

After this we went in together, to my *mother: we
5   tell her the matter: she rejoyseth: we recite unto her the whole order of the thyng: she exulteth and triumpheth, and blesseth thee (o Lorde, whiche art more strong and liberall than we can aske or understand,) for that she sawe now, much more graunted to her from thee, touch-
10   ing me, than she was wont to aske with her pittifull and lamentable sighes. For thou haddest so converted me now to thee, that I nether soght for wyfe, nor any other hope at all, of this world: lyving and abyding in that *rule of fayeth, in which thou dyddest reveale me unto
15   her, so many yeres before. And so thou diddest turne her sorow now, into more abundant joye, than she could wishe: and into muche more deare and chaste joye, than shee could require, by my childeren, her nepheues, yf I had taken wyfe. O Lorde, I am thy servant, I am now
20   thy servant, and chylde of thy handmayde: thou hast broken my chaynes, and I will sacrifice to thee therfore, a sacrifice of prayse. Let my harte and tongue prayse the: and let my bones say to thee. *O Lorde, whoe is lyke unto thee?* Lett them saye it (o Lord,) and doe thou
25   answere, (I beseeche thee,) and saye to my soule: *I am thy salvation.* Hither to are S. Austens woordes.

In this marvailous example of this famous mans con-version, there be divers things to be noted, bothe for our comfort, and also for our instruction. First is to be
30   marked, the great conflict he had with his ghostelye ene-mye, before he could gett owt of his possession and dominion: which was so much the more (no dowt) for that he was to be so greate a pillar afterward in Godes churche. And we see, Alipius founde not so great resist-

*Her name was Monica, a verie holy woman as he sheweth. Li.9. c.9.10.11. 12.13.

*This was the reli-gious rule of monas-ticall lyfe whiche S. Austen after pro-fessed. Possid.in vita Augu.

Anno-tations upon this conver-sion.

---

4 *omits* in together   5 the order   14 [* rule] *mn, replacing Persons's:* B. *Which was but a more careful endevor in the way of godlines, such as was not used of the common sort. And so is this example of his, no patronage to any of our latter monasteries or rules, that were laden with loosenes and superstition: which notwithstanding som would gladly defend by this rule of his.   25 make answer   28 to be noted the

ance: for that the enemye sawe there was muche lesse
in hym, to hurt his kyngdome, than in Austen: which
ought greatlie to animate them, that feele great resistance, and strong temptations, against their vocation, assur-
5   ing them selves that this is a signe, of more grace and
favoure, yf they manfullye goe throughe. So was S. Paul
called (as we reade) moste violentlie, beyng striken downe
to the grounde, and made blynde by Christ, before his
conversion: for that he was a chosen vessell, to beare
10 Christes name unto the Gentyles.

Those that are to bee best men, have greatest conflicte in their conver-sion.
Act.9.

Secondlye is to be noted, that althoghe this man had
moste strong passions, before his conversion, and that
in the greatest, and moste incurable diseases, which commonlie afflict worldlye men: as in ambition, covetousnes,
15 and sinnes of the fleshe, (as hym selfe before confesseth:)
which maladies possessed hym so stronglie in deede, as
he thought it unpossible (before his conversion,) ever to
subdue and conquer the same: yet afterwarde, he proved
the contrarie, by the help of Gods omnipotent grace.

Li.6. c.6.
& 15.

20 Thyrdlye also is to be noted, that he had not onelie the
victorie over these passions, but also founde great sweetnes in the waye of vertuous lyfe. For a litle after his
conversion, he writeth thus: I could not be satisfied (o
Lorde) in those dayes, with the marvailous sweetnes
25 which thou gavest me. How muche dyd I weepe in thy
hymnes and canticles, being vehementlie stirred up with
the voyces of thy churche, singyng moste sweetlye? Those
voyces dyd runne into my eares, and thy trueth dyd
melt into my hart, and thence dyd boyle out an affection
30 of pyetie, and made teares to runne from me, and I
was in moste happie state with them.

Li.9.c.6.

Fourethlie is to be noted for our instruction and imitation, the behaviour of this man about his vocation.
First in searching and tryeing out the same, by his repaire
35 to S. Ambrose, Simplicianus, and others: by reading of
good bookes, frequenting of good companie, and the

S. Austens diligence in tryeing owt his vocation.

---

1 for the enemie   5 sign of grace   20 only a good victorie   25
[* thy hymns] *mn*: B. *When the people of God did sing their psalms
of thanksgiving and praises to God.   35 reading the word of God,
frequenting

lyke: whiche thou oughtest also (good reader) to doe
when thou feelest thy selfe inwardlie moved: and not to
lye dead, as manye are wont, resisting openlie the holye
ghoste, with all his good motions, and not so muche as
5   once to geve eare to the knocking of Christ at the doore   Apoc.3.
of their consciences. Moreover, S. Austen (as we see)
refused not the meanes to know his vocation, but prayed,
wept, and often retired hym selfe alone from companie
to talke with God, in that matter. Whiche many of us
10   will never doe: but rather doe detest and flye all meanes
that maye bringe us in to those cogitations of our conversion. Finallie, S. Austen, after he had once seene
clearelie the will and pleasure of God: made no more
staye of the matter, but bracke of stronglie from all the
15   worlde and vanities thereof: gave over his rhetorike
lecture at Millane: left all hope of promotion in the   Li.9.c.2.
court: and betooke hym selfe to serve God throughlie:
and therfore, no marvayle, yf he receaved so great consolation and advauncement from God afterward, as to
20   be so woorthye a member in his churche. Whiche example is to be folowed of all them that desire perfection, so farforth as eche mans condition and state of lyfe
permitteth.

And heere by this occasion I may not lett passe to   Violence
25   advertise thee (good reader) and also by S. Austens exam-   to be
ple to forewarne thee, that who soever meaneth to make   used at
this resolution throughlie, must use some violence at the   the begyn-
beginning. For as a fire, yf you rushe in upon it with   ning of
force, is easilie put out: but yf you deale softlie, putting   our con-
30   in one hand after an other, you may rather hurt your   version.
selfe than extinguishe the same: so is it with our pas-
sions, who require manhode and courage for a time, at
the beginning. Whiche whoe soever shall use (together
with the other meanes sett doune in the second booke
35   of this treatise:) he shall moste certaynelie fynde that
thinge easie, whiche now he thinketh heavie: and that

---

4 al good motions   8 oftentimes   21 desire to keep a good conscience, so far   33 use, togither with the other means therunto appertaining, he shal

moste sweete, which now he esteemeth so unsavorye.
For proofe wherof, as also for conclusion of this chapiter,
I will alleage a shorte discourse out of S. Barnard: whoe
after his fashion, proveth the same most fyttlie out of
5   the scriptures.

     Christ sayeth unto us: *take my yoke, you shall fynd rest.*
This is a marvailous noveltie, but that it cometh from
him *which maketh all things new.* He that taketh upp a
yoke, findeth rest: he that leaveth all, findeth a hundred
10 tymes so muche. He knew well this (I meane that man
according to the hart of God) whiche sayed in his psalme:
Dothe the seate of iniquitie cleave to thee (o lorde) whiche faignest
a laboure in thy commaundement? Is not this a faigned laboure
(deare bretheren) in a commaundement: I meane a light
15 burden, a sweete yoke, an anoynted crosse? So in olde
time he sayed to Abraham, *take thy sonne Isaac, whome*
thou lovest, and offer hym to me in sacrifice. This was a faigned
labour in a commaundement. For Isaac being offered,
he was not killed, but sanctified therby. Thou therfore,
20 if thou heare the voyce of God within thy hart, willing
thee to offer up Isaac (whiche signifieth joye or laughter): feare not to obey yt faithefullye, and constantlie:
what so ever thy corrupt affection judgeth of the matter, be thow secure: Not Isaac, but the Ramme shall
25 die for yt: Thy Joie shall not perishe, but thy stubburnes
onelie, whose hornes are entangled with thornes, and
can not be in thee, without the prickynges of anxietie.
Thy lorde dothe but tempt the, as he dyd Abraham, to
see what thow wilt doe. Isaac (that is thy joye in this
30 lyfe) shall not die, as thow imaginest, but shall lyve:
onelie he must be lyfted upp, uppon the wood, to the
end, thy joye may be on highe, and that thow maiest
glorie, not in thy owne fleshe, but onelie in the crosse
of thy lorde, by whome thy selfe also art crucified:

Bernard.
in verba
Euangelii:
ecce nos
reliquimus
omnia.

Psal.94.

Gen.22.

---

3 out of Barnard   4 same fitly   7 but it commeth   11 [* said] *mn:*
B. *The place being better considered, it doth not appeere that
David so said. Nevertheles, that which Barnard doth gather out of
it doth stand very wel with those words of Christ that therwithal he
allegeth of the light burden and easie yoke.   13 *commandements*   15
burden, an easie yoke   17 *unto me a sacrifice*

crucified, (I saye) but crucified to the world: for unto   Gall.2.
God thow lyvest still, and that muche more, than thow
diddest before.

Of the second impediment, whiche is persecution, affliction,
5   *and tribulation, wherby many men are kept from the*
service of God.

CHAP. II

Many there are in the worlde abrode who (ether upon
these considerations before layde doune: or for that, they
10 see some good men to lyve as merylye as them selves)
are content to yeeld this muche, that in verye deed they
esteeme vertuouse lyfe to be pleasant enough, to such
as are once entered in therunto: and that in good soothe,
for their owne partes, they could be content to folowe
15 the same, yf they might doe it wyth quiet and peace of
all handes. Mary to request them unto yt in such tyme
or place, or with such order and circumstances, as tribulation, affliction, or persecution may fall upon them, for
the same: they think it a matter unreasonable to be
20 demaunded, and them selves verie excusable, bothe before
God, and man, for refusing it. But this excuse is no
better, than the other goyng before, of the pretended
difficultie: for that it standeth upon a false ground, as
also uppon an unjust illation, made uppon that grounde.
25 The ground is this, that a man maye lyve vertuouslie,
and serve God truelie, with all worldlie ease, and without any affliction, tribulation, or persecution: whiche is
false. For that, albeit externall contradictions and persecutions be more in one tyme than in an other: more
30 in this place, than in that: yet can there not be any
time or place without some, bothe externall and internall. Which althoghe (as I have shewed before) in
respect of the manyfolde helpes and consolations sent
from God in counterpoyze of the same, they seeme not

---

11 thus much

heavye nor unpleasant unto the godlie: yet are they in
them selves bothe great and weightie, as wolde appeare
yf they fell upon the wicked and impatient. Secondlie,
the illation made upon this grounde, is unjust: for that
5   it alleageth tribulation, as a sufficient reason to abandone Gods service, whiche God hym selfe hathe ordained
for a meane to the contrary effect: that is, to draw men
therby unto his service. For better declaration wherof
(the matter beyng of verie great importance) I will han-
10 dle in this chapiter, these fower pointes. First, whether
it be ordinarie for all that must be saved, to suffer some
kynde of persecution, tribulation or affliction? that is,
whether this be appoynted an ordinarie meanes of mans
salvation in this lyfe or no? Secondlie, what are the
15 causes whie God (loving us as he dothe) wold chuse and
appoynt these meanes of our salvation? Thyrdlie, what
principall reasons of comfort, a man maye have in tribulation? Fowerthlie, what is required at his handes in that
state? Whiche fower pointes, being declared, I doubt not
20 but great light shall appeare in this whole matter, whiche
seemeth to fleshe and bloode to be so full of darkenes
and improbabilities.

And touching the first, there needeth litle proofe: for
that Christ hym selfe sayeth to his Disciples, and by
25 them to all other his servantes: *In mundo pressuram sustinebitis.*
In the world you shall sustayne affliction: And in an
other place: *In your patience shall you possesse your soules:*
That is, by suffering patientlie in adversities: which S. Paul
yet uttereth more playnelie when he sayeth: *All those that*
30 *will lyve godlie in Jesus Christ, shall suffer persecution.* Yf all,
then none can be excepted. And to signifie yet further
the necessitie of this matter, bothe Paul and Barnabas
also dyd teache (as S. Luke reporteth) *that we of necessi-*
tie must enter into the kingdome of God, by many tribulations:
35 using the woorde *oportet,* whiche signifieth a certaine
necessitie. And Christ him selfe yet more revealeth this

Fower
pointes
to be
handled
in this
chapiter.
1.
2.

3.

4.

1. Whe-
ther all
good men
must
suffer
tribulation
or no.
Joh.16.
Luc.21.
2.Ti.3.

Act.14.

---

12 *omits* that is whether this be appoynted an ordinarie meanes of
mans salvation in this lyfe or no?   15 so loving us   16 appoint so
to deale with us heer in this life. Thirdlie

secret, when he sayeth to S. John Evangelist, *that he*   Apo.3.
chastyneth all those whome he loveth: Whiche woordes S. Paul
as it were expounding to the hebrewes sayeth, *flagellat*   Heb.12.
omnem filium quem recipit. He whippeth every childe whome
5   he receaveth. And S. Paul urgeth this matter so farre
in that place, as he affirmeth playnlie all those to be
bastardes, and no children of God, whiche are not   Ver.8.
afflicted by hym in this lyfe. The same position he holdeth to Timothie: *Si sustinemus & conregnabimus.* Yf we   2.Ti.2.
10   suffer with Christ, we shall raigne with Christ, and no
otherwyse. Wherin also concurreth holye David, when he
sayeth, *Multæ tribulationes iustorum*: The just are appointed   Psa.34.
to many tribulations.

The same might be proved by many other meanes,
15   as by that Christ sayeth. *He came not to bringe peace, but*   Mat.10.
the sword into the woorld. Also by that S. Paul saieth. *That*   2.Tim.2.
no man can be crowned except he fight laufullie. But how can
we fight, yf we have no enemie to oppugne us? The
same signifieth Christ in the Apocalips, when he repeateth   C.2. & 3.
20   so often, that heaven is onelie for hym that conquereth.
The verie same is signified by the shyppe, where into   Matt.8.
Christ entered with his disciples, whiche was tossed and
tumbled, as yf it wolde have bene drouned: this (I saie)
by all the auncient fathers exposition, was a figure of
25   the troubles and afflictions, that all those shoulde suffer,
which doe rowe in the same shyppe with Christ our
saviour. The same also is proved by that, the lyfe of
man is called a warfare upon earthe: and by that, he   Job.7.
is appointed to labour and travayle, whyle he is heere: Job.5.
30   also by that, his lyfe is replenished with many miseries,   Job.13.
even by the appointement of God after mans fall. The
same also is shewed by that, that God hath appointed
every man to passe throughe the paynes of deathe, before
he come to joye: Also, by the infinite contradictions and
35   tribulations, bothe within and without, left unto man in
this lyfe: as for example, within, are the rebellions of
his concupiscen ce and other miseries of his mynde,
wherewith he hath continualie to make warre, yf he will

---

2 *chastiseth*   8 Saint Paul holdeth   24 by the ancient   26 *omits* shyppe

save his soule. Without, are the world, and the devil, whiche doe never cease to assault hym, nowe by fayre meanes, and now by foule: now by flatterie, and now by threates: now alluring by pleasure and promotion,

5 now terrifieinge by affliction and persecution: Against all which the good Christian hathe to resist manfullie, or els he leeseth the crowne of his eternall salvation.

The verie same also may be shewed by the examples of all the moste renowmed saintes, from the begyning: The example of saintes.

10 whoe were not onelie assaulted internallye withe the rebellyon of their owne fleshe: but also persecuted and afflicted outwardlye: therby to confirme more manyfest-lye this purpose of God. As we see in Abell, persecuted   Gene.4. and slayne by his owne brother, as sone as ever he

15 beganne to serve God: Also in Abraham, afflicted divers-   Gen.22. lye after he was once chosen by God: and moste of all by makyng hym yeeld to the kylling of his owne deare   Judit.8. and onelie child. Of the same cuppe dranke all his chil-dren and posteritie that succeded him, in Gods favour:

20 as Isaac, Iacob, Joseph, Moyses, and all the prophetes: of whiche Christ hym selfe geveth testimonie, how their   Ma.5.23. blood was shed most cruellye by the world. The affliction   Luc.13. also of Job is wounderfull, seing the scripture affirmeth   Job.1. it to have come upon hym by Gods speciall appoynt-

25 ment, he beyng a moste just man. But yet more wounder-ful was the affliction of holie Tobias, whoe among other   Tob.2. calamities, was strycken blynde by the falling doune of swallowes dung into his eyes: of whiche the Angell Raphael tolde hym afterwarde: *Because thou were a man*   Tob.12.

30 *gratefull to God, it was of necessitie that this tentation should prove thee.* Beholde the necessitie of afflictions to good men. I might adde to this, the example of David and others: but that S. Paul geveth a generall testimonie of all the saintes of the olde testament, sayeing: That some   Heb.11.

35 were racked, some reproched, some whipped, some chained, some imprisoned: other were stoned, cutt in peeces, tempted, and slayne with the swoorde: some went about in heare clothe, in skynnes of goates, in

---

4 threat   29 *wert a man acceptable*

great neede, pressed and afflicted: wandering and hyd-
ing them selves in wildernesses, in hilles, in caves, and
holes under grounde, the worlde not beynge woorthie
of them. Of all whiche he pronounceth this comfortable
5   sentence, to be noted of all men: *Non suscipientes redemp-*
tionem, ut meliorem inuenirent resurrectionem: That is, God
wolde not delyver them from these afflictions in this lyfe,
to the end their resurrection and rewarde in the lyfe to
come might be more glorious. And this of the saintes
10   of the olde testament.

But now in the new testament, founded expresselie
upon the crosse, the matter standeth much more playne,
and that with great reason. For yf Christ could not goe   Luc.24.
into his glorie, but by suffering, as the scripture sayeth:
15   then by the moste reasonable rule of Christ, affirming,   Mat.10.
that the servante hathe not privilege above his maister: It must   Luc.6.
nedes folowe, that all have to drinke of Christes cuppe,   Mat.10.
whiche are appointed to be partakers of his glorie. And
for proofe hereof, looke upon the dearest freendes that
20   ever Christ had in this life, and see whether they had
parte therof or no? Of his mother, old Simeon prophesied and tolde her at the beginning, *that the swoorde of*   Luc.2.
tribulations should passe her harte, signifieing therby, the
extreme afflictions that she felt afterward in the death
25   of her sonne, and other miseries heaped upon her. Of
the Apostles it is evident, that besyde all the laboures,
travailes, needes, sufferinges, persecutions and calamities, which were infinite, and in mans sight intolerable,
(yf we beleeve S. Paul recounting the same:) beside all   1.Cor.4.
30   this (I saye) God wold not be satisfied, except he had   2.Cor.4.
their blood also: and so wee see that he suffered none   6.11.12.
of them to dye naturallie, but onelye S. John by a spe-   Act.20.
ciall privilege by name graunted him frome Christ: albeyt   Rom.8.
yf we consider what John also suffered in so long a lyfe   Joh.21.
35   as he lyved, beynge banished by Domitian to Pathmos: Ter.li.de
and at an other tyme, thrust into a tonne of hoate oyle   prescrip.
at Rome (as Tertulian and S. Jerome doe reporte:) we   hereti.

---

11 expressedly   21 mother, Simeon   23 *tribulation*   32 *omits* by a
speciall privilege by name graunted him frome Christ

shall see that his parte was no lesse than others in this
cuppe of his maister. I might reckon up heere infinite
other examples: but it needeth not: for it may suffice,
that Christ hathe geven this generall rule in the new
5 testament: *He that taketh not up his crosse and foloweth me,*
is not woorthie of me. By which, is resolved playnelie, that
there is no salvation now to be had, but onelye for them
that take up (that is doe beare willinglie) theyr proper
crosses, and therwith doe folowe theyr captaine, walk-
10 ing on with his crosse on his shoulders before them.

But heere perhappes some man may saye: yf this be
so, that no man can be saved without a crosse: that is,
without affliction, and tribulation: how doe all those that
lyve in peacible tymes and places, where no persecution
15 is, no trouble, no affliction, or tribulation? To which I
answere, first, that yf there were anye such time or place:
the men lyving therein should be in great daunger,
according to the sayeing of the prophet, *they are not in*
the laboure of other men, nor yet whipped and punished as others
20 *are. And therfore pryde possessed them, and they were covered*
with iniquitie and impietie: and their iniquitie proceeded of their
fatnesse, or abundance. Beside this, thoghe men suffered
nothing in this lyfe, yet (as saint Austen largelye proveth:)
yf they dyed out of the state of mortall sinne: they might
25 be saved by suffering the purgyng fire in the next, according to the sayeing of Saint Paul: that such as build not
golde, or silver uppon the foundation, but woode, strawe,
or stuble: shall receave dammage thereof at the daye of
our Lorde, to be reveyled in fire: but yet by that fire
30 they shall be saved. Secondlie, I answer, that there is
no suche tyme and place so voyde of tribulation, but
that there is allwayes a crosse to be founde, for them
that will take yt up. For ether is there povertie, siknesse,
slaunder, enemitie, injurie, contradiction, or some lyke
35 affliction offered continually. For that, those men never
want in the world, wherof the prophet sayed: *These that*

Jerome.li.
contr.
Jouin.

Mat.10.

An objec-
tion
answered.

Psal.73.

In ps.37.
& de vera
& falsa
penitentia
c.18.

1.Cor.3.

Psal.38.

---

11 *omits* perhappes   22 *omits* Beside this, thoghe men suffered nothing in this lyfe . . . but yet by that fire they shall be saved.   31 time
or place

doe render evill for good, dyd detract from me, for that I folowed goodnesse. At the least wyse, there never want those domesticall enemyes, of which Christ speaketh: I meane, ether our kynred and carnall freends, whiche commonlie resist Mat.10.
5 us, yf we beginne once throughlie to serve God: or els our owne disordinate affections, whiche are the moste perylouse enemies of all: for that they make us warre upon oure owne grounde. Agayn, there never want the temptations of the world and devill: the resisting wherof
10 is muche more difficult in time of peace and wealthe, than in time of externall affliction and persecution: for that these enemies are stronger in flatterie, than in force: whiche a godly father expresseth by this parable. The sunne and wynde (sayeth he) agreed on a day to prove
15 their several strengthes in takinge a cloke from a wayefarynge man. And in the forenoone, the wynd used all violence that he could to blowe of the saide cloke: But the more he blewe, the more fast held the travailer his cloake, and gathered it more closely about hym. At after
20 noone the sunne sent foorthe her pleasant beames, and by litle and litle so entered into this man, as he caused hym to yeeld and put of, not onelye his cloke, but also his cote. Whereby ys proved (sayeth this father) that the allurementes of pleasure are more strong, and harder to
25 be resisted, than the violence of persecution. The lyke is shewed by the example of David, whoe resisted easilie manye assaults of adversitie: but yet fell daungerouslie in tyme of prosperitie. Wherby appearethe that vertuous men have no lesse warre in tyme of peace,
30 than in time of persecution: Nor ever wanteth there occasion of bearing the crosse, and suffering affliction, to hym that will accept of the same. And this may suffice for this first poynt, to prove that every man must enter into heaven by tribulation as S. Paul sayeth.
35   Touching the second, whye God wolde have this matter so: yt were sufficient to answere, that yt pleased hym best so, without seeking any further reason of his meaninge

Time of peace more daungerous than of persecution.

A parable.

2.Re.11.

2. The cause whye

23 is ment (saith   30 persecution: and that never there wanteth occasion   37 [* without] *mn:* B. *There was great reason in it, for

heerein: even as it pleased him, without all reason in our syght, to abase his sonne so much, as to send hym hyther into this world to suffer and dye for us. Or yf we will needes have a reason hereof: this one myght be
5   sufficient for all: that seynge we looke for so great a glorie as we doe: we should laboure a litle first for the same, and so shewe our selves woorthie of Gods favoure, and exaltation. But yet, for that yt hath pleased his divine majestie, not onelye to open unto us his will and
10 determination for our suffering in this lyfe: but also divers reasons of his moste holy purpose and pleasure therin, for our further encouragement and consolation which doe suffer: I will in this place repeate some of the same, for declaration of his exceeding great love, and father-
15 lie care towardes us.

God sendeth affliction to the godlie.

    The first cause then, and the most principall, is to encrease therby our merite and glorie in the lyfe to come. For having appointed by his eternall wisdome and justice, that none shall be crowned there, but according
20 to the measure of his fight in this world: the more and greater combates that he geveth (together with sufficient grace to overcome therin:) the greater crowne of glorie prepareth he for us at our resurrection. This cause toucheth S. Paul in the woordes before alleaged of the
25 saintes of the olde testament: to witt, that they receaved no redemption from their miseries in this world, to the end they might find a better resurrection in the world to come. This also meant Christ expresselie when he sayed: *Happie are they which suffer persecution, for theyrs is the*
30 *kyngdome of heaven: happie are you when men speake evell, and*

1. Increase of glorie.

2.Tim.2.
Apoc.2.

Heb.11.

Mat.5.

---

that seing man had sinned by man was the justice of God to be satisfied, which notwithstanding no man, but he alone, could do. Wherby it may seem, that although God hath given to this our Author a very good gift in persuading to godlines of life (for which we have to æsteem of him accordingly:) yet hath he not given him therwithal so ful a knowlege of the mysterie of our redemption in Christ. So it is lesse marvel, that he is in matters of controversie further to seek, than otherwise by his godly disposition, we may think that he should.   7 and so be made somwhat woorthy of Gods   17 *omits* merite and   19 but such as endure (in some good measure) a fight in this world: the more   26 no deliverance from

persecute you &c. Rejoyse and be glad (I saye,) for that your rewarde is greate in heaven. Hither also doe appertaine all those promyses: of *gayning lyfe by leesing lyfe*: of *receaving a hundred for one,* and the lyke. Heere hence do proceede
5   all those large promyses to virginitie, and chastitie: and to such as geld them selves for the kyndome of heaven: to voluntarie povertie, and to the renowncing of our owne will by obedience. All which are greate conflictes agaynst the fleshe, woorld, and our owne sensualitie, and
10 can not be performed but by sufferinges and affliction. Finally S. Paul declareth this matter fullie, when he sayeth: that *a litle and short tribulation in this lyfe worketh a weight of glorie above all measure in the hyght of heaven.*

The second cause why God appoynted this, is to draw
15 us therby from the love of the world, his professed ene-mye: as in the next chapter shalbe shewed at large. This cause S. Paul uttereth in these wordes: *We are punished of God, to the end we should not be damned with this world.* Even then, as a Nurse, that to weane her child from
20 the lykyng of her mylke, dothe anoynte her teat with Alloes, or some other suche bytter thing: so our mercy-full father, that wolde retire us from the love of world-lie delytes, whereby infinite men doe perish dayly, useth to send tribulation: whiche of all other thinges hathe
25 moste force to woorke that effect: as we see in the exam-ple of the prodigall sonne, whoe could by no meanes be stayed from his pleasures, but onelye by affliction.

Thirdlie, God useth tribulation as a most present and soveraigne medicine to heale us of many diseases, other-
30 wyse almoste incurable. As first of a certayne blynde-nes, and careles negligence in our estate, contracted by wealth and prosperitie. In whiche sense the scripture sayeth, that *affliction geveth understanding.* And the wyse man affirmeth, that *the rodde bryngeth wisdome.* This was shewed
35 in figure, when the sight of Tobie was restored by the bytter gaule of a fishe. And we have cleare examples in Nabuchadonasar, Saul, Antiochus, and Manasses: all-

Mat.10.
Mat.19.
Esa.56.
Mat.19.
1.Cor.7.
Psal.68.
Mat.19.
Luc.12.
Pro.21.
Luc.9.
2.Cor.4.
2. Hate of the world.

1.Co.11.

Luc.15.

3. A medi-cin to cure our diseases.

Eccl.18.

Pro.29.
Tob.11.

Dan.4.

---

3 promises to mortification, and newnes of life. In both which are great conflicts   34 *wisdom*: as also the sight

which came to see their owne faultes by tribulation,   2.Mac.9.
which they wolde never have done in tyme of prosper-   2.Paral.33.
itie. The lyke we read of the brethren of Joseph, whoe
falling into some affliction in Egypt, presentlie entered
5   into their owne conscience, and sayd: *We suffer these thinges*   Gen.42.
woorthely, for that we synned against our brother. And as tribulation bryngeth this light, whereby we see our owne
defectes: so helpeth yt greatlie to remove and cure the
same: wherin it may be well lykened unto the rodde of
10   Moyses. For as that rodde strikinge the harde rockes,
brought foorth water, as the scripture saieth: so, this   Exo.17.
rodde of affliction falling upon stonye harted synners   Deut.8.
mollyfyeth them to contrition, and often times bringeth   Psal.78.
foorthe the fluddes of teares to repentance. In respect
15   wherof, holy Tobye sayeth to God: *In tyme of tribulation*   Tob.3.
thou forgevest sinnes. And for lyke effect, it is compared
also to a fyle of yron which taketh away the rust of the
soule: Also to a purgation that driveth out corrupt   Job.23.
humours: And finallie to a golde smythes fyre which   Prov.17.
20   consumeth away the refuse metalls, and fineth the golde   Eccle.2.
to his perfection. *I will trye thee by fyre to the quick* (sayeth   Esa.1.
God to a sinner by Esay the prophet) *and I will take*
awaye all thy tynne, and refuse metall. And againe by Jeremie,   Jer.9.
I will melt them, and trye them by fire. This he meant of the
25   fyre of tribulation, whose propertie is (according as the
scripture saythe) to purge and fyne the soule, as fyre   Sap.3.
purgeth and fineth golde in the fornace. For besides the   Zach.13.
purgyng and removing of greater sinnes, by consideration, and contrition (which tribulation woorketh, as hathe
30   bene shewed:) it purgeth also the ruste of infinite evill
passions, appetites, and humours in man: as the humour
of pryde, of vayne glorie, of slouthe, of choler, of delicate nysenes, and a thousand more, whiche prosperitie
ingendereth in us. This God declareth by the prophet
35   Ezechiel, sayeing, of a rustie soule: put her naked upon   Ezec.24.
the hoote cooles, and let her heate there, untill her brasse
be melted from her, and untill her corruption be burned
owt, and her ruste consumed. There hathe bene muche

---

6 *sin*

labour and sweate taken abowt her, and yet her over
muche ruste is not gone owt of her. This also signifieth
holy Job, when having sayed, that *God instructeth a man*   Job.33.
by discipline (or correction) *to the end he may turne hym from*
5   *the thinges that he hath done, and deliver hym from pryde*: (whiche
is understoode of his synfull actes,) he addeth a litle
after, the maner of this purgation, sayeing, *his fleshe being*   Ver.25.
consumed by punishementes, let hym returne agayne to the dayes
of his youthe: That is, all his fleshlie humours and pas-
10   sions being now consumed by punishementes and tribulations, let hym begynne to lyve agayne in suche puritie
of soule, as he dyd at the begynning of his youthe, before
he had contracted these evill humours and diseases.

Nether onelie is tribulation a strong medicine to heale   4. A pre-
15   sinne: and to purge awaye the refuse metalles in us of   servative.
brasse, tynne, yron, lead, and drosse, as God by Ezechiel   Eze.22.
sayeth: but also a most excellent preservative against
sinne for the time to come: According as good kyng
David sayed, *thy discipline (o Lorde) hathe corrected me for ever-*   Psal.118.
20   *more*: That is, it hathe made me wary, and wachefull,
not to committ sinne agayne, according as the scripture
sayeth in an other place: *A grevous infirmitie or affliction*   Eccl.31.
maketh the soule sober: For whiche cause the prophet Jeremie
calleth tribulation, *virgam vigilantem*: A wachefull rodde: Jere.1.
25   that is, (as S. Jerome expoundeth it) a rodde that makith
a man wachefull. The same signified God, when he saied
by Ose the prophet: *I wil hedge in thy waye withe thornes*:   Ose.2.
That is, I will so close thy lyfe on everie side with the
remembrance and feare of affliction, that thou shalt not
30   dare to treade a-wrie, lest thou treade upon a thorne.   Psal.119.
All whiche good David expresseth of hym selfe in these
woordes: before I was humbled and broght lowe by
affliction, I did sinne and offend the (o Lord:) but after
that tyme, I have kept thy commaundementes.

35   Of this also appeareth an other cause, why God   5. A pre-
afflicteth his elect in this lyfe: and that is, to prevent his   vention of
justice upon them, in the worlde to come. I mean that   the pun-

---

35 *mn: A prevention of punishment*   37 *omits* I mean that Justice . . .
whereof I spake before

Justice, whiche other-wise remayneth to be executed upon every one after their departure hence in that moste grevous fire, whereof I spake before: touching which S. Barnard sayeth thus: *Oh wold to God some man wolde* *now beforehand, provide for my head abundance of waters, and* *to myne eyes a fountayne of teares: for so happely the burning* *fyre should take no holde, where running teares had clensed before.* And the reason of this is, (as that holy man hym selfe noteth after) for that God hathe sayd by Naum the prophet, *I have afflicted the once, and I will not afflicte thee* *agayne: there shall not come from me a double tribulation.*

Sixthelie, God sendeth tribulation upon his servantes, to prove them therby, whether they be fathefull and constant or no: That is, to make them selves and other men see and confesse, how faythefull or unfaythefull they are. This in figure was signified, when Isaac wold grope and touche his sonne Jacob, before he wolde blesse hym. And this the scripture expresseth playnelie, when talking of the tribulations layed upon Abraham, it addeth, *tentauit deus Abraham*: God tempted Abraham, by these meanes to prove hym. And Moyses sayed to the people of Israell: *Thou shalt remembre how thy God ledde thee* *fortie yeres about the desert to afflict thee, and tempt thee: to the* *end it might appeare what was in thy hart: whether thou wold-* *est keepe his commaundementes or no.* And agayne, a fewe chapiters after: *Your God and Lorde dothe tempt you, to the* *end it may be manifest whether you love him or no, with all your* *hart and with all your soule.* In whiche sense also, the scripture sayeth of Ezechias, after many prayses geven unto hym, *that God left hym for a tyme to be tempted, that the* *thoughtes of his hart might therby be made manyfeste.* And that this is Gods fashion towardes all good men, kyng David sheweth in the persone of all, when he sayeth, *Thou hast* *proved us (o lord) thou hast examined us by fyre: thou hast layed* *tribulation uppon our backes, and hast broght men upon our heades.* And yet how well he lyked of this matter, he signifieth, when he calleth for more therof in an other place:

ishement
in purga-
torie.

Ser.55.in
cantic.

Naum.1.

6. To
prove us.

Gen.27.

Gen.22.

Deut.8.

Deu.13.

2.Paral.32.

Psal.66.

---

16 This after a sort was figured, when Isaac

sayeing, *Trye me (o Lorde) and tempt me: burne my reynes and*   Psa.26.
hart within me. That is, trye me by the way of tribulation and persecution: searche out the secretes of my hart
and reynes: let the world see whether I will sticke to
5   thee in adversitie or no. Thus sayed that holie prophet,
well knoweing that whiche in an other place the holie
ghoste uttereth: that *as the fornace tryeth the potters vesselles,*   Eccl.27.
so tribulation tryeth men. For as the sounde vesselles onelie,
do holde when they come to the fornace, and those
10   whiche are crased doe breake in peeces: so in tyme of
tribulation and persecution, the vertuous onelie stand to
yt, and the counterfeit bewraye them selves: according
to the sayeing of Christ: *In tempore tentationis recedunt*: They   Luc.8.
departe from me in tyme of temptation.
15   The seventh reason, whye God layeth tribulation uppon   7. To
the vertuous is, therby to make them runne unto hym   make
for ayde and helpe: even as the mother, to make her   men
chyld more to love her, and to runne unto her, pro-   runne to
cureth the same to be made afearde and terrified by   God.
20   others. This, God expresseth playnelie by the prophet
Ose, sayeing of those that he loved: *I will draw them unto*   Ose.11.
me, in the ropes of Adam, in the chaynes of love, and will seeme
unto them as thoughe I raysed a yoke upon their jaw bones. By
the ropes of Adam, he meaneth affliction, wherby he
25   drewe Adam to knowe hym selfe: as also appeareth by
that he addethe of the heavy yoke of tribulation, whiche
he will laye upon the heades and faces of his servantes,
as chaynes of love, therby to draw them unto hym. This
chayne had drawen David unto hym when he sayed, *O*   Psal.32.
30   *lorde thow art my refuge from the tribulation of sinners.* As also
those wherof Esay sayeth, *they sought the out (o lorde) in*   Esa.26.
theyr affliction. Also those of whome David sayed, *Infirmities*
were multiplied upon them, and after that, they made haste to   Psal.16.
come. And God sayeth generallie of all good men: *They*   Ose.6.
35   *will ryse betimes in the morninge, and come to me in their tribu-*
lation. Wherfore holy kyng David desiring to doe certayne men good, and to wynne them to God, sayeth in   Psal.83.
one of his psalmes: *Fyll theyr faces (o lorde) with shame, and*
confusion, and then will they seek unto thy name. And this is
40   true (as I sayde) in the elect and chosen servantes of

God: but in the reprobate, this rope draweth not, this
yoke holdeth not, nor dothe this chayne of love wynne
them unto God: wherof God hym selfe complaineth,
sayeing, *In vayne have I strycken your children, for they have*   Jere.2.
5 *not receaved my discipline.* And agayne the prophet Jeremie
sayethe of them to God, *thow hast crushed them and they*   Jere.5.
have refused to receave thy discipline: they have hardened theyr
faces even as a rocke, and will not returne to thee. Beholde, they
have rent the yoke, and broken the chaynes.

10   Of this now enseueth an eigthe reason, why God   8. To
bringeth his servantes into affliction: to wytt, therby to   manifest
shew his power and love in delyvering them. For as in   Gods
this worlde a princelye mynde desireth nothing more,   power
than to have occasion wherby to shew his abilitie and   and love
15 good will unto his deare freend: so God which hathe   in deliver-
all occasions in his owne handes, and passeth all his   ing.
creatures together in greatnesse of love and nobilitie of
mynde, woorketh purposelye divers occasions and opor-
tunities, wherby to shew and exercise the same. So he
20 broght the three children into the burning fornace, therby
to shew his power and love in delivering them. So he
broght Daniel, into the lyons denne: Susanna, unto the   Dan.3.6.
point of death: Job, into extreeme miserie: Joseph, into   13.
prison: Tobye unto blyndenes: therby to shew his power   Job.1.2.
25 and love in their deliverance. For this cause also dyd   Gen.39.
Christ suffer the shyppe to be almoste drowned, before   Tob.2.11.
he would awake: and S. Peter to be almoste under water,   Matt.8.
before he wolde take hym by the hande.   Mat.14.

     And of this one reason, many other reasones and   9. The
30 moste comfortable causes doe appeare of Gods dealyng   joye of
heerein. As first, that we being delivered from our afflic-   deliver-
tions, might take more joye and delite thereof, than yf   ance.
we had never suffered the same. For as water is more
gratefull to the wayefayring man, after a long drythe:
35 and a calme more pleasant unto passingers after a troublesome tempest: so is our delyverie more sweet after
persecution or tribulation: according as the scripture
sayeth: *Speciosa misericordia dei in tempore tribulationis*: The   Eccle.35.

---

2 neither doth

mercie of God is beautyfull and pleasant in tyme of tribulation. This signified also Christ, when he sayed, *your*   Joh.16.
sorowe shalbe turned into joye: That is, you shall rejoyse, that
ever you were sorowfull. This had David proved when

5   he sayed, *thy rodde (o Lorde) and thy staffe have comforted me*:   Psal.23.
that is, I take great comfort that ever I was chastyned
with them. And agayne, *according to the multitude of my*   Psal.94.
sorowes, thy consolations have made joyfull my mynde: That is,
for every sorow that I receaved in tyme of affliction, I

10   receave now a consolation after my delyverance. And
agayn, in an other place, *I will exult and rejoyse in thy mer-*   Psal.31.
cye o Lord. And wherfore (good kyng) wilt thou so rejoyse?
yt foloweth immediatlie: *For that thou hast respected my abase-*
ment, and hast delyvered my soule from the necessitie wherin shee

15   *was, nor hast not left me in the handes of myne enemye*. This
then, is one most graciouse meaning of our lovyng and
mercifull father, in afflicting us for a tyme: to the end,
our joye may be the greater after our delyverance, as
no doubt but it was, in all those whome I have named

20   before, delivered by Gods mercie: I mean, Abraham,
Joseph, Daniel, Sidrach, Misach, and Abdenago, Susanna,
Job, Thobias, Peter and the rest: whoe tooke more
joye after their deliverance, than yf they had never bene
in affliction at all. When Judith had delyvered Bethulia,   Judith

25   and returned thyther with Holofernes heade: there was   6.14.15.
more hartie joye in that citie, than ever there wolde
have bene, yf it had not bene in distresse. When S. Peter   Act.12.
was delyvered out of prison by the Angel: there was
more joye for his deliverance in the churche, then coulde

30   have bene, yf he had never bene in prison at all.

     Out of this great joye resulteth an other effect of our   10.
tribulation, muche pleasant to God, and comfortable to   Thankes-
our selves: and that is, a moste hartie and earnest thankes   geving for
geving to God for our deliverance: suche as the prophet   our deliv-
                                                 erance.

35   used when he saied, after his deliverance: *I for my part*
will syng of thy strengthe, and will exalt thy mercie betymes in   Psal.59.
the morning, for that thou hast bene my ayder and refuge, in the
daye of my tribulation. Suche hartie thankes and prayse

---

6 chastised

dyd the children of Israel yeelde to God for their delyverance, when they were passed over the read sea, in that
notable song of theirs, whiche begynneth *Cantemus domino*: Exo.15.
And is regestred by Moyses in Exodus. From lyke har- 1.Re.2.
5 tie affect came also those songes of Anna, Debora, and Judic.5.
Judith, moved therunto by the remembrance of their Judi.16.
afflictions past. And finally, this is one of the cheefest
things that God esteemeth and desireth at our handes:
as he testifieth by the prophet, sayeing, *call upon me* Psal.50.
10 *in the daye of tribulation: I will deliver thee, and thou shalt*
honoure me.

Besides all these, God hathe yet further reasons of 11.
layeing persecution upon us: as for example: for that by Embold-
suffering, and perceyving in deede Gods assistance and dening us
in Gods
15 consolation therin, we come to be so hardie, bolde, and service.
constant in his service, as nothing afterwarde can dis-
maye us: even as Moyses, thoghe he were first a feard Exo.4.
of the serpent made of his rodd, and fledd awaye from
it: yet, after by Gods commandemente he had once
20 taken yt by the tayle, he feared it no more. This the Psal.46.
prophet David expresseth notablie, when he sayeth: God
hathe bene our refuge, and strengthe, and helper in our
great tribulations: and therfore we will not feare yf the
whole earthe should be troubled, and the mountaines
25 cast into the middest of the sea. What greater confidence
can be imagined than this?

Agayne, by persecution and affliction God bringeth 12. The
his children to the exercise and perfect possession of all exercise
the vertues belonging to a Christian man. As for exam- of all the
vertues.
30 ple, faythe is exercised in tyme of tribulation, in con- Faithe.
sidering the causes of Gods permission, and beleeving Hope.
moste assuredlie the promises he hathe made for our
deliverance. Hope is exercised in conceaving and assuring her selfe of the rewarde promised to them that suffer
35 patiently. Charitie is exercised, in considering the love Charitie.

---

28 *omits* and perfect possession; *continues* of many of those vertues
that do belong to a Christian man, and to enter into some reasonable
possession of them. As for example   31 Gods exercising of us, and
beleeving

of Christ suffering for us, and therby provoketh the
afflicted to suffer againe for hym. Obedience is exer-   Obedience
cised in conforming our willes to the will of Christ.   Patience.
Patience, in bearing quietlye. Humilitie, in abasing our   Humilitie.
5   selves in the sight of God. And so lykewise all other
vertues, belonging to a good Christian, are stirred upp,
exercised, confirmed, strengthened, and establyshed in
man by tribulation, according to the sayeing of S. Peter:
God shall make perfect, confirme, and establishe those, whiche have   1.Pet.5.
10   *suffered a litle for his name.*

Finallie, Gods meaning is by layeing persecution and   13. To
affliction upon us, to make us perfect Christians: that is   make us
lyke unto Christ our captaine, whome the prophet call-   lyke unto
eth *Virum dolorum, & scientem infirmitatem*: A man of sorowes,   Christ.
15   and one that had tasted of all maner of infirmities: therby   Esa.53.
to receave the more glorie at his returne to heaven, and
to make more glorious all those, that will take his parte
therin. To speake in one worde: God wolde make us
by tribulation *crucified Christians*: Whiche is the moste hon-   Crucified
20   orable title that can be geven unto a creature: crucified   Christians.
(I saye) and mortified to the vanities of this worlde: to
the fleshe: and to our owne concupiscence and carnall
desires: but quicke and full of all lyvelie spirit, to vertue,
godlines, and devotion. This is the heavenlie meaning
25   of our Soveraigne Lord and God, in sending us persecution, tribulation, and affliction: in respect whereof holie
Job dowteth not to saye: *Blessed is the man that is afflicted*   Job.5.
by God. And Christ hym selfe yet more expresselie: *Happie*   Matt.5.
are they which suffer persecution. Yf they are happie and
30   blessed therby: then is the worldlie greatlie a-wrie, whiche
so much abhorreth the sufferance therof: then is God
but unthankfullie dealt withal by many of his children,
whoe repyne at this happines bestowed upon them: where
as in deede they should accept it with joye and thankes
35   geving. For proofe and better declaration wherof, I will
enter now into the third pointe of this chapiter, to examine what reasones and causes there be to induce us to
this joyfullnes and contentation of tribulation.

2 again with him   7 *omits* exercised, confirmed, strengthened   30
then are the worldly greatly awry, which so much abhor the sufferance

And first, the reasones layed downe alredie of Gods mercifull and fatherlie meaning in sending us affliction, might be sufficient for this matter: That is, to comfort and content any Christian man or woman, who takethe
5   delite in Godes holie providence towardes them. For yf God doe send affliction unto us, for the encrease of our glorie in the lyfe to come: for draweing us from infection of the worlde: for opening our eyes, and curing our diseases: and for preserving our soules from synne here-
10   after: as hathe bene shewed: whoe can be justely displeased therwith, but suche as are enemies unto their owne good? We see that, for the obtaining of bodilie healthe, we are content, not onelie to admitt many bytter and unpleasant medicines: but also (yf neede require)
15   to yeeld willinglie some parte of our bloode to be taken from us. And how muche more shoulde we do this, for the eternall healthe and salvation of our soule? But now further, yf this medicine have so many more commodities besides, as have bene declared: yf it serve heere for
20   the punishement of our synnes, due otherwyse at an other place, in farre greater quantitie and rigour of justice: yf it make a triall of our estate, and doe drawe us to God: yf it procure Godes love towardes us: yeeld matter of joye by our delyverance: provoke us to thanke-
25   fullnes: embolden and strengthen us: and finally, if yt furnishe us with all vertues, and doe make us lyke to Christ hym selfe: then is there singular great cause, why we should take comfort and consolation therein: for that, to come neare and to be lyke unto Christ, is the great-
30   est dignitie and preeminence in the world. Lastlie, yf Gods eternall wisedome hathe so ordayned and appointed, that this shalbe the meanes of his servantes salvation: the badge and lyverie of his sonne: the hyghe waye to heaven under the standarde of his crosse: then oughte
35   we not to abhorre this meanes, not to refuse this lyverie: not to flye this waye: but rather, with good Peter and John to esteeme it a great dignitie to be made woorthie

3. The third parte of this chapter: whie tribulations should be receaved joifullie.

Act.5.

16 this, to the end that we hazard not the eternal   20 of our sin
32 *omits* the meanes of his servantes salvation   35 *omits* not to abhorre
this meenes   35 this liverie; nor to

of the most blessed participation therof. We see that to weare the colours of the prince, is thoght a prerogative among courtiers in this world: but to weare the robe or crowne yt selfe, were to great a dignitie for anye infe-

5   riour subiect, to receave. Yet Christ our lord and king is content to imparte bothe of his, with us. And how then ought we (I praye you) to accept therof?

And now (as I have sayd) these reasons might be sufficient to comfort and make joyfull all those that are

10   called to suffer affliction and tribulation. But yet there want not some more particular considerations besides. Wherof the first and moste principall is, that this matter of persecution cometh not by chaunce or casualtie, or by any certaine generall direction from higher pow-

15   ers: but by the speciall providence and peculiar disposition of God: as Christ shewethe at large in S. Mathews gospell: That is, this heavenlie medecine or potion is made unto us, by Gods owne hand in particulare. Whiche Christe signifiethe when he sayethe: *Shall I not drinke the*

20   *cuppe which my father hathe geven me?* That is, seing my father hath tempered a potion for me, shall I not drynke yt? as whoe would saye, it were too muche ingratitude. Secondlie is to be noted, that the verie same hand of God, whiche tempered the cuppe for Christ, his owne

25   sonne, hathe done the same also for us, according to Christ his sayeing: *You shall drynk of my cuppe.* That is, of the same cuppe whiche my father hathe tempered for me. Heerof it foloweth, that, with what hart and love God tempered this cuppe unto his owne sonne: with the

30   same he hathe tempered it also to us: that is, altogether for our good and his glorie. Thirdlie is to be noted, that this cuppe is tempered withe suche speciall care (as Christ sayeth) that, what trouble or daunger soever it seeme to woorke: yet shall not one heare of our head perishe

35   by the same. Nay further, is to be noted, that whiche the prophet sayeth, *O Lord thou shalt geve us to drynke in teares, in measure.* That is, the cuppe of teares and tribulation shall be so tempered in measure by our heaven-

Special Consi-derations, of com-fort in affliction.

Mat.10.

Joh.18.

Mar.10.

Luc.21.
Mat.10.
Psal.80.

---

14 any general

lie phisition, as no man shall have above his strengthe.
The dose of Aloes and other bitter ingredientes shalbe
qualified withe manna and sufficient sweetnes of heav-
enlie consolation. *God is faithefull* (saieth S. Paul) *and will*   1.Co.10.
5   *not suffer you to be tempted above your abilitie.* This is a singular point of comfort, and ought alwayes to be in our
remembrance.

Beside this, we must consider, that the appointing and
tempering of this cuppe, being now in the handes of
10   Christ our Saviour, by the full commission graunted hym
from his father: and he having learned by his owne   Mat.28.
sufferinges (as S. Paul notifieth) what it is to suffer, in   Heb.5.
flesh and blood: we may be sure that he will not laye
upon us more, than we can beare. For, as yf a man
15   had a father or brother, a moste skyllfull physition, and
should receave a purgation from them, tempered with
their owne handes, he might be sure it wolde never hurt
hym, what rombling soever it made in his belye, for the
time: so and muche more may we be assured of the
20   potion of tribulation ministred us, by the hand of Christ:
thoughe (as S. Paul sayeth) it seeme unto us unpleasant   Heb.12.
for a time. But above all other comfortable cogitations,
this is the greatest and moste comfortable, to consider,
that he divideth this cuppe onelie of love, as hym selfe
25   protesteth, and S. Paul proveth: that is, he geveth out
portions of his crosse (the richest Jewell that he maketh   Apoc.3.
accompt of) as worldlie princes doe their treasure, unto   Heb.12.
none, but unto chosen and pycked freendes: and among   Godes
them also, not equally to eche man, but to everie one   measure of
30   a measure, according to the measure of good will, wher-   tribulation
with he loveth hym. This is evident by the examples   goethe
before sett downe of his dearest freendes, moste of all   accordinge
afflicted in this lyfe: that is, they received greater por-   to the
tions of this treasure, for that his good will was greater   measure of
35   towardes them. This also may be seene manifestly in   his love.
the example of S. Paul: of whome after Christ had sayed
to Ananias, *vas electionis est mihi,* he is a chosen vessell   Act.9.
unto me: he geveth immediatelie the reason therof: *For*
I will shew unto hym, what great thinges he must suffer for my
40   *name.* Loe heere: for that he was a chosen vessell, therfore

he muste suffer great matters. Doth not the measure of
suffering goe then according to the measure of Gods
love unto us? Surely S. Peter knew well how the matter
went, and therfore he writeth thus: *Yf you living well, doe*   1.Pet.2.
5   *suffer with patience, this is a grace (or privilege) before God.* And
agayne a litle after: *Yf you suffer reproche in the name of*   1.Pet.4.
Christ, you are happie: for that the honoure and glorye, and power
of God, and of his holy spirit, shall rest upon you.

Can there be any greater rewarde promised, or anie
10   more excellent dignitie, than to be made partaker of the
honour, glorie, and power of Christ? Is it marvayle now
yf Christ sayed, *Happie are you when men revile and perse-*   Matt.5.
cute you? Is it marvaile thoughe he sayed, *gaudete in illa*   Luc.6.
die, & exultate, rejoyse and triumphe ye at that daye? Is
15   it marvaile, thoughe S. Paul sayde, I take greate pleas-   2.Co.12.
ure, and doe glorie in my infirmities or afflictions, in
my reproches, in my necessities, in my persecutions, in
my distresses for Christ? Is it mervaile yf Peter and John   Act.5.
being reproched and beaten at the Judgement seat of
20   the Jewes, went away rejoysing that they were esteemed
woorthie to suffer contumelie for the name of Jesus? Is
it mervaile thogh S. Paul accounted this suche a highe
privilege geven to the Philippiens when he sayed, *It is*   Philip.1.
geven to you, not onelie to beleeve in Christ, but also to suffer for
25   *hym, and to have the same combate, whiche you have seene in*
me, and now heare of me? All this is no marvaile (I saye,)
seing that suffering withe Christ, and bearing the crosse
with Christ, is as great a preferment in the court of
heaven, as yt should be in an earthlye courte, for the
30   prince to take of his owne garment, and to laye yt on
the backe of one of his servantes.

Of this now foloweth an other consequent of singu-   Tribula-
lar consolation, in time of affliction: and that is, that   tion a
tribulation (especiallie when grace is also geven to beare   signe of
predesti-
35   it patientlie) is a great conjecture of our predestination   nation.
to eternall lyfe. For, so muche doe all those argumentes
before touched insinuat, as also in the contrary part, to
lyve in continuall prosperitie, is a dreadfull signe of ever-

---

28 great preferment   35 *omits* our

lasting reprobation. This pointe is marvailouslie proved
by Saint Paul unto the hebrewes, and greatlie urged.　Heb.12.
And Christ geveth a playne signification in S. Luke,　Luc.6.
when he sayeth: *Happie are you that weepe now, for you shall*
5　*laughe.* And on the other side: *Woe unto you that laughe*
now, for you shall weepe: woe unto you riche men, which have
your consolation heere in this lyfe. And yet more vehementlie
than all this, dothe the sayeing of Abraham to the riche
man in hell, (or rather Christs woordes parabolicallye
10　attributted unto Abraham) confirme this matter: For he
sayeth to the riche man complayning of his torment:
Remember child, that thou receavedst good in thy lyfe tyme: He　Luc.16.
dothe not saye (as S. Barnard well noteth) *rapuisti*, thou
tookest them by violence: but *recepisti*, thou receavest
15　them. And yet, this now is objected against hym as wee
see. David handleth this matter in divers places, but pur-
poselie in two of his psalmes, and that at large. And　Psal.28.
after long searche, and muche admiration, his conclu-　& 144.
sion of wicked men prospered above other in the worlde
20　is this: *Veruntamen propter dolos posuisti eis, deiecisti eos dum*　Psal.73.
alleuarentur. Thow hast geven them prosperitie (o lorde)　ver.18.
to deceave them withall: and thou hast in deed throwen
them downe, by exalting them: That is, thow hast throwen
them downe to the sentence of damnation, in thy secrete
25　and inscrutable determination. Heere the comparison of　Com.in
S. Gregorie taketh place: that as the oxen appointed to　Job.
the slaughter, are lett runne afatting at their pleasure,
and the other kept under dailie labour of the yoke: so
fareth it with evill and good men. In lyke maner, the
30　tree that beareth no fruite, is never beaten (as wee see)
but onelie the fruitefull: and yet the other (as Christ

---

20 [* *propter*] mn: *In this they vary from S. Jerom, who translateth
(according to the Hebrew) *In lubrico posuisti eos*: that is thou hast set
them in slipperie places. So in this also the old translation followeth
not the hebrew nor Jerom, but the Greek translation of the Seventie
interpreters: saving that it doth omit *Kaca*, Mala: and so maketh the
sense obscure. But so much as therin it swerveth from the purity of
the text: so much doth that which heeron they build, want sufficient
warrant in this place, which notwithstanding (being soberly understood) is agreeable to the justice of God, and standeth by warrant
of other places. *In appendice Tom.8 Hie. in eodem psal.*

sayeth) is reserved for the fyre. The syck man that is   Mat.3.7.
past all hope of lyfe, is suffered by the phisition to have   Ep.Jud.
what so ever he lusteth after: But he whose health is
not dispaired, can not have that libertie graunted. To
5   conclude, the stones that must serve for the glorious   3.Re.6.
temple of Salomon, were hewed, beaten, and polyshed
without the churche, at the quarrie side: For that no
stroke of hammer might be heard within the temple.
S. Peter sayeth, that the vertuous are chosen stones, to   1.Pet.2.
10   be placed in the spirituall building of God in heaven,
where there is no beating, no sorow, no tribulation.   Apo.21.
Heere then must we be polyshed, hewed, and made fytt
for that glorious temple: heere (I say) in the quarrie of
this world: heere must we be fined, heere must we feele
15   the blowe of the hammer, and be moste gladde, when
we heare or feele the same: for that it is a signe of our
election, to that moste glorious howse of Godes eternall
mansion.

Beside this matter of predestination and election, there   Tribula-
20   is yet an other thing of no small comfort to the godlie   tion
afflicted, fownded on these woordes of God: *cum ipso*   bringeth
sum in tribulatione: I am withe hym in tribulation. Wherby the com-
is promised the companie of God hym selfe in afflic-   panie of
tion and persecution. This ys a singular motive (saythe   God him
25   S. Barnard) to styrre men up withall to embrace tribu-   selfe.
lation, seing in this world for good companie, men adven-   Psal.91.
ture to doe any thing. Joseph was carryed captive into   Gen.37.
Egypt, and God went downe with hym (as the scripture   Sap.10.
sayeth:) yea more than that, he went into the dongeon,
30   and was in chaynes with hym. Sidrach, Misac, and
Abdenago were cast into a burning fornace, and presentlie
there was a fowerth came to beare them compagnie, of
whome Nabuchodonasar sayeth thus: dyd we not put
three men onelie bounde into the fyre? And his ser-   Dan.3.
35   vantes answered: yea verilie. But beholde (sayeth he) I
see fower men unbounde walking in the myddest of the
fyre: and the shape of the fowerth is lyke the sonne of
God. Christ restored, as he passed by, a certaine beg-   Joh.9.
gar unto his sight, whiche hadd bene blynde from his   Note this
40   nativitie. For whiche thing, the man being called in ques- example.

tion, and speaking somewhat in the prayse of Christ, for
the benefit receaved, he was cast out of the synagoge
by the Pharasies: Whereof Christ hearing, sought hym
out presentlie, and conforting his harte, bestowed uppon
5   hym the light of mynde, muche more of importance
than that of the bodie geeven hym before. By this and
lyke examples, it appeareth, that a man is no sooner in
affliction and tribulation for justice sake, but streight
waye Christ is at hand to beare him companie: and yf
10 his eyes might be opened, as the eyes of Elizeus his dis-   4.Re.6.
ciple was, to see his companions, the troupes of Angells
(I meane) whiche attend upon their lord in this his vis-
itation: no doubt but his hart wolde greatlie be com-   The assis-
forted therwithe.   tance of
15 But that which the eye can not see, the soule feeleth: Godes
that is, she feeleth the assistance of Gods grace amyd-   grace in
dest the depthe of all tribulations. This he hathe promised   tribula-
agayne and agayn: this he hathe sworne: and this he   tion.
performeth moste faythfullye to all those that suffer meek-
20 lie for his name. This S. Paul most certaynlie assured
him selfe of, when he sayed, that he dyd glorie in all
his infirmities and tribulations, to the end, that Christ
his vertue might dwell in hym: that is, to the end that
Christ should assist hym more abundantlie with his grace:
25 *Cum enim infirmor, tunc potens sum*: For when I am in moste   2.Co.12.
infirmitie, then am I moste strong, saythe he: That is,
the more tribulations and afflictions are layed upon me,
the more potent is the ayde of Christs grace unto me.
And therfore the same Apostle writeth thus of all the
30 Apostles together: *We suffer tribulation in all things, but yet*   2.Co.4.
we are not distressed: we are brought into perplexities, but yet we
are not forsaken: we suffer persecution, but yet we are not aban-
doned: we are flong downe to the grounde, but yet we perishe not.
This then ought to be a moste sure and secure staffe in
35 the hand of all Christians afflicted, that, what soever
befall unto them: yet the grace of God will never fayle
to holde them up, and beare them owt therein: for moste
true and certaine is that sayeing of S. Austen, so often   Ser.88.de

---

28 the stronger is   37 for in this case most

repeated by hym in his woorkes: that God never for-
saketh anye man, except he be rejected and first forsaken by man.

   For the last reason of comfort in affliction, I will joyne
5 two thinges together, of great force and efficacie to this
matter. The first wherof, is the expectation of rewarde:
the other is the shortnes of tyme wherein we have to
suffer: bothe are touched by S. Paul in one sentence,
when he saythe, *that a litle, and momentarie tribulation in this*
10 *world, worketh an eternall weight of glorie in the hyghth of heaven.*
By *momentarie* he shewethe the litle time we have to suffer:
and by *eternall weight of glorie* he expresseth the greatnes
of the rewarde prepared in heaven for recompence of
that suffering. Christ also joynethe bothe these comfortes
15 together, when he sayethe: *Beholde I come quicklie, and my*
rewarde is with me. In that he promiseth to come quick-
lye, he signifiethe that our tribulation shall not endure
long: by that he bringethe his rewarde with hym, he
assureth us that he will not come emptie handed, but
20 redie furnished, to recompence our labour throughelie.
And what greater meanes of encouragement could he
use than this? If a man did beare a verie heavy burden: yet yf he were sure to be well payed for his labour,
and that he had but a litle waye to beare the same: he
25 wold strayne hym selfe greatlie, to goe throughe to his
wayes end, rather than for sparing so shorte a labour,
to leese so large and so present a rewarde. This is our
lordes most mercyfull dealing, to comfort us in our
affliction, and to animate us to holde out manfullie for
30 a time, thoghe the poyse seeme heavye on our shoulders: the comming of our Lord is even at hand, and
the judge is before the gates, who shall refreshe us, and
wype awaye all our teares, and place us in his kyngdome to reape joye without fayntinge. And then shall
35 we proove the sayeing of holye S. Paul to be true: *That*
the sufferinges of this world are not woorthie of that glorie which
shalbe revealed in us. And this may be sufficient for the
reasones left us of comforte in tribulation and affliction.

   And thus having declared the first three pointes prom-
40 ised in this chapiter: there remayneth onelie to saye a

temp. &
de nat. &
gr. ca.26.

2.Co.4.

Apo.22.

Jac.5.
Mat.11.
Apoc.7.21.
Gal.6.
Rom.8.

The
fowerthe

woorde or twoo of the fowerth: that is, what we have
to doe for our partes in time of persecution and affliction.
And this might be dispatched in sayeing onelie that we
have to conforme our selves to the will and meaning of
God, uttered before in the causes of tribulation. But yet
for more ease and better remembrance of the same, I
will breeflye runne over the principall pointes therof.
First then we have to aspire to that (yf we can) which
Christ counsaileth, *Gaudete & exultate*, rejoyse and triumphe: Or, yf we can not arryve to this perfection: yet
to doe as the Apostle willeth, *omne gaudium existimate cum
in varias tentationes incideritis*, esteeme it a matter woorthie
of all joye, when yee fall into divers temptations: that
is, yf we can not rejoyse at it in deede: yet to thincke
it a matter in yt selfe woorthye of rejoysement: repre-
hendinge our selves, for that we can not reache unto it.
And if we can not come thus the high waye nether, (as
in deede we ought to doe:) yet in anie case to remember, what in an other place he sayethe: *patientia vobis
necesssaria est, ut reportetis promissionem*: You must of necessitie have patience, yf you will receave Godes promisse
of everlasting lyfe.

Secondlie, we ought to doe as the Apostles dyd, when
they were in the moste terrible tempest of the sea (Christ
beinge wyth them, but a sleepe:) that is, we must goe
and awake hym: we must crye unto hym with the prophet:
Exurge, quare obdormis domine? O Lord arise, whye doest
thou sleepe in our miserie? This wakening of Christ
dothe please him wonderfullie, as hathe bene shewed:
but speciallie yf it be done, with that assured confidence
of true affectioned children, wherwithe S. Marke describeth the Apostles to have awakened Christ. For their
woordes were these: *Maister: dothe it not appertaine unto you
that we perish here?* As whoe wolde saye, are not we your
Disciples and servantes? are not you our Lorde and
Maister? is not the cause yours? is not all our trust and
hope in you? how chaunceth it then, that you sleepe

parte of
this
chapiter.

1. To
rejoyse in
tribulation
or at
leastwyse
to have
patience.

Luc.6.
Jac.1.

Heb.10.

2. To
come to
God by
fervent
prayer.
Mat.8.
Psal.44.

Marc.4.

---

13 *we fal*   17 thus high neither   29 *omits* as hathe bene shewed: but
speciallie

and suffer us to be thus tossed and tombled, as yf we
appertained nothing unto you? With this affection prayed
Esaye, when he sayed. Attend (o Lord) from heaven: Esa.63.
looke hither from the holie habitation of thy glorie: where
5   is thy zeale? where is thy fortitude? where is the multitude of thy mercifull bowelles? Have they shutt them
selves up nowe towardes me? thow art our father:
Abraham hathe not knowen us, and Israel hathe bene
ignorant of us: thow art our father (o lord) turne thy
10   selfe about for thy servantes sake, for love of the trybe
of thyne inheritance. Thus I say we must call upon God:
thus we must awaken hym, when he seemeth to sleepe
in our miseries, with earnest, with devoute, with continuall prayer: allwayes having in our mynde that moste
15   comfortable parable of Christ, wherin he sayeth, that yf   Luc.11.
we should come to our neighboures dore, and knocke
at mydnyght, to borowe some bread, when he were in
bedde with his children, and moste lothe to ryse: yet yf
we persever in asking, and beating at his dore still,
20   thoughe he were not our freend, yet woulde he ryse at
lengthe, and geeve us our demaunde, therby at least to
be rydde of our cryeing. And how much more will God
doe this (sayeth Christ) who bothe lovethe us, and ten-
derethe our case, moste mercyfullye?

25   But yet heere is one thing to be noted in this mat-   An
ter: and that is, that Christ suffered the shyppe almoste   important
to be covered with waves (as the Evangelist sayeth) before   note.
he wold awake, therby to signifie that the measure of   Matt.8.
temptationes is to be left onelie unto hym selfe: yt is
30   sufficient for us to rest upon the Apostles woordes: *He*   1.Co.10.
is faithfull, and therfore he will not suffer us to be tempted above
our strengthe. We may not examine or mistruste his doeyngs:
wee maye not inquire why doth he this? or why suffereth
he that? or how long will he permitt these evills to
35   raygne? God is a great God in all his doeyngs: and
when he sendeth tribulation, he sendeth a great deale
together, to the ende he maye shewe his great power,
in deliveringe us, and recompence it after, with greate

---

12 awake him   38 recompenseth it after, with as great

measure of comfort. His temptations often times doe goe
very deepe, therby to trye the verie hartes and reynes
of men. He went farre with Elias, when he caused hym
to flye into a mountaine, and there moste desirous of
5   deathe, to saye: *They have kylled all thy prophettes (o Lord)*   3.Re.19.
and I am left alone, and now they seek to kyll me also. He
went farre with David, when he made hym crie out:
why doest thou turne thy face away from me (o Lorde?)   Psal.44.
whye doest thou forget my povertie and tribulation? And
10 in an other place againe: I sayed withe my selfe in the   Psal.31.
excesse of my minde: I am cast out from the face of
thy eyes, o Lord. God went farre with the Apostles,
when he enforced one of them to wryte, we will not   2.Cor.1.
have you ignorant (brethren) of our tribulation in Asia,
15 wherein we were oppressed above all measure, and above
all strengthe: in so much as it lothed us to lyve any
longer. But yet above all others, he went furthest with
his owne deare sonne, when he constrayned hym to
utter those pityfull and moste lamentable woordes upon
20 the crosse: *My God, my God, why hast thou forsaken me?*   Mat.27.
Who can now complayne of any proofe or temptation   Psal.22.
what soever layd upon hym, seing God wolde goe so
farre with his owne deare onelie sonne?

Heereof then enseweth the thyrd thing necessarie unto   3. Mag-
25 us in tribulation: whiche is magnanimitie: grounded upon   nanimitie
a strong and invincible faithe of Gods assistance, and of   with a
our finall deliverance, how long soever he delay the mat-   stronge
ter, and how terrible soever the storme doe seeme for   faithe.
the tyme. This God requireth at our handes, as maye
30 be seene by the example of the disciples, whoe cried
not, *we perishe*, before the waves had covered the ship,
as S. Mathew writeth: and yet Christ sayed unto them,   Matt.8.
ubi est fides vestra? where is your faithe? S. Peter also was   Luc.8.
not a fearde untill he was almoste under water, as the
35 same Evangelist recordeth: and yet Christ reprehended
him sayeing, *thou man of litle faythe, why diddest thou doubte?*   Mat.14.
What then must we doe in this case, deare brother?
surelie we must putt on that magnanimous faithe of

---

23 deer and only   38 that mightie faith

valiant king David, whoe upon the moste assured trust
he had of Gods assistance, sayed: *In deo meo transgrediar*   Psal.18.
murum. In the helpe of my God I will goe throughe a
wall. Of which invincible faithe S. Paul was also, when
5   he sayed: *Omnia possum in eo qui me confortat*: I can doe   Phili.4.
all thinges in hym that comforteth and strengtheneth
me: Nothing is unpossible, nothing is to harde for me,
by his assistance. We must be (as the scripture sayeth)
quasi leo confidens absque terrore. Lyke a bolde and confident   Prov.28.
10   lion whiche is without terrour: that is, we must not be
astonyed at anye tempest, anye tribulation, anye adversitie: we must saye with the prophet David, experienced
in these matters: I will not feare many thousandes of   Psalm.3.
people that shoulde environe or beseyge me together. If   Psal.23.
15   I shoulde walke amyddest the shadowe of deathe, I will
not feare. If whole armies should stand agaynst me, yet   Psal.27.
my harte should not tremble. My hope is in God, and   Psal.56.
therfore I will not feare what man can doe unto me.
God is my ayder, and I will not feare what fleshe can   Psa.118.
20   doe unto me. God is my helper, and protector, and
therfore I will despise and contemne myne enemyes.
And an other prophet in lyke sense: *Beholde, God is my*   Esa.12.
savioure, and therfore will I deale confidentlie, and will not feare.
These were the speeches of holye prophettes: of men
25   that knew well what they sayed, and had often tasted
of affliction, them selves: and therfore coulde saye of their
owne experience, how infallible Gods assistance is therin.

To this supreme courage, magnanimitie, and Christian   Christian
fortitude, the scripture exhorteth us, when it sayeth: *Yf*   fortitude.
30   *the spirite of one that is in authoritie, doe ryse againste thee: see*   Eccl.10.
thou yeelde not from thy place unto hym. And agayn, an other   Eccle.4.
scripture saithe: strive for justice, even to the losse of
thy lyfe: and stand for equitie unto deathe it selfe: and
God shall overthrow thyne enemyes for thee. And Christ
35   hym selfe yet more effectuallie recommendeth this mat-   Luc.12.
ter in these woordes: I saye unto you my freendes, be
not a fearde of them which kyll the body, and afterwarde have nothing els to doe against you. And S. Peter

---

3 *the wal*

addeth further, *neque conturbemini*: That is, doe not onelie,   1.Pet.3.
not feare them, but (whiche is lesse) doe not so muche
as be troubled for all that fleshe and bloode can doe
agaynst you.

5   Christ goeth further in the Apocalyps, and useth marvailous speeches to entyse us to this fortitude. For these
are his woordes: he that hathe an eare to heare, let hym   Apoc.2.
heare what the spirit sayth unto the churches. To hym
that shall conquere, I will geve to eate of the tree of
10   lyfe, whiche is in the paradise of my God. This sayeth
the first and the last: he that was deade, and now is a
lyve: I know thy tribulation, and thy povertie: but thow
art riche in deede, and art blasphemed by those that
saye they are true Israelites, and are not: But are rather
15   the Sinagoge of Satan. Feare nothing of that whiche you
are to suffer: beholde, the devill wil cause some of you
to be thrust into prison, to the end you may be tempted:
and you shall have tribulation for *tenne dayes. But be   *Those
faythefull unto deathe, and I will geve the a crowne of   tenne
20   lyfe. He that hathe an eare to heare, lett hym heare   dayes
what the spirit sayeth unto the churches: he that shall   some
overcome, shall not be hurt by the second deathe. And   thinke to
he that shall overcome, and keepe my woorkes unto the   have
end: I will geve unto hym authoritie over nations, even   bene the
25   as I have receaved it from my father: and I will geve   tenne
him besides, the morning starre. He that shall overcome,   generall-
shalbe appareled in whyte garmentes: and I will not   persecu-
blott his name owt of the booke of lyfe, but will con-   tions,
fesse his name before my father, and before his Angels.   within the
30   Beholde, I come quickelie: holde fast that thow hast, lest   first 300
an other man receave thy crowne. He that shall con-   yeres
quere, I will make him a pillar in the temple of my   after
God, and he shall never goe foorthe more: and I will   Christ.
wryte upon hym the name of my God, and the name   Cap.3.

---

29 *mn* [*following Persons's mn*]: B. *But others rather think that ten
doth heer signifie many (as in some other places of scripture) and
dais, as they are broken of by the nights that come betwixt, so to
signifie such times of trial as shuld now and then have times of
breathing likewise; that so the faithful may be refeshed, and gather
their strength against a fresh assalt ensuing.

of the citie of my God, which is new Jerusalem. He that
shall conquer, I will geve unto him to sitt withe me in
my throne: even as I have conquered, and doe sitt with
my father in his throne.

5   Hitherto are the woordes of Christ to S. John. And
in the end of the same book, after he had described the
joyes and glorie of heaven at large, he concludeth thus.
And he that satte on the throne sayde to me. Wryte
these woordes, for that they are moste faythfull and true.

10   *Qui vicerit possidebit hæc, & ero illi deus, & ille erit mihi filius:*   Cap.21.
timidis autem & incredulis &c. pars illorum erit in stagno ardenti,
igne & sulphure, quod est mors secunda. He that shall conquer, shall possesse all the joyes that I have heere spoken of: and I will be his God, and he shall be my sonne.

15   But they whiche shalbe fearfull to fight, or incredulous
of these thinges that I have sayed: theyr portion shall
be in the lake burning withe fire and brymstone, which
is the second deathe.

Heere now we see bothe allurement and threates:
20   good and evill: lyfe and deathe, the Joyes of heaven,   Eccl.15.
and the burning lake, proposed unto us. We maye
streache owte our handes unto whiche we will. Yf we
fight and conquer (as by Gods grace we maye) then are
we to enjoye the promises layd downe before. Yf we
25   shew our selves ether unbeleeving in these promises, or
fearefull to take the fyght in hande, being offered unto
us: then fall we into the daunger of the contrarie threates:
even as S. John affirmeth, in an other place, that certayne noble men dyd, among the Jewes, whoe beleeved
30   in Christ, but yet durst not confesse hym, for feare of   Joh.12.
persecution.

Heere then must ensewe an other vertue in us, moste   A firme
necessarie, to all tribulation and affliction, and that is,   resolution.
a strong and firme resolution, to stand and go throughe,
35   what opposition or contradiction soever we fynde in the
world, ether of fawning flatterie, or persecuting crueltie.
This the scripture teacheth, cryeing unto us, *esto firmus*   1.Co.15.
in via domini: Be firme and immovable in the waye of

---

19 allurements   33 al those that are to suffer tribulation

our lord. And agayne, *State in fide: viriliter agite*: Stand to 1.Co.16.
your faythe, and play you the men. And yet further,
confide in deo, & mane in loco tuo: Trust in God, and abyde Eccl.11.
firme in thy place. And finalie, *confortamini & non dis-* 2.Par.15.
5 *soluantur manus vestræ*. Take courage unto you, and let not
your handes be dissolved from the worke you have
begonne.

This resolution had the three children Sydrach, Misach,
and Abdenago, when having heard the flattering speeche,
10 and infinite threates of cruell Nabuchodonasar, they
answered with a quiet spirit. O kyng: wee may not answere you, to this long speeche of youres. For beholde Dan.3.
our God is able (yf he will) to delyver us from this furnace of fyre, whiche you threaten, and from all that you
15 can doe otherwyse against us. But yet yf it should not
please hym so to doe: yet you muste know (Syr king)
that we doe not woorshippe your goddes, nor yet adore
your golden ydole, whiche you have sett up.

This resolution had Peter and John, who being so
20 often broght before the councell, and bothe commaunded,
threatened, and beaten, to talke no more of Christ: answered styll: *Obedire oportet deo magis quam hominibus*, we Act.4.5.
muste obey God, rather than men. The same had S. Paul
also, when being requested with teares of the Christianes Act.21.
25 in Cesarea, that he wolde forbeare to goe to Jerusalem,
for that the holie ghoste had revealed to manye the troubles whiche expected hym there: he answered, what
mean you to weepe thus, and to afflict my hart? I am
not onelie readie to be in bondes for Christs name in
30 Jerusalem: but also to suffer deathe for the same. And
in his epistle to the Romanes, he yet further expresseth Rom.8.
this resolution of his, when he sayeth: what then shall
we saye to these thinges? yf God be with us, whoe will
be against us? who shall separate us from the love of
35 Christ? shall tribulation? shall distresse? shall hungar?
shall nakednes? shall perill? shall persecution? shall the
swoorde? I am certaine that nether deathe, nor lyfe,
nor Angels, nor principalities, nor powers, nor things

---

11 *we may not be careful to answer you,*

present, nor things to come, nor strengthe, nor hyghthe, nor depthe, nor any creature els, shalbe able to separate us from the love of God, whiche is in Jesus Christ, our Lord.

5   Finallye, this was the resolution of all the holye martyres and confessors, and other servantes of God: wherby they have withstoode the temptations of the devill, the allurementes of fleshe and bloode, and all the persecutions of tyrantes, exacting things unlaufull at their handes.

10   I will alleage one example more owte of the scripture, and that before the comming of Christ, but yet nighe unto the same, and therfore no marvaylle (as the fathers doe note) thoghe it tooke some heate of Christian fervour and constancie towardes martyrdome. The example is wounderfull, for that in mannes sight it was but

15   for a small matter required at their handes, by the tyrantes commaundement: that is, onelie to eate a peece of swynes fleshe: for thus it is recorded in the scripture.

It happened seven brethren to be apprehended together   2.Mac.7.

20   in those dayes, and to be broght (with their mother) to   A mar-
the kyng Antiochus, and there to be compelled with tor-   vailous
mentes of whipping, and other instrumentes, to the eat-   constancie
ing of swynes flesh against the law. At what tyme one   of the
of them, (whiche was the eldest) sayde: what doest thou   seven

25   seke? or what wilt thou learne oute of us o king? we   Macha-
are readie heere rather to dye, than to breake the aun-   bees and
cient lawes of our God. Wherat the king being greatlie   their
offended, commaunded the fryeing pannes and pottes of   mother.
brasse to be made burning hote: whiche being redie, he

30   caused this first mannes tongue to be cutt of, with the toppes of his fingers, and toes, as also with the skynne of his head, the mother and other brothers looking on,

---

10 out of the *second book of Maccabes, and that; *mn*: B. *Which book is not any part of canonical scripture: nevertheles this example may wel be tru, for that such constancie is often found in the children of God.   16 [* smal] *mn*: B. *It was a manifest breach of the law of God: and so no smal matter to them that knew it.   18 flesh, which then was forbidden. For thus it is recorded in the book aforesaid.   19 It came to passe that seven brethren were apprehended togither in those dais, and brought (with their mother) to the king Antiochus, and there compelled

and after that to be fried untill he was dead. Whiche
being done, the second brother was brought to torment,
and after his heare pluckt of from his head, together
withe the skynne, they asked hym whether he wolde yet
5   eate swynes fleshe or no, before he was put to the rest
of his tormentes? wherto he answered, Noe: and therupon
was (after many tormentes) slayne with the other. Who
being deade the third was taken in hand, and being
willed to putt forthe his tongue: he helde it foorthe quick-
10 lye together withe bothe his handes, to be cut of, sayeing
confidentlie: *I receaved bothe tongue and handes from heaven,*   A worthie
and now I despyse them bothe for the lawe of God, for that   sayeing.
I hope to receave them all of hym agayne. And after they
had in this sorte tormented and putt to deathe syx of
15 the brethren, everie one moste constantlie protesting his
faythe, and the joye he had to dye for Gods cause: there
remayned onelie the yongest, whome Antiochus (being
ashamed that he coulde pervert never a one of the former) endevoured by all meanes possible to drawe from
20 his purpose, by promising and swearing, that he should
be a riche and happie man, and one of his cheefe freendes, yf he wold yeelde. But when the youthe was nothing moved therwith: Antiochus called to hym the mother,
and exhorted her to save her sonnes lyfe, by persuad-
25 ing hym to yeeld: whiche she faigning to doe, therby to
have libertie to speake to her sonne: made a most vehement exhortation to hym in the hebrew tongue, to stand
to yt, and to dye for his conscience: whiche speeche
being ended, the youthe cryed owt with a lowde voyce,
30 and uttered this noble sentence woorthie to be remembred: *Quem sustinetis? non obtempero præcepto regis, sed præ-*
cepto legis: Whome doe you staye for? I doe not obey
the commaundement of the kyng, but the commaunde-
mente of the lawe of God. Where uppon both he and
35 his mother were presentlie (after many and sundrye tormentes) putt to deathe.

    This then is the constant and immovable resolution
whiche a Christian man should have in all adversitie of
this lyfe. Wherof S. Ambrose sayeth thus. *Gratia præparan-*   Li.1.offi.
40 *dus est animus, exercenda mens, & stabilienda ad constantiam:*   c.38.

ut nullis perturbari animus possit terroribus, nullis frangi molestiis,
nullis suppliciis cedere. Our mynde is to be prepared with
grace, to be exercised, and to be so established in constancie, as it may not be troubled withe anye terrours,
5   broken with any adversities, yeeld to anye punishementes
or tormentes what soever.

If you aske me heere how a man may come to this
resolution: I answere, that S. Ambrose in the same place,
puttethe two wayes: the one is to remember the endles
10 and intolerable paynes of hell, yf we doe yt not: and
the other is to think of the unspeakable glorie of heaven,
yf we doe yt. Whereto I will adde the thirde, whiche
with a noble hart, may perhappes prevayle, as much as
ether of them bothe: and that is, to consider what others
15 have suffered before us, especiallie Christ hym selfe, and
that onelie of meere love and affection towardes us. We
see that in this worlde, lovyng subiectes doe glorie of
nothing more, than of their daungers or hurtes taken
in battaile for their prince, thoghe he never tooke
20 blowe for them agayne. What then wolde they doe, yf
their prince had bene afflicted voluntarilie for them, as
Christ hathe bene for us? But yf this great example of
Christ seeme unto thee to highe for to imitate: looke
upon some of thy brethren before thee, made of flesh
25 and bloode as thou art: see what they have suffered
before they coulde enter into heaven: and thinke not
thy selfe hardlye dealt withall, yf thou be called to suffer
a litle also.

Saint Paul writeth of all the Apostles together: even
30 unto this hower we suffer hungar and thirst, and lacke
of apparell: we are beaten with mennes fistes: we are
vagabondes, not having where to staye: we laboure and
woorke with our owne handes: we are cursed, and we
doe blesse: we are persecuted, and we take it patientlie:
35 we are blasphemed, and we praye for them that blaspheme us: we are made as it were the verie owte castes
and purginges of this worlde even unto this daye: That
is, thoghe we be Apostles, thoghe we have wroght so

Marginal notes:

How a
man may
come to
an invin-
cible
resolution.

1.Cor.4.
The
sufferinges
of the
Apostles.

---

7 ask heer   13 *omits* perhappes

manye miracles, and converted so manye milions of people: yet even unto this daye are we thus used. And a
litle after, describing yet further their lives, he sayeth: 2.Cor.6.
we shew our selves as the ministers of God, in muche
5   patience, in tribulations, in necessities, in distresses, in
beatinges, in imprisonmentes, in seditions, in laboures,
in waches, in fastinges, in chastitie, in longanimitie, in   2.Co.11.
sweetenes of behaviour. And of hym selfe in particular   The par-
he sayeth, *In laboribus plurimis, &c.* I am the minister of   ticular
10 God in many laboures, in imprisonmentes more than   sufferinges
the rest, in beatinges above measure, and oftentymes in   of S. Paul.
deathe it selfe. Fyve tymes have I bene beaten of the
Jewes, and at every tyme had fortye lashes lacking one:
three tymes have I bene whipt with roddes: once I was
15 stoned: three times have I suffered shipwrake: A daye
and a nyght was I in the bottome of the sea: oftentymes
in journeyes, in daungers of fluddes: in daungers of
theeves: in daungers of Jewes: in daungers of Gentyles:
in daungers of the citie: in daungers of wildernes: in
20 daungers of sea: in daungers of false bretheren: in labour
and travayle: in muche waching: in hungar and thyrst:
in muche fasting: in colde and lack of clothes: and besyde
all these externall thinges, the matters that daylie doe
depend upon me, for my universall care of all churches.
25   By this we may see now whether the Apostles taught
us more by woordes, than they shewed by example,
aboute the necessitie of suffering in this lyfe. Christ might
have provyded for them yf he wolde, at least wyse thinges
necessarie to their bodies, and not have suffered them
30 to come into these extremities of lacking clothes to their
backes: meate to their mouthes, and the lyke. He that
gave them authoritie to doe so manie other miracles,
might have suffered them at least to have wroght sufficient
maintenance for theyr bodyes, whiche should be the first
35 miracle that worldlie men would woorke, yf they had
suche authoritie. Christ myght have sayed to Peter when   Mat.17.
he sent hym to take his tribute from owte of the fyshes
mouthe: take so muche more, as will suffice your necessarie expences, as you travayle the countrie: But he
40 wolde not, nor yet diminishe the great afflictions whiche

I have shewed before, thoughe he loved them as deare-
lie, as ever he loved hys owne sowle. All whiche was
done, (as S. Peter interpreteth) to geve us example, what   1.Pet.2.
to folowe, what to looke for, what to desire, what to
5   comfort our selves in, amyddest the greatest of all our
tribulations.

Saint Paul useth this, as a principall consideration,   Heb.12.
when he writeth thus to the hebrewes, uppon the recitall
of the sufferinges of other saintes before them: wherfore
10   we also (bretheren) having so great a multitude of wit-   A notable
nesses (that have suffered before us,) lett us laye of all   exhorta-
burdens of sinne hanging upon us: and lett us runne by   tion of
patience unto the battaile offered us, fyxing our eyes   S. Paul.
upon the authour of our faith, and fulfiller of the same,
15   *Jesus*, who putting the joyes of heaven before his eyes,
sustayned patientlie the crosse, contemning the shame
and confusion therof, and therfore now sitteth at the
right hand of the seate of God. Thinke upon hym (I
saye) which sustayned suche a contradiction against hym
20   selfe, at the handes of sinners: and be not wearie, nor
fainte not in courage. For you have not yet resisted
against sinne unto bloode: and you have forgotten (perhapps) that comfortable sayeing, whiche speaketh unto
you as unto children: *My sonne, doe not contemne the disci-*   Prov.3.
25   *pline of our Lorde, and be not wearie when thou art chastened*   Job.5.
of hym. For whome God loveth he chasteneth, and he   Apoc.3.
whippeth every sonne whome he receavethe. Persever
therefore in the correction layed upon you. God offerethe
hym selfe to you as to his children. For what childe is
30   there whome the father correcteth not? Yf you be out of
correction, wherof all his children are made partakers:
then are you bastardes, and not children. All correction, for the present time when it is suffered, seemeth unpleasant and sorowfull: but yet after, it bringeth foorthe
35   most quiet fruite of justice, unto them that are exercised
by yt. Wherfore strengthen upp your wearie handes, and
loosed knees: make waye to your feete: &c. That is, take

---

5 our selves withal, in amidst the greatest of our tribulations   20
nor faint in   22 and it seemeth you have forgotten that

courage unto you, and goe forwarde valiantlye under
the crosse laied upon you. This was the exhortation of
this holie captayne unto his countrie men, souldyers of
Jesus Christ, the Jewes.

5   Saint James the brother of our Lorde useth an other
exhortation in his Catholike epistle, to all Catholikes, not
muche different from this. Be you therfore patient my
brethren (saythe he) untill the comming of our lord. Beholde, the husbandman expecteth for a time, the fruite
10   of the earthe, so pretious unto hym, bearing patientlie
untill he may receave the same in his season: be you
therfore patient, and comfort your hartes, for that the
commyng of our lorde will shortlie draw neere. Be not
sadde, and complayne not one of an other. Beholde the
15   Judge is even at the gate. Take the prophetes for an
example of labour and patience, whiche spake unto us
in the name of God. Beholde, we account them blessed
which have suffered. You have hearde of the sufferance
of Job, and you have seen the end of our lord withe
20   him: you have seen (I saye) that our lord is mercifull
and full of compassion.

I might heere alleage many thinges more owt of the
scripture to this purpose, for that the scripture is moste
copious heerin: and in verie deed, yf it should all be
25   melted and poured owt, yt wolde yeelde us nothing els
almoste, but touching the crosse, and patient bearing of
tribulation in this lyfe. But I must end, for that this
chapiter ryseth to be long, as the other before dyd: And
therfore I will onelye, for my conclusion, sett downe
30   the confession, and moste excellent exhortation of olde
Mathathias, in the tyme of the cruell persecution of
Antiochus against the Jewes. The storie is thus reported
in the scripture.

At that tyme the officers of Antiochus sayd unto
35   Mathathias: thow art a prince, and of greatest estate in

Jac.5.
The
exhorta-
tion of
S. James.

1.Mac.2.
The con-

6 exhortation to al tru Catholiks, not much different from this in
that his epistle, which he writeth generally to al   31 Mathathias
unto his children in the time   32 *omits* The storie is thus reported . . .
sayed unto his children: [220.12] *continues* Now (saith he) is

this citie, adorned with children and bretheren: come
thow therfore first, and doe the kinges commaundement,
as other men have done in Juda and Jerusalem, and
thow and thy children shalbe the kynges freends, and
5 enryched with golde and sylver, and many guyftes from
hym. Wherto Mathathias answered with a lowde voyce:
yf all nations should obey Antiochus, to departe from
the obedience of the lawes of theyr auncestours: yet I,
and my children, and bretheren will folowe the lawes
10 of our fathers, Let God be mercifull unto us at his pleasure &c. And the dayes came of Mathathias his deathe,
and then he sayed unto his children: Now is the tyme
that pryde is in her strengthe: Now is the tyme of
chastisement towardes us: of eversion and indignation
15 come. Now therfore (o children) be you zelous in the
lawe of God: yeeld upp your lyves for the testament of
your fathers: remember the woorkes of your auncestours,
what they have done in theyr generations, and so shall
you receave greate glorie, and eternall name. Was not
20 Abraham fownde faythefull in time of temptation, and
yt was reputed unto hym for justice? Joseph in tyme of
his distresse, kept Gods commaundementes, and was
made Lord over all Egypt. Phinees our father, for his
zeale towardes the lawe of God, receaved the testament
25 of an everlasting preesthode. Josue for that he fullfilled
Gods woord, was made a captayne over all Israel. Caleb
for that he testifyed in the churche, receaved an inheritance. David for his mercie obteyned the seat of an
eternall kyngdome. Elias for that he was zealous in zeale
30 of the lawe, was taken up to heaven. Ananias Azarias
and Misael throughe their beleefe, were delyvered from
the flame of the fyre. Daniel for his simplicitie was delivered from the mouthe of lyons. And so doe you runne
over, by cogitation, all generations, and you shall see
35 that all those that hope in God shall not be vanquyshed.
And doe you not feare the woordes of a synfull man:
for his glorie is nothing els but dung and wormes: to
daye he is great and exalted, and tomorow he shall not
be fownde: for he shall returne unto his earthe agayne,
40 and all his fond cogitations shall perishe. Wherfore take

fession &
exhorta-
tion of
Matha-
thias.

Gen.15.

Gen.41.

Num.25.

Josue.1.
Jos.14.

2.Re.7.
4.Re.2.
Dan.3.
Dan.6.

courage unto you (my children) and playe the men in
the lawe of God. For therin shalbe your honour and
glorie. Hitherto are the wordes of scripture, which shall
suffice, for the end of this chapter.

5   *Of the thyrd impediment that letteth men from resolution:*
       whiche is, the love of the worlde

CHAP. III

As the two impedimentes removed before, be in deede
great stayes to many men from the resolution we talke
10   of: so this that now I take in hande, is not onelie of it
selfe a strong impediment, but also a greate cause and
common grounde (as it were) to all the other impedimentes that be. For yf a man could touche the verie
pulse of all those, whoe refuse, or neglect, or differre
15   this resolution: he should finde the foundation therof to
be the love of this world, what soever other excuse they
pretended besides. The noble men of Jewrie, pretended
feare to be the cause, whye they could not resolve,
to confesse Christ openlie: but S. John that felt their   Joh.12.
20   pulse, uttereth the true cause to have bene, *for that they*
loved the glorie of men, more than the glorie of God. Demas
that forsooke S. Paul in his bandes, even a litle before
his deathe, pretended an other cause of his departure to
Thessalonica, but S. Paul sayeth it was, *quia diligebat hoc*   2.Tim.4.
25   *seculum*: For that he loved this world. So that this is a
generall and universall impediment, and more in deede
dispersed, than owtwardlye appeareth: for that it bringeth
foorthe divers other excuses, therby to cover her selfe
in many men.
30   This may be confirmed by that moste excellent para-   Mat.13.
ble of Christ, recorded by three Evangelistes, of the three   Marc.4.
sortes of men which are to be damned, and the three   Luc.8.
causes of their damnation: wherof the third, and last,
and moste generall (including as it were bothe the rest)

---

3 words of Mathathias, which   17 pretend

is, the love of this worlde. For the first sorte of men, are compared to a highe waye, where all seed of lyfe that is sowen, either withereth presentlye, or els is eaten up by the byrdes of the ayer: that is, (as Christ expoundeth

5 it) by the devill in careles men, that contemne what soever is sayd unto them: as infidels, heretikes, and other suche obstinate and contemptuous people. The second sorte are compared to rockye groundes, in which, for lacke of depe roote, the seed continuethe not: wherby

10 are signified, light and unconstant men, that now choppe in, and now runne owte: now are fervent, and by and by, keye colde againe: and so in time of temptation, they are gone. The third sorte are compared to a feeld, where the seed groweth up, but yet there are so many

15 thornes on the same (whiche Christ expoundeth to be the cares, troubles, miseries, and deceyvable vanities of this life) as the good corne is choked up, *and bringeth foorth no fruite*. By whiche last woordes our Saviour sig-nifieth, that whersoever the doctrine of Christ groweth

20 up, and yet bringeth not foorthe due fruite: that is, wher-soever it is receaved, and imbraced (as it is among all Christians) and yet bringethe not foorthe good lyfe: there the cause is, for that it is choked with the vanities of this world.

25 This is a parable of marvailous greate importance, as may appeare, bothe for that Christ after the recitall therof, cryed owt withe a lowde voyce: *He that hathe eares to heare, let him heare*: As also, for that he expounded it hym selfe in secrete onelie to his Disciples: And princi-

30 pallie, for that before the exposition therof, he used such a solemne preface: sayeing, *to you it is geven to knowe the mysteries of the kingdome of heaven, but to others not: for that they seyng doe not see, and hearing doe not heare, nor understand*. Wherby Christ signifieth, that the understanding of this

35 parable, among others, is of singular importance, for conceaving the true mysteries of the kyngdome of heaven: and that many are blinde, which seeme to see: and many deafe and ignorant, that seeme to heare and knowe: for

The exposition of the parable of the seed.

The im-portance of this parable.

Mat.13.

---

6 *omits* heretikes; *continues* and al other obstinate   30 useth

that they understand not well the mysteries of this parable. For which cause also Christ maketh this conclusion
before he beginnethe to expounde the parable. *Happie
are your eyes that see, and blessed are your eares that heare.* After
5   whiche woordes, he beginneth his exposition, withe this
admonition: *Vos ergo audite parabolam*: Doe you therfore
heare and understand this parable.

And for that this parable dothe contayne and touche
so much in deede, as may or needeth be sayed, for
10 removinge of this greate and daungerous impediment,
of worldly love: I meane to staye my selfe onelye uppon
the explication therof in this place, and will declare the
force and truthe of certaine woordes heere uttered by
Christ, of the world and worldlie pleasures: and for some
15 order and methodes sake, I will drawe all to these six
pointes foloweing.

First how and in what sense all the world and commodities therof are vanities, and of no value, (as Christ
heere signifieth:) and consequentlie, ought not to be an
20 impediment, to lett us from so great a matter, as the
kyngdome of heaven and serving of God is.

Secondlie how they are not onelye vanities and tryfles
in them selves, but also, *Deceptions*, as Christ sayeth, that
is, deceytes, not performing to us in deede, those litle
25 tryfles which they doe promis.

Thyrdlie, how they are *spinæ*, that is, pricking thornes,
as Christ sayeth, thoghe they seeme to worldly men to
be most sweet and pleasant.

Fowerthlye how they are *ærumnæ*, that is, myseryes,
30 and afflictions, as also Christs woordes are.

Fyvethlie, *quomodo suffocant*, how they strangle or choke
us, as Christ affirmeth.

Sixthelie, how we may use them notwithstanding, without these daungers, and evills, and to our greate com-
35 fort, gayne, and preferment.

And touching the first, I doe not see how it may be
better proved, that all the pleasures and goodlie shewes
of this world are vanities, as Christ heere sayeth: than

The
partes of
this
chapiter.

1.

2.

3.

4.

5.

6.

1. The
first
parte:

---

21 the serving

to alleage the testimonie of one, whiche hathe proved
them all: that is of one whiche speakethe not of speculation, but of his owne proofe and practise: And
this is kyng Salomon: of whome the scripture report-

5   ethe wounderfull matters, touching his peace, prosperitie,
riches, and glorie, in this world: as that, all the kynges
of the earthe desired to see his face, for his wisdome
and renowmed felicitie: that all the princes lyving besides,
were not lyke hym in wealthe: that he had six hundred

10   sixtie and six talents of golde (which is an infinite summe)
brought hym in yerelie, besides all other that he had
from the kynges of Arabia, and other princes: that silver
was as plentifull withe hym as heapes of stones, and not
esteemed, for the greate store, and abundance he had

15   therof: that his plate and Jewelles had no ende: that his
seat of majestie, with stooles, lyons to beare it up, and
other furniture, was of golde, passing all other kyngely
seates in the world: that his pretious apparell and armoure
were infinite: that he had all the kinges, from the river

20   of the Philistians, unto Egypt, to serve hym: that he had
fortie thowsand horses in his stables to ride, and twelve
thousand chariottes, with horses and other furniture,
redye to them, for his use: that he had two hundred
speares of golde, borne before hym, and six hundred

25   crownes of golde, bestowed in everie speare: as also three
hundred buckelers, and three hundred crownes of golde,
bestowed in the guylding of every buckler: that he spent
everye daye in his howse, a thowsand, nyne hundred,
thirtie and seven quarters of meale, and flower: thirtie

30   oxen: with a hundred wethers: beside all other fleshe:
that he had seven hundred wives, as queenes, and three
hundred other, as concubynes. All this, and muche more
dothe scripture report of Salomons worldlye wealthe,
wisdome, ryches, and prosperitie: whiche he having tasted,

how all
the world
is vanitie.

2.Par.9.

The
worldlie
prosperi-
tie
of king
Salomon.

3.Re.4.
30 Cori
similæ: &
60 cori
farinæ.
& everie
corus is
21.quar-

----

18 armor was infinite   34 [mn: * 21.] mn: B. *For 21. I think he
ment but 11. for a Coras according to Josephus is rekoned to be
738. of our gallons: which make of our measure 11. quarters, four
bushels, one pek. So 900. being taken out of the total sum, the
residu that remaineth doth agree wel to this account: for it maketh
1037. quarters, six bushels, two peks. But of this kind of measure

and used to hys fyll, pronounced yet at the last, this
sentence of it all: *Vanitas vanitatum, & omnia vanitas*: Vanitie
of vanities, and all is vanitie: by vanitie of vanities meaning, (as S. Jerome interpreteth) the greatenesse of this
5   vanitie, above all other vanyties that maye be devised.

    Nether onelye dothe Salomon affirme this thing, but
dothe prove it also by examples of hym selfe. I have
bene kyng of Israel in Jerusalem (saithe he,) and I
purposed with my selfe, to seeke owt by wisdome all
10   thynges: And I have seene that all under the sunne, are
meere vanities, and affliction of spirit. I sayd in my harte,
I will goe and abounde in delites, and in every pleasure that maye be had: and I saw that this was also
vanitie. I toke great woorkes in hande, buylded howses
15   to my selfe, planted vineyardes, made orchardes and
gardens, and besett them withe all kynde of trees: I
made me fyshe pondes to water my trees: I possessed
servantes and hand maydes, and had a great familie,
great heardes of cattell, above any that ever were before
20   me in Jerusalem: I gathered together golde and sylver,
the riches of kynges and provinces: I appointed to my
selfe syngars, bothe men and women, whiche are the
delytes of the children of men: fyne cuppes also to drynke
wyne with all: and what soever my eyes dyd desire, I
25   denied it not unto them: nether dyd I lett my harte
from using any pleasure, to delite it selfe in these thinges
whiche I had prepared: And when I turned my selfe to
all that my handes had made, and to all the labours,
wherein I had taken suche paynes and sweate: I sawe
30   in them all, vanitie, and affliction of the mynde.

    This is the testimonie of Salomon, upon his owne
proofe, in these matters: and yf he had spoken yt uppon
his wisedome onelye (being suche as yt was:) we ought
to beleeve hym: but muche more, seyng he affirmeth
35   yt, of his owne experience. But yet, yf any man be not

Right margin notes:
ters and
odde.
3.Re.11.
Eccle.1.
In cap.1.
ecclesias.
Salomons
sayeing of
hym selfe.

Eccl.1.

Cap.2.

---

the judgment of the learned doth vary much, and it would aske a
long discourse to beat out the more likely opinion, by conference of
places and measures togither. By the account of Saint Jerom it commeth far short: that is, but to 232. quarters, six bushels, and a halfe.
27 I prepared

moved withe thys: lett us bryng yet an other witnesse owte of the new testament, and suche an one, as was pryvie to the opinion of Christ heerin: that is S. John the Evangelist, whose woordes are these: *Doe not love the* 1.Joh.2.
5 *world, nor those thinges that are in the world: yf any man love the world: the love of God the father, ys not in hym. For that, all whiche is in the world, is ether concupiscence of the fleshe, or concupiscence of the eyes, or pryde of lyfe.* In whiche woordes S. John, besyde his threate agaynst suche as love and
10 folow the world, reduceth all the vanities therof, unto three generall pointes or braunches: that is, to concu- Three piscence of the fleshe (wherein he comprehendeth all generall carnall pleasures,) to concupiscence of the eyes, (wherein poyntes he contayneth all matters of riches:) and to pryde of of world-
15 lyfe, wherby he signifiethe the humour and disease of ties. worldly ambition. These then are the three generall and principall vanities of this lyfe, wherin woorldlye men doe wearie owte them selves: Ambition, covetousnes, and carnall pleasure: wherunto all other vanities are addressed,
20 as to theyr superiours. And therfore it shall not be amisse to consider of these three, in this place.

And first to Ambition or pryde of lyfe, belongeth vain- Vain- glorie: that is a certaine disordinate desire to be well glorie. thoght of, well spoken of, praysed and glorified of men:
25 and this is as greate a vanitie, (thoghe yt be common to manye) as yf a man should runne up and doune the streetes, after a fether, flyeing in the ayer, tossed hyther and thyther, withe the blastes of infinite mennes mouthes. For, as this man might wearie owt hym selfe before he
30 gatt the thing whiche he folowed, and yet when he had yt, he had gotten but a fether: so a vainglorious man maye labour a good whyle, before he attaine to the prayse whiche he desirethe: and when he hathe it, it is not woorthe three chyppes, being but the breathe of a
35 fewe mennes mouthes, that altereth upon everye lyght occasion, and now maketh hym greate, nowe litle, now nothing at all. Christ hym selfe may be an example of

---

2 such a one

this: who was tossed to and fro in the speeche of men: some sayd he was a Samaritan, and had the devill: other sayd he was a prophet: other sayde he could not be a prophet, or of God: for that he kept not the Sabboth
5   daye: others asked, yf he were not of God, how he coulde doe so many miracles? So that there was a schisme or division amonge them, abowte this matter, as S. John affirmeth. Finallie, uppon Palme sundaye, they receaved hym into Jerusalem, withe triumphe of *hosanna*, casting
10   their apparell under his feete. But the thursedaye, and frydaye next ensueing, they cried *Crucifige* against hym, and preferred the lyfe of Barrabas, a wicked murderer, before his.

Now my freend, yf they delt thus withe Christ, whiche
15   was a better man, than ever thou wilt be: and dyd more glorious miracles, than ever thou wilt doe, to purchase the name and honour withe the people: whie doest thou so labour, and beate thy selfe about this vanitie of vain-glorie? whye doest thou cast thy travailes into the wynde
20   of mens mouthes? whye doest thou put thy riches in the lyppes of mutable men, where everie flatterer may robbe the of them? hast thou no better a cheest to locke them up in? S. Paul was of an other mynde, when he sayde: *I esteeme litle to be judged of you, or of the daye of man.* And
25   he had reason surelye. For what carethe he that run-neth at tylt, yf the ignorant people gave sentence against hym, so the Judges geve yt with hym? If the blynde man, in the waye to Jericho, had depended of the lyk-ing and approbation of the goers bye: he had never
30   receaved the benefit of his sight: for that, they disuaded hym from runnyng and cryeing so vehementlie after Christ. It is a miserable thyng for a man to be a wynde-mill, whiche makethe no meale, but according as the blast endurethe. If the gale be strong, he sourgeth about
35   lustelye. But yf the winde slake: he relentethe presentlie. So, prayse the vaynglorious man, and ye make hym runne: yf he feele not the gale blowe, he is owte of

Mat.27.
Joh.8.

Joh.9.
Matt.21.
Mar.11.

Mat.27.
Luc.23.

1.Cor.4.

Luc.18.

---

8 *omits* uppon Palme sundaye   10 *omits* the thursdaye, and   13 before him   16 purchase thee

harte: he is lyke the Babilonians, whoe withe a litle   Dan.3.
sweete musike were made to adore any thing what soever.

    The scripture saythe moste truelye, *As silver is tryed in*   Pro.27.
the fyre by bloweing to it: so is a man tryed in the mouthe of
5 *hym that prayseth.* For as silver, yf it be good, taketh no
hurt therby: but yf it be evill, it goethe all into fume:
so a vaine man, by prayse and commendation. How
manye have we seene puffed up withe mennes prayses,
and almoste put beside them selves, for joye therof:
10 and yet afterwarde brought downe, with a contrarye
wynde, and dryven full neare to desperation by contempt? how many doe we see daylie (as the prophet dyd   Psal.10.
in his dayes) commended in their sinnes, and blessed in
their wickednes? How manye palpable and intolerable
15 flateries doe we heare bothe used, and accepted daylie,
and no man cryethe withe good kyng David, *awaye with*   Psa.141.
this oyle, and oyntement of sinners, let it not come upon my heade?
Is not all this vanitie? Is it not madnes, as the scripture   Psal.40.
callethe it? The glorious Angels in heaven seeke no hon-
20 our unto them selves, but all unto God: and thow poore
worme of the earthe desyrest to be glorified? the fowre
and twentie elders in the Apocalips tooke of theyr crounes,   Apoc.4.
and cast them at the feete of the lamb: and thow woldest plucke fortye from the lamb to thy selfe, yf thow
25 couldest. O fond creature: how truelie sayethe the prophet,
homo vanitati similis factus est: A man is made lyke unto   Psa.144.
vanitie; that is, lyke unto his owne vanitie: as lyght as
the verie vanities them selves, whiche he foloweth. And
yet the wise man more expresselie, *In vanitate sua appen-*   Eccl.23.
30 *ditur peccator*, the sinner is weyghed in his vanitie: that
is, by the vanitie, whiche he foloweth, is seene how light
and vayne a synner is.

    The second vanitie that belongeth to Ambition, is   Worldlie
desire of worldlie honour, dignitie and promotion. And   honour,
35 this is a greate matter in the sight of a worldlye man: and pro-
this is a Jewell of rare price, and woorthie to be bought,   motion.
even with any labour, travaile, or perill what soever.
The love of this, letted the great men, that were Christians
in Jewrie, from confessing of Christ openlie. The love   Joh.11.
40 of this, letted Pilat from delyvering Jesus, according as

in conscience he sawe he was bounde. The love of this,   Joh.19.
letted Agrippa and Festus, from makyng them selves   Act.26.
Christians, albeit they esteemed Paules doctrine to be
true. The love of this, letteth infinite menne daylie from
5 embrasing the meanes of their salvation. But (alas) these
men doe not see the vanitie heerof. S. Paul sayth not
without just cause, *Nolite esse pueri sensibus*, be you not   1.Co.14.
children in understanding. It is the fashion of Children,
to esteeme more of a paynted bable, than of a riche
10 Jewell: And suche is the paynted dignitie of this worlde:
gotten with muche labour, maintayned withe great
expenses, and lost withe intolerable greefe and sorow.
For better conceaving wherof, ponder a litle withe thy   The vani-
selfe (gentle reader) any state of dignitie that thou wold-   tie of
15 est desire: and think how many have had that before   worldlye
thee. Remembre how they mounted up, and how they   honour.
descended downe agayne: and imagine withe thy selfe,
whiche was greater, ether the Joye in getting, or the
sorowe in leesing it. Where are now all those emper-
20 ours, those kynges, those princes and prelates, whiche
rejoysed so muche once, at their owne advancement?
where are they now, I saye? who talketh, or thynkethe
of them? are they not forgotten, and cast into their
graves, long agoe? And doe not menne boldelye walke
25 over their heades nowe, whose faces might not be looked
on, without feare, in this world? what then have their
dignities done them good?

It is a wounderfull thing to consider the vanitie of
this worldlie honour. It is like a mans owne shadowe,
30 which the more a man runneth after, the more it flyeth:
and when he flyethe from it, it foloweth hym agayne:
and the onelye waye to cache it, is to fall downe to the
grounde upon it. So we see, that those men which desired
honour in this world, are now forgotten: and those which
35 most fledd from it, and cast them selves lowest of
all men, by humilitie: are now moste of all honoured:
honoured (I saye) moste, even by the world it selfe,
whose enemies they were, whyle they lyved. For who is

---

13 *mn: omits* The vanitie of

honoured more now, whoe is more commended, and
remembred, than S. Paul, and his like, whiche so muche
despised worldlie honour in this lyfe, according to the
sayeing of the prophet, *thy freendes (o Lorde) are to too muche*   Psa.139.
5   *honored?* Moste vayne then is the pursuyte of this worldlie honour and promotion: seyng it nether contenteth
the mynde, nor continuethe withe the possessor, nor is
voyde of greate daungers, bothe in this lyfe, and in the
lyfe to come, according to the sayeing of scripture, *Moste*   Sap.6.
10   *severe judgement shalbe used upon those that are over other: the*
meane man shall obtaine mercie: but the greate and strong shall
suffer tormentes stronglye.

     The third vanitie that belongeth to ambition or pryde   The vani-
of lyfe, is nobilitie of fleshe and bloode: a great pearle   tie of
15   in the eye of the world: but in deede in it selfe, and in   worldlie
the sight of God, a meere trifle and vanitie. Whiche   nobilitie.
holy Job well understoode, when he wrote these woordes:
I sayde unto rottennesse, thou art my father: and unto wormes,   Job.17.
you are my mother and sisters. He that will beholde the gen-
20   trye of his auncestoures: Lett hym looke into their graves,
and see whether Job saythe truelie or no. True nobilitie was never begonne but by vertue: and therfore, as
it is a testimonie of vertue to the predecessours: so is it
an other of vertue unto the successours. And he whiche
25   holdethe the name therof by descent, without vertue, is a
meere monster, in respect of his auncestoures: for that,
he breaketh the limites of the nature of nobilitie. Of
which sort of men, God sayeth by one prophet: *They are*   Ose.9.
made abominable, even as the thinges whiche they love: theyr glorie
30   *is from theyr nativitie, from the bellye, and from theyr conception.*

     It is a miserable vanitie, to goe begge credit of deade
men, wher as we deserve none our selves: to seek up
olde titles of honoure from our auncestours, we beyng
utterlye uncapeable therof, by our owne base maners
35   and behavyour. Christ clearlie confounded this vanitie,
when being descended hym selfe of the greatest nobilitie, that ever was in this world: and besides that, being
also the sonne of God: yet called he him selfe ordinar-

---

32 when as

ilie, *the sonne of manne*: That is, the sonne of the virgin
Marie (for otherwyse he was no sonne of man) and further than this also, called hym selfe a shepeheard, whiche
in the world is a name of contempt. He soght not up
5   this and that olde title of honour, to furnishe his style
withall, as our men doe. Nether, when he had to make
a kyng first in Israell, dyd he seeke owt the auncientest
bloode: but tooke Saul, of the basest tribe of Jewes: and
after him, David the poorest sheephearde of all his
10   brethren. And when he came into the world: he soght
not owt the noblest men to make princes of the earthe:
that is, to make Apostles: but tooke of the poorest, and
simplest, therby to confound (as one of them sayeth)
the foolishe vanitie of this world: in making so great
15   account of the preeminence of a litle fleshe and bloode,
in this lyfe.

      The fourthe vanitie that belongeth to ambition, or
pryde of lyfe, is worldlie wisdome, wherof the Apostle
sayeth: *The wisdome of this world is folye with God.* If it be
20   folie, then greate vanite (no dowbt) to delite so in it, as
men doe. It is a straunge thing to see, how contrarie
the Judgementes of God are to the Judgementes of men.
The people of Israel wolde needes have a kyng (as I
have sayd:) and they thoght God wolde have geven them
25   presentlie some great mightie prince to rule over them:
but he chose owte a poore felowe, that sought asses
aboute the countrie. After that, when God wolde dis-
place this man agayne for his sinnes: he sent Samuel to
anoynt one of Isay his sonnes: and being come to the
30   house, Isay brought foorthe his eldest sonne, Eliab, a
lustie taule felowe, thinkyng hym in deed most fytte to
governe: but God answered, *respect not his countenance, nor*
hys taulnes of personage: for I have rejected hym: nor doe I judge
according to the countenance of man. After that, Isay brought
35   in his second sonne, Abinadab: and after hym, Samma,
and so the rest, untill he had shewed hym seven of his
sonnes: All whiche being refused by Samuel, they mar-
vayled, and sayde, there was no moe left but onelye a

Math.8.
20.24.26.
Joh.10.

1.Re.9.

1.Re.16.

Matt.4.
Psal.45.
1.Cor.1.

The vani-
tie of
worldlie
wisdome.

1.Cor.3.

1.Re.9.

1.Re.16.

---

8 of al Israel   28 sin   33 *neither do I judge*

litle read headed boye, that kept the sheep, called David:
whiche Samuel caused to be sent for. And as sone as
he came in sight: God sayd to Samuel, this is the man
that I have chosen.

5   When the Messias was promised unto the Jewes to
be a king: they imagined presentlie according to theyr
worldlye wisdome, that he should be some great prince:
and therfore they refused Christ, that came in povertie.
James and John being yet but carnall, seing the Samari-
10   tanes contemptuouslie to refuse Christes disciples sent to
them, and knoweing what Christ was, thoght streight-
waye, that he must in revenge, have called downe fyre
from heaven to consume them: But Christ rebuked them,
sayeing, *you know not of what spirit you are.* The Apostles   Luc.9.
15   preachyng the crosse, and necessitie of suffering, to the   1.Cor.1.
wyse Gentiles and Philosophers, were thought present-
lye fooles for theyr labours. Festus, the Emperours lieu-
tenant, hearing Paul to speake so muche of abandoning
the world, and foloweing Christ, sayd, he was madde.   Act.26.
20   Finallie, this is the fashion of all worldlie wyse men: to
condemne the wisdome of Christ, and of his saints. For
so the holye scripture reporteth, of theyr owne confession, being now in place of torment: *nos insensati vitam*   Sap.5.
illorum æstimabamus insaniam, we fond men esteemed the
25   lives of Saintes as madnes. Wherfore, this is also great
vanitie (as I have sayde) to make suche accoumpt of
worldlye wisdome: which is not onelye folye, but also
madnes, by the testimonie of the holye ghoste hym selfe.
Whoe would not thinke, but that the wyse men of
30   this world, were the fittest to be chosen to doe Christ
service in his churche? Yet S. Paul saythe, *non multi sap-*   1.Cor.1.
ientes, secundum carnem, God hathe not chosen many wyse
men according to the fleshe. Whoe wold not thinke, but
that a worldlye wyse man might easilye also make a
35   wyse Christian? yet S. Paul saythe, no: except first he
become a foole, *stultus fiat, ut sit sapiens*: If any man seeme   1.Cor.3.
wise amongst you: let hym become a foole, to the ende
he may be made wyse. Vayne then, and of no account,
is the wisdome of this world, except it be subiect to the
40   wisdome of God.

The fyfthe vanitie belonging to pryde of lyfe, is corporall beautie: wherof the wyseman saythe, *vayne is beau-*
tie, and deceaveable is the grace of countynance. Wherof also,
king David understoode properlie, when he sayde, *Turne*
5 *awaye my eyes (o lord,) that they beholde not vanitie*: This is a
singular great vanitie, daungerous, and deceatfull: but
yet greatlie esteemed of the children of men: whose propertie is, *to love vanitie*, as the prophet saythe. Beautie is
compared by holie men, to a painted snake, whiche is
10 fayre without, and full of deadlye poyson within. If a
man dyd consider what infinite ruynes and destructions
have come, by over lyght geving credit therunto: he
wolde beware of yt. And yf he remembred what foule
drosse lyethe under a fayre skynne: he wolde litle be in
15 love therwith, saythe one father. God hathe imparted
certaine sparckes of beautie unto his creatures: therby
to drawe us to the consideration, and love of hys owne
beautie: wherof the other is but a shadow: even as a
man fynding a litle issue of water, maye seek owt the
20 fountane therby: or happenyng upon a small vaine of
golde, may therby come to the whole mynne it selfe.
But we lyke babes, delyte our selves onelye withe the
fayre cover of the booke, and never doe consider what
is writen therin. In all fayre creatures, that man dothe
25 beholde, he ought to reade this, saythe one father: that
yf God could make a peece of earthe so fayre and lovelie,
withe imparting unto yt some litle sparke of his beautie: how infinite fayre is he hym selfe, and how woorthye of all love and admiration? And how happye shall
30 we be, when we shall come to enjoye his beautifull presence, wherof now all creatures doe take theyr beautie?

If we wolde exercise our selves in these maner of cogitations: we might easilye keepe oure hartes pure and
unspotted before God, in beholding the beautie of his
35 creatures. But for that we use not this passage from the
creature to the creator: but doe rest onelye in the eternall appearance of a deceatfull face: letting goe the bry-
dle to foule cogitations, and setting willfully on fyre our

The vani-
tie of
beautie.
Prov.31.

Psa.119.

Psal.4.

A lesson
to be
read in
the beau-
tie of all
creatures.

---

36 but rest

owne concupiscences: hence is it, that infinite men doe peryshe daylie by occasion of this fond vanitie. I call it fond, for that everie chylde may discrie the deceate and vanitie therof. For take the fairest face in the world,

5   wherwithe infinite folishe men fall in love, upon the sight: and rase yt over but with a litle scrache, and all the matter of love is gone: lett there come but an Ague, and all this goodly beautie is distroyed: lett the soule departe but one halfe hower from the bodye, and this

10   loving face is uglye to looke on: lett yt lye but two dayes in the grave, and those whiche were so hote in love withe yt before, will skarse abyde to beholde yt, or come neare yt. And yf none of those things happen unto yt: yet quicklie cometh on olde age, which riveleth the

15   skinne, draweth in the eyes, setteth owt the teethe, and so disfigurethe the whole visage, as yt becometh more contemptible now, than it was beautifull and alluringe before. And what then can be more vanitie than this? What more madnesse, than ether to take pride of it, yf

20   I see it my selfe: or to endaunger my soule for yt, yf I see it in others?

The sixthe vanitie belonging to pryde of lyfe, is the glorie of fyne apparell: against whiche the scripture saythe, *In vestitu ne gloriaris unquam*: See thou never take

25   glorie in apparelle. Of all vanities this is the greatest, which we see so common among men of this worlde. If Adam had never fallen: we had never used apparell. For that, apparell was devised to cover our shame of nakednes, and other infirmities contracted by that fall.

30   Wherfore, we that take pryde and glorie in apparell, doe as muche as yf a beggar should glorie and take pride of the olde cloutes that do cover his sores. S. Paul sayd unto a byshope, *Yf we have wherwithall to cover our selves, lett us be content.* And Christ touched deeplie the

35   daunger of nyce apparell, when he commended so muche S. John Baptist for his austere attire: adding for the contradictorie, *Qui mollibus vestiuntur in domibus regum sunt*: They which are apparelled in soft and delicate appar-

The vanitie of apparell.

Eccl.11.

1.Ti.6.

Mat.3.11.
Luc.7.

---

23 the wise man saith

ell, are in kynges courtes: In kynges courtes of this world, but not in the kynges court of heaven. For which cause in the description of the riche man damned, this is not omitted by Christ: *That he was apparelled in purple and sylke.*   Luc.16.

5   It is a wounderfull thing to consider the different proceeding of God and the world heerin. God was the first tayler that ever made apparell in the world: and he   Gen.3. made it for the most noble of all our auncestours, in paradise: and yet he made it but of beasts skynnes. And

10   S. Paul testifiethe of the noblest saintes of the olde testament, that they were covered onelye withe goates skynnes, and with the heares of Camelles. What vanitie is it then for us, to be so curious in apparell, and to take suche pryde therein, as we doe? We robbe and   Heb.11.

15   spoyle all creatures almoste in the worlde, to cover our backes, and adorne our bodies withall. From one, we take his woolle: from an other his skynne: from an other his furre: and from some other their verie excrementes, as the silk, which is nothinge els, but the excrementes

20   of wormes. Nor content with this, we come to fishes, and doe begge of them certaine pearles to hang about us. We goe doune into the grounde for golde and silver: and turne up the sandes of the sea, for pretious stones: and having borowed all this of other creatures,

25   we jett up and doune, provoking men to looke upon us: as yf all this nowe were our owne. When the stone shyneth uppon our fingar: we will seeme (forsoothe) therby to shyne. When the silver and silkes doe glyster on our backes: we looke bigge, as yf all that beautie

30   came from us. And so (as the prophet saythe,) we passe   Psal.78. over our dayes in vanitie, and doe not perceave our owne extreme folie.

The second generall braunche, whiche S. John appointeth unto the vanitie of this lyfe, is concupiscence

35   of the eyes: wherunto the auncient fathers have referred all vanities of riches and wealthe of this world. Of this S. Paul writeth to Timothie: *Geve commaundement to the*   1.Ti.6. *riche men of this world, not to be highe mynded, nor to put hope*

The extreme vanitie and povertie of man.

2. Concupiscence of the eyes.

---

7 *omits* tayler   12 with hairs   16 to adorn

in the uncertaintie of their riches. The reason of which speeche
is uttered by the scripture, in an other place, when it
sayeth: *Riches shall not profitt a man in the daye of revenge.*   Prov.11.
That is, at the daye of deathe and Judgement: which
5   thing, the riche men of this world, doe confesse them
selves, thoghe to late, when they crye, *diuitiarum iactan-*   Sap.5.
tia quid nobis contulit? what hathe the braverie of our riches   The vani-
profited us? All whiche dothe evidentlie declare the great   tie and
vanitie of worldlye riches, whiche can doe the posses-   perill of
worldly
10   soure no good at all, when he hathe most need of their   wealthe.
help. *Riche men have slept theyr sleepe,* (saythe the prophet)   Psal.76.
and have found nothing in theyr handes: that is, riche men
have passed over this lyfe, as men doe passe over a
sleepe, imaginyng them selves to have golden moun-
15   taines, and treasures: and when they awake (at the daye
of their deathe) they fynde themselves to have nothinge
in theyr handes. In respect wherof, the prophet Baruch   Cap.3.
asketh this question: *Where are they now, whiche heaped*
together golde and sylver, and whiche made no end of their scrapyng
20   *together?* And he answereth hym selfe immediatlie: *Exter-*
minati sunt, & ad inferos descenderunt: They are now rooted
owte, and are gone downe unto hell. To lyke effect   Jac.5.
saythe S. James. Now goe to, you riche men: weepe,
and howle in your miseries, that come upon you: your
25   riches are rotten: and your golde and sylver is rustie:
and the rust therof shall be in testimonie against you:
it shall feede on your fleshe as fire: you have hoarded
upp wrathe for your selves in the last daye.
       If wealthe of this world be not onelie so vaine, but
30   also so perilous as here is affirmed: what vanitie then is
yt for men to sett their myndes upon it, as they doe?
S. Paul sayeth of him selfe, that *he esteemed it all but as*   Phil.3.
dung. And he had great reason surely to say so, seing in
deed they are but dung: that is, the verie excrementes
35   of the earthe, and fownde onelie in the moste barraine   Job.28.
places thereof: as they can tell which have seene their
mines. What a base matter is this then for a man to
tye his love unto? God commaunded in the olde law,

---

8 which evidently declareth

that what soever dyd goe with his breast upon the ground,   Levi.11.
should be unto us in abhomination. How muche more
then, a reasonable man, that hathe glewed his hart and
soule unto a peece of earthe? *We came in naked unto this*   Cap.1.
5   *world, and naked we must goe foorthe again*, sayethe Job. The
mylle wheele stirrethe much aboute, and beateth it selfe
from daye to daye, and yet at the yeres end it is in the
same place, as it was in the begynning: so, riche men,
let them toyle and labour what they can, yet at their
10   deathe must they be as poore, as at the first daye wherein
they were borne. When the riche man dyeth (saythe Job)   Job.27.
he shall take nothing with hym, but shall close up his
eyes, and finde nothing. Povertie shall laye handes upon
hym, and a tempest shall oppresse hym in the night: a
15   burning wynde shall take hym awaye, and a hurle wynde
shall snatche hym from his place: yt shall rushe upon
hym, and shall not spare hym: it shall bynde his handes
upon hym, and shall hysse over hym. For that it seeth
his place whether he must goe.
20   The prophet David in lyke wyse forewarneth us of   Psal.49.
the same, in these woordes: be not afeard when thou
seest a man made riche, and the glorie of his house
multiplied. For when he dyeth, he shall take nothing
with hym, nor shall his glorie descend to the place
25   whether he goeth: he shall passe into the progenies of
his auncestoures (that is, he shall goe to the place where
they are, who have lived as he hathe done) and world
without end he shall see no more light.
    All this and muche more is spoken by the holie ghoste,
30   to signifie the dangerous vanitie of worldlie wealthe: and
the folie of those men, who laboure so muche to procure the same, with the eternall peril of their soules, as
the scripture assureth us. If so many phisitions, as I have
heere alleaged scriptures, should agree together, that
35   suche, or suche meates were venemous and perillsome:
I think fewe wold geve the adventure to eate them,
thoghe otherwyse in taste they appeared sweet, and pleasant. How then cometh it to passe, that so manie earnest

---

15 *whirl wind*   21 *afraid*

admonitions of God him selfe, can not staye us from
the love of this daungerous vanitie? *Nolite cor apponere,*   Psal.62.
saythe God by the prophet: that is, laye not your harte
unto the love of riches. *Qui diligit aurum non iustificabitur,*   Eccl.31.
5 saythe the wyse man: he that loveth gold shall never be
justified. *I am angrie greatelye uppon riche nations,* sayethe   Cap.1.
God by Zacharie. Christ saythe: *Amen dico vobis, quia diues*   Mat.19.
difficile intrabit in regnum cælorum: Truelie I saye unto you,
that a riche man shall hardlie gett into the kyngdome
10 of heaven. And agayne, *woe be to you riche men, for that*   Luc.6.
you have receaved your consolation in this lyfe. Finallie S. Paul
saythe generallie of all, and to all: *They which wilbe riche,*   1.Ti.6.
doe fall into temptation, and into the snare of the devill, and into
many unprofitable and hurtfull desires, whiche doe drowne men in
15 *destruction and perdition.*

Can any thing in the world be spoken more effectuallie,
to dissuade from the love of riches than this? must not
heere now the covetous men, ether denye God, or condemne them selves in their owne consciences? lett them
20 goe, and excuse them selves, by the pretence of wyfe   The pre-
and children, as they are wont: sayeing, they mean   tence of
nothinge els, but to provyde for their sufficiencie. Dothe   wife and
Christ, or S. Paul admitt this excuse? ought we so much   children
to love wyfe, or children, or other kynred, as to endaunger   refuted.
25 our soules for the same? what comfort may it be to an
afflicted father in hell, to remember, that by his meanes,
his wyfe and children doe lyve wealthelie in earthe? all
this is vanitie (deare brother) and meere deceate of our
spirituall enemye. For within one moment after we are
30 dead, we shall care no more for wyfe, children, father,
mother, or brother, in this matter, than we shall for a
meere straunger: and one penye geven in almes while
we lyved for Gods sake, shall comfort us more at that
daye, than thowsandes of poundes bestowed upon our
35 kynne, for the naturall love we beare unto our owne
fleshe and bloode: The whiche, I wold to Christ worldlye men dyd consider: And then (no dowte) they wolde
never take suche care for kynred, as they doe: especiallie

---

23 excusation

upon their deathe beddes: whence presentlie they are to departe to that place, where fleshe and bloode holdeth no more privilege: nor riches have any power to deliver: but onelie suche, as were well bestowed in the service of God, or geven to the poore for his names sake. And this shalbe sufficient for this point of riches.

The third braunche of worldlie vanities is called by S. John concupiscence of the fleshe: whiche conteyneth all pleasures and carnall recreations: as banquetting, laughing, playeing, and the lyke, wherewithe our fleshe is much delyted in this world. And albeit in this kinde, there is a certaine measure to be allowed unto the god-lie, for the convenient maintenance of their healthe: as also in riches it is not to be reprehended: yet, that all these worldlie solaces, are not onelie vain, but also daungerous, in that excesse and abundance, as worldlie men seek and use them: appeareth playnelie by these woordes of Christ. Woe be unto you whiche nowe doe laughe, for you shall weepe. Wo be unto you that now lyve in fyll, and satietie: for the tyme shall come, when you shall suffer hungar. And agayne, in S. Johns gospell, speaking to his Apostles, and by them to all other, he saythe: *You shall weepe and pule: but the world shall rejoyse*: making it a signe distinctive betwene the good and the badde: that the one shall mourne in this lyfe, and the other rejoyse, and make them selves merye.

The verye same dothe Job confirme both of the one, and the other sort: for of worldlinges he saythe: that they solace them selves with all kynde of Musicke, and doe passe over their dayes in pleasure, and in a verie moment doe goe doune into hell. But of the godlie he saythe in his owne persone: that they sighe before they eate theyr breade. And in an other place: that they feare all their woorkes, knoweing that God spareth not hym which offendeth. The reason whereof the wyse man yet further expresseth, sayeing: *That the workes of good men are in the handes of God: and no man knoweth whether he be woor-thie of love or hatred, at Gods handes: but all is kept uncertayne*

Side notes:

3. Of the vanitie of worldlie pleasures.

Luc.6.

Joh.16.

Job.21.

Job.3.
Job.9.

Eccle.9.

---

9 *mn: pleasure*   37 *knoweth (by outward things) whether love or hatred*

for the tyme to come. And olde Tobias insinuateth yet an   Tob.5.
other cause, when he saythe: *What joye can I have or receave,*
seing I sytt heer in darkenes? Speaking literallye of his corporall blyndenes, but yet leavinge it also to be under-
5   standed of spirituall and internall darkenes.

These are then the causes (beside externall affliction   Whye
whiche God often sendeth) whye the godlie doe lyve   good men
more sadde and fearefull in this lyfe, than wicked men   are sadd in
doe, according to the counsayle of S. Paul: and whie   this lyfe.
10   also they sighe often and weepe, as Job and Christ doe   1.Co.2.
affirme: for that they remember often the Justice of God: 2.Co.7.
theyr owne frayltie in sinning: the secrete judgement of   Philip.2.
Gods predestination uncertaine to us: the vale of mis-   Job.3.
erie and desolation, wherein they lyve here: whiche made   Joh.16.
15   even the Apostles to grone, as S. Paul saythe, thoughe   Rom.8.
they had lesse cause therof than we. In respect wherof   Ephe.4.
we are willed to passe over this life in carefullnes, wache-   Mat.24.
fullnes, feare and trembling, and in respect wherof also,   2.Cor.5.
the wyseman saythe: *It is better to goe to the house of sorow,*   & 7.
20   *than to the house of feasting.* And agayne: *Where sadnes is,*   Eccle.7.
there is the hart of wysemen: but where myrthe is, there is the
harte of fooles. Finallie, in respect of this the scripture
saythe: *Beatus homo qui semper est pauidus*: Happie is the   Prov.28.
man whiche alwayes is fearefull: Whiche is nothinge els,
25   but that whiche the holie ghoste commaundethe every
man, by Micheas the Prophet, *solicitum ambulare cum deo*:   Mich.6.
To walke carefull and diligent withe God, thynkynge
uppon his commaundementes, how we keepe and observe
the same, how we resist, and mortifie our members
30   uppon earthe and the like: whiche cogitations, if they
might have place withe us, wolde cutt of a greate deale
of those worldlie pastimes, wherwithe the careles sorte
of synners are overwhelmed: I meane of those good
feloushippes of eatings, drynkings, laughings, syngings,
35   disputings, and other suche vanities that distract us most.

Hereof, Christ gave us a moste notable advertisement,   Joh.11.

---

13 [* uncertain] *mn*: B. *Calling and justifieng, are verie plain and
infallible tokens therof. Rom.8.30. And so far is it not uncertain unto
the faithful.

in that he wept often: as at his nativitie: at the resusci- Luc.19.
tation of Lazarus: upon Jerusalem and upon the crosse.
But he is never redde to have laughte in all his lyfe.
Heerof also is his owne nativitie and deathe a signification:
5 which, being bothe in Godes handes, are appointed unto
us withe sorow and greefe, as we see. But the midle
parte therof, that is, our lyfe, being left in our owne
handes (by Gods appointement:) we passe it over withe
vayne delytes, never thinking whence we came, nor
10 whether we goe.

A wyse travailer passyng by hys Inne, thoughe he see A simili-
pleasant meates offered hym: yet he forbeareth, uppon tude.
consideration of the price, and the journey he hathe to
make: and taketh in nothing, but so muche, as he
15 knowethe well, how to discharge, the next morning, at
his departure: But a foole layethe handes on everie delicate bayte that ys presented to his sight: and playeth
the prince, for a night or two. Marie, when it comethe
to the reckening: he wisheth, that he had lyved onelie
20 with breade and drynke, rather than to be so troubled,
as he is, for the payment. The custome of Gods churche
is, to fast the even of everye feast, and then to make
merye the next daye: that is, upon the feastivall daye it
selfe: which representethe the abstinent lyfe of good men
25 in this world, therby to be merye in the world to come.
But the fashion of the world is contrarie: that is, to eate
and drincke merilie first, at the taverne: And after, to
lett the hoste brynge in his reckening. They eate, drynke,
and laughe: and the hoste, he skoreth upp all in the
30 mean space: And when the time cometh, that they must
paye: many a harte is sadde, that was pleasant before.

This the scripture affirmethe also, of the pleasures of
this world: *Risus dolore miscebitur & extrema gaudii luctus* Prov.14.
occupat: Laughter shal be myngled with sorowe: and
35 mourning shal ensue at the hynder end of myrthe. The
devill, that playeth the hoste, in this world, and will

---

21 custome of many churches yet is   24 which may represent unto
us, the   25 world, and the mirth that they have in the world to
come.   29 host scoreth

serve you withe what delyte or pleasure you desyre, wryt-
ethe up all in his booke: and at the daye of your departure, (that is, at your deathe) will he bring the whole
reckening, and charge you withe it all: and then shall
5 folow that, whiche God promiseth to worldlinges, by the
prophet Amos: *Your mirthe shalbe turned into mourning and*   Amos.8.
lamentation. Yea, and more than this, if you be not able   Tob.2.
to discharge the reckening: you may chaunce to heare
that other dreadfull sentence of Christ, in the Apocalips,
10 *quantum in deliciis fuit, tantum date illi tormentum*: Looke, how   Apo.18.
muche he hathe bene in hys delites, so much torment
doe you lay upon hym.

Wherfore, to conclude this point, and therwithall this
first parte, touching vanities: truelie may we saie with
15 the prophet David, of a worldlye minded man: *Uniuersa*   Psal.39.
vanitas omnis homo viuens: The lyfe of suche men con-
tayneth all kynde of vanitie: That is, vanitie in ambition, vanitie in riches, vanitie in pleasures, vanitie in all
thinges whiche they most esteeme. And therfore, I may
20 well ende with the woordes of God, by the prophet
Esay, *væ vobis, qui trahitis iniquitatem in funiculis vanitatis*:   Esa.5.
Wo be unto you, whiche doe draw wickednes in the
ropes of vanitie. These ropes are those vanities of vain-   The
glorie, promotion, dignitie, nobilitie, beautie, riches,   ropes of
25 delites, and other before touched: which allwayes draw   vanitie.
with them some iniquitie and sinne. For which cause
David saythe unto God: *Thow hatest (o Lord) observers of*   Psal.5.
superfluous vanities. And the scripture reporting the cause
why God destroyed utterlye the famylye and linage of
30 Baasa kyng of Israel, saythe, yt was, *For that they had pro-*   3.Re.16.
voked God in their vanities. And lastlye, for this cause the
holie ghoste pronounceth generallie of all men: *Beatus*
vir qui non respexit in vanitates, & insanias falsas: Blessed is   Psal.40.
that man, whiche hathe not respected vanities, and the
35 false madnes of this world.

Now come I then to the second part proposed in this   2. How
chapiter: to shew how this world, with the commodities   worldlie

---

28 *omits* And the scripture reporting the cause . . . *they had provoked*
God in their vanities.

therof, are not onelie vanities, but also deceytes: as Christ
termeth them: for that in deede, they performe not unto
their folowers, those ydle vanities which they doe promise.
Wherin, the world may be compared to that wreched,
5 and ungratefull deceyver, Laban: whoe made poore Jacob
to serve hym seaven yeeres for fayre Rachell, and in the
end deceyved hym with fowle Lia. What false promises
dothe the world make daylye? to one it promisethe long
lyfe and healthe: and cutteth hym of in the myddest of
10 his dayes: To an other it promiseth great wealthe, and
promotion: and after long service, performeth no parte
therof: to an other it promiseth great honour by large
expences: but under-hande it castethe hym into contempt, by beggarie: to an other it assureth great advaunce-
15 ment by mariage: but yet never geveth hym abilitie to
come to his desire. Go you over the whole world: beholde
countries: vewe provinces: looke into cities: hearken at
the doores and windowes of private houses, of princes
palaces, of secrete chambers: and you shall see, and
20 heare nothing, but lamentable complaintes: one, for that
he hathe lost: an other for that he hathe not wonne: a
thyrd for that he is not satisfied: tenne thowsand, for
that they are deceyved.

Can there be a greater deceite (for examples sake)
25 than to promis renowme, and memorie, as the world
dothe to her folowers: and yet to forget them as soone
as they are deade? who dothe remember now one, of
fortie thowsand jolye felowes in this worlde, captaines,
souldiars, counsaillers, Dukes, Erles, princes, prelates,
30 and Emperoures, kynges and quenes, Lordes and ladyes?
whoe remembrethe them (I saye?) who once thynkethe
or speakethe of them now? hathe not their memorie
perished with their sounde, as the prophet saythe? did
not Job promise truelye, *that their remembrance shoulde be*
35 *as ashes troden under foote?* And David: *That they shoulde be*
as dust blowne abrode with the wynde? S. Paul the first

vanities
are also
deceytes.

Mat.13.
Gen.29.
False
promises
of the
worlde.

The false
promises
of
renowme.

Psal.9.
Job.13.
Psal.1.
Jerom.in

---

36 *omits* abrode 36 *omits* S. Paul the first heremite ... the world
bothe remembreth, and honoreth his memorie; *substitutes* Divers men
there have been ere this, that have been very mean in common

heremite hydd hym selfe fowerskore and tenne yeeres
in a wyldernesse, without knowing, or speaking with any
man, or once shewing or revealing hym selfe to the
world: And yet now, the world bothe remembreth, and
5 honoreth his memorie. But many a kyng and Emperour
have stryved and laboured, all their lyfe, to be knowne
in the world, and yet are now forgotten: So that the
world is like, in this pointe, (as one saythe) unto a covetouse and forgetfull hoste, who, yf he see his olde gest
10 come bye, in beggarlie estate, all his money beyng spent:
he maketh semblance not to knowe hym. And yf the
gest mervayle thereat: and saye, that he hathe come
often that waye, and spent muche money in the house:
the other answereth: yt may be so, for there passe this
15 waye so manye, as we use not to keepe accompt therof.
But, what is the waye to make this hoste to remembre
you (saythe this Author?) the waye is (saythe he) to use
hym evill as you passe by: beate hym well, or doe some
other notable iniurie unto hym (as Paul, and his lyke
20 did unto the world:) and he will remember you, as long
as he lyveth, and many tymes will talke of you, when
you are farre of from hym.

Infinite are the deceytes, and dissimulations of the
world: It seemeth goodlye, fayre and gorgeous, in utter
25 shew: but when it cometh to handling, it is nothing but
a fether: when it cometh to sight, it is nothing but a
shadow: when it cometh to weight, it is nothing but
smoke: when it cometh to opening, it is nothing but an
image of playster woork, full of olde ragges and paches
30 within. To know the miseries of the world, you must
goe a litle out from yt. For, as they whiche walke in a
myst, doe not see it so well, as they which stand upon
a hyll from yt: so fareth it, in discerning the world:
whose propertie is, to blynde them that come to it, to
35 the ende they may not see theyr owne estate: even as

---

account: and yet bicause they have labored to be unknow to the
world, therfore the rather the world both remembreth, and honoreth
now the memorie of them. But many   17 the way is to use him ill
19 *omits* (as Paul, and his lyke did unto the world:)   24 outward
show

a Raven, first of all, strykethe owte the poore shepes
eyes, to the ende, she may not see the waye, to escape
from his tyranie.

After the worlde hathe once bereft the worldlyng of
5   his spirituall syght, that he can judge no longer, betwene
good, and evell, vanitie, and veritie: then, it rockethe
him a sleepe, at ease and pleasure: it byndethe hym
sweetelie: it deceyvethe hym pleasantlie: it tormentethe
him in great peace and rest: it hathe a prowde spirite
10   streightwayes, to place him in the pinnacle of greedie   Math.4.
ambition, and there hence, to shew hym all the digni-
ties, and prefermentes of the world: it hathe twentie false
marchantes, to shew him in the darke, the first and former endes of fayre and precious clothes: Marie, he may
15   not looke into the whole peeces, nor carie them to the
light: It hathe fower hundred false prophettes to flatter
hym, as Achab had, whiche must keepe him from the   3.Re.22.
hearing of Micheas his counsayle: that is, from the remorse of his owne conscience, which telleth him truethe:
20   It hathe a thowsand cunning fishers, to laye before him
pleasant baytes, but all furnyshed withe daungerous
hookes within: It hathe infinite strumpettes of Babilon,
to offer him drinke in golden cuppes, but all myngled   Apo.17.
withe moste deadlie poison: It hathe in everie doore an
25   alluring Jahel, to entise hym into the milke of pleasures   Judic.4.
and delites, but all have their hammers and nayles in
their handes, to murder him in the brayne, when he
fallethe a sleepe. It hathe in everie corner, a flattering
Joab, to embrace withe one arme, and kill withe the   2.Re.20.
30   other: A false Judas, to geve a kisse, and therwith to   Luc.22.
betraye. Finallie it hathe all the deceites, all the dissimulations, all the flatteries, all the treasons, that possiblie
may be devised. It hateth them, that love yt: deceiveth them, that trust it: afflicteth them, that serve yt: rep-
35   rocheth them, that honour it: damneth them, that folow
it: and moste of all forgetteth them, that labour and
travaile moste of all for it. And to be breefe in this
matter, doe you what you can for this worlde, and love

---

2 eie, and so bringeth to passe, that she

it, and adore it, as muche as you will: yet in the ende,
you shall finde yt a right Nabal: who after many benefits
receyved from David, yet when David came to have
neede of hym, he answered, *whoe is David? or who is the*   1.Re.25.
5   *sonne of Isay, that I should knowe him?* Upon greate
cause then sayd the prophet David, *O you children of men,*
howe long will you be so dull harted? Whie doe you love vani-   Psal.4.
tie, and seeke after a lye? He callethe the world, not a lyar,
but a lie it selfe: for the exceeding great fraude, and
10   deceit, whiche yt useth.

The third name or propertie that Christ ascribethe   3. How
unto the pleasures and riches of the world is, that they   pleasures
are thornes: of which, S. Gregorie writethe thus, who   of the
ever wolde have beleeved me yf I had called riches   worlde
are
15   thornes, as Christ heere dothe, seyng thornes doe pricke,   thornes.
and riches are so pleasant? And yet surelie they are   Hom.15.
thornes, for that, with the prickes of their carefull cog-   in evang.
itations, they teare, and make bloodye the myndes of
worldlye men. By whiche wordes, this holye father sig-
20   nifieth, that even as a mans naked bodye, tossed and
tumbled among many thornes, can not be but much
rent and torne, and made bloudie with the prickes therof:
so a worldly mans soule beaten with the cares and cogitations of this lyfe, can not but be vexed with restles
25   pricking of the same, and wounded also with many temptations of sinne, which doe occurre. This dothe Salomon
(in the places before alleged) signifie, when he dothe not
onelie call the riches and pleasures of this world, *vanitie*   Eccle.1.2.
of vanities, that is, the greatest vanitie of all other vani-   3.4.
30   ties: but also *affliction of spirite:* Geving us to understand,
that where these vanities are, and the love of them once
entered: there is no more the peace of God, whiche pass-   Phil.4.
eth all understanding: there is no longer rest, or quiet
of mynde: but warre of desires: vexation of thoughtes:
35   tribulation of feares: pricking of cares: unquietnes of

---

20 [* naked] *mn:* B. *But the words of Christ declare, that it is
another thing that he did specially respect therin: that is, the chok-
ing or destroieng of such corn as was sown among them; and the
utter extinguishing, or great hindering of al good motions of the
spirit of God, in al those that are worldly minded.

soule: which is in deede a moste miserable and pityfull affliction of spirite.

And the reason hereof is, that as a clocke can never stand still from runnynge, so long as the peazes doe 5 hang therat: so a worldlie man, having infinite cares, cogitations, and anxieties hanging upon his mynde, as peazes upon the clocke, can never have rest or repose daye or night, but is inforced to beat his braynes, when other men sleepe, for the compassing of those trifles, 10 wherewith he is incombred. Oh, how many riche men in the world do feele to be true, that I now saye? how many ambitious men doe prove it daylie, and yet will not deliver them selves owt of the same?

A comparison.

Of all the plagues sent unto Egypt, that of the flyes 15 was one of the most troublesome, and fastidious. For, they never suffered men to rest: but the more they were beaten of, the more they came uppon them. So, of all the miseries, and vexations, that God layeth upon world-linges, this is not the least, to be tormented with the 20 cares of that, which they esteeme theire greatest feli-citie: and can not beat them of, by anye meanes they can devise: They rushe upon them in the morning, as sone as they awake: they accompanye them in the daye: they forsake them not at night: they folow them to bedde: 25 they lett them from their sleepe: they aflict them in their dreames: and finallie, they are those importune and unmercyfull tyrantes, whiche God threatnethe to wicked men, by Jeremie the prophet, *qui nocte ac die non dabunt requiem*, which shal geve them no rest, eyther by daye 30 or night. And the cause hereof, whiche God alleageth in the same chapter, is, *quia abstuli pacem meam a populo isto (dicit dominus,) misericordiam, & miserationes.* For that I have taken away my peace from this kynde of people (saythe God) I have taken away my mercie, and com-35 miserations: a verie heavie sentence to all them, that lye under the yoke and bondage of these miserable vanities.

Exod.8.

Jere.16.

But yet, the prophet Esaye hathe a muche more ter-rible description of these mens estate: *They put their trust*

Esa.59.

---

26 are like to those

*in thinges of nothing, and doe talke vanities: They conceave laboure,
and bring foorthe iniquitie: they breake the egges of serpentes, and
weave the webbes of spyders: he that shall eate of theyr egges,
shall dye: and that whiche is hached thence, shalbe a Cocatrice:*
5   *their webbes shall not make clothe, to cover them: for that, their
woorkes are unprofitable: and the worke of iniquitie is in their
handes.* These are the woordes of Esay, declaring unto
us, by most significant similitudes, how daungerous thornes
the riches and pleasures of this world are. And first he
10 saythe, *they put theyr hope in thinges of nothing, and doe talke
vanities*: To signifie, that he meanethe of the vanities,
and vayne men of this worlde: whoe commonlie doe
talke of the thinges whiche they love best, and wherin
they place their greatest affiance. Secondlie he saythe,
15 *they conceave labour, and bring foorthe iniquitie*: alluding herein,
to the chyld-byrthe of women, whoe fyrst, doe conceave
in their wombe: and after a greate deale of travaile, doe
bring foorthe their infant: so, worldlie men, after a greate
tyme of travaile, and laboure in vanities, doe bring
20 foorthe no other fruite, than sinne and iniquitie. For
that is the effect of those vanities, as he speaketh in the
same chapiter, crieinge owte to suche kynde of men:
Woe be unto you, which doe drawe iniquitie in the ropes of vanitie.

    But, yet to expresse this matter more forciblye, he
25 usethe two other similitudes: sayeing, *they breake the egges
of serpentes, and doe weave the webbes of spiders*: Signifieing
by the one, the vanitie of these worldlie cares: and by
the other, the daunger therof. The spider we see, takethe
great paynes and labour many dayes together, to weave
30 her selfe a webbe: and in the ende, when all is done,
cometh a puffe of wynde, or some other litle chaunce,
and breaketh all in peeces: even as he in the gospel,
which had taken great travayle and care, in heaping
riches together, in plucking down his olde barnes, and
35 buylding up of new: and when he was come to saye to
his soule, *Now be merie*: That night his soule was taken
from him, and all his labour lost. Therfore Esay saithe

The
explica-
tion of
the
woordes
of Esay.

Luc.12.

---

31 little matter, and   34 barns, building

in this place, that *the webbes of these weavers shall not make them clothe to cover them with all: for that their woorkes are unprofitable.*

The other comparison contayneth matter of great
5   daunger and feare. For, as the bird that sitteth upon the egges of serpentes, by breaking and hatching them, bringeth foorthe a perilous broode, to her owne destruction: so those that sytt a broode uppon these vanities of the worlde (saythe Esay) doe hatche at last their owne
10 destruction. The reason wherof is, (as he saythe) *for that the worke of iniquitie is in their hande*: Still harping uppon this stringe, that a man can not love and folow these vanities, or intangle hym selfe with their ropes (as his phrase is) but that he must in deede drawe on muche
15 iniquitie there with: that is, he must mingle muche sinne and offence of God with the same: whiche effect of sinne, because it kylleth the soule, that consenteth unto it: therfor Esay compareth it unto the broode of serpentes, that kylleth the byrd which bringeth them foorthe
20 to the world. And finallie, Moyses usethe the lyke similitudes, when he saythe, of vayne and wicked men. *Their*   Deut.32. *vineyard is the vineyarde of Sodomites, their grape is the grape of gaule, and their clusters of grapes are moste bytter: their wyne is the gaul of dragons, and the poyson of cocatrices, uncurable.* By
25 which dreadfull and lothesome comparisons, he wolde geve us to understand, that the sweete pleasures of this worlde are in deede deceytes, and will prove them selves, one daye, most bytter and daungerous.

The fowerth point that we have to consider is, how   The
30 this woorde, *ærumna*, that is, miserie and calamitie, may   fowerth be verified of the world, and the felicitie therof. Whiche   part, thing, thoghe it may appeare sufficientlie, by that whiche   how the hathe bene sayd before: yet will I (for promise sake) discusse it a litle further in this place, by some particulars.   miserie.
35 And among many miseries which I might heere recount,   Brevitie. the first, and one of the greatest, is, the brevitie and uncertaintie of all worldlie prosperitie. Oh, how greate a miserye is this unto a worldlie man, that wolde have his pleasures constant and perpetuall? *O deathe howe bytter*   Eccl.41.

is thy remembrance (saythe the scripture) *unto a man that hathe peace in his riches?* we have seene many men advanced, and not endured two monethes in their prosperitie: we have heard of divers maryed in greate joye, and not have lyved six dayes in their felicitie: we have read of straunge matters happened owt in this kynde: and we see with our eyes no few examples daylie. What a greefe was it (think you) to Alexander the greate, that having subdewed, in twelve yeeres, the moste part of all the world, shoulde be then enforced to dye, when he was moste desirous to lyve? and when he was to take moste joye and comfort of his victories? what a sorowe was it to the ryche man in the gospell, to heare uppon the suddayne, *hac nocte*: Even this night thou must dye? what a miserie will this be to many worldlings, whan it cometh: whoe now buyld palaces, purchase lands, heape riches, procure dignities, make mariages, joyne kynredes: as though there were never an ende of these matters? what a doolefull daye, will this be to them (I saye) when they must forgoe all these things, which they so muche love? when they must be turned of, as princes mules are wont to be, at the journeys ende: that is, their treasure taken from them, and their gauld backes onelie, left unto them selves? for, as we see these mules of princes goe, all the daye long, loaden with treasure, and covered with fayre clothes, but at night shaken of, into a sorie stable, much brused and gauled with the cariage of those treasures: so riche men, that passe through this world, loaden with golde and silver, and doe gaul greatlie their soules in cariage therof: are despoyled of their burden at the daye of deathe, and are turned of, with their wounded consciences, to the lothesome stable of hell and damnation.

An other miserie joyned to the prosperitie of this world, is the grevous counterpeaze of discontentementes, that everie worldlie pleasure hathe with it. Runne over everie pleasure in this lyfe, and see what sawce it hath adjoyned. Aske them that have had moste proofe therof, whether they remayne contented, or no? The possession

Margins:
1.Mac.1.

Luc.12.

A comparison.

Discontentement.

---

1 (saith the wise man) *unto*   6 *omits* happened owt   16 heap up riches

of riches is accompanyed with so many feares, and cares, as hathe bene shewed: The advauncement of honoures is subjecte to all miserable servitude that may be devised. The pleasure of the fleshe, thoughe yt be laufull and honest: yet, is it called by S. Paul, *tribulation of the fleshe*: But, yf it be with sinne: tenne thousand times more, is it environed with all kynde of miseries.

Whoe can recken up the calamities of our bodye? so many diseases, so manie infirmities, so many mischances, so many dangers? whoe can tell the passions of our mynde that doe afflict us, now with angar, now with sorowe, nowe with envie, nowe with furie? who can re-counte the adversities, and misfortunes that come by our goodes? whoe can number the hurtes, and discon-tentations, that daylie ensewe upon us, from our neigh-boures? one calleth us into law for our goodes: an other pursueth us for our life: a third, by slaunder impugneth our good name: one afflicteth us by hatred, an other by envie, an other by flatterie, an other by deceyte, an other by revenge, an other by false witnes, an other by open armes. There are not so many dayes, nor howres in our lyves, as there are miseries and contrarieties in the same. And further than this, the evill hathe this pre-rogative above the good, in our lyfe, that one defect onelie overwhelmeth and drowneth a greate number of good things together: as yf a man had all the felicities heaped together, which this world could yeeld, and yet had but one toothe out of tune: all the other pleasures wolde not make him merie. Heerof you have a cleare example in Aman, cheefe counsailer of king Assuerus:

1.Cor.7.

Miseries of bodie.

Of minde.

Of goodes.

Of neigh-bours.

Heste.5.

---

4 [* plesure] *mn*: B. *It selfe is not so called: but it is said, that those that marrie should have tribulation in the flesh: which is in respect of the cares and molestations that commonly hang (or specially at that time, as the case stood with them) on the married estate. 9 [* mischances] *mn*: B. *Wheras chance and fortune are used of us in much like sense, though the sense and meaning of those that are instructed in the faith be good, referring al to the providence of God: yet seeing that Saint Augustine long since was sorie, that he had so much used such words (as appeereth, Retr.I.c.I.) it were good that we also should more warily decline such words, as others have so prophanely abused. And better were it a great deal to say, that such things are of the hand of God.   13 and miseries, that

who, for that Mardochæus the Jewe dyd not ryse to him
when he went by, nor dyd honour hym, as other men
dyd: he sayde to his wyfe and freendes, that all his other
felicities were nothing, in respect of this one affliction.

5   Add now to this the miserie of darkenes and blindenes, wherin worldlie men live, (as in parte I have touched
before) most fitlie prefigured by the palpable darkenes
of Egypte, wherin no man could see his neighboure, no
man could see his worke, no man could see his waie:
10   such is the darkenes wherin worldlie men walke. They
have eyes, but they see not, sayth Christ: that is, thoughe
they have eyes to see the matters of this world: yet they
are blinde, for that they see not the things they should
see in deed. The children of this world are wyser in
15   their generation, than the children of light. But that is
onelie in matters of this world, in matters of darkenes,
not in matters of light, wherof they are no children: for
that, the carnall man understandeth not the thinges
which are of God. Walke over the world, and you shall
20   finde men as sharp eyed as Egles in thinges of earthe:
but the same men as blinde as betles in matters of
heaven: heerof ensewe those lamentable effectes, that we
see daylie, of mans lawes so carefullie respected, and Godes
commaundementes so contemptuouslie rejected: of earth-
25   lie goods sought for, and heavenlie goodes not thought
upon: of so muche travayle taken for the bodye, and so
litle care used for the soule. Finallie, yf you will see in
what greate blindenes the world dothe lyve: remember
that S. Paul comming from a worldlinge to be a good
30   Christian, had skales taken from his eyes by Ananias,
whiche covered his sight before, when he was in his
pride and ruffe of the world.

      Beside all these miseries, there is yet an other mis-
erie, greater in some respect, than the former, and that
35   is, the infinite number of temptations, of snares, of in-
tisementes in the world, wherby men are drawen to
perdition daylie. Athanasius writeth of S. Anthonie the
heremite, that God revealed unto hym, one daye, the

The mis-
erie of
blindenes.

Exo.10.

Mat.13.

Luc.16.

1.Cor.2.

Act.9.

Tempta-
tions and
dangers.

Athan.
in vita

---

5 this miserie   20 of the earth   22 Therof

state of the world, and he sawe it all hanged full of Antonii.
nettes in every corner, and devilles sitting by, to watche
the same. The prophet David, to signifie the verie same
thing, that is, the infinite multitude of snares in this
5   worlde, sayeth, *God shall rayne snares upon sinners*: that Psal.11.
is, God shall permit wicked men to fall into snares:
which are as plentyfull in the world, as are the droppes
of rayne, which fall downe from heaven. Everie thing
almoste, is a deadly snare, unto a carnall and loose
10 harted man. Everie sight that he seeth, every woord that
he heareth, every thought that he conceaveth: his youthe,
his age: his freendes, his enemies: his honoure, his dis-
grace: his riches, his Povertie: his compagnie keeping:
his prosperitie, his adversitie: his meate that he eateth:
15 his apparell that he weareth: all are snares, to drawe
hym to destruction, that is not watchefull.

    Of this then, and of the blyndenes declared before, Facilitie
dothe folow the last, and greatest miserie of all, whiche of
can be in this lyfe: And that is, the facilitie wherby sinning.
20 worldlie men doe runne into sinne. For truelie sayeth
the scripture, *miseros facit populos peccatum*: Sinne is the Pro.14.
thing that maketh people miserable. And yet, how easilie men of the worlde doe committ sinne, and how litle
scruple they make of the matter, Job signifieth, when,
25 talking of suche a man, he sayeth, *bibit quasi aquam iniq-* Job.15.
uitatem: He suppeth up sinne, as it were water: that is,
with as great facilitie, custome, and ease, passeth he
downe any kynde of sinne, that is offered him, as a man
drinketh water, when he is a thirst. He that will not
30 beleeve the sayeing of Job: let hym prove a litle, by his
owne experience, whether the matter be so or no: let
hym walke owt, into the streetes, beholde the doeinges
of men, vewe their behavioure, consider what is done
in shoppes, in halles, in consistories, in judgemente seates,
35 in palaces, and in common meetinge places abroade:
what lyeinge: what slanderinge: what deceyvinge there
is. He shall finde, that of all thinges wherof men make
anye accompt, nothing is so litle accounted of, as to

---

37 men take any

sinne. He shall see justice solde, veritie wrested, shame
lost, and equitie despised. He shall see the Innocent condemned: the guiltie delivered: the wicked advaunced: the
vertuous oppressed. He shall see manye theeves florishe:
5 manye usurers beare greate swaye, many murderers and
extorsioners reverenced and honoured: many fooles putt
in authoritie: and divers which have nothing in them
but the forme of men, by reason of money, to be placed
in great dignities for the government of others. He shall
10 heare at everie mans mouthe, almoste, vanitie, pride,
detraction, envie, deceyte, dissimulation, wantonnesse,
dissolution, lyeing, swearing, perjurie, and blaspheming.
Finallie, he shall see the moste parte of men, to governe them selves absolutelie, even as beastes doe, by the
15 motion of there passions, not by lawe of justice, reason,
religion, or vertue.

The sin-
full state
of the
world.

Of this dothe ensue the fiveth point that Christ toucheth
in his parable, and whiche I promised heere to handle:
to witt, that the love of this world choketh up and stran-
20 gleth everie man, whome it possesseth, from all celestiall and spirituall lyfe, for that it filleth hym with a
playne contrarie spirite, to the spirite of God. The Apostle
saieth, *Si quis spiritum Christi non habet, hic non est eius*: Yf
any man have not the spirit of Christ, this felow belongeth
25 not unto hym. Now, how contrarie the spirite of Christ,
and the spirite of the worlde ys, maye appeare by the
twelve fruites of Christs spirite reckened upp by S. Paul
unto the Galathians: to witt, *Charitie*, whiche is the roote
and mother of all good woorkes: *Joye*, in serving God:
30 *Peace*, or tranquilitie of minde in the stormes of this
worlde: *Patience*, in adversitie: *Longanimitie*, in expecting
our rewarde: *Bonytye*, in hurting no man: *Benignitie*, in
sweete behavioure: *Gentlenes*, in occasion geven of anger:
Faythefullnes, in performing our promises: *Modestie*, with-
35 out arrogancie: *Continencie*, from all kynde of wickednes:
Chastitie, in conserving a pure minde in a cleane and
unspotted bodie. *Against these men* (saithe S. Paul) *there is
no lawe*. And in the verie same chapiter he expresseth

The
fyveth
part of
this
chapiter.

Rom.8.

Gal.5.
The
effectes
of the
spirite of
Christe.

Gal.5.

---

27 *omits* twelve

the spirite of the world by the contrarie effectes, sayeing, the worckes of fleshe are manifest, whiche are, fornication, uncleannes, wantonnes, lecherie, idolatrie, poysonninges, enemities, contentions, emulations, wrathe, strife,
5 dissention, sectes, envie, murder, dronkennes, gluttonie, and the like: of whiche I foretell you, as I have tolde you before, that those men whiche doe suche thinges shall never obteyne the kyngdome of heaven.

The effectes of the spirite of this world.

Heere now may every man judge of the spirit of the
10 world and the spirit of Christ: and (applieing it to him selfe) may conjecture, whether he holdeth of the one, or of the other. S. Paul geeveth two pretie shorte rules in the very same place to trye the same: The first ys, *They whiche are of Christ, have crucified their fleshe, withe the*
15 *vices and concupiscences therof*: That is, they have so mortified their owne bodies, as they committ none of the vices and sinnes repeated before, nor yeeld not unto the concupiscences or temptations therof. The second rule is, *yf we lyve in spirite, then let us walke in spirit*: That is, our
20 walking and behavioure is a signe whether we be alyve or dead. For yf our walking be spirituall, suche as I have declared before by the twelve fruites therof: then doe we lyve and have life in spirite: but yf our workes be carnall, suche as S. Paul now hathe described: then
25 are we carnall and dead in spirite, nor have we any thing to doe with Christ, or portion in the kingdome of heaven. And for that all the worlde is full of those carnall workes, and bringeth foorthe no fruites in deede of Christs spirit, nor permittethe them to grow or prosper
30 within her: thence is yt, that the scripture alwayes putteth Christ and the world for opposite and open enemies.

Two rules of S. Paul to knowe our spirite.

Gal.5.

Christ & the world enemies.

Christ hym selfe sayeth, that *the worlde can not receave the spirit of trueth*. And againe in the same Evangelist, he sayeth, that nether he, nor anye of his, are of the worlde,
35 thoughe they live in the world: And yet further, in his moste vehement prayer unto his father, *pater iuste, mundus*

Joh.14.
Joh.15.17.

---

16 they strive against al the vices and sins repeated before, and yeeld not to serve the concupiscences   22 by those fruits therof   25 neither have we   29 grow up

te non cognouit: Just father the world hathe not knowen   Joh.17.
thee. For which cause S. John writeth, *If any man love*   1.Joh.2.
the world the love of the father is not in hym: And yet further S. James, that *who soever but desireth to be freend of this*   Jac.4.
5   *world, is therby made an enemye to God.* What will worldly
men saye to this? S. Paul affirmeth plainlie, that this   1.Co.11.
world is to be damned: And Christ insinuateth the same
in S. Johns gospell: but moste of all, in that wonder-   Joh.12.
full fact of his, when prayeing to his father, for other
10 matters, he excepteth the world by name. *Non pro mundo*   Joh.17.
rogo, saithe he: I doe not aske mercie and perdone for
the world, but for those whiche thow hast geven me
owt of the worlde. Oh what a dreadfull exception is
this, made by the Savioure of the world, by the lambe,
15 that taketh awaye all sinnes, by hym that asked per-   Joh.1.
done, even for his tourmentoures and crucifiers, to except   Luc.23.
now the world by name from his mercie? Oh that world-
lie men wold consider but this one point onelie: they
wolde not (I think) live so voyde of feare as they doe.
20   Can any man marvayle now why S. Paul cryeth so
carefullie to us, *nolite conformari huic sæculo,* conforme not Rom.12.
your selves to this world? and agayne: that we should
renounce utterlie all secular desires? can anye marvayle   Tit.2.
whye S. John, whiche was moste privie, above all other,
25 to Christs holie meaning herein, sayeth to us in suche
earnest sorte: *Nolite diligere mundum neque ea quæ in mundo*   1.Joh.2.
sunt, Doe not love the world, nor any thing that is in
the world? If we maye nether love it, nor so muche as
conforme our selves unto it, under so great paynes (as
30 are before rehearsed) of the enemitie of God and eternall damnation: what shall become of those men that
doe not onelye conforme them selves unto it, and the
vanities therof: but also doe folowe it, seeke after it, rest
in it, and doe bestowe all theyr labours, and travailes
35 upon it?
    If you aske me the cause whye Christ so hateth and   Whie
abhorreth this world: S. John telleth you, *Quia mundus*   Christ
totus in maligno positus est, for that all the whole worlde   hateth the
                                                              world.

23 *al worldly desires?*

is set on naughtynes: for that it hathe a spirite contrarie   1.Joh.5.
to the spirite of Christ, as hathe bene shewed: for that
it teacheth pryde, vainglorie, ambition, envie, revenge,
malice, with pleasures of the fleshe, and all kynde of
5   vanities: And Christ, on the contrarie side, humilitie,
meekenes, perdonyng of enemyes, abstinence, chastitie,
sufferance, mortification, bearing the crosse, with contempt of all earthelye pleasures for the kyngdome of
heaven: for that it persecuteth the good, and advanceth
10   the evill: for that it rooteth owt vertue, and planteth all
vice: And finalie, for that it shutteth the doores against   Apoc.3.
Christ when he knocketh, and strangleth the harte that
once it possessethe.
     Wherfore to conclude this parte, seyng this world is   A
15   suche a thing as it is: so vaine, so deceytfull, so trou-   descrip-
blesome, so daungerous: seyng it is a professed enemye   tion of
to Christ, excommunicated and damned to the pitt of   the
hell: seyng it is (as one father sayeth) an arcke of tra-   worlde.
vaile, a schoole of vanities, a feire of deceite, a labirinthe
20   of errour: seing it is nothing els but a barraine wildernes, a stonye fyeld, a durtye Stye, a tempestuous sea:
seing it is a grove full of thornes, a medowe full of scorpions, a flourishing garden without fruite, a cave full of
poysoned and deadlie basiliskes: seyng it is finallie (as I
25   have shewed,) a fountaine of miseries, a ryver of teares,   Au.ep.32.
a faigned fable, a delectable frensie: seyng (as S. Austen
sayeth) the joy of this world hathe nothing els but false
delyte, true asperitie, certaine sorowe, uncertaine pleasure, travailsome labour, fearfull rest: greevous miserie,
30   vayne hope of felicitie: seyng it hathe nothing in it (as
S. Chrisostome saythe) but teares, shame, repentance,   Hom.22.
reproche, sadnes, negligences, labours, terrours, sicknes,   ad pop.
sinne, and deathe it selfe: seyng the worlds repose is   Antioch.
full of anguishe: his securitie without foundation: his
35   feare without cause: his travailes without fruite: his sorowe without profitt: his desires without successe: his
hope without rewarde: his myrthe without continuance: his
miseries without remedies: seyng these and a thousande

---

8 *omits* for the kyngdome of heaven

evills more are in it: and no one good thing can be
had from it: who will be deceyved with this visard, or
allured with this vanitie hereafter? who will be stayed
from the noble service of God by the love of so fond a

5   trifle as is this world? And this, to a reasonable man
may be sufficient, to declare the insufficencie of this third
impediment.

But yet for the satisfieing of my promisse in the begynning of this chapiter: I have to adde a woorde or two

10   in this place, how we may avoyde the daunger of this
world, and also use it unto our gayne and commoditie.
And for the first, to avoyde the daungers, seyng there
are so many snares and trappes, as hathe bene declared:
there is no other waye but onelie to use the refuge of

15   byrdes in avoyding the daungerous snares of fowlers:
that is, to mounte up into the ayer, and so to flye over
them all. *Frustra iacitur rete ante oculos pennatorum:* saythe
the wise man: that is, the nett is layde in vayne before
the eyes of suche as have wynges, and can flye. The

20   spyes of Hierico, thoghe many snares were layde for
them by their enemyes: yet they escaped all, for that
they walked by hilles, sayeth the scripture: whiche place
Origen expounding, sayeth, that there is no waye to
avoyde the daungers of this world, but to walke uppon

25   hylles, and to imitate David, that sayed, *Leuaui oculos meos
ad montes, unde veniet auxilium mihi.* I lyfted up myne eyes
unto the hylles, wherhence all myne ayde and assistance
came, for avoyding the snares of this world. And then
shall we saye with the same David, *Anima nostra sicut*

30   *passer erepta est de laqueo venantium:* Our soule is delivered
as a sparowe from the snare of the fowlers. We must
saye with S. Paul, *Our conversation is in heaven.* And then
shall we litle feare all these deceytes, and daungers upon
earthe. For as the fowler hathe no hope to cache the

35   byrde, excepte he can allure her to pyche, and come
downe, by some meanes: so hath the devill no waye to
entangle us, but to saye as he dyd to Christ, *mitte te deor-*

The last
part of
this
chapiter:
how we
may
avoide
the evill
of the
worlde.

Pro.1.

Ho.1.in
Josue.
Psa.121.

Psa.124.

Phill.3.

---

22 scripture: wherunto Origin alluding, saith   24 [* but] *mn*: B.
*Though the matter be good: yet hardly doth it stand by these places.

sum, throw thy selfe downe: that is, piche downe upon   Matt.4.
the baytes whiche I have layde: eate and devoure them:
enamour thy selfe with them: tye thyne appetite unto
them: and the lyke.

5   Whiche grosse and open temptation he that will avoyde,
by contemning the allurement of these baytes: by flyeing
over them: by placeyng his love and cogitations in the
mountaines of heavenlie joyes and eternitie: he shall easilie escape all daungers and perilles. Kyng David was
10   past them all when he sayed to God: *What is there for*   Psal.73.
me in heaven, or what doe I desire besides thee upon earthe? my
fleshe and my harte have faynted for desyre of thee. Thou art the
God of my hart, and my portion (o Lord) for ever.
Saint Paul also was past over these daungers, when
15   he sayed, that now he was crucified to the world, and   Gal.6.
the world unto hym: and that he esteemed all the wealthe   Phili.3.
of this world as meere dung: And that albeit he lyved   2.Co.10.
in fleshe, yet lyved hee not according to the fleshe. Which
glorious example yf wee wolde folow, in contemning and
20   despising the vanities of this world, and fixing our mindes
in the noble riches of Gods kyngdome to come: the snares
of the devill wolde prevayle nothing at all agaynst us in
this lyfe.
Touching the second pointe: how to use the riches   How to
25   and commodities of this world to our advantage: Christ   use world-
hathe layed downe playnlie the meanes: *Facite vobis ami-*   lie wealth
cos de Mammona iniquitatis: Make unto you freendes of the   to our
riches of iniquitie. The riche gloutton might have escapede   advantage.
his tormentes, and have made hym selfe a happie man   Luc.16.
30   by helpe of worldlye wealthe, yf he wolde. And so might   Luc.16.
manye a thousand which now lyve, and will goe to hell
for the same. Oh, that men wolde take warning and be
wise whiles they have time. S. Paul sayeth: *Deceive not*   Gala.6.
your selves: Looke what a man soweth, and that shall he reape.   2.Cor.9.
35   What a plentifull harvest then might riche men provide
them selves, yf they wolde: whiche have suche stoore of
seede, and so muche ground offered them daylie to sowe
it in? whie doe they not remember that sweete harvest
song: *Come ye blessed of my father, enter into the kingdome pre-*   Mat.25.
40   *pared for you: for I was hungrie, and you fedd me: I was thirstie,*

and you gave me to drinke: I was naked and you appareled me?
Or yf they doe not care for this: whie doe they not
feare at least the blacke *Sanctus* that must be chaunted
to them for the contrarie? *Agite nunc diuites, plorate, ulu-*   Jac.5.
5   *lantes in miseriis vestris quæ aduenient vobis:* goe to now you
riche men, weepe and howle in your miseries that shall
come upon you.

The holy father John Damascen reporteth a goodly   Dam.in
parable of Barlaam the heremite, to our purpose. There   hist.Bar-
10 was (sayeth he) a certaine citie, or common wealthe,   laam &
which used to chuse them selves a kyng from among   Josaphat
the poorest sorte of people, and to advaunce him to   cap.14.
great honour, wealthe, and pleasures for a time: But
after a while, when they were wearie of him, there fash-   A
15 ion was to rise against hym, and to dispoyle hym of all   parable.
his felicitie, yea the verie clothes of his backe, and so
to banishe him naked into an yland of a farre countrie:
where, bringing nothing with him, he should lyve in
greate miserie, and be putt to greate slaverie for ever.
20 Whiche practise one kyng at a certaine time considering, by good advise: (for all the other, thoughe they
knewe that fashion, yet throughe negligence and pleasures of their present felicitie, cared not for it,) tooke
resolute order withe him selfe how to prevent this mis-
25 erie: which was by this meanes. He saved everye daye
great sommes of moneye from his superfluities and idle
expences, and so, secretlie made over before hand a
great treasure unto that yland, wherunto he was in
daunger daylie to be sent. And when the time came,
30 that in deede they deposed him from his kingedome,
and turned him awaye naked, as they had done the
other before: he went to the yland with joye and confidence, where his treasure laye: and was receyved there,
with exceeding great triumphe: and placed presentlie in
35 greater glorie, than ever he was before.

This parable teacheth as muche as possiblie may be   The

---

8 a parable   12 sort of the people   36 This parable (drawing somwhat
neer to that which Christ put of the evil steward, teacheth as much
as at this present needs to be said in this point.

sayd in this point. For the citie or common wealthe is
this present worlde, which advauncethe to authoritie,
poore men: that is, suche as come naked into this lyfe:
and upon the sodaine when they looke least for it, dothe
5   it pull them downe agayne, and turneth them of naked
into theyr graves, and so into an other world: where
bringing no treasure of good workes with them, they
are like to finde litle favoure, but rather eternal miserie.
The wyse king that prevented this calamitie, is he, whiche
10   in time of wealthe in this life (according to the coun-
sayll of Christ) dothe seeke to laye up treasure in heaven
by almes deedes and other good workes, against the
daye of his deathe, when he must be banished hence
naked, as all the princes of that citie were. At whiche
15   time, yf their good deedes do folowe them (as God
promyssethe) shall they be happie men, and placed in
much more glorie, than ever this worlde was able to
geve them: But yf they come without oyle in their
lampes: then is there nothing for them to expect, but
20   *nescio vos*: I knowe you not. And when they are knowen:
Ite maledicti in ignem æternum, goe you accursed into fyre
everlasting.

applica-
tion of
this
parable.

Luc.12.

Apo.14.

Mat.25.

Of the fowerthe impediment: whiche is, to muche presuming
of the mercie of God.

25   CHAP. IV

There are a certaine kynde of people in the world, who
will not take the paynes to think of, or to alleage any
of the sayd impedimentes before: but have a shorter
waye for all, and more plausible, as it seemeth to them:
30   And that is, to lay the whole matter upon the backe of
Christ hym selfe, and to answere what soever you
can saye agaynst them, with this onelye sentence: *God*

---

5 them naked into their graves, and so sendeth them   7 *omits* of
good workes   10 *omits* in time of wealthe   12 *omits* by almes deedes
and other, good workes   16 then shal they be

is mercifull. Of these men Christ complayneth greevous-
lie by the prophet, sayeing: *Supra dorsum meum fabricauerunt*   Psa.129.
peccatores, prolongauerunt iniquitatem: Sinners have buylt upon   Building
my backe, they have prolonged their iniquitie. By whiche   on Gods
5   woordes he signifieth, that prolonging of our iniquities,   backe.
in hope of Gods mercie, is to buyld our synnes on his
backe. But what foloweth? will God beare it? no verilie: for the next woordes ensewing are: *Dominus iustus,*
concidet ceruices peccatorum: God is just, he will cutt in
10   sunder the neckes of sinners. Heere are two coolyng
cardes, for the two warme imaginations before. Meane
you (Syr) to prolong your iniquitie, for that God is mercifull? remember also, that he is just, sayeth the prophet.
Are ye gotten up, uppon the backe of God, to make
15   your nest of sinne there? take heede: for he will fetche
you downe agayne, and breake your necke downeward,
except ye repent: for that in deede there is no one thing
whiche may be so injurious to God, as to make hym
the foundation of our sinfull lyfe, whiche lost his owne
20   lyfe for the extinguishing of sinne.

But you will saye perhappes: and is not God then   How God
mercyfull? yes truelie (deare brother,) he is moste mercy-   is bothe
full, and there is nether ende nor measure of his mercie: mercifull
he is even mercie it selfe: it is his nature and essence: and just.
25   and he can no more leave to be mercyfull, than he can
leave to be God. But yet (as the prophet heere sayth)
he is just also. We must not so remember his mercie,
as wee forgett his justice. *Dulcis & rectus dominus*. Our
lord is sweet, but yet upright and just too, sayeth David:
30   And in the same place, *all the wayes of our lord are mercie*   Psal.25.
and trueth: Which woordes holye Barnard expounding in   Ser.52.
a certaine sermon of his, sayeth thus: there be two feete   paruorum.
of our lorde, wherby he walketh his wayes: That is, mer-   The two
cie and trueth: And God fastneth bothe these feete uppon   feete of
35   the hartes of them whiche turne unto him. And everie   God.

---

1 may Christ complain with the prophet, saieng   3 *mn* [*following*
Persons's]: B *Though it stand not on the natural sense of this place:
yet is it that in effect, which is rebuked, Rom.6.1.   5 words we may
account our selves charged, that prolonging of iniquities   21 *omits*
perhappes

sinner that will truelie convert him selfe, must laye hande
faste on bothe these feete. For yf he should laye handes
on mercie onelie, letting passe trueth and justice: he
wold perishe by presumption. And on the other syde,
5 yf he should apprehend justice onelie, without mercie:
he wolde perishe by desperation. To the end therfore
that he may be saved: he must humblie fall downe and
kisse bothe these feete: that in respect of Gods justice
he may retayne feare: and in respect of his mercie, he
10 maye conceive hope. And in an other place: happie is
that soule, uppon whiche our lord Jesus Christ hathe
placed bothe his feete. I will not sing unto thee, Judgement alone, nor yet mercie alone (my God:) but I will
sing unto thee, with the prophet David, mercie and
15 judgement joined together. And I will never forgett these
justifications of thyne.

S. Austen handleth this pointe moste excellentlie in
diverse places of his worckes. Lett them marke (sayeth
he) whiche love so muche mercie and gentlenes in our
20 lord: lett them marke (I saye) and feare also his trueth.
For (as the prophet saieth) God is bothe sweete and just.
Doest thou love that he is sweete? feare also that he is
just. As a sweete lorde he sayd, *I have held my peace at
your sinnes*: But as a just lord he addeth. *And thynke you
25 that I will holde my peace styll?* God is mercifull, and full
of mercies, saye you: it is moste certaine: yea add unto
yt, *that he beareth long*. But yet feare that which commeth
in the verses ende, *& verax*: That is, he is also true and
just. There be two thinges wherby sinners doe stand in
30 daunger: the one, in hoping to much, (whiche is presumption:) the other, in hoping to litle, whiche is desperation. Who is deceived by hoping to muche? He
whiche sayeth to him selfe, God is a good God: a mercifull God: and therfore I will doe what pleaseth me:
35 and why so? because God is a mercifull God: a good
God: a gentle God. These men runne into daunger by
hoping to much. Whoe are in daunger by despaire?
those, whiche seing their sinnes grevous, and thinking

Ser.6.in
cant.

Psa.111.
Psa.148.

Tract.33.
in John.

Psal.25.

Psa.103.

Two
daungers
of sinners.

---

33 unto himselfe

yt now unpossible to be perdoned, saye within them
selves: well, wee are once to be damned: whie doe not
we then, what soever pleaseth us best in this lyfe? These
men are murdered by desperation: the other by hope:
5   what therfore doeth God for gaininge of bothe these
men? To him whiche is in daunger by hope, he saieth:
Doe not saye with thy selfe: the mercie of God is greate, he will   Eccle.5.
be mercifull to the multitude of my sinnes: for the face of
hys wrathe ys uppon sinners. To hym that is in daunger by
10   desperation he sayeth: *At what tyme soever a sinner shall*   Ezec.18.
turne hym selfe to me, I wil forgett his iniquities: Thus farre
S. Austen, beside muche more whiche he addeth in the
same place, touching the great perill and folie of those,
whiche uppon vayne hope of Gods mercie doe perse-
15   ver in theyr evill lyfe.

It is a verie evill consequent and most unjust kinde
of reasoning, to saye: that for so muche as God is mercifull and long suffering, therfore will I abuse his mercie,
and continue in my wickednesse. The scripture teacheth
20   us not to reason so, but rather quite contrarie. God is
mercifull, and expecteth my conversion, and the longer
he expecteth, the more greevous will be his punishement when it commeth, yf I neglect this patience. And
therfore I ought presentlie to accept of his mercie. So
25   reasoneth S. Paul, whiche sayeth, doest thow contemne   Rom.2.
the riches of his long suffering, and gentlenes? Doest
thow not knowe that the patience of God towardes thee,
ys used to bring the to repentance? But thow throughe
the hardnes of thy hart, and irrepentant minde, doest
30   hoarde up to thy selfe wrathe, in the daye of vengeance,
at the revelation of Gods just judgement. In which
woordes S. Paul signifieth, that the longer that God
suffereth us with patience in our wickednes, the greater
heape of vengeance dothe he gather against us, yf we
35   persist obstinate in the same. Wherto S. Austen addeth
an other consideration of great dreade and feare: and   Tract.33.
that is, yf he offer thee grace (sayth he) to daye: thou   in Joan.
knowest not whether he will doe it to morow or no. If
he geve thee lyfe and memorie this weeke: thow knowest
40   not whether thou shalt enjoye it, the next weeke or no.

The holye prophet beginnyng his seventithe and second Psalme of the daungerous prosperitie of worldlie
men, useth these woordes of admiration: *How good a God,*
is the God of Israel unto them that be of a ryght hart? And yet

5 in all that Psalme, he dothe nothing els but shewe the
heavie justice of God towardes the wicked, even when
he geveth them moste prosperities, and worldlie wealthe:
and his conclusion is: *beholde (o Lord) they shall perishe which*
departe from thee: thou hast destroyed all those that have broken

10 *theyr faythe of wedlocke with the.* By which is signified, that,
how good soever God be unto the just: yet that pertayneth nothing to the releefe of the wicked, whoe are
to receyve just vengeance at his handes, amyddest the
greatest mercies bestowed upon the godlie. *The eyes of*

15 *our Lorde are upon the just,* (sayeth the same prophet,) *and*
his eares are bent to heare their prayers: but the face of our Lord
is upon them that doe evill, to destroye theyr memorie, from owt
the earthe.

It was an olde practise of deceyving prophettes, resisted

20 stronglie by the prophettes of God, to crye, peace peace,
unto wicked men: when in deed theyr was nothing
towardes them but daunger, swoord and destruction, as
the true prophetes fortolde, and as the event proved.
Wherfore, the prophet David geveth us a notable and

25 sure rule to governe our hope and confidence withall,
sacrificate sacrificium iustitiæ, & sperate in domino, doe you
sacrifice unto God the sacrifice of righteousnes, and then
trust in hym. Wherwith S. John agreeth when he sayeth,
yf our harte or conscience doe not reprehend us for wicked lyfe:

30 *then have we confidence with God:* as whoe wolde saye, yf
our conscience be guyltie of lewde and wicked lyfe, and
we resolved to dwell and continue therin: then in vaine
have we confidence in the mercyes of God, unto whose
just judgemente we stand subject for our wickednes.

35 It is most wounderfull, and dreadfull to consider, how
God hath used him selfe towardes his best beloved in
this worlde, uppon offence geven by occasion of sinne:
how easelye he hath chaunged countenance: how soone
he hath brocken of frendshype: how straitlie he hath

40 taken accompt: and how severelye he hath punished.

Gods
goodnes-
nothing
helpeth
those that
persever
in sinne.

Psa.73.

Psa.34.

Jer.6.8.

Ezec.13.

Psal.4.

1.Jo.3.

The
severitie
of Gods
punishe-
ment
upon
sinne.

The Angells that he created with so greate care and
love, and to whome he imparted so singular privileges,
of all kinde of perfections, as he made them almost verie
goddes, (in a certaine maner:) committed but onelie one
5   sinne of pride, against his majestie, and that onelie in
thought, as divines doe holde: and yet presentlie, all
that good will and favour was chaunged into justice: and
that also so severe, as they were throwen downe to
eternall tormentes, without redemption, chayned for
10   ever, to abyde the rigoure of hell fire and intollerable
darkenes.

After this, God made hym selfe an other newe freende
of fleshe and bloode, which was our father Adam in
paradise: where God conversed with hym, so freendlie
15   and familiarlie, as is most wounderfull to considere: he
called hym, he talked with hym, he made all creatures
in the world subject unto him: he brought them all
before hym, to the ende that he, and not God, should
geve them their names: he made a mate and compan-
20   ion for hym: he blessed them bothe: and finallie, shewed
all possible tokens of love, that might be. But what
ensewed? Adam committed but one sinne: and that, at
the entisement of an other: and that also a sinne of
small importance, (as it may seeme to mans reason,)
25   beyng but the eating of an aple forbidden: And yet the
matter was no soner done, but all frendship was broken betwene God and hym: he was thrust owt of paradise, condemned to perpetuell miserie, and all his
posteritie to eternall damnation, together with him selfe,
30   yf he had not repented. And how severelie this grevous
sentence was executed afterwarde, maye appeare by the
infinite millions that went to hell for this sinne, for the
space of fower thousand yeres, that passed before it was
ransomed: whiche finallie could not be done, but by the
35   comming downe of Gods owne sonne, the second per-

The
Angelles.

Esa.14.

2.Pet.2.
Ep.Jud.

Adam &
Eve.

---

23 sin not of so verie great importance   25 eating of the tree forbidden,   31 sentence is executed, may sufficiently appeer by this,
that infinite millions of people, even the whole race of mankind, is
for it, cast down unto the unspeakable torments of hel: excepting
those few, that since are ransomed by the comming down

sone in Trinitie, into this fleshe: and by his intollerable sufferinges and deathe in the same.

The two miracles of the world, Moyses and Aaron, were of singular authoritie and favour with God: in so 5 muche as they coulde obtayne any thyng at his handes for other men: And yet, when they offended God once them selves, at the waters of contradiction in the desert of Sin, for that they dowted somewhat of the miracle promised to them from God, and therby dyd dishon-10 oure his majestie before the people, as he sayeth: they were presentlie rebuked moste sharpelye for the same: and thoghe they repented hartilye that offence: and so, obtayned remission of the fault or guilt: yet was there layd upon them a grevous punishement for the same: 15 and that was, that they should not enter them selves into the land of promise: but should dye when they came within the sight therof. And albeit they entreated God moste earnestlie for the release of this penance: yet could they never obtayne the same at his handes: but 20 always he answered them: seing you have dishonoured me before the people, you shall dye for it, and shall not enter into the land of promise.

In what speciall great favour was Saul with God, when he chose hym to be the first kyng of his people? caused 25 Samuel the prophet so muche to honour hym, and to anoynt hym prince uppon Gods owne inheritance as he calleth it? when he commended hym so muche, and tooke suche tender care over him? And yet after-ward, for that he bracke Gods commaundement in re-30 serving certaine spoyles of warre, whiche he should have destroyed: yea, thoghe he reserved them to honour God withall, as he pretended: yet was he presentlie cast of by God, degraded of his dignitie, geven over to the handes of an evell spirite, brought to infinite miseries, 35 (thoghe he shifted owt for a tyme,) and finallie so for-saken and abandoned by God, as he slew hym selfe, his sonnes were crucified on a crosse by his enemies, and all his familie and linage extinguished for ever.

Moyses & Aaron.
Num.20.
27.33.
Deu.10.
32.34.

Saul.

1.Re.10.
& 11.
Act.13.

1.Re.13.
15.16.

1.Re.16.
1.Re.31.

1.Par.10.

---

5 obtain great things at   14 greevous chastisement for   24 of the peple   37 crucified or hanged on

David was the chosen and deare freend of God, and David.
honoured with the tytle of *one that was according to Gods* 2.Re.12.
owne hart. But yet, as soone as he had sinned: the prophet
Nathan was sent to denounce Gods heavie displeasure
5 and punishement upon hym. And so it ensued, not with-   Psal.35.
standing his greate and voluntarie penance that him selfe   69.109.
added for the pacifieing of Gods wrathe, by fasting,   102.
prayer, weeping, wearing of sacke, eating of ashes, and   Psal.30.
the lyke. By which is evident, that how great Gods mer-
10 cie is to them that feare hym: so great is his justice to
them that offend hym.

The scripture hath infinite examples of this matter,
as the rejection of Cain and his posteritie streight upon   Gen.4.
his murder. The pitifull drowning of the whole worlde   Gene.7.
15 in the time of Noe. The dreadfull consuming of Sodom
and Gomorra, with the cities about yt, by fire and brim-   Gen.19.
ston: the sending downe quicke to hell of Chore, Dathan   Num.16.
and Abyron, with the slaughter of two hundred and fiftie
their adherents, for rebellion against Moyses and Aaron:
20 The suddain killing of Nadab and Abiu, sonnes of Aaron,   Le.10.
and chosen preestes, for once offering of other fire on
the Aultar than was appointed them. The most terrible
striking dead of Ananias and Saphira, for retaining some   Act.5.
parte of their owne goodes, by deceit, from the Apostles:
25 with many mo such examples, whiche the scripture dothe
recounte.

And for the greevousnes of Gods justice, and heav-   The
ines of his hand, when it lighteth upon us, thoughe it   heavines
may appeare sufficientlie by all these examples before   of Gods
30 alleaged, wherin the particular punishementes (as you   hand.
see) are moste rigorous: yet will I repeat one act of God
more, owt of the scripture, whiche expresseth the same

---

5 notwithstanding that he sorrowed and humbled himselfe so much,
as he did for the sin that he had done: as may appeer by his fasting   8 [* eating] *mn*: B. *In this the sense is rather to be regarded:
than the words to be streitly urged.   16 cities about, by   19 adherents, and many thousands of the people besides, for rebellion   21
[* other] *mn*: B. *Wherin also we may see what those may look for
that worship God with mens traditions, or otherwise than he hath
appointed.

in wounderfull maner. It is well knowne that Benjamin
among all the twelve sonnes of Jacob, was the dearest
unto his father, as appeareth in the booke of Genesis,
and therfore also greatlie respected by God: and his
5   tribe placed in the best part of all the land of promise,
upon the division therof, having Jerusalem, Jericho, and
other the best cities within it. Yet notwithstandinge for
one onelie sinne committed by certayne private men in
the citie of Gabaa, uppon the wife of a Levit, God pun-
10   ished the whole tribe, in this order, as the scripture
recounteth. He caused all the other eleven tribes to ryse
against them: and first, to come to the house of God
in Silo, to ask his advise, and folow his direction in this
warre against their brethren. And thence having by Gods
15   appointement entered battaile twise with the tribe of
Benjamin, the third daye God gave them so greate a
victorie, as they slew all the living creatures, within the
compasse of that tribe, except onelie six hundred men
that escaped awaye into the desert: the rest were slayne
20   bothe man, woman, children, and infantes, together with
all the beastes and cattall, and all the cities, villages, and
howses burnt with fire: And all this, for one sinne committed onelie at one time, with one woman.

    And who will not then confesse with Moyses, *that God*
25   *is a just God, a great God, and a terrible God?* who will not
confesse with S. Paul, *It ys horrible to fall into the handes*
of the lyving God? Who will not say with holye David:
A Iudiciis tuis timui: I have feared at the remembrance
of thy judgementes? If God wolde not spare the de-
30   stroyeing of a whole tribe for one sinne onelie: yf he
wolde not perdon Chore, Dathan, and Abiron for once:
the sonnes of Aaron for once: Ananias, and Saphira,
for once: if he wold not forgyve Esau, though he demaunded it with teares, as S. Paul saieth: if he wold not
35   remitt the punishement of one fault to Moyses and Aaron,
thoughe they asked it with great instance: if he wolde
not forgyve one prowde cogitation, unto the Angells: nor

Gen.42.
43.

Josu.18.

Judi.19.
20.

Deu.10.

Heb.10.

Psa.119.

Heb.12.

---

33 though afterward he sought the blessing with tears as the apostle
saith;   37 nor once eating of the tree forbidden unto

one eatinge of an apple unto Adam, without infinite
punishement: nor wolde not passe over the cuppe of
affliction from hys owne sonne, though he asked it thrise
upon hys knees, with the sweate of bloode and water:
5   what reason hast thow to thinke that he will lett passe   Mat.26.
so many sinnes of thyne unpunished? what cause hast
thow to induce thy imagination, that he will deale extra-
ordinarilie with thee, and breake the course of hys justice
for thy sake? art thow better than those whome I have
10   named? hast thow any privilege from God above them?

If thou woldest consider the greate and straunge effectes   Greate &
of Gods justice, whiche we see daylie executed in the   straunge
world: thou shouldest have litle cause to persuade thy   effectes
selfe so favorablie, or rather to flatter thy selfe so daunger-   of Gods
15   ouslie, as thou doest. We see that, notwithstanding Godes   justice.
mercye, yea after the deathe and passion of Christ our
Saviour, for saving of the whole world: yet so many
infinite millions to be damned daylie, by the justice of
God: so many infideles, heathens, Jewes and Turkes,
20   that remayne in the darkenes of their owne ignorance:
and among Christians so many heretiques and misbe-
levers: and amonge Catholiques so many evell lyvers, as
Christ truelie sayde, that fewe were they whiche should   Mat.7.20.
be saved: albeit his deathe was payd for all, yf they
25   made not them selves unworthie therof. And before the
comming of our Savyour muche more we see, that all
the world went a-wrye to damnation for many thousand
yeres together, excepting a fewe Jewes, whiche were the
people of God. And yet among them also, the greater
30   part perhappes were not saved, as may be conjectured
by the speeches of the prophetes from tyme to time:
and speciallie by the sayeings of Christ to the Pharisees
and other rulers therof. Now then, yf God for the satisfieing of his justice, could lett so manye millions per-
35   ishe, throughe their owne sinnes, as he dothe also now

---

2 nor would passe   4 *omits* and water   15 yea, notwithstanding the
21 Christians, so many that hold not their profession truly, or otherwise are il livers therin, as that Christ truly   30 part (it seemeth)
were not

daylie permitt, without any prejudice or impechement
to his mercie: whye may not he also damne thee, for
thy sinnes, notwithstanding his mercie, seyng thou doest
not onelie committ them without feare, but also doest
5   confidentlie persist in the same?

But here perhappes some man may saye, yf this be
so, that God is so severe in punishement of everie sinne:
and that he damnethe so many thousandes for one that
he saveth: how is it true, *that the mercies of God are above*
10   *all his other woorkes,* (as the scripture saythe,) *and that it*
passeth and exalteth it selfe above his judgement? for yf the
number of the damned doe exceede so muche the number of those whiche are saved: it seemeth that the worcke
of justice dothe passe the worcke of mercie. To which
15   I answere, that touching the small number of those that
are saved, and infinite quantitie of suche as are damned,
we maye in no wyse dowte: for that beside all other
prophetes, Christ our Saviour hathe made the matter
certaine, and owt of question. We have to see therfore,
20   how, notwithstanding all this, the mercie of God dothe
exceede his other worckes.

And first, his mercie may be sayd to exceede, for that,
all our salvation is of his mercie, and our damnation
from our selves, as from the first and principall causes
25   therof, according to the sayeing of God, by the prophet,
Perditio tua Israel: tantummodo in me auxilium tuum. Thy onelie
perdition is from thy selfe (o Israel) and thy assistance
to doe good, is onelie from me. So that, as we muste

Whether
Gods
mercie be
greater
than his
justice.
Psal.145.
Jac.2.

Matt.7. &
20.

Ose.13.

---

6 *omits* perhappes   9 [* above] *mn:* B. *Spread foorth over al his
works: as both Augustine and Jerom do read; *In omnia,* or *In Vniversa*
opera eius. Tom.8.11. on behalfe of his children. For even they also
have their works so unperfect, and their faith so weak, that but in
the depth of the mercie of God, they cannot in any wise be saved:
no, not the best that ever was. But concerning that he doth so res-
olutely set down so many thousands to be damned for one that is
saved, it is somwhat more, than the word it selfe doth warrant; or
the proportion of the mercie of God (compared with his justice) may
seem to bear. And seeing that this whole treatise in these four next
sections, viz. 16.19. is grounded upon a wrong text, therfore it is to
be read so much more warily: and no further to be accounted of,
than it may be found to have the word of God to warrant the same.
11 *judgements*

acknowlege Gods grace and mercie for the author of
everie good thought and acte that we doe, and consequentlie ascribe all our salvation unto hym: so none of
our evill actes (for whiche we are damned) doe proceede
5   from hym, but onelie from our selves, and so he is no
cause at all of our damnation: and in this dothe his
mercie exceede his justice.

Secondlie his mercie dothe exceede, in that he desireth   2.
all men to be saved, as S. Paul teacheth, and hym selfe   1.Ti.2.
10   protesteth, when he sayeth, *I will not the deathe of a sin-*
ner, but rather that he turne from hys wickednes and lyve. And   Eze.18.
againe by the prophet Jeremie, he complayneth greevous-
lie that men will not accept of his mercie offered. *Turne*   Jere.3.
from your wicked wayes (saythe he,) *whye will ye dye, you*
15   *howse of Israel?* By which appeareth, that he offereth his
mercie most willinglie and freelie to all, but useth his
justice onelie upon necessitie (as it were:) constrained
therunto by our obstinate behavioure. This, Christ signifieth more plainlie, when he sayth to Jerusalem: O
20   Jerusalem, Jerusalem, whiche kyllest the prophetes: and   Mat.23.
stonest them to deathe that are sent unto thee: how
often wolde I have gathered thy children together, as
the henne clocketh her chickyns undernethe her wynges, but thou woldest not? beholde thy howse (for this
25   cause) shalbe made desert, and left withoute children.
Heere you see the mercie of God often offered unto the
Jewes: but, for that they refused it, he was enforced (in
a certaine maner) to pronounce this heavie sentence of   Joseph.
destruction and desolation upon them: which he fullfilled   de bello
30   within fortie or fiftie yeeres after, by the handes of Titus   Jud.li.1.
and Vespasian, Emperours of Rome: who utterlie dis-   c.1.2.3.
comfited the citie of Jerusalem, and whole nation of
Jewes, whome we see dispersed over the world at this
daye in bondage, bothe of bodie and soule. Whiche
35   worke of Gods Justice, thoghe it be moste terrible: yet
was his mercie greater to them, as appeareth by Christs
woordes, yf they had not rejected the same.

Thirdlie, his mercie exceedeth his Justice, even towardes   3.

---

30 hands of Vespasian, emperor of Rome, and Titus his son: who
utterly   38 [* justice] *mn*: B. *As afore: not as though the meaning

the damned them selves: in that he used many meanes
to save them in this lyfe, by geving them freewill, and
assisting the same with his grace to doe good: by moving them inwardlie with infinite good inspirations: by
5   alluringe them owtwardlie, with exhortations, promisses,
examples of other, as also by sickenes, adversities, and
other gentle corrections: by gevinge them space to repent,
with occasions, opportunities, and excitations unto the
same: by threatning them eternall deathe, yf they repented
10   not. All whiche thinges beinge effectes of mercie, and
goodnes towardes them: they must needes confesse amyddest theyr greatest furie and tormentes, that his judgementes are true, and justified in them selves, and no
wayes to be compared with the greatnes of his mercies.
15   By this then we see that to be true, which the prophet   Psal.84.
sayeth, *Misericordiam & veritatem diligit dominus.* God loveth
mercie and trueth. And again: *Mercie and trueth have mett*
together: Justice and peace have kyssed them selves. We see the   Psal.85.
reason why the same prophet protesteth of hym selfe: *I*
20   *will sing unto thee mercie and judgement* (o Lord,) not mer-   Psa.101.
cie alone, nor judgement alone, but mercie and judge-
ment together: that is, I will not so presume of thy
mercie, as I will not feare thy judgement: nor will I so
feare of thy judgement, as I will ever despayre of thy
25   mercie. The feare of Gods judgement is always to be
joyned with our confidence in Gods mercie: yea in verye
saintes them selves, as David sayeth. But what feare?
that feare trulie, whiche the scripture describeth, when   Psa.34.
it sayeth: the feare of our Lord expelleth sinne: the feare   Eccle.1.
30   of God hateth all evill: he that feareth God, neglecteth   Prov.1.
nothing: he that feareth God will turne and looke into   Eccle.7.
his owne hart: he that feareth God will doe good woorkes.   Eccle.15.
They whiche feare God, will not be incredulous to   Eccle.2.
that whiche he sayeth: but will keepe his wayes, and
35   seeke owt the things that are pleasant unto hym: They
will prepare theyr hartes, and sanctifie their sowles in
his sight.

---

shuld be, that God were more merciful, than just, holie, wise, or
such like.   2 life, by calling upon them, and assisting them with his
grace

274   THE FIRST BOOKE OF THE CHRISTIAN EXERCISE

This is the description of the true feare of God, sett
downe by the scripture. This is the description of that
feare, which is so much commended and commaunded
in everye part and parcell of Gods woorde: Of that feare
(I saye) which is called *Fons vitæ, radix prudentiæ, corona &*
plenitudo sapientiæ, gloria & gloriatio, beatum donum: That is,
the fountaine of lyfe, the roote of prudence, the crowne
and fulnes of wisedome, the glorie and gloriation of a
Christian man, a happie gyft. Of hym that hathe this
feare the scripture saythe, *happie is the man whiche feareth*
our Lorde, for he will place his mynde upon his commaunde-
mentes. And againe, *the man that feareth God shalbe happie at*
the last ende, and shalbe blessed at the daye of hys deathe. Finallie, of suche as have this feare, the scripture saythe, that
God is theyr foundation: God hath prepared great multitude of sweetnes for them: God hathe purchased them
an inheritance: God is as mercyfull to them, as the father
is mercifull unto his children: And (to conclude) *Voluntatem*
timentium se faciet: God will doe the will of those that
feare him with this feare.

This holie feare had good Job, when he sayd to God:
I feared all my workes: And he yealdeth the reason therof:
For that I knewe that thow sparest not hym that offendeth thee.
This feare lacked the other of whome the prophet sayeth:
The sinner hathe exaspered God, by sayeing, that God
will not take accompte of his doeings, in the multitude
of wrathe. Thy judgementes (o Lord) are removed from
his sight. And againe: wherfore hathe the wicked man
styrred up God against hym selfe, by sayeing, God will
not take account of my doeyngs? Yt is a great wickednes
(no dowt) and a greate exasperation of God against us,
to take the one halfe of Gods nature from hym, whiche
is, to make hym mercifull without justice: and to lyve
so, as though God wolde take no account of our lyfe:
wheras he hath protested most earnestlie the contrarie,
sayeing that he is a hard and covetous man, whiche will
not be content to receyve his owne againe, but also will

The
prayse of
true feare.
Pro.14.

Eccle.1.2.
5.

Psa.112.

Eccle.1.

Psal.25.
Psal.31.
Psal.61.
Psal.103.
Psa.145.

Job.9.

Psal.10.

Matt.25.

---

23 *I know that*   28 the man stirred   34 God would not take account
36 and a sore man,

have usurie: that he will have a reckening of all hys goodes lent us: that he will have fruite for all his labours bestowed uppon us: and finallie, that he will have account for every woorde that we have spoken.

5   Christ in the three score and eight psalme, which in sundrye places of the gospell he interpreteth to be writen of him selfe, amonge other dreadfull curses, whiche he setteth downe, against the reprobate, he hath these: lett theyr eyes be daseled in suche sorte as they may not
10 see: powre owte thy wrathe (my father) upon them: lett the furie of thy vengeance take hand fast on them: add iniquitie upon their iniquitie: and lett them not enter into thy justice: Lett them be blotted owt of the booke of lyfe: and lett them not be inrolled together with the
15 just. Heer (loe) we see, that the greatest curse, which God can laye upon us, next before our blotting owt of the booke of lyfe, is to suffer us to be so blinded, as to adde iniquitie upon iniquitie, and not to enter into consideration of hys justice. For whiche cause also, this
20 confident kynde of sinning upon hope of Gods mercie, is accounted by divines for the first of the six grevous sinnes against the holie ghoste, whiche our Savioure in the gospell, signifieth to be so hardlie perdoned unto men by his father: and the reason whye they call this
25 a sinne against the holye ghost, is, for that it rejecteth willfullye one of the principall meanes left by the holye ghost, to retyre us from sinne, whiche is the feare and respect of Gods justice upon sinners.

Luc.16.
Matt.7.
Luc.13.
Mat.12.

Mat.27.
Marc.15.
Joh.2.

D. Tho.
secunda
secundæ.
q.14. art.
1.2.3.

Whye
presump-
tion is a
sinne
against
the holie
ghoste.

---

13 *thy righteousnes: let*   21 [* six] *mn:* B. *Those six that Thomas there nameth, are desperation, presumption, impoenitencie, wilfulnes, impugning of the known truth, and envieng of the grace that is given to another. Al which may indeed be easily found to go against the spirit of God. But that they may be accounted to be that same, that in the scripture is called sin against the holie Ghost, and excluded al hope of pardon, that is not so easily to be granted; for that the properties therunto assigned do not seem to be so fully found in any of these. A wilful resisting of the known truth, not of infirmitie, for fear, or favor, but of meere malice for hatred of it, even only for that it is the truth, may seem to come much neerer unto it, than (al things considered) those others do. Neither doth he set down absolutely to be six several sorts of that sin, but in that sense that himselfe doth there limit.

Wherfore, to conclude this matter of presumption: me thinke, we may use the same kynde of argument touching the feare of Gods justice, as S. Paul useth to the Romanes of the feare of Gods ministers, which are tem- Rom.13.

5   porall princes: woldest thow not feare the power of a temporall prince, sayeth he? doe well then: and thow shalt not onelie not feare, but also receyve laude and prayse therfor. But if thow doe evill: then feare. For he beareth not the swoorde without a cause. In lyke

10 sort may we saye to those good felowes, whiche make God so mercifull, as no man ought to feare his justice. Wolde ye not feare (my brethren) the justice of God in punishement? lyve vertuouslie then: and you shall be as voyde of feare, as lyons are, sayeth the wiseman: *For* Prov.28.

15 *that, perfect charitie expelleth feare.* But yf you lyve wicked- 1.Joh.4.
lie: then have you cause to feare: for God called not 2.Ti.4.
hym selfe a just judge for nothing.

If the matter had bene so secure, as manye men by flatterie doe persuade themselves it is: S. Peter wold

20 never have sayde unto Christianes new baptized: *Walke* 1.Pet.1.
you in feare, during the time of this your earthelie habitation. Nor
S. Paul to the same men: *Woorke your owne salvation in* Philip.2.
feare and tremblyng. But here perhappes, some men will An objec-
aske, how then doeth the same Apostle in an other place tion

25 say: *That God hath not geven us the spirite of feare, but of* answered.
vertue, love, and sobrietie? to which I answere: that our 2.Ti.1.
spirite is not a spirit of servile feare: that is, to lyve in
feare, onelie for dreade of punishement, without love: Servile
but a spirite of love joyned with the feare of children, feare, and

30 wherby they feare to offend their father, not onelye in the feare
of chil-
respect of his punishement, but principallie for his goodnes dren.
towardes them, and benefites bestowed upon them. This
S. Paul declareth playnlie to the Romanes, putting the Rom.8.
difference betwene servile feare, and the feare of childeren:

35 *you have not receyved agayne the spirit of servitude* (saythe he)
in feare, but the spirite of adoption of children, wherby we crye
to God, Abba father. He saythe heere to the Romanes: you

---

23 *omits* perhappes   29 with fear of children

have not receyved againe the spirite of servitude in feare, for that their former spirite, (being gentiles,) was onelye in servile feare: for that they honoured and adored their Idoles, not for any love they beare unto them, being so

5 infinite as they were, and suche notable lewdnes reported of them (I meane of Jupiter, Mars, Venus, and the lyke:) but onelie for feare of hurt from them, yf they dyd not serve and adore the same.

How the feare of gentiles was servile.

Saint Peter also in one sentence expoundeth all this

10 matter. For having sayde, *timorem eorum ne timueritis,* feare not their feare: meaning of the servile feare of wicked men: he addeth presentlie, *Dominum autem Christum sanctificate in cordibus vestris, &c. cum modestia & timore, conscientiam habentes bonam:* That is, doe you sanctifie our Lord Jesus

15 Christ in your hartes: having a good conscience, with modestie and feare. So that the spirite of servile feare, which is grounded onelie upon respect of punishement, is forbidden us: but the loving feare of children is com-maunded. And yet also about this, are there two things

20 to be noted.

1.Pet.3.

The first, that albeit the spirite of servile feare be for-bidden us: (especiallie when we are now entered into the service of God,) yet is it most profitable for sinners, and suche as yet but begynne to serve God: for that it

25 moveth them to repentance, and to looke aboute them: for which cause it is called by the wyseman, *the begyn-nyng of wisdome.* And therfore, bothe Jonas to the Ninivites,

Two thinges to be noted.

Prov.1.

---

11 [* Meaning] *mn:* B. *Divers so take it: but it seemeth rather (in my judgement) that such as expound it, as if the apostle forbad them to fear those adversaries of theirs, do come somwhat neerer to the sense of the place. 26 [* cause] *mn:* B. *Truth it is, that such fear serveth wel to such a purpose. But the fear that in this place is spo-ken of, seemeth by the circumstances of the place, not to be the servile, but the childlike fear. As also another sense of this place may stand likewise, viz. that to fear the Lord is the first, or principal part, or greatest point of al wisdome. For that whosoever feareth the Lord, shal so govern his wais, and have al things fal out so wel, that al the wisdome in al the world besides, can never be able so to forecast for al events. For the Lord himselfe taketh upon him the protection and government of those that fear him: on whose behalfe he maketh al things to fal out to the best.

and S. John Baptist to the Jewes, and all the prophets   Jon.3.
to sinners have used to styrre up this feare, by threat-   Matt.3.
ning the daungers and punishementes which were imminent to them, yf they repented not. But yet afterward,
5   when men are converted to God, and doe goe forwarde
in his service: they chaunge everye daye this servyle feare
into love, untill they arrive at last, unto that state wherof
S. John saythe, *that perfect love or charitie expelleth feare.*   1.Joh.4.
Wherupon S. Austen sayeth, that feare is the servant   Tract.9.
10   sent before to prepare place in our hartes, for his mys-   in ep.1.
tres, whiche is charitie: Who beyng once entered in, and   Joh.
perfectlie placed: feare goeth owte againe, and geveth
place unto the same. But where this feare never entereth
at all, there is it impossible for charitie ever to come
15   and dwell, sayeth this holye father.

The second thing to be noted is, that albeyt this feare
of punishement be not in verie perfect men, or at leastwyse, is lesse in them, than in others, as S. John teacheth: yet beyng joyned with love and reverence: (as it
20   ought to be:) it is moste profitable, and necessarie for
all common Christianes, whose lyfe is not so perfect,
nor charitie so greate, as that perfection wherof S. John
speakethe. This appeareth by that, that Christ persuaded
also this feare, even unto his Apostles, sayeing, *feare you*   Luc.12.
25   *hym, whiche after he hath slayne the bodye, hath power also to*   Mat.10.
send bothe bodye and soule unto hell fyre: this I saye unto you,
feare hym. The same dothe S. Paul to the corinthians
whoe were good Christians, layeing downe first the justice of God, and therupon persuading them to feare: All
30   we (sayeth he) must be presented before the tribunal   2.Co.5.
seat of Christ, to receive eche man his proper desertes,
according as he hath done, good or evill in this lyfe. And
for that we knowe this: we doe persuade the feare of
our Lord unto men. Nay (that whiche is more) S. Paul
35   testifieth, that notwithstanding all his favours receyved
from God: he retayned yet him selfe this feare of Gods
justice, as appeareth by those wordes of his: *I doe chastyne*   1.Co.9.

---

19 [* love] *mn*: B. *Then is it not that servile fear.

*my bodie, and doe bring it into servitude, least perchaunce, when
I have preached to other, I become a reprobate my selfe.*

Now (my freend) yf S. Paul stoode in awe of the justice of God notwithstanding his Apostleshipp: and that
5   he was guiltie to hym selfe of no one sinne or offence,
as he protesteth: what oughtest thou to be, whose conscience remayneth guyltie of so many misdeedes, and
wickednes? *This knowe you* (sayeth S. Paul) *that no fornicator, uncleane persone, covetouse man, or the lyke can have inher-*
10 *itance in the kingdome of Christ.* And immediatlie after, as
thoghe this had not bene sufficient, he addeth, for pre-
venting the folye of sinners, whiche flatter them selves:
*Lett no man deceyve you with vayne woordes: for the wrathe of
God cometh for these thinges, upon the children of unbeleefe. Be*
15 *not you therfore partakers of them:* As yf he should saye, those
that flatter you and saye, tushe, God is mercifull, and
will perdone easilie all these and lyke sinnes: these men
deceyve you .(saythe S. Paul), for that the wrathe and
vengeance of God lyghteth upon the children of unbeleefe,
20 for these matters: that is, uppon those whiche will not
beleeve Gods justice, nor his threates against sinne: but
presuming of his mercie doe persevere in the same, untill
uppon the sodayne, Gods wrathe doe rushe upon them:
and then is it too late to amende. Wherfore (sayeth he)
25 yf you be wise: be not partakers of theyr folie: but amend
your lyves presentlie, while you have time. And this
admonition of S. Paul shall be sufficient to ende this
chapiter: against all those that refuse, or deferre theyr
resolution of amendement, uppon vayne hope of Gods
30 perdon, or tolleration.

The con-
clusion.

1.Cor.4.

Ephe.5.

---

1 *least it should come to passe, that when* 6 as (in one case) he protesteth

Of the fyveth impediment: which ys, delaye of resolution
from tyme to tyme, upon hope to doe it better, or with
more ease, afterward.

CHAP. V

5   The reasons hitherto alleaged, might seeme (I think)
sufficient to a reasonable man, for proving the necessitie of this resolution, we talke of: and for removing
the impedimentes that let the same. But yet, for that (as   Prov.18.
the wiseman sayeth) he which is minded to breake with
10 hys freend, seeketh occasions how to doe yt with some
coloure and shew: there be manye in the world, who
having no other excuse of their breaking and holding
of from God, doe seeke to cover it with this pretense,
that they meane, by his grace, to amend all in time:
15 And this tyme is driven of from daye to daye, untill
God, in whose handes onelie the momentes of time are,
doe shutt them owte of all tyme, and doe send them to
paynes eternall withoute tyme, for that they abused the
singular benefite of tyme in this world.
20   This is one of the greatest and most dangerous deceites,
and yet the moste ordinarie and universall, that the enemie of mankinde dothe use towardes the children of
Adam: and I dare say boldlye, that more doe perishe
by this deceyte, than by all his other guiles and subtil-
25 ities besides. He well knoweth the force of this snare
above all others, and therfore urgeth it so muche unto
everie man. He considereth, better than we doe, the
importance of delaye, in a matter so weightie, as is our   The
conversion and salvation: he is not ignorant how one   causes
30 sinne draweth on an other: how he that is not fitt to   whie the
daye, will be lesse fitt to morowe: how custome groweth   devil per-
into nature: how olde diseases are hardlie cured: how   suadeth
God withdraweth hys grace: how hys justice is redie   us to
to punishe everie sinne: how by delaye we exasperate   delaye.
35 the same, and heape vengeance on our owne heades,
as S. Paul sayeth. He is privie to the uncertaintie and   Rom.2.
perills of our lyfe: to the daungerous chaunces we passe
throughe: to the impedimentes that will come daylie

more and more, to let our conversion. All this he knoweth, and well considereth, and for that cause persuadeth so manye to delaye as he doeth. For being not able any longer to blinde the understanding of many Christians,
5 but that they must needes see clearlie, the necessitie and utilitie of this resolution, and that all impedimentes in the world are but trifles, and meere deceites, which keepe backe from the same: he runnethe to this onelie refuge, that is, to persuade men, that they deferre a litle, and
10 that in time to come they shall have better occasion and oportunitie to doe yt than presently they have.

This, S. Austen proved in his conversion, as hym selfe writeth. For that after he was persuaded, that no salvation could be unto hym, but by chaunge and amende-
15 ment of his lyfe: yet the enemie held hym, for a time, in delaye, sayeing unto him: *yet a litle staye: yet deferre for a time*: Therby (as he sayeth) to binde hym more fast in the custome of sinne, untill, by the omnipotent power of Gods grace, and his owne moste earnest endevoure,
20 he bracke vyolentlie from hym, crieing to God, *whie shall I longer saye to morow, to morow? why shall I not doe it even at this instant?* And so he did, even in hys verie yowthe, lyving afterward a moste holie and severe Christian lyfe.

But yf we will discovere yet further, the greatnes and
25 perill of this deceyt: let us consider the causes that may lett our resolution and conversion at this present: and we shall see them all increased, and strengthened by delaye: and consequentlie, the matter made more hard and difficult, for the time to come, than now it ys. For
30 first (as I have sayd) the continuance of sinne bringeth custome: whiche once having gotten prescription uppon us, is so harde to remove, as by experience we prove dayly in all habites that have taken roote within us. Who can remove, (for examples sake) without greate difficul-
35 tie, a longe custome of dronkennes? of swearing? or of any other evill habite, once setled upon us? Secondlie, the longer we persist in our synfull lyfe, the more God

Li.8.con-fess.ca.7. 12.

The causes which make our conversion harder by delaie.
1.

2.

---

6 al the impediments

plucketh his grace and assistance from us: whiche is the
onelie meanes that maketh the waye of vertue easie unto
men. Thirdlie, the power, and kingdome of the devill is   3.
more established, and confirmed in us by continuance:
and so, the more harder to be removed. Fowerthlie, the   4.
libertie of oure free will is more and more weakened,
and daunted by frequentation of sinne, thoughe not
extinguished. Fivethlie, the faculties of our mynde, are   5.
more corrupted, as the understanding is more darkened,
the will more perverted, the appetite more disordered.
Sixtelie and lastlye, our inferiour partes and passions are   6.
more styrred up and strengthened against the rule of
reason, and harder to be repressed, by continuance of
time, than they were before.

Well then, put all this together (my freend) and consider indifferentlie within thy selfe, whether it be more
likelie, that thow shalt rather make this resolution hereafter, than now. Hereafter, (I say) when, by longer custome of sinne, the habite shalbe more fastyned in thee:
the devill more in possession uppon the: Gods helpe
further of from thee: thy mynde more infected: thy judgement more weakened: thy good desires extinguished: thy
passions confirmed: thy bodie corrupted: thy strengthe
diminished: and all thy whole common wealthe more
perverted.

We see by experience, that a shypp which leaketh, is   The same
more easilye emptied at the beginninge, than afterwarde.   shewed
We see, that a ruinous palace, the longer it is lett runne,   by com-
the more charge and labour yt will require in the   parisons.
repayring. We see, that yf a man dryve in a nayle with
a hammer, the more blowes he geveth to yt, the more
harde it is to plucke it owt agayne. How then thinkest
thow to committ sinne uppon sinne, and by perseverance therein, to finde the redresse more easie hereafter,
than now? It is writen among the lyves of olde heremites,

---

2 only mean that   5 the good inclination of our wil   35 now? That
were much like as if a good fellow, that having made to himselfe a
great burden to carry, should assay it on his bak; and for that, it
sat uneasie, and pressed him much, should cast it down again, and
put a great deal more unto it, and then begin to lift it again: but

how that on a time, an Angel shewed to one of them, in the wyldernes, a certayne good felow that hewed downe wood, and having made to him selfe a great burden to carie thence, layed it on his backe: and for that,

5   it satte uneasie, and pressed hym muche: he cast it downe againe, and put a greate deale more unto yt, and then beganne to lyft at yt agayne. But when he felt it more heavie than before: he fell into a greate rage, and added twyse as muche more to yt, therby to make

10   yt lighter. Whereat when this holie man mused muche: the Angel tolde hym, that this was a figure of those in the worlde, who fynding it somewhat unpleasant to resist one or two vices at the beginning, do deferre their conversion, and doe adde twentie or fortie more unto them:

15   thinking to finde the matter more easie afterward.

In prato spirituale sanctorum patrum. An example.

Saint Austen expounding the miracle of our Saviour, in raysing Lazarus from deathe to lyfe, whiche had bene deade now fower dayes, as the evangelist sayeth: examineth the cause whye Christ wept, and cryed, and trou-

20   bled hym selfe in spirite, before the doeing of this acte, where as he raysed other with greater facilitie. And he concludeth, the misterie to have bene, for that Lazarus was now deade fower dayes, and also buried: which signifieth, the fower degrees of a sinner: the first, in vol-

25   untarie delectation of sinne: the second, in consent: the third, in fulfilling it by woorke: the fowerth, in continuance or custome therof: wherin, who soever is once buried (sayeth this holy father) he is hardlie raysed to lyfe againe, without a greate miracle of God, and many

30   teares of his owne parte.

Tract.49. in Joh. Joh.11. Matt.9. Luc.7.

The reason heerof is, that which the wise man sayeth, *languor prolixior grauat medicum*, an olde sickenes doeth trouble the phisition: *Breuem autem languorem præcidit medicus*: But the phisition cutteth of quicklie a newe or freshe

35   disease, whiche hathe endured but a litle time. The verie

Eccl.10.

---

when he felt it more heavie than before, he should fal into a great rage, and ad twise as much more to it, therby to make it lighter. For so do the children of the world: who finding it   21 facilitie: and out of it, giveth this lesson to us: that as Lazarus was dead four dais, and also buried, so are there four degrees of a sinner: the first,

bones of an olde wicked man shalbe replenished with
the vices of his yowthe: (sayeth Job) and they shall sleepe   Job.20.
with hym in the dust, when he goeth to his grave. We
reade that Moyses, in part of punishement to the peo-   Exo.32.
5   ple, that had sinned in adoring the golden calfe, broke
the same in peeces, and made them drinke it: So, the
vices, wherein we delyted during our youthe, are so dispersed, by custome, in our bodies and bones: that when
olde age dothe come on, we canne not ridde them at
10   our pleasure, without greate difficultie and paine. What
folye then is it, to deferre our amendement unto our
olde age, when we shall have more impedimentes and
difficulties, by a greate deale, than we have nowe?

If it seeme harde to thee to doe penance now: to fast,
15   to praye, and to take uppon thee other afflictions, whiche
the churche prescribeth to sinners at their conversion:
how wilt thow doe yt in thy olde age: when thy bodie
shall have more neede of cheryshing, than of punishement? Yf thow finde yt unpleasant to resist thy sinnes
20   now, and to roote them owte, after the continuance of
two, three, or fower yeeres: what will it be after twentie yeres more adjoyned unto them? How madde a man   A com-
woldest thow esteeme hym, that travayling on the waye,   parison.
and having great choyse of lustye strong horses, should
25   lett them all goe emptie, and laye all his cariage upon
some one poore and leane beast, that could skarse beare
yt selfe, and muche lesse stand under so many bagges
cast upon yt? And surelie no lesse unreasonable is that
man, who passing over idlely the lustie dayes and times
30   of his lyfe, reserveth all the labour and travaile unto
feble olde age.

But to lett passe the folie of this deceyte, tell me,   Ingra-
(good Christian) what ingratitude and injustice is this   titude.
towardes God, havinge receyved so many benefites from

---

3 *to the grave* 14 thee to amend thy life now: painfully to be occupied in thy calling, and withal (for thy better help) to fast, to pray,
and to take upon thee other exercises, which the word of God prescribeth to sinners to their conversion: how wilt thou do it in thine
old age? 18 of painful exercise? 27 selfe, or much 33 ingratitude and unrighteousnes is this

hym all redie, and expecting so greate a paye, as the
kyngdome of heaven ys, for thy service: to appoint owt,
notwithstanding, the least, and last, and worst part of
thy lyfe unto his service: and that, wherof thow art moste
5   uncertayne, whether it shall ever be, or never, or whether
God will accept yt, when it cometh? He is accursed by
the prophet, whiche having whole and sownde cattall,
dothe offer unto God the lame, or halting parte therof.   Malac.1.
How muche more shalt thow be accursed, that having
10   so many dayes of youthe, strengthe, and vigoure, doest
appoint unto Gods service, onelie thy lymping olde age?
In the law it was forbydden, under a moste severe threate,   Deu.25.
for any man to have two measures in his howse for his
neighbour: one greater, to hys freend: and an other
15   lesser, for other men. And yet thow art not ashamed,
to use two measures of thy lyfe, moste unequall, in
prejudice of thy Lorde and God: wherby thow alottest
to hym, a litle, shorte, maymed, and uncertayne tyme:
and unto hys enemie the greatest, the fayrest, the surest
20   parte therof.
O deare brother, what reason is there, why God should
thus be used at thy handes? what lawe, justice or equitie is there, that after thow hast served the world, fleshe,
and devill all thy youthe, and best dayes: in the ende
25   to come, and clappe thy olde bones, defiled and worne
owt with sinne, in the dyshe of God? his enemies to
have the best, and he the leavinges? Hys enemies the
wyne, and he the lyes and dreagges? Doest thow not
remember, that he will have the fatt and best parte   Levi.3.
30   offered to hym? Doest thow not thinke of the punishe-   Num.8.
ment of those, whiche offered the worst part of theyr   Mala.1.
substance to God? Folow the counsayle then of the holye
ghoste, yf thow be wyse, whiche warneth thee, in these   Eccle.12.
woordes: be myndefull of thy creator in the dayes of
35   thy youthe, before the tyme of affliction come on, and
before those yeeres draw neere, of whiche thow shalt
saye, they please me not.
How many hast thow seene cutt of in the myddest

---

1 as the kingdome of heaven is after: to appoint

of their dayes, whiles they purposed in tyme to come,
to chaunge theyr lyfe? How many have come to olde
age yt selfe, and yet then have felt lesse will of amendement than before? How many have dryven of, even unto
5   the verie howre of deathe, and then least of all have
remembred their owne state: but have dyed, as dumme
and sensles beastes, according to the sayeing of holie
S. Gregorie, *The sinner hathe also this affliction layed uppon*   Serm.10.
hym, that when he cometh to dye, he forgetteth hym selfe, which   de sanc-
10 *in his lyfe tyme dyd forgett God?* O, how many examples   tis.
are there seen hereof daylie? how many worldlie men,
that have lyved in sensualitie: how many great sinners,
that have passed theyr lyfe in wickednes: doe ende and
dye, as yf they went into some place insensible, where
15 no account, no reckeninge should be demaunded? they
take suche care in theyr testamentes for fleshe and bloode,
and commodities of this worlde, as yf they should lyve
styll, or should have theyr parte of these vanities when
they are gone. In trueth, to speake as the matter ys,
20 they dye as yf there were no immortalitie of the soule,
and that, in verie deede, is theyr inwarde persuasion.

But suppose now, that all this were not so, and that   The losse
a man might as easilie, commodiouselie, yea and as   of merite.
surely also, convert him selfe in olde age as in youthe,
25 and that the matter were also acceptable enough to God:
yet tell me, what greate tyme is their lost in this delaye?
what greate treasure of merit is there omitted, which
might have beene gotten, by labour in Gods service? yf   A com-
whiles the captayne and other souldiers did enter a rych   parison.
30 citie, to take the spoile, one souldier should saye, I will
staye and come in the next daye after, when all the
spoyle is gone: wolde you not thinke him bothe a cow-
ard, and also moste unwyse? So it is, that Christ our
Savyoure and all hys good souldiers, tooke the spoyle
35 of this lyfe: enryched them selves with the merites of
theyre labours: caried the same with them as bylles of
exchange, to the bancke of heaven, and there receyved

---

22 *mn: The losse of time.*   27 treasure of godlines is there   32 would
not you think   35 inriched themselves with their labors in time;

paye of eternall glorie for them. And is it not greate
folye and perversenes in us, to passe over this lyfe without the gayning of any merit at all? Now is the tyme
of fight for gayning of our crowne: now is the daye of
5   spoile to seise on our bootie: now is the market, to buie
the kingdome of heaven: now is the time of running to
gett the game and price: now is the daye of sowyng, to
provide us corne for the harvest that commeth on. If
we omitt this tyme: there is no more crowne, no more   Pro.20.
10   bootye, no more kyngdome, no more price, no more
harvest to be looked for. For as the scripture assureth
us, he that for slouthe will not sowe in the winter, shall
begge in the sommer, and no man shall geve unto hym.

But yf this consideration of gayne can not move thee
15   (gentle reader) as in deed it ought to doe, beyng of suche
importance as it is, and irrevocable when it is once past:
yet weyghe with thy selfe, what obligation and charge   The
thou drawest on thee, by every day whiche thou defer-   obligation
rest thy conversion, and lyvest in sinne. Thou makest   & charge
20   eche daye knottes, which thou must once undoe agayne: by delaye.
thou heapest that together, which thou must once dis-
perse agayne: thou eatest and drinkest that howrelie,
whiche thou must once vomyte up againe: I meane, yf
the best fall owt unto thee: that is, yf thou doe repent
25   in tyme, and God doe accept therof (for other wise, wo
be unto thee, for that thou hoardest (as S. Paul sayeth)   Rom.2.
wrathe, and vengeance on thine owne heade). But supposing that thou receave grace hereafter to repent, whiche
refusest it nowe: yet (I saye) thou hast to weepe, for that
30   thou laughest at now: thou hast to be hartilie sorie for
that wherin thou delytest now: thou hast to curse the
daye wherein thou ever gavest consent to sinne, or els
thy repentance will doe thee no good. This thou knowest now, and this thou beleevest now, or els thou art
35   no Christian. How then art thou so madde, as to offend
God now, bothe willinglie, and deliberatlie: of whome
thou knowest that thou must once aske pardon with

---

1 *omits* for them   2 life in so fruitles affairs? Now is the time of
fight for the obteining of our crown   8 If you omit

teares? If thou think he will pardone the: what ingratitude is it to offend so good a Lord? If thou think he
will not pardone thee: what folye can be more, than to
offend a prince without hope of pardone?

5   Make thyne account now as thou wilt: yf thou never
doe repent and chaunge thy lyfe: then every sinne thou
committest, and every daye that thou lyvest therein, is
encrease of wrathe and vengeance upon thee in hell, as
S. Paul proveth. If thou doe, by Gods mercie, hereafter   Rom.2.
10   repent and turne (for this is not in thy handes:) then
must thou one daye lament, and bewaile, and do penance
for this delay, whiche now thou makest: then must thou   Satisfac-
make satisfaction to Gods justice, ether in this lyfe, or   tion for
in the lyfe to come, for that which now thou passest   delaye.
15   over so pleasantlie. And this satisfaction must be so
sharpe and rigorous, yf we beleeve the auncient fathers,
and councells of Christ his churche: as it must be answerable to the weight and continuance of thy sinnes, as I   Li.de la.
shall have occasion to shew in the second booke, talk-   &. li.5.ep.
20   ing of satisfaction. So that, by how muche the more   5. ad cor.
thou prolongest, and encreasest thy sinne: so much greater
must be thy paine and sorow in satisfaction. *Alto vulneri
diligens & longa adhibenda est medicina: pænitentia crimine minor
non sit* (sayth S. Ciprian.) A diligent and long medicine
25   is to be used to a deepe sore: and the penance may not
be lesse than the fault. And then he sheweth in what
order it must be: with prayer, with teares, with waching, with lyeing on the ground, with wearing of heare
clothe, and the lyke. It is not enoughe (sayeth S. Austen)   Hom. ult.
30   to chaunge our maners, and to leave to sinne, except   ex 50 ho.
we make satisfaction also to God for our sinnes past,
by sorowfull penance, humble sighes, contrition of hart,
and geving of Almes. Our bodie that hath lyved in   Ep.27.ad
manye delytes must be afflicted: (sayeth S. Jerom:) our   Eustoch.
35   long laughing must be recompensed with long weepinge:

---

11 bewail, and be hartily sorrie for this delay, which   12 *omits*
then must thou make satisfaction . . . talking of satisfaction [line 20]
21 greater wil be thy pain and sorow in thine amendment. *Alto*   23
omits pænitentia crimine minor non sit   25 *omits* and the penance may
not be lesse . . . and geving of Almes [line 33]   34 our laughing

our soft lynnen, and fyne silke apparell, must be chaunged into sharpe hearclothe. Finallie, S. Ambrose agreeing with the rest sayeth, *Grandi plagæ alta & prolixa opus est medicina. Grande scelus grandem necessariam habet satisfactionem.* Unto a great wounde, a deepe and long medicine is needfull. A great offence requireth of necessitie a great satisfaction.

Marke heere (deare brother) that this satisfaction must be bothe great and long, and also of necessitie. What madnes is it then for the, now to enlarge the wounde, knoweing that the medicine must afterwardes be so paynfull? what crueltie can be more against thy selfe, than to drive in thornes into thine owne flesh, which thou must after pull owte againe with so many teares? woldest thou drink that cuppe of poysoned liquour for a litle pleasure in the taste, whiche wolde cast thee soone after into a burning fever, torment thy bowells within thee, and ether dispache thy lyfe, or put the in great jeoperdie?

But heere I know thy refuge will be, as it is to all them, wherof the prophet saieth, *mentita est iniquitas sibi:* Iniquitie hathe flattered and lyed unto her selfe: thy refuge (I saye) wilbe, to alleage the example of the good theefe, saved even at the last howre, upon the crosse, and caried to paradise that same day with Christ, without any further penance or satisfaction. This example is greatlie noted, and urged by all those whiche deferre their conversion, as surelye it is, and ought to be, of great comfort to everie man, which findeth hym selfe now at the last cast, and therfore commonlie tempted by the enemye to despaire of Gods mercie, which in no case he ought to doe. For the same God whiche saved that great sinner at that last howre, can also, (and will) save all them that hartilie turne unto hym, even in that

Ad virg. lapsam. c.8.

Psal.27.

The example of the theefe saved on the crosse discussed.

---

1 *omits* our soft lynnen, and fyne silke apparell, must be chaunged into sharpe hearclothe 2 agreeing therunto, saith 4 *omits Grande scelus grandem necessariam habet satisfactionem.* 6 *omits* A great offence requireth of necessitie a great satisfaction. 8 that the labor of thine amendement must be very great; and that it cannot be avoided. What 23 at the last hour 25 any further toil of amendement. This example

last howre. But (alas) many men doe flatter and deceyve
them selves with misunderstanding, or rather mysusing
of this example.

For we must understand (as S. Austen well noteth)
5   that this was but one particular acte of Christ, which
maketh no generall rule: even as we see, that a temporall prince perdoneth some tyme a malefactor, when
he is come to the verie place of execution: yet were it
not for everie malefactor to trust therupon. For that,
10 this is but an extraordinarie acte of the prince his favoure,
and nether shewed, nor promised to all men. Besides
this, this act was a speciall miracle reserved for the man-
ifestation of Christ his power and glorie, at that howre
upon the crosse. Agayne, this acte was upon a moste
15 rare confession made by the theefe, in that instant, when
all the world forsooke Christ, and even the Apostles
them selves, ether dowted, or lost their faithe of his godhead. Beside all this, the confession of this theefe was
at suche a time, as he could nether be baptized, nor
20 have further tyme of penance. And we holde: that at a
mans first conversion, there is required no other penance,
or satisfaction at all, but onelye to be baptised, for the
gayning of heaven. But it shall not be amysse perhappes,
to put to S. Austens verye woordes upon this matter.   Ser.120.
25 For thus he writeth.   de tem.

It is a remedyles perill, when a man gyveth hym selfe
over so muche to vices, as he forgetteth that he must
geve accompt therof to God: and the reason whye I am
of this opinion is, for that it is a greate punishement of
30 sinne, to have lost the feare and memorie of the judgement to come, &ce. But (dearlie beloved) least perhappes,
the newe felicitie of the beleeving theefe on the crosse,
doe make any of you too secure and remisse: least per-
adventure some of you saye in his harte, my guyltie con-

---

16 and * the apostles; *mn*: B. *The blessed virgin likewise, and other
godly women were by: but said nothing (that we read of) in his
defence: a plaine breach of the first, fift, sixt, and ninth commandements.   20 time of amendement. And   21 required nothing else,
but to beleeve, and to be baptised. But it shal not be amisse to put
to   23 *omits* perhappes   31 *omits* perhappes

science shall not trouble nor torment me: my naughtie lyfe shall not make me verie sadde, for that I see even in a moment all sinnes forgeven unto the theefe: we must consider first in that theefe, not onelye the short-

5 nes of his beleefe and confession, but his devotion, and the occasion of that tyme, even when the perfection of the just dyd staggar. Secondlie, shew me the faith of that theefe in thy selfe, and then promise to thy selfe his felicitie. The devill doeth put into thy heade this

10 securitie, to the ende he may bryng thee to perdition. And it is unpossible to number all them, which have perished by the shadowe of this deceitfull hope. He deceiveth him selfe, and maketh but a Jeste of his owne damnation, whiche thinketh that Gods mercie at the last

15 daye shall help or releeve hym. It is hatefull before God, when a man, upon confidence of penance in his olde age, dothe sinne the more freelie. The happie theefe wherof we have spoken, happie (I saye) not for that he layed snares in the waye, but for that he tooke holde

20 of the waye it selfe in Christ, layeing handes on the praye of lyfe, and after a straung maner, makyng a bootie of his owne deathe: he (I saye) nether dyd deferre the tyme of his salvation wittinglie, nether dyd he deceytfullie put the remedye of his state, in the last

25 moment of his lyfe: nether dyd he desperatlie reserve the hope of his redemption unto the howre of his deathe: nether had he any knowlege ether of religion, or of Christ before that tyme. For yf he had: perhappes he wold not have bene the last in number among the

30 Apostles, which was first in the kyndome of heaven.

By these woordes of S. Austen we are admonyshed, (as you see) that this particular facte of Christ maketh no generall rule of remission to all men: not, for that Christ is not allwayes redye to receyve the penitent, as

35 he promiseth: but, for that everie man hath not the tyme

---

7 [* stagger] *mn*: B. *The blessed virgin, S. John, and others, as afore: and this staggering must needs be sin. 16 of repentance in 28 For if he had, it may be, he would not have been the last among the apostles in number, which was made the former in kingdom.

or grace to repent, as he should, at that howre, according as hath beene declared before. The generall waye that God proposeth to all is that, whiche S. Paul sayeth: *Finis secundum opera ipsorum:* The ende of evill men is according to their workes. Looke how they lyve, and so they dye. To that effect sayeth the prophet. *Once God spake, and I heard theese two things from his mouthe. Power belongeth to God: and mercie unto thee, (o Lord) for that thou wilt render to everie man, according to his workes.* The wyse man maketh this playne, sayeing, the waye of sinners is paved with stones, and their ende is hell, darkenes, and punishmentes. Finallie, S. Paul maketh this generall and peremptorie conclusion: *Be not deceyved, God is not mocked: looke what a man soweth, and that shall he reape. He that soweth in fleshe shall reape corruption: he that soweth in spirit shall reape lyfe everlasting.* In whiche woordes, he doeth not onelie laye downe unto us the generall rule wherto we must trust: But also saieth further, that to persuade our selves the contrarie therof, were to mocke and abuse God, whiche hathe layed downe this law unto us.

The generall waye.

2.Co.11.
Psal.62.

Eccl.21.

Gala.6.

Notwithstanding (as I have sayd) this barreth not the mercie of God from using a privilege to some at the verie last cast. But yet miserable is that man, whiche placeth the Ancker of his eternall wealthe or woe, upon so tyclesome a point as this ys. I call it ticlesome, for that, all divines, whiche have writen of this matter, doe speake verie dowtfullie of the penance or conversion of a man, at the last ende. And althoughe they doe not absolutely condemne yt, in all, but doe leave it as uncertaine unto Gods secret judgement: yet doe they incline to the negative parte: and doe alleage fower reasons, for whiche that conversion is to be dowted, as insufficient for a mans salvation.

That the conversion made at the last daye is insufficient.

The first reason is, for that the extreeme feare and paines of deathe, being (as the philosopher sayeth) the moste terrible, of all terrible thinges, doe not permitt a man so to gather his spirites and senses, at that tyme, as is required, for the treating of so weightie a matter

The first reason.

---

27 *omits* penance or

with God, as ys our conversion and salvation. And yf
we see often, that a verie good man can not fyxe his
mynde earnestlie upon heavenlie cogitations, at suche
tyme as he is troubled with the passions of cholique, or
5   other sharpe diseases: how muche lesse in the anguishes
of deathe can a worldlie man doe the same, beinge un-
acquainted with that exercise, and loaden with the guilt
of many and greate sinnes, and cloyed with the love,
bothe of his bodie, and thinges belonginge therunto?

10   The second reason is, for that, the conversion, which   The
a man maketh at the last daye, is not (for the most parte)   second
voluntarie, but upon necessitie, and for feare: suche as   reason.
was the repentance of Semei, whoe having greevouslie
offended king David, in tyme of his affliction: afterward,   2.Re.16.
15   when he sawe hym in prosperitie againe, and hym selfe
in daunger of punishement: he came, and fell downe
before hym, and asked hym forgyvenes with teares. But   2.Re.19.
yet, David well perceyved the matter how it stoode: and
therfore, thoughe he spared him for that daye, wherein
20   he wolde not trouble the myrthe with execution of justice: yet, after he gave order, that he should be used   3.Re.2.
according to his desertes.

The thyrd reason is, for that, the custome of sinne,   The third
whiche hath continued all the life long, can not be re-   reason.
25   moved upon the instant, beinge growen into nature it
selfe, as it were. For whiche cause, God sayeth to evill
men, by the prophet Jeremie: yf an Ethiopian can chaunge   Jere.13.
his black skynne, or a leoparde hys spottes, that are on
his backe: then can you also doe well, having learned
30   all dayes of your life to doe evill.

The fowerth cause is, for that, the actes of vertue   The
them selves, can not be of so greate value with God, in   fowerth
that instant, as yf they had bene done in time of healthe   reason.
before. For, what greate matter is yt (for example sake)
35   to pardone thy enemies at that tyme, when thow canst
hurt them no more? to geve thy goodes awaye, when
thow cannest use them no more? to abandon thy con-
cubine, when thow cannest keepe her no longer? to leave

---

24 long, is seldome remooved

of to sinne, when sinne must leave thee? All theese
thinges are good and holie, and to be done by him,
whiche is in that last state: but yet, they are of no suche
value, as otherwise they wolde be, by reason of this cir-
5   cumstance of time, whiche I have shewed.

Theese are the reasons whie the holie fathers and
doctors of Christ his church, doe speake so dowtfullie
of this last conversion: not, for any want on Gods parte,
but on theirs whiche are to doe that great acte. I might
10   heere alleage greate store of authorities for this purpose:
But one place of S. Austen shall serve for all. Thus then   Hom.41.
he writeth of this matter in a certaine homilie of his: If   ex. ho.50.
a man have done penance truelie, and do dye, being
absolved from the bondes wherwith he was tyed, and
15   seperated from the bodie of Christ: he goeth to God,
he goeth to reste. But yf a man in the extreeme necessitie of his sickenesse, doe desire to receyve penance,
and doe receyve it, and doe passe hence reconciled: I
confesse unto you, that we doe not denye hym that,
20   whiche he demaundeth: but yet we presume not, that
he goeth hence in good case. I doe not presume (I tell
you playnelie,) I doe not presume. A faythefull man that
hathe lyved well, goeth awaye securelie. He that dyeth
the same howre he was baptized, goeth hence secure-
25   lie. He that is reconciled in his healthe, and doeth
penance, and afterwarde lyveth well: goeth hence securelie. But he that is reconciled, and doeth penance at the
last cast: I am not secure, that he goeth hence securelie. Where I am secure, I doe tell you, and doe geve se-
30   curitie. And where I am not secure, I may geve penance,
but I can geve no securitie. But heere perhappes some
man will saye to me: good pryest, yf you knowe not in
what state a man goeth hence: nor can not geve secu-

---

5 shewed. [*continued in main text*] B. *A fift reason might be taken of
experience: for that we see oft times, that such as repent after that
maner, if they recover again, they are afterward as bad as they were
before, and somtimes much woorse: which (without quæstion) was
not tru repentance in them. [*New paragraph*] These are reasons why
there is such dowt made of this last   9 *omits* I might heere alleage
great store ... and after penance better. [295.17] *continues* Mark wel
(saith one again) what I say: and (it may be) it shal

ritie that he is saved, to whome penance was assigned
at his death: teache us (I beseeche you) how we must
lyve after our conversion and penance. I saye unto you:
abstayne from dronkennesse, from concupiscence of the
5   fleshe, from thefte, from muche babling, from immod-
erate laughter, from ydle woordes, for whiche men are
to geve account in the daye of judgement. Loe how
small thinges I have named in youre sight. But yet, all   Mat.12.
these are great matters, and pestilent to those which
10   commit them. But yet, I tell you further: a man must
not onelie abstaine from these vices, and the lyke, after
penance: but also before, when he is in healthe. For yf
he dryve it of to the last ende of his lyfe: he can not
tell, whether he shalbe able to receyve penance, and to
15   confesse his sinnes to God, and to the pryest, or no.
Beholde the cause why I sayd unto you, that a man
should lyve well before penance, and after penance better. Marke well what I saye: and perhappes it shall be
needfull to expounde my meaning more plainlie, leste
20   any man mistake me. What say I then? that this man
whiche repenteth at the ende shalbe damned? I doe not
say so. What then? Doe I saye he shalbe saved? no. What
then doe I saye? I say, I know not: I say, I presume not:
I promise not: I know not. Wilt thow deliver thy selfe
25   foorthe of this dowte? wilt thow escape this daungerous,
and uncertaine point? doe penance then whiles thow art
hole. For yf thow doe penance while thow art in healthe,
and the last day chaunce to come upon thee: runne
presentlie to be reconciled: and so doeinge, thow art
30   safe. And whie art thow safe? for that thow diddest
penance in that tyme, wherein thow myghtest have
sinned. But yf thow wilt doe penance then, when thow   A notable
cannest sinne no longer: thow leavest not sinne, but   sayeing.

---

20 then? That a man which repenteth not, but at the end shal be
damned?   26 point? Repent then whiles thou art whole. For if thou
repent while thou art in health, whensoever the last day shal come
upon thee, thou art safe. And why art thou safe? For that thou didst
repent, in that time, wherin thou mightest have sinned. But if thou
wilt repent, then when thou canst sin no longer: thou leavest not
sin, but sin leaveth thee.

sinne leaveth thee. But you will saye to me: how knowest thow whether God will forgeve a mans sinnes at the
last howre, or no? you say well: I know it not. For, yf
I knewe that penance wold not profit a man at the last
5 howre: I wolde not geve yt hym. Agayne, yf I knewe
that it wold deliver him: I wolde not warne you, I wolde
not terrifye you, as I doe. Two thinges there are in this
matter: ether God perdoneth a man, doeing penance,
at the howre of deathe: or he doeth not pardone him.
10 Whiche of these two shalbe, I know not. Wherfore,
if thow be wise: take that whiche is certaine, and let
goe the uncertaine. Hitherto are S. Austens woordes of
the dowtfull case of those, whiche doe penance at the
last daye.
15   And heere now wolde I have the carefull Christian to
consider, (with me) but this one comparison that I will
make. If those whiche repent, and doe suche penance
as they may at the last daye, doe passe hence, notwithstanding, in suche daungerous dowtfullnes as S. Austen
20 sheweth: what shall we thinke of all those, whiche lacke
ether time or abilitie, or will, or place, or meanes, or
grace to doe any penance at all, at that howre? what
shall we saye of all those, whiche are cutt of before?
whiche dye suddenlie? whiche are stricken dumme, or
25 deafe, or senseles, or frentike, as we see manye are?
what shall we saye of those, which are abandoned by
God, and left unto vice, even unto the last breathe in
theyr bodie? I have shewed before owte of S. Paul, that   2.Cor.11.
ordinarilie, sinners dye, according as they live. So that,
30 it is a privilege for a wicked man, to doe penance at
his deathe. And then, yf his penance (when it is done)
be so dowtfull, as S. Austen hath declared: what a pitifull case are all other in? I meane the more parte, whiche

---

1 *omits* But you will saye to me ... whiche doe penance at the last
daye [line 14]   17 If those which do shew a kind of repentance at
the last day, do passe hence notwithstanding in such dangerous dowt-
fulnes: what shal we think of al those which lak either time, or abil-
ity, or wil, or grace to repent at al, at that hour?   24 *omits* dumme,
or deafe, or   30 it is as it were a privilege for a wicked man, to
have his repentance to be begun, when he is to die. And then, if
his repentance (when it doth come) be so dowtful, what a pittiful

repent not at all: but dye as they lived, and are forsaken
of God in that extremitie, according as he promiseth,   Pro.1.
when he sayeth: for that I have called you, and you   Jere.35.
have refused to come: for that, I have held owt my
5   hande, and none of you wolde vouchsafe to looke towardes me: I will laughe also at your destruction, when
anguyshe and calamitie cometh on you. You shall call
uppon me, and I will not heare: you shall ryse betymes
in the morning to see me, but you shall not fynde me.
10   It is bothe dreadefull and lamentable which the prophet
sayeth, of suche as deferre their conversion, from tyme
to tyme: *Conuertentur ad vesperam: & famem patientur ut canes,*   Psal.59.
& circuibunt ciuitatem: They will convert them selves to
God at the evenyng, and then shall they suffer hungar,
15   as dogges: and shall runne about the citie. The woordes
that goe immediatlie before, and doe immediatlie ensue
after, doe expresse more playnlie the greatnes of this
threate. For before, the verse is: *Attend (o Lord) to visit all*
nations: take no mercie upon all those, whiche woorke iniquitie.
20   That is, which woorke iniquitie unto the ende. And
immediatlye after enseweth: *These men shall speake with*
their mouthe, and a sworde shall be in their lyppes: for whoe
hath heard them? and thou (o Lord) shalt skoffe at them. That
is, these men in their last extremitie shall crye vehe-
25   mentlie for help: and their crye shall be as sharp to
pearse mens eares, as a swoord is: and yet notwithstanding, no man shall heare them: and thou (o Lord)
whiche onelie cannest help them, shalt be so farre of
from hearing or pityeing their case, as thou shalt also
30   laugh at their miserie and destruction. By all whiche is
signified, the greate calamitie of suche as deferre their
conversion unto the laste daye, expressed by three cir-
·   cumstances, in the former sentence alleaged.
       For first he sayeth, *they will turne at the evenyng*: that is,
35   at the howre of deathe. For as the evening is the ende
of the daye, and the begynning of night: even so is this

---

4 *I held*   10 *omits* It is bothe dreadefull . . . heate of all sunne beames
is past; *substitutes* When a worldling doth see that the brightnes of
his honor, vainglorie, and worldly pomp is consumed [298.8]

tyme, the ende of light, and the begynning of all darkenes unto the wicked. In whiche sense Christ sayd: *I*
must worke the workes of hym that sent me, whiles the day lasteth: Joh.9.
for night will come on, when no man can worke more. At this
5   tyme then, that is, at this evening, in this twye light,
betwene daye and darkenes, when the pleasant brightnes
and heate of all sunne beames is past: the brightnes (I
meane) of honour, of vainglorie, and of worldlie pompe
is consumed: when the heat of concupiscence, of car-
10   nall love, of delicate pleasures is quenshed: when the
beautyfull sommer daye of this lyfe is ended, and the
boysterous wynter night of deathe draweth on: then
(sayeth the prophet) will the wicked man turne unto
God, then will he repent, then will he resolve hym selfe,
15   and make his conversion.

But what? shall this be accepted? you have heard the
prophets request to God: *Non miserearis*: Doe not take
mercie on them: Not, for that the prophet wisheth God
to be unmercyfull: but for that he knewe Gods justice
20   towardes suche men. Whose miserie, in this extremitie,
he expresseth further, by sayeing, *they shall suffer hungar*
as dogges: whiche is, as yf he should have sayed: even as
dogges, when they are hungrie, are ravynous, and do
seeke by all meanes for meate, be it never so homelye:
25   and will refuse nothing that is offered, but will devoure
all those thynges most gredilie, which they contemned
whiles their bellies were full: so these men that wolde
not heare of penance, while they were in health, will
now admitt any thyng, and make straunge of nothing:
30   Now (I saye) when they can lyve no longer, will they
promyse any paynes: what prayer you will: what fasting

---

12 then will he turn unto God   16 *omits* But what? shall this be
accepted? ... Now (I saye) *continues* When he can live no longer, he
wil promise any pains: what hearing or studieng of the word of God
you wil; what toil or labor in his vocation you wil; what praier you
wil; what fasting you wil; what alms deeds you can desire; what austeritie you can imagin, he wil promise it (I say) upon a condition
that he might have life again: upon condition that the day might
be prolonged unto him: though if God should grant him his request
(as many times he doth) he would perform no one point therof: but
be as careles, as he were before.

you will: what almes deedes you can desire: what austeritie soever you can imagine, they will promyse it, (I
saye) upon condition they myght have lyfe agayne: upon
condition that the daye might be prolonged unto them:
5   thoghe, yf God should graunt them their request, (as
many tymes he doeth) they wolde performe no one point
therof: but be as careles, as they were before: yet for
the present, you shall see them as hungrie as dogges,
sayeth the prophet, most redye to devoure any thyng,
10   that may be devised, for their salvation.

And not contented with this, the same prophet addeth
yet a further clause of miserie: And that is, *that they shall*
circuite or runne about the citie: even as dogges doe, when
they are hungrie, putting in their heades at everie dore
15   for releefe, thoghe it be with great daunger to be beaten
owt agayne. This expresseth an unspeakable distresse
and calamitie of wicked men, at the last daye: when
they shall circuite, and runne about the whole citie of
God, bothe in heaven, and earthe, to seeke help, and
20   shall finde none: When they shall crie, with sighes and
groones, as pearsing as a swoorde, and yet shall not be
heard. For, whether will they turne them selves in this
distresse? unto their worldlie wealthe, power, or riches?
alas, they are gone: and the scripture sayeth, *riches shall*   Prov.11.
25   *not profitt in the daye of revenge.* Will they turne unto their
carnall freends? But what comfort can they geve, besides
onelye weeping, and comfortles mourning? Will they
aske helpe of the saints in heaven to praye for them in
this instant? it is good, surelie, so to doe: but yet, they
30   can not chuse but remember what is writen: *The saintes*   Psa.149.
shall rejoyse in glorie, exultation shalbe in their throotes, and two
edged swoordes in their handes, to take revenge upon nations, and
increpations upon people: to bynde kynges in fetters, and noble men
in manacles of yron: to execute upon them the prescript judgement

---

7 *omits* yet for the present . . . to seeke help, and shall finde none;
continues When such shal   20 when such shal   22 heard, what comfort then wil they hope for to find? For whither wil they   28 saints,
to praie   29 *omits* it is good, surelie, so to doe: but yet, they can
not chuse but   29 Then must they remember   31 *glorie, and exulta-*
tion shalbe in their mouthes, and

of God: and this is the glorie of all his saintes. Their onelye
refuge then must be unto God, who in deed is the onelie
surest refuge of all: but yet in this case, the prophet
sayeth here, that he shall not heare them: but rather
contemne, and laughe at their miserie. Not, that he is   Prov.1.
contrarie to his promise of receaving a synner, at what   Psa.59.
tyme soever he repenteth, and turneth from his sinne.
But, for that this turning at the last day is not commonlie true repentance and conversion, for the causes
before rehearsed.

To conclude then this matter of delaye, what wyse
man is there in the woorlde, who reading this, will not
feare the deferring of his conversion, thoughe it were
but for one daye? who doeth know whether this shalbe
the last daye, or no, that ever God will call him in?
God sayeth, I called, and you refused to come: I held
owt my hand, and you wolde not looke towardes me:
and therfore will I forsake you, in your extremitie. He
doeth not saye, how many times, or how long he dyd   Prov.1.
call and holde owt his hand. God sayeth, *I stand at the*
dore, and knocke. But he sayeth not, how often he doeth
that, or how many knockes he geeveth. Agayne, he sayde
of wicked Jezabel, the faigned prophetesse in the Apo-   Apoc.2.
calips: I have geven her time to doe penance, and she
wolde not, and therfore shall she perishe: but he sayeth
not, how long this time of repentance endured. We reade   HEROD.
of wounderfull examples heerin. HEROD the father
had a call geven him, and that a lowde one, when John
baptist was sent unto him, and when his harte was so
farre touched, as he willinglie heard him, and folowed
his counsaile in many thinges, as one evangelist noteth: Marc.6.
but yet, because he deferred the matter, and tooke not
time, when yt was offered: he was cast of agayne, and
his last doeings made worse than his former. HEROD   HEROD
tetrarche, the sonne, had a call also, when he felt that   the
desire to see Christ, and some miracle done by hym: second.
but, for that he answered not unto the call: it did him   Luc.9.
                                                               Luc.23.

---

2 only refuge of   24 *to repent, and*   26 endureth   30 and so followed

no good, but rather much hurt. What a great knocke,   Mat.14.
had PYLATE geven hym at his hart, yf he had beene   PILATE.
so fortunate, as to have opened the dore presentlie, when
he was made to understand the innocencie of Christ: as   Mat.27.
5   appeareth by washing his handes in testimonie therof,
and his wyfe also sent hym an admonition abowt the
same? No lesse knocke had kynge AGRIPPA at his dore,   AGRIPPA
when he cryed owt, upon the hearing of S. Paul: *O Paul,*   Act.26.
thow persuadest me a litle, to be a Christian. But, because he
10   deferred the matter: this motion passed away agayne.

     Twyse happie had PHARAO beene, yf he had resolved   PHA-
hym selfe presentlie, upon that motion that he felt, when   RAO.
he cryed to Moyses, *I have sinned, and God is just.* But by   Exod.9.
delay he became worse than ever he was before. S. Luke   Act.24.
15   reporteth how FELIX, the governour of Jewrie for the   FELIX.
Romanes, conferred secretlie oftentimes with S. Paul,
that was his prisonner: and heard of hym the faithe in
Christ: wherwithe he was greatlie moved, especiallie at
one tyme, when Paul disputed of Gods justice, and the
20   daye of judgement, whereat FELIX trembled. But yet,
he deferred this resolution, willing Paul to departe, and
to come agayne an other tyme: and so the matter by
delation came to no effect. How many men doe perishe daylie, some cutt of by death: some left by God,
25   and geven over to a reprobate sense: which might have
saved them selves, if they had not deferred theyr conversion from daye to daye, but had made their resolution presentlye, when they felte God to call within theire
hartes.

30   God is most bountifull to knocke and call: but yet,   The dan-
he byndeth him selfe to no time or space, but commeth   ger of
and goeth at his pleasure: and they whiche take not   passinge
their tymes when they are offered, are excuseles before   the day
his justice, and doe not know whether ever it shalbe   of our
35   offered them agayne, or no: for that, this thing is onelie   vocation.
in the will and knowlege of God alone: whoe taketh
mercie where it pleaseth him best, and is bound to none: Exo.33.

---

2 been so gratious as to   8 cried out at the hearing   17 was prisoner   25 might have found grace, if they

And when the prefixed time of calling is once past: wo
be unto that partie. For a thowsand worldes will not
purchase it agayne. Christ showeth wonderfullie the
importance of this matter: when, entering into Jerusalem
5   upon palme sondaye, a-middest all his mirthe and glorie of receyvinge, he coulde not chuse but weepe upon
that citie, considering (as moste men thinke) that this
was the last day of mercie and vocation, that ever should
be used to the same: and therfore he sayed with teares:
10   *O Jerusalem, if thow knewest also, those thinges whiche apper-*
taine to thy peace, even in this thy day: but now these thinges
are hydden from thee: As yf he had sayed, yf thow knewest
(Jerusalem) as well as I doe, what mercie is offered
thee, even this daye, whiche is the last day, that ever
15   suche offer shalbe made: thow woldest not doe as thow
doest: but woldest presentlie accept therof: but now this
secret judgement of my father is hidden from thee: and
therfore thow makest litle account therof, untill thy
destruction shall come suddenlie upon thee. As sone after
20   it did.

By this now may be considered the great reason of
the wise mans exhortation: *Forslow not to turne to God: nor*
doe not deferre it from day to daye: for his wrathe will come upon
the, at the suddain: and in time of revenge it will destroy thee.
25   It may be seene also upon what great cause, S. Paul
exhorted the Hebrewes so vehementlie, *Dum cognominatur*
hodie: To accept of grace even whiles that verie daye
endured: and not to lett passe the occasion offered.
Whiche every man applyeing to hym selfe, should folow,
30   in obeing the motions of Gods spirite within hym: and
acceptinge of Gods vocation without delaye: consideringe
what a greevous sinne it is to resist the holye ghost:
Everie man ought (I saye) when he feeleth a good motion
in his hart, to thincke with him selfe: now God knock-
35   eth at my doore: yf I open presentlie, he will enter, and

Rom.9.

Luc.19.

Eccle.5.

Heb.3.

Act.7.

Apoc.3.

---

5 *omits* upon palme sondaye   7 *omits* considering (as moste men
thinke) that this was the last day of mercie and vocation, that ever
should be used to the same: and therfore he sayed; *continues* crieng
out with teares   14 *omits* whiche is the last day, that ever suche offer
shalbe made

dwell within me: But yf I deferre it untill to morow: I
know not whether he wil knocke agayne, or no. Everie
man ought to remember still that sayeing of the prophet,
touching Gods spirite: *Hodie si vocem eius audieritis, nolite*   Psal.95.
5   *obdurare corda vestra*: yf you chaunce to heare his voyce
calling you to daye, doe not harden your hartes, but
presentlie yeelde unto hym.

   Alas (deare brother) what hope of gayne hast thou by
this perilous dilation, which thou makest? thy accounte
10   is increased therby, as I have shewed: thy debt of satisfaction is made more grevous: thy enemie more strong:
thy selfe more feeble: thy difficulties of conversion multiplied: what hast thou then to withholde thee one daye
from resolution? the gayning perhappes of a litle time
15   in vanitie. But I have proved to thee before, how this   Merit by
tyme is not gayned but lost, beyng spent without merit,   good
whiche is in deede the onelie true gayne of tyme. Yf it   deedes,
seeme pleasant to thee for the present: yet remember   the onely
what the prophet saieth, *iuxta est dies perditionis, & adesse*   gaine of
tyme.
20   *festinant tempora*: The daye of perdition is at hand, and   Deu.32.
the tymes of destruction make haste to come on. Whiche
daye beyng once come, I marvaile what hope thou wilt
conceive. Doest thou thinke (perchaunce) to crie *peccaui?*
it shalbe well truelie, yf thou cannest doe it: but yet,   Exod.9.
25   thou knowest, that Pharao dyd so, and gat nothing by
it. Doest thou intend to make a good testament, and to
be liberall in almes deedes, at that time? this (no doubt)
is verie commendable: but yet thou must remember also,
that the virgines which filled their lampes, at the verie   Mat.25.
30   instant, were shutt owt, and utterlie rejected by Christ.
Doest thou think to weepe, and mourne, and to move
thy judge with teares, at that instant? first, this is not
in thy handes to doe at thy pleasure: and yet thou must
consider also, that Esau found no place of penance,
35   thoghe he sought it with teares, as S. Paul well notethe.   Heb.12.

---

5 *If you hear his voice calling on you*   10 debt of amendement is   14
omits perhappes   15 *mn: Godlines the only*   16 spent without fruit of
godlines, which   23 *omits* (perchaunce)   27 This as the case may
be, is very   34 that Esau failed, though he sought it with tears, as
the apostle wel noteth.

Doest thou meane to have many good purposes, to make
great promises and vowes in that distresse? call to minde
the case of Antiochus in his extremities: what promises   2.Mac.9.
of good deedes, what vowes of vertuous lyfe made he
5   to God upon condition he might escape, and yet prevayled he nothing therby. All this is spoken, not to put
them in despayre whiche are now in those last calamities: but to disswade others from falling in to the same:
assuring thee (gentle reader) that the prophet sayd not
10 without a cause, *seeke unto God while he may be fownd:*   Esa.55.
call upon hym while he ys neare at hand. Now is the time
acceptable, now is the day of salvation, sayeth S. Paul.   2.Co.6.
Now is God to be fownd, and neare at hand to embrace
all them that truelie turne unto hym, and make firme
15 resolution of vertuous lyfe hereafter. If we deferre this
tyme: we have no warrant that he will ether call us, or
receyve us heerafter: but rather many threates to the
contrarie, as hath bene shewed. Wherfore I will ende
with this one sentence of S. Austen: that he is bothe a   Tract.33.
20 careles and most graceles man, whiche, knoweing all this,   in Joh.
will venture notwithstanding the eternitie of his salvation and damnation, upon the doubtfull event of his finall
repentance.

Of three other impedimentes that hynder men from resolution:
25 *whiche are slothe, negligence, and hardnes of harte.*

CHAP. VI

Besides all impedimentes which hytherto have bene
named, there are yet divers other to be founde: yf a
man could examine the particular consciences of all
30 suche as doe not resolve. But these three heere mentioned, and to be handeled in this chapiter, are so
publique and knowen: as I may not passe them over,
without discovering the same: for that, many tymes men
are evill affected, and know not their owne diseases: the
35 onelie declaration whereof (to suche as are desirous of
their owne healthe) is sufficient to avoyde the daunger
of the sickenes.

First then, the impediment of slouthe is a great and ordinarie let of resolution to many men: but especiallie in ydle and delicate people, whose lyfe hathe bene in all ease and rest, and therfore doe persuade them selves,

5 that they can take no paines, nor abyde no hardnes, thoghe never so fayne they wolde. Of whiche S. Paul sayeth, that nise people shall not inherite the kyngdome of heaven. These men will confesse to be true, as muche and more than is sayd before: and that they wolde also

10 gladlie put the same in execution, but that they can not. Their bodies may not beare it: they can not fast: they can not watche: they can not praye. They can not leave their disportes, recreations, and merye companions: they should dye presentlye (as they saye) with melancholy, yf

15 they dyd it: yet in their hartes they desire (forsoothe,) that they could doe the same, whiche seyng they can not: no doubt (say they,) God will accept our good desires. But lett them hearken a litle what the scripture sayeth hereof: desires do kyll the slothefull man (sayeth

20 Salomon:) his handes will not fall to any woorke: all the daye long he coveteth and desireth: but he that is just, will doe, and will not cesse. Take the slothefull and unprofitable servant (sayeth Christ) and flyng hym into utter darkenes, where shalbe weeping and gnashyng of

25 teeth. And when he passed by the way and founde a figge tree with leaves, without fruit (which signified desyres without woorkes:) he gave it presentlie an everlasting curse. Finallie, the prophet David detesteth those men, and sayeth also, they are detested of God, *qui in labore*

30 *hominum non sunt*, which are not in the laboures of men.

Of this fountaine of slouthe do proceede many effectes that hynder the slothefull from resolution. And the first is a certaine heavynes, and sleepie drowsienes towardes all goodnes, according as the scripture sayeth, *pigredo*

35 *immittit soporem*, slouthe doeth bryng drowsines. For which cause S. Paule sayeth, *surge qui dormis*, arise thou which

1. Of slothe.

1.Co.6.

Pro.21.

Matt.25.

Mat.21.

Psal.73.

Fower effectes of slouthe.
1.DROW-SYNES.
Pro.19.
Ephe.5.

---

5 any hardnes   11 it: they can take no pains in their several callings: and in general they cannot fast;   26 *omits* (Which signified desyres without woorkes:)   28 *omits* Finallie, the prophet David . . . in the laboures of men.   36 *thou that art*

art a sleepe: and Christ crieth owt so often, *videte, vigi-*   Marc.13.
late, looke about you, and wache. You shall see many   Mat.24.
men in the world, with whome if you talke of a cowe   & 25.
or a calfe, of a fatt oxe, of a peece of ground, or the
5   lyke: they can bothe heare and talke willinglye and freshe-
lie: but yf yow reason with them of their salvation, and
their inheritance in the kyngdome of heaven: they answere
not at all: but will heare, as yf they were in a dreame.
Of these men then sayeth the wyse man: how long wilt   Prov.6.&
10   thou sleepe o slouthefull felow? when wilt thou arise owt   24.
of thy dreame? A litle yet wilt thou sleepe: a litle longer
wilt thou slumber: a litle wilt thou close thy handes
together, and take rest: and so, povertie shall hasten
upon thee as a running poste, and beggarye as an armed
15   man shall take and possesse thee.

The second effect of slouthe, is fond feare of paines   2.
and labour, and casting of dowtes where none be, accord-   FEARE.
ing as the scripture sayeth, *pigrum deiicit timor,* feare dis-   Pro.18.
courageth the slothefull man. And the prophet sayeth
20   of the lyke, *they shake for feare where there is no feare.* These   Psal.53.
men doe frame unto them selves straunge imaginations
of the service of God, and daungerous eventes, yf they
should folow the same. One sayeth, If I should fast
muche: it wolde without dowte corrupt my bloode. An
25   other sayeth, yf I should pray, and be bareheaded muche:
I should dye moste certainlie with reume. A third sayeth,
yf I should kepe account of all my sinnes, to confesse
them: it wolde quicklie kill me with sadnes. And yet all
this is nothing els but slouthe, as the scripture testifieth
30   in theese woordes: *Dicit piger, leo est foris: in medio platearum*   Pro.22.
occidendus sum. The slouthefull man sayeth, sitting still in
his house: ther is a lyon without: if I should goe oute
of doores to labour, I should certainlie be slayne in the
middest of the streetes.

---

4 or a fat ox   10 rise   23 *omits* If I should fast muche . . . it wolde
quicklie kill me with sadnes; *substitutes* If I should give much; it would
without dowt make me a begger. Another saith; If I should stil
imploy my selfe to painful labor, it would kil me ere long. A third
saith; If I should humble my selfe as is required, every bodie would
tread me under their feete. And yet

A third effect of slouthe is pusillanimitie and faintnes
of hart: wherby the slouthefull man is overthrowen, and
discouraged by every litle contrarietie or difficultie whiche
he findeth in vertue, or whiche he imagineth to finde
5 therein. Which the scripture signifieth, when it sayeth,
in lapide luteo lapidatus est piger, the slouthefull man, is
stoned to death with a stone of durt: that is, he is over-
throwne with a difficultie of no importance. Agayne: *De
stercore boum lapidatus est piger*, the slouthefull man is stoned
10 dead with the dung of oxen: whiche commonlie is of
matter so soft, as it can hurt no man.

A fowerth effect of slouthe is ydle lazynes: whiche we
see in many men that will talke and consult of this and
that, about their amendement, but will execute nothing.
15 Whiche is moste fytlie expressed by the holie ghoste in
these woordes: *Sicut ostium vertitur in cardine suo, ita piger
in lectulo suo*. As a dore is tossed in and owte upon his
hyngells, so is a slouthefull man, lieing lazelie upon his
bedde. And agayne: *vult & non vult piger*: A slothefull
20 man will and will not: that is, he turneth him selfe to
and fro in his bedde, and betwene willinge and nilling
he doeth nothing. And yet further, in an other place
the scripture describeth this lazynesse, sayeing, *the slothefull man putteth his handes under his girdle, and will not vouche-
25 safe to lift them up to his mouthe, for that it is painfull.*

All these and many more are the effectes of slouthe:
but theese fower especiallie, have I thought good to
touche in this place: for that, they lett and hinder greatlie
this resolution whiche we talke of. For he that lyveth in
30 a slumber, and will not heare, or attend to any thing,
that is sayed of the lyfe to come: and beside this, imagineth fearefull matters in the same: and thirdlie, is thrown
downe by everie litle blocke, that he findeth in the waye:
and lastlie is so lazye, as he can beare no laboure at

3. PUSIL-
LANIMI-
TIE.

Eccl.22.

4. LAZY-
NES.

Pro.26.

Pro.13.

Pro.19.

---

5 Which the wise man * signifieth when he saith; *mn*: B. *The
vulgar translation so readeth: but now it is found, that therin it misseth the sense of the text in both these places heer alledged.
And yet the matter it selfe is tru, though it have no warrant hence.
18 *hindges*

all: this man (I saye) is past hope, to be gayned to any
suche purpose as we speake for.

To remove therfore this impediment, this sorte of men   Meanes
ought to laye before their eyes, the laboures of Christ,   to remove
5   and of his saintes: the exhortations they used to other   slothe.
men, to take lyke paines: the threates made in scripture
against them whiche laboure not: the condition of our
present warfare, that requireth travaile: the crowne prepared for it: and the miserie enseweing upon idle and
10   lazye people. And finallie, yf they can not beare the
labour of vertuous lyfe, whiche in deede is accompanyed with so many consolations, as it may not rightful-
lie be called a labour: how will they abyde the labour
and tormentes of the lyfe to come, whiche must be bothe
15   intollerable and everlasting?

Saint Paul sayeth of him selfe and others, to the   2.Thess.3.
Thessalonians: we dyd not eate our breade of free cost
when we were with you: but dyd woorke in labour and
wearynesse, bothe daye and night: therby to geve you
20   an example of imitation: denouncing further unto you,
that yf any man wolde not woorke he shoulde not eate.
Christ went foorthe into the streetes twyse in one day,
and still reprehended grevouslie those that stoode ydle
there: *Quid hic statis tota die otiosi?* Whye doe ye stand   Mat.20.
25   heere all the daye ydle and doeyng nothing? I am a
vyne, (sayeth Christ) and my father is a husband man: Joh.15.
every braunche that beareth not fruit in me, my father
will cut of, and cast into the fire. And in an other place: Luc.13.
Cutt downe the unprofitable tree: whie doeth it stand
30   here, and occupie up the grounde for nothing? And   Mat.11.
againe: the kingdome of heaven is subject to force: and
men do gayne it by violence and labour. For which
cause, the wyse man also sayeth: what soever thy hand   Ecc.9.
can doe in this lyfe, doe it instantlie: for after this, there
35   is nether tyme, nor reason, nor wisdome, nor knowlege
that we can employe. And agayne the same wyse man   Prov.10.
sayeth: The lazie hande worketh beggarie to it selfe, but

---

22 *omits* went foorthe into the streetes twyse in one day, and; *sub-*
stitutes in his parable   24 *do you stand*

the laboursome and valyant hande heapeth up greate
riches. And yet further to the same effect: The slothefull man will not sowe in the wynter, for that it is colde:
and therfore he shall begge in the somer, and no man
5   shall take pitie of hym.

    All this pertayneth to shew, how that this lyfe is a
time of labour, and not of ydlenes: and appointed unto
us for the gayning of heaven: it is the Marquet, wherein
we must buye: the battaille wherein we must fight, and
10   gayne our crowne: the winter wherin we must sowe:
the daye of labour wherin we must sweate) and gaine
our pennie: And he that passeth over lazilie this daye
(as the most parte of men doe) must suffer eternall
povertie and neede in the life to come: as in the first
15   parte of this booke more at large hathe bene declared.
Wherfore, the wise man (or rather the holie ghost by
his mouthe) geveth eche one of us a moste vehement
admonition and exhortation, in theese wordes. Runne
aboute: make haste: styrre up thy freend: geve no sleepe
20   unto thy eyes: lett not thine eye lyddes slumber: skyppe
owt as a doe from the handes of hym that held her:
and as a byrd owt of the hand of the fowler: goe unto
the Emmet (thow slothefull man,) and consider her
doeinges, and learne to be wise: she having no guyde,
25   teacher, or captaine, provideth meate for her selfe in
the sommer, and gathereth together in the harvest, that
whiche maye serve her to feed upon in the wynter. By
whiche woordes we are admonished in what order we
ought to behave our selves in this lyfe, and how dili-
30   gent and carefull we should be in doeinge of all good
woorkes, (as S. Paul also teacheth) consideringe, that as
the Emmet laboureth most earnestlie in the harvest time
to lay upp for the wynter to come: so we should for the
next world: And that slothefullnes to this effect, is the
35   greatest and most daungerous lett that may be. For,
as the Emmet should dye in the wynter most certainlie
for hunger, yf she should lyve ydelie in the sommer: so
without all dowte they are to suffer extreme neede and

Prov.20.

Ca.3.
pa.[21]
Prov.6.

Coloss.1.
Rom.12.
Gala.6.

---

8 for the attaining of heaven   9 and obtain our   11 and get our

miserie in the world to come, whoe now for slouthe doe
omitt to laboure.

The seconde impediment ys called by me, in the title
of this chapiter, negligence. But I doe understand therby
5   a further matter than commonlie this woorde importeth.
For I doe comprehend under the name of negligent, all
careles and dissolute people, whiche take to hart nothinge
that pertayneth to God or godlynes, but onelie attend
to woorldlie affaires, making their salvation the least
10   parte of their cogitations. And under this kynde of negligence is contained bothe Epicurisme, (as S. Paul noted
in some Christianes of hys dayes, whoe beganne onelie
to attend to eate and drinke, and to make their bellies
their God, as our Christians now doe:) and also a secret
15   kinde of Atheisme, or denieing of God: that is, of denieing him in life and behaviour, as S. Paul expoundeth it.
For albeit these men in wordes doe confesse God, and
professe them selves to be as good Christians as the rest:
yet secretlie in deed they doe not beleeve God: as theyr
20   lyfe and doeings doe declare. Whiche thing the scripture discovereth plainlie, when it sayeth, *væ dissolutis corde,*
qui non credunt deo: woe be unto the dissolute and careles in hart, whiche doe not beleeve God. That is, thoughe
they professe that they beleeve and trust in hym: yet by
25   theyr dissolute and careles doeings, they testifie that in
theyr hartes they beleeve hym not: for that, they have
nether care nor cogitation of matters pertayning to hym.

These kynde of men are those which the scripture
noteth, and detesteth for ploweyng with an oxe and an
30   Asse together: for soweing their grounde with myngled
seede: for wearing apparell of linsie woolsie, that is made
of flaxe and wooll together. Theese are they of whome
Christ sayeth in the Revelations. *I wold thou were ether*
colde or hoate. But for that thou art luke warme, and nether cold
35   *nor hoate: therfore will I beginne to vomite thee owt of my mouth*:
Theese are they which can accorde all religions together,
and take up all controversies by only sayeing, that ether

Right margin notes:
2. Of neg- ligence.

Epicu- risme, or lyfe of Epicures. Phili.3. Rom.16. Tit.1.

Eccl.2.

Of careles Atheistes. Deu.22.

Apoc.3.

---

6 negligence   14 as many of our   20 thing Ecclesiasticus discovereth plainly, when he saith

they are differences of small importance, or els that they
appertaine onelie to learned men to thinke upon, and
not unto them. These are they whiche can applie them
selves to anye companie, to any time, to any princes
5   pleasure, for matters of lyfe to come. These men for-
byd all talke of spirite, religion, or devotion in their presence: onelie they will have men eate, drinke, and be
merie with them: tell newes of the courte and affayres
abrode, sing, daunce, laugh, and playe at cardes, and
10   so passe over this lyfe in lesse consideration of God,
than the very heathens did. And hath not the scripture
reason then, in sayeing that these men in their hartes
and woorkes are Atheistes? yes surelie. And yt may be
proved by many rules of Christ. As for example: this is
15   one rule sett downe by hym selfe: *By their fruites yee shall*   Luc.6.
know them: For suche as the tree ys within, suche is the
fruit whiche that tree sendethe foorthe. Agayne, *the mouthe*   Mat.12.
speakethe from the abundance of the harte: and consequentlie,
seeing their talke is nothing but of worldlie vanities: yt
20   is a signe, there is nothing in their harte, but that. And
then yt foloweth also by a third rule, *where the treasure is,*   Matt.6.
there is the harte, and so, seeing their hartes are onelie
sett uppon the world: the world is their onelie treasure,
and not God. And consequentlie they preferre that before
25   God, as in deed Atheistes.

    This impedimente reacheth farre and wyde at this   Two
daye: and infinite are the men which are intangled ther-   causes of
with: and the causes therof are two especiallie. The first   Atheism
is heresye: which by moving many questions and dowts   at this
30   wearyeth out a mans witt, and in the ende bringeth hym   daie.
to care for no parte, but rather to contemne all. The
second is inordinate love of the world: which bringeth
men to hate God, and to conceyve enemytie against
hym, as the Apostle sayeth: and therfore, no marvayle   1.Joh.2.
35   thoghe in deed they nether beleeve, nor delite in hym.
And of all other men these are the hardest to be re-

---

25 Atheists do 26 *mn: The cheefe cause of* 28 *omits* and the causes
therof are two. . . . The second; *substitutes* and the cause therof esspecally
is inordinate love

claymed, and brought to any resolution of amendement: for that, they are insensible: and beside that, doe
also flye all meanes, whereby they may be cured. For, A com-
as there were small hope to be conceyved of that patient, parison.
5 which being grevouslie sicke should nether feele his disease, nor beleeve that he were distempered, nor abide
to heare of phisick, or phisition, nor accept of anie coun-
sail that should be offered, nor admitt any talke or consultation about his curing: so theese men are in more
10 daungerous estate than anie other, for that, they know
not their owne daunger, but persuading them selves to
be more wyse than their neighbours, doe remove from
their cogitations all things, wherby theyr healthe might
be procured.

15 The onelie waye to doe theese men good, (if there The waye
be any waye at all) is to make them know that they are to cure
sicke, and in great daunger: whiche in our case may be careles
done best (as it seemeth to me) by geving them to under- men.
stand, how farre they are of, from any one peece of
20 true Christianitie, and consequentlie from all hope of
salvation that may be had, therby. God requireth at our
handes, that we should love hym and serve hym, *with* Deut.6.
all our harte, with all our soule, and with all our streengthe. Mat.22.
These are the prescript woordes of God, sett downe Luc.10.
25 bothe in the olde and new law. And how farre (I praye
the) are these men of from this, whiche employe not
the halfe of theyr harte, nor the halfe of theyr soule,
nor the halfe of theyr strengthe in Gods service, nay,
not the least part therof? God requireth at our handes, Deut.6.
30 that we should make his lawes and preceptes our studie & 11.
and cogitations: that we should thinke of them contin- Psa.1.
uallie, and meditate upon them bothe day and night, at
home and abrode, early and late, when we go to bedde,
and when we rise in the morning: this is his com-
35 maundement, and there is no dispensation therin. But
how farre are these men from this, whiche bestowe not
the third parte of theyr thoughtes uppon this matter, no
not the hundreth parte, nor scarse once in a yeare do

---

7 physitions 36 those men

talke therof? can these men saye, they are Christians,
or that they beleeve in God?

Christ making the estimate of things in this lyfe, pro-   Luc.10.
nounced this sentence: *Unum est necessarium*, one onelie
5   thing is necessarie, or of necessitie in this world, meaning the diligent and carefull service of God. These men
finde many things necessarie beside this one thing, and
this nothing necessarie at all. How farre doe they differ
then in judgemente from Christ? Christes Apostle sayeth,
10   that a Christian *must nether love the world, nor any thing in*   1.Joh.2.
the world. These men love nothinge els but that whiche
is of the world: he sayeth, *That who soever is a freend to*
the world, is an enemie to Christ: These men are enemies
to who soever is not a freende to the worlde. How
15   then can these men holde of Christ? Christ sayeth, *we*   Luc.18.
should praye still. These men praye never. Christs Apostle
saieth, *that covetousnes, uncleanesse, or scurrilitie should not be*   Ephe.5.
so muche as once named amonge Christians: these men have
no other talke but suche. Finallie, the whole course and
20   canon of scripture runneth, that Christians should *be*   Luc.21.
attenti, vigilantes, soliciti, instantes, feruentes, perseuerantes sine   Mat.24.
intermissione: That is, attent, vigilant, carefull, instant, fer-   Mich.6.
vent, and perseverant without intermission in the serv-   Rom.11.
ice of God: but these men have no one of these pointes,   Rom.12.
25   nor any one degree of any one of these pointes: but in   Mat.10.
everie one the cleane contrarie. For they are nether
attent to those things whiche appertaine unto God, nor
vigilant, nor solicitouse, nor carefull: and much lesse,
instant and fervent, and least of all perseverant without
30   intermission: for that they never beginne. But on the
contrarie side, they are careles, negligent, lumpishe,
remisse, key colde, perverse, contemning and despising,
yea loothing and abhorringe all matters that appertaine
to the mortifieing of them selves, and true service of
35   God. What parte have these men then in the lott and
portion of Christians, beside onelie the bare name, whiche
profiteth nothing?

---

17 *or securitie, should*

And this is sufficient to shew how great and dangerous an impediment this careles, senseles, and supine negligence is, to the resolution wherof we entreate. For yf
Christ require to the perfection of this resolution, that   Mat.13.
5   who soever once espyeth owt the treasure hidden in the
fyeld: (that is the kyngdome of heaven, and the right
waye to gayne it) he should presently goe and sell all
that he hathe, and bye that fyeld: that is, he should
preferre the pursute of this kyngdome of heaven, before
10 all the commodities of this lyfe what soever: and rather
venture them all, than to omitt this treasure: yf Christ
(I saye) require this, as he doeth: when will these men
ever be brought to this point, which will not geve the
least parte of their goodes to purchase that fyeld? nor
15 goe foorth of dore to treate the byeinge therof? nor will
so muche as think or talke of the same, nor allow of
him whiche shall offer the meanes and wayes to compasse it?

Wherfore, who soever findeth hym selfe in this dis-
20 ease, I wolde counsaile him to reade some chapiters of
the first parte of this booke, especiallie the third and
fowerth, entreating of the causes for which we were sent   Pag.[21].
into this woorld: as also the fiveth, of the account, which   & [26].
we must yeeld to God, of our time here spent: and he
25 shall there by understand (I dowt not) the errour and
daunger he standeth in, by this damnable negligence
wherein he sleepeth, attending onelye to those thinges
which are meere vanities, and for whiche he came not
into this world: and passing over other matters, without
30 care or cogitation, whiche onelye are of importance, and
to have bene studyed and thought upon by hym.

The third and last impediment, that I purpose to han-   Of
dle in this booke, is a certaine affection, or evill dispo-   hardnes
sition in some men, called by the scriptures, hardnesse   of hart.
35 of harte, or in other woordes, obstinacie of minde.
Wherby a man is setled in resolution, never to yeeld
from the state of sinne wherein he lyveth, what soever
shall or may be sayd agaynst the same. And I have

7 to come to it)   22 treating

reserved this impediment, for the last place in this booke:
for that, it is the last, and worst of all other impedimentes discovered before, contayning all the evill in it
selfe that any of the other before rehearsed, have: and
5   adding besides, a most willfull and malitious resolution
of sinne, quyte contrarie to that resolution whiche we
so muche endevour to induce men unto.

    This hardnes of harte hathe diverse degrees in divers   Two
men, and in some muche more greevous than in other.   degrees of
10   For some are arrived to that hyghe and cheefe obdu-   hardnes
ration, which I named before, in such sort, as albeit   of hart.
they well know that they are amysse: yet for some worldlye respect or other, they will not yeeld, nor chaunge
their course. Such was the obduration of Pilate: though
15   he knew that he condemned Christ wrongfullie: yet, not   Mat.27.
to leese the favour of the Jewes, or incurre displeasure
with his prince, he proceeded, and gave sentence against
hym. This also was the obduration of Pharao: whoe,   Exod.6.7.
thoghe he sawe the miracles of Moyses and Aaron, and   8.
20   felt the strong hand of God upon his kyngdome: yet,
not to seeme to be overcome by suche simple people as
they were: nor that men should thynk he wold be enforced
by any meanes to relent: he persevered still in his willfull wickednes, untill his last and utter destruction came
25   uppon hym. This hardnes of hart was also in kyng   Act.26.
Agrippa, and Foelix gouvernour of Jewrie: whoe, thoghe
in their owne conscience they thoght that S. Paul spake
trueth unto them: yet, not to hazard their credit in the
world, they continued still, and perished in their owne
30   vanities. And commonlie this obduration is in all per-   Perse-
secutors of vertue, and vertuouse men: whome, thoghe   cutors.
they see evidentlie to be innocent, and to have equitie
on their side: yet, to maintayne their estate, credite, and

---

14 [* Pilate] mn: B. *It seemed to be of weaknes rather, than of
such obduration as was in Pharao, or is spoken of heer.   23 by any
mean   26 [* Agrippa] mn: B. *In these two also it seemeth rather
to have been ignorance, than obduration. But the example is notably
found in the Preests, Scribes, and Pharisies: who ever opposed themselves against the preaching of Christ; and at the length put him to
death.   31 men, and especially of those that professe the truth: whom
32 have the word of God, and equitie

favoure in the world, they persist, without ether mercie or release, untill God cutt them of, in the middest of their malice and furious cogitations.

Others there are, whoe have not this obduration in
5 so hygh a degree, as to persist in wickednes directly against their owne knowleige: but yet they have it in an other sorte: for that, they are setled in firme purpose to folow the trade, which all redie they have begunne: and will not understand the daungers therof: but doe seeke
10 rather meanes to persuade them selves, and quiet their consciences therein: and nothing is so offensive unto them, as to heare any thing against the same. Of these men holye Job sayeth: *Dixerunt deo, recede a nobis, & scientiam viarum tuarum nolumus*: They say to God, departe
15 from us, we will not have the knowlege of thy wayes. And the prophet David yet more expresselye: *Their furie is lyke the furie of serpentes, lyke unto cocatrices that stoppe their eares, and will not heare the voyce of the inchaunter.* By this inchaunter he meaneth the holy ghoste, whiche seeketh
20 by all meanes possible to charme them from the bewitching wherein they stand, called by the wyse man, *fascinatio nugacitatis*: The bewitching of vanitie: but (as the prophet sayeth) *they will not heare, they turne their backes, they stoppe their eares, to the ende they may not understand: they*
25 *put their hartes as an Adamant stone, leste perhappes they should heare Gods lawe, and be converted.*

The nation of Jewes is peculiarlie noted to have bene always geven to this great sinne, as S. Stephen witnesseth, when he sayed unto their owne faces. *You styffe*
30 *necked Jewes, you have allwayes resisted the holye ghoste*, meaning therby (as Christ declareth more at large) that they resisted the prophetes and Saintes of God, in whome the holie ghoste spake unto them from tyme to tyme, for amendement of their lyfe: and for that, through the
35 lyght of knowlege which they had by hearing of Gods lawe, they could not in truthe or shew condemne the things which were sayd, or avoyde the just reprehensions used towarde them: and yet resolved with them

A second degree of obduration.

Job.21.

Psal.58.

Sap.4.

Zach.7.

The hard harted Jewes.

Act.7.

Matt.5.
Luc.11.13.

---

25 *omits perhappes*

selves not to obey, or chaunge the custome of their proceedings: therfore fell they in fine to persecute sharplye
their reprehendors: wherof the onelie cause was hardnes of harte. *Indurauerunt facies suas supra petram, & nolue-*
5 *runt reuerti*: sayeth God by the mouthe of Jeremie: they   Jere.5.
have hardened their faces above the hardnes of a rocke,
and they will not turne to me. And in an other place
of the same prophet he complayneth greevouslie of this
perversenes: *Quare ergo auersus est populus iste in Jerusa-*
10 *lem, auersione contentiosa?* And why then is this people   Jere.8.
in Jerusalem revolted from me, by so contentious and
perverse an alienation, as they will not heare me any
more, &c? And yet againe in an other place: *Quare morie-*   Ezec.18.
mini domus Israel? why will you dye, you house of Israel?
15 why will you damne your selves? why are you so obstinate, as not to heare? so perverse, as not to learne? so
cruell to your selves, as you will not know the daungers
wherin you lyve? nor understand the miserie that hangeth
over you?
20   Doest thou not ymagine (deare brother) that God
useth this kynde of speeche, not onelye to the Jewes,
but also to many thousand Christians, and perhappes
also unto thy selfe many tymes everie daye: for that thou
refusest his good motions, and other meanes sent from
25 hym, to draw thee to his service, thou being resolved
not to yeeld ther unto, but to folow thy pursuite, what
soever persuasions shall come to the contrarie? Alas,
how many Christians be there, whoe saye to God daylie,
(as they dyd whome I have named before) *departe from*   Job.21.
30 *us, we will not have the knowlege of thy wayes?* How many
be there, which abhorre to heare good counsayle? feare
and tremble to reade good bookes? flye and detest the
frequentation of godlie companie, lest perhappes by suche
occasions they might be touched in conscience, con-
35 verted, and saved? how many be there, whiche saye with
those most unfortunate hard harted men, wherof the
prophet speaketh: *Percussimus foedus cum morte, & cum inferno*   Esa.28.
fecimus pactum: We have stricken a league with deathe,

---

29 whom I named   33 *omits* perhappes   36 most miserable hard

and have made a bargayne with hell it selfe: whiche
is as muche to saye, as if they had sayde: trouble us
not, moleste us not with thy persuations: spend not thy
woordes and labour in vayne: talke unto other whoe are
5   not yet setled: lett them take heaven that take it will:
we for our partes are resolved: we are at a pointe: we
have made a league that must be kept: we have made
a bargaine that must be perfourmed, yea thoghe it be
with hell, and death everlasting.

10   It is a wounderfull furie, the obduration of a hard
hart: and not without cause compared by the prophet
(as I have shewed before) to the willfull furie and rage
of serpentes. And an other place of scripture describeth
it thus: *Durus es, & neruus ferreus ceruix tua, & frons tua*
15   *ærea*: Thou art hard harted, and thy neck is a sinowe
of yron, and thy forehead is of brasse. What can be
more vehementlie spoken to expresse the hardnesse of
this mettall? but yet S. Barnard expresseth it more at
large, in these woordes: *Quid ergo cor durum?* and what is
20   then a hard harte? and he answereth immediatlie: A
hard hart is that, whiche is nether cutt by compunction,
nor softened by godlynes, nor moved with prayers, nor
yeeldeth to threatning, nor is any thing holpen, but
rather hardyned, by chastening. A hard hart, is that
25   whiche is ingreatefull to Gods benefites, disobedient to
his counsails, made cruell by his judgementes, dissolute
by his allurementes, unshamefast to filthines, feareles to
perils, uncourteous in humane affaires, recheles in matters pertayning to God, forgetfull of things past, negli-
30   gent in things present, improvident for things to come.

By this description of S. Barnard it appeareth, that a
hard harte is almost a desperate and remedyles disease,
where it falleth. For what will you doe (sayeth this good
father) to amend it? yf you laye the grevousnes of his
35   sinnes before hym: he is not touched with compunction.
Yf you alleage hym all the reasons in the world, why
we ought to serve God, and why we ought not to offend

The description of a hard hart.

Psa.58.
Esa.48.

Li.1.de consid. ad Eug.c.2.

The explication of S. Barnards wordes.

---

6 *omits* we have made a league that must be kept   34 greevousnes
of sin

and dishonoure hym: he is not mollified by this consideration of pietie. Yf you wold request hym and beseeche
hym with teares, even on your knees: he is not moved.
Yf you threaten Gods wrathe against hym: he yeeldeth
5   nothing therunto. Yf God scourge hym in deede: he
waxeth furious, and becommeth much more hard than
before. If God bestowe benefites on hym: he is ungratefull. Yf he counsaile hym for his salvation: he obeyeth
not. Yf you tell hym of Gods secrete and severe judge-
10   mentes: it dryveth hym to desperation, and to more
crueltie. Yf you allure hym with Gods mercie: it maketh
him dissolute. If you tell him of his owne filthines: he
blusheth not. If you admonishe him of his perils: he
feareth not. If he deale in matters towardes men: he is
15   prowde, and uncurteous. If he deale in matters towardes
God: he is rashe, light, and contemptuous. Finallie, he
forgetteth what soever hath passed before him towardes
other men, ether in rewarde of godlines, or in punishement of sinners. For the time present, he neglecteth
20   it, nor maketh any account of using it to his benefite.
And of things to come, ether of blisse or miserie, he is
utterlie unprovident: nor will esteeme therof, laye you
them never so often, or vehementlie before his face. And
what waye is there then, to doe this man good?

25   Not without greate cause surelie dyd the wyse man
pray so hartilie to God: *Animæ irreuerenti & infrumitæ ne*
tradas me: delyver me not over (o Lord) unto a shame-
lesse and unrulie soule: that is, unto a hard and obstinate harte. Wherof he geveth the reason in an other
30   place, of the same booke: *Cor enim durum habebit male in*
nouissimo: for that a hard hart shalbe in an evill case at
the last daye. Oh that all hard harted people wolde note
this reason of the scripture. But S. Barnard goeth on,
and openeth the terrour heerof more fullie, when he
35   sayeth: *Nemo duri cordis salutem unquam adeptus est, nisi quem*
forte miserans deus abstulit ab eo (iuxta prophetam) cor lapideum,
& dedit cor carneum: There was never yet hard harted
man saved, except perchaunce God by his mercie dyd

The dan-
ger of a
hard hart.
Eccle.23.
Eccle.3.

Li.1.de
consid.c.2.
Ezec.36.

---

33 of scripture   38 *omits* perchaunce

take awaye his stonye harte, and geve hym a harte of
fleshe, according to the prophet. By whiche woordes
S. Bernard signifieth, and proveth owt of the prophet,
that there are two kyndes of hartes in men: the one a
5   fleshie hart, which bleedeth yf you but prick it: that is,
it falleth to contrition, repentance and teares upon never
so small a checke for sinne. The other is a stony hart,
which yf you beate and buffet never so muche with
hammers, you may as soone breake it in peeces, as ether
10 bend it, or make it bleede. And of these two hartes in
this lyfe dependeth all our miserie, or felicitie for the
lyfe to come. For as God, when he wolde take vengeance
of Pharao, had no more grevous waye to doe it, than
to saye, *Indurabo cor Pharaonis*: I will harden the hart of
15 Pharao: that is, (as S. Austen expoundeth) I will take
awaye my grace, and so permitt hym to harden his owne
harte: so when he wolde shew mercie to Israel, he had
no more forcible meanes to expresse the same, than to
saye, *I will take awaye the stony hart owt of your fleshe, and*
20 *geve you a fleshie hart in steade therof.* That is, I will take
away your hard hart and geve you a soft hart, that wilbe
moved when it is spoken unto. And of all other blessings and benefites whiche God dothe bestowe upon
mortall men in this lyfe, this soft and tender hart is
25 one of the greatest: I meane suche a hart as is soone
moved to repentance, soone checked and controlled,
soone pearsed, soone made to bleede, soone styrred to
amendement. And on the contrarie parte, there can be
no greater curse or malediction layed upon a Christian,
30 than to have a hard and obstinate hart, which heapeth
every day vengeance unto it selfe and his maister also,
as S. Paul sayeth: and is compared by the same Apostle
unto the grownde whiche no store of rayne can make
frutefull, thoughe it fall never so often upon the same:
35 and therfore he pronounceth therof, *Reproba est & male-*
dicto proxima, cuius consummatio in combustionem: That is, it
is reprobate, and next doore to malediction, whose ende
or consummation must be fire and burning.

Two
kindes of
hartes in
men, with
their
proper-
ties.

Exo.4.7.
14.

Au.q.18.
super
exod. &
ser.88.de
temp.
Eze.36.

Heb.6.

---

22 spoken to   31 also. S. Paul saith it is   35 *est, maledicto*

Whiche thinge being so, no marvaile though the holie
scripture doe dehort us so carefullie from this obduration and hardnes of hart, as from the moste daungerous and desperate disease, that possiblie may fall uppon
5   the Christian, being in deed (as S. Paul signifieth) the
next doore to reprobation it selfe. The same Apostle   Heb.6.
therfore crieth, *nolite contristare, nolite extinguere spiritum dei*:   Ephe.4.
doe you not contristate or make sadde, doe you not   1.The.5.
extinguishe the spirit of God, by obduration, by resist-
10   ing and impugning the same. Agayne: *non obduretur*   Heb.3.
quis ex vobis fallacia peccati: Lett no man be hard harted
among you, throughe the deceit of sinne. The prophet
David also crieth, *hodie si vocem eius audieritis, nolite obdu-*   Psal.95.
rare corda vestra: Even this daye, if you heare the voyce
15   of God calling you to repentance: see you harden not
your hartes against hym. All whiche earnest speeches,
used by Gods holie spirite, doe geve us to understand,
how carefullie we have to flie this moste pestilent infection of a hard hart: whiche allmightie God of his mer-
20   cie geve us grace to doe, and indue us with a tender
hart towardes the full obedience of his divine Majestie:
suche a soft hart (I saye) as the wise man desired, when
he sayd to God: *Da seruo tuo cor docile*: Geve unto me   3.Re.3.
thy servant (o lord) a hart that is docible, and tractable
25   to be instructed: suche a hart as God hym selfe describeth to be in all them whom he loveth, sayeing, *ad quem*   Esa.66.
respiciam, nisi ad pauperculum & contritum corde, & timentem
sermones meos? To whome will I have regarde or shew
my favour, but unto the poore and humble of hart, unto
30   the contrite spirit, and to suche as tremblethe at my
speeches?

Beholde (deare brother) what a hart God requireth
at thy handes? A litle poore and humble hart: (for so
muche importeth the diminitive pauperculus.) Also a
35   contrite hart, for thy offences past: and a hart that trembleth at everie woord that cometh to thee from God,
by his ministers. How then wilt thow not feare at so

---

6 selfe. S. Paul therfore   8 *Do you not make sad*   19 God by his
mercie

many woordes, and whole discourses as have bene used
before, for thy a-wakening, for openyng thy perill, for
styrring the to amendement? how wilt thou not feare
the threates and judgementes of this great Lord for thy

5   sinnes? how wilt thou dare to proceede any further in
his displeasure? howe wilt thou deferre this resolution
any longer? surelie the least parte of that which hathe
bene sayde, might suffice to move a tender hart, an
humble and contrite spirite, to present resolution and

10   earnest amendement of lyfe. But yf all together, can not
move thee to doe the same: I can saye no more, but
that thou hast a verie hard hart in deede: whiche I
beseeche our heavenlye father to soften for thy salvation, with the pretious hoate bloode of his onelie sonne,

15   our saviour, who was content to shedde it for that effect
upon the crosse.

And thus now having sayd so muche as time per-   The con-
mitted me, concernynge the fyrst generall point required   clusion of
at our handes for our salvation: that is, concerning res-   this whole
                                                              booke.
20   olution, appointed by my division in the beginning, to   Pag.[10].
be the subject or matter of this first booke: I will ende
heere: deferring for a tyme the performance of my purpose for the other two bookes, upon the causes and reasons sett downe in an advertisement to the reader at

25   the verie first entrance unto this booke: nothinge dow-
tynge but yf God shall vouchesafe to woorke in any
mans hart by meanes of this booke, or otherwise, this
first point of resolution, the moste hard of all other: then
will he also geve meanes to perfite the worke begunne   Phil.2.

30   of hym selfe, and will supplie by other wayes the two
pointes foloweing: that is, bothe right beginning, and
constant perseverance, whereunto my other two bookes
promised, are appointed. It will not be hard for hym
that were once resolved, to fynde helpers and instruc-

35   tours enoughe, beside the holye ghoste, whiche in this

---

4 thy sin?   18 general part   20 [* division] *mn*: B. *As may appeer
in my preface to the reader.   23 [* upon] *mn*: B. *Which was, for
that either time, or health, or libertie did not permit   30 the two
principal parts   34 once reformed   35 ynow, the holie Ghost in this
case being alwais at hand

case will alwayes be at hande: there want not good bookes, and better men (God be glorified for it) in our owne countrie at this daye, whiche are well able to guyde a zealous spirite, in the right way to vertue: and yet as
5 I have promised before, so meane I (by Gods most holie helpe and assistance) to send thee (gentle reader) as my time and habilitie will permitt, the other two bookes also: especiallie, yf it shall please his divine Majestie to comforte me therunto, with the gayne or good of any
10 one soule by this whiche is alredie done: that is, yf I shall conceive or hope, that any one soule so dearlie purchased by the pretiouse bloode of the sonne of God, shalbe moved to resolution by any thing that is here sayd: that is, shalbe reclamed from the bondage of sinne,
15 and restored to the service of our maker and redemer: whiche is the onelie ende of my writing, as his majestie best knoweth.

And surelie (gentle reader) thoughe I must confesse that muche more might be sayde for this point of res-
20 olution, than is heere touched by me, or than anye man can well utter in any competent kinde of booke or vol- ume: yet am I of opinion, that ether these reasons heere alleaged are sufficient, or els nothing will suffice, for the conquering of our obstinacie, and beating downe of our
25 rebellious disobedience in this pointe. Heere thou mayest see the principall argumentes inducing thee to the serv- ice of God, and detestation of vice. Heere thou mayest see the cause and ende whye thou wast created: the occasion of thy comming hyther: the things required
30 at thy handes in particular: the account that will be demaunded of thee: the justice and severitie of God therein: his goodnes towardes thee: his wachefullnes over thee: his desire to wynne thee: his rewarde, yf thou doe well: his infinite punishement, yf thou doe evill: his calles:
35 his baytes: his allurementes to save thee. And on the con- trarie parte, heere are discovered unto thee, the vanities, and deceytes of those impedimentes, hynderances, or excuses, whiche any waye might lett, staye, or discourage

The effecte of that whiche hath bene said in this booke. In the first parte.

In the second parte.

---

31 *omits* the justice and severitie of God therein   34 his callings

thy resolution: the faigned diffyculties of vertuous lyfe
are removed: the conceyted feares of Gods service are
taken awaye: the alluringe flatteryes of worldlie vanitie
are opened: the foolyshe presumption upon Gods mer-
5   cye: the daunger of delaye: the dissimulation of slothe:
the desperate perill of careles and stony hartes are declared. What then wilt thou desire more to move thee?
what further argument wilt thou expect, to drawe the
from vice and wickednes, than all this is?

10   If all this styrre the not, what will stirre thee (gentle
reader?) yf when thou hast read this, thou laye downe
the booke againe, and walke on in thy careles lyfe as
quietlye as before: what hope (I beseeche thee) maye
there be conceived of thy salvation? wilt thou goe to
15   heaven living as thou doest? it is impossible: as soone
thow maiest drive God owt of heaven as gett thither
thy selfe, by this kind of lyfe. What then? wilt thow forgoe heaven, and yet escape hell too? this is lesse possible, what soever the Atheistes of this world doe persuade
20   thee. Wilt thow perhappes deferre the matter, and think
of yt heerafter? I have tolde thee my opinion heerof
before. Thou shalt never have more abilitie to doe it
than now, and perhappes never halfe so muche. If thou
refuse it now: I maye greatlie feare, that thou wilt be
25   refused hereafter thy selfe. There is no waye then so
good (deare brother) as to doe it presentlie whiles it is
offered. Breake from that tyrant, whiche detayneth thee
in servitude: shake of his chaynes: cutt a sunder his
bandes: runne violentlie to Christ, whiche standeth redye
30   to embrace thee, with his armes open on the crosse.
Make joyfull all the Angels, and court of heaven with   Luc.15.
thy conversion: strike once the stroke with God agayne:
make a manlye resolution: saye with that olde coura-
gious souldier of Jesus Christ S. Jerome, If my father   A notable
35   stoode weeping on his knees before me, and my mother   sayeing of
hanging on my necke behynde me: and all my bretheren,   S. Jerome.

---

11 lay down thy book again, and walk on thy carelesse life   20 *omits*
perhappes   23 and (it may be) never halfe so much again   28 his
bonds   33 with the old

sisters, children, and kynsefolkes howling on every syde
to retayne me in synfull lyfe with them: I wolde fling
of my mother to the grounde: dispyse all my kynred,
runne over my father and treade hym under my feete,
5   therby to runne to Christ when he calleth me.

Oh that we had suche hartes as this servant of God
had: suche courage, suche manhoode, suche fervent love
to our Maister. Who wolde lye one daye drowned in
sinne? who wolde lyve one daye in suche slaverie as we
10   doe? who wolde eate huskes with the prodigall sonne
amonge swyne, seeynge he may returne home, and be
soo honorablye receyved, and entertaynede by his olde
father, have so good cheere, and banquetinge, and heare   Luc.15.
soo greate melodie, joye, and triumphe for his returne?
15   I saye no more heerin, (deare brother) than thow arte
assured of, by the woorde, and promise of Godes owne
mouthe: from whiche can proceede nether falshode nor
deceyte. Returne then I beseeche thee: laye hande faste
on his promise, whoe will not fayle thee: runne to hym
20   now he calleth, whiles thow hast tyme: and esteeme not
all this worlde woorthe a strawe, in respect of this one
acte. For so shalt thow be a most happie, and thryse
happie man, and shalt blesse hereafter the howre and
moment that ever thow madest this fortunate resolution.
25   And I for my parte (I trust) shall not be voyde of some
portion of thy good happe and felicitie: At leastwise I
doubt not, but thy holie conversion shall treate for me
with our common father, whoe is the God of mercies,
for remission of my many folde sinnes, and that I may
30   serve and honoure hym together with thee all the dayes
of my lyfe: whiche ought to be bothe our petytyons: and
therefore in bothe our names I beseeche his divyne
Majestye to graunt it to us. For ever and ever. Amen.

The ende of the fyrst booke: touching resolution.

---

1 children, kinsfolks   8 *omits* drowned in sinne? who wolde lyve one
daye   24 this blessed resolution   26 *omits* thy good happe and   29
my many sins   34 The end of this booke of Resolution.

APPARATUS CRITICUS

SUMMARIE
3.8   THE FIRST *para. not indented R*

ADVERTISEMENT
3.34   *Loartes] loartes R*
4.12   *effect. Which M: effect Which R*
4.14   *Paragraph not indented R*
4.15   *send thee M: send thee R*
4.32   *thee. But M: thee, But R*

PREFACE
5.1   CHRISTIAN] CRISTIAN *R*
5.8   *Exercise] exercise R*
6.10   Churche *M*: Chuche *R*
6.18   Jaco.2.] Iaco.3. *R*
6.20   Heb.11.] Heb.12. *R*
6.37   same, *M*: same. *R*
7.3   John.5.] Ihon.5. *R*
7.24   leste] lesse *R*

INDUCTION
8.26   Apostles] Apoostles *R*
8.35   (saieth he)]] *(saieth he) R*
8.36   *hungrie] Hungrie R*
10.5   persever *M*: perseruer *R*

I.I
12.15   (I saye) is] (I saie) is *B*: (I saye, is *R*
13.17   worldlye] worldlie *B*: wordlye *R*

I.II
14.1   *consideration B, M: condesiration R*
14.25   within *B, M*: whithin *R*
14.38   necessarye: *Thes M*: necessarie: *These B*: necessarye *Thes R*
15.14   knowinge] knowing *B*: knownge *R*

16.3   auncient *M*: ancient *B*: annuncient *R*
16.29   digest *B, M*: disgest *R, R2*
17.20   infinite *B*: infinitie *R*
17.29   begyninge, that] beginning, that *B*: begyninge that *R*
17.37   negligences *R2, M*: negli*n*gences *R*
19.18   looden] loden *B*: Looden *R*
19.29   (I saye)] (I saie) *B*: I saye *R*
20.3   notwithstandinge] notwithstanding *B*: notwithstundinge *R*
20.11   without *B, M*: vithout *R*
20.16   commitethe] committeth *B*: committhe *R*

I.III

21.24   Deu.14.] Gen.14. *R*: Gen.14. Deut. *R2*: Gen.15. Deut.4. *R4*
21.26   Zacharie *B, R2: Zacharie R4*: zacharie *R*
22.26   lyke, then *R2*: lyke: then *R*: like; then *B*
23.20   fulfilled: as, *that*] fulfilled: as, that *B*: fulfilled as, *that R*: fulfilled.
         As among other thinges, that *R2*
23.29   Zacheus *B*: Zachæus *R2*: zacheus *R*
24.25   daunsinge, so] daunsing, so *B*: daunsinge; so *R2*: dauncing,
         so *R4*: daunsinge so *R*
24.36   studies, labours] studies, labors *B*: studies labours *R*
25.1   world: which *B*: world, which *R*
25.4   heaven, as S. Paule] heauen as, S. Paule *R*
25.17   worldlie wealthe *M*: worldly wealth *B*: worldlie, wealthe *R*
25.21   *foole, this B: foole this R*
25.31   also *B*: alsoo *R*
26.15   without *B, M*: wthout *R*

I.IV

27.6   Christ *B, M*: Cbrist *R*
27.23   as S. Peter] as .S. Peter *R*: as Saint Peter *B*
27.35   Phil.1. *B*: Pphil.1. *R*
28.14   heaven, no more than] Gods blisse, no more then *R4*: Godes
         blisse; no more then *R2*: godlines, no more than *B*: heauen
         no more, than *R*
28.30   fire, et ce.] fire. et ce. *R*: fire, &c. *B*
29.3   *Paragraph break R2, R4: no paragraph break R, B*
29.5   neede:) and] neede) and *R*: need) and *B*
29.15   Exod.20.] Exod.12. *R*
29.19   *What B, M: what R2, R4: Whas R*

29.21   Col.1.] Eccle.1. *R*

29.21   *woorke.* And againe] *woorke*: And againe *R*: *work*: and again *B*

29.21   sayeth: *Let*] saith: *Let B*: sayeth *Let R*

29.22   *men.* And agayne *M*: men. And again *B*: *men.* and agayne *R*

29.26   *worckes, knowinge*] works, knowing *B*: *worckes knowinge R*

29.26   *unprofitable. M, B*: vnprofitable, *R*

30.6   Whoe will not marvaile] Who wil not marvel *B*: whoe will now maruaile *R*

31.8   act, and *B*: act and *M*: act. and *R*

31.25   whoe *M*: who *B*: woe *R*

32.2   2.Tim.1.] 1.Tim.1. *R, B, R2*

32.5   the helpes *M*: tbe helpes *R*

32.16   gathered owt] gathered: owt *R*

32.28   sowles: and] souls: and *B*: sowles, and *R*

33.1   Jo.9.] Io.6. *R*

33.10   opportunitie *B, R2, M*: opportunity *R4*: oprortunitie *R*

34.14   *tremblinge*: And] *trembling*: and *B*: *trembling,* and *M*: *trembling,* And *R*

34.20   *woorld M*: world *B*: *voorld R*

35.29   The good *B, M*: the good *R*

36.3   encrease of] increase of *B*: encrease, of *R*

36.12   *Paragraph break at* And is it not reason *above (line 6) R*

36.18   greate *M*: great *B, R2, R4*: gteate *R*

I.V

37.30   testifyeth:) yet *M*: testifieth) yet *B*: testifyeth.) yet *R*

38.32   circumstances *R, B*: circumstance *R2, R4*

39.3   dewtie. *M*: dutie. *B*: dewtie *R*

39.9   drowninge *M*: drowning *B*: drowningo *R*

39.15   tollerate with us *R*: tollerate us *B*

39.26   purpose. For *B*: purpose, for *M*: purpose. for *R*

39.36   Mat.24. *moved from* 'and not accepting' *above*

40.4   jumpe] jump *B*: Iumpe *R*

40.14   Joh.14. *B*: Iho.14. *R*

40.19   sayeth he] saith he *B*: *sayeth he R*

40.19   1.Joh.2.] Ioh.2. *R*

41.2   out, yea *B*: out yea *R*

41.3   with *B, M*: whith *R*

41.9   *thow art hole B*: *thow are hole R*

41.26   accounte *M*: account *B*: accountc *R*

41.34 Joh.5. *B*: Iob.5. *R*
41.35 are:) wherof] are) wherof *R, B*
42.13 feare (as *B*: feare, as *R*
42.29 is, that *B*: is that *M*: is. that *R*: second reason is; for that *R2, R4*
43.17 To *B, M*: Te *R*
43.33 Esa.13. *moved up from* 'by reason of the confusion'
44.8 moment, in] moment in *R, B*
44.8 1.Cor.15.] 1.Cor.13. *R*
44.13 1.Cor.4.] 1.Co4r. *R*: 1.Co.4.2. *B*
44.29 kingdome *B, R2: Kingdome R4*: kindome *R*
44.30 hungry *B*: hungrie *R2: hungry R4*: Hungry *M*: Humgry *R*
44.35 donne thes *M*: done these *B*: donne, thes *R*
45.2 hungrie *R2*: hungry *B*: *hungry R4*: Hungrie *R*
45.13 doune? how manye] down? How many *B*: doune: how manye *M*: doune how: manye *R*
45.28 horse, and *M*: horse, and *R2, R4*: horse. & *R*
45.31 *hell*] *HEL R2, R4*: hell *R*
46.1 and the riche *R2, R4, M*: and the the riche *R*
46.1 stoute hid *R2, R4*: stoute, hid *R*
46.4 blast. At *R2, R4*: blast, at *R*
46.9 Absinthium] *Absinthium R2, R4*: absinthium *R*
46.10 torche, and] torch, and *R2*: torch, & *R4*: torche and *R*
46.28 destroyer. At *R4, M*: destroier. At *R2*: destroyer, At *R*
46.32 brymstone *M*: brimstone *R2, R4*: brymstome *R*
47.9 reade] redde *R2*: red *R4*: Reade *R*
47.12 tongues *R2, R4, M*: tougues *R*
48.9 ghost: and] ghost; and *B*: ghost? and *R*
48.10 life? *B*: life. *M*: life: *R*
48.20 *sainctes. Alas M: saints.* Alas *B: sainctes* Alas *R*
48.25 yelde cause *R*: yeeld them cause *B, R2, R4*
49.3 Mat.24.] Mar.24. *R*
49.23 and (that whiche] and (that which *B*: and that (whiche *R*
49.34 knee? all *M*: ? *inverted R*: knee; al *B*: knee? your *R4*: knee; your *R2*
50.6 riches, our *B*: riches our *R*: riches, offices *R2, R4*
50.12 *Paragraph break B, R2, R4: no paragraph break R*
50.12 The conclusion *R4: The conclusion B, R2*: the conclusion *R*
50.23 fulfilled *B, M*: fufilled *R*

50.23 Mat.24. *B*: Mat,24. *R*: Math.24. *R2*

50.26 *dronkennes R corr, M: dronkenes B: dronkenns R uncorr*

50.38 *Seinge] Seeing B: seinge R*

51.14 Our *B, R2, R4, M*: our *R*

I.VI

51.30 Sap.14. *R2, R4*: Psal.14. *R, B*

52.1 also, are *B, R2, R4*: also are *R*

52.4 mouthe, as] mouth, as *B, R2: mouth*, as *R4*: mouthe as *R*

52.23 marcke it not] marke it not *R2, R4*: mark it not *B*: marcke it anot *R*

53.18 contempt *B, R2, R4*: comtempt *R*

53.35 1.Joh.3. *B, R2*: 1,Ioh.3. *R*: 1 Ioh.3. *R4*

54.8 Esa.1. *R4: not in R, R2*

54.16 Psal.92. *R4*: Psal.90. *R, R2*

54.34 understandinge: yet *R2, R4*: understanding: yet *B*: vnder-standinge, yet *M*: vnderstandinge. yet *R*

55.23 Rom.1.] Rom.8. *R, R2, R4*

55.30 Of Adam *R4: Of Adam B, R2*: of Adam *R*

55.34 ofspring *B, R2*: of-spring *R4*: of spring *R*

56.3 hunger, thirst *B, R2, R4*: hunger thirst *R*

56.7 I say, (which *R2, R4*: (I say, which *R, B*

56.9 soone *R*: sonne *R2, R4*: son *B*:

56.17 offence] offences *R*

56.27 Mar.14. *B, R2, R4*: Mar.t4. *R*

56.28 Luc.22. *R2, R4*: Luc.12. *R*

56.29 *forsaken me?* Notwithstanding] *forsaken me.* Notwithstanding *R*

57.5 Of Saul *R4: Of Saul B*: of Saul *R, R2*

57.6 Agag *B, R2: Agag R4*: agag *R*

57.26 synne, as] sin, as *B*: synne as *R*: sinful state; As for example, where *R2*: sinful state. As for example, where *R4*

57.30 *sinners: brimstone] sinners, brimstone R*

57.31 Psa.9. *moved down from brimstone with tempestuous wyndes*

57.35 sinners: God *B*: sinners God *R*

57.35 Psal.3. *moved down from* let synners be turned into hell: *R has additional* Psal.9. *in this place*

58.2 hartes: thow] hartes, thow *R*

58.4 earth: desire] earth, desire *R*

58.24 *they R2, M: They B, R4: shey R*

58.32   noteth *B, R2, R4, M*: noteh *R*
59.3   without *B, R, R4*: with out *R*
59.8   *eares B, R2, R4, M: heares R*
59.13   consciences *B, R2, R4, M*: conscicnces *R*
59.19   dommages *R, R2*: dammages *R4*: damages *B*:
59.23   God can geeve *M*: God can give *B*: Cod can geeue *R*
59.28   enemies. Secondlie *M*: enimies. Secondlie *R2*: enemies. Sec-
         ondly *R4*: enimies. Secondly *B*: enemies Secondlie *R*
59.29   protection, care *B, R2, R4*: protection care *R*
60.18   sinne, and] sin; and *B*: sinne. and *R*
60.30   wordes *R2, M*: words *B, R4*: worldes *R*
60.32   Rom.6. *R4*: Rom.26. *R, R2*
61.15   all *R4, M*: al *B, R2*: aIl *R*
61.19   *boughes, take M: boughs, take B: boughes; take R2, R4: boughes.*
         take R
61.22   *but B, M*: but *R2, R4*: hut *R*
61.32   there to be *B, R2, M*: *there to be R4*: there to he *R*
61.36   beare *R2: beare R4*: bear *B*: heare *R*
62.1   wicked man *B*: *wicked man R4*: wickedman *R, R2*
62.5   recited *B, R2, R4, M*: reeited *R2*
62.15   world *B, R2, M*: wold *R2*: wosd *R*
62.26   worldly delytes?] worldly delites? *B*: worldly delytes. *R*: worldly
         contentations? *R2*: worldly contentations. *R4*
62.35   *praysed in M: praised in B: praysed iu R: praise the wicked man in*
         R2, R4
63.1   Psal.18. *R2, R4: not in R, B*
63.2   speaking of him selfe *M*: speaking of himselfe *B*: speaking
         him selfe *R*
63.6   againe, *I*] again; *I B*: againe *I R*
63.14   S. Peter *R2, M*: S. *Peter R4*: S: Peter *R*: Saint Peter *B*
64.8   world *B, M*: word *R*
64.10   Our *R2, R4*: our *R*
64.15   is content *B, R2, R4, M*: his content *R*

         I.VII
64.20   *towardes B: tovardes R*
64.28   *judgementes R2, M*: iudgements *B*: iudgmentes *R4*: sudgementes *R*
65.9   *omnipotent R2, R4, M*: ommipotent *R*
65.12   *longer B, R2, R4: longuer R*
65.16   saye, consider *R2*: say, consider *B, R4*: saye consider *R*

65.34 heavens, together with *R2: heauens, togeather with R4*: heauens together, with *R*: heavens togither, with *B*

65.35 Seraphins, doe] Seraphins, thrones . . . spirites, doe *R2: Seraphins, Thrones . . . spirites, doe R4*: Seraphins doe *R*: Seraphins do *B*

66.3 *light, which M: light: which B: light. which R*

66.32 contemplation *R4: contemplation B, R2*: contemplation tion *R*

66.33 chaire *B, R2, R4, M*: chairc *R*

67.24 thereof: and] therof: and *B*: therreof: and *M*: therreof. and *R*

67.27 This (I saye) yf] This (I say) if *R4*: This I saye, if *R2*: This I say, if *B*: This I saye yf *R*

68.15 injurie him. And *R2*: iniure him. And *R4*: iniurie him, & *R*: injurie him, and *B*

69.20 But yet consider] *new paragraph B, R2, R4: paragraph continues R*

69.23 2.Pet.] 1.Pet. *R, B*

69.27 the. O lorde *M*: thee. O Lord *B*: the O lorde *R*

70.4 Angels:) and] Angels) and *B*: Angels?) and *R*

70.12 justification *B, M*: Iustification *R2: Iustification R4*: iustificaton *R*

70.13 infidelitie *B, R2*: infidelity *R4*: infidelite *R*

70.19 justification *B, R2, M*: Iustification *R4*: iustifiication *R*

71.32 worldlye *M*: worldlie *R2*: worldly *B, R4*: wordlye *R*

72.24 which he eateth *B, R2, R4, M*: wich he eateth *R*

72.25 treadeth, the *R2*: treadeth; the *B*: treadeth the *R*: treadeth on, the *R4*

72.25 beholdeth, together] beholdeth; together *B*: beholdeth, the aire *R2, R4*: beholdeth together *R*

73.5 speeche, goe] speech, go *B*: speeche; goe *R2*: speeche goe *R*

73.13 earth? But *B, R2, R4*: earth? but *R*

73.19 What *B, R2, R4*: Vvhat *R*

74.6 purchase *B, R2, R4, M*: puchase *R*

74.7 infinite *B, R2, R4, M*: infiinte *R*

74.9 one: as *R2, R4*: one, as *B*: one? as *R*

74.30 benefites: wherin] benefits, wherin *B, R4*: benefites. Wherin *R2*: benefites? Wherin *R*

75.11 come: to which *B, R4*: come, to which *R, R2*

I.VIII

75.25 Genesis *B, R2: Genesis R4*: genesis *R*

75.33 whome all *R4*: whom al *R2*: whome, all *R*: whom, al *B*

76.9 Zacharie *B, R2: Zacharie R4*: zacharie *R*

76.9   matter, whoe saieth] matter, who saith *B*: behalf; who saieth
         R2: behalf, who saieth *R4*: matter whoe saieth *R*
76.18   *upp. M: up. B: vpp: R*
76.26   daye withe thes men also, when] *day with these men also, when*
         R4: daye, with thes men also, when *R2*: daye, withe thes
         men also when *R: day, with these men also when B*
76.30   *all men R4: al men B, R2: euill men R*
76.32   Isa.2.3.] Isa.2.13. *R, R2*: Esai.2.13. *B*
76.35   *lived*, as S. Paule sayeth: or] *liued*: as S. Paule sayeth, or *R*:
         lived: as Saint Paul saith, or *B*: *liued*: or *R2*: *liued*: Or *R4*
77.17   Sap.5. *B, R4*: Sap.8. *R, R2*
77.19   dishonorable: but *B, R2*: *dishonorable: but R4*: dishonorable,
         but *M*: dishonorable. but *R*
77.21   sainctes. We *R2*: *Saints. We R4*: sainctes? We *R*: saints? We *B*
77.22   trewth *M*: truth *B*: trueth *R2*: *truth R4*: trewsh *R*
77.23   sunne *R2*: *sunne R4*: sun *B*: sonne *R*
77.30   now, of matters: what *R*: mow, of al such matters: what *B*:
         now: what *R2, R4*
77.34   saye thes miserable men *R2*: say thes miserable men *B*: *saye*
         thes miserable men R
77.36   worldlinges *M*: worldlings *B*: wordlinges *R, R2, R4*
78.2   arrive at the last daie, to the gate of death, weryed] arriue
         at the last daie, to the gate of death, weried *R2*: arriue at
         the last day to the gate of death, wearied *R4*: arriue to, at
         the last daie, weryed *R*: arrive to, at the last day wearied *B*
78.31   selfe, though] self, though *R2, R4*: selfe though *R, B*
78.32   resistance. Which *R2, R4*: resistance: which *B*: resistance,
         which *R*
79.13   feare, anguishe, and *R2*: feare, anguish, and *R4*: fear, anguish,
         and *B*: feare anguishe and *R*
79.14   be in? how] be in? How *B, R2, R4*: be in: how *R*
79.38   *Paragraph break R2, R4: no paragraph break R, B*
80.17   them selves damned] themselues damned *R2, R4*: them selues
         often damned *R*: themselves often damned *B*
80.19   devill, the *R4*: deuil, the *R2*: devil; the *B*: deuill the *R*
80.20   lyke. And] like. And *B, R2, R4*: lyke, and *M*: lyke. and *R*
82.5   The third *R4*: *The third B*: the third *R*: The.3. *R2*
82.9   sowle. And] soule. And *R2, R4*: soul. And *B*: sowle, and *R*
82.10   *serpentes, beastes R2, R4*: serpents, beasts *B*: *serpentes beastes R*
82.12   vermen. That bodie, I meane, which] vermine. That bodie,

I meane, which *R2*: vermine. That body, I meane, which
R4: vermins: that bodie I mean, which *B*: vermen, that bodie
I meane which

82.21 discipline, must *B*: discipline must *R*: discipline at all, must
R4: discipline at al: must *R2*

82.22 wormes. Whiche *M*: worms. Which *B*: wormes, Whiche *R*:
wormes. Now the time *R2, R4*

83.2 as, if] as; *If B*: as if *R*

83.2 Mat.19. *B*: Mar.19. *R*

83.5 liar. Manie *M*: *liar. Manie B*: liar. manie *R*

83.6 &c. Not] *&c. Not B*: &c. not *R*

83.7 Goe *M*: Go *B*: goe *R*

83.8 Doe *M*: doe *R*: De *B*

83.14 God. Yf] *God. If B*: God. yf *R*

83.15 Gal.5. *B*: Cal.5. *R*

83.18 envie, murder] *envie, murder B*: enuie murder *R*

83.19 dronkenes, glouttonie *M*: *dronkenes, gluttonie B*: dronkenes glouttonie. *R*

83.22 the tribunall *M*: :he tribunall *R*: *the iudgment seat B*

83.24 evill: everye] *evil: every B*: euill, euerye *R*

83.27 judgement. If] *iudgement. If B*: iudgement, if *R*

83.29 appeare? Few *M*: *appeer? Few B*: appeare? few *R*

84.8 *out: why*] out: why *B*: *out why R*: *forth, why R2, R4*

85.11 loaden *R4*: loden *R2*: looden *R*

85.31 death. And *R2, R4*: death, and *R, B*

85.34 Ursinus *R2*: *Vrsinus R4*: vrsinus *R*

86.9 Ang.] Angl. *R2*: *Angl. R4*: Aug. *R*

86.13 hym *M*: him *R2, R4*: hvm *R*

86.18 he should *M*: de should *R*

86.22 sheweth] shevveth *M*: sheyveth *R*

86.28 *Paragraph break B, R2, R4: no paragraph break R*

86.38 perill? Yf] peril? If *B*: perill? If *R4*: perill? yf *R*: peril? if *R2*

87.36 the: o follye *M*: thee; O follie *B*: the? o follye *R*

87.37 myne: Loe] mine! Lo *B*: myne, Loe *R*

88.13 have left me *B*: haue left me *R2, R4*: hath left me *R*

88.16 behalfe. Woe *R2, R4*: *new paragraph B: (not indented) R*

88.25 *deathe of sainctes is precious*] *death of saincts is precious B*: *death of
Saints is pretious R4*: *deathe of sainctes are precious R*: *death of sainctes
are precious R2*

89.8 Psal.41.] Psal.40. *R4*: Psal.4. *R, B, R2*

I.IX

90.3   daunger *M*: danger *B, R2, R4*: dannger *R*

90.4   Jon.3.] Ion.1. *R4*: Ion.5. *R, B, R2*

90.7   maner: yet *R*: manner: yet *R4*: maner, yet *B*: maner yet *R*

90.26   perill, wherby *M*: peril, wherby *B, R2*: perill, whereby *R4*:
         perill. wherby *R*

90.28   shame, (which *R2, M*: shame (which *B, R4*: shame. (which *R*

90.38   hell. This *R4*: hel. This *B, R2*: hell, this *R*

91.2   Wherfore *R2, R4, R (catchword), M*: wherfore *R (text)*: sorrow,
         wherfore *B*

91.3   is, remember *B, R2, R4*: is remember *R*

91.12   Psal.76.] Psal.75. *R4*: Psal.71. *R, B, R2*

91.13   scripture, *deus iustitiæ*, God of justice: as also, *deus vltionum*,
         God of revenge] scripture, *Deus iustitiæ*, God of iustice: as
         also, *Deus vltionum*, God of reuenge *R2*: scripture, *Deus iustitiæ*,
         God of iustice: As also, *Deus vltionum*, God of reuenge *B*:
         scripture *deus iustitiæ*. God of iustice as also *deus vltionum*
         God of reuenge *R*: Scripture, both *God of iustice*: and *God of
         reuenge R4*

91.30   mercie: the whiche] mercie: the which *B*: mercie the whiche
         R: mercie; which *R2, R4*

91.32   these two are *B, R4*: these two, are *R, R2*

91.33   kyssinge *M*: kyssing *R2, R4*: kissing *B*: kyssnge *R*

91.34   saieth. Therfore *M*: saith. Therfore *R4*: saieth, Therfore *R*:
         saith, therfore *B*: saieth: And therfore *R2*

92.2   them, whome] them, whom *B*: them, whoe *R*

92.3   Rom.9. *R4: not in R, B, R2*

92.4   *furoris*: Vessels] *furoris: vessels B: furoris*. Vessels *R: furoris*; that
         is, vessels *R2, R4*

92.22   saithe: *Doest*] saith: *Doest R4*: saith; *Dost B*: saithe: *doest R*:
         saith: *doest R2*

92.27   He *B*: he *R*

92.29   covetous man doth *R4*: covetous man, doth *B*: couetous man,
         doth *R, R2*

92.35   *abhominations B, R2, R4, M: obhominations R*

93.2   *evill, let hym*] *euill, let him R4*: *euil, let him R2*: *evil, let him B*:
         euill let hym M: *euill let, hym R*

93.2   Apo.22.] Apoc.22. *R2, R4*: Apo. 221 *R*: Apoc.21. *B*

93.7   severitie *R2, R4*: severitie *B*: serueritie *R*

93.16   come, now] *come, now B*: come; now *R2, R4*: come now *R*

93.35 God *B, R2, R4, M*: Cod *R*

93.38 it is *M*: *it is R2, R4*: It is *B*: it is is *R*

94.12 deathe. An] deathe: An *R*

94.18 *tamen M*: *tamem R*

94.32 *hym*: and looke] *him*; and looke *R2, R4*: *hym*, & looke *R*

94.34 thorough: how] through; how *R2, R4*: thorough, how *R*

95.1 *coles, untill M*: *coles, vntil R2*: *coales, vntill R4*: *coles) vntill R*

95.8 c.18.] C 18. *R*: cap.18. *R2*: *cap*.18. *R4*

95.11 fire: and *R4*: fire, & *R2*: fire, and *M*: fire. and *R*

95.19 punishment *R2, R4*: punishmet *R*

95.21 Gregorie *R2*: *Gregory R4*: Gregoire *R*

95.34 beleeve] beeleue *R*

95.37 August. *R2*: *August. R4*: *not in R*

96.3 conclusion, *ista*] conclusion. *ista R*

96.14 water] water *R2, R4*: watters *R*

96.15 Serm.16.&55.] Serm.55. *R, R2*: *ser.de sex tribulationibus.16.&*
       55. R4

96.16 before. And *R2, R4, M*: before, And *R*

96.23 teares: they] teares; they *R2, R4*: teares they *R*

96.34 Serm.20.in Psalm.118.] *Serm.20.in Psal.118. R4*: Serm.2.in
       Psalm.118. *R*: Serm.2.in Psal.118. *R2*

97.8 imagine] Imagine *R, R2*

97.12 *that M*: *tbat R*

97.15 *wicked R2, R4, M*: *wrcked R*

97.32 Lucifer] *Lucifer R4*: lucifer *R, R2*

98.5 doune with suche contempt, and] doune with such contempt,
       and *R2*: downe with such contempt, and *R4*: down, with
       such contempt, and *B*: doune, with suche contempt and *R*

98.9 is *B, R2, R4, M*: *is R*

98.9 Mat.14. *appears between* Esa.14. *and* Apo.14. *in R, B, R2*: *not
       in R4*

98.11 *Dei*, the *R2*: *Dei*, The *R4*: *Dei, The B*: *dei* the *R*

98.12 Apo.21. *R, B, R2*: Apo.20. *R4*

98.14 is, *Hades*] is, HADES *R2*: is *Hades R4*: is: *Hades M*: is. *Hades*
       R: is, *Elades B*

98.15 Plutarche] Plutarch *B, R2*: *Plutarch R4*: plutarche *R*

98.18 2.Pet.2.] 2.Pet.4. *R, B, R2*

98.19 obscuritie. Also *R2*: *obscuritie. Also B*: obscurity. Also *R4*:
       obscuritie, Also *R*

98.22 2.Pe.2.] 2.Pe.4. *R*: 2.Pet.4. *B, R2*

98.27   (which *R2, R4*: which *R, B*
98.33   idolatrous *B*: Idolatrous *R, R2, R4*
98.37   therof, that the *B*: therof that, the *R*
99.2   place, the *B, R2, R4*: place the *R*
100.1   eyes, his *R2, R4*: eies, his *B*: eyes his *R*
100.23   afflicted with his particular *B, R2, R4*: afflicted, with this
         particular *R*
100.31   Imagination shalbe] imagination shalbe *B*: Imagination,
         shalbe *R*
100.37   calamities *B, R4*: calamites *R, R2*
101.9   damned, *cruciabuntur R2*: damned; *Cruciabuntur B*: damned:
         Cruciabuntur R4: damned. *cruciabuntur R*
101.11   *geve her torment*] geue her torment *R2*: giue her torment *R4*:
         Give hir torment B: *geue her, torment R*
101.11   Babilon *R2: Babilon R4*: Babylon *B*: babilon *R*
101.28   (as I have sayd) and *B, R4*: (as I haue sayd; and *R2*: (as I
         haue sayd & *R*
102.31   God, *thou R2*: God; *Thou B, R2*: God. thou *R*
103.6   place. As *B, R2, M*: place. *As R4*: place As *R*
103.14   drunkarde *R2, R4*: drunkards *R, B*
103.30   like. Which *B, R2*: like, Which *R, R4*
104.5   worldling was] worldling, was *R*
104.11   horriblie] horrible *R*
104.13   brimstone *M*: brimstome *R*
104.20   accustomed to *M*: accustomed: to *R*
104.26   also: And] also? And *R*
105.1   sayeth, *we*] saith; *We B*: sayeth *we R*
105.8   in so muche] in so much *R2, R4*: insomuch *B*: inso muche *R*
105.23   heaven withall: and now] heauen; and now *R2*: heauen;
         now *R4*: heauen withall & now *R*
106.6   into rage *B, R2, R4*: in to rage *R*
106.8   *R, R2 insert* Apo.23. *before* Luc.23.: Apo.13. *B*: Apo.23.&16. *R4*
106.18   Apo.20.&21. *R4*: Apo.21. *R, B, R2*
107.35   God and good men *B*: good and good men *R*
108.7   bodye *M*: bodie *B, R2*: body *R4*: dodye *R*
108.10   greater *B, R2, R4*: greate *R*
108.14   sufficient *B, R2, M*: sufficient *R*
108.15   nedes *R2, M*: needs *B*: medes *R*
108.19   away to hell, to] away to hel, to *R2*: *away to hel, to B*: away,
         to hell to *R*

108.22 blysse and Joye (as I have sayd,) of eternall] blysse, and
Ioye, (as I haue sayd) of eternall *R*: blisse, and joy (as I
have said) of eternal *B*: blisse and ioye; of eternal *R2*: blisse
and ioy, of eternall *R4*

108.23 societie with *B*, *R2*: society with *R4*: societie, with *R*

108.26 the other *B*: tbe other *R*

108.31 lyeth] lieth *B*, *R2*, *R4*: Lyeth *R*

108.34 Judit.16.] Iudit.6. *R*, *B*, *R2*, *R4*

109.1 calamities: as *B*: calamities. as *R*: calamities. To wit *R2*, *R4*

109.10 unfortunatlie *R2*: vnfortunatly *R4*: vnfortunallie *R*

109.13 worldlie *B*, *M*: wordlie *R*, *R2*: wordly *R4*

109.19 before us by our own conscience, shall] before us by our
own conscience, shal *B*: *before vs by our owne conscience; shal*
R2: *before vs by our owne conscience; shall R4*: before vs, by our
own conscience shall *R*

109.30 freat and *R2*, *M*: fret and *B*, *R4*: freat end *R*

109.34 scripture) *What*] Scripture) *What R4*: Scripture;) *What B*:
scripture) *what R*, *R2*

110.28 bene? Yf] byn? If *R4*: been? If *B*: bene? yf *R*: bene? if *R2*

110.33 heare. Afterward *R2*, *R4*, *M*: hear. Afterward *B*: heare Afterward *R*

111.17 good? We *B*, *R4*: good? we *R*, *R2*

112.13 daunger before *R2*, *R4*: daunger, before *R*: danger, before *B*

112.14 wary *R2*, *R4*: warie *B*: weary *R*

I.X

112.33 spoken. I *B*, *R2*, *R4*: spoken: I *R*

113.16 magnificence: so *R4*: magnificence; so *B*, *R2*: magnificence.
So *R*

113.24 sayed, doe] said; Do *B*: sayed doe *R*

113.30 paynes? King] paines? King *R4*: pains? King *B*: paynes?
king *R*: paines? king *R2*:

114.9 him selfe, *beholde*] him selfe; *behold R2*: himselfe; *Behold R4*:
himself: *Behould R4*: him selfe *beholde R*

114.16 sayeth in] saieth in *R2*: saith in *B*, *R4*: sayeth as in *R*

114.26 worldlie *M*: worldly *B*: wordlie *R*

114.28 able *B*, *R2*, *R4*: hable *R*

115.11 though *B*, *R2*, *R4*, *M*: thought *R*

116.26 *thousand B*, *R2*, *R4*: *thouusand R*

116.26 Dan.7. *R2*, *R4*: Dan.5. *R*: Dan.1. *B*

116.27   God) *B, R2, R4, M*: God) *R*
116.27   *hundred B, R4:* hundreed *R, R2*
116.27   *thowsand dyd*] *thousand did R4: thowsand, dyd R:* thousand, did
         B, R2
116.36   creation *R4: creation B, R2:* cteation *R*
117.3   power of] *power of B:* power.of *R*
117.23   be? Yf] be? If *B, R2:* shalbe? If *R4:* be? yf *R*
117.33   *Paragraph break R2, R4: no paragraph break R, B*
118.14   Assuerus *B, R2: Assuerus R4:* assuerus *R*
118.21   the joy *R2, R4:* a ioy *R:* a joy *B*
118.21   day? O *B:* day? o *R:* therof? O *R2, R4*
118.28   notwithstanding *B, R2, R4, M:* notwthstanding *R*
118.36   innumerable *B, R2, R4:* Innumerable *R*
119.28   joyfullie, that *R4:* ioifullie, that *R2:* joifullie, that *B:* ioyful-
         lie that *M:* ioyfullie. that *R*
120.3   even in *R2, R4:* even in *B:* euen, in *R*
120.6   14.20. *B, R2, R4:* 14:20. *R*
120.7   Pharao *B, R2: Pharao R4:* pharao *R*
120.18   Helias *B: Helias R:* helias *R, R2*
120.30   Luke *B, R2: Luke R4:* Lucke *R*
120.32   effect: and *R4:* effect; and *B, R2:* effect, and *R*
121.10   is *coelum*] is *Coelum B, R4:* is, *coelum R2: is coelum R*
121.13   that, Looke] that Looke *R:* that look *B*
121.25   witt, understanding] wit, vnderstanding *R2, R4:* wit, under-
         standing *B:* witt vnderstanding *R*
122.9   accedentall parte.] accedentall.parte. *R*
122.15   inconveniences: subject] inconueniences; subiect *R2, R4:* in-
         conveniences; subject *B:* inconueniences, subiect *R*
122.28   *Paragraph break R2, R4: paragraph continues R*
123.6   bodie is] bodie, is *R:* flesh is *R2, R4*
123.22   bodie: as] bodie as *M:* bodie? as *R:* bodies whatsoeuer; as
         R2: bodies whatsoeuer, as *R4*
123.24   corruptible bodie *R2, M:* corruptible body *R4:* corruptible,
         bodie *R*
123.25   resurrection *R2, R4, M:* resurrcction *R*
123.31   drinking, sleeping *R2, R4:* drinking sleeping *R*
124.2   his senses together finding *R2:* his senses togeather find-
         ing *R4:* the senses togither, finding *B:* their senses together
         finding *R*
124.5   after.) Now] after). Now *M:* after) Now *R*

124.10   pleasure: the] pleasure, the *R*, *B*: comfort; the *R2*, *R4*
124.11   hands, the *B*, *R4*: hands the *R*, *R2*
124.18   bodie shalbe] body shalbe *R4*: bodie, shalbe *R*, *R2*
124.28   This *M*: this *R*: And this *R2*, *R4*: Which *B*
124.35   end. These *M*: end, These *R*
125.8   worlde *R2*, *R4*, *M*: woalde *R*
125.15   happinesse: Yet *R4*: happinesse; Yet *R2*: happines: yet *B*:
          happinesse. Yet *R*
125.17   happie. *Hæc R2*: happy. *Hæc R4*: happie? *Hæc B*, *M*: hap-
          pie? *Hec R*
125.19   Which *B*, *R2*, *R4*: Vvhich *R*
125.29   than *B*, *M*: then *R2*, *R4*: han *R*
126.3   nobilitie *B*, *R2*, *M*: nobility *R4*: nobitie *R*
126.9   universall felicitie *R4*, *M*: vniuersal felicitie *R2*: universal
          felicitie *B*: vniuersall: felicitie *R*
126.16   thinges that *R4*: times that *R2*: times, that *R*, *B*
126.19   rejoyse, we] reioice, we *R2*, *R4*: rejoice; we *B*: reioyse we *R*
126.21   God, which *B*, *R2*, *R4*: God which *M*: God. which *R*
126.21   causes, natures *B*, *R2*, *R4*: causes natures *R*
126.22   Knowleige.] Knowledge. *R4: Knowledge. B*: knowleige. *R*:
          Knoledge. *R2*
126.23   bothe God] both God *B*, *R2*, *R4*: bothe, God *R*
126.23   infinite causes *B*, *R2*, *R4*: infinitie canses *R*
126.35   sayed, *goe*] sayd: *Goe R4*: said; *Go B*: sayed *goe R*, *R2*
127.4   *live in R2*, *R4: live in B*: liue, in *R*
127.7   *harte, for*] hart, for *R2*, *R2*: hart: for *B*: harte. For *R*
127.11   Co.2.] Co.3. *R*, *B*, *R2*, *R4*
127.18   sonne: we] sonne, we *R*, *R2*: Sonne, we *R4*: Son, we *B*
127.27   Phil.4. *R4*: Psal.4. *R*, *B*, *R2*
128.1   (sayeth he to Abraham).] saieth he to Abraham *R2*: saith
          he to Abraham *R4*: (sayeth he) to Abraham *R*: (saith he)
          to Abraham *B*
128.16   thee? O *B*, *R2*, *R4*: thee? o *R*
128.18   in whiche the soules] in which the souls *B*: in whiche, the
          soules *R*: wherin the soules *R2*: *wherin the soules R4*
129.19   2.The.] 1.The. *R*, *B*, *R2*, *R4*
129.20   Principalities, Powers, Vertues *R2: Principalities, Powers, Vertues*
          R4: principalities, powers, vertues *R*
129.24   God *B*, *R2*, *R4*, *M*: Cod *R*
130.7   value *R2*, *R4*: valure *R*, *B*

130.8   honorable is B, *R2*: honourable is *R4*: honorable, is *R*

131.3   rejoyse, to] rejoice, to *B*: reioyse to *R*: reioice and *R2, R4*

131.4   Lambe] LAMBE *R2*: *Lambe R4*: lambe *R*: lamb *B*

131.7   state? Yf] state? If *B, R2*: State? If *R4*: state? yf *R*

132.1   daylye] dailie *R2*: daily *B, R4*: dalye *R*: dayle *M*

132.12   world: an other] world: another *B*: world; an other *R2*: world; another *R4*: world an other *R*

134.7   Ser.37.de sanctis.] Ser.31.de sanctis. *R, R2: Ser.31.de sanctis. B: Ser.31.de Sanctis. R4*

134.9   heard before, that *B*: heard, before that *R*: heard, that *R2, R4*

134.11   joye. Good *R2*: joy? Good *B*: ioy? Good *R4*: ioye: Good *R*

134.33   glorie that heaven contayneth, shall] glorie that heauen contayneth, shal *R2*: glory that heauen contayneth, shall *R4*: glorie, that heauen contayneth shall *R*: glorie, that heaven conteineth shal *B*

134.34   Pet.3. *B, R2, R4*: Pet.3., *R*

134.35   Lambe *R2, R4*: lambe *R*: lamb *B*

134.40   Lambe] lambe *R, R2, R4*: lamb *B*

135.7   Matt.5.&19.] Matt.5.&9. *R*

135.10   2.Co.] 1.Co. *R, B*

135.20   worlde *M*: wuorlde *R*

135.29   Christ:) I] Christ.) I *R*: Christ) *I B*

136.4   wickedst *B, R2, R4*: whickedest *R*

136.8   brother,)] brother) *B*: brother.) *R*

136.28   same. But *B, M*: same But *R*

137.1   Cor.9.] Cor.6. *R, B, R2, R4*

138.11   deathe to come] deathe, to come *R, B*

138.36   salvation *R2, R4, M*: salvation *B*: salauation *R*

     II.I

141.21   ys, that vertuouse] is, that vertuous *B*: ys that, vertuouse *R*

141.31   seeme: yet] seem: yet *B*: seeme; yet *R2, R4*: seeme yet *R*

142.3   S. Austen, that] *S. Augustine,* that *R4*: S. Austen; That *B*: S. Augustine; That *R2*: S. Austen, That *R*

142.5   imprysonementes, losse] imprisonmentes, losse *R2*: imprisonments, losse *B, R4*: imprysonementes losse *R*

142.10   2.Pet.3.] 2.Pet.2. *R, B, R2, R4*

142.32   Mat.11.] Mat.12. *R, B, R2, R4*

143.1   subtiltie *B*: subtilitie *R*

143.4   difficulties *R4: difficulties R2: difficultie B:* difficulti *R:*

143.4   same: they] same; they *R2:* same: They *R4:* same. They *B:* same, they *R*

143.4   Rom.7. *not in R, B, R2, R4*

144.9   compleyneth under] compleyneth, vnder *R:* complaineth, vnder *R2, R4:* complaineth under *B*

144.13   able to *B R2, R4:* hable to *R*

144.19   *worlde? And] world? And R2, R4: worlde. And R: world.* And *B*

144.37   woords grace and mercie] words, Grace & Mercie *R2:* words *Grace* and *Mercie R4:* woord grace and mercie *R:* word grace, and mercy *B*

145.1   Matt.1. *moved up from* from sinne to come

145.10   ghoste, and with the vertues infused: to] Ghost, and with the vertues infused; to *R2, R4:* ghoste? and with the vertues infused, to *R:* Ghost, and with divers special graces, to *B*

145.22   Christianitie *B:* Christiantie *R*

145.29   is of *B, R2, R4:* is, of *R*

146.2   Eze.ca.11.] Eze.11. *B:* Exo.ca.11. *R, R2:* Exo.11. *R4*

146.3   *bowelles, that]* bowels, that *B: bowelles; to the end R2, R4: bowelles that R*

146.6   *New paragraph at equivalent place in R2, R4; paragraph continues R, B*

146.10   *know, that R2, R4: know that R, B*

146.11   *crucified also, to B: crucified, to R2, R4: crucified also to R*

146.22   a feard, for] *afraid, for R4:* afraid, for *B:* a feard for *R, R2*

146.25   just man *M:* iust (man,) *R:* iust (MAN,) *R2: iust (MAN,) R4:* just (man) *B*

147.9   diligence, doe *R2, R4:* diligence: doe *R*

148.26   burden shoulde] burden should *B, R2, R4:* burden, shoulde *R*

148.31   *with us, who R2, R4: with vs, whoe M: with us, who B: with, vs whoe R*

148.31   us? sayeth the Apostle.] *us* (saith the Apostle.) *B: vs,* sayeth the Apostle? *R, R2: vs* saith the Apostle? *R4*

149.4   S. John, in that (having] Saint Iohn, in that (having *B: S. Iohn:* in that (hauing *R4:* S. Iohn; in that, (hauing *R2:* S. Iohn in that. (hauing *R*

150.19   sweete, this *R4:* sweet, this *B, R2:* sweete: this *R*

151.12   Imprisonmentes, tormentes *R2, R4, M:* Imprisonments, torments *B:* Imprisonmentes tormentes *R*

151.28 maketh even] maketh even *B*: maketh, euen *R*: doe make euen *R2, R4*

151.30 Psa.1.] Psa.6. *R, B, R2*: Ps.6. *R4*

152.17 Whiche S. John] Which Saint Iohn *B*: Whiche, S. Iohn *R*

153.31 righteousnes, for that they are made able to discerne for] righteousnes, for that they are made able to discern for *B*: rightetousnes for that they are made able to discerne, for *R*

153.38 joye, comfort] joy, comfort *B*: ioye comfort *R*

153.40 parte? For] part? For *B*: parte? for *R*

154.3 paynfull? Doeth] painful? Doth *B*: paynfull? doeth *R*

154.5 walke: consider] walke: Consider *R*: walk? Consider *B*

154.9 Esa.59.] 59 *inverted R*: Esa.65. *B, R2, R4, M*

154.10 *groped B, R2, R4: grooped R*

154.29 *manna, knowen R2, R4*: manna, known B: *manna knowen R*

155.14 hartes and spirites *R2, R4*: harts and spirits *B*: hartes, and spirites *R*

155.30 Psa.89.] *not in R, B, R2, R4*

156.16 Idole Dagon] Idoll *Dagon R4*: idole Dagon *R2*: idol Dagon *B*: Idole dagon *R*

156.29 before *B, R2, R4, M*: hefore *R*

156.32 thorowghly] thoroughly *B*: throughly *R4*: thorowgly *R*: throughly *R2*

157.9 *Philistines B, R2*: Philisthines *R4: philistines R*

157.18 easie, pleasant *B*: easie: pleasant *R*

157.29 allwayes in] alwaies in *R2, R4*: alwais in *B*: allwayes, in *R*

158.2 Sap.17.] Sap.7. *R*

158.8 wicked *B, R2, R4*: wiked *R*

158.9 *proved: R2, R4: prooved B: prowed R*

158.21 his owne *R2, R4, M*: his own *B*: his, owne *R*

158.25 suspect *B, R2, R4*: supect *R*

159.16 *hope B, R2, R4: hoope R*

159.27 prosperitie *B, R2*: prosperity *R4*: prospertie *R*

160.4 againe, *præstolatio R2*: againe: *Præstolatio R4*: again; *Præstolatio B*: againe *præstolatio R*

160.23 wherein in deede] wherein in deed *R2*: wherin indeed *B, R4*: wherein, in deede *R*

160.29 Pharao: accursing them for the same, and] Pharao, accursing them for the same, & *R2*: *Pharao*, accursing them for the same, and *R4*: Pharao, accursing them for the same: and *R, B*

160.32   worldlie *R2, M*: worldly *B, R4*: wordlie *R*

161.5   seeke to *B*: seeke too *R*

161.8   prosperities? When *B, R2, R4*: prosperities? when *R*

161.12   honour? Yf] honour? If *R4*: honor? If *B*: honour? yf *R*: honour? if *R2*

161.30   lost: great, for *B, R2, R4*: lost: great for *R*

162.4   woorkes: that is] workes; that is *R4*: works, that is *B*: woorkes that is *R, R2*

162.25   *S. Paul R4*: S. Paul *R2*: S. *Paul R*: Saint Paul *B*

162.27   agayne, *Every*] again; Every *B*: agayne. *Euery R, R2*: againe. *Euery R4*

162.34   *New paragraph] Paragraph continues R, B, R2, R4; R2, R4 begin new paragraph at 163.4 after* declare the same according to their dignities

164.17   sensualitie.] *sensualitie. B, R2*: sensualitie: *R*: sensuality. *R4*

164.19   tyrannie? Remember *B, R2*: Tyranny? Remember *R4*: tyrannie? remember *R*

164.20   Jud.16.] Iud.14. *R*

164.22   Hercules *B, R2*: *Hercules R4*: hercules *R*

164.25   further *B, R2, R4, M*: futher *R*

165.12   looketh *B, R2, R4*: Looketh *R*

165.30   creature: that is *R4*: creature; that is *R2*: creature, that is *R*: creature that is *B*

166.13   Psal.116.] Psal.90. *R, B, R2, R4*

166.32   same men *B, R2, R4, M*: same, men *R*

166.32   Rom.3.] Psal.13. *R, B, R2, R4*

166.35   diversitie of *R2*: diuersity of *R4*: diuersitie, of *R*: diversitie, of *B*

167.2   sweetly and calmely *R2*: sweetly and calmly *B*: sweetly & calmely *R4*: sweetly, and calmely *R*

167.4   lyfe. But *M*: life. But *B, R2, R4*: lyfe But *R*

167.9   Jac.4.] Iac.3. *R, R2, R4*: Iaco.3. *B*

167.15   say *hoe*] say *Hoe R4*: say, *Hoe R2*: say hoe *R*: never ho *B*

167.33   sayeth, *spend*] saith; Spend *B*: sayeth *spend R*: saieth to his maister, *spend R2, R4*

168.3   *contradictionem B, R2, R4: coniradictionem R*

168.8   other in their *B, R2, R4*: other their *R*

168.10   as *B, R2, R4, M*: *as R*

168.20   towardes God *R2, R4, M*: towards God *B*: towardes, God *R*

169.1   dominions against *B, R4*: dominions, against *R, R2*
169.22   mention or remembrance *B, R2, R4*: mention, or remem-
          brance *R*
169.24   Pro.11. *R2*: Prou.11. *R4*: Pro.12. *B* Pro.12 *R*
170.6   for that thou *B*: for that, thou *R*: for that perhaps thou
          R2, R4
170.16   Churche *M*: Church *R2, R4*: Curche *R*
170.19   *woorke M*: *worke R2, R4*: *work B*: *voorke R*
170.28   heavenlie *R2, M*: heauenly *R4*: heavenly *B*: heanenlie *R*
171.5   Gofr.in vita Barn.] *Gofr.in vita Barn. B*: Gofr: in vita barn.
          R: Gofr. in vita Bern. *R2*: *Gotfr. in vita Bern. R4*
172.9   least prove *R4*: least proove *B*: least, proue *R, R2*
173.8   adorat.] orat. *R*
173.10   Levit.] *Leuit. R4*: leuit. *R, R2*: *Leu. B*
173.12   Hill.in Psa.118.] Hill.in psa.118. *R, R2*: *Hil. in psal.*118. *R4*:
          *Hi. in ps.*118. *B*
173.14   Eccle.2. *R2*: Eccl.2. *B*: Eccle.1. *R*: Eccl.22. *R4*
173.30   devill. *B, R2, R4, M*: deuill *R*
173.31   example *B, R2, R4*: examples *R*
174.3   Austen.] Austen, *R*: *Aust. B*: August. *R2*: *Augustine. R4*
174.5   bookes of his confessions *R2*: Bookes of his *Confessions R4*:
          books of his confessions *B*: bookes, of his confessions *R*
175.2   and the *R, M*: and the *R*: & the *R4*
175.7   Millan] *Millan R2, R4*: millan *R*
175.33   saieng: *Demittes*] saieng; *Demittes B*: saieng? *Demittes R*
176.1   Austen,) O] Austen) O *B*: *Austen.) O R*: Augustin) O *R2*:
          Augustine. O R4
176.6   a marvailous *R2, R4*: a marvelous *B*: maruailous *R*
176.8   hym selfe on] himselfe on *B*: hym self upon *R2*: himself
          upon *R4*: on hym selfe, on *R*
176.9   scope *B, R2, R4*: scoope *R*
176.23   thus *M*: this *R, B*: in this sort *R2*: in this sorte *R4*
177.8   had *B, R4, M*: lad *R, R2*
177.30   doutefulnes unto me] doutfulnes vnto me *R2*: doubtfulnes
          vnto me *R4*: dowtfulnes vnto me *B*: doutefulnes, vnto me *R*
178.6   Monica] *Monica B, R2, R4*: monica *R*
178.10   sheweth.Li.] *sheweth.Li. R4*: *sheweth.*Li *R2*: *sheweth.li. B*: shew-
          eth Li. *R*
178.21   Possid.] *Possid. R4*: possid. *R*: *possid. R2*
178.25   (I *B, R2, R4, M*: *(I R)*

178.32   dowt) for *B, R2*: doubt) for *R4*: dowt:) for *R*
179.25   How *M*: how *R*: me: how *B*: O how *R4*: O, how *R2*
179.33   vocation. First *B, R2, R4, M*: vocation First *R*
181.12   *lorde) M: Lord) B, R2, R4: lorde(R*
181.13   *commaundement? Is not this] commandement? Is not this R4: com-mandements? Is not this B: commaundement? is not this R: commandement? is not this R2*
181.14   commaundement: I meane a] commandement; I meane a *R2*: commandement, I meane a *R4*: commandement? I mean a *B*: commaundement (I meane) a *R*
181.15   crosse? So *R2, R4*: crosse? so *R*: crosse. So *B*
182.1   Gall.2.] Gall.3. *R, R2*: Gal.3. *B, R4*

II.II

182.8   who (ether . . . as them selves) are content] who, (either . . . as them selues) doe yeld *R2*: who either . . . as themselves, are content *B*: who either . . . as themselues, doe yeeld *R4*: who: ether . . . as them selues, are content *R*
182.13   therunto: and that *B*: thervnto: And that *R4*: thervnto. And that *R*: therunto. And that *R2*
182.16   handes. Mary] hands. But *B*: handes. But yet *R2, R4*: han-des: Mary *R*
182.19   unreasonable to R2, R4: vnreasonable, to *R*: unreasonable, to *B*
182.25   may lyve] may liue *R2, R4*: may live *B*: maye, lyue *R*
183.12   is, whether *R2, R4*: is whether *R*
183.19   state? Whiche] state. Which *B, R4*: state? whiche *R*: state. which *R2*
183.28   Joh.16.] Iohn.16. *B*: Ioh.26. *R, R2*: Ioan.26. *R4*
183.29   Luc.21.] Luc.11. *R, B, R2, R4*
184.11   when he *B, R2, R4, M*: when be *R*
184.15   by that Christ sayeth] by that our Sauious sayeth *R2*: by that our Sauiour said *R4*: by that, Christ sayeth *R*: by that, Christ saith *B*
184.31   fall. The same *R4*: fal. The same *B, R2*: fall: The same *R*
185.18   child. Of the same *B*: chosen by almightie God. Of the same *R2*: chosen by almighty God. Of the same *R4*: child: Of the same *R*
185.22   world. The affliction *B, R2, R4*: world: the affliction *R*
185.25   man. But *B, R2, R4*: yet man: But yet *R*

186.14   his glorie *R2: his glory R4*: this glorie *R, B*

186.15   Christ, affirming *R2, R4*: Christ affirming *R, B*

186.27   calamities, which *R2, R4*: calamities which *B, M*: calamities' which *R*

186.35   Domitian *B, R2: Domitian R4*: domitian *R*

186.35   Pathmos *B, R2: Pathmos R4*: pathmos *R*

187.3   Jouin. *R2: Iouin. R4*: Iauin. *R: Ia.vin. B*

187.36   Psal.38.] ps.73. *R, R2: Psal.73. R4*

188.3   Mat.10.] Matt.7. *R, B*: Mat.7. *R2, R4*

188.13   parable. The sunne *R2, R4*: parable. The sun *B*: parable: The sunne *R*

188.19   cloake *R4*: cloke *B*: clocke *R*: clock *R2*

189.3   us. Or yf] us. Or if *B*: vs: Or yf *R*

190.1   *Rejoyse R4: Reioice B: reioyse R, R2*

190.3   of *receauing R4: of receiuing* B: of, *receauing R, R2*

190.32   wealth and prosperitie *R2*: wealth and prosperity *R4*: wealth, and prosperitie *R, B*

190.32   Eccl.18.] Eccl.28. *R, B, R2, R4*

190.35   Tob.11.] Tob.12. *R, R2, R4*: Tobi.12. *B*

191.5   *these thinges R4: those thinges R, R2: those things B*

191.11   brought *B, R2, R4, M*: hrought *R*

191.18   Job.23.] *moved down from* And for lyke effect

192.4   (or correction) *R2, R4: (or correction) R, B*

192.19   *thy discipline R2: Thy discipline B, R4: the discipline R*

192.19   Psal.118.] Psal.17. *R, B, R2, R4*

192.30   Psal.119.] Psal.18. *R, B, R2, R4*

193.19   Abraham, it *R2, M: Abraham, it R4*: Abraham. It *B*: Abraham, It *R*

193.28   sense also, the *R2, R4*: sense also the *M*: sense, also the *R, B*

193.33   Psal.66.] Psal.63. *R, B, R2, R4*

195.25   Gen.39.] Gen.31. *R*

195.26   Tob.2.11.] Tob.2.12. *24R*

196.11   place *B, R2, R4, M*: plaee *R*

196.14   *soule R2, R4, M*: soul *B: foule R*

196.22   Peter *B, R2: Peter R4*: peter *R*

196.37   *morning, for B, R2, R4: morning for R*

197.6   Judi.16.] Iudi.12. *R*

197.10   *shalt B, R2, R4: shall R*

197.25   What *B, R2, R4*: what *R*

199.2 mercifull and fatherlie] merciful and fatherly *R2*: mercifull and fatherly *R4*: mercifull, and fatherlie *R*: merciful, and fatherly *B*

199.5 chapter: whie] *chapter, why B*: chapter whi *R*: chapter which *M*

199.9 joyfullie *R2*: *ioifully B*: *ioyfully R4*: laufullie *R*

199.12 good? We see *B*: welfare? We see *R2, R4*: good? we see *R*

199.36 Peter *B, R2*: *Peter R4*: peter *R*

200.6 with us *R, B*: unto us *R2, R4*

200.8 might be *B, R2, R4, M*: might he *R*

200.13 chaunce *R4*: chance *B, R2*: chaunces *R*

200.26 Mar.10.] Mat.10. *R*

202.26 *me? All R4*: *me?* Al *B*: me? Al *R2*: me: All *R*

203.12 *thou receavedst R2, R4*: *thou receivedst B*: *thou receauest M*: *thou receauest R*

203.13 *rapuisti, thou R2, R4*: *Rapuisti, thou B*: *rapuisti thou R*

203.20 Psal.73. *B*: Psal.37. *R, R2, R4*

205.3 Pharasies *B, R4*: pharasies *R, R2*

205.10 disciple was *R, B, R2, R4*

205.11 4.Re.6.] 4.Re.16. *R*

205.25 2.Co.12.] *not in R, B, R2, R4*

207.12 matter *B, R2, R4, M*: mattter *R*

207.18 doe:) yet *R4*: doe) yet *R2*: do) yet *B*: doe: yet *R*

207.30 confidence of *R2, R4*: confidence, & of *R*: confidence, and of *B*

208.2 you? With *B*: thee? With *R4*: the? with *R2*: you? with *R*

208.7 towardes me? *R*: *towards me? B*: *towardes vs? R4*: towards vs? *R2*

208.18 with his *B, R2, M*: *with his R4*: with, his *R*

208.25 An important *R4*: *An important B, R2*: 4.An important *R*

209.8 Psal.44.] *not in R, B, R2, R4*

209.26 stronge faithe] strong faith *R2, R4*: *strong faith B*: stronge. faithe *R*

209.31 *perishe, before B, R4*: *perish; before R2*: *perishe before R*

209.34 under *B, R2, R4, M*: vndet *R*

210.2 sayed: *In deo*] said: *In deo R4*: saied, *In deo R2*: said; *In Deo B*: sayed *In deo R*

210.6 comforteth *R2, R4, M*: *comforteth B*: comforteh *R*

210.9 *confidens B, R2, R4, M*: *cenfidens R*

210.14 Psal.23.] Psal.21. *R*

210.27 experience *B, R2, M*: exeperience *R4*: exporience *R*

210.36 freendes, be] *freendes, be R2: friendes, be R4: frinds, be B*: freendes be *R*

211.29 yeres after] *yeers after B*: yeres, after *R*: *yeres, after R2: yeares, after R4*

212.5 S. John. *R2: S.Iohn. R4*: Saint Iohn *B*: S.Ioh. *R*

212.8 satte on] sate on *R2: sate on R4*: sat on *B*: satte, on *R*

212.37 teacheth, cryeing] teacheth, crieng *B*: teacheth, crying *R4*: teacheth cryeing *R*: teacheth crying *R2*

212.37 1.Co.15.] Eccl.9. *R, B, R2, R4*

213.19 Peter *B, R2: Peter R4*: peter *R*

213.29 Christs name *R2: Christs name B, R4*: Christ name *R*

215.8 taken *B, R2, R4, M*: take *R*

215.11 *tongue R2, R4, M: toong B: tougne R*

216.3 constancie *B, R2*: constancy *R4*: constantie *R*

216.5 adversities *R2, R4, M*: adversities *B*: aduersiities *R*

216.29 1.Cor.4.] 2.Cor.4. *R, B, R2, R4*

217.1 miracles *B, R2, R4, M*: miracles *R*

217.7 2.Co.11.] 2.Cor.11. *B*: 1.Co.11. *R*: 1.Cor.11. *R4*: 1.Co.11. *R2*

217.18 Gentyles: in] Gentiles: in *R2*: gentils: in *B*: Gentiles; in *R4*: Gentyles, in *R*

217.31 mouthes *R2, R4, M*: mouths *B*: moutes *R*

217.35 worldlie *M*: worldly *B, R2, R4*: wordlie *R*

218.5 our selves in, amyddest] our selues in, amiddest *R2, R4*: our selues, in amyddest *R*: our selves withal, in amidst *B*

218.7 consideration *B, R2, R4, M*: consiration *R*

218.16 shame and confusion *R2*: shame & confusion *R4*: shame, and confusion *B*: shame: and confusion *R*

218.30 not? Yf] not ? If *B, R4*: not? yf *R*: not? if *R2*

218.37 feete: &c.] feete, &c. *B*: feete &c. *R4*: feete. &c. *R2*: feete? &c. *R*

220.19 Gen.15.] Gen.12. *R, B, R2, R4*

220.22 distresse *B, R2, R4, M*: didistresse *R*

220.23 Egypt. Phinees *B, R2, M: Egypt. Phinees R4*: Egypt Phinees *R*

220.26 Jos.14.] Iud.14. *R, R2 R4*: Iudg.14. *B*

220.29 2.Re.7.] 2.Re.2. *R, B, R2, R4*

220.32 Dan.6.] Dan.9. *R, B, R2, R4*

II.III

221.17 pretended feare *R2, R4*: pretended, feare *R*: pretended, fear *B*

222.32 *mysteries of B, R4, M: mysteries if R: misteries if R2*

223.20 chapiter./ 1.] Chapter./ 1. *R4: chap./* 1. *R2*: 1./ The partes of this chapiter. *R*: 1/ *The parts of this chapter. B*

223.22 Secondlie *R2, M*: Secondly *B, R4*: Sccondlie *R*

223.26 pricking thornes *R2: pricking-thornes R4*: pricking thorns *B*: princking thornes *R*

224.4 this is kyng] this is king *B*: this is the wise and mightie king *R2*: this is the wise and mighty King *R4*: this, is kyng *R*

224.18 apparell and armoure] apparel and armour *R2*: apparell and armour *R4*: apparell, and armoure *R*: apparel, and armor *B*

224.20 Philistians *B, R2: Philisthines R4*: philistians *R*

225.2 sentence of *B, R2, R4*: sentence, of *R*

225.25 dyd I *M*: did I *B, R2, R4*: dyd: I *R*

226.1 witnesse *R2, R4*: witnes *B*: wyitnesse *R*

226.14 contayneth all] containeth al *B*: contayneth, all *R*

226.15 humour and disease] humour, and disease *R*: humor, & di ease *B*

226.16 worldly *B, R2, R4, M*: wordly *R*

226.20 superiours. And *R2, M*: superiors. And *B*: Superiours. And *R4*: superiours, And *R*

226.23 desire *B, R2, R4, M*: destre *R*

226.28 mouthes. For *R2, R4, M*: mouths. For *B*: mouthes For *R*

226.31 so a *B, R2, R4, M*: so. a *R*

227.11 cried *Crucifige* against *B, R4*: cried, *Crucifige* against *R, R2*

227.31 runnyng and cryeing] running and crying *R2, R4*: runnyng, and cryeing *R*: running, and crieng *B*

227.36 vaynglorious *M*: vainglorious *B, R2*: vain=glorious *R4*: waynglorious *R*

228.1 whoe withe] who with *R2, R4*: whoe, withe *R*: who, with *B*

228.7 commendation. How *B, R2, R4, M*: commendation How *R*

228.31 foloweth, is *R2*: followeth, is *B, R4*: foloweth is *R*

228.40 Pilat *B, R2: Pilate R4*: pilat *R*

229.2 Agrippa and Festus *R2: Agrippa* and *Festus R4*: Agrippa, & Festus *B*: Agrippa, and festus *R*:

229.17 imagine *R2, R4*: imagin *B*: Imagine *R*

229.19 those emperours, those kynges, those princes and prelates] thos emperours, thos kings, thos princes & prelates *R2*: those Emperours, those Kings, those Princes and Prelats *R4*: these emperours, these kynges, these princes, and prelates *R*: these emperors, these kings, these princes, and prelates *B*

229.29   worldlie *M*: worldly *B*, *R2*, *R4*: wordlie *R*

230.14   fleshe and bloode] flesh and blood *B*: flesh & blood *R2*:
         flesh & bloud *R4*: fleshe, and bloode *R*

231.9   all his brethren *R4*: al his brethren *B*, *R2*: all his breethren *R*

231.20   vanite *R*: vanitie *B*, *R2*: vanity *R4*

232.16   Gentiles and Philosophers *R2*: Gentiles, and Philosophers *R*:
         gentils, and philosophers *B*

232.18   Paul *B*, *R2*: paul *R*

232.24   men esteemed] men, esteemed *R*, *R2*: *men, esteemed B*

232.29   that the *B*, *R2*, *R4*: that, the *R*

232.34   that a *B*, *R2*, *R4*: that, a *R*

233.11   ruynes and destructions] ruines and destructions *R2*, *R4*:
         ruynes, and destructions *R*: ruins, and destructions *B*

233.30   come to *B*, *R2*, *R4*: come, to *R*

234.37   Mat.3. *B*: Ma.3. *R*, *R2*, *R4*

234.37   *regum B*, *R2*: *Regum R4*: *regni R*

235.8   auncestours *M*: ancestors *B*, *R4*: auncestous *R*, *R2*

235.10   Heb.11.] Heb.12. *R*, *B*, *R2*: Hebr.12. *R4*

235.14   doe? We robbe *R4*: do? We rob *B*: doe? we robbe *R*, *R2*

235.15   creatures almoste] creatures almost *B*: creatures, almoste *R*

235.33   appointeth unto] appointeth unto *B*: appointeth, vnto *R*

235.36   riches and wealthe] riches and wealth *B*: riches, and wealthe
         R: riches, and wealth *R2*: riches, & wealth *R4*

235.36   world. Of *B*, *R2*, *R4*, *M*: world Of *R*

237.20   Psal.49.] *not in R*, *B*, *R2*, *R4*

238.10   *woe be to you riche men R2*: *Woe be to you riche men R4*: *wo be
         to you riche men R*: *Wo be to you rich men B*

238.24   refuted. *R4*: *refuted. R2*: refuted, *R*: *refused. B*

239.18   Woe *R2*, *R4*: Wo *R*, *B*

239.19   Luc.6. *R4*: Ioh.16. *R*, *R2*: Iohn.16. *B*

239.23   saythe: *You M*: saith: *You R4*: saith; *You B*: saith; *you R2*:
         saythe. *You R*

239.28   saythe: that they] solace saith: *That they solace R4*: saythe;
         that they solace *R*: saith; that they solace *R2*: saith; *That
         they solace B*

240.4   understanded] vnderstood *R2*, *R4*: understood *B*: vnder-
         stande *R*

240.5   spirituall and internall *R4*: spiritual and internal *B*, *R2*: spir-
         ituall, and internall *R*

240.16 Ephe.4. *R2*: Eph.4. *B*: Ephe:4. *R*: Ephes 4 *R4*

240.20 agayne: *Where M*: againe: *Where R4*: again; *Where B*: agayne. *Where R*: againe. *Where R2*

240.32 worldlie *M*: worldly *B, R2, R4*: wordlie *R*

240.33 overwhelmed: I *R2*: overwhelmed: I *B*: ouerwhelmed; I *R4*: ouerwhelmed. I *R*

240.36 Joh.11.] Ioh.10. *R, R2*: Iohn.10. *B*: Ioan.10. *R4*

241.5 appointed unto us withe] appointed vnto vs in *R2, R4*: appointed vnto vs, withe *R*: appointed unto us, with *B*

241.16 layethe] layeth *R2, R4*: laith *B*: Layethe *R*

241.19 lyved onelie] liued onelie *R2*: liued only *R4*: lyued, onelie *R*: lived, only *B*

241.21 Gods *R2, R4*: gods *M*: goods *R*: many churches *B*

242.1 serve you withe] serve you with *B*: serue you at an inche with *R2*: serue you at an inch with *R4*: serue you, withe *R*

242.6 Amos.8.] Amos.2. *R, B, R2*: Amos 2. *R4*

242.7 be not *B, R2, R4, M*: he not *R*

242.10 *deliciis B, R4: delitiis R, R2*

242.15 worldlye *M*: worldlie *R2*: worldly *B, R4*: wordlye *R*

242.21 Esa.5.] Esa.59. *R, R2*: Esai.59. *B*: Esa.56. *R4*

242.27 Psal.5.] Psal.3. *R, B, R2, R4*

242.30 3.Re.16.] 4.Re.17. *R, R2*: 1.Reg.17. *R4*

244.5 kyng and Emperour] king and Emperour *R2*: King & Emperour *R4*: king and emperor *B*: kyng, & Emperour *R*

245.4 worldlyng of] worldling of *B, R2, R4*: worldlyng, of *R*

245.14 endes of *R2, R4*: endes, of *R*: ends of *B*

246.5 him? Upon] *him?* Vpon *B, R2, R4*: him? vpon *R*

246.19 worldlye *M*: worldly *B, R2*: *worldly R4*: wordlye *R*

246.20 even as *R2, R4*: even as *B*: euen, as *R*

246.29 vanitie of *B, R2*: vanity of *R4*: vanitie: of *R*

246.35 cares: unquietnes] cares; unquietnes *B* cares, vnquietnes *R, R2*: eares, vnquietnes *R4; B, R2 and R4 retain consistency of punctuation in the list*

247.7 rest or repose *R2, R4*: rest or repose *R, B*

247.12 yet will *R4*: yet wil *B, R2*: yet, will *R*

247.13 them selves owt] themselues out *R2, R4*: themselves out *B*: them selues, owt *R*

247.16 more they *B, R2, R4, M*: more. they *R*

247.17 them *B, R2, R4*: hym *R*

247.36 yoke and bondage *R2*, *R4*: yoke, and bondage *R*, *B*
250.12 joye and comfort *R2*: ioy and comfort *R4*: ioye, and comfort *R*: joy, and comfort *B*
250.15 worldlings] worldlinges *B*, *R4*: wordlings *R*, *R2*
250.27 brused and gauled with *R4*: brused & gauled, with *B*, *R2*: brused, & gauled, with *R*
250.29 golde and silver] gold and siluer *R2*, *R4*: golde, and siluer *R*: gold, and silver *B*
250.29 greatlie their *R2*: greatly their *B*, *R4*: greatlie, their *R*
251.7 environed with *R2*, *R4*: environed with *B*: enuironed with *R*
252.1 for that Mardochæus *R2*: for that *Mardochæus* *R4*: for that, Mardochæus *R*: for that, Mardocheus *B*
252.16 onelie in] only in *B*: onelie, in *R*, *R2*
252.32 pride and ruffe *R2*: pride, and ruffe *R*: pride, and ruff *B*
253.9 carnall and loose harted] carnal and loose harted *R2*: carnall and loose-harted *R4*: carnall, and loose harted *R*: carnal, and loose harted *B*
253.16 watchefull. *M*: watchful. *B*, *R2*: watchefull: *R*
253.24 when *B*, *R2*, *R4*, *M*: vhen *R*
254.28 witt, *Charitie*] wit, *Charitie* *R2*: wit, *Charity* *R4*: wit; *Charitie* *B*: witt. *Charitie* *R*
254.30 *Peace* *B*, *R4*: peace *R*, *R2*
255.3 idolatrie *R2*: *idolatrie* *B*: *idolatry* *R4*: Idolatrie *R*
255.5 dronkennes, gluttonie *R2*: *dronkennes, gluttony* *R4*: *droonkennes, gluttonie* *B*: dronkennes gluttonie *R*
255.6 foretell you, as] *fortel you, as* *R2*: *for-tell you, as* *R4*: *foretel you, as* *B*: foretell you: as *R*
255.10 spirit of Christ *B*, *R2*, *R4*: spirit of Christ *R*
255.15 *vices and concupiscences* *R4*: *vices, and concupiscences* *R*, *B*: *vices, & concupiscences* *R2*
255.30 world enemies. *R4*: *world enemies.* *R2*: *world enimies.* *B*: world.enemies. *R*
255.31 Christ and the world *R2*, *R4*: Christ, and the world *R*, *B*
256.2 1.Joh.2.] Ioh.2. *R*, *R2*: Iohn.2. *B*: Ioan.2. *R4*
256.11 *rogo*, saithe he: I] *rogo*, saith he: I *R4*: *rogo*, saith he: *I* *B*: *rogo* saithe he: I *M*: *rogo* saithe he? I *R*: *mundo*, saith he; I *R2*
256.11 mercie and perdone *R2*: mercy and pardon *R4*: mercie, and perdone *R*: *mercie, and pardon* *B*
256.12 but *B*, *R2*, *R4*: But *R*
256.16 tourmentoures and crucifiers *R2*: tormentors & crucifiers

R4: tourmentoures, and crucifiers *R*: tormentors, and crucifiers *B*

256.22 your selves *R2*, *R4*: *your selves* *B*: your selfes *R*

256.25 meaning herein, sayeth] meaning herein, saieth *R2*: meaning herin, saith *R4*: meaning heerin, saith *B*: meaning, here
in sayeth *R*

256.26 sorte: *Nolite*] sort: *Nolite* *B*, *R4*: sorte, *Nolite* *R2*: sorte. *Nolite* *R*

256.28 world? If] world. If *R*, *R2*, *R4*: *world*. If *B*

256.34 travailes upon it?] trauailes vpon it *R*, *R2*, *R4*: travels upon
it *B*

256.36 Whie] Why *R4*: *Why* *B*, *R2*: Whi *R*

257.19 feire of deceite] feare of deceite *R*: marcket of deceit *R2*:
market of deceipte *R4*: feat of deceit *B*

257.25 shewed,) a] shewed) a *B*, *R2*, *R4*: shewed, a *R*

257.25 Au.ep.32.] Au.ep.39. *R*, *R2*: *Au.ep.39.* *B*: *Aug.ep.39* *R4*

258.6 sufficient, to *B*, *R2*, *R4*: sufficient to *R*

258.9 chapiter: how] *chapter, how* *B*: chapiter how *R*

258.36 devill no waye] deuil no way *R2*: diuell no way *R4*: deuill,
no waye *R*: divel, no way *B*

259.20 fixing our mindes in] fixing our mindes on *R2*, *R4*: fixing
our mindes, in *R*: fixing our minds, in *B*

259.33 Gala.6.] Gala.4. *R*: Gal.4. *B*, *R2*, *R4*

260.6 men, weepe *R4*: *men, weep* *B*: men; weepe *R2*: men weepe *R*

260.7 come upon you. *R4*: come vpon you? *R*, *R2*: *come upon you?* *B*

260.26 superfluities and idle expences *R2*, *R4*: superfluities, & idle
expences *R*: superfluities, and idle expenses *B*

261.12 other good *R2*, *R4*: other, good *R*

II.IV

262.7 verilie] verily *B*, *R4*: verelie *R2*: verlie *R*

262.9 cutt in sunder the neckes] *cut in sunder the neks* *B*: cut in sunder the neckes *R2*, *R4*: cutt the neckes *R*

263.34 me: and why] me: and why *R2*: me. And why *B*, *R4*: me,
& why *R*

264.3 lyfe? These men life? These men *B*, *R4*: life? Thes men *R2*:
lyfe? these men *R*

264.25 reasoneth S. Paul *B*, *R2*: reasoneth *S. Paul* *R4*: reasoneth,
S. Paul *R*

264.40 thou shalt *B*, *R2*: *thou shalt* *R4*: thou shall *R*

265.14 mercies bestowed *R2*, *R4*: mercies, bestowed *R*, *B*

265.17   *memorie, from* R, R2, R4: *memorie from* B
265.24   us a R2, R4: us a B: vs, a R
265.26   Psal.4. *R4: no sidenote in* R
266.29   posteritie B: prosperitie R, R2: prosperity R4
267.2   sufferinges and deathe] sufferinges and death R4: sufferinges,
         & deathe R: sufferinges, and death R2: sufferings, and death B
267.24   people? caused R2: people? Caused R4: people: caused R:
         peple: caused B
267.28   And yet afterward B, R2, R4, M: an yet afterwad R
268.6   greate and voluntarie R2: great and voluntary R4: greate,
         and voluntarie R
268.20   Le.10.] Leu.10. R4: Leui.10. B: 1.Le.10. R, R2
269.3   Genesis B, R2: *Genesis* R4: genesis R
269.9   Levit R2: *Leuite* R4: leuit R: leuite B
269.21   beastes and cattall] beastes and cattel R4: beastes, and cat-
         tel R2: beasts, and cattel B: beastes: and cattall R
269.28   *Iudiciis]* Iudicijs R2: iudicijs B, R4: Iuditiis R
269.29   judgementes? If] iudgementes. If R, R2, R4: *iudgements. If* B
269.34   as S. Paul saieth R2: as *S. Paul* saith R4: as S Paul saieth R
270.7   thy imagination B, R2, R4: the imagination R
270.23   Mat.7. B, R4: Ma.7. R, R2
270.32   Pharisees] Pharisies B, R4: pharisees R
271.10   Psal.145.] Psal.144. B: Psal.14. R, R2, R4
272.2   thought and acte R2: thought and act R4: thought, and
         acte R: thought, and act B
272.2   consequentlie M: consequently B, R2, R4: consequenlie R
272.18   by B, R2, R4, M: hy R
272.20   Mat.23. R2: Mat 23. R4: Mat.25. R, B
272.26   the mercie of God B: the mercy of God R4: thee mercie
         of God R, R2
272.30   fortie or fiftie R2: forty or fifty R4: fortie, or fiftie R, B
272.30   Titus and Vespasian R2: *Titus & Vespasian* R4: Titus, and
         Vespasian R
272.31   discomfited B: discomfaited R: ouerthrewe R2
272.37   same R2: sonne R: Son B: same mercy R4
273.12   furie and tormentes R2: fury of desperation & tormentes
         R4: furie, and tormentes R: furie, and torments B
273.24   feare of thy R: feare thy R2, R4: fear thy B
273.25   mercie. The B, R2, M: mercy. The R4: mercie The R
273.31   *R, B, R2 insert redundant additional* Eccle.7. *after* Eccle.15.: *R4 omits*

274.5   *corona & plenitudo sapientiæ, gloria R2, R4: corona, & sapientiæ*
        gloria R: corona; & plenitudo sapientiæ; gloria B

274.18 Psal.103.] Psal.62. *R, B, R2, R4*

274.24 lacked *B, R2, R4, M:* backed *R*

274.29 sayeing, God] saieng; God *B: saying, God R4: saying God R2:*
        sayeing god *R*

274.30 doeyngs? Yt] dooings? It *B: doings? It R2, R4:* doeyngs? yt *R*

274.32 whiche is, to] which is, to *R2, R4:* which is; to *B:* whiche
        is: to *R*

275.12 lett them not] *let them not R4:* lett hym not *R:* let him not
        B: let him not R2

275.16 Tho.secunda] Tho, secunda *R, R2: Thomas secunda B: D.Tho.*
        2.2. R4

275.21 divines for *R2:* Deuines for *R4:* diuines, for *R:* divines, for *B*

275.23 signifieth to be *B, R2, R4:* signifieth, to be *R*

276.20 new *R4, M:* now *R, B, R2*

277.8   serve and adore *B:* serue, and adore *R:* serue adore and
        honour *R2:* serue, adore, and honour *R4*

277.10 sayde, *timorem*] said, *timorem R2:* said: *Timorem R4:* said;
        Timorem B: sayde *timorem R*

277.13 *vestris, &c. cum modestia & timore R4: vestris, &c. cum modestia,*
        & timore R2: vestris & cum modestia, & timore B: vestris &c cum
        modestia, & timore R

278.1   Jon.3. *R4:* Ion.13. *R, B, R2*

278.8   *love or charitie R2: loue, or charitie R: love, or charitie B: perfect*
        charity R4

278.14 all, there is] al, there is *B, R2, R4:* all, there, is *R*

278.20 be:) it *M:* be,) it *R2:* be) it *B, R4:* be: (it *R*

278.31 receive eche] *receiue ech R4: receive ech B:* receiue, eche *R:*
        receiue, ech R2

279.8   wickednes *B, R2, R4, M:* wickcdnes *R*

279.13 *deceyve you with]* deceiue you with *R2, R4:* deceyue you, with *R:*
        deceive you, with B

279.16 tushe, God] Tush, God *B, R2: Tush, God R4:* tushe God *R*

II.V

280.5   The] THe *B, R2, R4, M:* THthe *R*

280.29 conversion and salvation *R2, R4:* conuersion, and saluation
        R: conversion, & salvation *B*

280.31 groweth into *B, R2, R4:* groweth, into *R*

281.5   necessitie and utilitie *R2*: necessity and vtility *R4*: necessi-
          tie, and vtilitie *R*: necessitie, and utilitie *B*

281.14   unto hym] vnto him *R2, R4, M*: unto him *B*: vnto, hym *R*

281.21   *to morow, to morow R2*: to-morrow, to-morrow *B*: *to morow to
          morow R*: *to morrow R4*

282.12   styrred up and strengthened] stirred vp and strengthened
          R2, R4: styrred vp and strengthened *R*: stirred up, and
          strengthened *B*

282.27   emptied *R2, R4*: empted *R*: empited *B*

283.14   twentie or fortie *R2*: twenty or forty *R4*: twentie, or fortie
          R, B

284.20   continuance *B, R2, R4, M*: continunace *R*

284.29   idlely *B, R2, R4*: Idlely *R*

284.29   dayes and times] daies and times *R2, R4*: dais and times
          B: dayes, and times *R*

284.33   this towardes God] this towards God *B*: this towardes
          almighty God *R4*: this, towardes God *R*: this, towardes
          almightie God *R2*

285.28   dreagges? Doest] dregges? Doest *R2, R4*: dregs? Dost *B*:
          dreagges? doest *R*

285.32   God? Folow *R2*: God? Follow *B, R4*: God? folow *R*

285.33   Eccle.12.] Eccle.5. *R*: Eccl.5. *B, R2, R4*

286.6   state: but] state? but *R*: state? But *B*: estate; but *R2*: estate,
          but *R4*

286.13   wickednes: doe] wickednes; doe *R2*: wickednes, doe *R, R4*:
          wickednes, do *B*

287.27   heade). But supposing] head. But supposing *R2*: head for
          euer. But supposing *R4*: heade) but supposing *R*; head) but
          supposing *B*

288.3   will not *R4. M*: wil not *B, R2*: vill not *R*

288.30   ex 50] *ex 50 R4*: & 50 *R, R2*

289.25   penance or satisfaction *R2*: pennance or satisfaction *R4*:
          penance, or satisfaction *R*

291.21   praye of lyfe, and] pray of life, and *R4*: praie of life; and
          R2: praye of lyfe: and *R*: pray of life: and *B*

292.6   effect *B, R2, R4*: affect *R*

292.13   *deceyved, God is not mocked: looke*] *deceiued, God is not mocked;
          looke R2, R4*: *deceyued: God is not mocked, looke R*: *deceived: God
          is not mocked, looke B*

292.37   man so] man, so *R, B*: man commonlie so *R2*

293.25 instant, beinge] instant, being *B, R2*: instant beinge *R*

293.26 were. For *M*: were, for *B*: were, For *R*

293.27 Jere.13. *B, R2*: Iere:13. *R*

293.36 goodes awaye] goodes awaie *R2*: goods away *B*: goodes, awaye *R*

294.11 Hom.41.ex.ho.50.] *Hom.41.ex 50 R4*: Hom.47.ex.ho.50. *R*: Hom.47.est.ho.50. *R2*

294.16 reste. But *R2*: rest. But *R4*: reste: But *M*: reste But *R*

294.17 sickenesse *R2, R4, M*: sicknenesse *R*

294.29 Where I am secure, I *R2, R4*: Where I am secure: I *R*

296.10 not. Wherfore *R2, R4*: not, wherfore *R*

296.22 penance at *R2*: pennance at *R4*: penance, at *M*: penance 'at *R*

296.28 Cor.11. *B*: Co.11. *R2*: Cor.11, *R*: Cor.11 *R4*

297.18 threate. For *R2, M*: threat. For *R4*: threate For *R*

298.6 brightnes and heate *R4*: brightnes, and heate *R, R2*

298.24 meanes for meate *R2*: meanes, for meate *R*

299.27 mourning? Will] mourning? Wil *R2*: moorning? Wil *B*: mourning? will *R*

299.30 writen: *The*] written; *The B*: writen, *The R2*: writen *The R*

299.31 *shalbe R2, M: shal be B: shalhe R*

300.8 that this *B, R2*: that, this *R*

300.11 wyse man] wise man *R2*: wise-man *R4*: wyse men *R*: wise men *B*

300.22 knockes *R2, R4, M*: knoks *B*: kuockes *R*

300.34 HEROD the] HEROD *the R2*: Herod the *R4: Herod the B*: HEROD.the *R*

300.36 Luc.9.] Luc.11. *R, B, R2, R4*

302.10 Luc.19.] Luc.21. *B, R2, R4*: Luc.21 *R*

303.10 therby, as *B, R2*: therby as *M*: therby. as *R*

303.18 onely gaine] *only gain B*: onely, gaine *R*

304.2 vowes *B, R2*: voues *R*

II.VI

305.26 fruit (which *R2, R4*: fruit (Which *R*

306.4 peece *B, R2, R4*: pece *R*

306.13 povertie *R2: povertie B: pouerty R4*: prouertie *R*

306.16 feare of *R2, R4*: feare, of *R*: fear, of *B*

306.18 Pro.18.] Pro.19. *R, B, R2*: Prou.19. *R4*

308.1 gayned to] gained to *R2, R4*: gayned, to *R*: gained, to *B*

308.16   2.Thess.3.] 1.The.3. *B*: Thess.3. *R, R2, R4*

308.31   kingdome] *kingdome B, R2: Kingdome R4*: kindome *R*

308.34   instantlie *R2, M: instantly B, R4*: instanlie *R*

308.34   for after this, there is nether] for after this, there is neither
         *R2: for after this, there is neither R4: for after it, there is neither
         B*: for there is nether *R*

308.35   nor knowlege] nor knowledge *R2: nor knowledge R4*: or knowl-
         ege *R: or knowledge B*

309.14   povertie and neede *R2*: pouerty and need *R4*: pouertie, and
         neede *R*: povertie, and need *B*

309.23   man,) *M: man,) R2: man) B, R4*: man,(*R*

310.7   careles and dissolute *R2*: carelesse and dissolute *R4*: care-
         les, and dissolute *R, B*

310.33   Revelations *B, R4*: reuelations *R, R2*

311.30   bringeth *R2, R4, M*: brinheth *R*

312.12   neighbours *R2, R4*: neighbors *B*: neigbours *R*

312.31   Psa.1.] Ioh.1. *R*: Iohn.1. *R2*: Ioan.1. *R4*

313.17   *should not be so muche as once named amonge Christians*] italics *B,
         R4: roman R, R2*

314.1   to shew *B, R2, R4, M*: te shew *R*

315.25   Act.26.] Act.26.27. *R, R2*: Act 26.27. *R4*: Acts.26.27. *B*

315.26   Foelix *R2*: Felix *B: Felix R4*: foelix *R*

316.1   persist, without ether *R2*: persist, without either *B, R4*: per-
         sist without, ether *R*

316.13   *nobis, & B, R2, R4: nobis. & R*

316.28   harted Jewes. *R4: harted Iews. B*: harted.Iewes. *R: harted.Iewes. R*

317.1   chaunge the custome] change the custom *B*: change the
         custome *R2, R4*: chaunge custome *R*

317.13   more, &c?] *more, &c? B*: more, &c. *R4*: more &c? *R, R2*

318.1   whiche is as muche to saye, as if *R*: Which is as much to
         say, as if *B*: which is in effect as much, as if *R2*: Which is
         in effect as much, as if *R4*

318.2   trouble us *R2, R4, M*: Trouble us *B*: trouble: vs *R*

318.14   Psa.58.] Psa.75. *R*: Psal. 75. *B*

319.12   dissolute. If *B, R2, R4, M*: dissolute If *R*

320.15   (as *B, R2, R4, M*: (as *R*)

321.7   *dei: doe*] Dei: doe *R4: Dei: Do B*: Dei; doe *R2: dei doe R*

321.10   Agayne: *non*] Againe: *Non R4*: Againe; *non R2*: Again; *Non B*:
         Agayne *non R*

321.17   spirite, doe] spirit, doe *R2, R4*: spirit, do *B*: spirite doe *R*

321.27 *respiciam, nisi* B, R2, R4: *respiciam nisi* R

321.34 pauperculus.) Also] *Pauperculus.) Also* R2, R4: *Pauperculus:)* also B: pauperculus) Also R

323.28 thou wast B: thou was R

324.30 embrace thee, with R2, R4: imbrace thee, with B: embrace, thee with R

COMMENTARY

For scriptural and patristic references given by Persons in the side-notes, and for a list of parallel passages in Luis de Granada, see the appendices. This commentary supplements these identifications where necessary, notes difficulties in tracing sidenote references, discusses textual cruces and glosses, records Persons's responses to Bunny in the *R2* sidenotes, and draws attention to certain features of the *R2* and *R4* revisions.

Title page. *RESOLUTION*. For the precise meaning of this word, as the settlement of inner conflict over obedience to God's call, see the Introduction, 'Sources and Influences'. A contemporary psychological explanation is offered by William Meissner, *Ignatius of Loyola: The Psychology of a Saint* (New Haven: Yale UP, 1992): 'In the case of the pilgrim of Manresa, the difficult psychic crisis he endured undoubtedly brought about a regressive state, marked by severe suicidal depression, a loss of ego boundaries in which the capacity to differentiate self and object was undetermined, and acute identity diffusion. As the conversion process continued, the *resolution* allowed for the shaping of a new identity, now cast specifically in religious and spiritual terms.' (p. 36, my italics)

PREFACE

5.2. *TWO EDITIONS OF THIS BOOKE*. 'This booke' is Gaspar de Loarte's *Esercitio della vita christiana*; the two 'editions' are Brinkley's translation (1579) and the *Resolution*, planned as an expansion of Loarte, adding, as it is put below, 'two partes of three'. Originally Persons designed a three-part work, the third part to consist of an adaptation of Loarte: hence Persons's title *The firste booke of the Christian exercise*. See the Introduction, 'Stages of Composition'.

6.7. *our dayes, most unhappie*. This lament, blaming the Reformation for time-wasting 'jangling abowte the foundation', is omitted by Bunny. He abridges the preface and converts it into the third person, explaining that 'we might have heard [it] in his own words, but that he interlaceth other things withal, that I dare not in conscience and dutie to God comment unto thee' (sig. *5v). The other objectionable matter is the argument that virtuous life is the best way to come to true faith.

R2 emphasizes even more strongly that an undivided church fosters devotion; previous generations 'receav[ed] with humilitie one uniforme faith without contention or contradiction, from their mother the holie Catholique Church' (fol. 6v).

7.29. *under indurance.* Stephen Brinkley, Persons's printing assistant and the translator of Loarte, was arrested in July 1581 when their press was seized at Stonor Park. He was imprisoned in the Tower until mid-1583, after which he rejoined Persons in France. See *Persons Notes*, pp. 30–31.

INDUCTION

8.13. *speculatyve.* The rest of the Induction implies that *R* is concerned with the 'praktike' part, virtuous life, rather than 'theorike', right belief. Yet the Preface to *R2* (fols. 6v–7) advertises that the first book of the *Christian Directorie* would form the 'Speculative' part, with the projected second and third books forming the 'Practive'. This reflects a shift in the meaning of 'speculative' from 'theological' or 'doctrinal', as here, to 'motives for resolution'. The latter sense, of course, applies well to *R*.

PART I CHAPTER I

13.30. *praye for theym.* The old dative form (ME *eym*) is used.

PART I CHAPTER II

14.1. *consideration. R2*, omitting the chapter on the purposes of the book, commences with a much expanded discussion of consideration, which emerges as a more reflective process. Early reference (p. 14) is made to the *Treatise on Consideration* by Bernard, which is only mentioned incidentally at the very end of *R* (pp. 421, 23). E.B. Broderick, *Robert Persons: The Christian Directory: Prolegomena to an edition* (Unpublished Ph.D. thesis, Fordham University, 1951) pp. 180–81, quotes Bernard's definition: 'The first effect of consideration is to purify the mind which has given it birth. Then it regulates the affections, directs the actions, cuts away all excessives, forms the character, orders and ennobles the life, and lastly, it endows the understanding with a knowledge of things divine and human. It is consideration which distinguishes what is confused, unites what is divided, collects what is scattered, discovers what is concealed, searches out what is true, examines what is probable, exposes what is false and deceptive. It is consideration which preordains what we have to do, and passes in review what has been accomplishes, so that nothing disordered may remain in the mind, nor anything requiring correction. It is consideration, finally, which in prosperity makes provision for adversity, and thus endures misfortune, as it were, without feeling it, of which the former is the part of prudence, and the latter the function of fortitude.' (tr. anon., Dublin: Brown and Nolan, 1921, p. 20: Latin text in the Cistercian edition of the *Opera*, Vol. 3: 403–04) For the importance of 'consideration' in continental meditative works, see Ceri Sullivan, *Dismembered Rhetoric: English Recusant Writing, 1580–1603* (Madison, NJ: Fairleigh Dickinson UP, 1995), pp. 42–44, 53.

Shakespeare uses the term 'consideration' in a description (by the Archbishop of Canterbury) of the process by which Prince Hal is transformed into Henry V:

> Consideration like an angel came,
> And whipp'd the offending Adam out of him. . . .
>
> (*Henry V*, I.i.28–29)

J.H. Walter discusses the term in some detail in his introduction to the play, referring to Bernard and to the sermons of John Donne and Lancelot Andrewes (New Arden edition; London: Methuen, 1954, pp. xviii–xix).

PART I   CHAPTER III

21.1. *the ende for which man was created*. Ignatius defines it thus: 'to praise, reverence and serve God Our Lord, and by so doing to save his or her soul' (*The Spiritual Exercises*, 23, in *Personal Writings*, ed. and tr. Joseph A. Munitiz and Philip Endean, Harmondsworth: Penguin, 1996, p. 289). *R2* inserts an extremely long chapter on the proofs for God's existence; an equivalent to this chapter follows, commencing with a philosophical and scriptural exposition of the purpose of human life, based on the argument that all earthly creatures are designed to serve a higher end. The chapter ends with detailed examples of famous men, such as Herod, Agrippa, Alexander the Great, Julius Caesar and Belshazzer, who neglected their divine calling to pursue worldly ends.

21.24. *condition of our creation*. *R4* continues (p. 25): 'the condition of our creation upon earth, as Moyses wel expresseth; *that we should be a holy people to serve our God*' (Deut 14:2): hence my emendation of the sidenote from Gen 14 to Deut 14.

21.28. *holynes and justice*. *R2* and *R4* adopt Bunny's '*holines and righteousnes*', but reinforce references to salvation by works, e.g. (cf. lines 31–4 below): 'our ende and final cause of being in this worlde, is to serve God, and therby to worke our owne salvation'.

22.34. *contrarie case*. There but for the grace of God, in Persons's view, might many young Catholic men have gone, who, instead, were constant even to martyrdom: 'learned men brought up in thadversaries owne scooles, and to whom yf they would have folowed the pleasures of the world or yeelded in any one little poynt against the truthe it had byn lawfull to have lived both in favor and credit' (*Persons Letters*, 121–22; letter attributed to Persons, 26 Nov. 1581).

PART I CHAPTER IV

26.22. *two speciall thinges required*. *R2* defers these two obligations, to resist sin and practise virtue, for two chapters. In answer to the question 'what service this is that God requireth' (p. 132), he simply identifies: 'Religion', and proceeds to demonstrate the supremacy of the Christian religion. There follows a chapter explaining 'How a man may judge or discerne of him self, whether he be a true Christian or not', referring to the two parts of Christian profession: belief and life. This recalls some of the matter in *R*'s Induction. Only then does *R2* consider the two obligations of shunning sin and practising virtue.

31.32. *marye*. Here and elsewhere, *R2* silently replaces the expression to which Bunny objected, obscuring the concession by an expansion:

'albeit he were assaulted with many strong and violent temptations of the flesh, by Satans suggestion: yet by his owne diligent resistance together with the assistance of Gods holy grace . . . he preserved his minde so pure and unspotted'. (p. 328)

31.34. *externall helpes*. 'These thinges Bunney clippeth as not so necessarie for Ministers'. (*R2*, p. 329)

32.8. *greate store of examples*. 'Bunney doubteth whether S. Anthonie had sufficient groundworke of his doinge; but Athanasius doubted not' (*R2*, p. 329; referring to Bunny's mn to p. 184.11 below).

33.14. *infinite monumentes*. 'All thes things donne for the Church Bunny leaveth out as no good deeds, though he doe dedicate the booke to an Archbishop, and doe feed of the rentes hym self. So leaveth he out also hospitals. &c.' (*R2*, pp. 342–43). *R2* accordingly adds more instances, e.g. 'Monasteries . . . Conventes . . . Cells, Oratories', and sharpens the political point, 'we make no scruple at all, to spoile the poore and godlie of thes benefites and releefes, which were left unto them by our holie forefathers'.

35.22. *encreaseth his merit*. 'Note that Bunny thrusteth out this word MERIT not onlie here, but in al the booke besides, which is almost in everie leafe of auncient fathers wrytinges, as also expresselie Eccles. 16. v.15. and the value thereof, which is retribution for good workes, is in everie place of scripture. Gen. 4. v.4. Exod. 1.20. Lev. 11.43. Psal. 118.112. Mat. 5.12. 2.Tim. 4.8. Heb. 11.26. &c.' (*R2*, p. 346)

PART I CHAPTER V

43.12. *the paines of the wicked are . . . augmented*. *R2* provides several examples of harmful writers such as heretics and 'dissolute Poets and other loose writers' (p. 354). This passage in *R2* made Sir John Harington feel uneasy about his translation of Ariosto's *Orlando Furioso* (see the edition by Robert McNulty, Oxford: Clarendon Press, 1972, p. 558).

43.17. *second judgement*. Before giving the continuous account of the Second Coming from Revelation, Persons creates a unified image of the Day of Judgement from material dispersed throughout the rest of the Bible: the two accounts in the synoptic gospels of Christ's 'Eschatological Discourses' (Mark 13; Matt 24–5, interpreting the 'abomination of desolation' as the Last Judgement), Luke, 1 and 2 Cor, Eccl and Isa.

In contrast, *R2*, instead of structuring the material according to biblical sources, gives a more comprehensive and analytical account of the final day of judgement, divided into three parts: 'preparations', 'thinges that must passe in this judgement' (the arrival of the judge and the gathering of the people) and 'the end and that which shal ensue' (the passing of sentence). The gospel accounts are replaced with passages from Dan and Ezek, prophesying the tribulations and the appearance of the Antichrist before the Last Judgement, under the heading 'Of preparations'. Persons quotes from Gregory: 'it behoveth that many transitorie calamities should goe before; to denounce unto us the endles woes which are to come after' (*R2*, p. 357). *R2* also moves the gospel passage about the sheep and goats to the third section, to represent the delivery of the verdict.

44.13. *tribunall of Christ*. Presumably Bunny found this term too closely associated with ancient Rome; Persons re-affirmed it in a new passage in *R2* emphasizing its awefulness: 'And finally, that this accompt or day of reconning, (for declaration of the terrour and maiestie that shalbe vsed therin,) is called here by Christ, a judgment and tribunal, wherin sentence of life or death is to be pronounced'. (pp. 351–52)

47.31. *most terrible and fearce preparations*. *R2* greatly expands the description of the actual process of judgement. A particularly effective addition is a paragraph about the coming together of soul and body for judgement: 'Good God, what a marvailous daie shal this be, when we shal see al the children of Adam gathered together from al corners and quarters of the earth; when (as S. John saieth) the sea and land shal yeeld their dead bodies, and both hel and heauen shal restore the soules which they possesse, to be united to thos bodies? What a wonderful meeting wil this be, (deare Christian,) how joyful to the good, and how lamentable, doleful, and terrible to the wicked? The godlie and righteous, being to receyve the bodies wherin they lived, into the league & felowship of their eternal blisse; shal embrace them with al possible sweetnes and delight, singing with the prophet; *Behold, how good and pleasant a thing it is, for brethern (or parteners) to dwel together in unitie.* But the miserable damned spirites, beholding the carcases which were the instruments and occasions of their sinne; & wel knowing that their inspeakable tormentes, shalbe encreased by their mutual conjunction and association: shal abhorre and utterly detest the same, & curse the daie that ever they were acquainted together; inveighing most bitterly against all the partes and senses therof, as against the eies, for whos curious delighte so many vanities were sought; the eares, for whos pleasure and daliance so great varietie of sweet sounds and melodie was procured; the mouth and taste, for whos contentement and fond satisfaction, so innumerable delicacies were deuised. And to be short, the backe and belly with other sensual partes, for contentation of whos riotous volupteousnes, both sea and land were sifted and turmoiled.' (pp. 368–9)

48.21. *take no paine for their salvation.* Unusually, *R2* adopts Bunny's alteration to 'in the service of God', as well as several others in this paragraph: 'On the right hand . . . on the left hand . . . al damned soules bewailing' (p. 371). Since Persons claimed to respond to Bunny only in his marginal notes, the presence of Bunny variants in the main text of *R2* is hard to explain. For a more detailed discussion, see my note 'Persons Cannibalized Again', *Notes and Queries*, 242 (1997): 32–33.

49.4. *drie up for verie feare.* Actually in Luke 21:26, in a passage paralleled in Matt 24:29–30 (sidenote).

51.4. *dewe examination.* Where Bunny glosses this as a subjective experience with the preface 'an earnest longing after [the day of judgement], which never is had until first there go before a du examination', Persons in *R2* expands 'amendment of lyfe' to include 'the workes of pietie and holy conversation'. (p. 377)

PART I CHAPTER VI

51.16. *nature of sinne.* This consideration is central to the First Week of *The Spiritual Exercises*, 46–54. See Ignatius of Loyola, *Personal Writings*, pp. 294–96.

56.15. *every litle dropp of bloode.* This sentiment, omitted by Bunny, appears in Sir Henry Wotton's lyric, 'A Hymn to my God in a night of my late Sicknesse' as a Protestant repudiation of Catholic 'helps':

No hallowed oyls, no grains I need,
No rags of Saints, no purging fire,

One rosie drop from Davids Seed
Was worlds of seas, to quench thine Ire.
O pretious Ransome! which once paid,
That Consummatum Est was said. . . .

(*The Metaphysical Poets*, ed. Helen Gardner, Harmondsworth: Penguin, 1957, p. 45.)

56.22. *never left to laye on. R2* intensifies this passage considerably: 'he never ceased to add affliction to affliction, and to heape tormentes upon the bodie and flesh of this his most deare and blessed sonne, (for by Esaye, he sayeth, that him self was the doer therof;) until he had brought him unto that most rueful plight, that his flesh being all mangled and most lamentably torne in peeces, retained no one droppe of blood within it'. (p. 386)

57.1. *the sinne of Esau.* Esau's inability to repent haunted Bunyan in *Grace Abounding*: see paragraphs 141, 145, 163, 191, 216, 225–27. Persons uses it simply to enforce the heinousness of sin and the necessity of grace.

57.14. *weepinge, fastinge, watchinge.* 'All thes bodilie punishmentes Bun. leaveth out, notwithstanding they be set doune in scripture.' (*R2*, p. 387)

PART I CHAPTER VII

69.31. *some greate man. R2* clarifies the analogy with the angels by substituting 'some of his principal Peres'.

PART I CHAPTER VIII

78.1. *to the gate of death. R*'s 'arriue to, at the last daie, weryed' is evidently corrupt. *R2*'s reading may be a revision rather than a correction, but I have adopted it as an extant, plausible reading in preference to the alternative, 'arrive to the gate of death at the last daie'.

80.17. *often . . . thinke them selves damned. R* repeats 'often' in 'often damned', probably in error, as Augustine's original reads: '*pro quibus etiam se damnatos existimant*', where *etiam* means 'repeatedly'.

82.9. *for his bodie.* This passage echoes Augustine, *Sermo ad fratres in eremo,* c. 50, which is cited in error later in this chapter. (p. 90.14)

84.11. *Saint Cyprian.* 'Note here that Bun. rejecteth not only thes authorities of S. Cyprian and Possidonius, but also the whole discourses folowing of S. Augustine, S. Gregorie, and of venerable Bede: for that they talke of apparitions.' (*R2,* p. 432)

86.38. *Yf thow be a Christian.* The following passage, probably the best-known in the book, is an extensive elaboration of Luis de Granada, *The Sinners Guide,* I, 7.9: 'Remember, therefore, that you are a man and a Christian. As man, you know you are to die, and as a Christian, you know you are to give an account of your life as soon as dead. Daily experience will not permit us to doubt the one, nor the faith we profess let us call the other into question. Every one of us all lies under this necessity. Kings and popes must submit to it. The day will come when you shall not live to see night, or a night when you shall not survive till day. The day will come, and you know not whether it may not be this very day or tomorrow, when you yourself, who are now reading this treatise in perfect health, and who perhaps think the number of your days will be answerable to your business and wishes, shall be stretched out in your bed, with a taper in your hand, expecting the last stroke of death, and the execution of that sentence which is passed upon all mankind, and from which there is no appeal.' (anon. tr. Philadelphia: Eugene Cummiskey, 1833, pp. 55–56.) Persons's version is quoted from *R2* by Louis Martz, *The Poetry of Meditation* (New Haven: Yale University Press, 1954), pp. 134–35.

88.21. *flootinge.* 'unstable, uncertain' (*OED* fleeting 4).

88.34. *prevent it.* Subsequent versions expand this brief exhortation. *R2* elaborates on the comfort of past good deeds on the day of death, and expounds six benefits of regular meditation on death. *R4* commends alms-giving as a special defence against a bad conscience in the hour of death, citing examples of divine favour to benefactors. Several pages on the use of the death's head follow (pp. 194–201). For an analysis of the revision of this chapter, see my article 'A Jesuit *memento mori*: The Passage of Death in the *Resolution* of Robert Persons', *Southern African Journal of Medieval and Renaissance Studies,* 5 (1995): 75–96.

PART I CHAPTER IX

95.30. *a hundred like sayinges.* 'Note that Bun. turneth of here, thes and al other fathers that speake of Purgatorie. He is not of their opinion.' *R2*, p. 453. Accordingly, *R2* reinforces the traditional authorities for Purgatory in the next paragraph: 'And *truly* it is *verie* straunge *and wonderful* to consider, how great feare *and terrour* holie men *of auncient time* conceyved *at the verie cogitation of* this fire, and how *slenderly* we passe the same over now a daies, having *infinite* more cause to feare then they had. Among other *that blessed devout man* S. Bernard, *who lead so examplar and strict a life as the world doth know; entering into contemplation of this matter, broke forth into thes words ensuing . . .*' (p. 454; additions to *R* in italics) *R4* interpolates several pages of examples and admonitions concerning purgatory, drawn from various passages in Augustine. (pp. 215–27)

95.38. *the place before.* This refers to 'Hom. 16 ex Homiliis 50' (sidenote, p. 94.27), whereas 'in the same place' (line 39 below) refers to the *Enarratio in Ps 37* mentioned in the sidenote here.

96.26. *discussed to his handes. OED* sense 5, 'made known, declared', is probably meant here.

97.29. *the old fathers. R4*, p. 229, refers us to Augustine, *Retractiones*, II.24 (*PL* 32: 640; *FC* 60: 169).

98.33. *hinnom.* See Lev 18:2 and Jer 19:5–6, for child sacrifice.

99.9. *the names. R2* adds Tophet, citing Isa 30:33.

99.32. *his teeth.* The attempt to make hell frightening by projection from the temporary and particular to the eternal and universal is commonplace. Cf. a reference to Persons's contemporary William Perkins in *The Life and Death of Mr Vavasor Powell* (1671): 'At this time the Lord visited me with a very sore and great pain of the toothache . . . and by another good providence I met with a little book of Mr. Perkins, and in that, with this expression, if the pains of one little bone, or tooth, be so grievous for a few days, what then will the pains of the whole body and soul be in hell for evermore? Upon this my terrour began in Conscience to that degree, that it made the other pain to seem somewhat more easier.' (p. 4)

103.8. *Ephraem.* Not traced in the works of Ephraem of Syria.

109.13. *worldlie*. The fact that *R*'s 'wordlie' is repeated in *R2* and *R4* indicates that they were printed from marked-up copy, not from a new ms.

112.17. *remedies*. *R4* adds several pages commending the practice of the sacrament of confession and absolution (pp. 251–60). The Jesuits were renowned for administering this sacrament in such a way as to promote an inner change of heart as the prelude to the serious practice of religion. This material would be appropriate in Persons's projected second book of resolution: how to begin well. See O'Malley, *The First Jesuits*, p. 137.

PART I   CHAPTER X

112.22. *motives*. *R2* makes so much concession to Bunny, who prefers 'reasons' to 'motives', as to include 'motives, reasons and considerations', thus turning a substitution into an expansion.

116.15n. *The creation of Angels*. *R4* cites Aquinas, *Summa Theologiae*, 1a, 50, 3 (Blackfriars ed., London: Eyre & Spottiswoode, Vol. 9: 16–21) and Dionysius Areopagitica, *De caelesti hierarchia*, I.14 (*PL* 122: 1064).

117.14. *like veins in the bodie*. In view of Persons's association with the Spanish cause, particularly strong from 1588, it is worth noting that John Donne, in 'Elegy XI: The Bracelet', uses this image to describe Spanish gold, which corrupts all Europe: 'As streames, like veines, run through th'earth's every part' (*Poems*, ed. H.J.C. Grierson, 1912, I:97). Grierson's commentary (II:77) quotes Ralegh: 'It is his Indian gold that endangers and disturbs all the nations of Europe; it creeps into councils, purchases intelligence, and sets bound loyalty at liberty in the greatest monarchies thereof.'

119.20. *number of thy wisdom*. This is a literal rendering of Augustine's '*numerus sapientiae tuae*'; *R2* offers a more elegant expansion: 'number of thy merits, nor depth of thie wisdome'. (p. 490)

121.28. *horrour . . . to turne into his mothers wombe again*. An exception was the 'brave infant of Saguntum' who, horrified at the prospect of his city devastated by Hannibal, returned immediately to the womb (Pliny, *Natural History*, VII.iii.40–42). See Ben Jonson's 'To the Immortal Memory and Friendship of That Noble Pair, Sir Lucius Cary and

Sir H. Morison', lines 1–8 (*Selected Poetry*, ed. G. Parfitt, Harmondsworth: Penguin, 1992, p. 139).

122.18. *made gloriouse.* See Aquinas, *Summa Theologia*, 3a, 54, 1–2 (Blackfriars ed., Vol. 55: 18–27).

124.35. *seven qualities.* 'Al thes thinges Bun. either rejecteth, or mangleth: perhappes, as not appertaining to the bodies of Protestantes.' (*R2*, p. 498)

125.23. *seing God, as he is.* See 1 John 3:2.

126.18. *doctor.* Not traced in Hugo de Folieto, *De anima claustro* (*PL* 176) or Augustine, *De anima et eius origine* (*PL* 44).

131.26. *meet with all her godlie freendes in heaven.* 'Bun. rejecteth here this beleefe of S. Cyprian touching knowledge in heaven, of fathers and mothers &c. But everie man of reason, can put a difference betwene a Cyprian and a Buney.' (*R2*, p. 509)

135.5. *The kyngdome of heaven suffereth violence.* 'Note that Bun. thrusteth out, as wel thes wordes of Christ, as thos that issue of S. Augustine: and therby sheweth, that he spareth th'Evangelist no more then th'ancient fathers, when he misliketh their writinges.' (*R2*, p. 514)

136.2. *pudle water.* Richard Crashaw develops a contrast between the puddle water of earthly pleasure and the wine of heaven in 'An Apologie for the precedent Hymne' [to St Teresa]:

> . . . let others swimme
> In puddles, we will pledge this Seraphim
> Bowles full of richer blood then blush of grape
> Was ever guilty of, change wee our shape,
> My soule, some drinke from men to beasts; o then,
> Drinke wee till we prove more, not lesse then men. . . .

(*Works*, ed. L.C. Martin, 1927, p. 137.)

PART II CHAPTER I

141.1. *THE SECOND PART. R2* has a Preface to Part Two, explaining Satan's role in countering the motives dealt with in Part One, and then inserts an entirely new chapter on 'the mistrust and diffidence in Gods mercies'. The reason given in the earlier Preface, fol. 20v, is that he was criticized for emphasizing God's justice at the expense of His mercy.

142.3. *holy S. Austen.* The material in this paragraph has not been traced in Hom. 16 ex 50 (*PL* 39: 2210–12), although Augustine does suggest that the pains of purgatory may be avoided by putting out the fire of concupiscence.

142.33. *My yooke is sweete.* On this theme, cf. Antonio de Guevara, *Epistolae familiares*, 4, reprinted in *The Spirit of the Spanish Mystics*, ed. Kathleen Pond (New York: P.J. Kenedy and Sons, 1958), pp. 10–16.

145.28. *S. Paul.* 'This grace geven to S. Paul, Bun. striketh out; for fear, least by S. Pauls example, any man should think himself able (with the helpe of Gods grace) to resist such temptations.' (*R2*, p. 580) *R2* also clarifies 'grace' by adding two paragraphs on 'the manifold and sundry helpes [sc. Catholic ceremonies and disciplines], that almightie God doth lend to man, for the facilitating of the way of his holie commandementes'. (p. 578)

146.25. *just man. R*'s 'iust (man)', followed by *R2*, may represent Persons's uncertainty how to translate the Vulgate's '*dextera iusti mei*' (Isa 41:10).

147.11. *choler or angre.* 'Here Bun. besides al other patching and cobling, maketh a long and idle annotation how that we doe hold, that the soule doth follow the temperature of the body; and therupon doe build that our B. Ladie was conceaued without sinne. And other like doctrine: wherin the poore man lieth fondlie not knowing what we hold, nor what him self saith.' (*R2*, p. 582)

148.33. *whome shall I . . . tremble?* OED cites Thomas Stapleton, *A fortresse of the faithe* (1565), p. 104, for the meaning 'tremble at': 'That which the devil, above al thinges, trembleth'.

153.28. *light of understandinge. R2* elaborates: 'For as in bodilie sight and in viages of this world, it falleth out, that he which hath good eyes and seeth perfectelie, goeth on his way with far greater alacritie, joy, and securitie, then doth an other that either lacketh that sense, or hath it very dimme: So in the course of our soule in this life, it is of no lesse importance and comfort . . . for a man to have this celestial understanding . . .; that is, to know what he doth, see wher he walketh, discerne wither he goeth, conceave what he expecteth. . . .' (pp. 591–92)

156.34. *newlye to his service*. On the immediate rewards given to the newly resolved, Ignatius writes (in a letter to Teresa Rejadell, 1536): '[the enemy] does not get us to think about the abundant comforts and consolations normally given by the Lord if the new servants of the Lord shatter these difficulties by choosing to desire to suffer with their Creator and Lord' (*Personal Writings*, p. 130). In *The Spiritual Exercises*, 316, he defines 'consolation' as 'all interior happiness that calls and attracts a person towards heavenly things and to the soul's salvation, leaving the soul quiet and at peace in her Creator and Lord'. (*Personal Writings*, p. 349)

157.33. *tormented with in it selfe*. R2 makes it clear that 'it' refers to the conscience: 'the wicked man, having his conscience vexed with the privitie and guilt of many sinnes, the same is alwaies tormented within it selfe; as we reade that the conscience of wicked Cain was'. (p. 597)

166.13. *affectuouse*. Fervent, earnest.

170.17. *sacrament of confession*. 'Here Bun. is inforced to mangle extremly.' (*R2*, p. 615). The 'excessive consolations' referred to below (p. 171.7) were commonly associated with the early Jesuit ministry of confession. See O'Malley, *The First Jesuits*, pp. 134–52.

170.31. *Effrem*. Not traced in Joannes Moschus, *De vitis patrum* (*PL* 74), commonly known as the *Pratum spirituale*. Similarly, the reference to Geoffrey of Auxerre's *S. Bernardi vita* (*PL* 185) is untraced.

171.22. *large discourse*. *R4*, pp. 392–94, provides the discourse from Cyprian in full.

174.3. *many . . . poyntes*. 'Here Bun. maketh an impious note upon this conversion' (*R2*, p. 620)—or rather, on Persons's interpretation of Augustine's conversion.

174.23. *finding by chaunce*. 'Al this storie Bun. cutteth out, saving certaine ragges of his owne making.' (*R2*, p. 621)

181.3. *discourse out of S. Barnard*. The source is in fact Geoffrey of Clairvaux, *De colloquio Simonis cum Jesu ex sermonibus Bernardi*, xlvii, 'De labore ficto' (*PL* 184: 467), reporting a sermon by Bernard.

PART II CHAPTER II

186.37. *Jerome.* Not traced in Jerome, *Adversus Jovinianum* (*PL* 23).

191.5. *these thinges.* *R4*'s correction from 'those thinges' (*R*) is supported by the Vulgate reading: *'merito haec patimur'* (Gen 42:21).

195.1. *this rope draweth not.* An interesting gloss on George Herbert's 'The Collar', lines 22–24, where the speaker claims, like Persons's reprobate here, that God's rope is a 'rope of sands' and not 'good cable, to enforce and draw' (*Works*, ed. F.E. Hutchinson, 1941, p. 153).

200.6. *imparte both of his, with us.* Although *R2* and *R4* correct to the more familiar 'unto us', I have retained *R*'s reading, taking it to mean 'in our case'.

203.20. *propter dolos.* As Bunny points out, Persons consistently uses the Vulgate's Latin translation of the Psalms according to the Septuagint rather than the Hebrew. Jerome, *Breviarum in Psalmos* (*PL* 26: 1031), *pace* Bunny, gives the same reading (*'propter dolos'*).

203.26. *Gregorie.* Not traced in Gregory the Great, *Moralia, sive expositio in librum Job* (*PL* 75).

207.33. *unto you.* A rare example of 'you' when addressing Christ, pursued for several lines in *R* but corrected to 'the' in *R2*, p. 669.

220.14. *eversion.* Overthrowing or overturning of the past.

PART II CHAPTER III

228.18. *madnes.* Ps 39:5 in the Vulgate (following Septuagint) has *'vanitates et insanias falsas'* where English translations (Ps 40:4) favour the Hebrew, *'superbias pompasque mendacii'*. Similarly, at 230.4 below, the Septuagint text, *'nimis honorificati sunt amici tui'*, differs materially from the Hebrew.

233.23. *fayre cover.* J.H. Crehan, 'The Prose of Robert Parsons', *The Month*, 175 (1940): 373, quotes this passage to explain why Persons uses a plain style.

240.4. *understanded.* The substitution of 'understood' in *B, R2* and *R4* bears witness to the obsolescence of this form, which was common, claims *OED*, until 1575. A frequently quoted instance is in Article XXIV of the *Thirty-Nine Articles of Religion*, rejecting the use, in public worship, of a language 'not understood of the people'.

243.36. *first heremite*. 'This example Bunnie thrusteth out in despite of heremites.' (*R2*, p. 722)

251.5. *tribulation*. *R2* appears to recognize the justice of Bunny's objection, namely that sexual intercourse in marriage is not itself a tribulation, and expands the clause to read: 'yet is it accompanied (as S. Paul saith) *with tribulation*'. (p. 732)

251.9. *mischances*. Bunny refers us to Augustine, *Retractationes*, I.1 (*PL* 32: 585; *FC* 60: 6–7), who regrets appearing to attribute to a goddess (Fortune) what is owing to divine Providence. The Latin words he mentions—*forte, forsan, fortisan, fortasse, fortuito*—are more closely associated with Fortune than their English equivalents.

252.37. *Athanasius*. Although the *Life of St Anthony* (*FC* 15; *PL* 73) is full of references to the wiles and temptations of the devil, there is nothing that corresponds closely to this anecdote.

257.19. *feire of deceite*. *R2*'s 'marcket' makes it plain that Persons meant a fair rather than a fear: hence my emendation. This striking list is not found in the *Epistolae* of Augustine, although the basic argument occurs in Letter 32.

259.20. *fixing our mindes in*. An early use of the phrase, recorded (as 'fix on') from 1663 in *OED*.

261.21. *fyre everlasting*. *R2*, followed by *R4*, inserts a new chapter at this point, of 'examples of true resolution', interrupting the sequence of impediments.

PART II CHAPTER IV

266.6. *divines*. *R4*, p. 580, refers us to Aquinas, *Summa Theologia*, 1a, 63,2 (Blackfriars ed., Vol. 9: 250–55).

271.9. *above all his other works*. Persons follows the Septuagint's '*super omnia opera tua*', where the Hebrew has '*in universa opera eius*'. Bunny cites Augustine (*Enarrationes in Psalmos*, *PL* 37: 1877) and Jerome in support of his argument that this verse has little to do with the relative status of God's justice and mercy. However, Jerome (*Breviarum in Psalmos, PL* 26: 1247) reads '*super omnia opera eius*'.

272.29. *destruction*. Described in detail in Josephus, *De bello Judico*, Bk VI, but also mentioned several times in the initial survey in Bk I (as given in the sidenote).

273.24. *will I . . . feare of thy judgement*. Cf. Shakespeare's Sonnet 115: 'Fearing of love's tyranny'; I have therefore retained *R*'s reading against *B*, *R2* and *R4*.

275.10. *powre owte thy wrathe*. See Ps 69: 23–28.

276.27. *servile feare*. For the value of both servile and filial fear, see *The Spiritual Exercises*, 370 (Ignatius of Loyola, *Personal Writings*, p. 358).

PART II CHAPTER V

282.4. *established, and confirmed*. Unusually, *R2* and *R4* retain the strong pointing throughout the rest of this paragraph, suggesting that the pauses are deliberate. But 'more harder' (line 5), is revised to 'more hardely'.

282.35. *lyves of olde heremites*. Not traced in Joannes Moschus, *De vitis patrum* (*PL* 74—see note to 170.31 above).

286.8. *Gregorie*. Not traced in the works of Gregory the Great.

288.16. *auncient fathers*. 'Al the authorities of S. Cyprian, Aug. & Hierom. following Bun. leaveth out and mangleth most impudently.' (*R2*, p. 830)

288.19. *second booke*. The word 'satisfaction' suggests that confession and penance would feature prominently in the proposed second book of resolution, 'how to begin well'.

290.16. *Apostles*. 'Here Bun. wil needes bring in our lady also: affirming her to have broken three commandmentes at once, for that she defended not her sonne. God help the fond man.' (*R2*, p. 832)

294.10. *authorities*. 'Al this discourse of S. Augustin Bun. striketh out.' (*R2*, p. 838) For good measure, *R4* cites Duns Scotus, Hugh of St Victor, Suarez, Cyprian, and others. (pp. 614–22)

295.18. *Marke well.* 'Here Bun. putteth in a peece of S. Aug. againe, but suppresseth his name.' (*R2*, p. 839)

296.1. *sinne leaveth thee.* The 'notable sayeing' in the original Latin is: '*Si autem vis agere poenitentiam ipsam, quando jam peccare non potes; peccate te dimiserunt, non tu illa*' (*PL* 39: 1715).

298.27. *these men.* R4 cuts this satirical passage, possibly felt to be redundant in view of the multiplication of examples of delay. (pp. 628–55)

300.27. *HEROD the father.* In fact, these events all relate to Herod the tetrarch, who had John the Baptist beheaded (Matt 14; Mark 6), was curious about Jesus (Matt 14, Luke 9), and later tried him (Luke 23).

PART II   CHAPTER VI

306.18. *pigrum deiicit timor.* This phrase is added to Prov 18:8 in some texts of the Vulgate but is normally omitted.

306.23. *fast.* 'Bun. here striketh out the first two members of fasting and praying.' (*R2*, p. 855)

311.4. *any princes pleasure.* This glances at the church papists (Catholics who attended Anglican worship) for adapting their religious principles to please the prince.

311.29. *heresye.* 'This Bun. leaveth out.' (*R2*, p. 862)

323.27. *Heere thou mayest see.* R2 indicates how its major additions support or amplify the basic argument of the *Book of Resolution*: 'Here thou maiest behold ... first, that of necessitie thou must confesse there is a God that made thee and al the rest; the end and cause whie he created thee, which was to serve him; the only true way of which service, to be by fulfilling Christs holy commandementes; then, what things are required at thy handes in particular. . . .' (pp. 879–80)

325.34. *The ende.* R2 appends, first, a 'Breefe methode how to use the former treatise' (advising the reader which sections to consult in various states of mind); second, a ten-day cycle of meditation on the arguments for the existence of God and the supremacy of Christ; and, third, a two-week programme of meditation on 'matter more proper to stirre up our affections to pietie and devotion'.

SCRIPTURAL INDEX

The abbreviations used are those of the *OED*. Where appropriate, Persons's abbreviations are given in brackets. For the Psalms, Persons uses the Vulgate numbering, which I have adjusted to the standard system throughout. The numbers in brackets refer to page numbers in this edition of the *Book of Resolution*.

Judg 16:4–20 (164)
Judg 19–20 (269)

1 Sam (1 Re) 2:1–10 (197);
   30 (119)
1 Sam 5:3–5 (156)
1 Sam 9 (231b):21 (231a)
1 Sam 10–11 (267)
1 Sam 10:1 (57)
1 Sam 13:7–15 (267)
1 Sam 15 (57):9–23 (267)
1 Sam 16 (57, 231b):11 (231a);
   14 (267)
1 Sam 25:10 (246)
1 Sam 28:15–19 (39)
1 Sam 31:4 (267)

2 Sam (2 Re) 7 (220):1–3 (113)
2 Sam 11:2–27 (164, 188)
2 Sam 12 (39, 268):13–14 (57)
2 Sam 16:5–14 (293)
2 Sam 19:15–24 (293)
2 Sam 20:9–10 (245)

1 Kgs (3 Re) 2:8–9, 36–46 (293)
1 Kgs 3:9 (321)
1 Kgs 4:22 (224)
1 Kgs 6:7 (204)
1 Kgs 11 (225):1–13 (164)
1 Kgs 16:7 (242)
1 Kgs 17:1 (120)
1 Kgs 19:10 (209)
1 Kgs 22 (245)

2 Kgs (4 Re) 2:1–12 (220)
2 Kgs 5:1–14 (120)
2 Kgs 6:15–17 (143, 205)
2 Kgs 13:21 (120)

1 Chr (1 Para) 10:1–14 (267)

2 Chr 9 (2 Para) 224)
2 Chr 15:7 (213)
2 Chr 32:31 (193)
2 Chr 33:11–13 (191)

Tobit 2 (195):6 (242); 11 (185)
Tobit 3:6 (191)
Tobit 4:6 (58)
Tobit 5:12 (240)
Tobit 11:7–14 (190); 17 (195)
Tobit 12:6, 14 (185); 10 (58, 141)

Judith 6, 14, 15 (196)
Judith 8:21–26 (185)
Judith 16:1–21 (197); 21 (108)

Esther 1:1–4 (117)
Esther 5:9–13 (251)

1 Macc 1:1–10 (250)
1 Macc 2:17–21 (219)
1 Macc 6:8–13 (157)

2 Macc 7 (214)
2 Macc 9:11–28 (304); 18–27 (191)

Job 1, 2 (195)
Job 1:1–12 (185); 21 (237)
Job 3:24 (239, 240)
Job 5:7 (184); 17 (198, 218)
Job 7:1 (27, 184)
Job 8:13 (160)
Job 9:2–9 (65); 28 (31, 239, 274)
Job 10:21–22 (98a); 22 (98b)
Job 11:7–8 (97); 11 (51); 20 (160)
Job 13:12 (243); 115 (159); 13–28 (184)
Job 15:16 (253); 20–24 (158)
Job 17:14 (230)
Job 20:11 (284); 14–16 (103)
Job 21:12–13 (239); 13–14 (12); 14
   (316, 317)
Job 23:10 (191)
Job 27:19–23 (237)
Job 28:1–11 (236)
Job 33:16–17, 25 (192)

Ps 1:2 (15, 151, 312); 4 (159, 243)
Ps 3:6 (210); 7 (57)
Ps 4:1 (91); 2 (134, 233, 246); 5 (265)
Ps 5:5 (51, 242)
Ps 6 (57):1 (95)
Ps 7:9 (53); 13 (92)
Ps 9:5–6 (243); 16 (76); 16–17 (57);
   17 (94)
Ps 10:3 (58); 5 (62); 9 (228); 11, 13 (274)
Ps 11:5 (58); 6 (57, 253)
Ps 14:1–3 (52)
Ps 15:2 (137)
Ps 16:4 (194); 11 (153)
Ps 18:21 (63); 29 (210)
Ps 19:8–10 (151); 9 (64); 10 (144)
Ps 21:3 (128)
Ps 22:1 (56, 209)
Ps 23:4 (148, 196, 210)
Ps 25:8 (263); 8, 10 (262); 11 (74);
   12–14 (274)
Ps 26:2 (194)
Ps 27:1–3 (148); 3 (210); 12 (289)
Ps 28:4 (102); 5 (203); 7 (148)
Ps 30 (57, 268)
Ps 31:1 (97); 7 (196); 19 (119, 154,
   274); 22 (209)
Ps 32:7 (194)
Ps 34:9 (273); 15–16 (265); 19 (184);
   21 (88)

Wisd 9:15 (122)
Wisd 10:13 (204)
Wisd 14:9 (51)
Wisd 17:9 (130); 11 (158)

Ecclus 1:11, 13 (274); 21 (273)
Ecclus 2:1–2 (173); 5 (191); 8 (274); 15–17 (273); 13 (310)
Ecclus 3:26 (319)
Ecclus 4:28 (210)
Ecclus 5:1–10 (274); 6–7 (264); 8–9 (302)
Ecclus 7:19 (108); 29–36 (273); 36 (91)
Ecclus 10:10 (283); 13 (82)
Ecclus 11:4 (234); 21 (213)
Ecclus 12:6 (43)
Ecclus 14:20–23 (15)
Ecclus 15:1 (273); 6 (212); 9 (52)
Ecclus 18:14 (190); 19–20 (51)
Ecclus 21:2 (58); 10–11 (292)
Ecclus 22:1–2 (307)
Ecclus 23:6 (319); 8 (228); 19 (106)
Ecclus 27:5 (194)
Ecclus 31:2 (192); 5 (238)
Ecclus 35:26 (195)
Ecclus 40:9 (57)
Ecclus 41:1 (81, 249)

Isa 1:2 (73); 3 (76); 5 (191); 10–20 (28, 52); 16–17 (27); 24 (54)
Isa 2:10–22; 3:6–22; 34:1–10; 37:21–36; 61:1–3 (76)
Isa 4:4–6 (73)
Isa 5:14 (97); 18 (242)
Isa 6:2 (129)
Isa 10:27 (145)
Isa 11:1–5 (70); 2 (59); 2–9 (145)
Isa 12:2 (210)
Isa 13:3 (92); 9 (58); 13–14 (43)
Isa 14:9 (98); 12 (97); 12–15 (266)
Isa 25:6 (118)
Isa 26:10 (108); 16 (194)
Isa 27:8 (92, 102)
Isa 28:15 (20, 160, 317); 17 (102)
Isa 29:9–10 (155)
Isa 30:1–3 (160)
Isa 35:10 (128)
Isa 36:6 (160)
Isa 38:8 (120); 14 (15); 17–18 (97)
Isa 40:4 (145)
Isa 41:10–13 (146)
Isa 48:4 (318); 22 (166)
Isa 51:11 (128)
Isa 53:3 (198); 4–10 (56)
Isa 54:13 (153)

Isa 55:6 (304)
Isa 56:4–5 (190)
Isa 57:20 (167); 21 (166)
Isa 59:4–6 (247); 10 (154)
Isa 63:15–17 (208)
Isa 64:4 (114)
Isa 66:1 (65); 2 (321); 11 (156); 24 (108)

Jer 1:11 (192)
Jer 2:9 (83); 12 (73); 13 (136); 19 (102); 30 (195)
Jer 3:12 (272)
Jer 5:3 (317); 3, 5 (195); 22 (91)
Jer 6:14 & 8:11 (265)
Jer 8:5 (317)
Jer 9:7 (191)
Jer 12:11 (14, 17)
Jer 13:23 (293)
Jer 16:5, 13 (247); 18 (92)
Jer 17:5 (160)
Jer 31:33 (153)
Jer 35:14–17 (297)
Jer 48:7 (160)

Baruch 3:16–19 (236)

Ezek 7:7–9 (93)
Ezek 11:19–20 (146)
Ezek 13:10 (265)
Ezek 18:21–22 (264); 23 (272); 32 (317)
Ezek 22:18–22 (192)
Ezek 24:11 (191); 14 (103)
Ezek 34:27 (166)
Ezek 36:26 (319, 320); 26–27 (146)

Dan 3 (220)
Dan 3, 6, 13 (195)
Dan 3:7 (228); 16–18 (213); 25 (204)
Dan 4:28–37 (190)
Dan 6 (220)
Dan 7:9–10 (66, 116); 9–27 (104); 10 (94)

Hos (Ose) 2:8 (192); 14 (154)
Hos 4:6 (12)
Hos 6:1 (194)
Hos 9:11 (230)
Hos 11:4 (194)
Hos 12:2 (103)
Hos 13:9 (271)

Amos 8:10 (242)

Jonah 3:4–5 (14, 90); 4 (278)

Mic 6:8 (240, 313)

Luke 19:1–10 (23); 41 (241); 42 (302)
Luke 21:18 (200); 19 (183); 25–28 (43);
    28 (88, 129); 34 (313)
Luke 22:30 (35, 119); 41–44 (56);
    47–48 (245); 69 (134)
Luke 23:8–12 (300); 20–23 (227); 30
    (44, 106); 31 (97); 34 (256)
Luke 24:26 (186)

John 1:9 (153); 29 (256)
John 2:17 (275)
John 5:14 (41a); 29 (41b); 44 (7)
John 7:7 (26)
John 8:23 (26, 156); 31–32 (163); 32,
    36 (148); 34 (165); 48 (227)
John 9 (204):4 (25, 33, 298); 13–17 (227)
John 10:10 (144); 11 (231)
John 11:35 (240, 283); 45–46 (228)
John 12:31 (26, 256); 42 (212); 43 (221)
John 14:15 (40, 152); 17 (156, 255); 21
    (135, 137); 27 (168)
John 15:1–2 (308); 18–19 (156); 19
    (255)
John 16:11, 20 (156); 20 (196, 239,
    240); 33 (183)
John 17:3 (125, 128); 9 (256b); 14–16
    (255); 15 (168); 25 (256a)
John 18:11 (200); 36 (121)
John 19:12 (229)
John 20:19 (123)
John 21:20–23 (186)

Acts 1:14 (19); 16–20 (157)
Acts 4:19 (213); 21 (145)
Acts 5:1–11 (268); 16 (120); 29 (213);
    41 (199, 202)
Acts 7:38 (38); 51 (11, 302, 316)
Acts 9:15 (179); 15–16 (201); 18 (252)
Acts 10:5 (6)
Acts 12:1–17 (196)
Acts 13:21–22 (267)
Acts 14:22 (183)
Acts 19:12 (120)
Acts 20:23 (186)
Acts 21:13 (213)
Acts 24:22–27 (301)
Acts 26:24 (232); 24–32 (229, 315); 28
    (301)

Rom 1:5, 17 (162); 21–22 (55); 22
    (20); 28 (11, 141)
Rom 2:4–5 (264); 4–6 (92); 5 (280,
    287–88); 13 (83); 15 (37)
Rom 3:16–17 (166)
Rom 5:1–11 (70); 3–5 (159); 10 (53);
    10, 15, 17 (144)

Rom 6:1–6 (60b); 6 (146, 166b); 15
    (27); 16–23 (166a); 23 (60a)
Rom 7:13 (37); 23 (143); 24–25 (148)
Rom 8:6 (77, 83); 9 (254); 14–15
    (276); 17 (134, 137); 18 (142, 206);
    18–30 (35); 18, 35 (186); 23 (240);
    27 (53); 28–30 (70); 31 (148); 31,
    35–39 (213); 37–39 (143)
Rom 9:2 (92); 15 (302)
Rom 11:9–11 (167); 20–21 (61); 21
    (313)
Rom 12:2 (256); 11 (309, 313)
Rom 13:3–4 (276); 8 (152); 13–14
    (177)
Rom 14:1 (177)
Rom 16:18 (310)

1 Cor 1:2, 26–31 (70); 18 (77, 232a);
    18–20 (55); 19, 26 (231); 20 (20);
    21 (6); 26 (232b); 27 (134)
1 Cor 2:3 (19, 240); 9 (99, 114, 127,
    136b); 14 (20, 77, 134, 136a, 252);
    14–15 (153–54)
1 Cor 3:9–11 (6); 12–15 (96, 187);
    15 (94); 18 (232); 19 (20, 134, 231)
1 Cor 4:3 (227); 4 (31, 279); 5 (44);
    11–12 (19); 11–13 (216); 11–15 (186)
1 Cor 5:11 (19)
1 Cor 6:2 (134); 3 (120); 9–10 (83,
    305)
1 Cor 7:1 (190); 9 (251)
1 Cor 9:7 (19); 24 (137); 24–27 (25,
    32); 27 (7, 130, 278)
1 Cor 10:13 (201, 208)
1 Cor 11:31 (51); 32 (191, 256)
1 Cor 13:1 (162); 2 (7); 12 (125, 127);
    13 (70)
1 Cor 14:20 (229)
1 Cor 15:2 (162); 52 (44); 53 (122); 58
    (29, 212)
1 Cor 16:13 (213)

2 Cor 1:8 (209); 12 (157)
2 Cor 3:17 (163)
2 Cor 4:7 (18); 8–9 (205); 8–10 (19,
    145, 186); 16–18 (145); 17 (190,
    206)
2 Cor 5:10 (42, 44, 76, 83, 90); 10–11
    (278); 11 (63, 240)
2 Cor 6:2 (304); 4–6 (31, 217); 5 (19,
    186)
2 Cor 7:1 (135); 4 (155); 5–13 (240a);
    11 (240b)
2 Cor 9:6 (259)
2 Cor 10:3 (259); 4 (27)

PATRISTIC AND CLASSICAL INDEX

Abbreviations

FC   *Fathers of the Church* (Catholic University of America)
PG   *Patrilogia Graeca*
PL   *Patrilogia Latina*

[Homiliae] *Sermones*, Appendix, 252, alias Hom. 16 ex Homiliis 50 (*PL* 39: 2212): pp. 94, 142; Appendix, 393, alias Hom. 41 ex Homiliis 50 (*PL* 39: 1714–15): p. 294; Appendix, 351, alias Hom 50 ex Homiliis 50 (*PL* 39: 1549): p. 288

Quaestiones in Heptateuchum, Bk 2, q. 8 (*PL* 34: 601–02): p. 320

Sermo ad Fratres in Eremo, c. 48 (*PL* 40: 1331): p. 80; c. 50 (*PL* 40: 1335): p. 84

Sermo de vanitate seculi (*PL* 40: 1213): p. 84

Sermones, [de sanctis 37] Appendix, 209 (*PL* 39: 2136): pp. 131, 134, 135; [de tempore 88] Appendix, 22 (*PL* 39: 1786–87): pp. 205, 320; [de tempore 120] Appendix, 154 (*PL* 39: 2046–47): p. 290; [de tempore 209] Appendix, 81 (*PL* 39: 1904): p. 145; [de verbis Domini 9] Serm. 70 (*PL* 38: 443–44): p. 150

Soliloquia animae ad Deum, c. 21 (*PL* 40: 881–82): p. 118; c. 35 (*PL* 40: 894–95): p. 128; c. 36 (*PL* 40: 896): p. 127

Tractatus in epistolam Joannis ad Parthos, 4.5 (*PL* 35: 2008): p. 127; 9.4 (*PL* 35: 2047): p. 278

Tractatus in Joannis Evangelium, 26.4 (*PL* 35: 1608; *FC* 79: 263): p. 151; 33.7–8 (*PL* 35: 1650–51; *FC* 88: 57–59): pp. 263, 264; 33.8 (*PL* 35: 1651; *FC* 88: 59): p. 304; 49.3, 18–19 (*PL* 35: 1747–48, 1754–55; *FC* 88: 240–41, 252–54): p. 283; 49.9–10 (*PL* 35: 1751; *FC* 88: 247): p. 42

Bede, the Venerable

Historia ecclesiastica gentis Anglorum, Bk 5, c. 13 (*PL* 95: 252–54; tr. Leo Sherley-Price as *A History of the English Church and People*, Harmondsworth: Penguin, 1968: 295–97): p. 86; c. 14 (*PL* 95: 254–55; Sherley-Price, 297–98): p. 86

Bernard of Clairvaux

Sermones de diversis, 12, 'De primordiis, mediis, et novissimis, in illud Ecclesiastici, vii, 40' (*PL* 183: 572–73): p. 90; 88, 'Alias, 52 ex Parvis' (*PL* 183: 703): p. 262

Sermones in Cantica, 6 (*PL* 183: 803): p. 263; 16 (*PL* 183: 852): p. 96; 55 (*PL* 183: 1046): pp. 96, 193

Sermones in Psalmum 'Qui habitat', 16.2 (Cistercian ed. Vol. 4: 482): p. 173; 16.3 (Vol. 4: 483): p. 204

Tractatus de consideratione, Bk I, c. 2 #3 (Cistercian ed. Vol. 3: 396): pp. 318, 319

Cyprian

Epistolae, 1 ad Donatum (*PL* 4: 198–202; *FC* 36: 8–10): p. 171; *ibid.* (*PL* 4: 202–04; *FC* 36: 10–11): p. 172; ?59 ad Cornelium (*PL* 3: 812–17; *FC* 51: 184–86): p. 288

Liber de lapsis, c. 35 (*PL* 4: 492; *FC* 36: 86–87): p. 288

Liber de mortalitate, c. 19 (*PL* 4: 596–97; *FC* 36: 214–15): p. 84; c. 26 (*PL* 4: 601–02; *FC* 36: 220–21): p. 131

Cyril of Alexandria

De adoratione et cultu in spiritu et veritate (*PG* 68: 134 ff.): p. 173

Homélies sur Josué, I.5 (*Sources Chrétiennes*, 71: 106): p. 258; XI.2 (71: 284): p. 173

Plutarch

Moralia, 'An recte dictum sit latenter esse vivendum', 1129F–1130B: p. 98

Possidius

Vita sancti Augustini, c. 5 (*PL* 32: 37–38; *FC* 15: 78–79): p. 178; c. 27 (*PL* 32: 57; *FC* 15: 107–08): p. 84

Tertullian

De Praescriptione Haereticorum, c. 36 (*The Ante-Nicene Fathers* (Grand Rapids: Wm Eerdmans) 3: 260): p. 186

LUIS DE GRANADA

This index records clear derivations from the works of Luis de Granada; in some cases Persons follows Luis quite closely. References to this edition of the *Book of Resolution* are given in the right hand column.

A memoriall of a Christian life. Trans. Richard Hopkins. Rouen: George L'Oyselet, 1586

Treatise I, i.5	p. 103: 'A vision of the handling of a wicked man in hell.'
Treatise II, I.iii.3	p. 65: 'everie offence is so muche the greater. . . .'
—, I.iii.4	p. 52: 'And for the understandinge of this injurie. . . .'
—, I.iii.5	p. 54: 'Godes hatred infinite against sinners.'
—, I.iii.7	p. 72: 'The intollerable ingratitude of a synner.'
Treatise IV (prologue)	p. 27: 'Two partes of our ende in this lyfe.'

Of prayer, and meditation. Trans. Richard Hopkins. Paris: Thomas Brumeau, 1582

Prologue	p. 16: 'Beleef in grosse.'
Sunday night, fols. 262–76	p. 67: 'A consideration of the benefites of God.'
Wednesday night, fol. 182	p. 78: 'The first matter of miserie in deathe.'
—, fol. 192	p. 82: 'The third matter of miserie in death.'
Thursday night, fols. 207–26	p. 43: 'Of the generall day of judgement.'

The Sinners guide. Trans. Francis Meres. London: James Robert, 1598

Book I	
c. 1.3	p. 65: 'The majestie of God.'
cc. 2–6	p. 67: 'A consideration of the benefites of God.'
c. 3.7	p. 72: 'There is not so feerse or cruell. . . .'
c. 7.3	p. 87: 'A veri profitable consideration.'
	p. 79: 'A similitude expressinge the paynes of death.'

c. 7.4	p. 80: 'The second matter of miserie in deathe.'
c. 7.9	p. 84: 'Now then, if good men and saintes. . . .'
	p. 87: 'The cogitation & speeche of the sowle at the last daye.'
	p. 81: 'The sorow of leavinge all.'
c. 8.2–3, 5	p. 47: 'The demandes at the last day.'
c. 8.5	p. 109: 'Now onelie is the time of weeping. . . .'
c. 9.1	p. 117: 'The greate king Assuerus. . . .'
c. 9.4	p. 113: 'God commaunded Abraham. . . .'
c. 9.6	p. 116: 'The creation of the worlde to expresse the power of God.'
c. 9.7	p. 121: 'The three places wherto a man is appointed.'
c. 9.8	p. 125: 'The essentiall felicitie of the soule.'
c. 9.9	p. 74: 'Causes of love in God besides his benefites.'
	p. 135: 'Nothing greeveth this our Saviour more.'
c. 10.2–6	p. 91: 'Gods majestie . . . mercye . . . patience.'
c. 10.12	p. 106: 'A wonderfull sayeing.'

INDEX OF SUBJECTS

INDEX OF PEOPLE AND PLACES

Studies in the History
of Christian Thought

EDITED BY HEIKO A. OBERMAN

46. GARSTEIN, O. *Rome and the Counter-Reformation in Scandinavia.* 1553-1622. 1992
47. GARSTEIN, O. *Rome and the Counter-Reformation in Scandinavia.* 1622-1656. 1992
48. PERRONE COMPAGNI, V. (ed.). *Cornelius Agrippa, De occulta philosophia Libri tres.* 1992
49. MARTIN, D. D. *Fifteenth-Century Carthusian Reform.* The World of Nicholas Kempf. 1992
50. HOENEN, M. J. F. M. *Marsilius of Inghen.* Divine Knowledge in Late Medieval Thought. 1993
51. O'MALLEY, J. W., IZBICKI, T. M. and CHRISTIANSON, G. (eds.). *Humanity and Divinity in Renaissance and Reformation.* Essays in Honor of Charles Trinkaus. 1993
52. REEVE, A. (ed.) and SCREECH, M. A. (introd.). *Erasmus' Annotations on the New Testament.* Galatians to the Apocalypse. 1993
53. STUMP, Ph. H. *The Reforms of the Council of Constance (1414-1418).* 1994
54. GIAKALIS, A. *Images of the Divine.* The Theology of Icons at the Seventh Ecumenical Council. With a Foreword by Henry Chadwick. 1994
55. NELLEN, H. J. M. and RABBIE, E. (eds.). *Hugo Grotius – Theologian.* Essays in Honour of G. H. M. Posthumus Meyjes. 1994
56. TRIGG, J. D. *Baptism in the Theology of Martin Luther.* 1994
57. JANSE, W. *Albert Hardenberg als Theologe.* Profil eines Bucer-Schülers. 1994
59. SCHOOR, R.J.M. VAN DE. *The Irenical Theology of Théophile Brachet de La Milletière (1588-1665).* 1995
60. STREHLE, S. *The Catholic Roots of the Protestant Gospel.* Encounter between the Middle Ages and the Reformation. 1995
61. BROWN, M.L. *Donne and the Politics of Conscience in Early Modern England.* 1995
62. SCREECH, M.A. (ed.). *Richard Mocket, Warden of All Souls College, Oxford, Doctrina et Politia Ecclesiae Anglicanae.* An Anglican Summa. Facsimile with Variants of the Text of 1617. Edited with an Introduction. 1995
63. SNOEK, G.J.C. *Medieval Piety from Relics to the Eucharist.* A Process of Mutual Inter-action. 1995
64. PIXTON, P.B. *The German Episcopacy and the Implementation of the Decrees of the Fourth Lateran Council, 1216-1245.* Watchmen on the Tower. 1995
65. DOLNIKOWSKI, E.W. *Thomas Bradwardine: A View of Time and a Vision of Eternity in Fourteenth-Century Thought.* 1995
66. RABBIE, E. (ed.). *Hugo Grotius, Ordinum Hollandiae ac Westfrisiae Pietas (1613).* Critical Edition with Translation and Commentary. 1995
67. HIRSH, J.C. *The Boundaries of Faith.* The Development and Transmission of Medieval Spirituality. 1996
68. BURNETT, S.G. *From Christian Hebraism to Jewish Studies.* Johannes Buxtorf (1564-1629) and Hebrew Learning in the Seventeenth Century. 1996
69. BOLAND O.P., V. *Ideas in God according to Saint Thomas Aquinas.* Sources and Synthesis. 1996
70. LANGE, M.E. *Telling Tears in the English Renaissance.* 1996
71. CHRISTIANSON, G. and T.M. IZBICKI (eds.). *Nicholas of Cusa on Christ and the Church.* Essays in Memory of Chandler McCuskey Brooks for the American Cusanus Society. 1996
72. MALI, A. *Mystic in the New World.* Marie de l'Incarnation (1599-1672). 1996
73. VISSER, D. *Apocalypse as Utopian Expectation (800-1500).* The Apocalypse Commentary of Berengaudus of Ferrières and the Relationship between Exegesis, Liturgy and Iconography. 1996
74. O'ROURKE BOYLE, M. *Divine Domesticity.* Augustine of Thagaste to Teresa of Avila. 1997
75. PFIZENMAIER, T.C. *The Trinitarian Theology of Dr. Samuel Clarke (1675-1729).* Context, Sources, and Controversy. 1997
76. BERKVENS-STEVELINCK, C., J. ISRAEL and G.H.M. POSTHUMUS MEYJES (eds.). *The Emergence of Tolerance in the Dutch Republic.* 1997
77. HAYKIN, M.A.G. (ed.). *The Life and Thought of John Gill (1697-1771).* A Tercentennial Appreciation. 1997
78. KAISER, C.B. *Creational Theology and the History of Physical Science.* The Creationist Tradition from Basil to Bohr. 1997
79. LEES, J.T. *Anselm of Havelberg.* Deeds into Words in the Twelfth Century. 1997
80. WINTER, J.M. VAN. *Sources Concerning the Hospitallers of St John in the Netherlands, 14th-18th Centuries.* 1998

81. TIERNEY, B. *Foundations of the Conciliar Theory*. The Contribution of the Medieval Canonists from Gratian to the Great Schism. Enlarged New Edition. 1998
82. MIERNOWSKI, J. *Le Dieu Néant*. Théologies négatives à l'aube des temps modernes. 1998
83. HALVERSON, J.L. *Peter Aureol on Predestination*. A Challenge to Late Medieval Thought. 1998. ISBN 90 04 10945 5
84. HOULISTON, V. (ed.). *Robert Persons, S.J.: The Christian Directory (1582)*. The First Booke of the Christian Exercise, appertayning to Resolution. 1998
85. GRELL, O.P. (ed.). *Paracelsus*. The Man and His Reputation, His Ideas and Their Reputation. 1998